RESEARCH
in the
ANTARCTIC

RESEARCH IN THE ANTARCTIC

A symposium presented at the
Dallas meeting of the
American Association for the
Advancement of Science—December, 1968

LOUIS O. QUAM, *Editor*
HORACE D. PORTER, *Associate Editor*

AMERICAN ASSOCIATION FOR
THE ADVANCEMENT OF SCIENCE
WASHINGTON, D.C. 1971 PUBLICATION NO. 93

International Standard Book Number (ISBN) 087168-093-9
Library of Congress Catalog Number 71-147118

Printed in the United States of America
The Horn-Shafer Division of
Geo. W. King Printing Co.
Baltimore, Maryland, U.S.A.

Preface

Antarctica is the only major landmass on earth that remained largely unexplored and unspoiled only two decades ago. Because of this, scientists from all over the world have found it unequalled as a treasury for research in a multitude of disciplines.

"Hostile" is a word that has often been used to describe this wild continent which surrounds the South Pole. It has always resisted man's efforts to explore it, or even to find out that it existed, for that matter. It still resists man. Antarctica discouraged navigators by barricading itself with weather so ferocious that it was impenetrable by early sailing ships. The intense cold and winds of unheard-of velocity made it impossible for early explorers to make anything more than brave and sporadic attempts to investigate this forbidding, but breathtakingly beautiful, continent at the bottom of the world.

It was not until modern techniques and equipment were developed that men were able to pursue specialized and intensive research. When they found that they could, workers from all branches of science and from more than a dozen nations moved in to explore, discover, learn, and share their knowledge, regardless of their national politics or boundary lines. It is heartening to know that international understanding may succeed through science when treaties and negotiations through military strength fail so dismally.

The papers in this volume are primarily the results of research by the United States Antarctic Research Program (USARP). It is an outgrowth from, but not a complete record of, the Antarctic Research Symposium held in Dallas, Texas, December, 1968, at the 135th Annual Meeting of the American Association for the Advancement of Science (AAAS).

USARP was established in the spring of 1958 to continue the Antarctic Program of the International Geophysical Year (IGY) beyond its termination in December, 1958. In May of that year, the United States invited the governments of the other 11 countries participating in IGY activities in Antarctica to consider a treaty which would provide for freedom of scientific investigation in the Antarctic by citizens, organizations, and governments of all countries, and to continue the international scientific cooperation carried out so successfully during the IGY. At that time President Eisenhower stated, "The United States is dedicated to the principle that the vast uninhabitable wastes of Antarctica shall be used only for peaceful purposes."

In the United States, the administration of the scientific effort was transferred from the U.S. National Committee for the IGY in the National Academy of Sciences to the National Science Foundation. The promulgation, planning, and funding of the scientific programs are the responsibility of the Foundation's Office of Polar Programs. The Department of Defense provides logistic support through the U.S. Naval Support Force, Antarctica.

Plans for scientific programs are formulated on five-year projections of the requirements of the scientific and academic communities; these plans are reevaluated annually to incorporate new ideas and directions for research.

The cause of science in Antarctica was given new impetus in 1961 when the Antarctic Treaty was ratified by all 12 of the IGY "Antarctic Nations": Argentina, Australia, Belgium, Chile, France, Japan, New Zealand, Norway, the Republic of South Africa, the United Kingdom, the United States, and the U.S.S.R. Four nations—Czechoslovakia, Denmark, The Netherlands, and Poland—have since acceded to the Treaty.

The Treaty reserves Antarctica for peaceful purposes, banning the use of the land area and ice shelves south of 60°S for military operations, nuclear testing, or the disposal of atomic wastes. The free exchange of scientific information is provided for; the exchange of scientists between expeditions and the right of inspection of scientific installations are also stipulated.

When it was established that the Antarctic Program would continue after the IGY, the Foundation asked the National Academy of Sciences to form a Committee on Polar Research (CPR) to determine the antarctic interests of university scientists, and to develop objectives and trends for a continuing antarctic program. The CPR also serves as the U.S. representation to the non-governmental Scientific Committee on Antarctic Research (SCAR) of the International Council of Scientific Unions. Dr. Laurence M. Gould is Chairman of CPR and Past President of SCAR. His paper in this volume broadens this perspective of U.S. participation in the Antarctic.

The United States had seven research stations on the continent when the National Science Foundation assumed the management of the programs: Little America, McMurdo, Byrd, South Pole, Hallett, Wilkes, and Ellsworth. Subsequently Little America was abandoned. Custody of Wilkes was turned over to Australia and of Ellsworth to Argentina. The United States and New Zealand agreed to operate Hallett jointly as a summer station.

The U.S. IGY program has concentrated on synoptic observations and on glaciology in order to understand better the influence of this great ice mass on atmospheric circulation. Under the new long-term program of scientific investigations, mapping and programs of geology and biology were added. Oceanography was soon included with the acquisition of the USNS *Eltanin* which was converted from an arctic cargo vessel to a research ship and put in operation in February, 1962.

Research in the Antarctic is divided into seven parts: an introduction to the continent (including the amazing story of James Eights) and recent research efforts, ecosystems, glaciology, cold poles and heat balances, conjugate phenomena, ocean dynamics, and Gondwanaland. Except for the first part, each is preceded by a brief introduction and, so far as is possible, includes representative papers reporting some of the findings of work that has been accomplished. It is impossible to cover, with any degree of completeness, the vast amount of research that has been carried out in Antarctica, but perhaps this sampling may spark the reader into delving further into the literature which is accumulating. If the reader leaves this book with a better understanding of the research being done in the Antarctic, the editors will be satisfied.

Most, but unfortunately not all, copies of the volume will be accompanied by a recent large-scale map of Antarctica which should be helpful as a reference aid. Arrangements for including the map have been made through the cooperation of the American Geographical Society.

The editors are grateful to the American Association for the Advancement of Science for making it possible to produce this volume; we especially thank Dr. William T. Kabisch, Dr. Walter G. Berl, and Dr. Richard Trumbull for their advice and encouragement.

Many of our co-workers contributed substantially to the production of this book. We acknowledge, particularly, George A. Llano, Ray R. Heer, Jr., and Mort D. Turner of the Foundation's Office of Polar Programs, Albert P. Crary of the Foundation's Division of Environmental Sciences, and Morton J. Rubin of the National Oceanic and Atmospheric Administration for their skillful assistance in organizing and evaluating the papers. Walter R. Seelig of the Office of Polar Programs was most helpful in arranging for the production of the maps. We are indebted also to Edythe S. Schirnhofer for her patient and efficient handling of the administrative details, to Mary Porter for editing manuscripts and performing countless editorial and art chores, and to Margit Friedrich for her expert and painstaking preparation of the index.

Louis O. Quam

Horace D. Porter

Washington, D.C.

May, 1971

Contributors

JOHN O. ANNEXSTAD, Manned Spacecraft Center, National Aeronautics and Space Administration, Houston, Texas

JAMES R. BARCUS, Department of Physics, University of Denver, Denver, Colorado

ALBERT E. BELON, Geophysical Institute, University of Alaska, College

JOHN L. BOWEN, Department of Meteorology, Massachusetts Institute of Technology, Cambridge

COLIN BULL, Institute of Polar Studies and Department of Geology, The Ohio State University, Columbus

ROY E. CAMERON, Bioscience Section, Jet Propulsion Laboratory, California Institute of Technology, Pasadena

EDWIN H. COLBERT, Museum of Northern Arizona, Flagstaff

A. P. CRARY, Division of Environmental Sciences, National Science Foundation, Washington, D.C.

JOHN C. CROWELL, Department of Geology, University of California, Santa Barbara

PAUL C. DALRYMPLE, Earth Sciences Laboratory, U.S. Army Natick Laboratories, Natick, Massachusetts

T. NEIL DAVIS, Geophysical Institute, University of Alaska, College

ROBERT B. ELDER, Polar Projects Section, U.S. Coast Guard Oceanographic Unit, Washington Navy Yard, Washington, D.C.

SAYED Z. EL-SAYED, Department of Oceanography, College of Geosciences, Texas A&M University, College Station

ROBERT E. FEENEY, College of Agricultural and Environmental Sciences, University of California, Davis

LAWRENCE A. FRAKES, Department of Geology, University of California, Los Angeles

THOMAS O. FROSTMAN, Earth Sciences Laboratory, U.S. Army Natick Laboratories, Natick, Massachusetts

T. P. GANNUTZ, Department of Biology, Clark University, Worcester, Massachusetts

NEEL W. GLASS, Los Alamos Scientific Laboratory, University of California, Los Alamos, New Mexico

ARNOLD L. GORDON, Lamont-Doherty Geological Observatory of Columbia University, Palisades, New York

LAURENCE M. GOULD, Department of Geology, College of Mines, The University of Arizona, Tucson

A. J. GOW, U.S. Army Cold Regions Research and Engineering Laboratory, Hanover, New Hampshire

MARTIN HALPERN, The University of Texas at Dallas

B. LYLE HANSEN, U.S. Army Cold Regions Research and Engineering Laboratory, Hanover, New Hampshire

JOEL W. HEDGPETH, Marine Science Center, Oregon State University, Newport

RAY R. HEER, JR., Atmospheric Physics Programs, Office of Polar Programs, National Science Foundation, Washington, D.C.

J. R. HEIRTZLER, Woods Hole Oceanographic Institution, Woods Hole, Massachusetts

R. A. HELLIWELL, Radioscience Laboratory, Stanford University, Stanford, California

T. O. JONES, National and International Programs, National Science Foundation, Washington, D.C.

C. C. LANGWAY, JR., U.S. Army Cold Regions Research and Engineering Laboratory, Hanover, New Hampshire

HEINZ LETTAU, Department of Meteorology, University of Wisconsin, Madison

GEORGE A. LLANO, Polar Biology Programs, Office of Polar Programs, National Science Foundation, Washington, D.C.

DIETLAND MÜLLER-SCHWARZE, Department of Wildlife Resources, Utah State University, Logan

Robert L. Nichols, Department of Geology, Tufts University, Medford, Massachusetts

David T. Osuga, College of Agricultural and Environmental Sciences, University of California, Davis

Martin A. Pomerantz, Bartol Research Foundation of The Franklin Institute, Swarthmore, Pennsylvania

Louis O. Quam, Office of Polar Programs, National Science Foundation, Washington, D.C.

George C. Reid, National Oceanic and Atmospheric Administration, Boulder, Colorado

Morton J. Rubin, Office of Special Studies, National Oceanic and Atmospheric Administration, Rockville, Maryland

Emanuel D. Rudolph, Institute of Polar Studies, The Ohio State University, Columbus

James M. Seabrooke, U.S. Coast Guard Oceanographic Unit, Washington Navy Yard, Washington, D.C.

Jay T. Shurley, Veterans Administration, Oklahoma City; University of Oklahoma School of Medicine, Oklahoma City

Henry Stommel, Department of Meteorology, Massachusetts Institute of Technology, Cambridge

Paul Tasch, Department of Geology, Wichita State University, Wichita, Kansas

Mort D. Turner, Earth Sciences Programs, Office of Polar Programs, National Science Foundation, Washington, D.C.

Harry van Loon, National Center for Atmospheric Research, Boulder, Colorado

Bruce A. Warren, Woods Hole Oceanographic Institution, Woods Hole, Massachusetts

Charles R. Wilson, Geophysical Institute, University of Alaska, College

Contents

PART I—Introduction to Research in the Antarctic

PART II—Biology

PART III—Glaciology

PART IV—Cold Poles and Heat Balances

PART V—Conjugate Phenomena

PART VI—Ocean Dynamics

PART VII—Gondwanaland

PART I

Introduction to Research in the Antarctic

James Eights of the Antarctic (1798-1882)

JOEL W. HEDGPETH

Marine Science Center, Oregon State University, Newport

The story of James Eights, the first qualified naturalist to set foot on land south of the Antarctic Convergence, is one of unfulfilled promise, of a life destroyed by circumstances. The bad luck that befell Eights in his own lifetime seems to have carried over to the records of his aborted scientific career, to say nothing of all other records of his long life, and we do not know the reasons for his eclipse after one brief and promising antarctic orbit. James Eights was born in Albany, New York, in 1798, and died in Ballston, not many miles away, in 1882. Most of his 84 years, except for his participation in Captain Edmund Fanning's expedition to South America and the Antarctic in 1829-1831, was spent in obscurity in his native Albany. Even the meaning of his name, which apparently died with him, is obscure, other than that it was of Dutch derivation.

No record has yet been found of how James Eights, trained as a physician, perhaps in part by his father Jonathan Eights, won assignment as naturalist of our first "official" or at least morally supported exploring expedition. Nor is there any clear record whether he sailed on the *Annawan,* Nathaniel B. Palmer, captain, or the *Seraph,* Benjamin Pendleton, captain, except that in his application for a post on the U.S. Exploring Expedition he mentioned having been on the *Annawan.* In any event, Eights did sail, and visited Tierra del Fuego, Staten Island, and the South Shetlands, including Deception Island. Eights was a keen and accurate observer and a competent artist, and between the years 1833 and 1852 five papers were published on his antarctic observations and collections. These papers, four of which are reprinted here, constitute the only solid record of the exploring expedition, and, probably, had a great deal to do with gaining support for the United

States Exploring Expedition under the command of Charles Wilkes. James Eights was appointed geologist to this expedition in 1837, and was granted funds for outfitting and advance pay. Yet he was omitted from the official company and remained at home when the expedition sailed in 1838. In the years following this setback Eights apparently worked as artist and geologist for the Natural History Survey of New York and prepared a few papers on aspects of the geology of upstate New York. He also evidently went to North Carolina sometime before 1854, as he wrote several reports on the mines and geology of North Carolina. After this, however, Eights quietly faded away; he never married; and as late as 1915 John M. Clarke of the State Museum could gather together only a few scattered impressions from persons who dimly remembered an old man living in poverty, and nothing much more.

Were it not for this handful of remarkable papers on the life and geology of the South Shetlands, Eights would have been completely forgotten. Two of the animals he found and described, with illustrations that cannot be improved upon today, are the characteristic antarctic isopod *Glyptonotus antarctica* and the ten-legged pycnogonid *Decolopoda australis.* His account of the South Shetlands, appended to his description of *Serolis trilobitoides,* is a fresh, vivid, and significant account by a field naturalist of high ability. By the standards of his day as well as ours these papers were fundamental contributions and his demonstrated ability to produce publishable results would probably have ensured him a place on any similar modern expedition. Why Eights perished in spite of publishing we will probably never know. There has been some allusion to personal squabbles and personality differences among the principals of the time, but there is no evidence that Eights was passed over because of a disagreeable personality. The circumstances of his life would suggest the contrary, for disagreeable personalities usually manage to make some sort of splash as they go down, but Eights sank quietly, almost without a ripple. We do not even have a description of the sort of person he was, or what he looked like.

Editors' Note: The papers of James Eights which follow have been set in approximately the same type and format as his original publications. Some variations have been necessary because of modern requirements of spacing and the difficulty in obtaining type faces which were used over a century ago. An attempt has been made, however, to maintain the general appearance and typographical similarity of the initial works. His spelling and punctuation have been retained, but it has not been possible to retain the original pagination.

ON THE ICEBERGS OF THE ANT-ARCTIC SEA.

BY JAMES EIGHTS

To the voyager, whose adventurous inclination has conducted to almost every clime and distant shore, to which the ocean rolls its wave, there is perhaps no scene in all his wide wanderings, that so powerfully arrests his attention, and calls forth those feelings of admiration in so sublime a degree as that produced by his earliest prospect of the polar seas. In approaching these dreary and uninhabitable regions, the chilling influences of the land are sensibly felt, long ere it becomes visible; but when the curtain of mist that enshrouds its glories, discloses the sublime spectacle, all the feebler sensations of the mind are at once lost in the all-absorbing sentiment of delight which pervades his breast.

The vast masses of snow and ice that lie piled over the uneven superficies of the land, and the numerous icebergs that drift through the Southern ocean, and are every where strewed along its surface, are, in a peculiar manner, adapted to create feelings of awe and admiration in the bosom of the beholder, not alone from the majesty of the size, but likewise, by the variety of the forms and everchanging hues that they assume, throughout the different hours of the long-continued light in these high latitudes.

From the shapeless mass of comparatively small dimensions, to that of some miles in extent, these icebergs are not unfrequently seen, elevated to the height of between two and three hundred feet above the ocean's level; they are then swept along with an inconceivable grandeur, borne by the powerful currents, and aided by the almost ceaseless winds, they move steadily onward until they finally become dissolved, and entirely disappear, in the warmer regions much farther to the north.

It is almost impossible to conceive anything more delicately beautiful than the effect produced by these icebergs, when the sky is free from clouds, and the ocean is at rest; it is then there can be traced, among the numerous angles and indentations by which they are impressed, all those mingling gradations of color, from the faintest tinge of emerald green to that of the most intense shades of blue; and when the sky is filled with clouds—which is most generally the case—the scene, though equally as picturesque, exhibits a much severer aspect; these clouds being all over torn into rough and irregular patches, by the powerful winds that here prevail; while the sun, having but a moderate altitude, and almost encircling the heavens but a few degrees above the horizon, pierce with its rays the numerous openings between, and light up both cloud and ice, into a most magnificent glow. These changing hues are again brought to the eye of the spectator, in mild and beautiful reflections, so that, throughout the hours of the long summer day, the entire scene presents the ever-varying aspect of a most gorgeous sunset.

But when seen amid the turbulence of cloud and storm, the scene becomes sternly sublime. The dense masses of heavy vapor that deadens the entire face of the heavens, and roll rapidly along its surface, together with the dashing of the wild waves against the icebergs' slippery sides, sometimes sending the spray far beyond their loftiest tops, where, soon becoming dissipated in clouds of silvery mist, it gradually descends and envelopes the distant view as with a soft transparent veil of light. But it is only when, under these circumstances, these masses of ice are seen through the gloomy twilight of the midnight hours, that they assume a strangely terrific aspect; their huge forms then loom in the hazy atmosphere that surrounds them, and fall upon the vision shadowy and indistinct, like fragmentary spectres of a disruptured world.

These icebergs at all times derive their origin from the land; being merely detached fragments from the huge glaciers which every where fill the numerous valleys, and cover the hills from the water's edge upward, until they attain their greatest eminence. These glaciers are all formed from the accumulating snows of ages, this being almost the only form that moisture ever assumes in falling in these elevated regions; scarcely a day occurred while we were in the vicinity of these southern lands—even though at mid-summer—that snows did not descend, and water congeal into ice upon our decks.

The powerful winds which prevail in these high latitudes, acting with their usual energy upon such portions of the land as are freely exposed to their sweeping influence, have a direct tendency in the first instance, to drift up and fill the valleys and other depressions with snow, until they become almost even with the adjoining hills; it is then, by the pressure of the enormous weight, that it is speedily condensed into solid ice. During this process it is, that those numerous shrinkage fissures are also produced, that are to be seen traversing the glaciers in almost every possible direction.

In passing along the surfaces of these glaciers, the journey ofttimes becomes one of extreme peril to the incautious traveller, from the circumstance that the fissures are not unfrequently crusted over by a thin and fragile covering of snow, which readily yields to his footstep, and suddenly precipitates him some hundreds of feet below.* It is in this manner that animals sometimes perish, and when at length discovered, firmly imbeded in the drifting ice, give rise to no small degree of surprise and varied speculation.

The carcasses of penguins and seals, which in the greatest profusion inhabit the southern lands, were, in several instances, observed in such positions; and it is in this way that the remains of animals are frequently conveyed to distant shores, and deposited in climes in every way uncongenial to their species.

From the constantly increasing weight of accumulating snows above, these glaciers are silently and almost imperceptibly encroaching on the sea, so as, in many places, to project far over its foaming waves. Sometimes they are seen gradually to approach from opposite directions, and eventually to bridge over some of the narrower straits that in various places divide the land; in most instances, however, they are observed to encompass the land by a

* This, but to an unimportant depth, occurred to one of the officers of our ship, and it was only after a considerable time had elapsed, and some exertion on our part, that he was ultimately relieved.

series of precipitous cliffs, which have an extent for miles together, presenting a naked wall or barrier of ice to the sea. Huge masses of these, particularly during the season of summer, are continually breaking off with an astounding report, and after falling into the waves beneath are carried onward, and constitute the vast icebergs of the Southern ocean.

These icebergs, when first detached from the land, are of a rudely tabular form, but by the continued action of the oceanic waters about their bases, penetrating into their fissures, and wearing them away in such a manner as to destroy their equilibrium, they suddenly topple over, and then exhibit all those strange and imitative forms which have so often been described in most glowing terms, by the many voyagers whose good or evil fortunes have hitherto led within their influence.

Embraced within these drifting icebergs, rocky fragments, varying greatly in size, are not unusually to be seen, sometimes rounded into the boulder form, but for the most part angular, and so arranged as to present a dark striped, or partially stratified appearance, strikingly visible from the contrast of their darker hues, with those of the lighter tints of the ice in which they are inclasped. The origin of these last is extremely obvious, and admit of a simple explanation. In many places, isolated masses of the rock that constitute the land, are observed to penetrate and protrude far above the general level of the surrounding snows; portions of these are almost continually falling, from the expansive power of the congealing water among their fissures: these fragments are thrown upon the indurated surface of the snows, and are then slidden to some considerable distance from whence they were derived; upon these the falling snows soon accumulate to a sufficient depth to retain them in their places, until they become firmly embraced within the mass. When portions of these glaciers are detached, and tumble into the sea, icebergs bearing rocky fragments are then produced. These fragments, like the animal remains, are frequently borne along, and deposited in regions far remote from the parent rock, from whence they were detached.

The largest drifting iceberg that we saw, during a period of three months in their vicinity, was estimated at about two miles in extent, and elevated between two and three hundred feet in the air. Should we take into consideration the specific gravity of ice, which allows about eight parts beneath, to one above the sea, we will be able to form some conception of the vast magnitude of these floating mountains. One of these larger ones was seen drifting along at the rate of two and a half knots an hour, at which speed, on approaching Cornwallis island—one of the South Shetland group—it suddenly became arrested in its course, the anterior portion grounding, and remaining attached, while that which followed, submitting to the powerful impulse of the current, was swept around, describing a complete semicircle ere it again became free. Should this part of the ocean's bottom, at any future time, be elevated into dry land by the active energies so peculiar to volcanic regions, the impressions made by this iceberg would furnish to the world a highly interesting subject for geological speculation. When agitated by the waves, these mountains of ice are frequently rent assunder with terrific explosion, scattering their fragments far and wide over the surrounding surface of the deep. In fine weather too, they are not unusually seen covered with penguins, whose chattering noise is often heard at an incredible distance over the silent sea.

DESCRIPTION

Of a New Animal belonging to the CRUSTACEA, *discovered in the Antarctic Seas, by the author,* JAMES EIGHTS.

[Cabinet of the Albany Institute.]

GENUS GLYPTONOTUS. (EIGHTS.)

Animal composed of a head, thorax, and post-abdomen or tail, constituting in all thirteen distinct segments.

Head deeply inserted into the cephalic segment of the thorax. *Eyes* sessile, and finely granulate. *Antennae* two pairs, placed one above the other, with an elongate multiarticulated filament. *Mouth* as in the ordinary *Isopods,* mandibles not palpigerous; the two superior foot-jaws expanded into a well defined lower lip, bearing palpi.

Thorax separated into seven distinct segments, the three posterior ones biarticulate near their lateral extremities; each segment giving origin to a pair of perfect legs, terminating with a strong and slightly curved nail.

Post-abdomen, or tail, divided into five segments, provided with neither styles nor swimmerets; the under surfaces each supporting a pair of branchial leaflets, longitudinally arranged, and covered by two biarticulated plates attached to the outward edges of the last segment, closing over them much in the manner of an ordinary bivalve shell.

SPECIES G. ANTARCTICA. (EIGHTS.)

ANTARCTIC SCULPTURE-BACK.

Animal perfectly symmetrical, ovate, elongate, and depressed.

Teguments solid and calcareous. Color, brown sepia. Length, from the insertion of the antennae, three and a half inches; width, one and three-quarters.

Head transversely elliptical, terminating at its lateral and anterior corners acutely, and incurved; anterior margin obtusely elevated, and arched each way to its centre. Superior surface of the head ornamented with an imperfectly sculptured "fleur-de-lis;" posterior portion obtusely elevated, producing a marginal rim. *Eyes* small, reniform, indigo blue, and placed near the lateral and anterior portion of the head, so deeply impressed in the margin of the shell as to be easily distinguished from beneath. Inferior pair of *antennae* longer than the superior, corresponding in length to the width of the head, transversely, from spine to spine; articulations four in number; last segment longest, the remaining three gradually diminishing in length as they proceed to the place of insertion; segments triangulate, with angular projections on their surfaces; edges of the angles, and articulating extremities rigidly spined. Terminating filament about the length of the basal articulations, gradually attenuated until it diminishes to a finely pointed apex. Superior *antennae* half the length of the inferior, three-jointed, and terminating with an attenuated filament whose articulations are indistinct; segments angular, external one much the longest; extremities and angles likewise spined. *Mouth* with the labrum or upper lip hard and massive, resembling in form a reversed heart. The mandibles are without palpi, stout and osseous, tipped with a hard and black enamel. The maxillae are furnished with the usual palpi. The lower lip, or superior foot-jaws when united, sub-cordate; its palpi five-jointed, snugly embracing the manducatory organs along their base, like a row of ciliated leaflets.

The *thorax* is composed of seven distinct segments, each one being beautifully ornamented on its superior surface by an elongated and sub-conic insculptation, forming a series, whose pointed apices almost unite along the longitudinal dorsal ridge. These segments are finely bordered along their posterior articulating edges by an elevated and continuous marginal rim, extending to the lateral extremities of the shell. The cephalic depression is likewise margined by an obtusely elevated border. Each segment of the thorax gives origin, beneath, to a pair of ponderous angulated legs, composed of the ordinary parts. The three anterior pairs project themselves forward, and are closely compressed upon the inferior surfaces of the three foremost segments; they are monodactyle, with the nails incurved upon the anterior edges of the rather largely inflated penultimate joint. Each joint is furnished at its articulating extremity with rigid spines; the inner edges of the penultimate joint, together with those of the three adjoining, are provided with a double row of tufted cilia, disposed diagonally, and much resembling in appearance the arrangement of hairs in an ordinary brush. The four posterior pairs of legs are directed backwards, strongly triangulate, stout and ponderous, terminating by a slightly curved nail; their length is nearly equal, but they gradually increase in thickness as they recede toward the tail. The basal joints are large and inflated; the remainder regularly angulate. The extremities of the articulating joints, and edges of the two inferior angles, are each provided with a series of tufted and rigid spines.

The *post-abdomen* is composed of five segments. The four anterior ones are much smaller than those which constitute the thorax, but greatly resemble them in form, being ornamented on their superior surfaces with similar insculptations, though but slightly defined. Each of these segments is provided beneath with a pair of articulated pedicels, which furnish a support to the bifoliated bronchial leaflets. These leaflets are arranged longitudinally one upon the other, and are entirely concealed by the biarticulated plates of the caudal segment; they are subovate and elongate; the outward ones smaller than those which they cover, and are nearly surrounded by a fringed cilia, most conspicuously developed along their inner margins. The second pair are each supplied with an elongated style, extending almost to the termination of the caudal segment. The terminating segment is large and triangular, giving attachment to the biarticulated plates at a single point on its outer margins near the base, which enables the animal to close them together in a line along its centre beneath. These plates are about the length of the segment, and of a triangulate form, each one having near its termination a small oval articulation. The segment and marginal plates are slightly inflated along their external edges, producing an obtusely elevated border.

The segments constituting the thorax and post-abdomen are supplied by a central, angular, and elongated knob, which, when united, form a prominent dorsal ridge, gradually diminishing in its backward course, and forming a sharp elevated line along the caudal segment, terminating at its extremity in a short and obtusely pointed spine.

This beautiful crustacean furnishes to us another close approximation to the long lost family of the *Trilobite*. I procured them from the southern shores of the New South Shetland Islands. They inhabit the bottom of the sea, and are only to be obtained when thrown far upon the shores by the immense surges that prevail when the detached glaciers from the land precipitate themselves into the ocean.

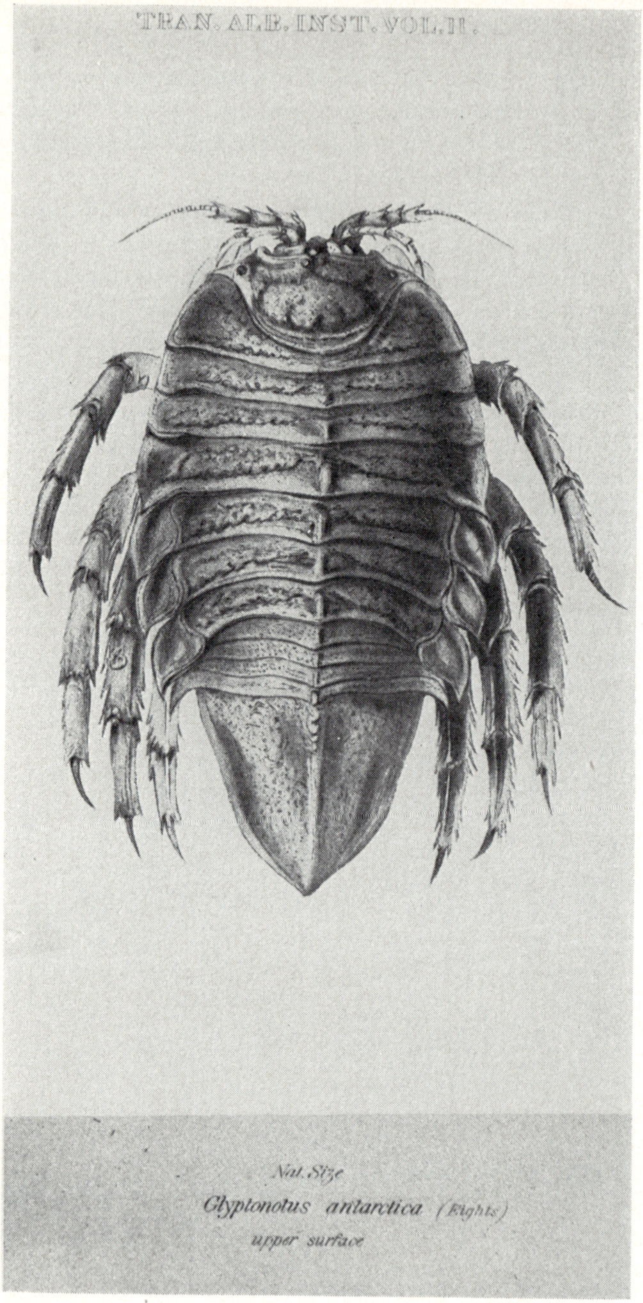

Nat. Size
Glyptonotus antarctica (Eights)
upper surface

TRAN. ALB. INST. VOL. II.

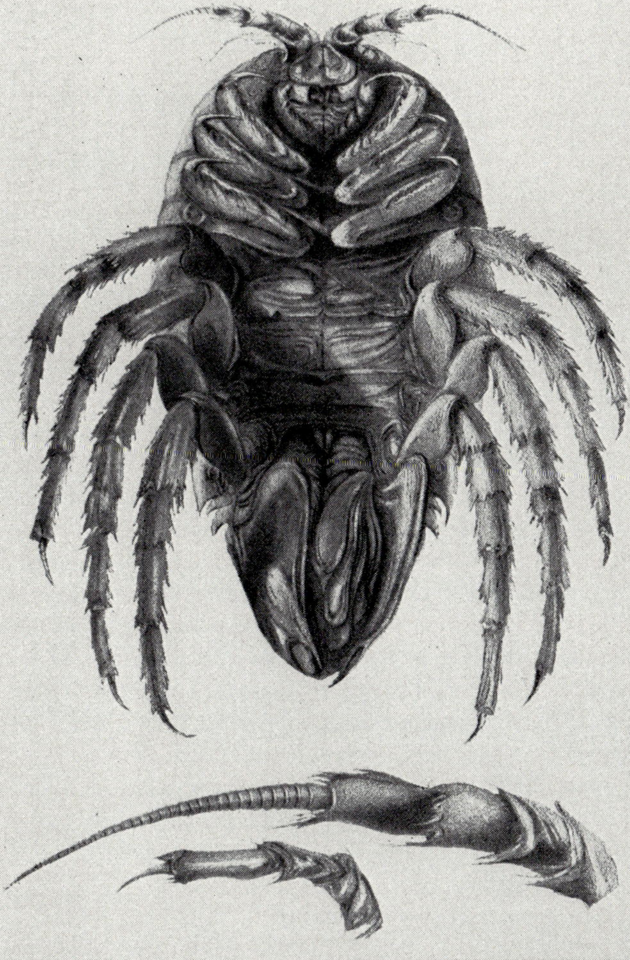

Nat. Size

Glyptonotus antarctica (Eights)

under surface

1 Inferior antennae }
2 Superior antennae } *Magnified*

ART. XI.—DESCRIPTION OF A NEW ANIMAL BELONGING TO THE ARACHNIDES OF LATREILLE; DISCOVERED IN THE SEA ALONG THE SHORES OF THE NEW SOUTH SHETLAND ISLANDS. By JAMES EIGHTS, M. D. (Communicated September 17, 1834.)

ARACHNIDES.

Gen. DECOLOPODA.*

Thorax. Elliptical, composed of five segments, separated from each other by slightly impressed articulations; anterior one produced into a head-like process. Contracted behind, and having on its superior surface a subconic tubercle with two eyes placed on each side; segments terminated at each extremity by a tubular joint, to which are attached ten perfect legs. *Rostrum* longer than the thorax, tubular, clavate, arcuated downward, with a triangular aperture at its apex; inserted into the anterior portion of the head-like process below. *Chelicerae* rather longer than the rostrum, inserted on each side of its base, above, biarticulate, and terminated by a forceps composed of a finger and thumb, much curved, and meeting only a short distance along their tips, the superior finger, alone movable. *Palpi* setaceous, ten jointed, longer than the rostrum, inserted beneath the chelicerae. *Egg-bearing organs* attached to a process at the base of the palpi, ten-jointed, with a terminal incurved nail. *Legs* cylindrical, composed of a three-jointed coxa, one-jointed femur, and a two-jointed tibia and tarsus, the latter terminated by a simple, slightly curved claw. *Abdomen?* attached to the posterior segment of the thorax by a movable articulation, small, sub-clavate, and perforated at its extremity by an anal incision.

---

*From δεχα, *ten*, ‘ολος, *perfect*, ποδα *feet*.

PLATE VII.

Fig. 1. Superior view of the animal, natural size.
" 2. Inferior " " " deprived of the legs near the coxae.

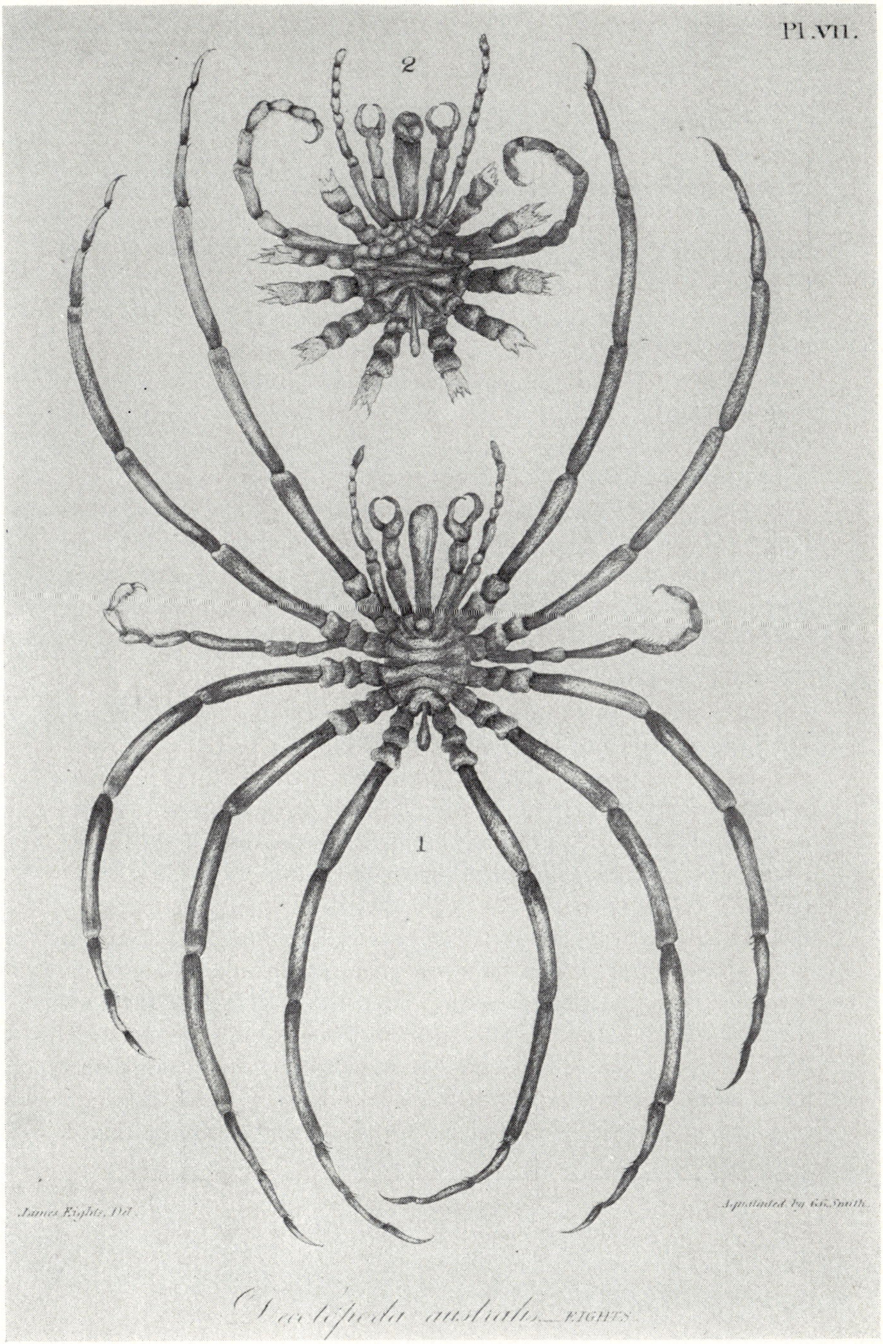
Pl. VII.
2
1
James Eights, Del.
Aquatinted by G.G. Smith.
Decolopoda australis—EIGHTS.

D. Australis.

Entire animal of a bright scarlet; disk of the thorax convex, beneath, slightly so; on the superior surface of the tubular joints, near the margin, are situated about four very small, rigid spines; basal joint of the chelicerae, elongated. *Palpi* with the third and fifth joints elongate, the former of greater length than the latter. *Egg-bearing organs* with the three first joints small and sub-equal, fourth and sixth elongate, the remainder nearly equal: the four terminal joints are prehensile, and have their inner margins dentated, the teeth arranged in about four longitudinal rows. *Legs* long and nearly equal, posterior pair rather smaller; joints of the coxae short and subequal. *Thighs* about twice the length of the coxae, furnished with small spines at their superior extremity. The first joint of the tibia equal in length to the thigh, the other rather longer. *Tarsi* as long as the thigh; the last joint of the tibia, and those of the tarsi, each armed at their extremities beneath, with four rigid spines. *Eyes* very small. *Teguments* pergamineous.

Habitat: sea in the vicinity of the New South-Shetland Islands.

Cabinet of James Eights.

I have placed this interesting animal in the class *ARACHNIDES,* in consequence of its close approximation to Latreille's second family *Pycnogonoides,** of his order Tracheariae; it possesses all of the characters, besides which, it has a segment supporting two additional legs, making in all *five perfect pairs;* this latter circumstance would doubtless bring it in the preceding class *CRUSTACEA,* being a character which strikingly distinguishes the animals that compose it; at all events, I think it will certainly form a connecting link in the great chain of the animal kingdom, between these two classes, passing from the *CRUSTACEA* into the *ARACHNIDES* by the genera Nymphon, Phoxichili, Pycnogonum, &c. Their mode of respiration I could not determine, as no appearance of the stigmata, through which they are supposed to breathe, were visible. Of the many specimens that I

* Cuvier, Regne Animal.

obtained, I saw none but such as were furnished with what are termed the egg-bearing organs, consequently, if those are the females that are thus distinguished, they prove much more numerous than the males.

The tegument covering the body is soft and yielding, the appearance of segments and articulations are necessarily faint, indicating that little motion of the parts is required.

They are to be found in considerable numbers in connexion with the fuci, thrown up by the waves along the shores of the islands, after being detached by the motion of the large masses of ice, from the bottom of the sea.

Art. IV. *Description of a new Crustaceous Animal found on the Shores of the* South Shetland *Islands, with Remarks on their Natural History. By* James Eights, *Naturalist to the Exploring Expedition of* 1830, *and Corresponding Member of the Albany Institute.*

Communicated July 10, 1833.

CRUSTACEA.

MALACOSTRACA.

BRONGNIARTIA.

Animal broad-oval, much depressed, trilobate, lobes formed by a slightly impressed sulcus; divided from the head downwards into eight articulations, and a terminal cordiform tail: *teguments* solid and calcareous. *Eyes* two, superior, sessile and immoveable. *Antennae* four, on a line with the margin of the shell. *Mouth* inferior, composed of a labrum, two mandibles bearing palpi, two pair of maxillae, tongue, and a labium formed of the first foot-jaws. *Feet* fourteen, anterior four with a dilated hand, and an incurved moveable finger, remaining ten unguiculate. *Branchiae* situated under the post-abdomen in pairs. *Tail* with foliaceous fin-like appendages on its lateral edge, inferiorly it supports four pairs of diaphanous laminae.

B. TRILOBITOIDES.

Head approaching the segment of a circle, descending from the vertex to its anterior portion, and laterally to the edge of the margin, which is slightly serrate; anterior extremity terminated by a broad sinus, having a narrow, raised and reflected rim, furcate at each extremity: posterior edge gently elevated, sinuous, and corresponding to the articulation of the abdomen. *Eyes* elevated and prominent: cornea oblong, lunulate, reticulate, composed of an infinite number of facets, distinctly visible to the naked eye: colour blue, the superior surface covered by an irregular calcareous incrustation: from the posterior and external angle of the eye extends a suture forward and outward, dividing the front and anterior portion of the head from its lateral expansion; at the origin of the suture commences a transverse furrow, overshadowed by a narrow reflected rim, which gradually becomes obliterated at the outward margin, giving to the posterior portion of the head somewhat the appearance of a distinct segment: a second narrow rim commences near the termination of the suture, extending backwards until it almost bisects the transverse one near the margin. The *Front* between the eyes is raised to a line with them, assuming in appearance somewhat the figure of a corona in high relief; posterior to it is an elevated angle bearing a small tubercle of a dark colour, resembling an ocellus; between the anterior angles of the eyes is also a reflected sinuous rim, rising to the same height. *Antennae* four, inserted one above the other by a tri-articulated peduncle into the sinus of the anterior portion of the head, contiguous at the base, setaceous, a three-jointed clavola with a terminal pluri-articulated stem, the inferior projects forward and rises to an equal height, so that the four antennae appear as if situated on the same line: superiorly, the segments are longitudinally grooved, inferiorly crossed, the shortest by three, the second six, and the external one by five ciliate elevations; superior one two thirds, and inferior one half, the length of the animal. *Labrum* attached to the nasi anteriorly, triangulate, slightly punctate, with two central depressions. The body of the *Mandibulae* are somewhat trapezate, with an angular dental process, armed, the one on the left with two corneous teeth, placed one within the other, that on the right contains but one, they are convex externally and internally concave, with a small foramen at their base. A pediform three-jointed palpi is inserted into the base of the mandible, the first segment about equal in length to its body, lies in a deep groove on its anterior margin, the middle one corresponds in size, terminal one half its length, subovate, dilated and compressed, with a ciliate inferior edge. *Maxillae,* two pair, inserted at the side of the mentum; superior one simple, apex armed with six rigid spines, arranged in a triple series: inferior, compound, the upper lobe covering the lower externally, and is cleft almost to its first articulation, giving to the maxillae the appearance of being three-lobed: the apex of each is furnished with flexile spines. *Tongue* linguiform, with an acute apex, cartilaginous, short and retractile. The appendages corresponding to the first foot-jaws approximate closely to a true lip, each being furnished with a palpus, they rise up to the mandibles, meeting each other at a line in the centre, so as to close effectually the lower portion of the mouth; they are somewhat rhomboidal in form, and divided into four subequal portions by both a longitudinal and transverse articulation: the palpus is situated superiorly near its inner margin and is composed of a small peduncle supporting a sub-triangulate, dilated segment, the anterior edge of which is fringed with cilia, and a terminal subovate one containing a row of hairs on its extreme edge: when these two lips meet in the centre the parts are osseous and triangular; the apex is armed with a small rigid tooth. The first pair of feet corresponding to the second foot-jaws, are attached to the head a short distance from the lower lip, laterally; they are directed forward and laid on the mouth in such a manner as if constituting one of the organs of manducation, six-jointed: the second, third and fourth nearly equal, short and irregular, seeming to form a kind of wrist for supporting a rather large, subovoid, dilated hand, with a terminal incurved finger reflected on its inner ciliate edge. *Abdomen* with five transverse articulations, somewhat arcuated backwards, their posterior margin is slightly elevated so as to suffer the anterior edge of the following ones to pass under them; the three first segments have their lateral portions divided at the sulcus by a deeply impressed line, or suture, which may be disunited by macerating the parts in water, otherwise they are immovable; the remaining two are entire: the lateral parts are falcate and separated from each other by an incisure extending to the longitudinal sulcus, near which, both on their anterior and posterior edges, is situated a small tooth-like process; a narrow elevated rim runs along the anterior margin until it becomes obsolete near the external slightly serrated edge. The second pair of feet corresponding to the third foot-jaws, are attached to the first segment after the head, and also seem to assist in the process of manducation; they are more slender than any of the other feet, the first joint is longest, the penultimate one slightly dilated, forming a hand with an incurved moveable finger. The four remaining segments are each furnished with a pair of six articulated coriaceous feet, resembling each other both in size and appearance, being largest at the base, and gradually attenuated to the slightly curved terminal nail; the first segment is much compressed, the succeeding ones tubular and armed at the apex, both forward and behind, with a number of small moveable spines; on their anterior edge are one, two or more small processes armed in like manner. The sexual organs are double, and situated near the origin of the posterior pair of the last mentioned feet. The *Post-Abdomen* is divided into three articulations, and a terminal cordiform appendage constituting a tail proper. The anterior segment has no lateral elongation, in place thereof its extremities are produced inferiorly, giving insertion to the posterior pair of true feet; these feet differ only from the preceding ones, in being rather smaller and having the terminal nail more curved. The two last segments are somewhat similar to those of the abdomen, though inferior in size. The three segments have on their under sides each a pair of pediform appendages, composed of a single compressed joint, to which are attached one about midway, the other terminal, two subovate vesicular bursae, fringed with branchial fibres: the inferior ones of the middle pair have inserted along their inner edge a flexile setaceous style, extending backwards about twice the length of the whole appendage. *Tail* cordiform: a raised and reflected rim terminating in an acute spine near the outward margin, gives the anterior part the appearance of a distinct segment; longitudinally through the centre is an elevated, sharp, muricate ridge, terminating the end of the tail with an attenuated spine; at its base are situated a pair of short and reflected teeth: the posterior margin is slightly elevated, having its edge armed with a row of sharp spines pointing backwards; on the outer edge are two narrow, rather thick, serrate and acuminate leaflets, inserted into a moveable peduncle; their motion is lateral, and when at rest the superior shuts over the inferior one like the sticks of a fan. At the origin of the tail inferiorly, on each side of the vent so as to conceal it, are inserted in pairs eight membranous laminae, meeting each other by a longitudinal line in the centre, when they form the perfect figure of a heart; they are entirely covered by the external pair, which is rather thicker, and is diagonally articulated.

Males more numerous than females.

Females carry their ova between scales under the thorax. *Ova* orbicular, nearly a line in diameter, of a fine orange colour.

Colour of the animal, an olivaceous green.

Length two and three quarter inches. Breadth two and one quarter.

Hab. Seas, along the coast of Patagonia, Cape Horn, New South Shetlands.

Cabinet of the Albany Institute.

Profesor Eaton, in his Geological Text-Book, has created a genus of Trilobites, to which he applies the name *Brongniartia;* comprising B. isotela, (Isotelus gigas. De Kay.) B. carcinodea, (Triarthus Beckii. Green.) and B. platicephala, (Asaphus platycephalus. Stokes.) Dr. Green in his Monograph of Trilobites, has justly thought proper to retain the genus of Dr. De Kay. His second species is the head of either an Asaphus or Paradoxide of Brongniart, and was previously described by Green, leaving the A. Platycephalus, which is well known to come under the genus Isotelus. The name of *Brongniartia* then, being unoccupied, I have employed it for this interesting animal, in honor of Professor Alexander Brongniart, not only for the eminence he has attained in science, but in consideration of his having been the first individual that ever attempted a systematic arrangement of the trilobites; and *trilobitoides,* from its resemblance both in form and appearance to these fossils.

During one of those calms which most generally succeed to the celebrated "Pamparos" along the coast of Patagonia, the seamen employed themselves in catching some of the fine bottom fish, that are so abundantly to be obtained after making soundings. They comprise chiefly the whole of Cuvier's family of Gadites. On examining the contents of the stomach of several of an undescribed species of Phycis, I was struck by the resemblance of some Crustacea that I obtained, to the *Paradoxus boltoni,* figured and described in the fourth volume of the Journal of the Academy of Natural Science of Philadelphia. On referring to that work, which I fortunately had on board, I was convinced that this animal came nearer to the long lost family of Trilobites than any thing hitherto discovered. They were scarcely more than an inch in length, and most of them partially decomposed. That part which particularly attracted my attention, was the lu-

EXPLANATION OF THE PLATES.

Plate I.

Figure 1. Superior view of the animal, natural size
Inferior, do do do

Plate II.

1. Head deprived of appendages.
2. A transverse section, through the first articulation after the head.
3. Mandible with the Palpus.
4. Maxillae. a. superior. b. inferior.
5. Tongue.
6. Labium.
7. Branchial appendages.*
8. Paradoxus Boltoni.

* From 3 to 7, enlarged.

Plate I.

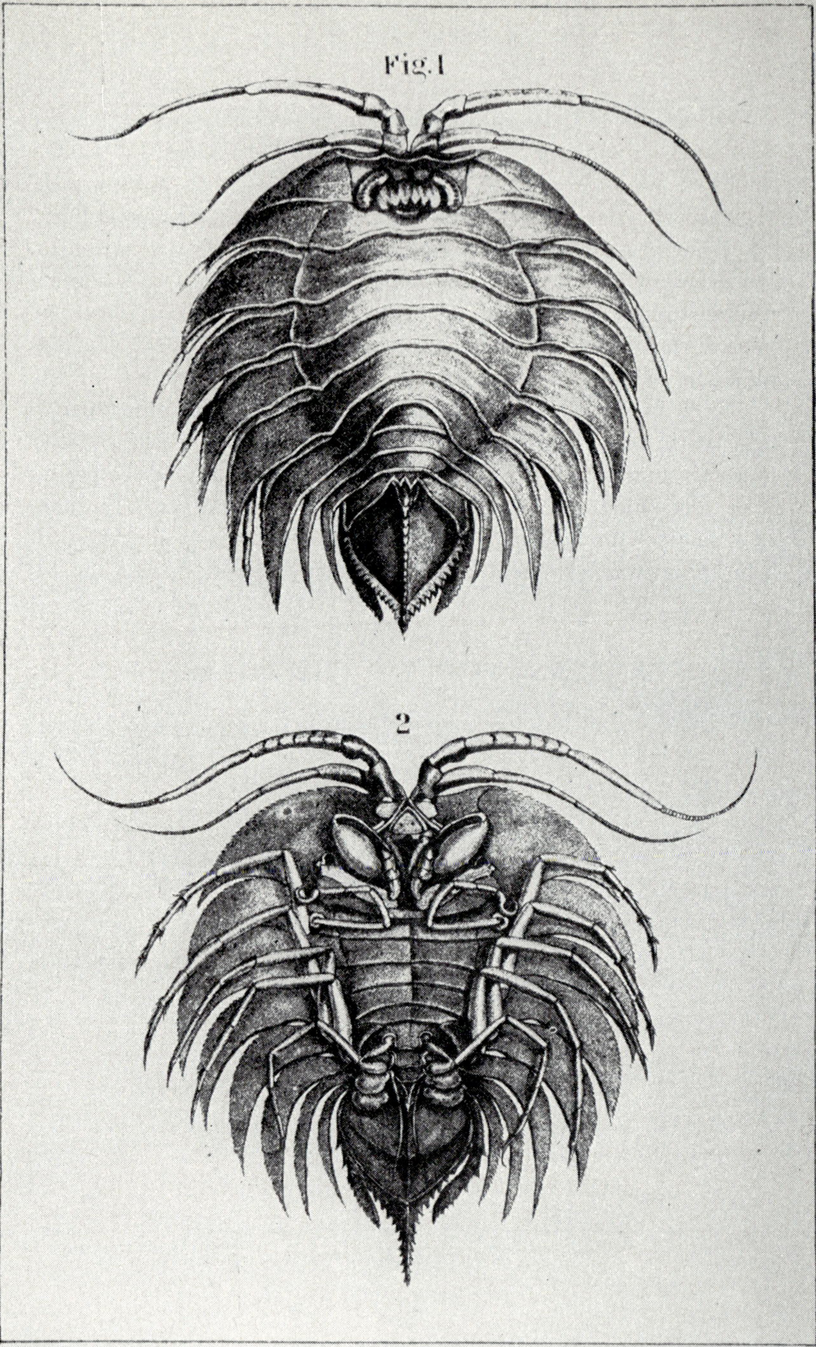

James Eights, del.

Pendletons Lith.

Plate II.

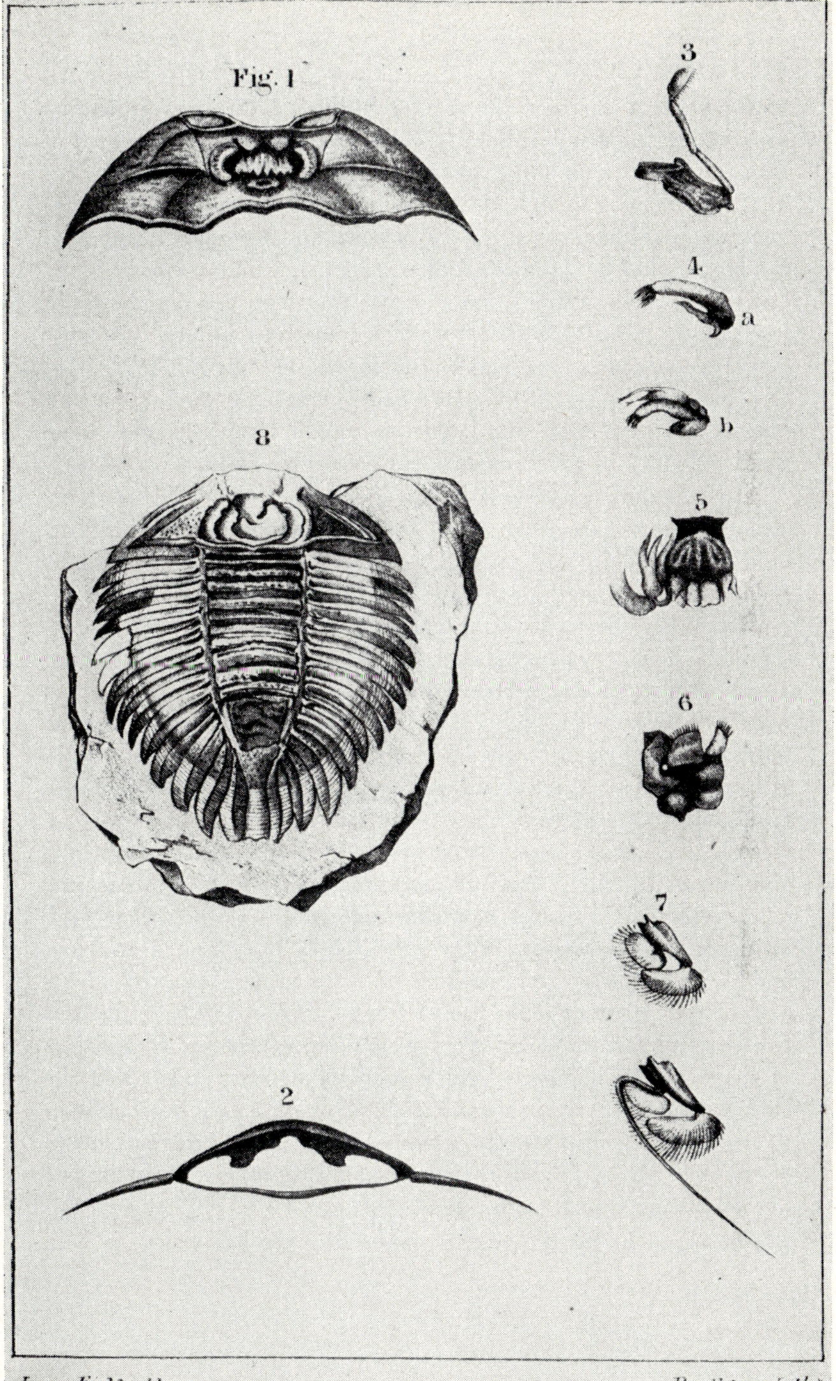

James Eights, del.

Pendletons Lith.

nate markings on the head of Dr. Bigsby's figure, corresponding in a wonderful manner, both in form and situation, to the eyes of this animal, although the fossil is represented as being deficient in these organs. In fact, I think it doubtful if any of the trilobites were destitute of eyes, the circumstance of their never having been found in some of the few fragments that we possess any knowledge of, is certainly no evidence that they did not exist. In some of the Crustacea that I collected in the southern ocean the eyes are extremely small and situated on the external margin of the head, very near to its edge: had but a small portion of this part of the shell been mutilated, we should have been put to no small difficulty in assigning to them organs of vision.

After landing at several places along the coast and spending some days at Staaten Land, we proceeded to the new South-Shetland islands, which are situated between 61 and 63° of south latitude, and west longitude 54 and 63. They are formed by an extensive cluster of rocks rising abruptly from the ocean, to a considerable height above its surface. Their true elevation cannot easily be determined, in consequence of the heavy masses of snow which lie over them, concealing them almost entirely from the sight. Some of them however, rear their glistening summits to an altitude of about three thousand feet, and when the heavens are free from clouds, imprint a sharp and well defined outline upon the intense blueness of the sky: they are divided every where by straits and indented by deep bays, or coves, many of which afford to vessels a comfortable shelter from the rude gales to which these high latitudes are so subject. When the winds have ceased to blow and the ocean is at rest, nothing can exceed the beautiful clearness of the atmosphere in these elevated regions. The numerous furrows and ravines which every where impress the snowy acclivity of the hills, are distinctly visible for fifty or sixty miles, and the various sea-fowl, resting upon the slight eminences and brought in strong relief against the sky, ofttimes deceive the experienced eye of the mariner by having their puny dimensions magnified in size to those of the human form.

The ocean in the vicinity, as far as the eye has vision, is here and there studded with ice bergs, varying in magnitude from a few feet to more than a mile in extent, and not unfrequently rising two hundred feet in the air, presenting every variety of form, from the snug whitewashed cottage of the peasant, to the enormous architectural pile, containing either broadly expanded Grecian domes, or having the many lofty and finely attenuated spires of some Gothic structure.

The sun, even at midsummer, attains but a moderate altitude in these dreary regions, and when its horizontal beams illumine these masses of ice, their numerous angles and indentations catching the light as they move along, exhibit all the beautiful gradations of colour from an emerald green to that of the finest blue. Some of them whose sloping sides will admit of their ascent, are tenanted by large assemblages of Penguins, whose chattering noise may be heard on a still day at an incredible distance over the clear smooth surface of the sea. When the storms rage and the ocean rolls its mountain wave against their slippery sides, the scene is truly sublime. Tall columns of spray shooting up far above their tops, soon become dissipated in clouds of misty white; gradually descending, they envelope the whole mass for a short space of time, giving to it much the appearance of being covered with a veil of silvery gauze. When thus agitated they not unfrequently explode with the noise of thunder, scattering their fragments far and wide over the surrounding surface of the deep. These hills of ice are borne onwards at a considerable rate by the power of the wind and the velocity of the current—when so, they sweep along with a majesty that nothing else can equal.

The sky too in these latitudes presents a very singular aspect; being, most generally filled with innumerable clouds, torn into ragged and irregular patches by the wild gales which every where race over the Antarctic seas: the sun as it rises or sets, slowly and obliquely in the southern horizon, sends its rays through the many openings between, tinging them here and there with every variety of hue and colour, from whence they are thrown in mild and beautiful reflections upon the extensive fields of snow which lie piled on the surrounding hills, giving to the whole scene for a greater part of the long summer day, the ever varying effect of a most gorgeous sunset.

Although many of the scenes about these islands are highly exciting, the effect produced on the mind by their general aspect is cold and cheerless to an unusual degree, for on their lonely shores the voice of man is seldom heard: the only indication of his ever having trod the soil, is the solitary grave of some poor seaman near the beach, and the only wood that any where meets the eye, are the staves that mark its dimensions; no sound for years disturbs the silence of the scene, save the wild screech of the sea-birds as they wing their way in search of their accustomed food—the incessent chattering of the congregated Penguins—the rude blasts, tearing among the icy hills—the sullen roar of the waves, tumbling and dashing along the shores, or the heavy explosions of the large masses of snow falling into the waves beneath, to form the vast ice-bergs which every where drift through the southern ocean.

The shores of these islands are generally formed by perpendicular cliffs of ice frequently reaching for many miles, and rising from ten feet, to several hundred in height. In many places at their base, the continued action of the water has worn out deep caves with broadly arched roofs, under which the ocean rolls its wave with a subterranean sound that strikes most singularly on the ear, and when sufficiently undermined, extensive portions crack off with an astounding report, creating a tremendous surge in the sea below, which as it rolls over its surface, sweeps every thing before it, from the smallest animal that feeds on its shallow bottom, to those of the greatest bulk. Entire skeletons of the whale, fifty or sixty feet in length, are not unfrequently found in elevated situations along the shores many feet above the high water line, and I know of no other cause capable of producing this effect. Whales are very common in this vicinity, and in calm weather great numbers of them may be seen breaking the surface of the ocean in the many intervals which occur between its numerous ice-bergs, sometimes sending forth volumes of spray, at others, elevating their huge flukes in the air to descend head first, as it were, to fathom the ocean's depth. When they perish either from accident or some more natural cause, their carcasses in drifting towards the shore are overtaken by these billows and thrown thus far upon the land, here they are left by the retiring wave, and in a few hours their bones become perfectly denuded by the numberless sea-birds that feed upon the flesh. It is after these waves have subsided that the animal here described, together with several other equally interesting crustacea may be obtained in considerable numbers.

The geological features that these islands present in those highly favored situations, where the continuous power of the winds has swept bare the rocks, correspond in a great measure with their desolate and dreary aspect. They are composed principally of vertical columns of basalt, resting upon strata of argillaceous conglomerate; the pillars are united in detached groups, having at their bases sloping banks constructed of materials which are constantly accumulating by fragments from above. These groups rise abruptly from the irregularly elevated plains, over whose surface they are scattered here and there, presenting an appearance to the eye not unlike some old castle crumbling into ruin, and when situated upon the sandstone promontories that occasionally jut out into the sea, they tower aloft in solitary grandeur over its foaming waves; sometimes they may be seen piercing the superincumbent snow, powerfully contrasting their deep murky hues with its spotless purity. Ponds of fresh water are now and then found on the plains, but they do not owe their origin to springs, being formed by the melting of the snow.

The rocky shores of these islands are formed by bold craggy eminences standing out into the sea at different distances from each other, from whose bases dangerous reefs not unfrequently lie out for several miles in extent, rendering it necessary for navigators to keep a cautious watch, after making any part of this coast: the intervals between these crags are composed of narrow strips of plain, constructed of coarsely angulated fragments of every variety of size, which at some previous period have fallen from the surrounding hills. They slope gradually down to the water terminating in a fine sandy beach: a few rounded pieces of granite are occasionally to be seen lying about, brought unquestionably by the ice-bergs from their parent hills on some far more southern land, as we saw no rocks of this nature in situ on these islands. In one instance, I obtained a boulder nearly a foot in diameter from one of these floating hills. The action of the waves has produced little or no effect upon the Basalt along this coast, as its angles retain all the acuteness of a recent fracture, but when the conglomerate predominates, the mass is generally rounded.

The ocean about these shores is generally of great depth, the materials which constitute its bottom are finely comminuted particles having their origin from the decomposition of the neighbouring rocks. Our stay at these islands occupied a period of four weeks, during which time we observed but one ebb and flow of the tide in twenty-four hours. I know not if this be universal, but have been informed by mariners familiar in these seas, that they have generally found it so; if it should prove to be the case, it is a very singular phenomenon.

Not a day occurred that snow did not fall or ice make on our decks, and during the time we spent between the latitudes of 60 and 70° south, and 54 & 101 west longitude, which was more than two months, we found the current setting with considerable velocity from the south-west to the north-east. The prevailing winds were also westerly, most commonly from the south-west and north-west.

The colour of the basalt is generally of a greenish black. The prisms are from four to nine sided, most commonly however of but six, and from three to four feet in diameter; their greatest length in an upright position above the subjacent conglomerate is about eighty feet. Their external surfaces are closely applied to each other, though but slightly united, consequently they are continually falling out by the expansive power of the congealing water among its fissures. When they are exposed to the influence of the atmosphere for any length of time, they are for a small depth of a rusty brown colour, owing no doubt to the iron which they contain becoming partially oxydized: sometimes they are covered by a thin coating of quartz and chalcedony.

Clusters of these columns are occasionally seen reposing on their side in such a manner as to exhibit the surfaces of their base distinctly, which is rough and vesicular. When this is the case they are generally bent, forming quite an arch with the horizon. When they approach the conglomerate for ten or twelve feet, they lose their columnar structure and assume the appearance of a dark coloured flinty slate, breaking readily into irregular rhombic fragments: this fine variety in descending, gradually changes to a greenish colour and a much coarser structure, until it passes into a most perfect amygdaloid, the cavities being chiefly filled with quartz, amethyst, and chalcedony. Sometimes an interval of about forty or fifty feet occurs between these columns, which space is occupied by the amorphous variety elevated to some considerable height against them, their edges in this case are not at all changed by the contact.

The basalt is very tough and hard, the effect produced upon it by the action of the file is very slight: the steel elicits no sparks: the fragments are angular with an imperfect conchoidal fracture: its structure is coarsely granular and uneven, and is composed essentially of hornblende, feldspar, and a greenish substance in grains much resembling epidote: crystals of leucite of a yellow and reddish tinge are disseminated throughout the mass whose fractured surfaces strongly reflect the rays of light to the eye: in some places it sensibly affects the needle, owing no doubt to its iron. Veins of quartz frequently traverse the fine variety, some of them containing beautiful amethysts.

The basis rock of these islands, as far as I could discover, is the conglomerate which underlies the basalt. It is composed most generally of two or three layers, about five feet in thickness each, resting one on the other and dipping to the south east at an angle of from twelve to twenty degrees. These layers are divided by regular fissures into large rhombic tables, many of which appear to have recently fallen out, and now lie scattered all over the sloping sides of the hills, so that the strata when seen cropping out from beneath the basalt, present a slightly arched row of angular projections of some considerable magnitude and extent.

These strata are chiefly composed of irregular and angular fragments of a rock, whose principal ingredient appears to be green earth, arranged with both a granular and slaty structure, united by an argillaceous cement; the whole mass when moistened by the breath giving out a strong odour of that earth. The upper portion of this conglomerate for a few feet, is of a dirty green colour, and appears to be constructed by the passage of the amygdaloid into this rock, the greenish fragments predominating, and they are united to each other principally, by zeolite of a beautiful light red, or orange colour, together with some quartz and chalcedony; a few crystals of lime cause it to effervesce slightly in some places. These minerals seem in a great measure to replace the earthy cement. In descending a few feet further, the green fragments gradually decrease in number and become comparatively rare, the minerals also give place to the cement until the whole mass terminates below in a fine argillaceous substance, with an imperfect slaty structure and a spanish-brown aspect.

This rock being much softer in its nature than the basalt and more affected by decomposing agents, the number of fragments are consequently greater in proportion, and much more finely pulverised, forming the little soil, which supports some of the scattered and scanty patches of the vegetation of these islands.

The minerals embraced in this rock are generally confined to its upper part where it unites and passes into the incumbent amygdaloid, many of them are also in common with that rock. They consist chiefly of quartz, crystalline and amorphous, amethyst, chalcedony, cachalong, agate, red jasper, felspar, zeolite, calcareous spar in rhombic crystals, sulphate of barytes, a minute crystal resembling black spinelle, sulphuret of iron and green carbonate of copper.

The only appearance of an organized remain that I any where saw, was a fragment of carbonized wood imbedded in this conglomerate. It was in a vertical position, about two and a half feet in length and four inches in diameter: its colour is black, exhibiting a fine ligneous structure, the concentric circles are distinctly visible on its superior end, it occasionally gives sparks with steel, and effervesces slightly in nitric acid.

There are a number of active volcanoes in the vicinity of these islands, indications of which are daily seen in the pieces of pumice found strewed along the beach. Capt. Weddel saw smoke issuing from the fissures of Bridgeman's island, a few leagues to the N. E. Palmers land, situated one degree south: what little is known of it, which is only a small portion of its northern shore, contains several. Deception island also, one of this group, has boiling springs, and a whitish substance like melted felspar, exudes from some of its fissures.

The rocky fragments on these islands are generally very hard and little liable to the disintegrating influence of the atmosphere, and rarely indeed are they subject to a power capable of agitating them sufficiently to remove even the acuteness of their angles, consequently but a small quantity of soil can any where be found, and when discovered, being destitute of the necessary ingredients that give fatness to the earth elsewhere, it affords but a few scattered patches of vegetation, which appear to struggle hard for the small portion of vitality they enjoy. The *Usnea fasciata,* Torrey,* is most common. A species of Polytrichum resembling the alpinum of Lin. one or two lichens and a fucus found in the sea, along the shores—when you add to these an occasional plant of a small species of avena, you complete the botanical catalogue of the islands.

The only vertebral animals ever observed on these islands are very few in number, and confined to the amphibia carnivora of Cuvier; all being embraced in the genus Phoca. The P. leonina, Lin. (sea elephant) is the largest of the species, sometimes attaining the length of twenty-five feet, and is regularly proportioned. These animals are remarkable for the powerful strength of their jaws. When attacked, and wounded in such a manner as to be unable to reach the sea, in the struggle, either through agony or rage, they not unfrequently take up considerable sized stones with their mouth, and break them into a number of fragments between their teeth: sometimes they seize upon the lance, breaking it instanta-

* Silliman's Journal, vol. 6, page 104. Imperfectly described in consequence of the badness of the specimen.

neously, or else, bending it in such a manner as to render it perfectly useless. The sea leopard is not so large, but is a far more beautiful animal. P. vitulina, Lin. (fur-seal.) This beautiful little animal was once most numerous, but was almost exterminated by the sealers at the time these islands were first discovered. There is also a fourth species, which I have no recollection of ever seeing the slightest notice of. It is probably not common, as I saw but one; it was standing on the extremities of its fore-feet, (flippers) the head and chest perfectly erect, abdomen curved and resting on the ground, the tail was also in an upright position: the animal in this attitude bore a striking resemblance to the representations we frequently meet with of the "mermaid," and I think it was undoubtedly one of the animals of this genus that first gave origin to the fable of the maid of the sea. I regret that I could not obtain a nearer view of this interesting animal. When I approached within one hundred feet, it threw itself flat and made rapidly for the sea: it appeared about twelve or fifteen feet in length, and distinctly more slender in proportion than any of the other species, so much so that the motion of the body when moving seemed perfectly undulating. Some of the seamen had seen them frequently on a former voyage, and mentioned that they were known among sealers by the name of sea-serpent, from this circumstance. Some of the teeth were brought to me which had been picked up on the beach. The crown of the grinders is deeply and singularly five lobed.

When these animals resort to the shores for the purpose of breeding or shedding their hair, they are in fine condition. During this time they require no food, existing by the absorption of their fatty matter: if killed at this period, you generally find a quantity of small stones in the stomach, swallowed most probably for the purpose of keeping that organ distended and preventing its internal surfaces from adhering to each other. When the season for returning to the sea arrives, these stones are ejected on the beach, and they proceed in search of their ordinary food, which is chiefly penguins. A singular character in the habit of these animals is the faculty they possess of shedding tears when in any way molested. The eyes becoming suffused and the large tear-drops chasing each other in quick succession over their wrinkled faces, creates quite a sympathy in the breast of the beholder. Of the Cetacea inhabiting the ocean among these islands, the Balaena physalis (fin whale) with a smooth belly, is very numerous: the B. mysticetus (right whale) is occasionally seen. The Grampus and Dolphins are quite common, and a species of Porpoise which I had not before seen, occurs in great numbers. From their appearance in the water their colour seemed dark, with a broad, somewhat waved white line, extending from the posterior and inferior part of the head, backward and upward to the dorsal fin: a second and similar one commences on the abdomen immediately below the termination of the first, and ends at the origin of the tail above: these marks are distinctly visible as they glide through the sea. They are called sea skunks by the sailors. I am told they are confined to high southern latitudes.

The birds which frequent these islands are much more numerous than any of the other classes of animals; of penguins there are five species. The Aptenodytes patagonica, Gm.* (king penguin) is the largest and by far the most beautiful of the species, and may be seen in great numbers covering the shores for some considerable extent. They are remarkably clean in their appearance, not a speck of any kind is suffered for a moment to sully the pure whiteness of the principal part of their plumage: their upright position, uniform cleanliness, and beautiful golden yellow cravat, contrasts finely with the dark back-ground by which they are relieved, so that the similitude is no unapt one, which compares them to a regiment of soldiers immediately after parade. The females lay but one egg on the bare ground, which is rather larger than that of a goose, and of about equal value as an article of food, but differs a little in shape, being more tapering at its smaller end. The egg lies between the feet, the tail being sufficiently long to

* For a further account of the animals and birds here mentioned, I must refer to the four voyages of Capt. B. Morrell, jr. and those of Capt. Edmund Fanning, two popular works recently published in New-York.

conceal it effectually from the sight. When approached they move from you with a waddling gait, rolling it along over the smooth surface of the ground, so that a person not acquainted with the fact might pass through hundreds of them without discovering it. The Spheniscus antarcticus, Shaw. (rookery penguin) is more numerous than any of the other species, assembling together in vast congregations, occupying the smooth strips of plain for a mile or more in extent; passing through them, they barely give you sufficient space, picking at your legs, and keeping up a continual chatter. Their whole appearance as you walk along, brings powerfully to your recollection the story of Gulliver, striding among the Lilliputians. The Chrysocoma saltator, C. torquata, C. catarractes, Shaw, are occasionally found along the beach, and scattered among the others. These birds swim with great velocity through the sea and may be seen several feet in depth shooting along in every direction, at short intervals rising to its surface, darting out and in again, at the same time, uttering a quick sound very similar to that produced by a single blast on a split quill. Phalacrocorax graculus, Shaw. Sterna hirundo ? Lin. Diomedea exulans, Lin. and fuliginosa, Lath. Daption capense—antarcticum—niveum, Shaw. Fulmarius giganteus, and antarcticus, Shaw, are all very common. Procellaria pelagica ? Lin. This is much smaller than any I observed in other parts of the ocean, and may probably prove a distinct species. Larus eburneus ? Gmel. Lestris catarractes, Tem. arc also common. Chionis Forsteri, Shaw. (sheath bill.) This is the white pigeon so often mentioned by mariners as inhabiting the islands of the southern ocean, it is easily caught by the hand, and soon becomes domesticated. We kept a number of them several days after leaving these islands, they ran about the decks of the vessel apparently without any disposition to leave them, feeding from the hand of any individual that offered them food.

The mollusca are very few, though unique. An interesting species of Pholas; a beautiful Nucula, and a fine Patella, neither of which I think have been described, comprise all that we saw.

The existence of a southern continent within the antarctic circle is, I conceive, a matter of much doubt and uncertainty, but that there are extensive groups, or chains of islands yet unknown, I think we have many indications to prove, and were I to express an opinion, I would say, that our course from the south Shetlands to the southwest, until we reached the 101° of west longitude, was at no great distance along the northern shores of one of these chains. The heavy clouds of mist which encircled us so often, could arise from no other cause than that of the influence of large quantities of snow or ice, on the temperature of the atmosphere: the hills of floating ice we encountered, could not form elsewhere than on the land. The drifting fuci we daily saw, grow only in the vicinity of rocky shores, and the penguins and terns, that were almost at all times about us, from my observation of their habits, I am satisfied, never leave the land at any great distance. During our cruize to the southwest above the 60° of south latitude, we found the current setting continually at a considerable rate towards the northeast, bearing the plants and ice along in its course, some of the latter embracing fragments of a rock, the existence of which, we could discover no where on the islands we visited. When the westerly winds drew toward the south, we were most generally enveloped in banks of fog, so dense that it was with difficulty we could distinguish objects at the distance of the vessel's length. When Palmer's land becomes properly explored, together with the known islands situated between the longitude of Cape Horn and that of Good Hope, I think they will prove to be the north eastern termination of an extensive chain, passing near where Capt. Cook's progress was arrested by the firm fields of ice in latitude 71°10′ s. and west longitude about 105°; had that skilful navigator succeeded in penetrating this mass of ice, he would unquestionably in a short time have made the land upon which it was formed. Capt. Weddel after passing the icy barrier to the east of the South Shetlands, succeeded in reaching the 74°15′ south, (the highest latitude ever attained by man,) and found in crossing this chain and progressing towards the south, that the sea became more free of ice, and the weather almost as mild as summer, evidently proving I think, that the south pole can be nearly approached, without incurring any great degree of hazard in the attempt. But for further information on the practicability of reaching the south pole, I must refer to the judicious remarks of Capt. Edmund Fanning of New-York, contained in his account of several voyages to the southern ocean, with which I perfectly coincide; and will conclude with the regret that the government of the United States, with a population whose daring enterprize has already carried our flag into the remotest corners of the globe, could not be induced to forward an expedition, the expense of which would little exceed that of a vessel doubling Cape Horn. They might thus settle this interesting question, and also determine with certainty the situation, magnitude, and extent of these lands, and by that means open a new source of revenue to the country in the oil and fur animals which must necessarily exist in these high southern regions.

NOTES

Sources for the Introduction

Calman, W. T., 1937. James Eights, a pioneer antarctic naturalist. *Proc. Linn. Soc. London, 149* (4) : 171–184.
Based in large part on Clarke (1916), with some additional material and a discussion of Eights' contributions to carcinology.

Clarke, J. M., 1916. The reincarnation of James Eights, antarctic explorer. *Sci. Monthly, 2* (2) : 189–202.
The principal source, including extensive quotes from Eights' description of the South Shetlands.

Martin, L., 1940. Early explorers of southern South America from the United States (Abstract). *Nature, 146:* 238–239.

Martin, L., 1940. Early explorations and investigations in southern South America and adjacent antarctic waters by mariners and scientists from the United States of America. *Congr. Rec., 86, Appendix:* 3194–3195.

Martin, L., 1943. Early explorations and investigations in southern South America and adjacent antarctic waters by mariners and scientists from the United States of America. *Section VII, Eighth Am. Sci. Congr.,* Washington, D. C. (1940) : 43–46.

On the Icebergs of the Ant-Arctic Sea

Published in 1846 in *American Quarterly Journal of Agriculture and Science;* vol. 4, no. 1, pp. 20–24.

In this paper the transport of rocks and animals by drifting ice is clearly discussed, and, apparently the term tabular is first used in reference to the characteristic shape of antarctic icebergs.

Description of a New Animal Belonging to the CRUSTACEA

Published in 1833 in *Transactions of the Albany Institute;* vol. 2, pp. 331–334.

This description was reprinted by J. D. Dana in the *American Journal of Science, Series 2;* vol. 22, no. 66, pp. 391–397, 1856. The description itself occupies pages 391–394; the rest of the reprint consists of selected paragraphs on the geology of the South Shetlands from Eights' first paper. It is curious, when it is remembered that Eights was passed over in favor of Dana for the Wilkes Expedition, that he seems to have been treated by Dana as if he were no longer alive, for no mention is made of him other than that he is the author of the material quoted. But Dana acknowledged the kindness of one Mr. J. E. Gavit, the engraver, for making the plates (drawn by Eights) available for reprinting!

There are a number of minor errors and changes in Dana's reprinting, and a line was omitted (apparently by the printer), so that the reprinted description is not exactly the same as the original version.

Glyptonotus ("sculpture back") is one of the common animals of shallow antarctic waters. It fills the ecological role that crabs do in temperate waters, being both predatory and a scavenger. Its voracious habits, however, mean that it should not be placed in aquaria with other study material. *Glyptonotus* belongs to the Idotheidae, and is related to the somewhat similar arctic *Mesidothea.* It is fitting that Eights' generic and specific names should still stand for this characteristic antarctic animal.

Description of a New Animal Belonging to the Arachnides of Latreille

Published in 1835 in *Boston Journal of Natural History;* vol. 1, no. 2, pp. 203–206.

There has been some confusion about the date of this paper, probably because most copies do not carry the front page with the 1834 date.

Decolopoda australis was the first member of the Colossendeidae to be described, but the genus *Colossendeis* was not described until 1874 and *Decolopoda* was not found again until 1905. In that same year J. C. C. Loman, the Dutch specialist in pycnogonids, considered *Decolopoda* a mistake, since by that time several hundred eight-legged pycnogonids had been described including several giant *Colossendeis* from the *Challenger* expedition. The French specialist E. L. Bouvier considered the extra legs of his specimens of *Decolopoda* from the French Antarctic Expedition an insignificant anomaly and at first assigned the specimens to *Colossendeis. Decolopoda* is one of several species of extra-legged pycnogonids related to the "normal" generic stocks *Colossendeis, Nymphon,* and *Pycnogonum.* Except for the added legs (and persistent chelae in *Decolopoda*) the forms are indistinguishable from those of the stem genera.

In 1931 a giant 12-legged form, the largest of all pycnogonids,

Dodecolopoda mawsoni (obviously related to *Decolopoda*) was found by the BANZAR Expedition in 219 m at 66°45′S, 62°03′E, and in 1959 the New Zealanders found another specimen in the Ross Sea. A third specimen was recently collected by the *Eltanin* in the Ross Sea in 1968. Another 12-legged pycnogonid, *Sexanymphon mirabilis,* was collected in deep water west of the South Shetlands by the *Eltanin* in 1962. Except for two species from the tropical western Atlantic, these polymerous pycnogonids are most characteristic of antarctic waters.

Eights evidently presented some of his material, including at least one specimen of *Decolopoda,* to the museum of the Boston Society of Natural History, from whence it found its way to the Museum of Comparative Zoology at Harvard. The single remaining specimen of *Decolopoda australis* at the M.C.Z. collected by Eights was designated Neoholotype No. 12271 by Fenner A. Chace some years ago.

Decolopoda australis is not a rare anomaly; every season several specimens are collected somewhere in the Antarctic and it ranges from South Georgia through the Ross Sea to Heard Island.

Description of a New Crustaceous Animal Found on the Shores of the South Shetland Islands

Published in 1833 in *Transactions of the Albany Institute;* vol. 2, no. 1, pp. 53–69.

Later Eights suspected that his *Brongniartia trilobitoides* was possibly a *Serolis,* and published a short note in 1852 (*Trans. Albany Inst., 2:* 354), commenting on the similarity. The species is now known as *Serolis trilobitoides* (Eights) (See E. Sheppard, *Discovery Reports, 7:* 326–329).

The record of king penguins in the South Shetlands, where they are unknown today, was accepted by R. C. Murphy in his *Oceanic Birds of South America.* Along with the frequent comments on falling ice, this record suggests a somewhat warmer temperature regime in the South Shetlands at the time of Eights' visit. Yet he does say that "not a day occurred that snow did not fall or ice make on our decks."

As Calman and others have noted, Eights evidently found the first plant fossils in Antarctica. Several of his bird, mammal, and plant names have been superseded; Calman makes some note of these, but they are for the most part obvious.

A Bibliography of James Eights' Writings

A complete bibliography of James Eights is not possible at this late date. Although he published comparatively little in his long lifetime, some of that was in the form of anonymous scientific and nature notes in a popular periodical called *The Zodiac*. Probably a fair amount of his writing was in the form of official reports published under the names of his superiors (e.g., see 1837, 1842). This listing is primarily from that of Calman (1937) with minor corrections. Publications not seen are indicated by an asterisk.

*1829. Specimens of a singular variety of quartz crystal from Palestine. Read before Lyceum of Natural History of New York. *Am. J. Sci., 16* (2) : 355.

1833. Description of a new crustaceous animal found on the shores of the South Shetland Islands, with remarks on their natural history. *Trans. Albany Inst., 2* (1) : 53–69.

1835. Description of a new animal belonging to the Arachnides of Latreille; discovered in the sea along the shores of the New South Shetland Islands. *Boston J. Nat. Hist., 1* (2) : 203–206.

*1835–6. (1) A synopsis of the rocks of the State of New York. (2) Notes of a pedestrian [geological notes on southeastern New York]. *Zodiac* (Albany, N. Y.), *1:* 27–28, 111–112, 113–116, 141–143, 146–147, 177–178.

*1837. First Annual Report of the Geological Survey of the 4th District of the State of New York. [Signed at end 'Lardner Vanuxem, State Geologist, James Eights, Assistant'.] In: *First Ann. Rept. Geol. Surv. New York, 1837;* pp. 187–212.

1842. Description [of *Sphaeroma bumastiformis*] furnished by Dr. James Eights. In: *Natural History of New York;* vol. iv, Geology, pt. 2, by E. Emmons, pp. 390, 433–434.

According to Calman, this isopod is *Exosphaeroma gigas* [Leach, 1818].

*1846. Outlines of the geological structure of Lake Superior mineral region belonging to the N. Y. and L. S. Mining Co. Albany, N. Y. 21 pp. (Appendix to first Amer. [? Ann.] Rept. of the Company)

1846. Notes on natural history. *Am. Quart. J. Agr. Sci., 3* (2) : 219–223.

1846. On the ice-bergs of the Ant-Arctic Sea. *Am. Quart. J. Agr. Sci., 4* (1) : 20–24.

1846. On the elevated temperature of the waters of the Gulf Stream. *Am. Quart. J. Agr. Sci., 4* (8) : 210–211.

1847. Notes on natural history. *Am. Quart. J. Agr. Sci., 5* (5) : 248–259.

This article concerns the natural history and geological formations of Patagonia. In large part it is based on Darwin's *Journal of Researches* (published in 1845), which is in fact mentioned by Eights. Some of the article appears to be direct quotation, other parts are paraphrase, of Darwin, but there is no specific indication of this usage, which in these times would be considered unethical.

It is interesting to note that there is less correspondence between the geological parts of this article and Darwin's observations than in the passages on natural history. Eights was more of a geologist by training than Darwin, and evidently depended more on his own notes in discussing geological formations. It would appear that they did not visit exactly the same localities. One also gets the impression, by comparing corresponding passages, such as those on phosphorescence in the sea, that Eights was a better seafarer than Darwin; certainly he preferred a more purple variety of prose and was making more of an effort to entertain his readers. This article was published years after the Wilkes' Expedition, and obviously had no bearing on the decision to leave Eights behind. I am indebted to Michael T. Ghiselin and Joseph G. Gregory for enlightening comments on this problem.

1852. Description of a new animal belonging to the Crustacea, discovered in the Antarctic Seas by the author. *Trans. Albany Inst., 2:* 331–334.

1852. Observations on the geological features of the Post-Tertiary formation of the city of Albany and its vicinity. *Trans. Albany Inst., 2:* 335–353.

1852. Explanation to Article IV in this volume. *Trans. Albany Inst., 2:* 354.

*1854. Report in relation to the Fisher Hill and Puckett mines in Guilford Co. N.C. Fisher Hill, N.C., 7 pp.

*1855. A report on the geological, mineralogical and other resources of the Hiatt tract of land, containing 2000 acres and situated in the county of Surry, N.C. Greensboro, N.C., 8 pp.

1856. Description of an isopod crustacean from the antarctic seas, with observations on the New South Shetlands. *Am. J. Sci., Ser. 2, 22* (66): 391–397.

*1858. North Carolina: its geology, mining regions, scenery . . . *Mining Mag. J. Geol. . . . New York and New Haven, 10* (3): 183–188; (4) 268–273; (5) 369–373; (6) 423–427.

The History of the Scientific Committee on Antarctic Research (SCAR)

LAURENCE M. GOULD

Department of Geology, College of Mines, The University of Arizona, Tucson

Though SCAR is but thirteen years old, its period of gestation goes back nearly a century. The seeds of international scientific cooperation in high southern latitudes goes back to the year of the transit of Venus, 1874–1875. In that year France, Germany, the United Kingdom, and the United States set up observatories in the Subantarctic to study the phenomena characteristic of this polar area.

In 1882–1883 the first International Polar Year was born. Most of the activities were confined to the arctic and subantarctic regions. During the second International Polar Year in 1932–1933 major activities again took place in the Arctic with Argentine scientists carrying on observations on subantarctic islands.

As originally conceived, International Polar Years were to be organized at fifty-year intervals. However, there had been such great progress in the geophysical science since 1933 that it seemed wise not to wait that long but hold another International Polar Year in 1957–1958. Solar activity would be near its maximum then whereas it had been near its minimum in 1932–1933.

In 1950 a formal proposal was placed before the International Council of Scientific Unions (ICSU) "that the third International Polar Year be nominated for 1957–1958 and that in view of the length of time necessary for adequate organization of the complex physical equipment now potentially available, an International Polar Year Commission be appointed in 1951 to supervise planning." The resolution was approved and the Special Committee was convened in 1952. The World Meteorological Organization (not a member of ICSU) was invited to participate and wisely pointed out that the concept be extended to include the entire earth. The suggestion was warmly received and thus what was to be the third International Polar Year became a much greater enterprise—The International Geophysical Year (IGY), which Hugh Odishaw, Executive Secretary of the United States National Committee, has aptly called "the greatest peacetime activity in man's history." ICSU created a special committee to organize and manage the IGY—Comité Special de l'année Geophysique Internationale (CSAGI). The first CSAGI Antarctic Conference was held in Paris, July 6 to 10, 1955, with representatives from the nations which planned to mount antarctic programs. Ing.-Gén. G. R. Laclavére was elected President, and in his opening remarks emphasized the technical character of the conference, excluding problems of finance and politics. Tensions due to overlapping political claims in Antarctica which had been evident were laid to rest by Gen. Laclavére's pronouncements and the following motion was unanimously adopted: "The Antarctic Conference entirely endorses M. Laclavére's statement of purposes of the opening session, and specifically his affirmation that the overall aims of the Conference are entirely scientific."

This attitude was the guiding light throughout the IGY and has distinguished the continuing international activities in Antarctica ever since. It was this highly successful scientific cooperation which led to the creation of the Antarctic Treaty.

Working groups were formed for several disciplines with special emphasis on logistics and communications.

The recommendations of the conference led to the location of sites of the new scientific stations occupied by the various participating countries.

Three further CSAGI Antarctic Conferences were held, with the last in Paris, June 13 to 15, 1957, at which final arrangements were made for the IGY.

Fifty-five stations, including some already established by Argentina, Chile, and the United Kingdom in the Antarctic Peninsula carried out programs under the administration of the following 12 participating nations: Argentina, France, Australia, Belgium, Chile, Japan, New Zealand, Norway, South Africa, United Kingdom, United States, and the Soviet Union.

It was clear at the last CSAGI Antarctic Conference, which preceded the official opening of the IGY on July 1st by only a few weeks, that a single "year," even eighteen months long, would do little more than permit the scientists to scratch the surface of man's ignorance of Antarctica. It was, therefore, recommended at this fourth CSAGI Antarctic Conference that the Executive Board of ICSU set up an ad hoc committee to examine the merits of further general scientific investigations in Antarctica. The committee met in Stockholm in September, 1957, and resolved that there was a need for continuing international organization of scientific activity in Antarctica. They recommended that ICSU should establish a committee to undertake this task. The Special Committee on Antarctic Research (SCAR) was to consist of delegates from each nation actively engaged in antarctic research and representatives of various scientific committees, which would have overlapping interests in antarctic scientific activity. The first meeting of the Special Committee on Antarctic Research was held at The Hague, February 3 to 5, 1958, and here the foundations were laid from which the committee has developed and which changed its name in 1961 to Scientific Committee on Antarctic Research.

The following business was transacted at that first meeting:

1. A constitution was formed and adopted which was later ratified at the Eighth General Assembly of ICSU in October, 1958.
2. A president, vice president, and secretary were elected.
3. A budget was framed for the work of the committee and a finance committee was appointed.
4. A plan for the scientific exploration of Antarctica in the years following the IGY was prepared. This plan has been amended from time to time as the scope of scientific activities in Antarctica has increased.
5. It was agreed that for the purposes of SCAR Antarctica shall be bounded by the Antarctic Convergence. In addition certain subantarctic islands, which lie outside the Antarctic Convergence, are to be included in SCAR's area of interest.
6. Three working groups were formed for special disciplines of antarctic activity.

In the approved constitution SCAR is described as "a scientific committee of ICSU charged with furthering the coordination of scientific activity in Antarctica with a view to framing a scientific program of circumpolar scope and significance."

SCAR ORGANIZATION AND PROGRAMS

Membership

SCAR membership falls into four categories:

1. One scientific delegate from each country actively engaged in antarctic research; to be "actively engaged" involves wintering-over operations. There are 12 member countries: Argentina, Australia, Belgium, Chile, France, Japan, New Zealand, Norway, South Africa, United Kingdom, United States, and the Soviet Union.
2. One representative from each of the scientific unions federated in ICSU which has indicated its interest in antarctic research.
3. The World Meteorological Organization, which is not a member of ICSU.
4. In addition, interested international organizations and committees of ICSU may be invited to designate observers to attend the meetings.

Operating Procedures

The Executive Committee of SCAR consists of the president, vice president, and secretary. It is responsible to ICSU for the coordination of the scientific programs adopted by SCAR. In the operation of SCAR from the beginning, the secretary is in effect the executive officer.

The SCAR constitution provides that participating countries will be invited to form national antarctic committees for their respective national programs. All twelve nations have created such committees or have assigned SCAR duties to existing committees. In the United States the responsible participating committee is the Committee on Polar Research of the National Academy of Sciences which, as indicated by its name, is responsible for planning scientific programs not only in the Antarctic but in the Arctic as well.

The bulk of the work of SCAR is carried out through its working groups. Three such groups were organized at the first meeting of SCAR. Since that time this number has been increased to 12 as follows: biology, communication, geodesy, cartography, geology, geomagnetism, glaciers, logistics, meteorology, oceanography, solid-earth geophysics, and upper atmosphere physics.

Normally each national committee nominates a member for each working group. In addition, at the Santiago meeting in 1966 it was recommended that a group composed of members of other working groups be established to investigate the use of space vehicles in antarctic research.

Most of the business of the working groups is conducted by correspondence and for this reason the secretaries of the various groups play key roles. They are expected to see that the work of their various groups progresses satisfactorily and three months in advance of a SCAR meeting they report to the Secretary of SCAR on progress being made and plans for the future.

The working groups have the principal responsibility in the whole program of SCAR because the SCAR scientific programs in Antarctica are a composite of the various programs being conducted there. Meetings of the various working groups are normally held in conjunction with plenary sessions or executive committee meetings of SCAR. In addition to the normal exchange of information and other business, working groups are responsible for the organization of symposia in their various fields. Such symposia are usually but not necessarily held along with SCAR meetings.

International Weather Central

During the International Geophysical Year an antarctic weather central was established at Little America. After the IGY the station was moved to Melbourne, Australia, and reformed as the International Antarctic Analysis Center under the sponsorship of SCAR, with the assistance of the Australian Bureau of Meteorology. The center provided operational forecasts and supported meteorological research. Early in 1966 the Southern Hemisphere analysis center of the World's Meteorological Organizations World Weather Watch took over the operational functions of the center. The center continues its activities under the name of the International Antarctic Meteorological Research Center.

Finances

From its beginning SCAR has operated on a very modest budget, most of which is derived from annual assessments made upon member nations. The amount of the assessment depends on the size of the wintering-over party and ranges from a low of $500 to $1,000 for Argentina, the United States, and the Soviet Union.

This provides an income of $15,000 per year which fortunately has been supplemented from time to time by the treasury of ICSU.

Meetings

In addition to the organization meeting at The Hague in February, 1958, a second meeting was held in Moscow in August of the same year. After 1958, meetings were held annually as follows: Canberra—March, 1959; Cambridge—August–September, 1960; Wellington—October, 1961; Boulder, Colorado—August, 1962; Cape Town—September, 1963; and Paris—August, 1964.

It was decided at the Paris meeting that in the future full plenary sessions would be held every two years with the Executive Committee meeting in alternate years. The ninth plenary session was held in Santiago, Chile, in September, 1966, and the tenth in Tokyo in 1968. The eleventh meeting was held in Norway in 1970. Meetings of the Executive Committee are held in Cambridge, England, at the Scott Polar Research Institute.

Scientific Meetings

A *Symposium on Antarctic Research* was held in Wellington, New Zealand, February, 1958, to provide scientists just returning from Antarctica an opportunity to discuss informally the first phase of the IGY. Ninety-three scientists attended and 52 papers were presented covering current scientific programs and plans for future antarctic reseach. There were no formal publications of the proceedings of this symposium.

A second comprehensive *Antarctic Symposium* was held in Buenos Aires in November, 1959, at the invitation of the Argentine government. It was a natural sequel to the Wellington symposium and enabled scientists to discuss the results of the IGY which had ended on December 31, 1958. Fifty scientists, including representatives from all the SCAR nations, attended and presented 188 papers.

A *Symposium on Antarctic Meteorology* was held in Melbourne in February, 1959, under the aegis of the Australian Commonwealth Bureau of Meteorology supported by the Australian Academy of Science, CSAGI, and SCAR. Seven sessions dealing with particular subjects provided the most comprehensive coverage of antarctic meteorology and its problems for continuing research that had ever been held. *Antarctic Meteorology*, including copies of papers presented and summaries of discussions, was published by Pergamon Press, London, in 1960.

Following this pattern symposia have been organized by SCAR as follows: *Logistics,* Boulder, Colorado, August, 1962; *Biology* (in conjunction with International Union of Biological Sciences) in Paris, September, 1962; *Geology* (in conjunction with International Union of Geological Sciences) in Cape Town, September, 1963; *Polar Meteorology* (in conjunction with World Meteorological Organization and International Association for Meteorology and Atmospheric Physics) Geneva, September, 1966; *Antarctic Oceanography* (in conjunction with Scientific Committee on Oceanographic Research, International Union of Biological Sciences, and the International Association of Physical Oceanography, International Union of Geodesy and Geophysics) Santiago, Chile, September, 1966; Second *Biology Symposium on Antarctic Ecology,* Cambridge, July–August, 1968; *International Symposium on Antarctic Glaciological Exploration* (in conjunction with U.S. Army Center for Terrestrial Sciences, Dartmouth College, and Commission on Snow and Ice of the International Association of Scientific Hydrology), Hanover, N.H., September, 1968; and *Antarctic Geology and Solid-Earth Geophysics,* Oslo, Norway, August, 1970.

Publications

SCAR publishes a bulletin three times a year, in January, May, and September, which is printed in the *Polar Record* by the Scott Polar Research Institute of Cambridge, England. In addition it is available in reprint form, and a Spanish edition is published by the Argentine Antarctic Institute. The bulletin contains news of SCAR meetings and activities, short articles on matters of general interest, and abstracts of papers delivered at SCAR symposia. From time to time SCAR also sponsors the publication of its symposia.

Science is no respecter of political boundaries, and SCAR has played an important role in all of the international scientific projects involving worldwide observation. It is particularly concerned with the coordination of these programs in Antarctica and with overcoming the problems peculiar to the region. Since the International Geophysical Year, SCAR has been interested in the antarctic contributions to such projects as the International Years of the Quiet Sun, the World Magnetic Survey, the Upper Mantle Project, the International Biological Program, and the International Hydrological Decade.

The SCAR recommendations are transmitted by members to their respective national antarctic committees and scientific unions for study. These are referred to national committees and forwarded to appropriate scientific bodies or government agencies in the development of their national antarctic programs.

SCAR recommendations are advisory and not binding either on scientific organizations or government.

Relations to Antarctic Treaty

The Antarctic Treaty was the first such document in history formed to protect a scientific program, namely that coordinated by SCAR. It is, therefore, natural that the Treaty Organization and SCAR should have a close relationship. This has worked out well since many of the objectives of the treaty, such as the exchange of information and personnel and encouragement of cooperative working relations with organizations having scientific or technical interests in Antarctica, parallel those of SCAR.

It has become the practice for meetings of SCAR to make recommendations to the Treaty Organization concerning subjects appropriate to their responsibilities. At each of their meetings the treaty powers have generously acknowledged their debt to SCAR and its working groups. This has been particularly true in the fields of scientific exchanges, logistics, communications, and especially conservation. The last is one of the most productive results of the friendly cooperation between SCAR and the Treaty Organization. At its third consultative meeting the Treaty Organization adopted a series of agreed measures based on SCAR recommendations on the important subject of conservation.

Because of its non-governmental status, SCAR and its various working groups provide an easy mechanism through which representatives of the national antarctic committees and international scientific unions can meet informally and discuss freely the problems involved. They have been able to make adjustments and arrive at recommendations that have been both reasonable and effective.

The best characterization of SCAR which I know of was made by Dr. Henry M. Dater of the History and Research Division of U. S. Naval Support Force, Antarctica, in a report to the Commanding Admiral of Task Force 43, in April, 1967:

> Much of the success of SCAR has resulted from the character and stability of its membership and that of its

working groups. Included are most of the world's leading experts in Antarctic affairs, both scientific and logistic. For 10 years they have met together frequently and have established an air of mutual respect and confidence. Many of them, because of their positions in their respective national organizations or international scientific bodies, can powerfully affect decisions. The influence of SCAR lies, therefore, not in the authority of the organization itself, but in the authority of its members. SCAR plays a part in Antarctic affairs that transcends its unofficial character, limited budget, restricted activities, and purely advisory functions.

OFFICERS OF SCAR

President

1958–1963	G. R. Laclavére, *France*
1963–1970	L. M. Gould, *U.S.*
1970–	G. deQ. Robin, *U.K.*

Vice President

1958–1962	K. E. Bullen, *Australia*
1962–1968	R. N. Panzarini, *Argentina*
1968–	C. A. Avsiuk, *U.S.S.R.*

Secretary

1958–1958	V. Schytt, *Sweden*
1958–1970	G. deQ. Robin, *U.K.*
1970–	R. W. WILLETT, *N.Z.*

The Antarctic Treaty

T. O. JONES

National and International Programs, National Science Foundation, Washington, D.C.

Science does not come immediately to mind as a prime consideration in international relations, but in Antarctica science has been the lever which pried loose a peaceful solution of national rivalries.

A brief review of the history of Antarctica over the past thirty years should help us to see how science has aided in bringing national aspirations into closer international harmony. When World War II broke out, the Antarctic was being rapidly cut up like a great pie by the interested powers—Argentina, Australia, Chile, France, New Zealand, Norway, and the United Kingdom—which had claimed wedges of antarctic territory. Belgium, Germany, and Japan all possessed potential rights by exploration. The Soviet Union, long preoccupied with the development of its hinterland and with European politics, indicated that its interests must be considered in reaching a settlement in Antarctica. The United States continued publicly not to recognize the territorial claims of other countries and to reserve its territorial rights in accordance with the policy, first enunciated by Secretary of State Charles Evans Hughes in 1924, that:

> The discovery of lands unknown to civilization, even when coupled with a formal taking of possession, does not support a valid claim to sovereignty unless the discovery is followed by an actual settlement of the discovered country.

Those concerned with antarctic affairs wondered whether or not the United States could long maintain this position.

World War II served only to further the disintegration of the integrity of Antarctica as a *terra nulla.* German military activities in antarctic waters showed how operations around Antarctica could dominate portions of the southern sea routes, particularly in the region of the Drake Passage. The United Kingdom's moves to counter German activities and the inevitable rivalry with Argentina over these areas further complicated the problem. Only the preoccupation of the European powers in recovering from World War II allowed the antarctic problem to recede.

The United States in the decade after 1945 hoped to resolve its own dilemma on a proper stance in Antarctica by seeking some international solution to the problem. One object was the peaceful settlement of differences among the involved nations and another was freedom of access to carry on scientific investigations. Discussions with leaders in antarctic activities, including Laurence M. Gould, indicated that in the foreseeable future, the main resource in Antarctica would be its location as a site for fundamental research on geophysical problems. In the meantime, the United States undertook major expeditionary activities, such as *Operation Highjump* and *Operation Windmill,* under the leadership of Rear Admiral Richard E. Byrd and others.

These efforts carried U.S. aerial explorers over much of Antarctica. The prospect that these efforts would develop international accord or resolve the dilemma of our stance regarding a claim, however, did not presage success. Other governments with antarctic territorial interests were, at this time, reluctant to enter into international agreements on Antarctica as they were suspicious of U.S. intentions. Much of the force behind the U.S. expeditions came from the personal zeal of a few explorers, while the general attitude was one of indifference. It was obvious that something was needed which would develop a wider scale of interest in antarctic affairs in the United States—something which would create a national purpose to support a long-term presence in Antarctica and provide sufficient cause and reason to finance and support antarctic activities. The International Geophysical Year (IGY) did just this.

In the perspective of more than a decade since the IGY ended, we can see clearly that the significance of the IGY in Antarctica was the commitment of national resources to the exploration of the continent and the opportunity it provided to obtain international accord on certain vital questions. The allotted time for the IGY was too short to do more than begin the exploration of Antarctica, but the national expeditions to which governments committed themselves for the IGY continue today, twelve years later. Vicissitudes of budgets forced Belgium, Japan, and Norway to close their stations. Japan, however, was able to return in 1965 after a new capital commitment of millions of dollars to modernize its transport and the station. Norwegian parties took to the field in 1968–1969 for the first time since 1959. The Belgians still hope to reopen their station. None intend to drop out permanently. All of the other countries which participated in the IGY have expanded their efforts to varying degrees over the last ten years. Antarctica has become an item of national policy for all these countries. It is no longer just a dream in the mind of explorers.

The IGY Antarctic Program was the first large-scale international effort in which the needs of science dominated the relationships among the governments concerned. The scientific forum became the vehicle to reach accord on several critical non-scientific matters. The chief coordinating group was the Antarctic Committee of the Special Committee for the International Geophysical Year of the International Council of Scientific Unions (ICSU).

In this forum, scientific representatives spoke for their respective scientific communities with the tacit consent of their governments. The desire for a better understanding of our earth assumed ascendancy over the more parochial and divisive national objectives which had previously dominated antarctic affairs.

The critical issues on which accord was achieved were:

1. The distribution of stations
2. The meteorological telecommunications network
3. The exchange of data, results, and personnel
4. Freedom of movement to pursue scientific programs

These issues were contentious if approached from the point of view of national interest. But scientific requirements provided a neutral ground on which to discuss them. Thus, for scientific reasons the Soviet Union and the United States resolved the matter of occupancy of the geographic and geomagnetic poles. New Zealand and the United States found *modus operandi* on Ross Island and at Hallett Station. The Australians accepted, albeit guardedly, the presence of Soviet stations in East Antarctica. A network of radio stations and procedures were agreed upon for the relay of scientific traffic and the great volume of meteorological data needed for operational purposes in particular. Although these arrangements were never embodied in any formal agreement, the present-day array of antarctic stations remains basically the same. Changes that have occurred have been dictated by the requirements of science and the need to make possible the exploration of the remaining unknown areas. The communications network has survived with only a few changes and has become a recognized system within the World Meteorological Organization.

The exchange of certain data and results was actually formalized into a series of ICSU agreements, while freedom of movement of scientists was assumed as a principle and observed as a matter of tacit consent.

The importance of the settlement of these matters in the Special Committee for the International Geophysical Year forum can be seen when one considers the Washington Treaty Conference of 1959. Insofar as the United States was concerned, the IGY had dramatically allowed a change in the U.S. position with respect to Antarctica. It provided a comparatively long period (1955 to 1959) of widespread U.S. presence not dependent upon the efforts of a single explorer or upon military ventures. Scientific exploration brought in a clientele with a legitimate long-term interest plus regularized financial and management support through the National Science Foundation. The erosion of rights which had worried the normally nationalistic planners and policymakers since 1939 had stopped and the United States found itself in an advantageous position as the IGY came to an end.

Pursuing the efforts begun in 1947 to find an international solution for Antarctica, and encouraged by a parallel interest on the part of the British Commonwealth, the United States issued an invitation in 1958 to the IGY nations involved in Antarctica to meet in Washington in 1959 to negotiate a treaty for Antarctica.

The text of the note delivered on May 2, 1958, to the other IGY antarctic nations stressed heavily the progress which scientists had made in cooperation with one another in Antarctica. The last paragraph concluded:

> The International Geophysical Year comes to a close at the end of 1958. The need for coordinated scientific research in Antarctica, however, will continue for many more years into the future. Accordingly, it would appear desirable for those countries participating in the Antarctic program of the International Geophysical Year to reach agreement among themselves on a program to assure continuation of the fruitful scientific cooperation referred to above. Such an arrangement could have the additional advantage of preventing unnecessary and undesirable political rivalries in that Continent, the uneconomic expenditure of funds to defend individual national interests, and the recurrent possibility of international misunderstanding. It would appear that if harmonious agreement can be reached among the countries directly concerned in regard to

> friendly cooperation in Antarctica, there would be advantages not only to those countries but to all other countries as well.

At the same time, President Eisenhower released a statement which said:

> We do not want Antarctica to become an object of political conflict. Accordingly, the United States has invited eleven other countries, including the Soviet Union, to confer with us to seek an effective joint means of achieving this objective.
>
> We propose that Antarctica shall be open to all nations to conduct scientific or other peaceful activities there. We also propose that joint administrative arrangements be worked out to ensure the successful accomplishment of these and other peaceful purposes.
>
> The countries which have been invited to confer are those which have engaged in scientific activities in Antarctica over the past nine months in connection with the International Geophysical Year. I know of no instance in which international cooperation has been more successfully demonstrated. However, the International Geophysical Year terminates on December 31, 1958. Our proposal is directed at ensuring that this same kind of cooperation for the benefit of all mankind shall be perpetuated after that date.
>
> I am confident that our proposal will win the wholehearted support of the peoples of all the nations directly concerned, and indeed of all other peoples of the world.

It is interesting that in the note to other governments the United States implied that the IGY had been a regime. In the text of his remarks, President Eisenhower also enunciated the principal U.S. policy objectives in Antarctica.

Representatives of the twelve nations met in Washington on October 15, 1959, and after a month's work the Antarctic Treaty was signed, on December 1, 1959. The treaty provided that Antarctica be used for peaceful purposes only; that nuclear explosions and the dumping of nuclear wastes be prohibited; that open, unannounced inspections for conformity of activities with the provisions of the treaty be carried out. Furthermore, a formula was devised to place in abeyance for a period of time claims or rights of the Antarctic Treaty nations, and to negate as a basis for future claims any activities conducted in Antarctica while the treaty was in force. The treaty furthermore made provision for representatives of governments to meet periodically to consult together on matters of mutual concern and to recommend to their governments measures in furtherance of the principles and purposes of the treaty. Such measures, when approved by all the governments, become part of the binding agreements under the treaty.

Perhaps some of the most significant and interesting parts of the Antarctic Treaty are those that deal with science. Article II of the treaty says:

> Freedom of scientific investigation in Antarctica and cooperation toward that end as applied during the International Geophysical Year shall continue subject to the provisions of the present Treaty.

It is interesting to reflect that the drafters of the treaty, with the experience of the International Geophysical Year freshly in mind, had a clear idea of what was meant by scientific investigation and cooperation toward that end as applied during the IGY. It meant, among other things, agreement on those critical issues of station locations, radio networks, and freedom of movement which had been settled in the international scientific planning forum for the International Geophysical Year. It meant patterns of cooperation and mutual assistance which had been practiced in the past several years by expeditions in Antarctica. One wonders whether new generations of antarctic scientists and politicians will find it useful to draft a new protocol to formalize for a broader area the established and accepted procedures of the scientific world.

Article III of the treaty gave the substance of working regulations to Article II by formalizing principles of the exchange of personnel, data, and results.

It is interesting finally to note that, to the limited extent to which the treaty deals with jurisdiction, it specifies that exchange scientists and other persons attached to expeditions will remain under the jurisdiction of their countries of origin. From this provision can be inferred the right of those involved in the scientific program to move about freely in Antarctica without fear of interference from jurisdictions centered on territorial claims. This freedom of movement applies to observers carrying out inspections in Antarctica.

The treaty is, therefore, a triumph for science, and since it came into force in August, 1961, further steps have been taken under the consultative provision of the treaty to advance scientific interests. The arrangements for the exchange of scientific data among the signatory nations have been improved. Efforts are being made to regulate non-scientific activities, such as tourism, to produce the minimum interference with ongoing scientific programs.

Perhaps the most significant measures to be approved since the treaty has come into force are those dealing with conservation of living resources. These measures establish uniform practices to limit harmful interference to plant and animal life and to give special protection to ecological systems in selected areas of Antarctica against the careless inroads of human activities. Regulations have been implemented to prevent the introduction of exotic animals, plants, and diseases. Further measures are being considered to protect seals on the drifting pack ice surrounding Antarctica and to ensure that the relatively undisturbed environmental conditions of Antarctica are preserved for the benefit of mankind. It should be noted that this is probably the first time in history that steps have been taken in conservation before it is too late.

It is interesting to note that the Antarctic Treaty was the first of a number of important international measures which deal with the limitation of the use of nuclear explosions and with the regulation of human activities in areas other than the continents on which man normally lives—the Nuclear Nonproliferation Treaty and the Moon and Celestial Bodies Treaty, commonly known as the Space Treaty. Many articles of these latter agreements were drawn directly from the Antarctic Treaty.

The U.S. Government has made it a point to carry out cooperative scientific activities with the other treaty nations in Antarctica as part of the U.S. Antarctic Research Program. The most frequent of these is the exchange of scientists between expeditions. Last year, for example, U.S. exchange scientists joined the Japanese, United Kingdom, and the U.S.S.R. expeditions. Scientists from Belgium, Chile, Norway, South Africa, the Soviet Union, and the United Kingdom joined U.S. Antarctic Research Program field parties in Antarctica. These are cooperative programs in the sense that one nation extends its services and facilities to accommodate a scientist from another country.

There are, however, more involved programs of international cooperation. Last year (1969–1970), Argentina, Norway, and the United States continued for the third summer the exploration of the Weddell Sea, utilizing icebreakers of Argentina and the United States, and underwater buoys supplied by Norway. In addition to logistic cooperation between the two icebreakers, scientists cooperated in the analysis and reduction of the data. As part of a long-term exchange of scientists between the Soviet Union and the United States, the United States has maintained a series of upper-atmosphere observations at the Soviet station, Vostok, at the geomagnetic south pole. The northern conjugate of this station, Kanak in Greenland, is operated cooperatively by Denmark and the United States. The results of this program, with the addition of other programs in Scandinavia, will be the subject of a joint publication by Danish, Finnish, Norwegian, Soviet, and U.S. scientists.

Four years ago, a U.S. scientist was invited by the French to join the rocket team at Dumont d'Urville, where he contributed significantly to the successful firing of three rockets during a major solar flare, a program in which he was able to contribute to the success not only in the field but in the subsequent analysis of results.

The United States two years ago provided the logistic support to a Norwegian field party of six which explored a heretofore unvisited mountain range in Queen Maud Land. This group represented the first return of Norwegian scientists to Antarctica since 1959; the United States was proud to have been able to assist the Norwegians in this effort, which was repeated again in the last antarctic summer (1969–1970).

The largest and longest program of cooperation in Antarctica is that between New Zealand and the United States. The United States uses New Zealand's facilities to mount our efforts in Antarctica and in return, under terms of a memorandum of agreement, New Zealand receives certain logistic support and assistance. Cooperation between New Zealand and the United States has gone beyond mutual logistic support and scientific collaboration. It has expanded into cooperation in establishing and administering Specially Protected Areas in Antarctica, and in the preparation of compatible regulations to govern activities of tourists at adjacent New Zealand and U.S. stations.

The history of the last sixteen years in Antarctica shows clearly that persistent and earnest cooperation can influence relationships among nations. We have seen that science can provide the grounds to initiate agreements which can circumvent causes of potential division and acrimony.

The history of Antarctica since the beginning of the International

Geophysical Year has been a story of the influence of science on national policy. Cooperation in international activities through national research programs has been shown not to spark aggressive national policies but rather to give vent to the national will to peace.

The success which has been achieved in Antarctica through the marriage of science and diplomacy should serve as a beacon for other areas. I do not mean to suggest that the precise way of operation or the agreements which have been entered into in Antarctica are directly applicable elsewhere. But good science pursued in its own international forums and conducted with an appreciation of the objectives and problems of international relations can serve to open routes for diplomacy. As science becomes increasingly concerned with the very big problems of man and his environment, the scientist must learn to accept responsibilities for the politics of his art, and the diplomat would do well to recognize that science is another avenue by which accord and agreement can be reached.

PART II

Biology

PART II

Biology

As Dr. Hedgpeth's interesting vignette of James Eights documents so well, the United States' scientific roots in Antarctica appeared almost with the birth of the young nation. The early studies of Eights in antarctic biology were for a long time overlooked and in recent times further obscured by the more dramatic events of the Heroic Age of Exploration. Indeed, the traditions of the United States in antarctic biology established by Eights were sustained for over a century only by the scientific reports of A. A. Lindsey and Paul Siple of the Second Byrd Antarctic Expedition of 1933–1935. From 1935 until the end of the 1957–1958 International Geophysical Year, with the exception of studies carried out by H. M. Bryant and Carl Eklund during the U.S. Antarctic Service Expedition of 1939–1941, there was little U.S. activity in antarctic biology.

With the inception of the U.S. Antarctic Research Program, formal studies began into life phenomena in Antarctica. The superb logistic and fiscal organization which carried out the geophysical programs of the IGY, as much as the absence of biological activity, did much to focus the attention of life scientists on the polar regions. Biologists saw in the successful IGY expedition the pattern for a similar worldwide international effort in biology and this effort, in a sense, has been recently concluded as the International Biological Program (IBP). However, since the major thrust of the IBP is directed toward the problems of the Northern Hemisphere, the basic coordination in the Southern Hemisphere continues to come from cooperation among the Antarctic Treaty nations. In this regard, the U.S. Antarctic Research Program since 1959 has functioned as a similar international activity through exchange of personnel and data with scientists of 11 other nations, and by its extensive biological programs conducted across a broad disciplinary front in Antarctica and on the southern ocean. The studies ashore utilize the facilities of modern laboratories and equipment at McMurdo and Palmer Stations. The marine studies on the *Eltanin,* a research vessel which is at sea almost two-thirds of the year, are already outstanding for the biological surveys which have been carried out almost around Antarctica.

Over 300 biologists from the United States have participated in antarctic research; the current participants include "second generation" scientists, that is, graduate students who have achieved their doctorates in antarctic research. It is obvious that the papers in this volume are an inadequate measure of the scope of work conducted under the National Science Foundation's national program in Antarctica. For a more thorough review, the reader is referred to the *Antarctic Bibliography* published by the Library of Congress and to the *Antarctic Research Series* published by the American Geophysical Union of the National Academy of Sciences.

The program objectives in biology are basically the support of worthwhile research which will contribute to a more complete understanding of the southern polar region. Participation in the national antarctic program has been directed toward regional involvement by U. S. institutions commensurate with their departmental interests and capabilities for a truly representative national effort. Encouragement has been directed toward broad interdisciplinary research for the purpose of developing a qualified cadre of polar specialists with firsthand knowledge of antarctic environmental conditions and actual experience in polar expeditionary planning. Information of topical interest in the annual development of research plans is reported bimonthly in the *Antarctic Journal of the United States.* This journal is available on a subscription basis from the Superintendent of Documents, U.S. Government Printing Office. In addition to descriptions of approved programs and schedules for the seasonal field work, the *Antarctic Journal* also reports accomplishments at the conclusions of the field period, often with preliminary results of unusual scientific interest. Projection of long-range plans, new concepts and techniques, international cooperative activities, and similar items of interest to the national and international community of antarctic workers are also reported n the *Antarctic Journal.*

Not the least of the resources of the program are the vast collections of specimens and related materials maintained by the Smithsonian Oceanographic Sorting Center and their ready accessibility as both worked and unworked data through modern computer recording and retrieval methods.

The U.S. Antarctic Research Program has since its inception depended on the U.S. Navy for logistic support in Antarctica. Through the Commander, Naval Support Force, Antarctica, it has provided for all basic needs essential to the comfort and safety of a large number of civilian workers and scientists, for the most part lacking in experience or knowledge of the severity or hazards of polar field work. With the U.S. Navy, the U.S. Air Force's Military Airlift Command has provided intercontinental transportation during the austral summer season. The Coast Guard icebreakers and their helicopters have functioned efficiently as scientific platforms for the support of oceanographic and terrestrial research. The Military Sealift Command, Pacific, has supported USNS *Eltanin* operations for ten years, with a degree of safety and reliability which has helped establish *Eltanin's* outstanding records for almost continuous scientific work at sea. The assistance of the Services and the contractual support of Holmes & Narver, Inc., 828 So. Figueroa Street, Los Angeles, California 90017; Marine Acoustical Services, Inc., 1975 N.W. South River Drive, Miami, Florida 33125; and Alpine Geophysical Associates, Inc., 65 Oak Street, Norwood, New Jersey 07648, represent a particularly important and successful development of the National Science Foundation, U.S. Antarctic Research Program.

GEORGE A. LLANO

Polar Biology Programs
Office of Polar Programs
National Science Foundation
Washington, D.C.

Dynamics of Trophic Relations in the Southern Ocean

SAYED Z. EL-SAYED

Department of Oceanography, College of Geosciences, Texas A&M University, College Station

Although biological exploration of the Antarctic Ocean dates back to the expedition of the *Erebus* and *Terror* (1839–1843), it was not until the initiation of the *Discovery II* investigations in 1925 that a new era in the scientific exploration of the Antarctic Ocean began. In this era, the cataloging or purely descriptive phase was less emphasized, and instead, the dynamic aspect of antarctic marine biology was stressed. Although the *Discovery II* investigations were primarily concerned with whales and whaling, studies of practically all the factors influencing their migration, food and feeding habits, breeding cycle, etc., led to an intensive program of physical, chemical, and biological oceanography of the southern ocean.

Antarctic marine biology, as in the case of biological research elsewhere, has undergone successive phases of extensive collecting, biogeographical survey, and descriptive ecology (Holdgate, 1968). While these studies have provided very valuable information on the taxonomy, distribution, and abundance of the organisms in the southern ocean, there is a dearth of knowledge about the relationship between the trophic levels and the flow of energy through the antarctic marine ecosystem. This is primarily due to a paucity of data on estimates of biomass of the different trophic levels and to our almost complete lack of knowledge of the metabolic rates and turnover rates of the antarctic marine organisms. The deficiencies in our knowledge of the antarctic marine ecosystem, together with the potential richness of its oceanic resources, are now ushering in a new phase of antarctic biology—a phase in which population dynamics and metabolic studies must be stressed.

The study of the antarctic marine ecosystem holds more than

a casual or academic interest. With the burgeoning of the human population and its increased demand for more animal protein, there is great interest in harvesting more of the marine living resources. With the deplorable decline (about 85–90 percent) of the stock of baleen whales in the past 40 years, attention is now being shifted to the krill, *Euphausia superba,* the potential catch of which has been estimated by Moiseev (1968) to be well in excess of the 1967 total harvest of 60.5 million tons of fish from all the oceans (FAO, 1967). If the krill resource is to be exploited wisely, it must first be inventoried and its population dynamics understood. The great tragedies perpetrated on the plaice fishery in the North Sea, the California sardine, and the antarctic baleen whales are testimonies of poor management of natural resources. Lack of knowledge about natural resources makes it difficult to reach international agreements, and encourages irresponsible exploitation of valuable resources.

THE PHYSICAL ENVIRONMENT

The areas between 40°S and Antarctica can be divided into several well-defined circumpolar frontal zones of which the Antarctic Convergence is the most stationary. The Antarctic Convergence forms one of the major boundary zones of the world's ocean, dividing the southern waters into the antarctic and subantarctic regions.

The main transport of water between 40° and 60°S is from west to east in what is known as the Circumpolar Current. Close to the continent easterly or southeasterly winds prevail that cause transport in a westerly direction. Because of the earth's rotation, the westerlies and easterlies produce, respectively, northerly and southerly transports in the upper layer, resulting in a surface divergence (the Antarctic Divergence), and consequent upwelling, along the boundary of these two wind belts (Fig. 1). Superimposed upon this eastward circumpolar movement are north-south components. At its northern limit the Antarctic Surface Water sinks beneath the less dense south-flowing Subantarctic Water. The region in which this phenomenon occurs is called the Antarctic Convergence or "Antarctic Polar Front." The principal property by which its location can be mapped is the steep temperature gradient at the sea surface. Across the Convergence surface temperature change in summer is from 3° to 5.5°C and in winter from 0.5° to 3°C. One of the most remarkable features of the Antarctic Convergence is that its position changes very little from season to season and year

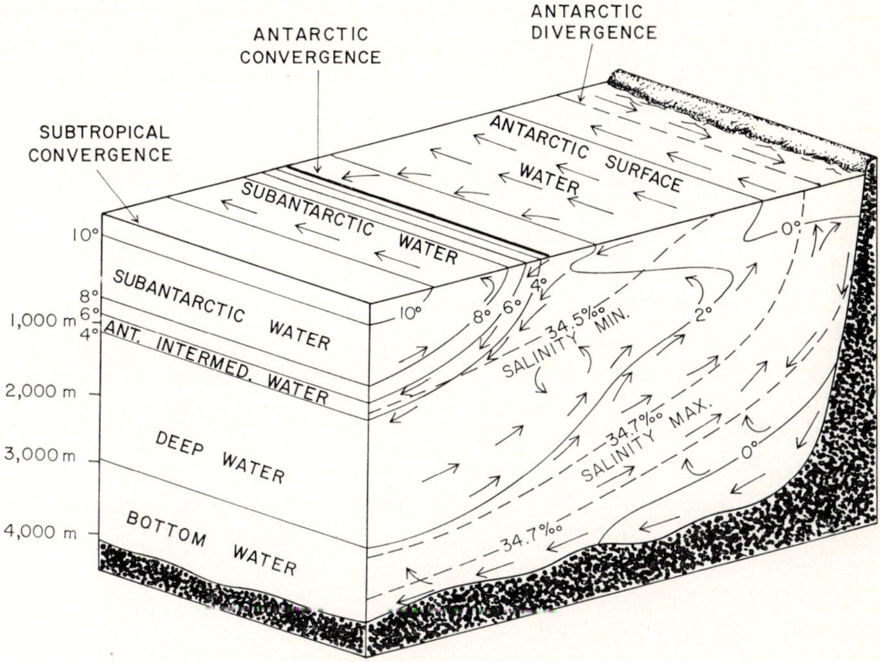

Fig. 1. Schematic representation of the currents and water masses of the southern ocean and the distribution of temperature and salinity. Temperatures shown are in Centigrade (Modified from Sverdrup *et al.*, 1942).

to year. The Convergence position has been regarded by Deacon (1964) as fixed by the thermohaline circulation. As the Antarctic Surface Water sinks below the surface at the Convergence, and continues northward, mixing with the water above and below, it forms the Antarctic Intermediate Water, which is characterized by a salinity minimum and a relatively oxygen maximum. At the edge of the continent (the Weddell Sea in particular), very cold water sinks and moves northward along the shelf and into the deep, forming the Antarctic Bottom Water. This water is found all around the Antarctic Continent and even beyond the equator in the Atlantic Ocean but is of more limited extent in the Pacific and Indian Oceans.

Immediately above Antarctic Bottom Water is an exceptionally thick, warm water mass—the "Deep Water"—that is formed in the North Atlantic and perhaps in the northern Indian Ocean by the cooling and sinking of high-salinity water. This deep water moves southward and ultimately spreads into all the world's oceans. The upward movement of the Deep Water creates a zone of upwelling which supplies to the surface water vast quantities of nutrients which contribute to the luxuriant phytoplankton growth close to the antarctic coasts.

One unique aspect of the Antarctic Ocean is its nearly homoiothermic nature. Sea temperature south of the Convergence is very low; its variation with depth and season barely exceeds 4° or 5°C. Variations in salinity are also small—only some 0.1 percent. Thus from the surface to the bottom, the conservative properties of the antarctic waters show a high degree of uniformity (Currie, 1964).

For a region which lies in relatively high latitudes, the extreme variations in incoming solar radiation between summer and winter, certainly have a pronounced effect on marine plant life. This is illustrated in Figure 2, in which the mean monthly values of radiant energy (with average cloudiness) measured at the Norwegian station "Maudheim" (71°03′S, 10°56′W) are plotted against primary production and standing crop of phytoplankton collected in antarctic waters. It is clear from this figure that the rise and fall of the chlorophyll *a* and C^{14} uptake are in direct response to the amount of energy received.

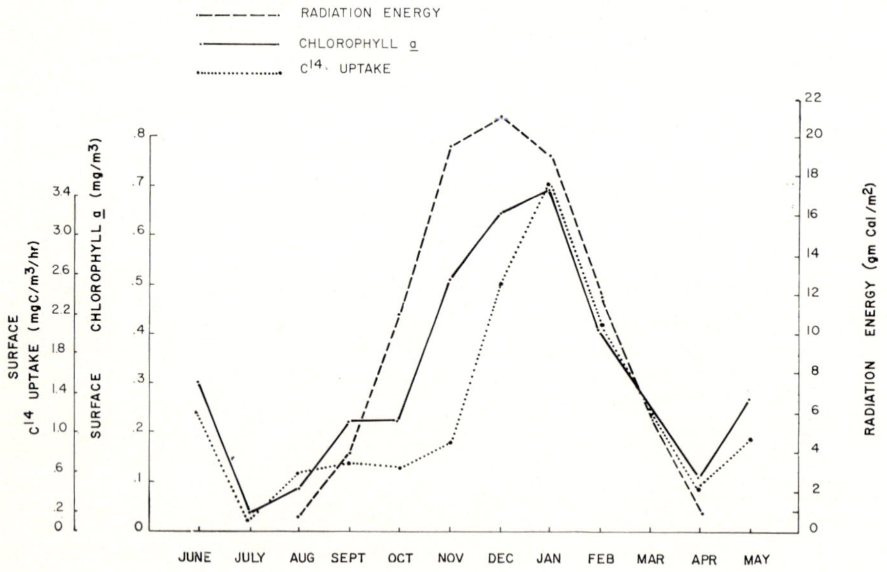

Fig. 2. Monthly variation of radiation energy (with average cloudiness) at Maudheim Station (71°03′S, 10°56′W) compared with monthly changes in surface chlorophyll *α* and C^{14} uptake in antarctic waters.

Further, light penetration in antarctic waters is determined not only by its intensity, angle of incidence, surface reflectance, absorption by suspended particles, and so forth, but also by the presence of thick fast ice and pack ice which appreciably reduces the amount of submarine illumination. The biological implication of the extent of pack ice assumes great significance when it is realized that the open surface water of the ocean south of the Antarctic Convergence is approximately halved by the extensive coverage of sea ice in winter. According to Mackintosh and Brown (1956), this area is reduced from $2.38 \times 10^7 km^2$ in February to $1.18 \times 10^7 km^2$ in September.

The nutrient salts in the antarctic waters appear to be in excess of phytoplankton requirements. This is primarily owing to the mechanism of upwelling, which ensures abundant supply of these salts. Even at the peak of phytoplankton growth, the concentration of nutrients remains well above the limiting values. For instance, during a very heavy phytoplankton bloom which covered an area more than 15,500 km^2 off the Filchner Ice Shelf, in southern Weddell Sea (El-Sayed, 1970), the nutrient salts still exhibited high concentrations—e.g., phosphates: 2.02 μg at./l; nitrates: 24.9 μg at./l; and silicates: 68 μg at./l. No discernible seasonal variations in the nitrate values were observed in antarctic waters. Phosphate distribution, on the other hand, showed a marked decline during late spring and early summer. However, the low values encountered in the latter period are higher than some of the maximum values reported in temperate regions.

THE BIOLOGICAL SETTING

Enough data and observations have been accumulated through the investigations of several antarctic expeditions to allow us to draw up a tentative food chain diagram such as that of Hart (1942) shown here in Figure 3. This figure illustrates some of the important links in the antarctic food chains. It also shows the significant role played by the krill, *Euphausia superba,* and the oceanic squid in the trophic relationships in the Antarctic. The major biotic components in the antarctic ecosystem (Fig. 4) will be discussed below.

The Phytoplankton

Antarctic phytoplankton, in general, is dominated by the diatom population. Scattered among the diatoms are the dinoflagellates.

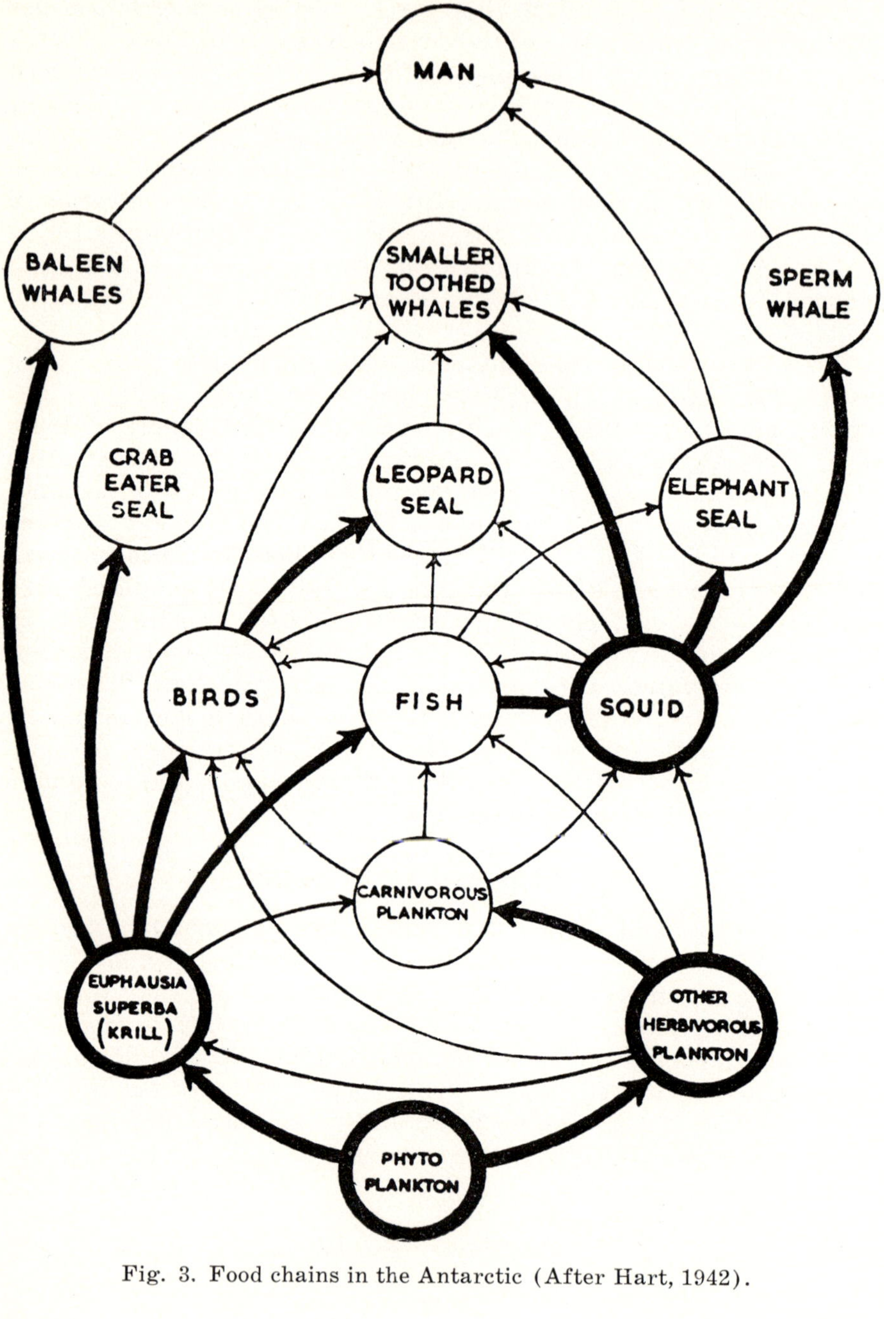

Fig. 3. Food chains in the Antarctic (After Hart, 1942).

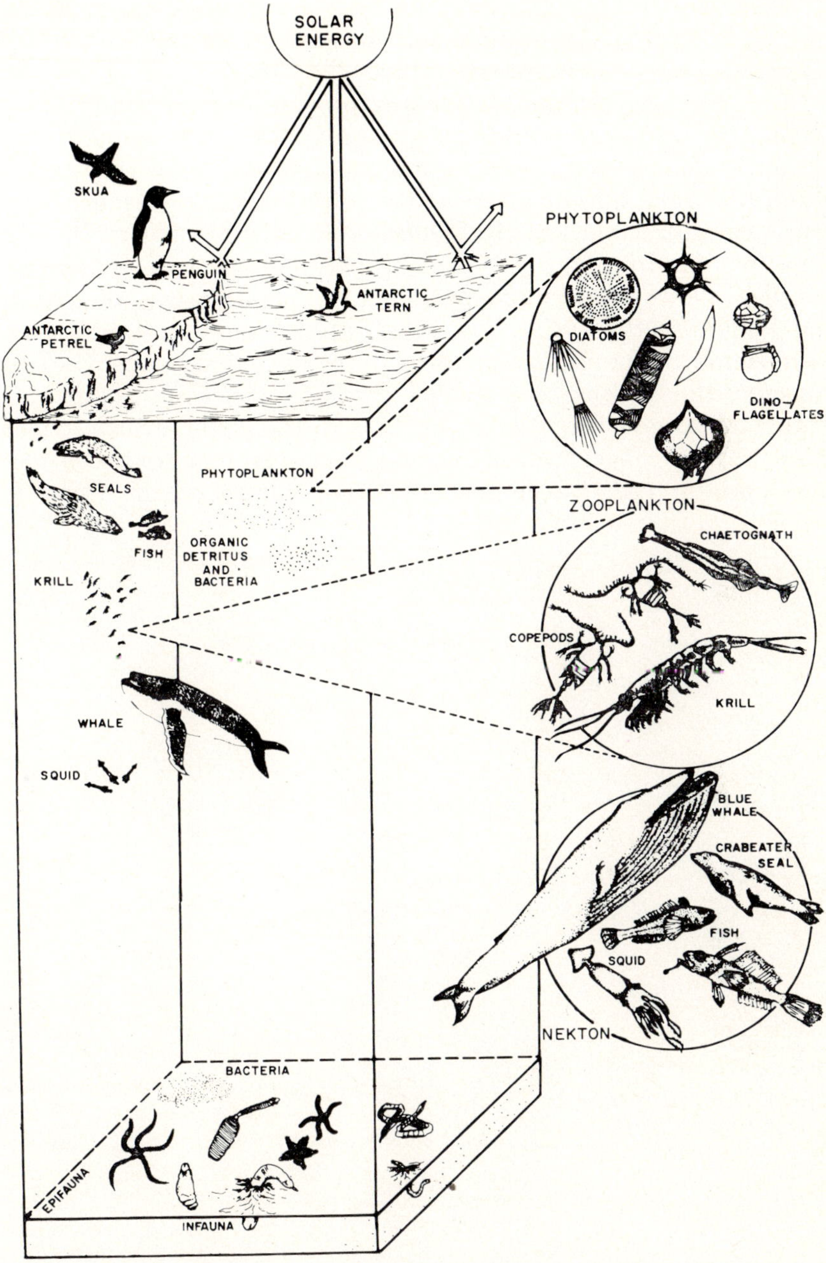

Fig. 4. Major biotic components in the antarctic marine ecosystem.

However, since the flagellate numbers are small compared to the number of diatoms, the dinoflagellate biomass in the Antarctic has generally been underestimated (Balech, 1968).

Our knowledge of the phytoplankton standing crop and primary production and distribution of diatoms and dinoflagellates in the antarctic and subantarctic waters is summarized in the *Antarctic Map Folio Series, Folio 10,* recently published by the American Geographical Society (El-Sayed, 1968b). The distribution of the phytoplankton standing crop (in terms of chlorophyll *a*) in surface-water samples shows discernible geographic variations in the Atlantic and Pacific sectors (Fig. 5). Small phytoplankton standing crops were found in the region of the Antarctic Convergence, the Drake Passage, the Bellingshausen Sea, and in the Pacific sector of the Antarctic, except for isolated pockets in the latter where moderate chlorophyll *a* concentrations ranging between 0.50 and 0.99 mg/m^3 were encountered. Large phytoplankton standing crops were found

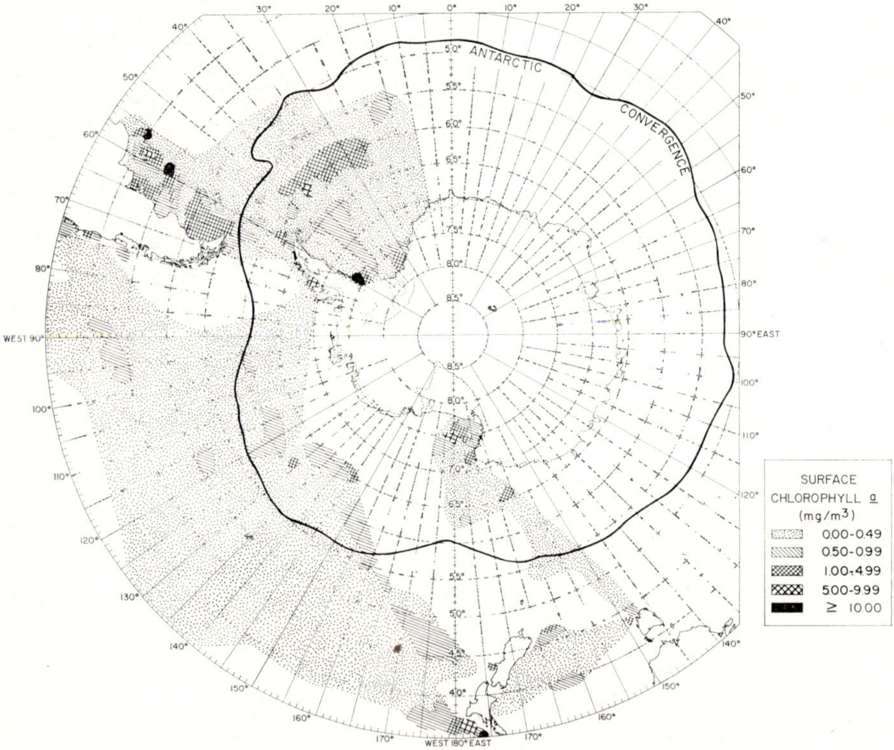

Fig. 5. Distribution of chlorophyll *a* (surface) in the Atlantic and Pacific sectors.

in the Scotia Sea, southwestern Weddell Sea, west of the Antarctic Peninsula, and in the Ross Sea. Substantial differences between surface phytoplankton standing crops in the Atlantic and the Pacific sectors were found by the author (1.40 and 0.36 mg/m^3, respectively). Integrated values (i.e., values integrated from the surface to the depth of 1 percent light penetration), on the other hand, showed slightly higher chlorophyll *a* values in the Atlantic sector (14.92 mg/m^2) than in the Pacific sector (11.55 mg/m^2).

Primary productivity of surface-water samples in both the Atlantic and Pacific sectors (Fig. 6) showed a picture more or less similar to that of the distribution of the phytoplankton standing crop. The primary productivity of surface-water samples in the Atlantic sector was four times the Pacific value (4.87 mg C/m^3 per hr, compared to 1.22 mg C/m^3 per hr). However, carbon assimilation in the euphotic zones in the Atlantic stations was not substantially higher than the Pacific stations (42.82 and 32.01 mg C/m^2 per hr, respectively).

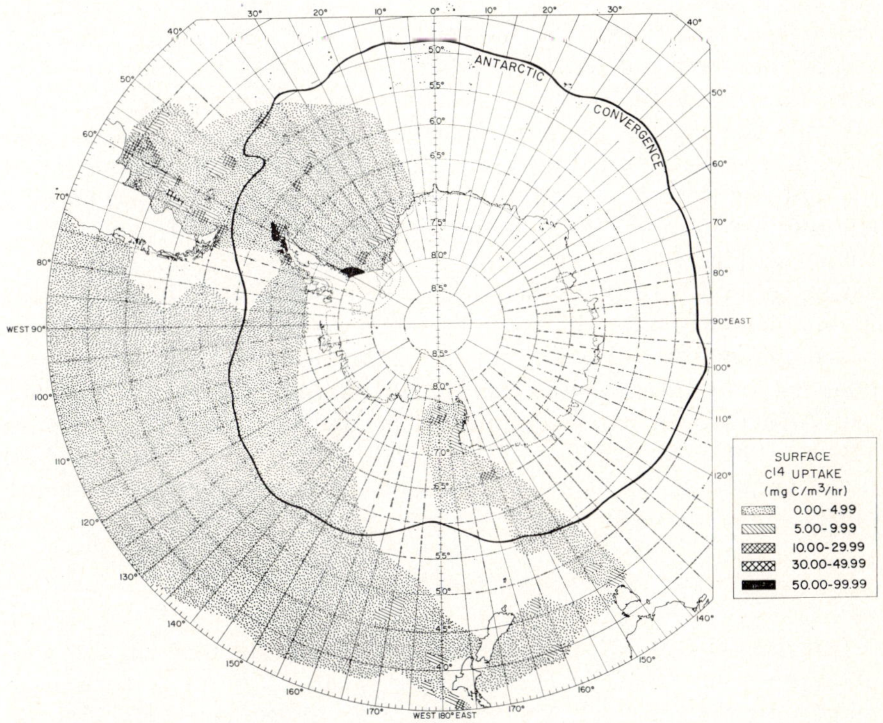

Fig. 6. Distribution of C^{14} uptake (surface) in the Atlantic and Pacific sectors.

Despite the vastness of the areas studied in the Atlantic and Pacific sectors, it is safe to say that we now have a fair knowledge of the basic productivity of both. Although the Indian Ocean sector was not studied by the author, the few published data from there, obtained by Russian and Japanese investigators, indicate that its productivity is intermediate between the other two sectors.

Our observations in the southern ocean demonstrated the marked differences between the productivity values of the antarctic and subantarctic waters, and showed the effect of the Antarctic Convergence on the distribution and concentration of the productivity parameters and nutrient salts (El-Sayed, 1968a). Our studies also underscored conspicuous differences between the productivity of the oceanic and neritic regions. This led to the conclusion that the extreme richness of the antarctic waters exists only in the coastal and inshore regions, and not in the oceanic regions (El-Sayed, 1970).

In studying the trophic relationships in the antarctic ecosystem, it is imperative to know the amount of carbon fixed annually by the phytoplankton. Based on 153 stations occupied south of the Antarctic Convergence in the Atlantic and Pacific sectors, and using Mackintosh and Brown's (1956) estimate of the mean surface area of open water south of the Antarctic Convergence as $1.78 \times 10^7 km^2$, the annual primary production of antarctic waters was calculated as 3.03×10^9 tons of carbon. This figure is arrived at by multiplying the average photosynthetic rate (mg C/m^2) per hour by the number of hours of sunshine per year for each of the 153 stations occupied in both the Atlantic and Pacific sectors. It is interesting to note here the close similarity between the 3.03×10^9 tons given above and 3.3×10^9 tons of carbon given by El-Sayed (1968a) based primarily on data from the Atlantic sector. This estimate does not take into account the amount of algal production in pack ice. Although our knowledge of this production is still fragmentary (Bunt, 1968), Burkholder and Mandelli (1965) estimated one-half ton of carbon per day for the microalgae under ice in the area south of the Antarctic Convergence.

The Zooplankton

Our knowledge of the distribution and abundance of the zooplankton populations in the southern ocean (Fig. 7) is based primarily on the work of the *Discovery II* expedition (Mackintosh, 1934; Foxton, 1956; Marr, 1962) and, more recently, on the investi-

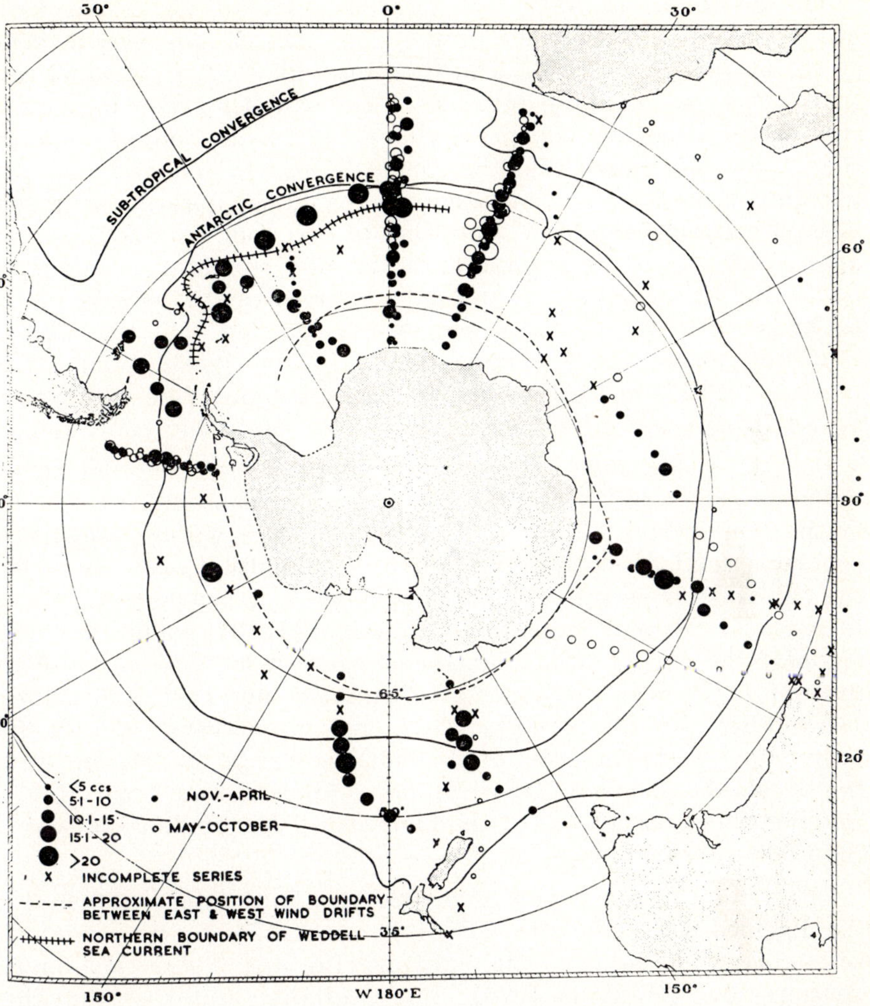

Fig. 7. The total volume of the zooplankton (1,000–0 m) at each station plotted according to the position of the station. A few observations in 0°, 20°E, and 80°W have had to be omitted for clarity (After Foxton, 1956).

gations of the USNS *Eltanin* (Hopkins, 1966, 1970). It is clear from these investigations that although most, if not all, the zooplankton species are circumpolar in distribution, they frequently show centers of concentration at different depths or in different latitudes. As a result, there are both quantitative and qualitative differences.

The dominant organism in antarctic zooplankton is the krill, *Euphausia superba,* which in the past has supported enormous stocks of whales. According to Hopkins (1970), the principal contributors to zooplankton biomass in the samples taken in the Pacific sector were the copepods, chaetognaths, and euphausiids, in that order. He found that the copepods contributed 67.7 and 59.6 percent respectively of the standing crop in the antarctic and subantarctic regions sampled. Voronina (1966) found similar percentages (72.8 and 61.5) for the antarctic and subantarctic plankton in the Indian Ocean sector. Hopkins attributes the paucity of the euphausiids in his plankton samples to the fact that the *Eltanin* collections were made farther north in the West Wind Drift. Naumov (1964) has also indicated that the Juday nets used by the Soviet investigators were poorly suited for capturing adult krill.

Despite the extensive zooplankton investigations carried out in the southern ocean, it is difficult to arrive at reasonable estimates of the zooplankton standing crops in antarctic waters because of problems related to sampling, patchy distribution, ease by which the euphausiids escape the sampling nets, and problems pertinent to seasonal vertical migration. Hopkins (1970) noted that over one-half the zooplankton biomass of the upper 1,000 m occurred in the top 250 m in the late spring, summer, and early fall months (November through April), while during the remainder of the year (May–October), most of the biomass was below 250 m. As to the organisms below 1,000 m, Hopkins showed that from May to October, 23 to 30 percent of the biomass of the top 2,000 m was in the 1,000 to 2,000 m zone.

The annual total biomass of zooplankton in the upper 1,000 m in the Pacific sector averaged 3.5, 2.55, and 2.76 g dry weight/m^2 respectively in the antarctic, subantarctic, and Antarctic Convergence regions (Hopkins, 1970). In the Atlantic sector, on the other hand, Hopkins (1966) found an average zooplankton/micronekton abundance of 5 to 9 g dry weight/m^2 in the upper 1,000 m. If we take the minimum estimates of the zooplankton biomass as 50 cm^3/m^2, as calculated by Foxton (1956), the equivalent dry weight estimate per m^2 would be 8 to 10 g/m^2, which is not substantially different from the estimates given by Hopkins for the Atlantic sector.

As to the annual production of zooplankton, no reliable data are available at present. If we assume that the life span of most of the zooplankton organisms exceeds one year, however, the total annual production might be of the same order as the average standing crop, or 10 g/m^2. If we take this value as representative of the Antarctic, and if we multiply this figure by the mean surface area of open water south of the Convergence, we obtain a biomass (dry weight) value which is equivalent to 0.178×10^9 tons. This figure should be regarded as the low estimate of zooplankton biomass since there is some uncertainty about the amount of open water in the pack ice, and we know very little about the distribution and abundance of zooplankton in the area covered permanently by pack ice.

Fish and Squids

Virtually no figures are available concerning the standing crop of the pelagic fish and squids. These organisms depend ultimately on phytoplankton, and probably feed on krill and other crustacea. The squids, in turn, are eaten by larger animals such as whales, seals, and seabirds. Despite the importance of the squids as predators and prey, they remain largely unstudied.

As to the pelagic, plankton-eating fish, little is known about their biology, distribution, and abundance. We are still uncertain as to whether there are substantial concentrations of pelagic species which might provide a food supply for higher animals.

Seals

Some data are available on the stock size of the seal population in the Antarctic. Rough estimates of the crab-eater seals range between 5 to 8×10^6 seals; and taking the mean body weight as 300 kg (Holdgate, 1967), this yields a total stock of about one million tons. It is believed that the maximum sustained yield does not exceed 10 percent of the virgin stock.

Whales

The only marine pelagic organisms in the Antarctic for which reliable estimates of the stocks are available are the whales. If we take the population of baleen whales in the thirties to be 340,000 specimens, and if we use Mackintosh and Brown's (1956) mean weight of each whale as 53 metric tons, the total stock was 18×10^6 tons.

Birds

Assessment of the biomass of the plankton-eating birds in the southern ocean is exceedingly difficult. Further, census data for bird populations at sea are virtually nonexistent. Estimates of bird populations in breeding colonies are rough estimates at best. Despite their overwhelming numbers, however, it is reasonable to assume that such breeding birds represent a very small biomass per square meter of ocean surface. Of this biomass, perhaps 60 percent are plankton-feeders, while the remainder eat fish and squids, are predatory on other birds, or are scavengers (Holdgate, 1967).

Benthos

Unlike the plankton and nekton in the Antarctic, the benthos consists mainly of slow-growing organisms such as sponges and echinoderms.

Dense benthic communities have been reported on the shelf of Antarctica and its islands. A standing crop of 400 to 500 g/m^2 on the continental shelf region in 100 to 500 m depth has been reported by Belyaev (1958) and Ushakov (1962). At 2,000 m, the standing crop of benthos falls to 2.8 g/m^2, and at 3,500 m, to 1.4 g/m^2.

Belyaev (1958) estimated that as much as 60 percent of the standing crop of the benthos may not be directly available as food for other organisms—the so-called dead end in the food chain. However, other investigators contend that recycling in the general web of life takes place despite the low temperature at the depths sampled.

For the most part, the abyssal bottom fauna remain largely unsampled. We know very little about their nature and contribution to the antarctic marine ecosystem.

TROPHIC RELATIONSHIPS AND ENERGY FLOW IN THE ANTARCTIC ECOSYSTEM

It is clear that there are enormous gaps in our knowledge of biomass and of the relative abundance of even the more accessible populations in the antarctic ecosystem. Considerable caution should be exercised in using the above biomass estimates of the different trophic levels and in drawing conclusions as to the ecological efficiency of the system.

In the study of tropho-dynamic relationships, one is interested in assessing the net trophic efficiency, that is, the percentage of organic matter in one trophic level incorporated in the next higher trophic level. However, given the state of our knowledge of the antarctic ecosystem, this cannot be readily calculated. For instance, although the primary production in antarctic water (3.03×10^9 tons of carbon) has been estimated, it is difficult to arrive at a reliable estimate of the phytoplankton biomass. Further, estimates of standing crop and biomass of zooplankton given above are crude at best. The situation is further complicated by our limited knowledge of carnivore/herbivore ratios in antarctic waters. Hopkins (In press) showed that based on the zooplankton samples collected in the Pacific sector of the Antarctic, the carnivore/herbivore ratio exceeded 15 percent in every month in which samples were taken except January (14 percent) in the subantarctic region (Table 1).

Hopkins's observations seem to be at variance with Slobodkin's (1960) view that net trophic efficiency does not exceed 10 to 15 percent. Hopkins further stated that the carnivore fraction has probably been underestimated, since predaceous micronekton (mostly fishes, squids, and decapods), megaplankton (e.g., coronate scyphomedusae), and the predominantly carnivorous animals living below 1,000 m (Vinogradov, 1962) were not included in his calculations. Hopkins concluded that the carnivore/herbivore ratio appears too high throughout the year to mirror net trophic efficiency. It is doubtful, therefore, that biomass estimates alone would

Table 1. Carnivore/herbivore ratio of biomass in the upper 1,000 m of Antarctic Convergence Zone, and subantarctic areas in the Pacific sector. The number of series of hauls is in parentheses (From Hopkins, 1970).

	Antarctic	Convergence	Subantarctic
January	0.21(4)	0.19(3)	0.14(2)
February	—	—	—
March	0.19(1)	—	0.18(2)
April	0.27(7)	0.26(2)	0.53(4)
May	0.21(1)	0.36(1)	0.54(1)
June	0.38(4)	0.50(1)	0.51(5)
July	0.28(1)	0.38(5)	0.99(1)
August	0.35(6)	0.36(1)	0.43(4)
September	—	0.23(1)	—
October	0.33(2)	0.53(2)	—
November	0.29(5)	0.39(3)	0.61(1)
December	—	—	0.38(1)

give us a realistic picture of trophic level efficiency. What is needed is knowledge of rates of turnover.

As to the trophic efficiency at levels higher than the secondary producers, our knowledge of standing crop and biomass of these organisms is too fragmentary, or totally lacking, to give us a realistic picture of tropho-dynamic relationships.

There is a dearth of knowledge of life history, physiology, behavior, and population dynamics of even the major components of the antarctic organisms. Very little is known about the food and feeding habits of even the easily accessible organisms in the Antarctic.

Because of the great significance of the krill (*Euphausia superba*) in the antarctic marine ecosystem, and since, sooner or later, the krill will be the subject of commercial exploitation, it is imperative that realistic data on the density, dimensions, frequency, and distribution of its swarms be made. It would be of great interest to gain some idea of how the krill distributes itself under the ice, if swarms are found under the floes, and if the distribution of krill under ice is in some way different from what we find in open water.

There is a striking lack of knowledge of the metabolism of the key organisms at the different trophic levels. Except for McWhinnie and Marciniak's (1964) respiration studies on *Euphausia superba,* and Wohlschlag's (1964), Everson and Ralph's (1968), and Morris's (1968) studies on the metabolism of antarctic fish, very little is known concerning the metabolic rates of zooplankton and micronekton in the Antarctic. Metabolic studies are thus needed, not only for the phytoplankton, zooplankton, seals, winged birds, penguins, fishes, and squids, but also for the ultraplankton and the microbenthic flora and fauna. For instance, Pomeroy and Johannes (1968) have shown that most of the energy turnover in the pelagic environment is accomplished by the ultraplankton passing through the meshes of plankton nets. It is interesting to note in this respect that during an all-biological cruise (*Eltanin* Cruise 38), studies were made to estimate as quantitatively as possible the total metabolism of selected water columns in the antarctic, subantarctic, and Convergence regions. Such studies are urgently needed for a thorough understanding of how the biological system works and how it relates to the physical and chemical milieu within which it operates.

In order to understand how the system works, the following specific studies are suggested:

1. An inventory of the diversity, magnitude, and distribution of the living components of the system should be made. Such data should be accumulated in correlation with appropriate measurements of the physical and chemical parameters of the environment.
2. Measurements of the rates of production, storage, and release of energy by key components of the system should be taken.
3. Estimates of the organic inputs and outflows of the system, as well as from one part of the system to another, should be made.

In other words, it is critical that the biological system be approached as a single functional unit. Isolated studies of one component or another cannot be relied upon to provide the kind of coherent and correlated data required for computer simulation and prediction.

Author's Note: I thank Dr. T. L. Hopkins for the opportunity of reading and quoting from his manuscript, "Zooplankton standing crop of the Pacific sector of the Antarctic." Grateful acknowledgment is extended to the Office of Polar Programs, National Science Foundation, for the financial support of this study (G-915 and G-1487) under the U.S. Antarctic Research Program.

References

Balech, E., 1968. Dinoflagellates. In *Antarctic Map Folio Series, Folio 10,* edited by V. Bushnell; pp. 8–9. Am. Geograph. Soc., New York.

Belyaev, G. M., 1958. Some patterns in the quantitative distribution of the bottom fauna in the Antarctic. *Soviet Antarctic Inform. Bull., 1:* 119–121.

Bunt, J. S., 1968. Microalgae of the antarctic pack ice zone. In *Proceedings of the Symposium on Antarctic Oceanography;* pp. 198–218. Scott Polar Res. Inst., Cambridge, England.

Burkholder, P. R., and E. F. Mandelli, 1965. Productivity of microalgae in antarctic sea ice. *Science, 149* (3686) : 872–874.

Currie, R. I., 1964. Environmental features in the ecology of the antarctic seas. In *Biologie Antarctique,* edited by R. Carrick, M. W. Holdgate, and J. Prevost; pp. 87–94. Hermann, Paris.

Deacon, G. E. R., 1964. Antarctic oceanography: the physical environment. In *Biologie Antarctique,* edited by R. Carrick, M. W. Holdgate, and J. Prevost; pp. 81–86. Hermann, Paris.

El-Sayed, S. Z., 1968a. On the productivity of the southwest Atlantic Ocean and the waters west of the Antarctic Peninsula. In *Antarctic Research Series, 11, Biology of the Antarctic Seas, III,* edited by G. A. Llano and W. L. Schmitt; pp. 15–47. Am. Geophys. Union, Washington, D. C.

El-Sayed, S. Z., 1968b. Productivity of antarctic and subantarctic waters. In *Antarctic Map Folio Series, Folio 10,* edited by V. Bushnell; pp. 1–6. Am. Geograph. Soc., New York.

El-Sayed, S. Z., 1970. On the productivity of the Southern Ocean. In *Antarctic Ecology,* edited by M. W. Holdgate; vol. 1, pp. 119–135. Academic Press, London and New York.

Everson, I., and R. Ralph, 1968. Metabolism of antarctic fish in relation to growth. *Abstracts of Symposium on Antarctic Ecology, 29 July–2 August, 1968.* Cambridge, England.

FAO, 1967. *FAO Yearbook Fish Statistics;* vol. 25. U.N. Food Agr. Org., Rome.

Foxton, P., 1956. The standing crop of zooplankton in the Southern Ocean. *Discovery Repts., 28:* 193–235.

Hart, T. J., 1942. Phytoplankton periodicity in antarctic surface waters. *Discovery Repts., 21:* 261–336.

Holdgate, M. W., 1967. The antarctic ecosystem. *Phil. Trans. Roy. Soc. London, Ser. B, 252* (777) : 363–383.

Holdgate, M. W., 1968. Antarctic biological research in prospect and retrospect. *Abstracts of Symposium on Antarctic Ecology, 29 July–2 August, 1968.* Cambridge, England.

Hopkins, T. L., 1966. Zooplankton standing crop in the Atlantic sector of the Antarctic Ocean. In *Second International Oceanographic Congress Abstracts,* edited by A. P. Vingradov; p. 160. Nauka, Moscow.

Hopkins, T. L., In press. Zooplankton standing crop in the Pacific sector of the Antarctic. In *Antarctic Research Series 16, Biology of The Antarctic Seas, IV,* edited by G. A. Llano. Am. Geophys. Union, Washington, D. C.

Mackintosh, N. A., 1934. Distribution of the macroplankton in the Atlantic sector of the Antarctic. *Discovery Repts., 9:* 67–158.

Mackintosh, N. A., and S. G. Brown, 1956. Preliminary estimates of the southern populations of the larger baleen whales. *Norsk Hvalfangstiid, 5:* 469–480.

McWhinnie, M. A., and P. L. Marciniak, 1964. Temperature responses and tissue respiration in antarctic crustacea with particular reference to the krill *Euphausia superba.* In *Antarctic Research Series 1, Biology of the Antarctic Seas,* edited by M. O. Lee; pp. 63–72. Am. Geophys. Union, Washington, D. C.

Marr, J. W. S., 1962. The natural history and geography of the Antarctic krill (*Euphausia superba* Dana). *Discovery Repts., 32:* 33–464.

Moiseev, P. A., 1968. Some aspects of commercial utilization of the Antarctic *Euphausia* resources. *Abstracts of Symposium on Antarctic Ecology, 29 July–2 August 1968.* Cambridge, England.

Morris, R. W., 1968. Thermogenesis and its possible survival value in fishes. *Abstracts of Symposium on Antarctic Ecology, 29 July–2 August, 1968.* Cambridge, England.

Naumov, A. G., 1964. Some features of the distribution and biology of *Euphausia superba* Dana. *Soviet Antarctic Expedition, Inform. Bull., 4:* 191–194.

Pomeroy, L. R., and R. E. Johannes, 1968. Occurrence and respiration of ultraplankton in the upper 500 m of the ocean. *Deep-Sea Res., 15*(3): 381–391.

Slobodkin, L. B., 1960. Ecological energy relationships at the population level. *Am. Naturalist, 194*(876): 213–236.

Sverdrup, H. U., M. W. Johnson, and R. H. Fleming, 1942. *The Oceans, Their Physics, Chemistry, and General Biology.* Prentice-Hall, Englewood Cliffs, N.J.

Wohlschlag, D. E., 1964. Respiratory metabolism and ecological characteristics of some fishes in McMurdo Sound, Antarctica. In *Antarctic Research Series 1, Biology of the Antarctic Seas,* edited by M. O. Lee; pp. 33–62. Am. Geophys. Union, Washington, D. C.

Ushakov, P. V., 1962. Some characteristics of the distribution of the bottom fauna off the coast of East Antarctica. *Soviet Antarctic Expedition Inform. Bull., 4:* 287–292.

Vinogradov, M. E., 1962. Feeding of the deep-sea zooplankton. *Rapports et Procès-Verbaux Des Reunions, Conseil Permanent International pour l'Exploration de la Mer, 153:* 114–120.

Voronina, N. M., 1966. The zooplankton of the Southern Ocean: some study results. *Oceanology, 6:* 681–689.

Perspectives of Benthic Ecology in Antarctica

JOEL W. HEDGPETH

Marine Science Center, Oregon State University, Newport

This paper is not intended to be a summary of all that has been done in studies of the benthic animals of the antarctic seas, but is rather an effort to focus on some of the questions raised by our still incomplete knowledge of antarctic benthic ecology. Some of these questions have been discussed by Dunbar (1968) in his concise book on ecological development of polar regions. His orientation, however, was primarily toward the Arctic, and he did not do justice to the differences in the environment and ecology of the Antarctic.

We always seem to be in danger of forgetting the obvious, and we need to be constantly reminded that in discussing the differences and similarities of the polar regions we are trying to compare the conditions of a cold mediterranean sea subject to coastal dilution and sedimentation from large rivers with a colder, oceanic ring around a central land mass. Fluctuations in salinity and deposition of sediment are greater in the arctic regions, and the environment as a whole is physiographically less stable through time. To put it simply, we may be trying to compare an estuary with an ocean, at least in the absence of adequate information on the deep arctic basins.

We are nevertheless indebted to Dunbar for his forceful reminder that low temperature in itself is not a limiting environmental factor, that in general an environmental factor with a narrow range is not limiting to the development of life. This is certainly obvious with respect to the benthic fauna of antarctic seas (and to a lesser degree of abyssal depths), which may indeed be as rich and diverse as that of tropical areas. Of course such comparisons depend on the groups or areas from which the data are selected, or, as the statisticians quaintly put it, on the size of the universe being considered. Information based on penguins, for example, would show that the equator is a much more severe and limiting environment than the icebound edge of Antarctica, for are there not hundreds of thousands if not millions of several species of penguins in that part of the world, and a dwindling population of perhaps 1,200 Galapagos penguins hiding from the heat of the sun in caves and beneath mangroves in one small spot of the entire equatorial region of the world? On the other hand, comparison of the brachyuran fauna of the same regions leads to the conclusion that the Antarctic is indeed the most severe and inhospitable of environments because there are no crabs there. (But we must remember that brachyuran crabs are absent from the arctic basin also.) Factors other than temperature may govern both cases.

At this time we are only beginning to obtain information to bear on these problems of evolution and ecological diversity in antarctic seas, yet at the same time we have initiated a global experiment in marine ecology by removing the top of the food pyramid of antarctic seas; in the absence of whales from the top what is going to happen to *Euphausia superba*, the key animal in the system? Or are we to place ourselves in the position of the whales, and if so, what would be the effect of our different pattern of levying upon these populations? It seems typical of our approach to nature that we have precipitated this vast unplanned experiment at the same time that a careful, limited experiment in the field to determine the effect of predation on bottom communities is being carried out in McMurdo Sound.

Another, much more pervasive and significant and equally unpremeditated experiment (experience is the better term for this sort of thing) is that of the release of lethal substances in our environment. The detection of pesticides in antarctic penguins indicates the global scale of our interference with the natural system, even if the amounts detected are as yet below "dangerous" levels at least as far as penguins may be concerned (Sladen *et al.*, 1966; George and Frear, 1966; Tatton and Ruzicka, 1967). The impact of our present unconscionable dispersal of pesticides on the antarctic benthos may hopefully be minor, but we cannot be certain in view of the growing suspicion that many pesticides may be more lethal in sea water than on land or in fresh water (or perhaps marine organisms may be more susceptible). Certainly marine crustacea appear to be more susceptible than freshwater crustacea to noxious chemicals designed to kill terrestrial arthropods (Eisler, 1969).

While we may not have reached the stage of seriously affecting antarctic ecosystems, the early warning signs are apparent, and it is obvious that protection of antarctic ecosystems must begin in other parts of the world.

INTERTIDAL LIFE

Our knowledge of the shore and shallow-water life of the antarctic regions begins with the pioneer observations of the ill-fated James Eights (see Clarke, 1916; Calman, 1937). Eights visited the South Shetlands region as surgeon and naturalist on Captain Fanning's expedition of 1829–1830, and collected two of the most characteristic antarctic invertebrates which he later described, *Glyptonotus antarcticus* and *Decolopoda australis.* Neither of these animals occurs intertidally, but were cast upon the shore or trapped in tide pools by the surge from ice breaking off the permanent ice caps (Eights, 1833). In this vivid first account of antarctic shores nothing specifically was said of life between the tides other than a passing reference to "a fine Patella" (obviously *Patinigera*), although Eights did observe the diurnal tide cycle of the South Shetlands.

The tidal difference in some parts of the Antarctic is approximately two to three meters; during January and February of 1969 it was about six feet or two meters at Palmer Station on Anvers Island. In his summary of studies of the tides and intertidal zones of the Antarctic Knox (1968) inferred from the literature a "basic pattern" for intertidal (littoral) zonation that places the seasonal growth of diatoms and filamentous green algae characteristically but vaguely between high- and low-tide levels, and the limpet *Patinigera* in the "upper sublittoral," or the highest part of the subtidal, although its occurrence in tide pools is mentioned. Probably *Patinigera polaris* should be considered a characteristic intertidal animal, if not the only large intertidal invertebrate, on the shores of the antarctic islands, and it seems odd that Neushul (1964) observed it only in tide pools, since it does not appear to be rare on exposed rock surfaces. It may move upward during the summer to feed upon the seasonal bands of diatoms and filamentous green algae, but at Palmer Station it occurs in many places well above this seasonal growth which is obvious to about 0.25 m or a foot above the low-tide level (Fig. 1). Below tide level (the "upper sublittoral") this limpet is evidently the characteristic mass species (Gruzov and Pushkin, 1970), with densities of about 200

Fig. 1. The filamentous alga zone at Palmer Station; the water level is approximately at mean low tide and the staff reading should be lowered so that zero is at water level. (Photograph taken January 16, 1969, by the author.)

per m^2 at 1.5 to 3 m below low water in the Palmer Station area (McCain and Stout, 1969). It remains to be demonstrated whether its intertidal occurrence is seasonal or whether it frequents locations that are free from ice action the year around. To judge from the diagram of ice cover at Hope Bay (Fig. 2), fast ice is variable and sporadic and it is possible that many parts of the rocky intertidal area at lower levels may be free from fast ice because of surge and tidal action beneath the ice. The limiting factor for the intertidal occurrence of *Patinigera* may not be winter ice but predation by the Dominican gull. Holdgate (1967) observed that "among the sublittoral/littoral benthos in the shallowest water the limpet, *Patinigera polaris* is an important element in the diet of gulls, *Larus dominicanus*." In the Palmer Station area there are extensive middens of limpet shells marking the feeding stations of the gulls, which, according to B. Stonehouse (personal communication), feed only from surfaces exposed at low water. This would suggest that where the gulls are abundant the limpets may be cropped off as they move upwards. Most of the limpets in the intertidal region, to judge from personal observations and various accounts in the literature, occur in crevices and similar sheltered situations (e.g.,

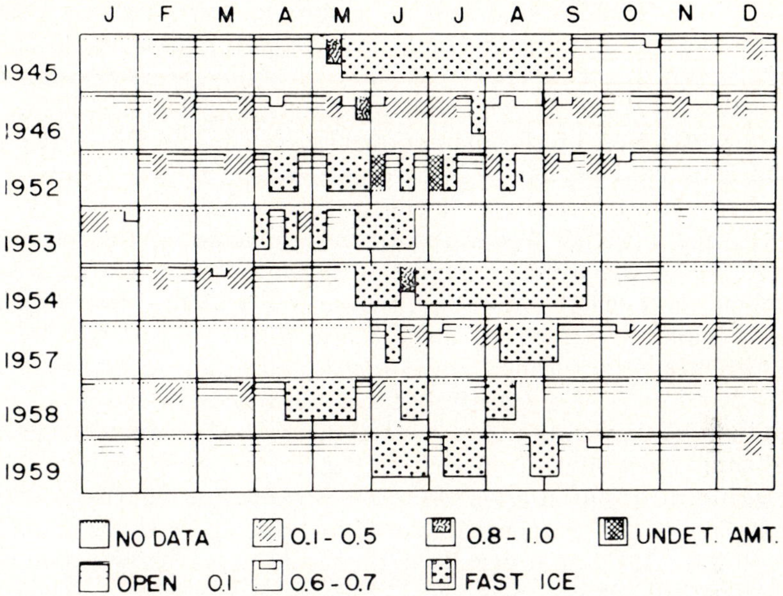

Fig. 2. Ice cover for various months at Hope Bay, Antarctica, for the indicated years (From Neushul, 1968).

Price and Redfearn, 1968), when they are not in the standing water of tide pools. Air temperatures at exposed situations occupied by limpets were about 8° to 10°C. Two specimens were observed in a splash pool high above the ordinary tide levels; the obvious vegetation of this pool was *Enteromorpha intestinalis* (according to R. Schuster), and the temperature of the water in daytime was about 11°C. Other specimens of *Patinigera* were observed on sheer rock faces of a narrow cove on Litchfield Island well above high-tide level. Quite possibly this is a situation relatively free from the action of brash ice during the summer months.

A number of small crustaceans and worms are associated with the seasonal belt of filamentous algae (which include representatives of *Ulothrix, Cladophora, Enteromorpha,* and *Monostroma*) and diatoms, but the larger invertebrates occasionally found in tide pools or exposed on rocks are adventitious, cast up by surge or wave action from falling ice, as Eights observed so long ago. At Palmer Station these included a pycnogonid, the sea urchin *Sterechinus,* and an asteroid (*Cryptasterias* sp.). The more common diatoms forming the brown fur-like growth in tide pools and on intertidal surfaces just below the filamentous green algae include (in order of abundance in a sample from Palmer Station determined by N. Ingram Hendey): *Achnanthes subsessilis, Licmophora belgicae* var. *minor, Fragilaria planctonica, F. islandicae* var. *stricta, Achnanthes parvula,* and *Navicula directa.*

This restriction of the filamentous algae zone to the lower part of the intertidal region is in strong contrast to the zonation observed at Petrel Island and vicinity (about 66°40′S) by Delépine and Hureau (1963). According to these observers, the green belt extends from the average high-tide level to about mid-tide level, a vertical distance of one meter, where it is replaced by the brown zone of colonial diatoms for about 0.5 m to the mean low-tide level. This difference may reflect differences in physiographic conditions in the two localities, or possibly the later season of observation by Delépine and Hureau, or the conditions and consequently the seasonal zones may vary from year to year. Obviously we are only at the beginning of our study of zonation on antarctic shores.

Observed water temperatures at the surface near shore at Palmer Station were 1.0°C, not greatly higher than those of the upper 30 m investigated by divers. Levring (1966) suggested that in the spring when light is a more significant factor than temperature, algae may grow faster because the water is still too cold for respiration to increase and inhibit rapid growth. With special reference to filamentous greens "perhaps mainly where differences in temperature of the surface water are considerable," Levring stated, "the development of such seasonal communities is certainly favored by the balance between radiant energy and water temperature. . . . Further investigations in this field would be most valuable." In antarctic regions where air temperature may be more variable than water temperature, especially during the spring and summer, the development of a filamentous green algal community is an intertidal phenomenon.

Above the filamentous algal and diatom zone the intertidal rocks are apparently bare, at least at Palmer Station. There may be sparse growths of microscopic algae, but the general appearance of the exposed regions is that of polished barren granite surfaces, even on those surfaces occupied by a sparse scattering of limpets. Here and there along with the limpets is a sparse scattering of various red algae such as *Leptosomia simplex, Iridaea,* and *Curdiea racowitzae* in crevices and on sheltered rock surfaces up to perhaps mid-tide levels (Fig. 3). The plants are small and evidently seasonal. In all, this is obviously the simplest of intertidal zones, devoid of barnacles, littorines, and such roaming crustaceans as crabs and isopods (*Ligia,* etc.).

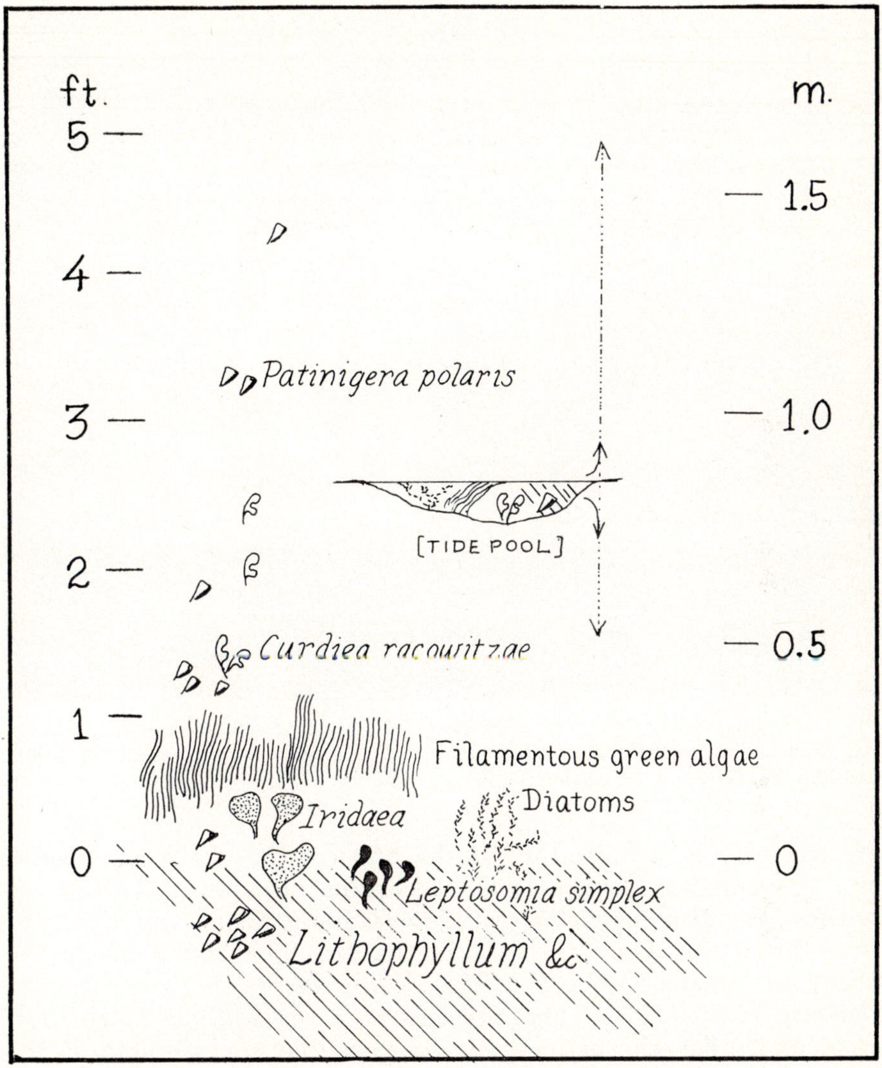

Fig. 3. Diagram of zonation at Palmer Station, Antarctica.

Although most of the observations of littoral and sublittoral situations in the antarctic and subantarctic islands so far reported have been made by botanists, little emphasis has been placed on the wide occurrence of encrusting red alga except that it is characteristic of the bottom of permanent tide pools (Fig. 4). In various locations around the Palmer Station area (Hedgpeth, 1969c), and in much of Antarctica for that matter, crustose red or coralline algae

Fig. 4. A small tide pool (about 15″ long) at Palmer Station, showing crustose red algae, diatom growth, and specimen of *Patinigera*. (Photograph taken January 14, 1969, by the author.)

are characteristic indicators of the upper level of the sublittoral, or of the extreme low-tide level. According to Zaneveld (1968) the crustose red *Hildenbrandia* is the most abundant alga of this type from Ross to Balleny Islands. In the Melchior Island group the abundant crustose alga is *Lithophyllum aequabile,* according to Delépine *et al.* (1970). The presence of *Lithophyllum, Lithothamnion,* and other encrusting red and coralline algae is one of the most reliable indicators of the lowest part of the intertidal, or the uppermost extension of the subtidal zone for most parts of the world, including the Galapagos Islands (Hedgpeth, 1969b). In favorable conditions of wave action and exposure, modified by such factors as humidity and shelter from insolation, the "Lithothamnia zone," as termed by Gauld and Buchanan (1959) may extend above the extreme low-water levels, especially in regions of reduced tidal range, and constitutes a universal zonation marker. One of the striking features of the situation at Palmer Station, where there is no surf but irregular surge from falling ice, is the almost diagrammatic upper limit of the encrusting gray-lavender growth of red algae at what appears to be the extreme low-water line (Fig. 5). This is probably the same algal complex that is referred to as "*Lithophyllum aequabile,* etc." in the Melchior Islands. The limit does not appear to change with exposure, and although encrusting algae do occur in the tide pools well above the low-water line, they do not occur on surfaces exposed at low tide at either Palmer Station or Port Lockroy. Perhaps this distribution is controlled in part by winter ice conditions. The zone of encrusting red algae is obviously higher on the shores of subantarctic islands; at Macquarie, where there is heavy wave action, it is evidently well above low tide (Kenny and Haysom, 1962) and Knox (1968) indicates it as occurring to the upper part of the intertidal zone in the Magellanic region. In such regions the lithothamnia zone proper appears to be that of *Lithothamnion-Lithophyllum-Melobesia* of the lower littoral of Knox's Table 5, rather than of *Hildenbrandia*. Indeed, in some parts of the world, such as the eastern North Pacific, a species of *Hildenbrandia* may be part of the black encrustation on rocks of the higher tidal zones (Southward, 1958).

Similar displacement of *Lithothamnion* with exposure to wave action occurs in arctic regions, to judge from the diagrams pre-

Fig. 5. View of intertidal area at Palmer Station, showing low tide line of crustose algae (*Lithophyllum, etc.*) and cluster of *Patinigera polaris;* a patch of green alga to the left. (Photograph taken January 16, 1969, by the author.)

sented by Gurjanova (1968), but it is difficult to compare the "high arctic" and antarctic patterns of zonation in the absence of more comprehensive information. Because of the current patterns of the Northern Hemisphere, boreal conditions extend proportionately much farther north than subantarctic conditions to the south, with consequent northward extension of many common elements of the north temperate or boreal flora and fauna. Much of the intertidal life and zonation patterns described in the literature as subarctic or arctic are those familiar to students of the shores of northern Europe and the British Isles (See Lewis, 1964).

Madsen (1936, 1940) suggested that the arctic littoral zone can be characterized by the absence of *Balanus balanoides* and littoral mollusks, especially *Mytilus* and *Littorina*. In Greenland the northern limit of these animals is about 74°N but their absence from localities considerably south of this limit may be related, according to Madsen, to local productivity conditions. Barnacles are absent from the littoral of Macquarie Island, which Kenny and Haysom (1962) considered to be at the limit of the subantarctic. This absence is attributed to the inability of the pelagic larvae of barnacles to cross the strong currents of the westerly drift. However, it should be noted that *Chthamalus* has not colonized the Galapagos Islands, although they lie directly in the path of the strong currents from the mainland. Perhaps the long trip weakens some larvae beyond reasonable chance of survival, even if their normal span of pelagic life would theoretically enable them to make such a voyage; the distance is simply beyond their safety factor.

While the intertidal life of the Antarctic is obviously minimal, it is possible that the conditions under which *Patinigera* lives are not as extreme as those of the boreal Arctic, where exposure at low tide in winter may result in freezing of the animal, with the formation of ice crystals (Kanwisher, 1955, 1959). While this may be a normal event in the lives of organisms in such an environment, it does restrict their feeding and reproduction. It will be interesting to find out if *Patinigera* is actually caught within the ice, or lives beneath it during winter, protected from the winter air extremes, in view of Kanwisher's observation that animals in a constant environment of −1.7°C cannot withstand freezing.

THE SHALLOW SUBLITTORAL REGION

Since the feasibility of free diving in antarctic waters was demonstrated a decade ago (Neushul, 1959, 1964), this method of studying the shallow, sublittoral benthos to depths of 35 to 50 m has steadily increased, and has now reached the stage of experimental ecology, although only preliminary information on the experiments is available at this time (Dayton *et al.*, 1970). As a result of these efforts by investigators of many nations we now have some knowledge of the qualitative distribution of some of the more conspicuous benthic organisms, especially the larger algae, in the region of the Antarctic Peninsula (Neushul, 1964; Delépine and Hureau, 1963; Etcheverry, 1968; Price and Redfearn, 1968; Gruzov and Pushkin, 1969; McCain and Stout, 1969) and of the rocky to coarse gravel and stony bottoms of the Antarctic Continent at Mirnyy (Gruzov *et al.*, 1967; Andriashev, 1968; Propp, 1970) and at McMurdo Sound (Dayton *et al.*, 1969). Some account of the general distribution of the flora of the extreme southern antarctic regions is provided by Zaneveld (1966, 1968) and Neushul (1968).

Two somewhat different regions are involved in these studies, although the fauna of the muddy bottoms at the base of the rocky granite shores of some parts of the Antarctic Peninsula appears to consist of the same species as that of the coarse basaltic to muddy bottoms of McMurdo Sound, such as *Odontaster validus, Sterechinus neumayeri, Laternula elliptica, Glyptonotus antarcticus,* and various pycnogonids. On the steep or vertical slopes of the rocky regions of the Antarctic Peninsula there are dense growths of algae a few meters below the surface. The largest and most conspicuous species is *Phyllogigas grandifolius,* a large laminarian that may attain a length of 3 m. Delépine and Hureau (1963) did not find this alga in fertile or fructifying condition during the antarctic summer, but M. Neushul (personal communication) found it "completely covered by reproductive cells during the summer." However, the life cycle is not yet worked out, and may have some similarity to that of *Laminaria hyperborea* in northern waters which reproduces during the winter months (Kain, 1966), and the larger plants could be ten years or more old. This may be verified if, like *Laminaria hyperborea, Phyllogigas* lays down annual growth rings in the stipe. *Ascoseira mirabilis* is another alga that may germinate at some other time than summer, or have particular requirements as yet unascertained. According to Neushul (1968) there is no evidence that larger antarctic algae are heterotrophic during the winter, but Wilce (1967) considered that this may be a significant factor in deep water perennial algae in the Arctic.

There are local differences in the occurrence of the various larger algae, but most of the available reports are preliminary and it is not possible to state what may be the "typical" or "characteristic" zonation of the sublittoral flora and perhaps there is none. Neushul (1964) found dense growths of *Phyllogigas* more characteristic of islands south of the South Shetlands group during his pioneer study, and Delépine and Hureau observed well-developed growths of this species at the Pointe Geologie Archipelago. In general, there is first a zone of red algae such as *Leptosomia, Iridaea,* a lower and often dense band of brown algae consisting of dense bushy growths of *Desmarestia,* and the foliose thalli of *Phyllogigas,* ending at around 20 m on steep slopes. Below this are patches of red algae and occasional bushes of *Desmarestia* in some localities. Some examples of algal zonation are represented in Figure 6.

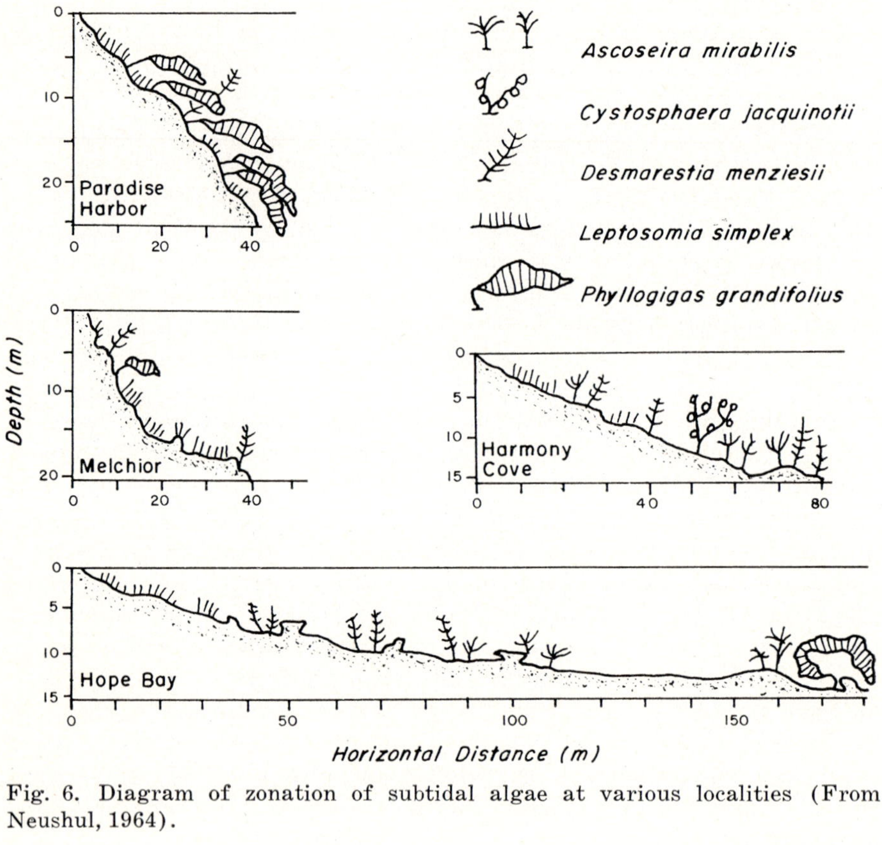

Fig. 6. Diagram of zonation of subtidal algae at various localities (From Neushul, 1964).

Zaneveld (1968) considered the limit of the sublittoral in the Antarctic to be about 37 m; various algae occur below that to depths of at least 600 m, but he did not believe that such algae are heterotrophic.

The dense growths of macroscopic algae in the Antarctic Peninsula area are apparently associated with very high levels of primary production. Horne *et al.* (1969) estimated a productivity of 130 g C/m^2 for the season (about 90 days) near Signy Island. This value is comparable to measurements made by El-Sayed (1968) in the Bransfield and Gerlache Straits, but as the authors pointed out, it is difficult to compare the shipboard measurements with the *in situ* procedures carried out in a small boat at Signy Island.

In contrast to the region of the Antarctic Peninsula and the Scotia Arc, where most of the diving investigations have been made by botanists, observations of Mirnyy and at McMurdo have been made primarily by zoologists. This is appropriate since the benthos of these regions is predominantly animal. At both Mirnyy and McMurdo nearshore life is restricted by the Ice Shelf and heavy winter ice formation, and at McMurdo the phenomenon of anchor ice influences the distribution of benthic life above 33 m (Dayton *et al.*, 1969). The general patterns of sublittoral zonation and assemblages of organisms is similar at both McMurdo and Mirnyy (Fig. 7). There is a shallow zone inhabited principally and sparsely by motile organisms, in which large perennial sessile animals are not established. In the Mirnyy area two biocoenoses or communities are recognized, the diatom-*Odontaster validus*-*Tubularia ralphy* community, of the shallowest depths (2 to 10 m depending on type of substrate, slope, and relation to ice cover), and the *Sterechinus neumayeri*-*Phyllophora antarctica* community, which may extend to 15 or 20 m, but seems to be absent from vertical rocky slopes. The biomass of these two groups is calculated at 20–25 g/m^2 and 450 g/m^2 respectively. These two assemblages are roughly comparable to the first zone recognized at McMurdo Sound (Fig. 8). The third community recognized at Mirnyy is characterized by the presence of alcyonarians, and its zonation appears to be similar to the second zone, predominantly of sessile coelenterates at McMurdo, and at both localities its lower limit is slightly below 30 m. The average biomass of this assemblage at Mirnyy is estimated at 1,000 g/m^2. (It is possible that the *Eunephthya* sp. of Soviet workers and *Alcyonium paessleri* at McMurdo are the same

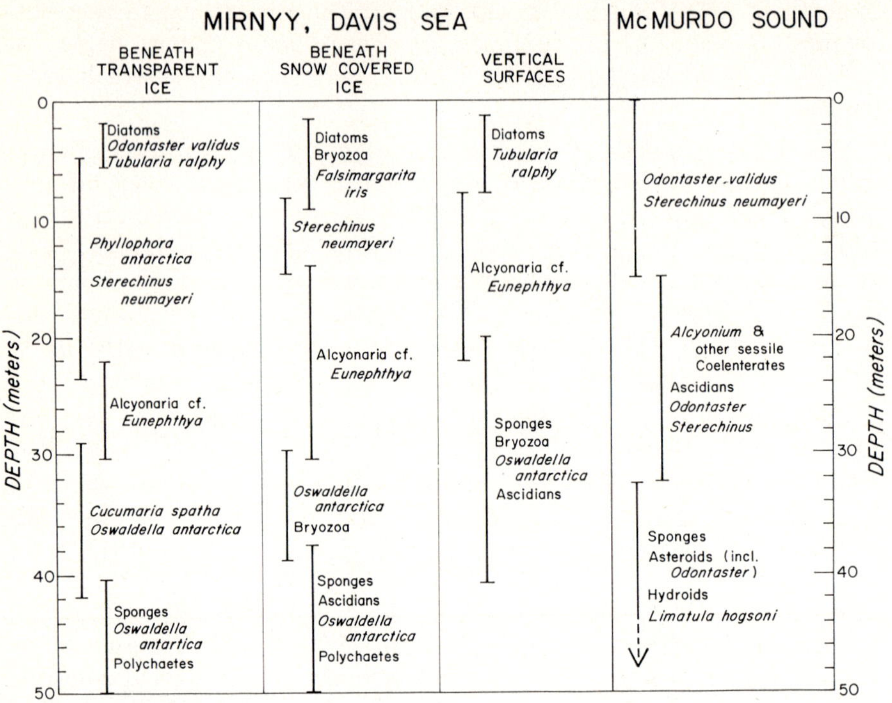

Fig. 7. Zonation of benthos at various situations in the Davis Sea (left) and at McMurdo Sound (right) (Compiled from Gruzov *et al.*, 1967; Dayton *et al.*, 1970).

animal; marine ecology is beginning to suffer badly from the dearth of competent, active specialists in all groups of coelenterates.)

Below thirty meters or so (33 at McMurdo) the well-known sponge community is developed. Soviet workers estimate the biomass in the order of 3 kg/m^2. It seems apparent that at both McMurdo and Mirnyy the zone of relative stability or freedom from seasonal ice action is about 30 m. This suggests also that the differences in associations and their depths between the two localities may be due in part to local physical differences and in part to methodology, but that the associations or communities are the same. The research at McMurdo has been concerned with detecting biological interactions and field experimentation with the effect of predation upon community stability, whereas the Mirnyy studies have been primarily of a quantitative-cataloging nature aimed at estimating and understanding the trophic structure of the communities. Both approaches are necessary if we are to understand antarctic bottom communities.

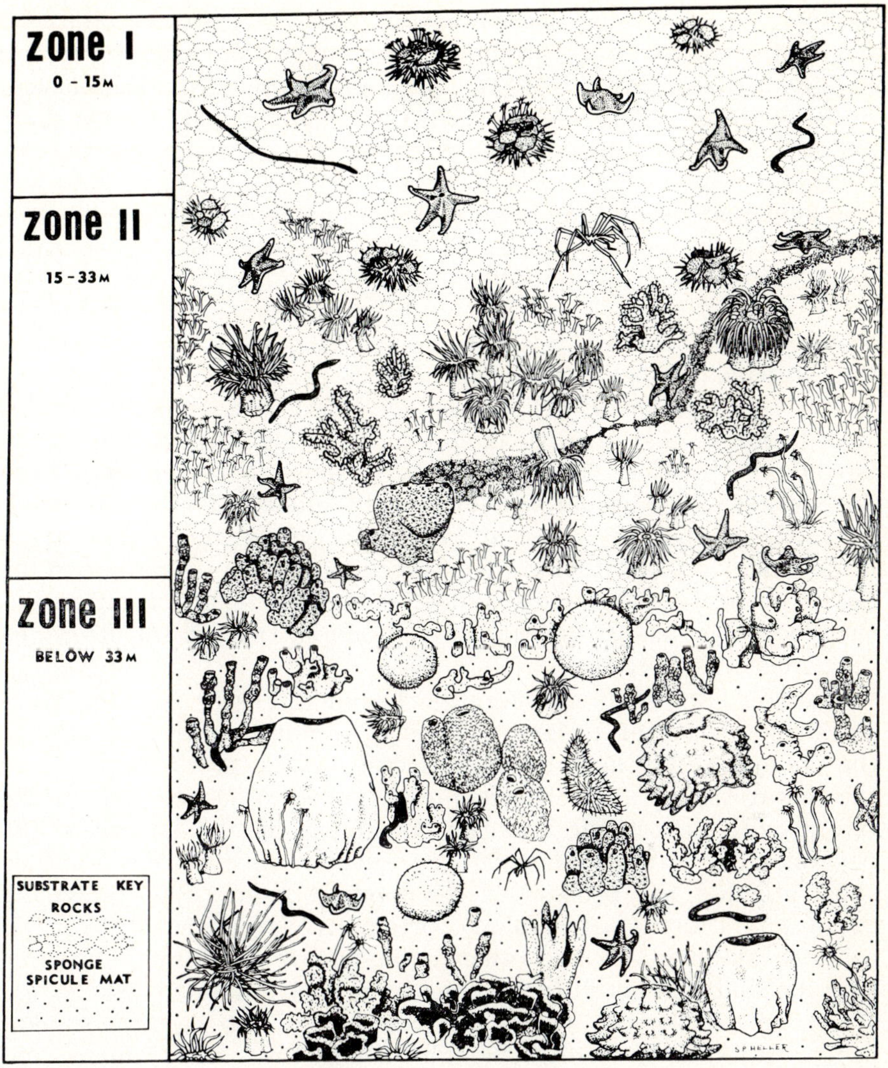

Fig. 8. General view of distribution of shallow benthos in McMurdo Sound (Drawing courtesy Paul Dayton).

THE DEEPER BENTHOS

Beyond the range of diving our knowledge of the composition of the benthos depends on the results of dredging, bottom grabbing, or trawling and photography (Bullivant, 1967; Dearborn, 1968). All of these methods are frustratingly incomplete in one way or another, especially in the Antarctic with its great diversity of taxonomic entities. (It is interesting to note that after writing a review of the situation in 1964, Longhurst moved from the benthos to the plankton.) Andriashev (1968), for example, stated that there are at least 500 different species of invertebrates in the shallow benthic assemblages of antarctic coastal regions. So far, however, the principal studies of antarctic bottom fauna in quantitative terms have been undertaken by Soviet workers, using the same methodology they have applied to studies of arctic bottom fauna since the 1930's. The large corpus of quantitative benthic ecology of the arctic seas of the U.S.S.R. is summarized by Zenkevitch 1963); the comparable work in other parts of the Arctic is that of Thorson (1933, 1934), Vibe (1937), Einarsson (1941), and Spärck (1937). It is probable that conditions similar to those encountered in the Greenland fjords by Thorson and Vibe exist in the region of the Antarctic Peninsula, but so far the only quantitative benthic studies reported upon are those at Foster Bay, Deception Island (Gallardo and Castillo, 1968). The Davis Sea area investigated by Soviet workers (Uschakov, 1963), is a more open situation, although the fauna is essentially the same as that of the Ross Sea on comparable bottoms.

The volcanic events at Deception Island in Foster Bay and those at Surtsey south of Iceland suggest a miniature mirror image of the obvious differences between arctic and antarctic regions—in the Antarctic we are concerned with an enclosed bay and in the Arctic with an oceanic situation around a central landmass, the new island of Surtsey (Fig. 9). At Surtsey the situation is a new substrate and the process of colonization from the neighboring ocean and established shallow bottoms (Nicolaisen, 1968). Deception Island is, on the other hand, a site of chronic volcanic activity that has recently become more active (Valenzuela *et al.*, 1968) and ecological studies are concerned with reestablishment during quiescent periods, although in both cases the primary concern is the reaction of organisms to new environments. In Port Foster (the bay of Deception Island) the volcanic activity is on a smaller scale than at Surtsey. According to the observations of Gallardo and Castillo (1968), volcanic activity eliminated or severely reduced the bottom fauna on the east side of Port Foster, but a pocket of comparatively undisturbed benthos was left on the western side of the bay (approximately indicated by Station 8 in Fig. 9). A photograph of this area at a depth of 109 m taken by the *Hero* in February, 1969, shows an ophiuroid assemblage

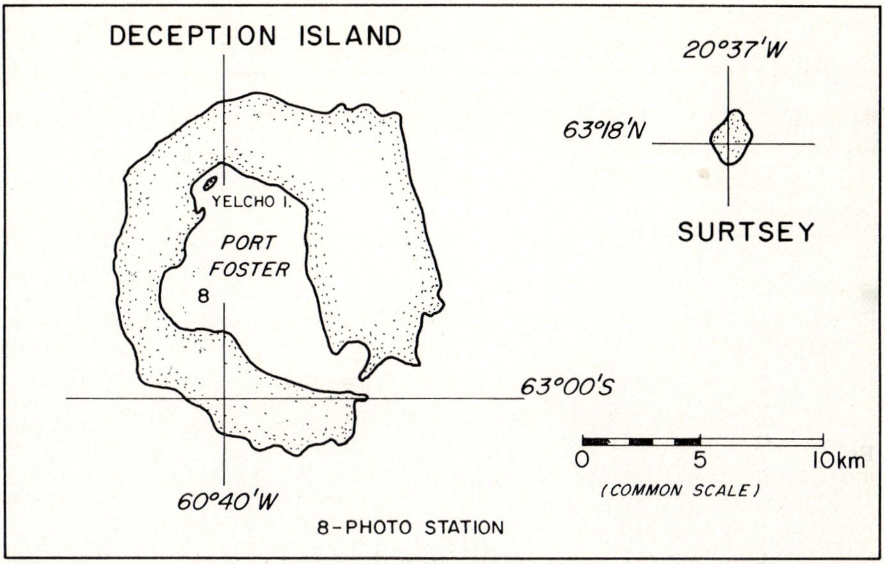

Fig. 9. Location map of Deception Island and Surtsey, to approximately same scale.

superficially reminiscent of northern latitude shallow bottom assemblages (Fig. 10).

In the area of the Davis Sea, or East Antarctic, there is a very high nearshore biomass; the averages are much higher than for similar depths in the Bering Sea, but at about 500 m the concentrations fall off and at depths of 1,000 m and below they are less than in similar depths in the Bering Sea (Fig. 11). The antarctic bottom assemblages differ from those of the Arctic not only in their greater biomass but also in their comparative composition. There are usually more sponges and other epifaunal types in the antarctic assemblages, and fewer bivalves (Fig. 12).

Studies in the Ross Sea have been based on qualitative dredge and trawl hauls, supplemented by excellent photographs (Figs. 13, 14). Bullivant (1967) recognized three major assemblages in the Ross Sea at depths of 200 to 400 m. The first of these is the Deep Shelf Mixed Assemblage, associated with fine sediment with erratic boulders, consisting for the most part of tubiculous polychaetes, rooted bryozoa, various echinoderms, mollusks, and large nemerteans. The second is the Deep Shelf Mud Bottom Assemblage, occurring on mud or sandy bottom with erratic boulders; tubiculous polychaetes are again abundant, along with sipunculids, a forami-

Fig. 10. Bottom photograph taken from R/V *Hero* in the comparatively undisturbed part of Foster Bay (See Fig. 9), 109 m (Courtesy John C. McCain).

nifer, and ophiuroids. The third assemblage is that associated with a bottom of cobbles embedded in muddy sand, consisting for the most part of hard bottom animals such as bryozoans, gorgonaceans, stylasterine corals and tunicates, several species of ophiuroids, and pycnogonids. A number of minor assemblages were noted, including the McMurdo Sound glass sponge assemblage in depths of 69 to 180 m, on a bottom of "unsorted debris." These assemblages were not well defined quantitatively, but the photographs convey an adequate impression of both the richness and patchiness of the bottom assemblages of the Ross Sea.

Some elements of the fauna evidently occur some distance beneath the permanent shelf ice; Littlepage and Pearse (1962) found amphipods and actiniarians to be abundant at depths of 40 to 75 m beneath the shelf ice some 28 km from the ice edge. Some of the most common animals found near McMurdo Station were absent, including *Limatula hodgsoni, Odontaster validus, Lineus corrugatus,* and *Trematomus bernacchii.* Their sampling was done by grabs and traps lowered through cracks in the ice, but the tech-

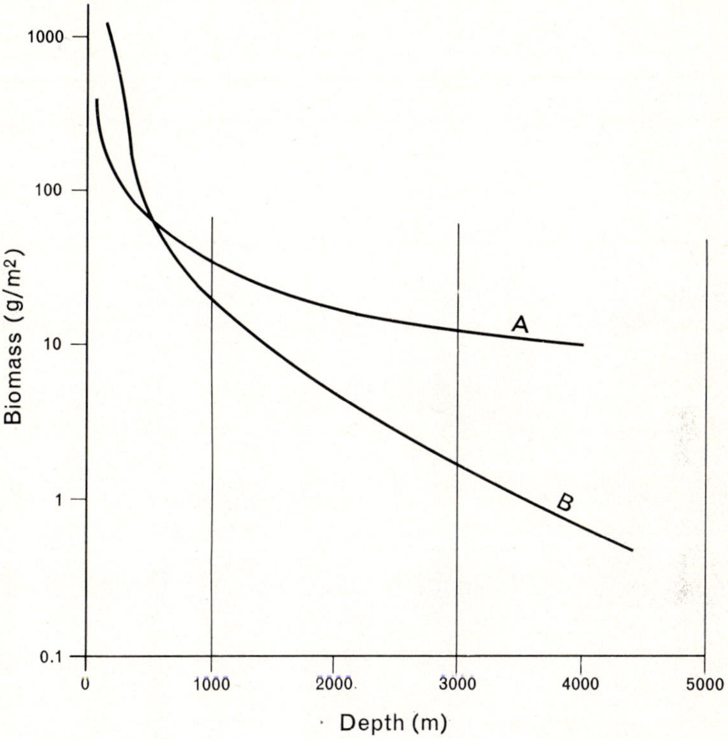

Fig. 11. Comparative biomass profiles for the Davis and Bering Seas (From Uschakov, 1963).

nique has not been followed up, and nothing has been added to this preliminary study.

As a whole the Ross Sea benthos consists primarily of sessile, filter, or particle feeding invertebrates attached to numerous rocks, and bears no clear relationship to the shallow soft or level bottom communities of European waters. If there is any "parallel community" in Thorson's (1957) sense, it would be the assemblage associated with cobble bottoms off Point Barrow. This was already suggested by Bullivant (1967) ; the only account of the Point Barrow assemblages of "the rubble zone" is that by MacGinitie (1955). Unfortunately it is impossible, because of the different manners of presenting data, to compare the assemblages in any detail, except that it appears that sponges and asteroids are less significant in the arctic assemblage. The most significant difference between the general ecological situations of Point Barrow and McMurdo Sound is the considerable freshwater drainage and associated deposition

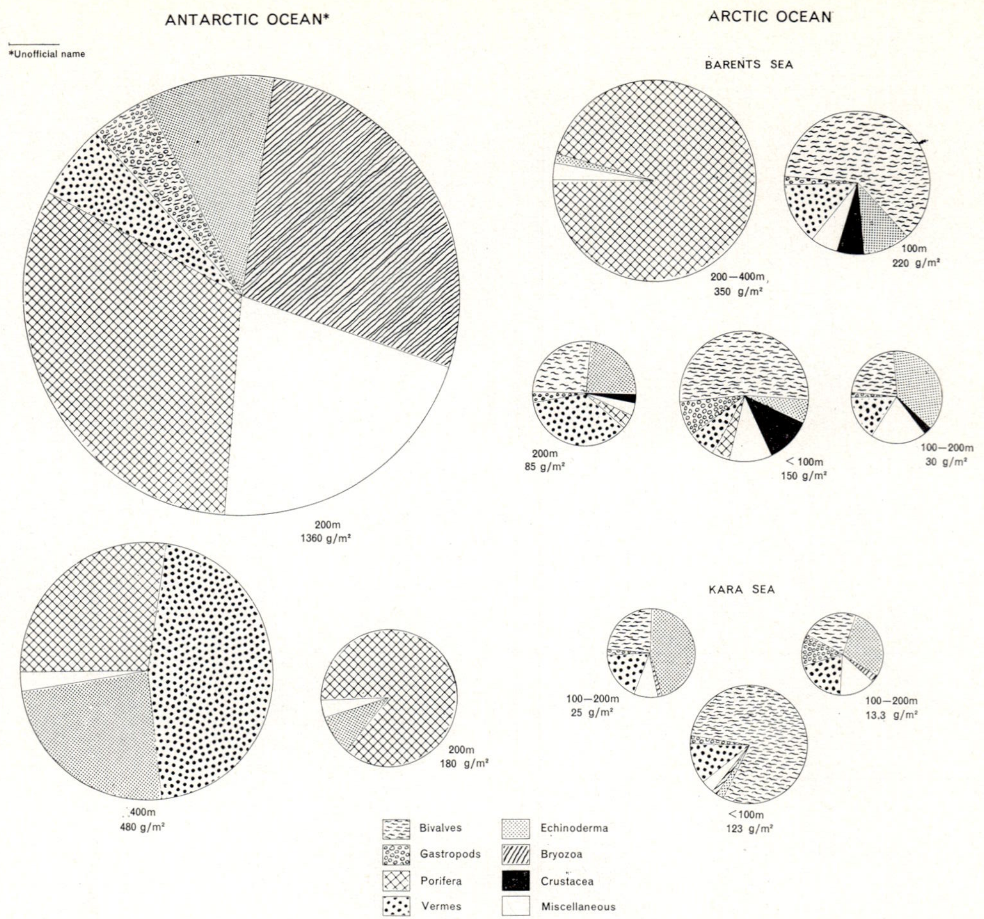

Fig. 12. Percentage composition of various elements of the benthic fauna in the Antarctic and Arctic (Modified from Uschakov, 1963, and Zenkevich, 1963; courtesy American Geographical Society).

Fig. 13. View of association of large sponges in the Ross Sea, east of Beaufort Island, Endeavour Station A468, 110 m, 76°59′S, 166°36′E, 26 Jan. 1959 (Courtesy J. S. Bullivant).

of mud in the Point Barrow area. The area is consequently unfavorable for observations by divers and photography. Similar epifaunal assemblages uninfluenced by river drainage may occur in the high arctic areas of northern Canada and Greenland, but we have no information about them. Most of the "arctic" epifaunal assemblages described in the literature (e.g., Vibe, 1939; Einarsson, 1941) are actually boreal assemblages in which *Modiolus* is the most abundant larger animal. The information on these assemblages is based primarily on quantitative bottom grabs and, as the authors pointed out, the grab is not a suitable instrument for sampling stony bottoms. Some direct comparisons between antarctic

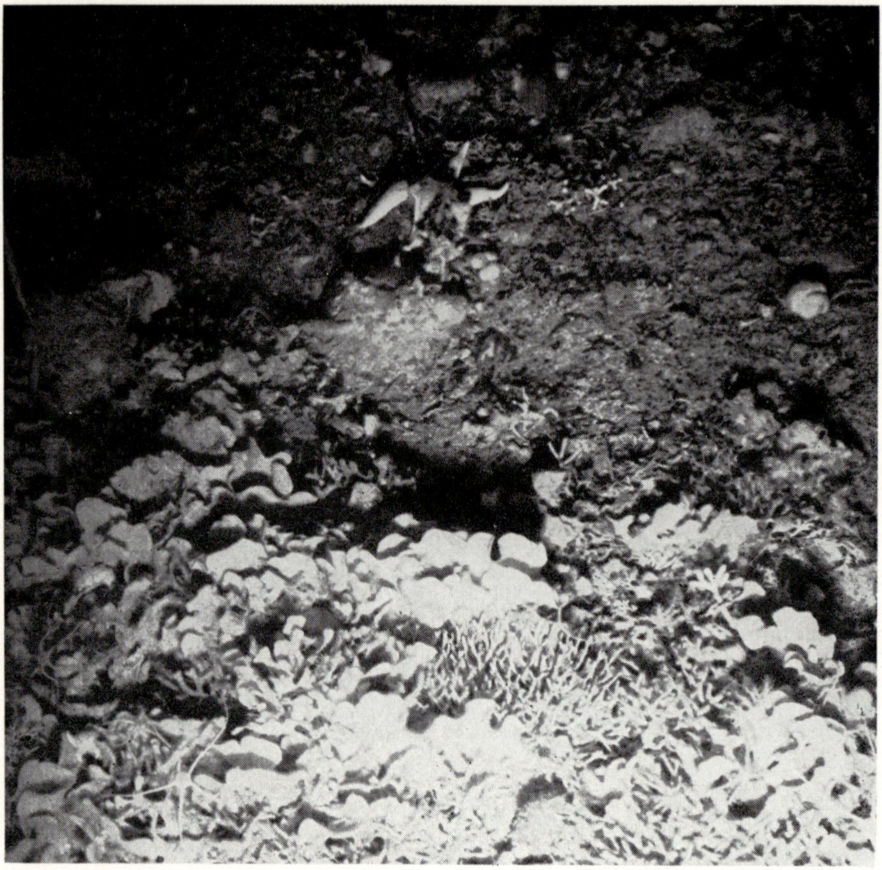

Fig. 14. View of bryozoan-sponge association (Pennell Bank assemblage) in the Ross Sea, Endeavour Station A528, 274-265 m, 74°23′S, 179°26′W, 7 Feb. 1960 (Courtesy J. S. Bullivant).

and arctic hard bottom communities have been made by Soviet investigators but their results are not yet available in detail (Propp, 1970).

TOWARD A BIOGEOGRAPHIC SYNTHESIS

Since Ekman's worldwide synthesis of zoogeography in 1935 (revised and translated in the 1953 edition), there has been a renewed emphasis on the collection of antarctic material and a corresponding increase in monographs and reports on various taxa from antarctic waters. While much remains to be done, especially with more difficult groups such as coelenterates and bryozoa, and with smaller organisms of the "meiofauna," a coherent picture of distribution of taxonomic entities in antarctic seas (or the southern ocean) is emerging.

Subject to further refinement of detail, there are basically two broad regions, the Antarctic and the Subantarctic, with some tendency towards regional differences in the Kerguelen and Magellanic areas of the Subantarctic, and the Antarctic Peninsula, Western Antarctic, and South Georgia areas. This is essentially as surmised by Ekman, although he preferred the term "Antiboreal" to Subantarctic, a usage which has not been kindly received, especially by oceanographers, who still refer to the Subtropical rather than Antiboreal Convergence. As far as the basic distributions are concerned, there seems to be little to argue about among biogeographers except the terminology to be used for them. The term "notal" in place of Subantarctic has, as far as I am concerned, little to recommend it (Hedgpeth, 1969a,c), since it is basically an anatomical term pertaining to the back or dorsum of some organism or another. It has had a certain vogue among Soviet workers, and in the *Soviet Atlas of Antarctica* (Bakayev, 1966) "Notalian" is used for distributions in the southern temperate zone by several of the contributors for special maps (see Plate 128), including the general map for phytobenthos (Plate 129, V), but in several others and in the summary map for zoogeography (Plate 132, No. XII) the term Subantarctic is used. Although Webster III acknowledges the existence of the term "notalian," I am unaware of any usage in the American English, and the source of the definition as the "south temperate marine biogeographic realm that is bounded by the southern isocrymes of 68° and 44°F." is not stated. In any event, most workers using the English language obviously prefer Subantarctic, although Fleming (1963) would prefer to use "Neoaustral" and "Paleoaustral" and suggests "Neonotian" and "Paleonotian" as alternatives.

Part of this terminological problem arises from the application of terms established for terrestrial circumstances (e.g., boreal) to marine conditions. As Dunbar (1968) emphasized, the "Subarctic" and "Subantarctic" of the sea are two very different environments, but he obviously prefers to refine the definitions rather than concoct new terms (and we obviously agree) :

> ... *subarctic* refers to the region with mixed Arctic and non-Arctic water in the upper 200 to 300 meters. *Pacific*

> *Subarctic* as used by Sverdrup, Johnson and Fleming ... refers to the waters of the North Pacific in the Gulf of Alaska region, which contain no Arctic water at all; the *Subantarctic* is usually understood to mean the broad zone between the Antarctic Convergence and the Subtropical Convergence to the north, which is innocent of any Antarctic water in the upper layers.

Ekman divided the Antarctic into a high antarctic region and a low antarctic region. The high antarctic was subdivided into the West Antarctic, including the Weddell Sea and the Antarctic Peninsula, and the East Antarctic, including the Ross Sea. The low antarctic region included South Georgia. His antiboreal region was divided into the South American region with a strong antarctic component, Kerguelen, and the other oceanic islands. In Ekman's English edition (1953) the usages of "region" and "province" are inconsistent, and may possibly represent the vagaries of the translator, but das Gebiet of the original edition is also an imprecise term. In any event the term province has never been precisely defined in biogeography and since it may nevertheless imply somewhat more knowledge than we have at present for most antarctic localities, it seems best to avoid it. Our knowledge of the deeper benthos of all oceans of the Southern Hemisphere is still very incomplete; as Knox (1970) put it, "Over the greater part of the vast expanse of the South Pacific there is very scanty information concerning the distribution of the benthic animals." He pointed out that studies in deeper water around New Zealand have turned up an interesting array of species represented in Tertiary deposits but no longer found nearshore in New Zealand.

Support for a distinct east and west biogeographic subdivision of the Antarctic is diminishing as systematic work with recent collections proceeds, and few workers now support this division of Ekman's (See Bushnell and Hedgpeth, 1969) as more and more benthic invertebrates are demonstrated to have circumpolar distributions in the antarctic waters close to the continent. The benthic fauna and flora of the Antarctic Peninsula appear to be somewhat different in composition from that of the "high antarctic" region because of the interchange of elements between the Peninsula and the Magellanic region of South America. This may be a result of the different emphases in collection, however, since deeper water species seem for the most part to be limited in their northward extension south of the Convergence. Although some workers (e.g., Kussakin, 1967) consider South Georgia to merit separate division from the rest of the "western" Antarctic, Ekman's original opinion that it could not be considered independent of the rest of the region is substantiated by most subsequent studies.

The subantarctic region includes the oceanic area south of the Subtropical Convergence, most of the area north of the Antarctic Convergence, and the shallow waters of the tip of South America; but the northern limits on the two sides of South America are not clearly defined (e.g., Dahl, 1960). Southern New Zealand is not considered strictly "subantarctic" but "subantarctic cold temperate," by Knox (1960), and there is less evidence of interchange between New Zealand and the subantarctic islands than there is between South America and the nearby antarctic regions. The islands from Kerguelen to Macquarie are usually regarded as comprising a Kerguelen subregion or district; Macquarie is subantarctic in its flora and fauna although at present it does lie south of the Antarctic Convergence.

There are nevertheless various degrees of affinity between the outlying subantarctic islands and New Zealand, South America, and South Africa, especially of the littoral fauna (Holdgate, 1960). The source of the colonizing species seems to be the nearest larger neighbor to the west; this applies especially to Tristan da Cunha as related to South America. Fell (1967) postulated New Zealand as the region of active speciation that has sent its colonists eastward along the West Wind Drift. This can also be explained on the grounds that New Zealand, a eurythermal region extending into the subtropics, has a greater variety of species and that such eurythermal species would have a better chance of colonizing than species from a limited, stenothermal environment of one of the smaller islands. The smaller islands have proportionately fewer species to contribute to the eastward migration. It is difficult to see how this sort of evidence can be used to estimate centers of speciation in the past, even by invocation of the Coriolis parameter.

A general scheme for littoral regions of the southern regions was proposed by Knox (1960). Since this scheme of biogeographic divisions was concerned primarily with littoral or shallow water organisms, it did not take into consideration the distribution of benthos in depths below the first hundred meters or so. In this system South Georgia is considered a separate province, the Antarctic Peninsula and Scotia Arc are considered to be the Scotian sub-province, and the Ross Sea is given independent provincial status. As already indicated, these various regions cannot be easily separated. Certainly the Ross Sea cannot be defended as a separate region; as work progresses with collections from other parts of the Antarctic Ross Sea "endemics" fall by the wayside. Insofar as the broad patterns are concerned, the scheme of biogeographic divisions adopted for the *Antarctic Map Folio Series* is substantially in agreement with that of Knox and also with the *Soviet Atlas of Antarctica* (Fig. 15).

This zonal pattern of circumpolar species is, as might be expected, more characteristic of the Antarctic than it is of the Arctic. While there are ubiquitous circumpolar or pan-arctic species, there is also a significant distribution pattern of so-called "high arctic" species that are absent from a large part of the Arctic Basin (Fig. 16). The species indicated are fairly large, stenohaline pycno-

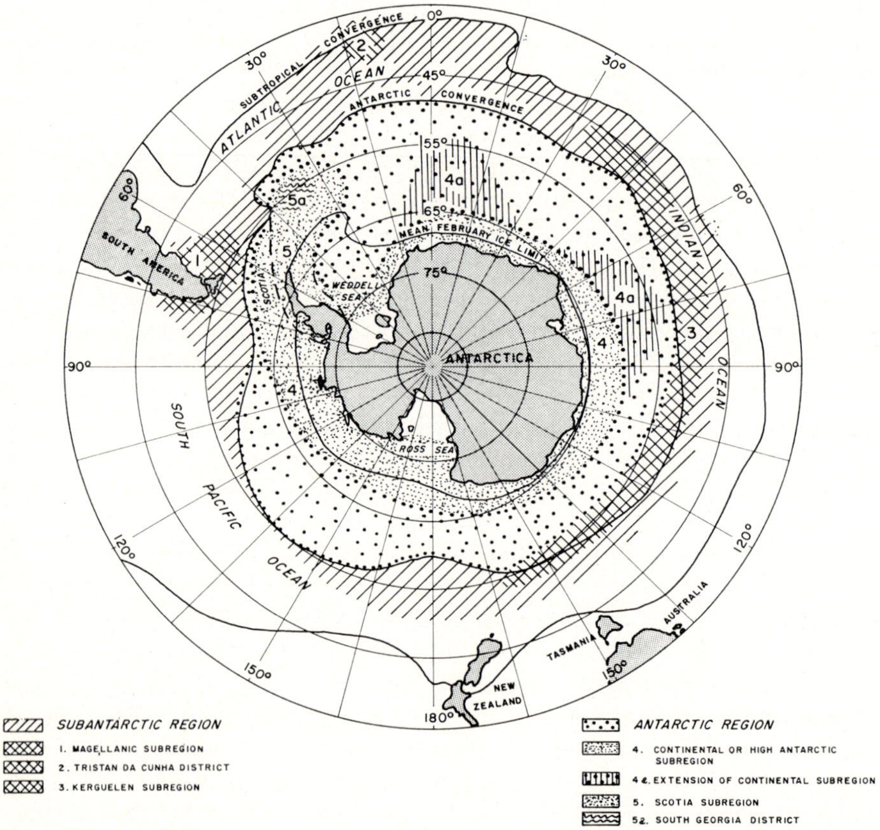

Fig. 15. Biogeographic zones of the Antarctic and Subantarctic (From Hedgpeth, 1969a; courtesy American Geographic Society).

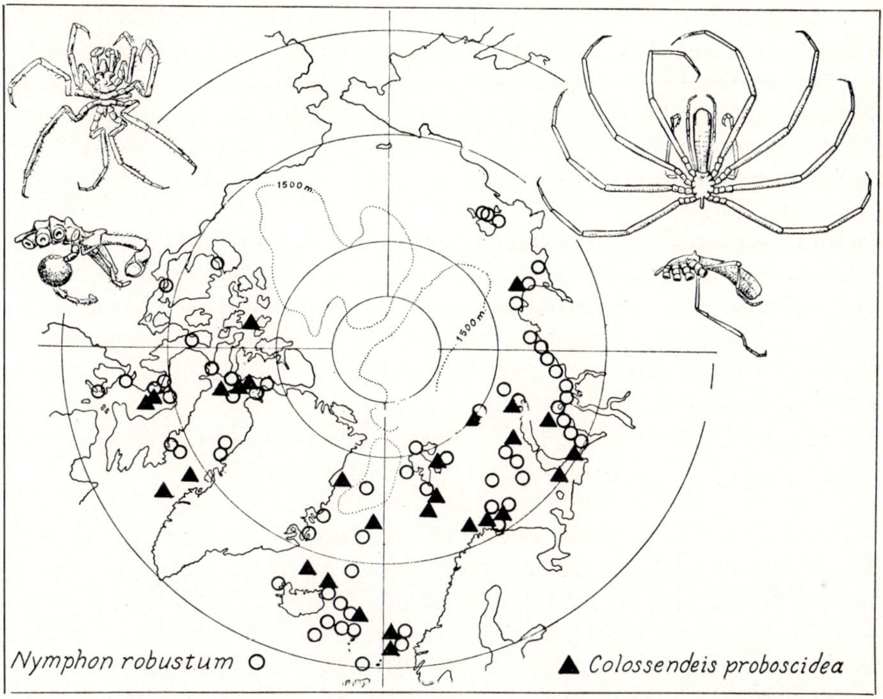

Fig. 16. Distribution of two "high arctic" pycnogonids (Hedgpeth, 1963).

gonids. These distributions include parts of the subarctic region in Dunbar's sense, a circumstance also noted for bryozoa by Powell (1968) ; but it must also be pointed out that there appear to be very few high arctic endemics of any kind. Most of the species extend somewhat outside of the region, and for many groups there are no significant endemic genera. The comparative impoverishment of the arctic bryozoan fauna as contrasted with that of the Antarctic remarked upon by Powell is additional evidence that the faunas of the two polar regions have little in common (See Bushnell and Hedgpeth, 1969). As far as the bryozoa are concerned "the group has not furnished any significant evidence in support of the bipolar theory" (Powell, 1968).

It is becoming increasingly difficult to recognize true bipolar taxa in the sense of identical species found only in the two polar regions and nowhere else. There are probably some, but the original idea that there were extensive polar faunas separated by the warming oceans since glacial times is not supported by present evidence. Most of those now considered to be identical bipolar are species in difficult groups or in groups whose systematics are in an uncertain state. The classic example that still lingers in popular literature is *Priapulus*, a peculiar worm of uncertain zoological affinities. As antarctic material became more available, the specimens were considered at first a variety, and then a separate species. Now, as more specimens turn up from unlikely places, it appears that neither the Northern or Southern Hemisphere forms (which may indeed be closely related) are restricted to the cold regions, but may occur in temperate regions in shallow water (Fig. 17). There are, nevertheless, some phenotypic resemblances between arctic and antarctic benthos. The absence of brachyuran crabs and their ecological replacement by large idotheid isopods is a striking parallel, for example.

ECOLOGICAL SPECULATIONS

Diversity is one of the currently fashionable themes in ecology. There are all sorts of diversity and most of the discussions tend to be subjective and theoretical (Pianka, 1966). The most objective way to judge diversity is by taxonomic groups or species: whether there are more or fewer kinds of organisms in different but comparable situations or places. There is an extensive literature on specific diversity gradients and latitude (Fischer, 1960), yet we have few figures for this diversity in any reasonably defined natural system or area, and our impression of a decreasing diversity gradient with increasing latitude from the equator is based on all sorts of information of varying provenance or systematic sophistication for imprecisely defined areas, both terrestrial and marine. This is not intended to deny that systematic diversity is greater in the tropics than toward the poles, for this is obvious (Stehli, 1968). Further, it is obvious that some of these taxonomic gradients indicate greater variety in the Antarctic than in the Arctic (Fig. 18). Groups in addition to bivalves showing a greater variety in the Antarctic than the Arctic include sponges, bryozoa, and pycnogonids. The most recent information is that concerning gammaridean amphipods, which according to Barnard (1969) are represented by 56 genera and 110 species in the antarctic-subantarctic regions, and 25 genera and 71 species in the arctic-subarctic regions.

One gradient of particular interest to us is that of penguins in the Southern Hemisphere and alcids (auks, puffins, etc.) in the Northern Hemisphere. For these ecological counterparts, diversi-

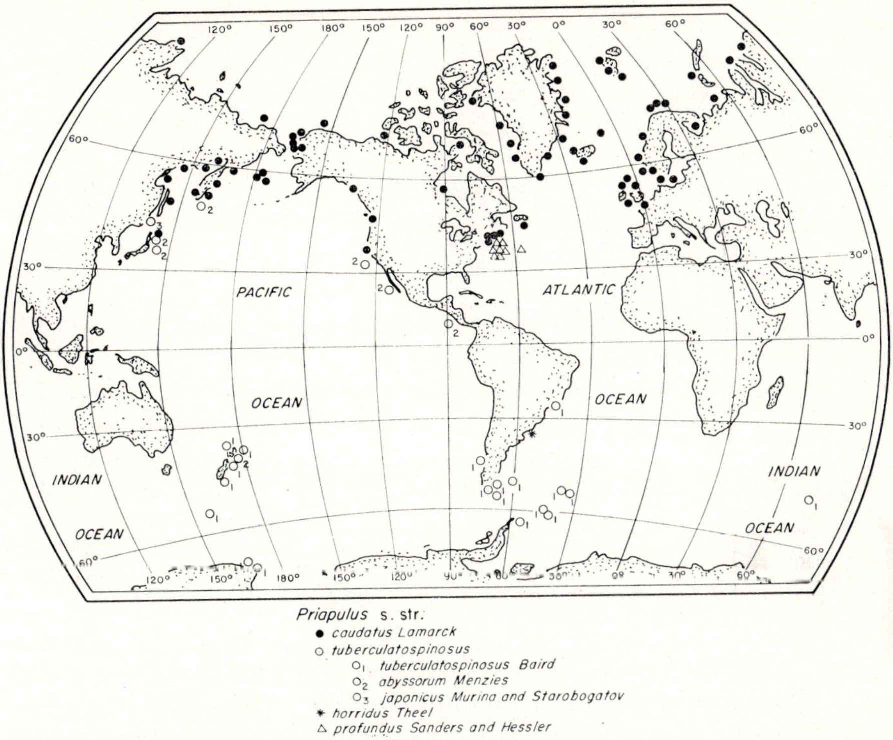

Fig. 17. Distribution of species of *Priapulus* s. str. (From Hedgpeth, 1969a; courtesy American Geographical Society).

fication is greatest in middle latitudes. Penguins, at least, were probably birds of warm temperate or tropical environments that have become adapted to the conditions of the Antarctic and Subantarctic (Stonehouse, 1969). Possibly this is the result of response to the abundant food supply, associated with adaptations for reducing heat loss (Stonehouse, 1967).

Systematic or taxonomic diversity is not of itself as interesting to the ecologist as the diversity of function or ecological role within an interrelated system. How many of the 700-odd species of Indo-Pacific corals are really different in the sense of function and requirements in the place in which they live, or do they (and how many of them) constitute a sort of functional mosaic, perhaps changing in composition from reef to reef? What are the average numbers of species of coral in a given location or atoll; how does one evaluate in ecological terms such an observation as that of Wells (1957) who found 80 species of hermatypic corals on a "few

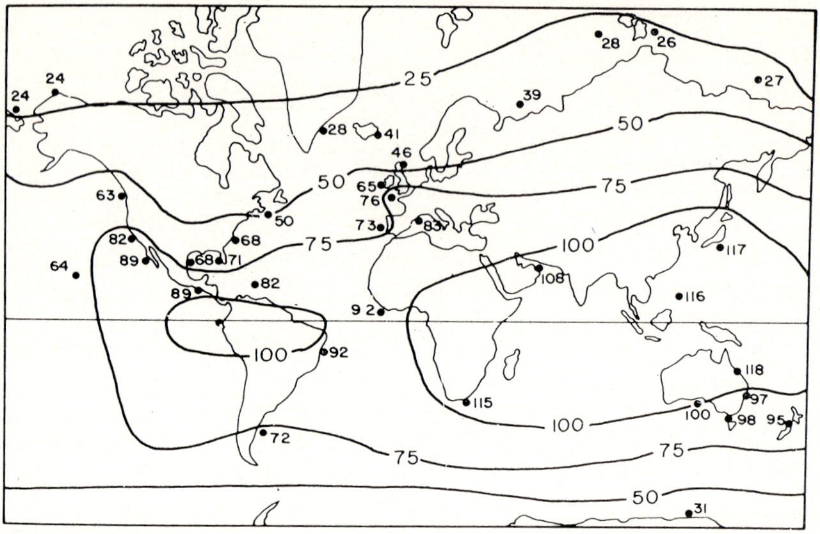

Fig. 18. Diversity contours for genera of Recent bivalves (From Stehli, 1968).

acres" of Arno Atoll? How really different are all those 300 species of antarctic sponges or a similar number of antarctic bryozoa? Questions of this sort cannot be answered by compiling diversity indexes of taxa versus abundances yet they do bear upon the question whether the tropic seas are really more diverse as ecological systems than other parts of the world. With reference to pelagic organisms, as already suggested (Hedgpeth, 1969a), we may be dealing with limited diversity of large populations and a representation of other species of considerably less ecological significance as a sort of ecological "noise." Obviously environments which produce an excess of energy over requirements to keep the system going can afford such ecological noise, which might be looked at in terms of more different kinds of specialized predators, as observed for the genus *Conus* by Kohn (1959, 1968). Perhaps there are just as many, albeit less spectacular, predator relationships among antarctic pycnogonids, as intimated by the study by Fry (1964, 1965); Nesis (1966) has incidentally touched upon this aspect for pycnogonids of the subarctic regions of Labrador and Newfoundland although he attributes the primary response to the same hydrographic factors which also select the variety of food organisms. There are evidently several hundred kinds of antarctic polychaetes (Hartman, 1967); what are they all doing there? (Or anywhere else in the sea, for that matter; perhaps it is not without significance that the investigators who find the most diversity in marine bottom communities are for the most part polychaete specialists.)

A true diversity comparison for different parts of the sea, in which strictly equivalent areas or systems would be compared for the entire flora and fauna of the selected entities, is a philosophical ideal which will not be achieved in our time. The basic problem has been neatly stated by Margalef (1968), and it would appear from this discussion that one of the chief architects of diversity indexes in ecology is wavering in his faith, or at least is warning us that diversity may also be diverse, that it is a parameter that must be carefully qualified, especially as related to sample or "universe" size, and that "it is a bad beginning to assume that we are working with samples from a 'uniform universe'." This would seem obvious, but while theoretical ecologists may be willing to admit that they are dealing with concepts whose end results are numbers that are at best approximations, derived "despite the handicap of insufficient ecological data, or perhaps because of it" (Pianka, 1966), they leave behind them equations that delude more practically minded but ecologically unsophisticated persons into fluttering around like the proverbial moths at a candle flame. While the problem of incautious acceptance of diversity indexes by pollution engineers is not yet a matter of concern in studies of antarctic benthos, it may soon be if we attempt to assay the effects of human occupation on the Ross Sea benthos at McMurdo Sound in quantitative terms.

In any event, the current controversy over diversity in level bottom communities in various parts of the world is based in large part on differences in sampling and concepts of what constitutes the statistical universe being considered. The concept of relatively stable, low-diversity level bottom communities from the arctic to the tropics, contrasted with an increasing gradient of epifauna, was developed by Thorson (1957), primarily on the basis of certain types of organisms caught by a 2 mm mesh sieve from grab samples. At the time Thorson's experience with the tropics was restricted to the anomalous situation of the Persian Gulf. A number of workers, using smaller mesh sizes, and attempting to consider all infaunal groups, especially polychaetes and small arthropods, have taken issue with this generalization (Day, 1963; Hartman, 1955, 1966; Knox, 1961; Sanders, 1968). Insofar as the comparisons involve grab samples by unit area, the criticisms have validity, but they may be on less firm ground when the samples are based on material gathered by dragging much more extensive areas (Sanders *et al.*, 1965; Hessler and Sanders, 1967). While it may be possible to derive a diversity index independent of sample size (Sanders, 1968) this is not quite the same as an index independent of area or "community" (whatever that may be), or duration of sampling time. In other words, Margalef's warning against assuming that we are working with a uniform universe applies. Nevertheless it is obvious that consideration of the smaller animals in the sediments (the meiofauna) will produce a very different picture of diversity than the "classic" one based on larger invertebrates. Thorson (1966) has responded to his critics by admitting that apparently not all soft bottom communities fit his "parallel community" scheme, and while the meiofauna may well be a very numerous and diverse part of the community, it nevertheless constitutes a small percentage of the biomass. He also conceded that these small organisms may well be a controlling influence on the composition of the macrobenthos, but the "radical revision" of his concept of parallel infaunal communities for the exceptional tropical and warm temperate areas is not available at this time.

Quantitative benthic ecology in antarctic seas has not yet produced a body of data to contribute to this argument one way or another. For that matter, quantitative knowledge of the epifauna is still meager. Andriashev's (1968) estimate of 500 species encountered in the Davis Sea area refers primarily to epifaunal groups (and plants), but this figure does compare with Riedl's (1966) tabulation of upwards of 500 species encountered in various cave systems in the Tyrrhenian Sea. Riedl's grand total of 905 (or more) species refers to all organisms characteristic of undersea caves and grottoes in the Mediterranean, including burrowers, nestlers, epizoics, fishes, and all. The observations by Pequegnat (1964) on reef epifauna in southern California sound very similar to Andriashev's description of "very dense, often multistory settlements of invertebrates especially sestonophagous, not leaving 'bare places' on the bottom" of antarctic rocky bottoms. Pequegnat found between 300 and 400 "described" species on an area of 1,385 m^2, but within recognized subzones there were considerably fewer species (Table 1).

The numbers of species per zone are in the same order of magnitude as observed for various depth zones off Point Loma (Turner *et al.*, 1968).

It will be of interest to compare such results with those of studies

Table 1. Comparative abundances of epifaunal zones on a siltstone reef, Southern California (Modified from Pequegnat, 1964).

Zone	Area (m^2)	Depth (m)	No. of species with max. pop. in zone	No. of species in zone	Mean of species (per $0.1m^2$)
Reef top	550	9.5–12.5	131	189	89
Mid-reef	400	12.5–14.5	87	144	80
Reef base	250	14.5–16.5	51	114	49
Mixed bottom	185	16.5–18.5	31	47	23

of antarctic shallow epibenthos. Perhaps more fruitful analysis of work now in progress will be gained if one proceeds on the hypothesis that antarctic and tropical epibiotic communities are of the same order of ecological diversity. Certainly it is dangerous to assume simplicity; Glynn (1965) began the study of an apparently simple association of barnacles and a red alga at Monterey, and found after several years of careful study that he was dealing with more than 93 species, of which 35 were common and 28 made up more than 98 percent of the total number of individuals.

In a general way, concepts of diversity provide a useful frame for discussion, even if we do not have really comparable numbers for more or less similar situations for arctic:antarctic and antarctic:tropical systems. One of the more popular ideas concerning diversity in its broad subjective sense is that increased diversity is an indication of the complexity of a community and of its stability in time. That is, a more diverse community is developed in situations where environmental conditions do not fluctuate significantly. Or, conversely, communities or assemblages of low diversity and comparatively high biomass of the few species involved are associated with relatively unstable or fluctuating conditions and are relatively younger in the stage of ecological evolution. This is one of the central themes of Dunbar's book (1968) on ecological development in polar regions.

It may not be really true, however, that complex systems are more stable than simple ones; some simple systems are probably very old and presumably stable within environmental limits (Hedgpeth, 1964). Dunbar's idea is based in part on conditions in the Arctic, an environment in oscillation which tends to prevent the establishment of complexity, and therefore he assumes that the system is still young and in the process of evolving towards complexity and stability. Margalef (1968), however, made the interesting suggestion that the most stable systems should be those of cold temperatures:

> In a system at high temperature, a higher amount of entropy is produced in the exchange of a fixed amount of energy. In consequence, a system at high temperature cannot go as far (cannot reach the same degree of maturity) as an equivalent system at a lower temperature. Anything that accelerates change and energy flow in an ecosystem causes a reduction in potential maturity. Nevertheless, it happens that at the present time the most stable environments are found in the tropics.

Apparently Margalef was thinking primarily of the tropical rain forest in this context. In an entertaining comment on the problem of longevity as related to community stability, Frank (1968) suggested that in the sea the organisms that promote stability in a community are not plants, but the animals with relatively long life spans and high fecundity. It remains to be determined how long lived the more conspicuous elements of the antarctic benthos may be; Pearse (1969a) suggested that the common sea star of shallow antarctic waters, *Odontaster validus,* may live a hundred years. Reproduction and growth may be very slow in antarctic organisms, if the data for *Odontaster validus* may be accepted as typical: gametogenesis begins 18 months or two years before spawning, and spawning may occur when the animal is three to six years old; larval development is comparably slow and growth after metamorphosis may be at the rate of 1 to 2 g per year (Pearse, 1965). As asteroids go, *Odontaster validus* is small, but there are "giant" forms of several invertebrate groups in antarctic waters, perhaps more so than in the Arctic. Little is known about growth rates of antarctic animals other than whales, seals, euphausiids, and penguins, but large size in invertebrates is usually considered to be associated with the slow growth, long life, and prolonged fecundity ascribed to *Odontaster validus.* Obviously more such work with antarctic invertebrates is necessary. Many of the giant pycnogonids of antarctic waters and the deep sea (*Colossendeis, Decolopoda, Dodecolopoda*) are still a riddle, as there is no information on reproduction whatever (Fig. 19). One is almost tempted to suggest they reproduce only sparingly and that reproduction has simply not yet been observed, although they are comparatively

Fig. 19. *Dodecolopoda mawsoni,* the giant 12-legged pycnogonid. This specimen was from Endeavour Station A459, 534–549 m (Photograph by J. Bahler; courtesy New Zealand Oceanographic Institute).

abundant. Like the sea stars, these giant pycnogonids could be many decades old, and replacement may be slow. Casual aquarium observations and some bottom photographs of these giant pycnogonids with large proboscides and long sensory palpi whose terminal segments are carried parallel to the bottom in front of the mouth lead to the suspicion that the possibility of dependence upon meiofaunal elements of the upper sediment layers should be examined. Dependence upon such a food supply could be associated with very slow growth and replacement.

Connell and Orias (1964) suggested that in a stable environment less energy is needed to cope with the environment and therefore more energy can be devoted to growth and reproduction, which in turn means larger populations may be supported. From large populations there follows genetic variety and ultimately greater specific diversity. The theory that the greater the productivity, the greater the diversity "may have some validity," according to Sanders (1968), although he did not find it applicable to the deep-sea benthos, where high diversity values are associated with "regions of low productivity." Yet there is obviously both high diversity and high productivity in antarctic waters, and the very slow rates of reproduction of many of the benthic animals may be a means of adjusting to the comparatively high phytoplankton productivity. Gametogenesis is so slow in *Odontaster*, for example, that it may require two years and there may be several generations (or "year classes") of oocytes in an individual sea star. This implies a steady year-round use of resources, although the production of young is adjusted to the summer period of phytoproduction (Pearse, 1965, 1969b).

It has been suggested by Preston (1969) that fluctuation in numbers may be necessary to stability, that "stability lies in the ability to bounce back, not in the ability to hold tenaciously to ground once taken or numbers once achieved." Margalef (1969) has discussed the two aspects of stability as: (1) survival of many changes while retaining "a certain recognizably similar structure" and (2) persistence essentially without change. Comparing these alternatives to a continuous serpent, Margalef remarks, "Perhaps it would be wiser to refer to the two ends by separate names, for instance, by *adjustment* or *lability* to one, and by *conservatism, endurance,* or *persistence* to the other."

Little is yet known of rates of replacement in the antarctic benthos, but fluctuation in numbers does not necessarily imply rapid oscillation; the time scale may be in the order of decades instead of years. We may be somewhere near the middle of Margalef's serpent.

While natural replacement may be slow, there appears to be no dearth of predators of various levels or orders among antarctic invertebrates: nemerteans large enough to eat fish, anemones that engulf passing urchins and sea stars that may chew off large fragments of sponges, according to the observations of Dayton and others. Some of these animals may be necrophagous rather than predaceous, others may feed on the dead only during the winter (Arnaud, 1969). It is in this environment at McMurdo Sound that Paine's hypothesis that diversity is enhanced by the reduction of mass species by predation is being tested; the experiment is still under way (Dayton *et al.*, 1970). According to this hypothesis "local species diversity is directly related to the efficiency with which predators prevent the monopolization of the major environmental requisites by one species" (Paine, 1966). This hypothesis was developed specifically in application to rocky intertidal situations where space is the prime requisite involved. The presence of several kinds of predators in an environment where space is not a potentially limiting factor is a complication that suggests influences other than direct predation may be operative in maintaining diversity in such a situation. Even where space is the principal factor of increased predation, "additional factors must be invoked to explain the existence of the resources which support these additional species" (Spight, 1967).

In dealing with a comparatively simple laboratory system, a group of eight investigators (Hairston *et al.*, 1968) found that two species of *Paramecium* consistently had larger populations in longer-lived cultures without the third species, suggesting some interaction between this pair and the third species, and that two species (less diversity) are better than three (more diversity) in this experimental case. Perhaps so, but as the eight authors said, "We conclude that much more experimental and observational work is necessary before the nature of any functional relationship between diversity and stability can be claimed with confidence." At best this experimental situation is considerably less diverse than most conditions in nature, except perhaps those of a brine spring.

Recently we have become aware of extensive changes in the coral reef community of the western Pacific. It is suggested that one possible cause of this change is the increase of the coralliphagous sea star *Acanthaster,* possibly by removal of the predator assumed to control sea star numbers, the large gastropod *Charonia.* According to a number of newspaper stories and almost equally uninformative scientific reports (e.g., Chesher, 1969), the sea stars, now abundant, are eating up the reefs so that what remains is in danger of being destroyed by wave action. This aspect of the situation has been oversensationalized by ecological entrepreneurs, with a resulting public reaction to the starfish comparable to the terrestrial sportsman's attitude towards "vermin." Later observations (Vine, 1970) suggest that "the recent outbreak of reports about *Acanthaster* may perhaps be explained by great public attention and increase in the number of divers rather than of starfish." This same author discounts the idea that populations are controlled by the predatory gastropod *Charonia.* On the reefs of Molokai in the Hawaiian Islands *Acanthaster planci* appears to be a preferential feeder and may actually benefit the reef structure (Branham *et al.,* 1970); in the Gulf of California the activities of another species, *Acanthaster ellisi,* do not appear to be eliminating corals (Wolfson and Dana, 1970). Some laboratory studies of *Acanthaster* suggest that when they get enough, they stop eating: ". . . satiety in the starfish may potentiate the withdrawal reflex." (Barnes *et al.*, 1970). In commenting on the preliminary information about *Acanthaster* in Guam and on the Barrier Reef, Paine (1969) remarked, "Whatever, then, the significance of ecologic complexity may be, it seems to have exercised little influence in ameliorating significant, short-term changes . . . and hence has contributed minimally to stability." It may turn out that something other than decreased diversity is really the cause of the outbreaks of *Acanthaster* in various parts of the Pacific, but in any event something may be changing the supposedly stable system of coral reefs in some parts of the Pacific. Possibly the cause is allochthonous. Margalef may be right, nevertheless, in suspecting that the uniformly cold environments are more mature and ultimately more stable. The experiments under way at McMurdo Sound may become even more significant than anticipated, although if there is anything to the idea of cold-related stability, we may expect no significantly observable changes in the experimental plots from which predators have been excluded, or at least unspectacular results.

Author's Note: This paper was made possible through support provided by NSF Grants GA 1217 and GA 18348. I am indebted to John S. Pearse and Bernard Stonehouse for helpful comments and criticisms, some of which have influenced me to make changes in the manuscript. However, this does not absolve me from errors and misinterpretations.

References

Andriashev, A. P., 1968. The problem of the life community associated with the antarctic fast ice. In *Symposium on Antarctic Oceanography, Santiago, Chile, 13–16 September, 1966;* pp. 147–155. Scott Polar Res. Inst., Cambridge, England.

Arnaud, P., 1969. Frequency and ecological significance of necrophagy among the benthic species of antarctic coastal waters. In *Antarctic Ecology,* edited by M. Holdgate; vol. 1, pp. 259–267. Academic Press, London.

Bakayev, V. G. (Editor), 1966. *Atlas Antarktikii;* vol. 1, pp. 1–22. Main Administration of Geodesy and Cartography, Ministry of Geology, Moscow. [Text and legend matter publ. in English as a *Special Issue of Soviet Geography,* Review and Translation; vol. 7, nos. 5–6, pp. 261–507. Am. Geograph. Soc., New York.]

Barnard, J. L., 1969. The families and genera of marine Gammaridean Amphipoda. *Bull. U. S. Nat. Museum, 271.*

Barnes, D. J., R. W. Brauer, and M. R. Jordan, 1970. Locomotory response of *Acanthaster planci* to various species of coral. *Nature, 228* (5269: 342–343.

Branham, J. M., J. H. Bailey, J. Caperon, and S. A. Reed, 1970. Coral-eating Crown-of-Thorns sea stars in Hawaii. *Abstracts, Western Soc. Naturalists, Honolulu, Hawaii;* pp. 32–33.

Bullivant, J. S., 1967. Ecology of the Ross Sea benthos. The fauna of the Ross Sea, Part 5. *New Zealand Oceanog. Inst. Memoir, 32:* 49–75.

Bushnell, V. C., and J. W. Hedgpeth, 1969. Distribution of selected groups of marine invertebrates in waters south of 35°S latitude. *Antarctic Map Folio Series, Folio 11.* Am. Geograph. Soc., New York.

Calman, W. T., 1937. James Eights, a pioneer antarctic naturalist. *Proc. Linn. Soc. London, 149* (4) : 171–184.

Chesher, R. H., 1969. Destruction of Pacific corals by the sea star *Acanthaster planci. Science, 165* (3890) : 280–283.

Clarke, J. M., 1916. The reincarnation of James Eights, antarctic explorer. *Sci. Monthly, 2* (2) : 189–202.

Connell, J. H., and E. Orias, 1964. The ecological regulation of species diversity. *Am. Naturalist, 98* (903) : 399–414.

Dahl, E., 1960. The cold temperate zone in Chilean seas. *Proc. Roy. Soc., London, Ser. B, 152* (949) : 631–633.

Day, J. H., 1963. The complexity of the biotic environment. *Systematics Assoc., Publ. 5:* 31–49.

Dayton, P. K., G. A. Robilliard, and A. L. DeVries, 1969. Anchor ice formation in McMurdo Sound, Antarctica, and its biological effects. *Science, 163;* 273–274.

Dayton, P. K., G. A. Robilliard, and R. T. Paine, 1970. Benthic faunal zonation as a result of anchor ice at McMurdo Sound, Antarctica. In *Antarctic Ecology,* edited by M. Holdgate; vol. 1, pp. 244–258. Academic Press, London.

Dearborn, J. H., 1968. Benthic invertebrates. *Australian Nat. Hist., December, 1968:* 134–139.

Delépine, R., and J. C. Hureau, 1963. La végétation marine dans l'Archipel de Point Géologie. (Terre Adélie) (Aperçu préliminaire). *Bull. Mus. Natl. Hist. Nat., (2) 35* (1) : 108–115.

Delépine, R., I. Mackenzie Lamb, and M. H. Zimmermann, 1970. Preliminary report on the marine vegetation of the Antarctic Peninsula. In *Antarctic Ecology,* edited by M. Holdgate; vol. 1, p. 268. Academic Press, London.

Dunbar, M. J., 1968. *Ecological Development in Polar Regions. A Study in Evolution.* Prentice-Hall, Englewood Cliffs, N. J.

Eights, J. 1833. Description of a new crustaceous animal found on the shores of the South Shetland Islands, with remarks on their natural history. *Trans. Albany Inst., 2* (1) : 53–69.

Einarsson, H., 1941. Survey of the benthonic animal communities of Faxa Bay (Iceland). *Medd. Komm. Danmarsk Fisk.–havunders., Fiskeri, 11:* 1–46.

Eisler, R., 1969. Acute toxicities of insecticides to marine decapod crustaceans. *Crustaceana, 16* (3) : 302–310.

Ekman, S., 1953. *Zoogeography of the Sea.* Sidgwick and Jackson, London.

El-Sayed, S. Z., 1968. On the productivity of the southwest Atlantic Ocean and the waters west of the Antarctic Peninsula. In *Antarctic Research Series 11, Biology of the Antarctic Seas, III,* edited by G. A. Llano and W. L. Schmitt; pp. 15–47, 230. Am. Geophys. Union, Washington, D.C.

Etcheverry, H., 1968. Distribution of the benthic algae on the continental platform of the Antarctic Peninsula. In *Symposium on Antarctic Oceanography, Santiago, Chile, 13–16 September 1966.* Scott Polar Res. Inst., Cambridge, England.

Fell, H., 1967. Resolution of Coriolis parameters for former epochs. *Nature, 214:* 1192–1198.

Fischer, A. G., 1960. Latitudinal variations in organic diversity. *Evolution, 14* (7) : 64–81.

Fleming, C. A., 1963. Paleontology and southern biogeography. In *Pacific Basin Biogeography, A Symposium,* edited by J. L. Gressitt; pp. 369–385. Tenth Pacific Sci. Congr., Honolulu, Hawaii. Bishop Museum Press, Honolulu.

Frank, P. W., 1968. Life histories and community stability. *Ecology, 49* (2) : 355–357.

Fry, W. G., 1964. The pycnogonid fauna of the antarctic continental shelf. In *Biologie Antarctique,* edited by R. Carrick, M. W. Holdgate, and J. Prevost; pp. 263–270. Hermann, Paris.

Fry, W. G., 1965. The feeding mechanisms and preferred foods of three species of Pycnogonida. *Bull. Brit. Museum (Nat. Hist.), Zool., 12* (6) : 197–223.

Gallardo, V. A., and J. G. Castillo, 1968. Mass mortality in the benthic infauna of Port Foster resulting from the eruptions in Deception Island (South Shetland Is.). *Publ. Inst. Antarctico Chileno, 16:* 1–13.

Gauld, D. T., and J. B. Buchanan, 1959. On the principal features of the rocky shore fauna in Ghana. *Oikos, 10* (1) : 121–132.

George, J. L., and D. E. H. Frear, 1966. Pesticides in the Antarctic. *J. Appl. Ecol., 3 (Suppl.):* 155–167.

Glynn, P., 1965. Community composition, structure, and interrelationships in the marine intertidal *Endocladia muricata-Balanus glandula* association in Monterey Bay, California. *Beaufortia, 12:* 1–198.

Gruzov, E. N., M. V. Propp, and A. F. Pushkin, 1967. Biologischeskie soobschchestva pribrezhnikh raionov morya Deivisa (po rezul'tatam vodolaznikh nablyudenii). *Byul. Sov. Antarkt. Eksp., 65:* 124–141.

Gruzov, E. N., and A. F. Pushkin, 1970. Bottom communities of the upper sublittoral of Enderby Land and South Shetland Islands. In *Antarctic Ecology,* edited by M. Holdgate; vol. 1, pp. 235–238. Academic Press, London.

Gurjanova, E. F., 1968. The influence of water movements upon the species composition and distribution of the marine fauna and flora throughout the arctic and north Pacific intertidal zones. *Sarsia, 34:* 83–94.

Hairston, N. G., J. P. Allan, R. K. Colwell, D. J. Futuyma, J. Howell, M. D. Lubin, J. Mathias, and J. H. Vandermeer, 1968. The relationship between species diversity and stability: an experimental approach with protozoa and bacteria. *Ecology, 49* (6) : 1091–1101.

Hartman, O., 1955. Quantitative survey of the benthos of San Pedro Basin, Southern California, Part I. Preliminary results. *Allan Hancock Pac. Exp., 19* (1) : 1–185.

Hartman, O., 1966. Quantitative survey of the benthos of San Pedro Basin, Southern California, Part II. *Allan Hancock Pac. Exp., 19* (2) : 187–456.

Hartman, O., 1967. Benthic zonation in Antarctica, as displayed by marine annelids (Polychaeta) based on published and new records, from intertidal to hadal depths. *Japanese Antarctic Res. Exp., Sci. Repts., Special Issue 1:* 192–204. National Science Museum, Tokyo.

Hedgpeth, J. W., 1964. Evolution of community structure. In *Approaches to Paleoecology,* edited by J. Imbrie and N. Newell; pp. 11–18. John Wiley and Sons, New York.

Hedgpeth, J. W., 1969a. Introduction to antarctic zoogeography. In *Antarctic Map Folio Series, Folio 11,* edited by V. C. Bushnell and J. W. Hedgpeth; pp. 1–9. Am. Geograph. Soc., New York.

Hedgpeth, J. W., 1969b. An intertidal reconnaissance of rocky shores of the Galapagos. *Wasmann J. Biol., 27* (1) : 1–24.

Hedgpeth, J. W., 1969c. Preliminary observations of life between tidemarks at Palmer Station, 64°45′S, 64°05′W. *Antarctic J. U.S., 4* (4) : 106–107.

Hedgpeth, J. W., 1969d. Marine biogeography of the antarctic regions. In *Antarctic Ecology,* edited by M. Holdgate; vol. 1, pp. 97–104. Academic Press, London.

Hessler, R. R., and H. L. Sanders, 1967. Faunal diversity in the deep sea. *Deep-Sea Res., 14:* 65–78.

Holdgate, M. W., 1960. The fauna of the mid-Atlantic islands. *Proc. Roy. Soc. London, Ser. B, 152* (949) : 550–567.

Holdgate, M. W., 1967. The antarctic ecosystem. *Phil. Trans. Roy. Soc. London, Ser. B, 252* (777) : 363–383.

Horne, A. J., G. E. Fogg, and D. J. Eagle, 1969. Studies *in situ* of the primary production of an area of inshore antarctic sea. *J. Marine Biol. Assoc., 49* (2) : 393–405.

Kain, J. M., 1966. The role of light in the ecology of *Laminaria hyperborea.* In *Light as an Ecological Factor;* pp. 319–334. British Ecol. Soc. Symposium 6. John Wiley and Sons, New York.

Kanwisher, J. W., 1955. Freezing in intertidal animals. *Biol. Bull., 109* (1) : 56–63.

Kanwisher, J. W., 1959. Histology and metabolism of frozen intertidal animals. *Biol. Bull., 116* (2) : 258–264.

Kanwisher, J. W., 1966. Photosynthesis and respiration in some seaweeds. In *Some Contemporary Studies in Marine Science,* edited by H. Barnes; pp. 407–420. Allen and Unwin, London.

Kenny, R., and N. Haysom, 1962. Ecology of rocky shore organisms at Macquarie Island. *Pacific Sci., 16* (3) : 245–263.

Knox, G. A., 1960. Littoral ecology and biogeography of the southern oceans. *Proc. Roy. Soc. London, Ser. B, 152* (949) : 577–624.

Knox, G. A., 1961. The study of marine bottom communities. *Proc. Roy. Soc. New Zealand, 89* (1) : 167–182.

Knox, G. A., 1968. Tides and intertidal zones. In *Symposium on Antarctic Oceanography, Santiago, Chile, 13–16 September 1966;* pp. 131–146. Scott Polar Res. Inst., Cambridge, England.

Knox, G. A., 1970. Biological oceanography of the South Pacific. In *Scientific Exploration of the South Pacific,* edited by W. S. Wooster; pp. 155–182. Natl. Acad. Sci., Washington, D.C.

Kohn, A. J., 1959. The ecology of *Conus* in Hawaii. *Ecol. Monographs, 29* (1) : 47–90.

Kohn, A. J., 1968. Microhabitats, abundance and food of *Conus* on atoll reefs in the Maldive and Chagos Islands. *Ecology, 49* (6): 1046–1062.

Kussakin, O. G., 1967. Isopoda and Tanaidacea from the coastal zones of the Antarctic and Subantarctic. *Rez. Biol. Issl. Sov. Ant. Eksp., 3:* 220–380.

Levring, T., 1966. Submarine light and algal shore zonation. In *Light as an Ecological Factor. Brit. Ecol. Soc. Symp. 6;* pp. 305–318. John Wiley and Sons, New York.

Lewis, J. R., 1964. *The Ecology of Rocky Shores.* English Univ. Press, London.

Lewis, J. R., 1968. Water movements and their role in rocky shore ecology. *Sarsia, 34:* 13–36.

Littlepage, J. L., and J. S. Pearse, 1962. Biological and oceanographic observations under an antarctic ice shelf. *Science, 137:* 679–681.

Longhurst, A. R., 1964. A review of the present situation in benthic ecology. *Bull. Inst. Oceanog., Monaco, 63* (1317): 1–54.

McCain, J. C., and W. E. Stout, 1969. Benthos zonation on submarine cliffs in the vicinity of Arthur Harbor, Antarctica. *Antarctic J. U.S., 4* (4): 105–106.

MacGinitie, G. E., 1955. Distribution and ecology of the marine invertebrates of Point Barrow, Alaska. *Smithsonian Misc. Colls., 128* (9): 1–201.

Madsen, H., 1936. Investigations on the shore fauna of east Greenland with a survey of the shores of other arctic regions. *Medd. Grønland, 100* (8): 1–79.

Madsen, H., 1940. A study of littoral fauna of northwest Greenland. *Medd. Grønland, 124* (3): 1–24.

Margalef, R., 1968. *Perspectives in Ecological Theory.* Univ. Chicago Press.

Margalef, R., 1969. Diversity and stability: a practical proposal and a model of interdependence. In *Diversity and Stability in Ecological Systems. Brookhaven Symposium in Biology;* vol. 22, pp. 25–37. Brookhaven National Lab., Upton, N.Y.

Neushul, M., 1959. Biological collecting in antarctic waters. *Veliger, 2* (1): 15–17.

Neushul, M., 1964. Diving observations of sub-tidal antarctic marine vegetation. *Botan. Marina, 8* (24): 234–243.

Neushul, M., 1968. Benthic marine algae. In *Antarctic Map Folio Series, Folio 10,* edited by E. Balech *et al.;* pp. 9–10. Am. Geograph. Soc., New York.

Nicolaisen, W., 1968. Marine biological studies of the sublittoral bottoms around Surtsey. *Surtsey Res. Prog. Rept., 4:* 89–94. (Surtsey Res. Soc., Reykjavik. Mimeo.).

Paine, R. T., 1966. Food web complexity and species diversity. *Am. Naturalist, 100* (910): 65–75.

Paine, R. T., 1969. A note on trophic complexity and community stability. *Am. Naturalist, 103* (929): 91–93.

Pearse, J. S., 1965. Reproductive periodicities in several contrasting populations of *Odontaster validus* Koehler, a common antarctic asteroid. In *Antarctic Research Series 5, Biology of the Antarctic Seas II,* edited by G. A. Llano; pp. 39–85. Am. Geophys. Union, Washington, D. C.

Pearse, J. S., 1969a. Antarctic sea star. *Australian Nat. Hist., September, 1969:* 234–238.

Pearse, J. S., 1969b. Slow developing demersal embryos and larvae of the antarctic sea star *Odontaster validus*. *Marine Biol. Intern. J. Life Oceans Coastal Waters, 3* (2) : 110–116.

Pequegnat, W. E., 1964. The epifauna of a California siltstone reef. *Ecology, 45* (2) : 272–283.

Pianka, E. R., 1966. Latitudinal gradients in species diversity: a review of concepts. *Am. Naturalist, 100* (910) : 33–46.

Powell, N. A., 1968. Bryozoa (Polyzoa) of Arctic Canada. *J. Fish. Res. Bd. Canada, 25* (11) : 2269–2320.

Preston, F. W., 1969. Diversity and stability in the biological world. In *Diversity and Stability in Ecological Systems. Brookhaven Symposium in Biology;* vol. 22, pp. 1–12. Brookhaven National Lab., Upton, N. Y.

Price, J. H., and P. Redfearn, 1968. The marine ecology of Signy Island, South Orkney Islands. In *Symposium on Antarctic Oceanography, Santiago, Chile, 13–16 September 1966;* pp. 163–164. Scott Polar Res. Inst., Cambridge, England.

Propp, M. V., 1970. The study of bottom fauna at Haswell Islands by scuba diving. In *Antarctic Ecology,* edited by M. Holdgate; vol. 1, pp. 239–241. Academic Press, London.

Riedl, R., 1966. *Biologie der Meereshölen. Topographie, faunistik und Ökologie eines Unterseeischen Lebensraumes.* Verlag Paul Parey, Hamburg.

Sanders, H. L., 1968. Marine benthic diversity: a comparative study. *Am. Naturalist, 102* (925) : 243–282.

Sanders, H. L., R. R. Hessler, and G. R. Hampson, 1965. An introduction to the study of deep-sea benthic faunal assemblages along the Gay Head-Bermuda transect. *Deep-Sea Res., 12:* 845–867.

Sladen, W. J. L., C. M. Menzie, and W. L. Reichel, 1966. DDT residues in Adélie penguins and a crabeater seal from Antarctica. *Nature, 210* (5037) : 670–673.

Southward, A. J., 1958. The zonation of plants and animals on rocky sea shores. *Biol. Rev., 33:* 137–177.

Spärck, R., 1937. The benthonic animal communities of the coastal waters. *Zool. Iceland, 1* (6) : 1–45.

Spight, T. M., 1967. Species diversity: a comment on the role of the predator. *Am. Naturalist, 101* (922) : 467–474.

Stehli, F. G., 1968. Taxonomic diversity gradients in pole location: the recent model. In *Evolution and Environment,* edited by E. T. Drake; pp. 163–227. Yale Univ. Press, New Haven.

Stonehouse, B., 1967. The general biology and thermal balances of penguins. *Advan. Ecol. Res., 4:* 131–196.

Stonehouse, B., 1969. Environmental temperatures of Tertiary penguins. *Science, 163:* 673–675.

Tatton, J. O'G., and J. H. A. Ruzicka, 1967. Organochlorine pesticides in Antarctica. *Nature, 215* (5099) : 346–348.

Thorson, G., 1933. Investigations on shallow water animal communities in the Franz Joseph Fjord (East Greenland) and adjacent waters. *Medd. Grønland, 100* (2) : 1–70.

Thorson, G., 1934. Contributions to the animal ecology of the Scoresby Sound fjord complex (East Greenland). Hydrography by H. Ussing. *Medd. Grønland, 100* (3) : 1–69.

Thorson, G., 1957. Bottom communities (sublittoral or shallow shelf). In *Treatise on Marine Ecology and Paleoecology. Geol. Soc. Am. Mem., 67* (1): 461–534.

Thorson, G., 1966. Some factors influencing the recruitment and establishment of marine benthic communities. *Neth. J. Sea Res., 3* (2): 267–293.

Turner, C. H., E. E. Ebert, and R. R. Given, 1968. The marine environment offshore from Point Loma, San Diego, California. *Calif. Fish Game, Fish. Bull., 140:* 1–79.

Uschakov, P. V., 1963. Quelques particularités de la bionomie benthique de l'Antarctique de l'Est. *Cahiers Biol., 4:* 81–89.

Valenzuela, E., L. Chavez, and F. Munizaga, 1968. Informe preliminar sobre la erupción de Isla Decepción ocurrida en diciembre de 1967. *Bol. Inst. Antarct. Chileno, 3:* 5–16.

Vibe, C., 1939. Preliminary investigations on shallow water animal communities in the Upernavik- and Thule-districts (Northwest Greenland). *Medd. Grønland, 124* (2): 1–44.

Vine, P. J., 170. Densities of *Acanthaster planci* in the Pacific Ocean. *Nature, 228* (5269): 341–342.

Wells, J. W., 1957. Coral reefs. In *Treatise on Marine Ecology and Palaeoecology, Geol. Soc. Am., Mem. 67* (1): 609–631.

Wilce, R. T., 1967. Heterotrophy in arctic sublittoral seaweeds: an hypothesis. *Botan. Marina, 10* (3/4): 185–198.

Wolfson, A., and T. Dana, 1970. Eastern Pacific Crown-of-Thorns sea star populations in the lower Gulf of California. *Abstracts, Western Soc. Naturalists, Honolulu, Hawaii;* p. 33.

Zaneveld, J. S., 1966. Vertical zonation of antarctic and subantarctic benthic marine algae. *Antarctic J. U.S., 1* (5): 211–212.

Zaneveld, J. S., 1968. Benthic marine algae. Ross Island to Balleny Islands. In *Antarctic Map Folio Series, Folio 10,* edited by E. Balech *et al.;* pp. 10–12. Am. Geograph. Soc., New York.

Zenkevitch, L. A., 1963. *Biology of the Seas of the U.S.S.R.* (Translated by S. Botcharskaya). Allen and Unwin, London.

Antarctic Soil Microbial and Ecological Investigations

Roy E. Cameron

Bioscience Section, Jet Propulsion Laboratory, California Institute of Technology, Pasadena

During the austral summers of 1966 to 1970, soil microbial and ecological investigations were undertaken in the Antarctic, primarily in the dry valleys of southern Victoria Land, but also on the Antarctic Peninsula and in the Transantarctic Mountains. Some of these studies were made in cooperation with Virginia Polytechnic Institute (Benoit and Cameron, 1967; Benoit and Hall, 1970; Cameron *et al.,* 1970a,b; Cameron and Benoit, 1970). The primary objective for these investigations was to determine the relationships of edaphic, climatic, microclimatic, topographic, and geographic factors with the habitat, numbers, distribution, kinds, and activities of microorganisms in the cold deserts of Antarctica. In addition to the main objective, subordinate goals were to obtain information on the ecology of cold, polar, temperate, and hot desert areas before searching for possible life on Mars (Cameron, 1963, 1966, 1969b; Horowitz *et al.,* 1969; Hubbard *et al.,* 1968, 1970). Although Antarctica does not possess a Martian environment, it can serve as a useful model of ecology for design, testing, and extrapolation. The naturally harsh environmental conditions of the Antarctic provide a valuable testing ground for space exploration and manned bases (Johnson and Smith, 1970; Matthews and Madden, 1968; Stuhlinger, 1969).

RESEARCH METHODS

For our studies in the dry valleys, five field sites were established for approximately one-week periods during the austral summers of 1966–1968 in McKelvey, Victoria, Taylor, Wheeler, and Conrow (King and David) Valleys. In the austral summer of 1968–1969 a site was also established on the cinder cones within the sunken caldera of Port Foster, Deception Island (62°57′S, 60°38′W). For the 1969–1970 field season, our most southerly site was established in the large moraine just north and below the talus slopes west of Coalsack Bluff (84°14′S, 162°25′E), designated hereafter as "Berg Moraine." Environmental measurements for soil and air temperature, relative humidity, dew point, wind direction and velocity, solar and environmental radiation flux, net thermal exchange, evaporation rate, ultraviolet (UV) and visible light intensity, barometric pressure, and cloud cover were usually made either continuously or every three hours. Additional sites in other dry valleys and the surrounding vicinities also were investigated and 290 samples were collected from 135 sites. Samples were usually collected from the surface to depths of hard, icy permafrost using aseptic techniques developed for sampling, handling, and processing of desert soils (Cameron, 1967, 1968; Cameron *et al.*, 1966). Care was taken to sterilize the collecting instruments before and after each sample was obtained from the surface or at lower depths of the soil pit. A portion of each sample was put into sterilized plastic tubes, sacks, or glass jars for microbiological determinations, and additional samples were taken for soil moisture, porosity (voids), and bulk density. All samples were kept frozen at −25° to −30°C following collection, transport, and storage at McMurdo Station and the Jet Propulsion Laboratory, California Institute of Technology (JPL). At JPL they were processed in a cold isolation booth or "antarctic simulator" (Cameron and Conrow, 1968). For most purposes, each sample was homogenized by passing it through a sterilized stainless steel 2 mm sieve (No. 10 mesh), unless particles or aggregates were already $\leq$2 mm in diameter, which constitutes the size range of soil. For physical, physicochemical, and chemical analyses a fraction of each sample was air-dried, and a subsequent fraction was powdered by mortar and pestle when necessary. For microbiological determinations, a frozen portion was processed at below freezing temperatures and retained, usually at the *in situ* moisture content, for culture studies.

Soil physical and chemical analyses, including mineralogy, mechanical analysis, bulk density, porosity, moisture content, weight loss on ignition, cation exchange capacity, buffer capacity, pH, Eh, electrical conductivity, elemental chemical abundance, concentrations of prominent water soluble cations and anions, organic carbon and nitrogen, and their ratios were performed for many of the samples. These properties were determined by standard procedures or other methods developed especially for desert soils or other similar geological materials from harsh environments (Cameron, 1969a, 1970; Cameron and Blank, 1963).

Abundance and distribution of general and specific groups of soil microorganisms were determined by direct inoculation of 1 to 10 grams of soil onto agar plates, or by spread plate and dilution culture techniques designed for the investigation and study of low abundances of desert soil microflora (Benoit and Hall, 1970; Cameron, 1967, 1970; Hall, 1968). Tests were performed at various temperatures ranging from +2° to +55°C for aerobic, microaerophilic, and anaerobic bacteria; lactose fermenters; nitrate reducers; sulfate reducers; and coliforms (Allen, 1957). Additional media were used to detect and enumerate streptomycetes, molds, and yeasts. Details of algal determinations have been given previously (Cameron, In press; Cameron *et al.*, 1970c), and included incubation of soil crusts in moist chambers or dilution cultures in weak salt solution at 25 to 200 foot candles at approximately 20°C. Some soils were tested for microbial activity by a method utilizing assimilation of $C^{14}O_2$ into organic compounds (Hubbard *et al.*, 1968, 1970).

ENVIRONMENT AND THE NATURE OF SOILS

Environmental Characteristics

Except for the Antarctic Peninsula, during the summer months when there is a period of continuous daylight there are diurnal fluctuations of environmental parameters for most of the area within the dry valleys and in other exposed areas of moraine and outcrops, such as in the vicinity of the Transantarctic Mountains. These occur not only because of the low angle of incident solar radiation, but because of the interference of mountains and the depth of the valleys which have been deepened by glaciation. These fluctuations greatly influence the microclimate of the soil ecosystem and its dependent biota.

Typical midsummer measurements of incident solar radiation, plotted at 3- or 1-hour intervals, are shown in Figures 1 through 5 for McKelvey, Victoria, Taylor, Wheeler, and Conrow Valleys. Figure 6, "Berg Moraine," illustrates a similar diurnal phenomenon, although the site was relatively open, and shielded from the

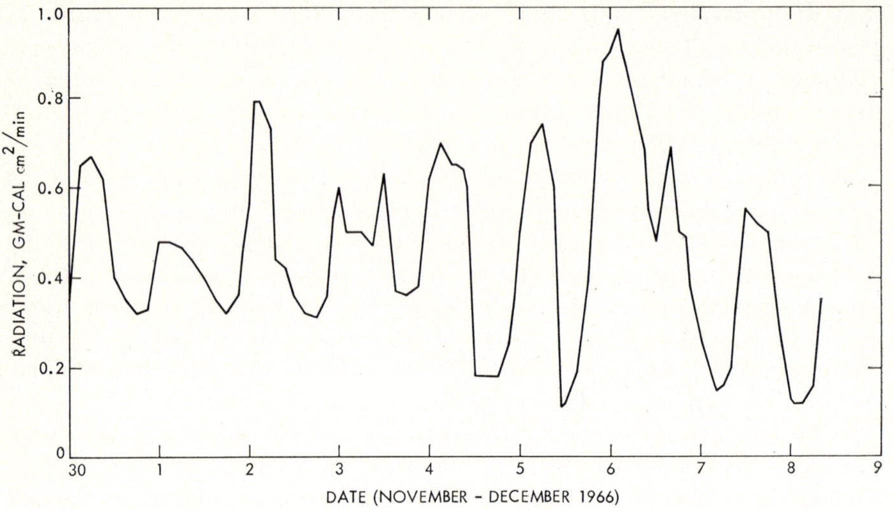

Fig. 1. Solar radiation at normal incidence, McKelvey Valley, Antarctica.

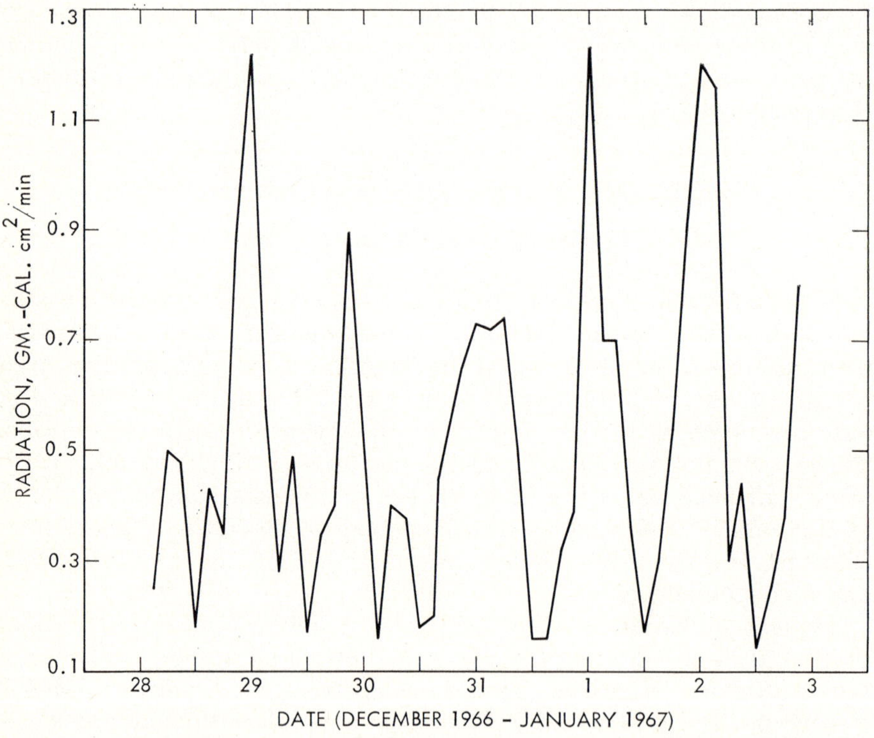

Fig. 2. Solar radiation at normal incidence, Victoria Valley, Antarctica.

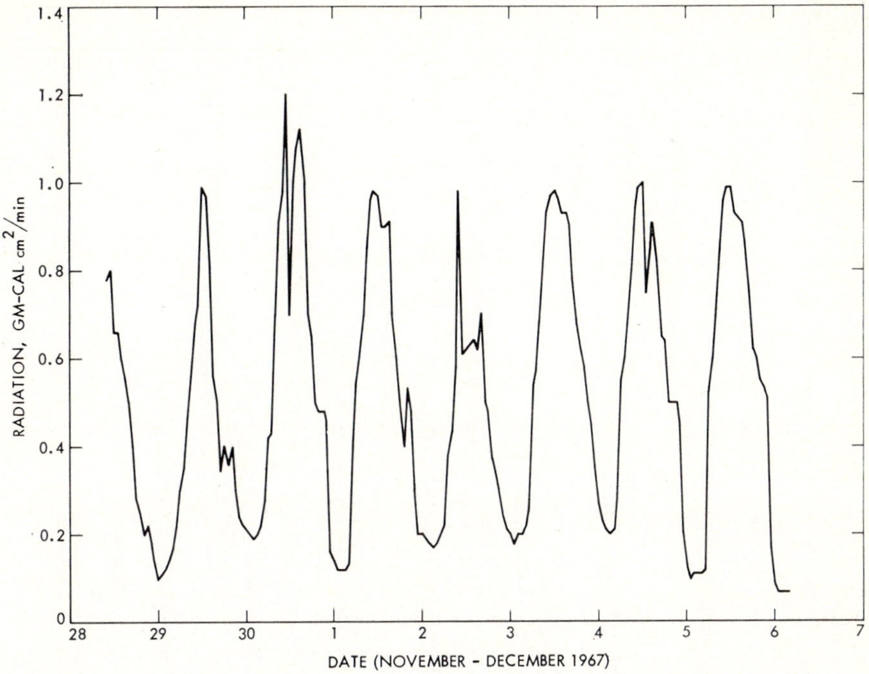

Fig. 3. Solar radiation at normal incidence, Taylor Valley, Antarctica.

sun only shortly after 12 midnight. For the site at Deception Island, north of the Antarctic Circle, there was no solar radiation received during midnight hours (Fig. 7). The site was located in the west and at the base of a cinder cone. As is usual on the peninsula, the weather was frequently cloudy and full intensity of solar radiation was seldom received at this site. For the site at "Berg Moraine," the soil surface did not usually receive peak intensity of radiation because of interfering afternoon cloud cover. Irregularities in increments of solar radiation received at the soil surface were commonly the result of intermittent clouds or extensive cover, and maximum highs and lows of incident radiation were seldom received at some sites such as McKelvey Valley (Fig. 1). Rapid changes in incident radiation were noted at most sites as shown by the overall steepness of the curves. Similar diurnal characteristics were noted for temperature, relative humidity, light intensity, evaporation rate, and wind profile (Cameron, 1969b, In press; Cameron and Conrow, 1969a; Cameron *et al.*, 1970a). This same phenomenon of a diurnal cycle has been noted for temperature by

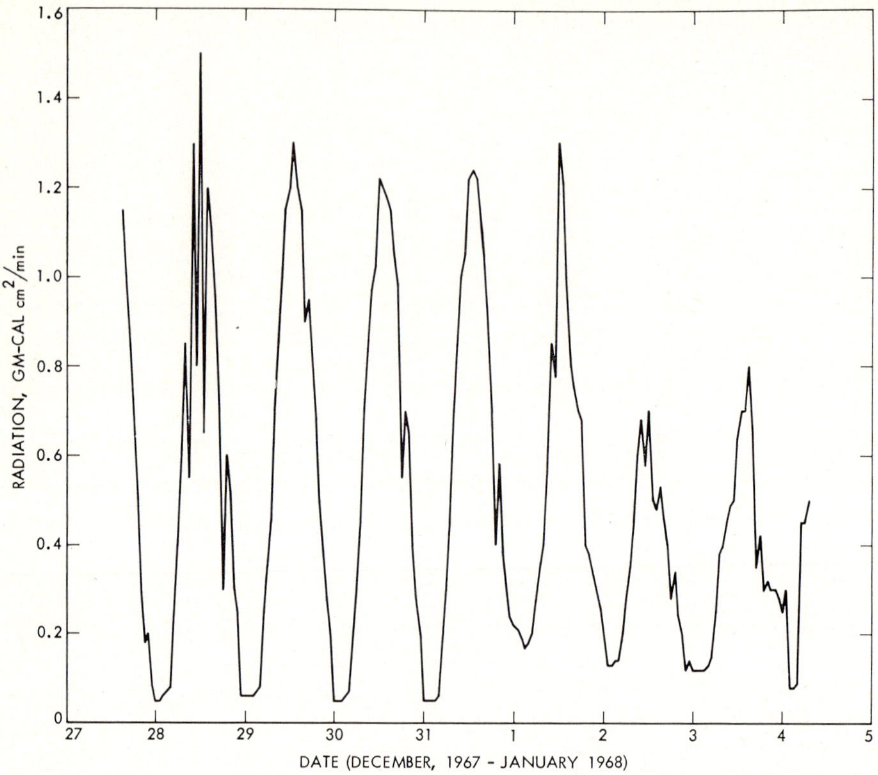

Fig. 4. Solar radiation at normal incidence, Wheeler Valley, Antarctica.

other investigators (Janetschek, 1967; Rudolph, 1966; Ugolini, 1963).

Profiles of soil and air temperatures for the site at "Berg Moraine" (Figs. 8, 9) show that only the soil surface was warm enough to permit the growth of microorganisms, and then only for that part of the diurnal cycle when the temperature was at or above 0°C. An unusually high soil surface temperature of +26°C was measured on a north-facing slope near this site; but in general the air temperatures above the soil usually showed very little variation between 15 cm and 1 m, and showed great similarity to temperature curves obtained for the shaded soil surface and at depths of 2.5 and 5 cm in the soil. The hard, ice-cemented permafrost, which was a rather distinctive ice layer, started at 5 cm. For drier soils, and above the ice-cemented permafrost layer, there may be negligible temperature effects at 25 to 30 cm.

A comparison of the measured and observable environmental

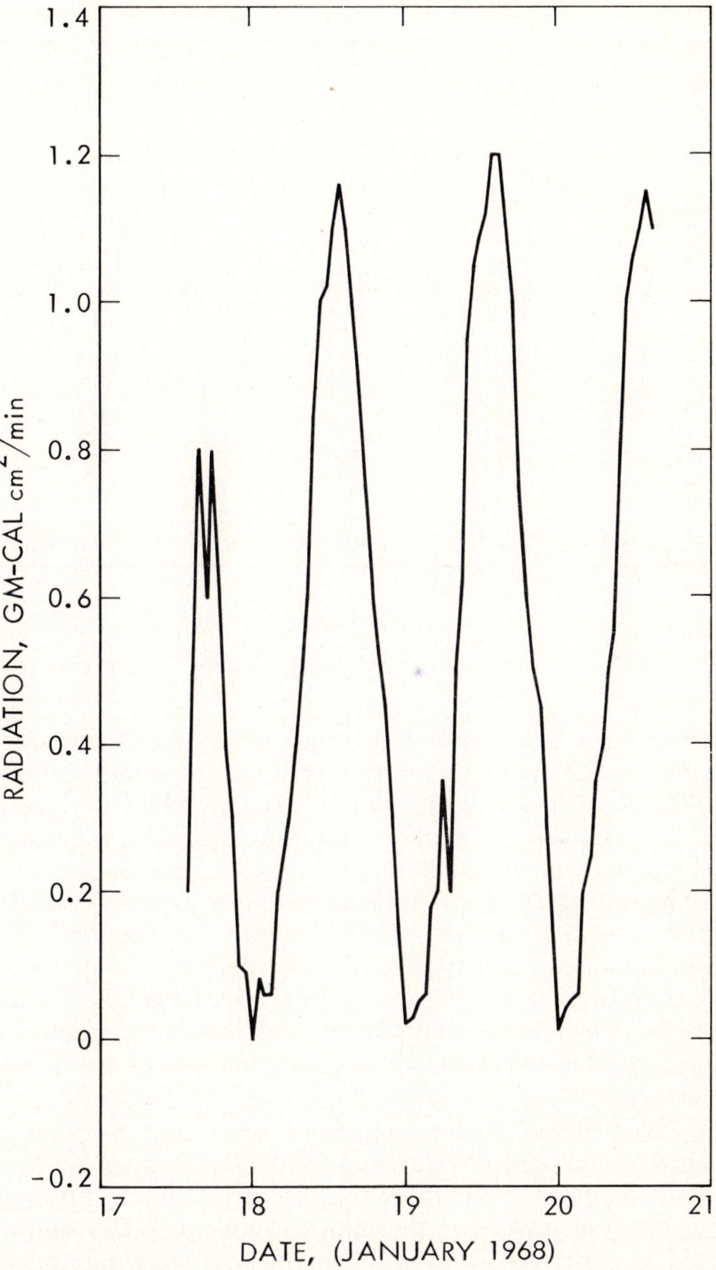

Fig. 5. Solar radiation at normal incidence, Conrow Valley (King-David Junction), Antarctica.

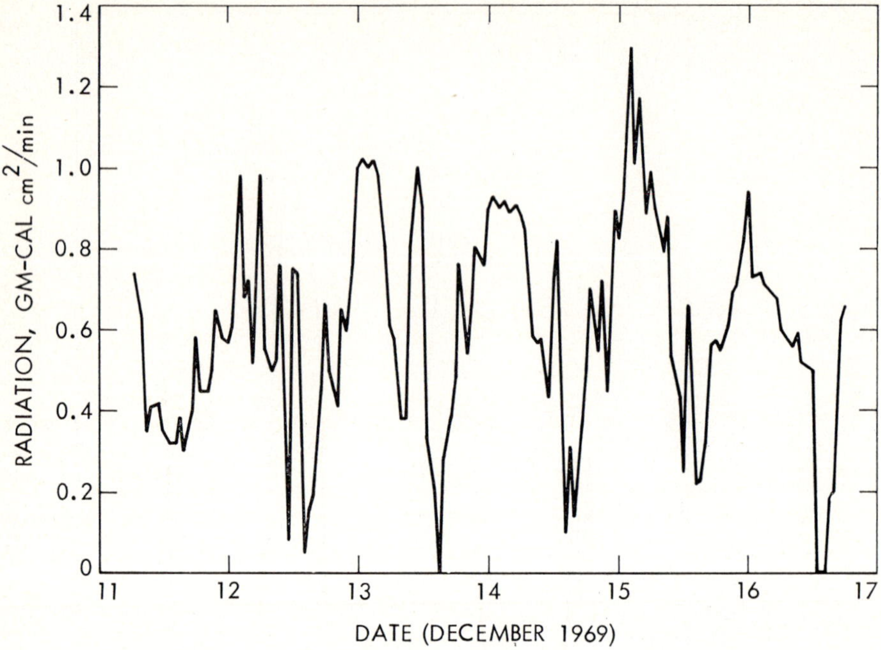

Fig. 6. Solar radiation at "Berg Moraine," Antarctica.

parameters at a given site with other sites has shown the importance of these phenomena for the existence of microorganisms. A higher soil relative humidity, which may be offset by adverse salt effects, provides for a higher standing crop of microorganisms (Cameron and Conrow, 1969a). As indicated previously (Rudolph, 1966), vegetation in the Antarctic is more likely to survive if it can withstand the sudden environmental changes and if it also can grow during the short, fragmented periods when the environmental conditions are favorable. For microorganisms, this must be a period when both temperature and moisture conditions provide for available moisture for the time necessary for growth and reproduction.

It has been shown under some conditions that bacteria can not only survive but grow following diurnal freezing and thawing (Young *et al.*, 1963) ; but there can be lethal effects (Hawrylewicz *et al.*, 1965) and even for mesophilic sporeforming bacilli in soil subjected to controlled diurnal freezing and thawing there was a gradual decrease in viability (Hagen and Hawrylewicz, 1969).

There are a number of reports of studies on effects of freezing

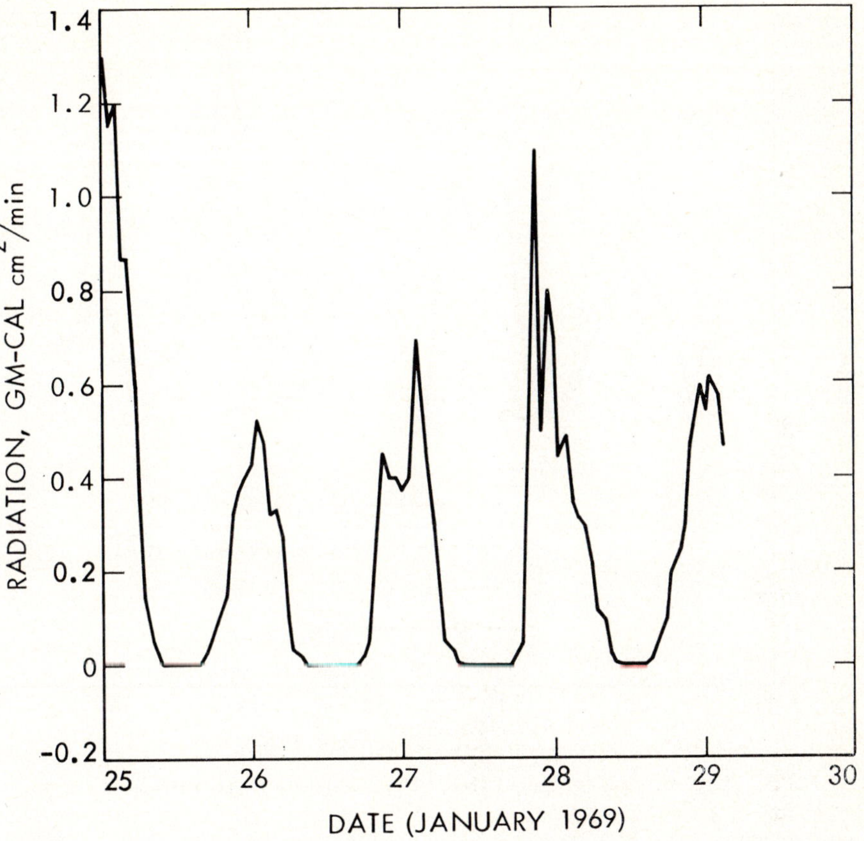

Fig. 7. Solar radiation at normal incidence, Deception Island, Antarctica.

and thawing on survival and growth of bacteria (Saunders, 1969), but the results are not conclusive. Laboratory experiments must be correlated with naturally occurring field conditions, as shown by early work on studies of survival and growth of bacteria in frozen soils in Quebec (Lochhead, 1924). The rate and degree of freezing and thawing, moisture content and activity, and the *in situ* association of bacteria with soil particles are important factors to be considered, as well as the nature of the bacteria themselves and their cryotolerance.

For the Antarctic, it has been found that there is a seasonal change in numbers of soil microorganisms, with peaks reached during midsummer (Boyd and Boyd, 1963a). For approximately three to four weeks during midsummer, many antarctic soils are subjected to diurnal freeze-thaw cycles. The increase in micro-

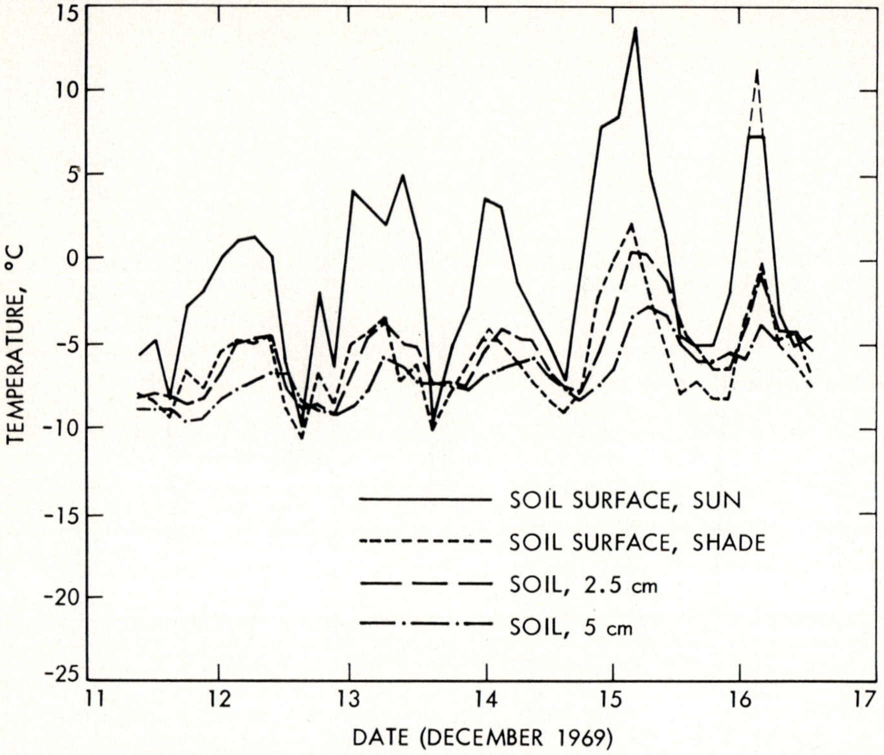

Fig. 8. Soil temperatures, "Berg Moraine," Antarctica.

organisms must be considered in terms of the undisturbed soil ecosystem, which acts as a protective shield for the microorganisms. When the same microorganisms are in dislodged soil sprinkled on agar plates and subsequently subjected to freezing and thawing, they are either drastically reduced in numbers or totally dead. This was determined for most dry valley sites examined during the austral summers of 1966–1967 and 1967–1968. Under similar circumstances of controlled freezing and thawing, bacteria cultured in agar from temperate semiarid soils did not show severe reductions in numbers following diurnal freezing and thawing (Cameron *et al.*, 1969–1970).

Soil Properties

Antarctic soils are primarily weakly or poorly developed sandy materials of shallow depth (Calkin, 1964; Claridge, 1965; McCraw,

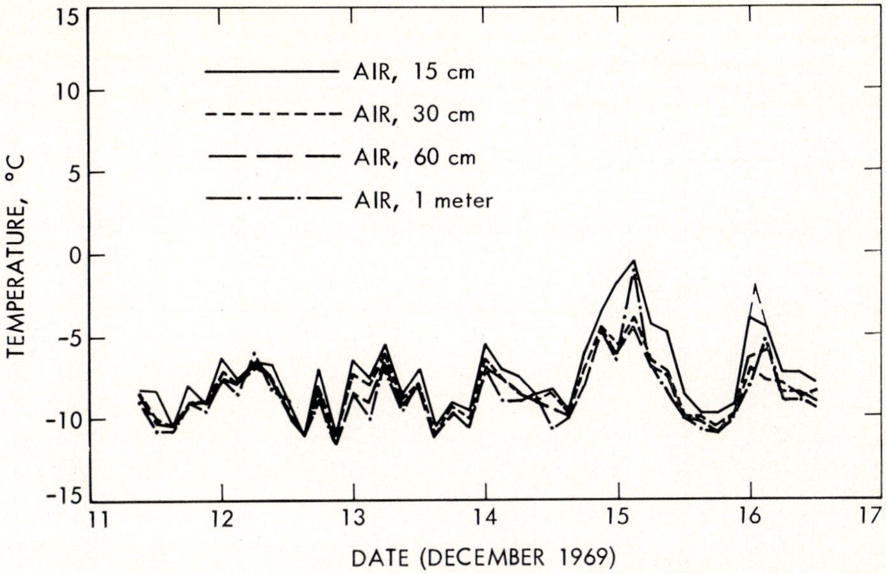

Fig. 9. Air temperatures, "Berg Moraine," Antarctica.

1967; Tedrow and Ugolini, 1966; Ugolini and Bull, 1965). Soils are frequently overlain by a desert or lag pavement if pebble- and gravel-sized fragments and cobbles in a gently to increasingly rolling terrain of barren swales and depressions which may be intersected by various stages of sorted and nonsorted frost-crack polygons. Almost without exception, the soils are coarse materials, although a small percentage (usually <10 percent) of silt and clay-sized particles are present, either in older, surface soils, or as glacial fines near the permafrost boundary layers. Older soils are commonly overlain by a pavement showing desert varnish, as in McKelvey Valley, and surface colors of brown or yellowish brown (Tedrow and Ugolini, 1966). Frost-crack polygons may be present regardless of altitude, but in older and drier areas they may be absent or nonsorted and characterized by sand wedges (Black and Berg, 1963; Berg and Black, 1966). Polygon characteristics may be used for dating and show that various of the dry valleys are from 3,000 to 10,000 years old (Berg and Black, 1966). Based on the chloride content of lakes, however, some areas may be more than 60,000 years old, for example, Lake Vanda in Wright Valley (Wilson, 1970).

In situ moisture contents of soils tested showed a wide range (Table 1) which has been summarized previously for a number of

Table 1. Physical and physicochemical properties of antarctic soils.

Soil No.	Sample depth (cm)	Location and remarks	Texture	H_2O (in situ wt. %)	pH sat. (paste)	Elect. Cond. (ECX 10^{-6} mhos/ cm^2 at 25°C 1:5 extract)	Cation Exchange Capacity (meq/100 gm)	Buffer Capacity (meq/100 gm)
713	Surf. 2→5	Antarctic Peninsula, Deception Is. 1967 cinder cones.	gravelly sand	12. 2	5. 9	30	0. 5	0. 3
718	Surf. 2→5	Antarctic Peninsula, Deception Is. Main Island.	gravelly sand	21	7. 3	170	2. 0	0. 3
740	Surf. 2	Dunlop Is. Algae in low areas, around stones.	sand	34. 5	7. 4	1.2×10^4	11	6. 0
741	2→5	Skuas nesting nearby. Wet, salty soil.	sand	37. 1	7. 4	275	5. 0	4. 5
562	Surf. 2	Marble Pt. Algal crusts near algal "peat" deposit	loamy sand	1. 37	8. 9	375	10	3. 0
735	Surf. 2	Strand Moraines. Several cm of loose, dried	gravelly sand	0. 35	7. 5	235	3. 0	3. 0
736	2→5	algal material on surface. Skuas nesting nearby.	gravelly sand	3. 3	8. 6	108	4. 0	3. 5
737	30	Algae also in partially "thawed" ice.	gravelly sand	6. 1	8. 4	81	2. 0	2. 5
522	Surf. 5	Balham Valley. Wet, spongy, salty depres-	sand	13. 6	7. 7	3.8×10^4	1. 5	16. 5
523	5→15	sion. Soil did not freeze at -25°C.	sand	13. 6	7. 6	1.5×10^4	1. 5	2. 5
524	30	Vacuum dried.	sand	12. 3	7. 4	1.5×10^4	3. 5	4. 0
625	Surf. 5	Barwick Valley. Duplicate sample, Lunar Receiving Lab.	sand	1. 74	8. 3	49	0. 5	1. 5
571	Surf. 2	Bull Pass. Dry, ventifacted glacial moraine.	sand	1. 12	7. 4	4400	3. 0	2. 8
572	2→5		sand	1. 60	7. 1	2900	1. 5	1. 8
573	30		sand	1. 86	7. 6	360	2. 0	0. 7
638	Surf. 2	Conrow Valley (King-David Junct.) Some algal	sand	3. 7	8. 1	180	4. 0	2. 5
639	2→8	soil crusts in vicinity.	sand	4. 4	7. 5	68	6. 0	2. 0
640	10→15		sand	6. 6	7. 4	63	4. 0	2. 0
632	Surf. 5	King Valley. Dry site. Duplicate sample, Lunar Receiving Lab.	sand	1. 47	7. 6	2400	2. 0	0. 5

Table 1 (continued)

Soil No.	Sample depth (cm)	Location and remarks	Texture	H_2O (in situ) wt. %	pH sat. (paste)	Elect. Cond. (ECX 10^{-6} mhos/ cm^2 at 25°C 1:5 extract)	Cation Exchange Capacity (meq/100 gm)	Buffer Capacity (meq/100 gm)
664	Surf. 2	Matterhorn Valley. Moist area. Soil friable.	sandy loam	5.0	8.9	8400	11	47
647	Surf. 2	Pearse Valley. Some soil algal crusts and algae in nearby pond.	sand	0.63	7.6	4620	3.0	1.5
648	2 → 15		sand	0.78	7.5	1.3×10^4	4.0	1.5
600	Surf. 2	Taylor Valley. Island near Lake Bonney Hut. Subject to extensive field party contamination. Algae in ice surrounding island.	sand	0.51	7.9	4560	2.5	12.5
601	2 → 15		sand	0.63	8.0	4800	2.5	9.7
602	30		sand	0.73	7.9	4480	2.5	12.6
603	60		sand	3.0	8.2	3280	2.5	8.6
649	Surf. 2	Turnabout Valley. High-ridged frost-crack polygons.	loamy sand	1.52	7.0	4320	7.0	2.0
650	2 → 15		sand	1.39	6.8	3780	4.0	1.5
634	Surf. 5	Victoria Valley. Dune sand. Duplicate sample, Lunar Receiving Lab.	sand	0.14	8.0	2400	2.5	2.6
629	Surf. 5	Wright Valley, Labyrinth Dias. Crustose lichens at site. Duplicate sample, Lunar Receiving Lab.	sand	3.6	7.8	1480	2.5	1.3
621	Surf. 2	Wheeler Valley. Sparse crustose lichens, moss, algae.	sand	5.1	8.8	215	3.0	1.5
725	Surf. 2	Coalsack Bluff, West. Transantarctic Mts.	sand	0.92	5.2	1700	2.0	1.5
726	2 → 10		sand	1.27	5.3	2700	2.0	1.5
742	Surf. 2	Berg Moraine, below Coalsack Bluff, West. Transantarctic Mts.	sand	1.58	6.5	1040	2.0	5.0
743	2 → 7		sand	1.77	6.6	920	3.0	7.5

soil profiles (Cameron and Conrow, 1969a). *In situ* moisture values were usually higher for coastal areas, where there was greater influence from glacial melt, runoff, and subsequent surface moisture accumulation than in the dry valley areas. The usual trend was a perceptible increase in moisture from the surface to depth of permafrost. Within the ice table, the percentage of moisture could exceed that of soil, especially in areas where there were moraine deposits over ice or an influx of moisture from glacial melt. In general, the driest antarctic cold desert soils had moisture contents approaching or similar to the driest desert soils from temperate or hot desert regions (Cameron, 1969b). Despite a greater subsurface moisture content than at the surface, a comparison of temperature measurements at many soil sites showed that the subsurface soils were nearly always below freezing near the permafrost layer even during austral midsummer, and therefore this water was essentially unavailable for microorganisms. With increasing relative humidity more microorganisms were found in subsurface soils (Cameron and Conrow, 1969a). Some diurnal fluctuations of soil relative humidity are concurrent with temperature fluctuations. Radioactive tracers have shown that subsurface moisture moves to the surface (Ugolini and Grier, 1969).

The pH values of saturated soil pastes were usually above 7.0, and commonly between 7.5 and 8.5. Some pH and Eh values were measured *in situ* for moist soils and found to be similar to values obtained later in the McMurdo laboratory (Cameron, In press). The pH values were generally indicative of slightly to strongly saline soils and similar to many other saline desert soils (Cameron, 1969a, b). Only one soil, No. 562 from Marble Point, pH 8.9, could be classified as alkaline.

Some low pH values were obtained. Volcanic cinders and ash of sample No. 713 from Deception Island had a pH of 5.9, but this value will probably increase following additional leaching, despite the nature of the volcanic materials. Relatively low pH values also were obtained for samples collected from "Berg Moraine" (Fig. 10), and also in the vicinity of the bluffs west of Coalsack Bluff (Fig. 11). In regard to these latter samples, it should be remembered that the Antarctic once had a much more favorable climate than today. Endemic biota (Adie, 1970; Doumani and Long, 1962), fossil plant, and animal remnants in exposed outcrops show that approximately 100 to 200 million years ago the region near Beardmore Camp, where some of our samples were collected, had a much milder climate than at present and the biota included big-leaf fern

Fig. 10. Microbial air samples near snow remnant, "Berg Moraine." Site 740–741, December, 1969.

Fig. 11. Profile of tropical relict soil near stromatolites, Coalsack Bluff, west. Site 725–726, November, 1969.

(*Glossopteris*), an amphibian (*Lystrosaurus*), and calcareous blue-green algae (stromatolites) (Discussions and observations with W. Breed, N. Colbert, D. Elliott, J. Jensen, J. Schopf, P. Tasch, and others). Near the stromatolite find (by W. Breed), a distinct soil profile was evident (Fig. 11) in a protected hollow which was an ancient reddish-brown relict soil showing arid tropical influences, but it has been modified by calcareous (orthid) efflorescences and subsurface permafrost of the cold antarctic desert. The acid pH values of this soil were obtained for both the saturated paste and 1:5 water extract.

Molecular Characteristics

Electrical conductivity (EC) values, in conjunction with pH and percentages of extractable ions, are typical of normal, saline, or calcareous cold desert soils. Electrical conductivities for the 1:5 extract were $>250 \times 10^{-6}$ mhos per cm^2, for 25 of 37 soils (Table 1) and could be osmotically detrimental for organisms under normal conditions of a favorable moisture-temperature regime (Richards, 1954). Values of $>2{,}000 \times 10^{-6}$ mhos per cm^2 indicate a very high proportion of total soluble salts (Metson, 1961), and would provide an environment for halotolerant or osmophilic organisms (Hall, 1968; Hall and Benoit, 1968). Most of the antarctic soils containing algae have EC values $<250 \times 10^{-6}$ mhos per cm^2 (Cameron, In press). The osmotic pressure of the environment is increased in antarctic soils because of aridity and desiccation (Boyd, 1967). In this regard, it should be noted that a decrease in soil moisture also reduced the *in situ* pH, as has been shown for temperate desert soils (Cameron, 1966). This would provide a more favorable environment for acid-tolerant microorganisms, such as yeasts and molds.

The cation exchange capacity (CEC) of antarctic cold desert soils is dominated by the mono- and divalent ions listed in Table 1. Approximate relationships can be shown between the CEC, total extractable ions, and electrical conductivity (Metson, 1961). The relatively low CEC can be expected for coarse-textured soils having only small amounts of fines and organic matter. The values for CEC are comparable to determinations obtained for a large variety of temperate desert soils and leached volcanic materials, ranging between 3 and 10 milliequivalents (meq) per 100 g soil, but higher than for soils from the Chilean Atacama Desert, which were mostly zero or <0.1 meq/100 g soil (Cameron, 1970). For ground pumice, kaolin, siliceous sand, and limonite, the CEC is between 4.0 and 6.0 meq per 100 g (Cameron, 1970). The highest values were usually obtained for soils having finer-textured fractions or organic matter in the form of viable algae. Coarse-textured salty soils from the Matterhorn Valley have been found with no measurable CEC (Cameron, In press).

Buffer capacities are dependent upon many of the same factors as cation exchange capacity, but, in addition, they are greatly influenced by the kinds and amounts of salts. Absence or paucity of clays and colloidal organic matter, a neutral pH, and presence of carbonates and phosphates are indicated by low buffer capacities in many antarctic soils. Sandy soils from temperate desert areas show a similar range of buffer capacities, but those areas where very calcareous soils are present, as in southwestern United States and the Moroccan Sahara, may show considerably higher values. Sandy Chilean Atacama Desert soils, which lack fines and salts, have values similar to those for the least buffered antarctic soils, with an average of 2.2 meq per 100 g soil for 35 soils. For our antarctic samples, the soils with the highest buffer capacities generally did not provide optimum conditions for microorganisms, even if sufficient moisture was present. For example, soil sample No. 664 from Matterhorn Valley had the highest buffer capacity, 47 meq per 100 g, and did not contain any detectable microorganisms. However, more than one limiting factor for microorganisms characterized this soil, which also was medium textured, moist, and had high concentrations of sodium, potassium, chloride, bicarbonate, nitrate, and boron on a moderate CEC at a high pH level.

Chemical Ions

The principal anions and cations in cold desert soils are Ca^{++}, Mg^{++}, Na^{+}, and K^{+}. A few ppm of NH_4^{+}, as well as Fe^{+++}, were detected in some samples (Table 2). Only in areas subjected to contamination by sea birds, for example, Dunlop Island (surface sample No. 740), was there a significant level of NH_4^{+}. Ammonia is characteristic for bird-derived (ornithogenic) soils (Boyd and Boyd, 1963b; Ugolini, 1965). Tests for Al^{+++} were generally negative, as would be expected for normal or saline desert soils. High concentrations of Na^{+} and Mg^{++}, as found at Site 522–524 in Balham Valley, are unfavorable soil properties, and the soil was highly hydrated, dispersed, and showed a depressed freezing point.

Table 2. Chemical properties of antarctic soils.

Soil No.	Sample Depth (cm)	H_2O Soluble Ions in 1:5 extract											Organic C (wt. %)	Organic N (wt. %)	Carbonate C (wt. %)	C/N (organic)
		Ca^{++}	Mg^{++}	Na^{+}	K^{+}	MH_4^{+}	$SO_4^{=}$	Cl^{-}	HCO_3^{-}	NO_3^{-}	NO_2^{-}	$PO_4^{\equiv}$				
713	Surf. 2 → 5	1	0.2	2	0.05	0.0	4	4	0	0	0.00	0.00	0.01	0.002	0.01	5
718	Surf. 2 → 5	1.5	0.6	8	0.05	0.0	4	7	18	0	0.00	0.50	0.02	0.002	0.04	10
740	Surf. 2	150	180	2300	3	26	520	4260	82	50	0.05	0.40	4.62	0.589	0.04	7.8
741	2 → 5	3	25	400	2.5	1.3	52	639	24	4	0.00	0.25	1.10	0.139	0.09	7.9
562	Surf. 2	0.2	1	89	9	0.7	24	46	134*	3	0.01	2.2	0.25	0.027	0.26	9.4
735	Surf. 2	24	1	20	2	1.1	12	36	67	10	0.00	0.35	0.15	0.020	0.24	2.5
736	2 → 5	9	0.5	8	1.5	0.7	4	11	70	4	0.00	0.25	0.14	0.007	0.33	20.0
737	30	3	0.4	10	1.5	1.0	0	12	55	4	0.00	0.15	0.06	0.005	0.37	12.0
522	Surf. 5	500	750	8000	3	0.0	30	8875	52	900	0.08	0.06	0.61	0.114	0.04	5.3
523	5 → 15	350	1000	2000	8	0.0	20	3018	64	600	0.04	0.00	0.07	<0.000	0.16	---
524	30	200	1050	1800	10	0.0	17	3330	43	700	0.02	0.05	0.16	0.001	0.05	160
625	Surf. 5	1	0.5	4	0.3	0.8	3	5	18	1	0.00	0.15	0.02	0.004	0.01	50
571	Surf. 2	220	190	420	30	0.0	700	900	24	320	0.02	0.00	0.02	<0.000	0.02	---
572	2 → 5	230	90	220	20	0.0	500	565	24	240	0.02	0.00	0.01	<0.000	0.02	---
573	30	12	7	47	5	0.6	36	89	34	13	0.00	0.07	0.01	0.001	0.02	10
638	Surf. 2	0.2	1.0	29	7	0.2	20	18	34	4	0.05	1.20	0.03	0.008	0.02	3.7
639	2 → 8	0.2	0.5	6	4	0.1	1	2	15	1	0.02	0.90	0.02	0.006	0.04	3.3
640	10 → 15	0.3	0.4	3	0	0.1	0	4	9	1	0.03	0.40	0.04	0.005	0.01	8.0
632	Surf. 5	520	20	98	16	1.8	1080	209	3	80	0.10	0.10	0.01	0.002	<0.00	5

Table 2 (continued)

Soil No.	Sample Depth (cm)	H_2O Soluble Ions in 1:5 extract											Organic C (wt. %)	Organic N (wt. %)	Carbonate C (wt. %)	C/N (organic)
		Ca^{++}	Mg^{++}	Na^{+}	K^{+}	MH_4^{+}	$SO_4^{=}$	Cl^{-}	HCO_3^{-}	NO_3^{-}	NO_2^{-}	$PO_4^{\equiv}$				
664	Surf. 2	37	100	1550	245	0.8	450	2340	61	130	0.01	0.80	0.01	0.002	0.25	5
647	Surf. 2	200	15	260	8	0.1	400	515	30	12	0.02	0.10	0.06	<0.000	0.01	---
648	2 → 15	210	80	410	9	0.1	650	850	18	16	0.03	0.10	0.01	<0.000	0.01	---
600	Surf. 2	55	100	200	75	0.5	8	835	30	5	0.05	0.00	0.02	0.003	0.28	6.6
601	2 → 15	89	85	230	9	0.4	120	800	30	5	0.04	0.10	0.02	0.003	0.19	6.6
602	30	52	60	200	9	0.4	130	600	30	4	0.04	0.10	0.02	0.002	0.18	10
603	60	22	80	130	10	0.5	190	320	30	3	0.04	0.10	0.02	0.001	0.14	20
649	Surf. 2	230	95	160	8	0.2	600	355	24	48	0.02	0.00	0.05	0.007	0.01	7.1
650	2 → 15	290	60	116	7	0.1	290	640	21	32	0.03	0.10	0.05	0.007	0.01	7.1
634	Surf. 5	140	80	240	21	1.0	6	834	37	2	0.03	0.05	0.02	0.003	0.04	6.6
629	Surf. 5	200	25	92	1.3	0.9	680	21	24	17	0.00	0.06	0.05	0.011	0.02	4.5
621	Surf. 2	0.6	1	14	3	0.2	0	2	43	0	0.00	0.04	0.03	0.004	0.02	7.5
725	Surf. 2	240	35	90	2.5	0.2	700	75	18	140	0.01	0.00	0.02	0.009	<0.00	22.0
726	2 → 10	280	60	200	3	0.1	700	186	21	340	0.00	0.15	0.03	0.003	<0.00	10.7
742	Surf. 2	50	15	150	2	1.0	120	110	24	250	0.00	0.00	0.38	0.024	0.03	16.2
743	2 → 7	45	10	130	2	1.0	140	91	21	210	0.00	0.00	0.05	0.019	0.03	26.3

* 3ppm $CO_3^{=}$

The principal anions were $SO_4^=$ and Cl^-, lesser concentrations of HCO_3^-, and sometimes NO_3^-. Only one soil, algal crust sample No. 562 from Marble Point, contained any $CO_3^=$. Both NO_2^- and $PO_4^{\equiv}$ were either undetectable or present in low concentrations and comparable to values obtained for other arid regions. At some sites, the presence of surface salt accumulations and powdery decayed undersurfaces of surface stones indicated the overall aridity of the area; but at other sites, the variable distribution of salts indicated the influence of topography, slope, drainage, and exposure.

Only a few samples showed limitations in the determined ions, although some showed either an imbalance or presence of high concentrations. A few samples (No. 632 from King Valley and No. 664 from Matterhorn Valley) showed no detectable microorganisms either because of the aridity of the site and its location with regard to a moisture source, or high concentrations of the major ions and toxic levels of trace elements, such as boron (Cameron *et al.*, 1968a). Boron toxicity can occur in arid regions where sodium and calcium borates accumulate in surface soils and water-soluble B is >2 ppm (Mitchell, 1964). Other toxic trace elements could include nitrites, sulfides, chromates, or lead. Eight to 30 ppm nitrite and 2 to 10 ppm sulfide were detected in some McKelvey and Victoria Valley soils not air-dried before analysis. Nitrites are known to accumulate in frozen soils. Iodate also may be present in Antarctica in concentrations similar to that found in Chilean deposits (Claridge and Campbell, 1968). In some antarctic soils, as in the Chilean Atacama Desert soils, it has been found that soils with high concentrations of nitrate may have few or no culturable microorganisms (Cameron, 1969b), and biotic activity as well as leaching may be absent (Claridge and Campbell, 1968). Nitrate deposits are indicators of extreme aridity. They are undetectable or present in trace quantities in most nondesert soils because of leaching and/or biotic activity.

Carbon and Nitrogen

A completely satisfactory explanation for the origin of nitrate deposits, whether in the Antarctic or Chile, has not yet been established. Atmospheric formation and precipitation of nitrates has been shown for South Polar snow (Wilson and House, 1955) and apparently some nitrate, as well as ammonia, is formed in the aurora australis (Claridge and Campbell, 1968). Subsequent evaporation and sublimation of snow deposits must be considered for some accumulations of nitrates, but the biological origin is also likely. In the Antarctic, higher plants either were not present since ancient times or there were algae in a number of lakes, and complete mineralization followed decomposition, and denitrification did not take place. For photosynthetic organisms, nitrate is the end product of the oxidation of nitrogen compounds (Olson, 1970). It should also be considered that a substantial proportion of our desert bacterial isolants will grow on nitrogen-free media (Johnson, 1970), and also can contribute to the formation and accumulation of nitrate during the nitrogen cycle. High concentrations of nitrates are toxic for many microorganisms and the absence or low abundance of microorganisms in soils may be either because of aridity or because they are precluded from colonizing the site unless leaching or denitrification can occur. Although leaching is highly unlikely because of low temperatures, high salt concentrations, especially of NaCl, probably could be tolerated by denitrifying bacteria (Ingram, 1957).

Despite unfavorable ionic balance or high concentrations of ions, water is usually a more critical factor for growth of microorganisms in antarctic soils than is the factor of soil chemical composition (Boyd, 1967; Boyd *et al.*, 1966; Benoit and Cameron, 1967; Benoit and Hall, 1970; Cameron and Conrow, 1969a, b; Cameron *et al.*, 1968a, 1970a).

Organic carbon and nitrogen, except for algal crust samples, were extremely low (Table 2). The organic carbon, in general, corresponded to the lowest values obtained for typical harsh desert soils of the temperate regions of western United States, the Egyptian Sahara, Negev, Patagonian, and Atacama Deserts (Cameron, 1969b). They were higher than values obtained for scrub deserts in Upper Sonora, Moroccan Sahara, and central Australia. The organic carbon was usually not more than 0.05 percent in most of the antarctic soils. Such low values are outside the range of "normal" or arable soils. This can account for the "ahumic" status reported for a number of antarctic soils (Tedrow and Ugolini, 1966) and would correspond to recent criteria established for recently defined antarctic cold desert zonal (frigic) soils (Campbell and Claridge, 1969). The small amount of organic carbon present in some antarctic soils may have been anthracite coal (Horowitz *et al.*, 1969). In most antarctic soils, except where algae were abundant, the amounts of carbonate carbon were similar to organic carbon.

Organic nitrogen values, as for organic carbon, were correspondingly low, except where algal mats or crusts were present. These values were in the same range as soils from harsh or relatively barren temperate deserts, and a few negligible values were obtained, as for some soils from the Atacama Desert. On the basis of their organic nitrogen and carbon content, the antarctic soils tested were relatively infertile.

Nostoc commune has been considered as the primary synthesizer of organic matter for the dry valleys (Boyd *et al.*, 1966), although autotrophic bacteria, lichens, and mosses, as well as algae, also are considered to be primary producers (Janetschek, 1967). Other likely sources of organic matter in the dry valleys are wind-borne organic matter from the sea, windblown debris from the McMurdo Sound Station, Scott Base, and penguin rookeries on Ross Island, skua nesting sites, a few mummified or desiccated seals and penguins within the valleys, and debris from field parties and logistic support groups.

Organic carbon-organic nitrogen (C:N) ratios are exceptionally narrow for most antarctic soils, regardless of whether the organic matter is either highly decomposed or of a microbial nature. The C:N ratio for microorganisms is narrow, usually between 4:1 and 9:1 (Buckman and Brady, 1960). The C:N ratio for antarctic cold desert soils is similar to that for temperate aridic soils, and the narrow ratio for samples taken throughout the soil profile generally corresponds to values reported for subsoils occurring in favorable climatic regions (Buckman and Brady, 1960). Unless organic matter of wide C:N ratio, for example 50:1, is added to the soil, there will not be a rapid change in the activity and growth of the heterotrophic microflora (bacteria, streptomycetes, yeasts, and molds), and nitrate can build up. As a general rule, critical ratios for nitrogen transformations are between 20:1 and 25:1 and values above this will favor immobilization, while narrower ratios will favor mineralization (Stevenson, 1964). Hence, the buildup of nitrates in antarctic soils is substantiated by the narrow C:N ratios, and nitrate accumulation will be stabilized by absence of denitrifiers, aridity, oxidized conditions, low temperatures, lack of organic matter, and leaching; and the deposits will not be volatilized despite their exposure on basic soil at pH values >7.

Thermal Luminescence

Some antarctic soils were analyzed by means of thermal luminescence (Cameron *et al.*, 1969) and an attempt was made to establish correlations with the abundance and distribution of microorganisms. The natural thermoluminescence for some antarctic soils is shown in Figure 12. These were soils collected with R. Benoit during a traverse made in Matterhorn Valley, an east-west oriented valley in Asgard Range (77°41′S, 162°24′E) descending into Taylor Valley near Lake Bonney. In general, the natural glow curves show a change in peak intensity with a change in sample location, and a good correlation with the total abundance of microorganisms. The soils with the highest natural thermoluminescence generally contained the fewest or no microorganisms as determined by cultural and radiorespirometric methods. Plots of glow curves following irradiation of these soils with 50K rad CO_{60} are shown in Figure 13 for comparison. Similar studies were performed for soils collected on a traverse of Wheeler Valley, St. John's Range, another high-altitude valley, but located farther north at 77°12′S, 162°42′E. This valley contained a much greater abundance of microflora, had a north-south orientation, a more favorable microclimate, better soil properties, and all soils showed a relatively low natural thermoluminescence. Additional information on the soil microbiological, physical, and chemical properties for the Matterhorn-Taylor Valley and Wheeler Valley traverses

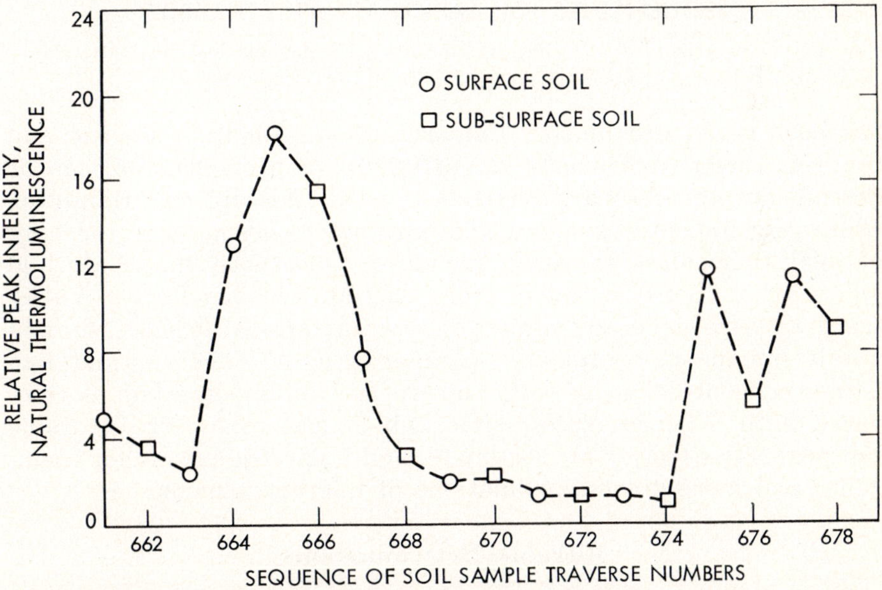

Fig. 12. Relatively high natural thermoluminescence of surface and subsurface soils collected from Matterhorn-Taylor Valley traverse.

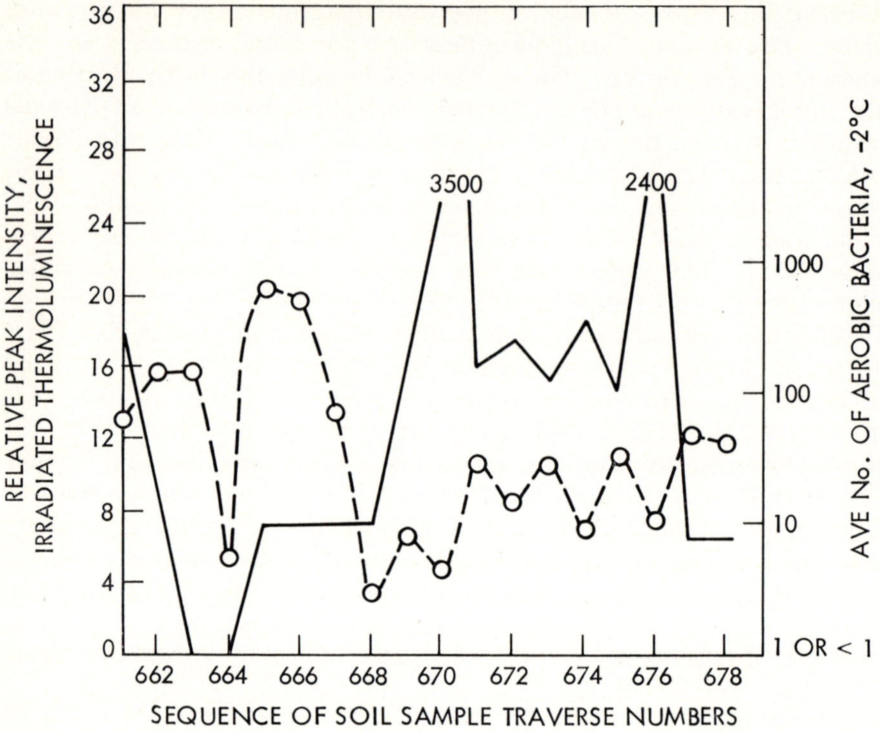

Fig. 13. Comparison of CO_{60}-irradiated soils with aerobic bacterial abundance of samples collected from Matterhorn-Taylor Valley traverse.

has been given previously (Cameron *et al.*, 1968b; Cameron and Conrow, 1969a; Cameron *et al.*, 1970a, b). A previous study on the thermoluminescent characteristics of soils (Nishita and Hamilton, 1968) has indicated some of the parameters responsible for high natural thermoluminescence, including calcareous materials and other salts. Soils collected from the Matterhorn-Taylor Valley traverse were generally higher in concentrations of salts, showed a salt imbalance or toxicity (Cameron *et al.*, 1968a), and had higher concentrations of total and water-soluble potassium as compared with Wheeler Valley sites, which had relatively favorable soil properties, better microclimate, and a consequent higher abundance and more diverse populations of microorganisms.

Microbial Determinations

Soil microbiological properties are given in Tables 3 and 4 for bacteria, streptomycetes (actinomycetes), fungi (yeasts and molds), algae, and protozoa. The total of all groups of microorganisms as determined for a given sample ranged from zero (undetectable) to approximately 10^7 per g of soil, with the largest part of the biomass generally provided by bacteria and algae. Although cultural techniques were commonly used to detect and determine the presence and abundance of microorganisms, radiorespirometric techniques utilizing C^{14}-labelled substrates have confirmed the presence (or absence) of small numbers of microorganisms in our soil samples (Table 5) (Hubbard *et al.*, 1970). This method permitted the detection of CO_2 produced from the catabolism of a small amount of substrate. However, subsurface soils did not show as positive a correlation (Hubbard *et al.*, 1968), which may indicate that the subsurface microorganisms are not the same kinds as the surface microflora or possibly that they have been relatively inactive and in the freeze-dried condition for a number of years. Freeze-drying is a natural phenomenon in the Antarctic, and apparently increases the ability of antarctic microorganisms to survive subsequent exposure to high temperatures (Holm-Hansen, 1967). A longer incubation time is usually required to culture microorganisms in subsurface soils than in surface soils, which further supports the belief that the subsurface microorganisms are either different kinds or have been quiescent for a longer period than surface microbiota. In the drier sites, it is unlikely that the subsurface microorganisms were recently deposited through leaching, not only because of subfreezing temperatures, which would not permit infiltration and percolation of liquid water (if there was an available supply), but also because of the upward movement of moisture (Ugolini and Grier, 1969) and resulting evidence of surface salt efflorescence and evaporites.

Some subsurface soils may have a greater abundance of microorganisms than surface soils (Benoit and Hall, 1970; Cameron *et al.*, 1970a,b), especially near the boundary layer of the hard ice-cemented permafrost (site Nos. 571–573, 638–640, 600–603, and 649–650, Tables 3 and 4). Polar soils usually have fewer organisms in the upper horizons (Boyd, 1967), although where algal surface crusts are present (Fig. 14) there are larger and more diverse populations, similar to communities found in other arid regions (Cameron and Devaney, 1970).

Most of the soil microorganisms were aerobic or microaerophilic heterotrophic bacteria, with abundances comparable to that found in typical temperate or hot desert soils (Cameron, 1969a). As noted previously (Boyd, 1967), arctic polar soil populations are

Table 3. Aerobic, anaerobic, and microerophilic bacteria in antarctic soils. Microorganisms per g of soil.

Soil No.	Sample depth (cm)	Aerobic bacteria and streptomycetes					Anaerobes	Microaerophiles
						Positives at highest dilution		Positives at highest dilution
		+ 2(+5) °C	+ 20 °C	+ 45 °C	+ 20 °C	+ 20 °C	Room temp. 20 °C (±3 °C)	+ 20 °C
713	Surf. 2 → 5	1.6×10^{3}	1.1×10^{4}	10**	3×10^{4}	10^{7}	0	10^{3}
718	Surf. 2 → 5	2.5×10^{5}	3.1×10^{5}	0	10^{5}	10^{6}	<10	10^{6}
740	Surf. 2	2.4×10^{4}	1.6×10^{5}	0	0	10^{5}	0	10^{5}
741	2 → 15	4×10^{3}	1.2×10^{3}	4.5×10^{5}	250	10^{4}	0	10^{4}
562	Surf. 2	5.5×10^{5}	4.4×10^{5}	0*	3.1×10^{5}	10^{5}	1.5	1.5
735	Surf. 2	2.1×10^{6}	1.8×10^{5}	0	9.4×10^{5}	10^{6}	0	10^{6}
736	2 → 15	9.8×10^{4}	1.2×10^{5}	0	8.3×10^{4}	10^{6}	0	10^{6}
737	30	8.3×10^{4}	1.6×10^{5}	0	1.1×10^{5}	10^{4}	0	10^{3}
522	Surf. 5	9.2×10^{4}	1.9×10^{5}	0	<10	10^{5}	0	10^{4}
523	5 → 15	2.9×10^{4}	1.8×10^{5}	0	<10	10^{6}	0	10^{4}
524	30	10^{4}	1.2×10^{5}	0	8.7×10^{3}	10^{5}	0	10^{3}
625	Surf. 5	5.2×10^{4}	6.8×10^{4}	0	8.5×10^{4}	10^{4}	0	10^{7}
571	Surf. 2	80	200	<10	280	10^{3}	0	10^{3}
572	2 → 15	30	60	0	30	10^{3}	0	10^{3}
573	30	1.2×10^{3}	300	0	410	10^{3}	0	10^{3}
638	Surf. 2	8.8×10^{3}	6×10^{3}	0*	8×10^{3}	3.2×10^{3}	0	3.2×10^{3}(7)*
639	2 → 8	1.5×10^{4}	1.4×10^{5}	0	2×10^{5}	1.3×10^{6}	0	6.4×10^{4}(1)*
640	10 → 15	1.7×10^{4}	5×10^{4}	0	3×10^{5}	1.3×10^{6}	0	6.4×10^{4}(6)*
632	Surf. 5	0	0	0	0	0	0	0

Table 3 (continued)

Soil No.	Sample depth (cm)	Aerobic bacteria and streptomycetes					Anaerobes	Microaerophiles
						Positives at highest dilution		Positives at highest dilution
		+ 2(+5) °C	+ 20 °C	+ 45 °C	+ 20 °C	+ 20 °C	Room Temp. 20 °C (+ 3 °C)	+ 20 °C
664	Surf. 2	0	0	0	0	0	0	0
647	Surf. 2	1	60	0*	0	10	<10	0
648	2 → 15	0	1.7×10^3	0*	1.3×10^3	10	<10	0
600	Surf. 2	200	50	0	<10	10	0	10^2(1)*
601	2 → 15	<10	10	0	<10	10	0	10^2(1)*
602	30	100	20	0	<10	10^3	0	10^2
603	60	10^3	7×10^3	0	<10	10^3	0	10^2(3)*
649	Surf. 2	30	460	0*	580	10	0	0
650	2 → 15	1.6×10^3	4×10^3	0*	8.6×10^3	10^4	0	10^3
634	Surf. 5	50	0	0	0	0	0	0
629	Surf. 5	2×10^3	2.5×10^5	0	2.1×10^4	10^6	0	10^5
621	Surf. 2	1×10^3	3×10^3	0	3×10^3	3.2×10^3	0	6.4×10^4(4)*
725	Surf. 2	9	0	0	0	0	0	0
726	2 → 10	0	0	0	0	0	0	0
742	Surf. 2	2.9×10^3	400	0	375	10^3	0	10^3
743	2 → 7	2.7×10^3	1.5×10^3	0	250	100	0	10^3
Media		Trypticase soy agar			Actinomycete agar	Trypticase soy broth	TSA in CO_2 or "Gas-pak"	Fluid thioglycollate medium
Remarks		*Tested only at 55 °C **Growth also at 55 °C			Count includes bacteria	Growth also checked by staining	Incubation period 4 to 6 weeks	*Colony count

Table 4. Specialized bacteria, algae, fungi, and protozoa in antarctic soils. Microorganisms per g of soil.

Soil No.	Sample depth (cm)	Lactose fermenters	Nitrate reducers	Nitrogen fixers	Fungi			Algae	Protozoa
					molds	yeasts		Positives at highest dilution	Positives at highest dilution
		+ 20°C	+ 20°C	+ 20°C	+ 20°C	+ 2°C	+ 20°C	Room temp. or + 20°C	Room temp. or + 20°C
713	Surf. 2 → 5	10^7	10^6	1.6×10^5	10	0	1	10^4	0
718	Surf. 2 → 5	10^7	10^7	1.5×10^5	140	0	0	10^3	100
740	Surf. 2	10^3	10^3	0	0	0	0	10^5	10^3
741	2 → 15	0	100	0	0	0	0	100	0
562	Surf. 2	10^5	10^5	4.7×10^3	10	0	1.3×10^3	10^6	100
735	Surf. 2	10^6	10^5	9.5×10^4	2×10^2	4×10^3	4.6×10^3	10^5	10^3
736	2 → 15	10^5	10^6	2.1×10^5	0	0	0	100	10
737	30	10^3	10^3	2×10^4	0	0	0	100	0
522	Surf. 5	10^3	10^3	0	0	0	0	10	0
523	5 → 15	10^4	10^3	0	0	0	90	0	0
524	30	10^3	10^3	0	0	0	0	0	0
625	Surf. 5	10^4	10^5	1.4×10^4	0	0	300	100	0
571	Surf. 2	10^3	10^4	200	0	0	0	0	0
572	2 → 15	10^3	10^4	20	0	0	0	0	0
573	30	10^3	10^4	0	0	0	0	0	0
638	Surf. 2	3.2×10^3	6.4×10^4	172	0	0	0	180	0
639	2 → 8	3.2×10^3	6.4×10^4	1.5×10^4	10	<10	0	18	0
640	10 → 15	6.4×10^4	3.2×10^3	5.1×10^4	0	0	0	2	0
632	Surf. 5	0	0	0	0	0	0	0	0

Soil No.	Sample depth (cm)	Lactose fermenters	Nitrate reducers	Nitrogen fixers	Fungi: molds	Fungi: yeasts		Algae: Positives at highest dilution	Protozoa: Positives at highest dilution
		+ 20°C	+ 20°C	+ 20°C	+ 20°C	+ 2°C	+ 20°C	Room temp. or + 20°C	Room temp. or + 20°C
664	Surf. 2	0	0	0	0	0	0	0	0
647	Surf. 2	100	100	0	0	0	0	0	0
648	2 → 15	100	10	2×10^3	0	0	0	0	0
600	Surf. 2	10	100	<10	0	0	0	0	0
601	2 → 15	0	10	<10	0	0	0	0	0
602	30	0	100	<10	0	0	0	0	0
603	60	10	10^3	<10	0	0	0	0	0
649	Surf. 2	100	100	580	0	0	0	0	0
650	2 → 15	100	10	8.6×10^3	0	0	0	0	0
634	Surf. 5	0	0	12×10^3	0	0	0	0	0
629	Surf. 5	10^5	10^4	0	0	0	9.4×10^3	100	0
621	Surf. 2	160	160	5×10^3	0	4	0	1.6×10^3	2
725	Surf. 2	0	0	0	0	3	5*	0	0
726	2 → 10	0	0	0	0	0	0	0	0
742	Surf. 2	10^3	10^3	6.5×10^4	0	1.1×10^3	5.1×10^3	0	0
743	2 → 7	100	100	1.3×10^6	0	105	500	0	0
Media		Lactose broth	Nitrate reduction broth	Burk's N-free "Ion agar"	Rose bengal agar (less antibiotics)	diMenna's dextrose-neopeptone agar, pH 4.5		Thornton's salt medium (without organics) Sylvania "Gro-lux" fluorescent lights, 250 ft. c. intensity (or less)	
Remarks		Growth also checked by staining		Does not exclude N in soil dilution	Count also substantiated by growth on other media	*Count on TSA at 20°C		Incubation period up to 6 months	

Table 5. CO_2 assimilation by surface soils from Wheeler and King-David Dry Valleys.

Soil	Viable microorganisms per gm soil: Algae Positive at highest dilution	Bacteria (+ 20°C)	$C^{14}O_2$ exposure[a]	Pyrolysis CO_2, cpm[c]	Trapped organics, cpm
Wheeler 609	300	2×10^4	light[b]	8,354	3
			light	7,023	165
			dark	16,832	78
Wheeler 613	800	2×10^4	light[b]	10,853	7
			light	14,600	773
			dark	37,841	83
Wheeler 615	6.4×10^6	1.2×10^5	light[b]	11,989	9
			light	11,818	1,643
			dark	27,206	122
Wheeler 619	40	8×10^3	light[b]	4,355	8
			light	4,729	43
King-David 641	0	8×10^3	light[b]	29,391	11
			light	20,860	93
			dark	36,918	51
King-David 643	1.8×10^5	5×10^3	light[b]	11,272	13
			light	23,072	7,212
			dark	17,016	175
King-David 638	180	6×10^3	light[b]	3,552	5
			light	2,348	29

[a] Soils were exposed to $C^{14}O_2$ for 22 hr at room temperature; 15 mg aliquots were used for pyrolysis.
[b] Sterilized before exposure.
[c] Carrier $C^{12}O_2$ was added during pyrolysis.

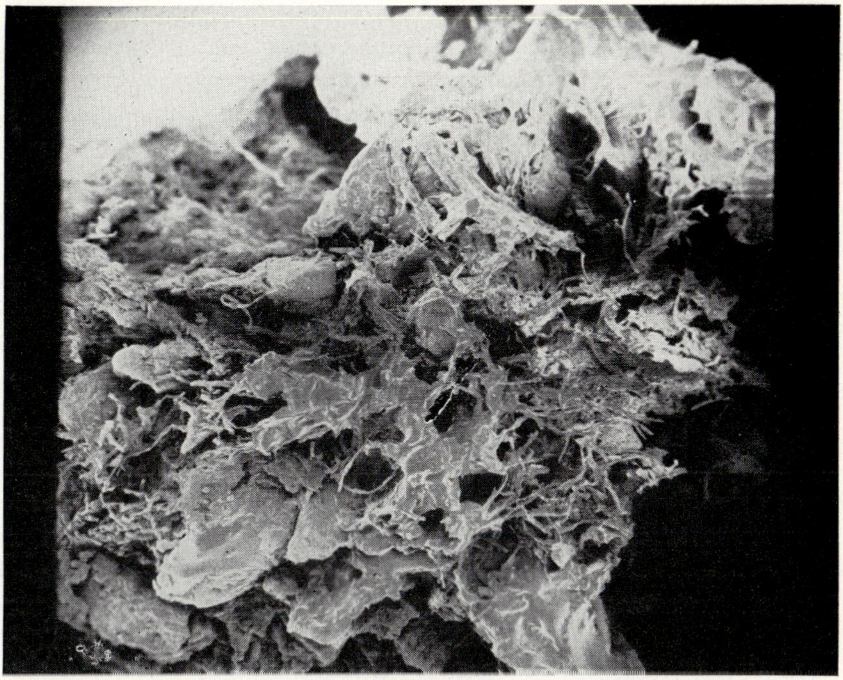

Fig. 14. Scanning electron photomicrograph of heterogeneous community of coalesced blue-green algal sheaths and imbedded filaments of molds and soil particles. Algal soil crust sample No. 562 from Marble Point. x 85.

primarily mesophilic bacteria. These same observations were substantiated for antarctic bacteria, and they grew as well, if not better, and more rapidly at 20°C than at 2° or 5°C. However, temperatures above 28° to 30°C are frequently inhibitory, and therefore the great majority of antarctic soil bacteria can be categorized as mesophiles, but with optimum growth in the minimum mesophilic range of 5° to 25°C (Jacobs *et al.,* 1957). No obligate psychrophilic bacteria were found. Tests performed by other workers for obligate low-temperature forms have shown that they are uncommon or absent (Benoit and Hall, 1970; Sinclair and Stokes, 1965). Many antarctic bacterial isolants are osmophiles or halotolerants, but their salt tolerance is lowered as temperatures are lowered (Hall and Benoit, 1968).

Although trypticase soy agar was the primary culture and isolation medium used for our studies, organically enriched Taylor Valley soil extract (R. Benoit's medium "M-12"), and an organically enriched salt medium based on Taylor Valley soil extract have also shown excellent, but sometimes variable results (Benoit and Hall, 1970; Cameron *et al.*, 1968a, 1970a; Hall, 1968).

It may not be necessary to add any enrichments, and the soil itself may supply sufficient nutrients, as shown by an increase in microbial abundance following moist soil incubation (Cameron and Conrow, 1969b). However, this test did not simulate actual field conditions because the soils were not subjected to diurnal freeze-thaw cycles. In general, similar abundances of bacteria were obtained, frequently within one logarithm unit, whether the culture medium was trypticase soy agar, trypticase soy broth, fluid thioglycollate, lactose broth, or nitrate-reduction broth. Growth in fluid thioglycollate was usually at the surface and subsurface of the tube at low dilutions, but only subsurface at higher dilutions. Frequent growth in nitrate broth indicates the ability of the soil population to reduce nitrate to nitrite and substantiates the occurrence of nitrite in some soils.

Excellent results also were obtained with actinomycete isolation agar and Burk's nitrogen-fixation agar. Bacteria and some streptomycetes grew on both of these media. Some soil diphtheroids may be favored by actinomycete isolation agar because it contains glycerol. A single population of fastidious, glistening red diphtheroid colonies grew only on this medium. Growth on Burk's nitrogen-fixation agar is not a definite indication of nitrogen-fixation ability unless the soil also lacks nitrogen. As shown for temperate desert soils (Johnson, 1970), however, it is quite likely that many of the antarctic soil bacteria may have this capability. A large abundance of microorganisms cultured on this medium does not necessarily mean that many nitrogen fixers are present, but the presence of ammonia (site No. 740–741) apparently decreases the possibility of finding nitrogen fixers in the microbial community as has been noted for arable soils.

Some groups of bacteria were either not present or relatively scarce as determined by cultural methods. These included several specific physiological groups. Coliforms apparently survive for only a short time in the Antarctic (Boyd and Boyd, 1963b), and this also has been observed for other desert soils, unless the organic contamination is recent, heavy, or continual, and left moist (Cameron, 1969a). Thermophiles may survive longer in arctic and antarctic soils (Boyd and Boyd, 1962, 1963b), but no thermophiles were detected in our samples, except as probable contaminants, or where favored in thermal environments around fumaroles (sample No. 713).

Anaerobes were essentially absent and only several possible anaerobes per gram of soil were obtained as from Deception Island (sample No. 718), and other areas subject to skua contamination (Nos. 562 and 647) and also from an ice-cemented permafrost sample (Cameron *et al.*, 1970b). The occurrence of anaerobes, such as *Clostridium*, is relatively rare (Meyer *et al.*, 1963). It has been indicated that sulfate-reducing bacteria (Table 4) may be widely distributed in Antarctica (Barghoorn and Nichols, 1961), and this has been substantiated (Boyd, 1967; Cameron *et al.*, 1970b). Our previous tests were performed with Van Delden's sulfate-reduction agar in an aerobic environment, however, and the use of a modified Starkey's medium has not shown the presence of obligate sulfate reducers in our typical cold desert soils. It has been shown previously that sulfur oxidizers, methane producers, and photosynthetic bacteria are absent from polar soils (Boyd *et al.*, 1966), and, except for sulfur oxidizers in the Deception Island samples, our work verifies these results.

In some areas, streptomycetes (actinomycetes) are reported to be the dominant microbiota, exceeding that of other bacteria (Benoit and Hall, 1970), but they are rare at other sites or low in abundance (Flint and Stout, 1960; Meyer *et al.*, 1967). In some valleys, they are widely distributed, in surface as well as subsurface soils, as was found in Wheeler Valley, which has a relatively favorable environment (Cameron *et al.*, 1970b), and also in Conrow, King, and David Valleys. In contrast to other antarctic bacteria, streptomycetes are a negligible part of the aerial microflora (Meyer, 1962), which is usually composed of microorganisms similar to that in the surrounding soils (Benoit, personal communication; Meyer, 1962; Rudolph, 1970).

Fungi

Antarctic fungi are cosmopolitan and of wide geographical distribution (Llano, 1965), but they are not generally present in antarctic soils unless the environment is relatively favorable and also supports algae (Table 1). Molds and yeasts are obviously more abundant around lakes and other sites supporting algal growth and higher cryptogams (di Menna, 1966; Sugiyama *et al.*, 1967; Tubaki, 1961) and it also includes areas contaminated by exogenous sources of organic matter such as skuas and refuse dumps. Both yeasts and molds may be isolated at temperatures of +2° and +20°C. However, some of the yeasts were isolated only at +2°

or +5° and not at +20°C, indicating their psychrophilic nature. Other workers also have established that only within the yeasts are there any true obligate antarctic soil psychrophiles (di Menna, personal communication; Goto *et al.*, 1969; Sinclair and Stokes, 1965; Straka and Stokes, 1960). Many antarctic yeasts apparently grow better at low temperatures, as shown by isolation of three times as many yeast strains at 10° as at 25°C (Goto *et al.*, 1969). Some may be osmophilic, but the relevance of pH to adaptation and isolation of yeasts is debatable (di Menna, 1966; Goto *et al.*, 1969).

Algae

In terms of biomass, the algae are the most abundant plants in the Antarctic (Llano, 1962). In the vicinity of lakes, ponds, and especially drainage areas receiving meltwater, they may be especially prominent, sometimes forming "peat" beds and an interjacence similar to that observed for the high arctic polar desert-tundra soils of northwest Greenland (Tedrow, 1968). When moisture is available to moisten the soil during most of the short summer season, algal soil crusts can form (Fig. 14) which are similar to those occurring in temperate deserts (Cameron and Blank, 1966). As in other desert areas, the antarctic soil algae are distributed primarily in the soil surface a few centimeters deep, but they also occur at subsurface depths in lesser abundance (Table 4) and even in the hard, ice-cemented permafrost (Cameron *et al.*, 1970b) where they must exist in the freeze-dried state. Freezing is not especially deterimental for antarctic algae (Holm-Hansen, 1963a), nor is it detrimental to algae from hotter areas (Cameron and Blank, 1967). However, the morbidity rate is tremendously increased when loose mats of growing algae, formed on the soil surface on shores of lakes and ponds, are subsequently caught in an unfavorable freeze. Despite the exposure of antarctic algae to relatively high light intensities measured at the soil surface (Cameron, In press; Cameron *et al.*, 1970a), they grow better at light intensities of <100 to 200 ft-c.

The algae were never found except in association with other microorganisms. Bacteria were always present in association with the algae and undoubtedly preceded them in the colonization of an area. Algae served as indicator organisms of a favorable habitat, and their presence generally provided for survival and growth of additional populations of microorganisms, including not only special groups of bacteria, but also fungi and protozoa. Molds were rarely encountered unless algae also were present, but yeasts were sometimes isolated without any discernible algae present (sample Nos. 725 and 742–743), possibly indicating a previous history of algae at those sites or transport and movement of preformed organic materials to those sites.

Our southernmost samples, mentioned in the preceding paragraph, were representative of many other samples in the same area which also were devoid of discernible or culturable algae. Algae have been reported previously from lower altitudes at similar latitudes (Wise and Gressitt, 1965). The most southern lichens were crustose forms in a sheltered niche on a north-facing slope of granitic basement rock in the Horlick Mountains at 86°9′S and 131°14′W (J. Mercer, personal communication). These lichens may represent relict forms. Lichens usually form under conditions of more favorable moisture. Algae in both hot and cold deserts tend to become parasitized and subsequently lichenized, depending on moisture supply, light, and other factors.

Other Microorganisms

Viable protozoa occasionally occurred with the algae and grew well in algal dilution cultures (Table 4). Protozoa were recorded only if active forms were observed. Cysts were undoubtedly present in some of the cultures, but were not always easily discernible from senescent or dying coccoid algal cells. Cysts were also observed in much of the dried algal material collected from the Antarctic (F. Drouet, personal herbarium). The protozoa are much more abundant and diversified in meltwater ponds (Dillon *et al.,* 1968) and moist areas enriched by organic contamination from transitory sea animals.

Groups of microorganisms identified from our samples are given in Table 6. These include members of the bacteria, streptomycetes, fungi (yeasts and molds), algae, and protozoa. This table presents only a partial list of identifiable microorganisms, and many isolants, especially bacteria and molds, are still under investigation. Isolation, maintenance, and culture of fastidious microorganisms, and the present state and evolution of taxonomy, particularly for the diphtheroid group of bacteria, yeasts, and coccoid green algae, are important factors which have presented difficulties in the identification and enumeration of species. Correct or at least acceptable taxonomy of microorganisms, as it is for macrobiota, is necessary for soil microbial and ecological studies (Cowan, 1968). It is

Table 6. Microorganisms identified in antarctic soils.

BACTERIA. (Identifications primarily by K. Byers-Kemper. Others by T. d'Arc.)

DIPHTHEROIDS
- *Arthrobacter* Conn. & Dimm.
- *Brevibacterium* Breed
- *Corynebacterium* Lehm. & Neum.
- *Jensenia* Biss. & Moore
- *Mycobacterium* Lehm. & Neum.
- *Mycobacterium brevicale* Krass.
- *Mycobacterium rupertinctum* Krass.
- *Mycococcus* Krass.
- *Mycococcus* Krass., thermophile
- *Mycococcus albus* Krass.
- *Mycococcus ruber* Krass.
- *Nocardia* Trev.

MICROCOCCI
- *Micrococcus* Cohn
- *Micrococcus freundreichii* Guill.
- *Sarcina* Good.

SPOREFORMING RODS
- *Bacillus cereus* Frank. & Frank.
- *Bacillus circulans* Jord.
- *Bacillus megaterium* d By.
- *Bacillus pumilus* Gott.

NONSPOREFORMING RODS
- *Azotobacter* Beij.
- *Nitrobacter* Winogr.
- *Pseudomonas* Mig.

STREPTOMYCETES. (Identifications by S. Nishikawa.)
- *Streptomyces* Waks. & Henr.
- *Streptomyces exfoliatus* (Waks. & Curtis) Waks. & Henr.
- *Streptomyces longisporoflavus* Waks.

ALGAE.

Blue-Greens

COCCOID SPECIES
- *Anacystis dimidiata* (Kuetz.) Dr. & Daily
- *Anacystis marina* (Hansg.) Dr. & Daily
- *Anacystis montana* (Lightf.) Dr. & Daily
- *Coccochloris aeruginosa* (Naeg.) Dr. & Daily
- *Coccochloris elabens* (Breb.) Dr. & Daily
- *Coccochloris stagnina* Spreng.

FILAMENTOUS SPECIES
- *Microcoleus vaginatus* (Vauch.) Gom.
- *Nostoc commune* Vauch.
- *Oscillatoria lutea* Ag.
- *Oscillatoria submembranacea* Ard. & Straft.
- *Porphyrosiphon Notarasii* (Menegh.) Kuetz.
- *Schizothrix calcicola* (Ag.) Gom.

Table 6 (continued)

Greens

COCCOID—NONFILAMENTOUS SPECIES

Bumileriopsis brevis Pasch.
Chlorella ellipsoidea Gern.
Chlorella vulgaris Beij.
Chlorococcum humicola (Naeg.) Rabenh.
Chlorococcum humicola (Naeg.) Rabenh., thermophile
Chlorococcum miniatum Starr
Dictyococcus varians Gern.
Neochloris aquatica Starr.
Palmogloea protuberans (Sm. & Sow.) Kuetz.
Phytoconis botryoides (L.) Bory

Diatoms

PENNATE SPECIES

Diatoma anceps (Ehr.) Kirchn.
Diatomella Grun.
Gyrosigma Hass.
Navicula Bory
Synedra Ehrenb.

FUNGI. (Mold identifications primarily by C. Benjamin. Others by R. Benoit, G. Lacy, and E. Staffeldt. Yeast identifications primarily by M. di Menna.)

MOLDS

Aspergillus (Mich.) Corda
Aureobasidium pullulans (d By.) Arn.
Beauveria Viull.
Camposporium Harkn.
Cephalosporium Corda
Chrysosporium pannorum (Link) Hughes
Chrysosporium verrucosum Tubaki
Dendryphiella salina (South.) Pugh & Nicot
Epicococcum Link
Fusarium Link
Gliocladium Corda
Penicillium Link
Penicillium brevi-compactum Dierc.
Penicillium duclauxi Delarc.
Penicillium martensii Biour.
Penicillium purpurgenum Stoll
Phialophora Medlar.
Sartorya Vuill.
Tritirachium album Link

YEASTS

Candida Berkh.
Cryptococcus albidus (Saito) Skinn.
Cryptococcus Lodd., psychrophile
Pullularia pullulans (d By.) Berkh.
Rhodotorula Harr. em. Lodd

Table 6 (continued)

Rhodotorula graminis diMenna
Rhodotorula minuta (Saito) Harr.
Rhodotorula mucilaginosa (Jorg.) Harr.
Saccharomyces Rees
Sporotrichum Link
Torulopsis sp. (?)

PROTOZOA

ZOOFLAGELLATES
Anisonema emerginatum Stokes
Bodo edax Kuehn.
Bodo minimus Klebs.
Bodopsis godboldi Lack.
Cercomastix parva Hart.
Polytoma uvella Ehrenb.
Spiromonas angusta (Dujard.) Alex.

AMOEBOIDS AND AMOEBOID FLAGELLATES
Amoeba guttula Dujard.
Dimastigamoeba gruberi
Pelomyxa palustris Leidy
Polychaos dubia Schaeff.
Trichamoeba limax Kudo
Valkampfia limax Dujard.

ACTINOPODS
Actinophyrs sol Ehrenb.

needed for comparison with what other antarctic investigators have found and to compare cold desert species with those from hotter deserts and other harsh environments. It is difficult, therefore, to determine if antarctic species are endemic, disjunct, or cosmopolitan. Many species have been named as distinct taxa merely because they have been observed or isolated from antarctic habitats, although some *in situ* studies indicate species specificity and adaptation (Ahmadjian, 1970; Gannutz, 1967). A detailed study of available materials, as has been done for blue-green algae (Drouet, 1968; Drouet and Daily, 1956), is rarely attempted. Inept taxonomic treatments have probably exaggerated the degree of antarctic endemism (Lamb, 1970).

The most frequently occurring bacteria found in our samples (Table 6) were members of the diphtheroid group. This may include bacteria of the following genera: *Achromobacter, Brevibacterium, Corynebacterium, Jensenia, Mycobacterium, Mycococcus, Nocardia,* and *Proactinomyces.* The taxonomy and relationships of these microorganisms has not yet been established, but they represent primarily a pleomorphic group of coccirods with some showing gradients into the streptomycetes. Most of the members of these groups are heterotrophic, aerobic gram variable to gram negative, catalase positive, non-sporeforming, and cream, ivory, or translucent colored colonies. They occur at the soil surface, as well as subsurface, and may be the only microorganisms occurring subsurface as a single population at the drier sites. The micrococci, *Micrococcus* spp., were more prominent at the soil surface where the moisture status was more favorable, such as around lakes, ponds, and meltwater pools and around sites subject to increments of organic contamination from birds. They usually appeared as chromogenic colonies when cultured. The sporeforming bacteria, various *Bacillus* spp., were either not prominent or absent, unless environmental conditions were favorable, as for the micrococci and *Streptomyces* spp. Heat-shocking and other methods were attempted to obtain sporeforming bacteria from our soils, but results were the same as for culture methods indicated above. A predominance of gram negative soil bacilli has been reported by other workers (Benoit and Hall, 1970), but also a high proportion of chromogenic micrococci (Flint and Stout, 1960; Meyer *et al.*, 1963). For cool temperate deserts, our isolants have been primarily *Micrococcus* spp. and gram negative bacilli (Johnson, 1970). *Pseudomonas* may make up a significant proportion of the microflora when bacterial counts are high (Meyer *et al.*, 1963). It is generally recognized that sporeforming bacteria or *Bacillus* spp. are rare (Benoit and Hall, 1970; Flint and Stout, 1960; Cameron *et al.*, 1970a,b; Meyer *et al.*, 1963, 1967). *Bacillus* spp. were more common in hot temperate desert soils than in cool temperate desert samples (Johnson, 1970). *Azotobacter* spp. were found in favorable environments in the Antarctic. They were not isolated from the dry valleys of southern Victoria Land, nor Mirnyy, a similar area (Meyer *et al.*, 1967). *Nitrobacter* was isolated from only one of several dry valley soils tested. The dry valleys appear to have a microflora that is endemic to the area, and markedly different from that of nearby Ross Island (Boyd *et al.*, 1966) which has a much more favorable environment and one with relatively heavy increments of contamination from sea animals and man. Birds can be considered an important factor in the distribution of antarctic microorganisms (Meyer *et al.*, 1967) and they are not common in the dry valleys or further inland, although they are sooner or later observed at locations where field party sites are active. Skuas may subsequently contribute to the spread of microorganisms in Antarctica, as man also makes further investigations.

The soil streptomycetes are infrequently identified from the Antarctic except as *Streptomyces* spp., and they generally show overlapping characteristics with *Nocardia* (Waksman, 1967). One species, however, identified as *S. longisporoflavus* was found to be widespread in both surface and subsurface soils in Wheeler Valley (Cameron *et al.*, 1970b). It was also the only species found in favorable habitats in King, David, and Conrow Valleys, although *S. exfoliatus* was isolated from the Victoria Valley complex. *S. longisporoflavus* may have a more widespread distribution in the dry valleys than is realized. It is not considered one of the more notable of numerous species (Waksman, 1967), and it was not isolated from any soils from hotter deserts (Bollen and Nishikawa, 1968, 1969). *Streptomyces* spp. were more commonly isolated from hot temperate desert soils than from cool temperate desert samples (Johnson, 1970). The *S. longisporoflavus* isolants were studied in detail (Bollen and Nishikawa, 1969) and found to produce a whitish or yellowish aerial mycelium with long, loose screw-formed sporophores containing smooth spores (Figs. 15, 16). No soluble pigment was produced and growth could be obtained at 5° to 26°C, with sporulation occurring from 10 to 12 days at 20° to 26°C.

A variety of fungi were obtained from many of our samples that also contained algae. Most of the molds belonged to a single order, the *Moniales,* and especially in the family Monialaceae. A similar observation has been made for mold isolants from desert soils from warmer areas (Staffeldt, 1969). As observed previously, most of the antarctic molds are represented by a few genera of many species (Llano, 1965).

Penicillium spp. were the most frequently encountered isolants in our antarctic samples (approximately 20 percent) and are apparently one of the predominant fungi, at least in the coastal area (Rudolph, 1970). It is a component of both the aerial and soil microflora, although it may have been introduced by man (Rudolph, 1970). *Penicillium* and *Aspergillus* spp. were the only two mold genera represented by isolants from Lake Vanda or other moist areas in Wright Valley (Sugiyama *et al.*, 1967). *Penicillium* spp. were the most frequently isolated molds from our soils in other desert areas, followed by *Mycelia sterilia* and *Aspergillus* spp. (Staffeldt, 1969).

Chrysosporium pannorum and *C. verrucosum* were the next most frequently isolated molds from our antarctic samples. *C. pannorum*

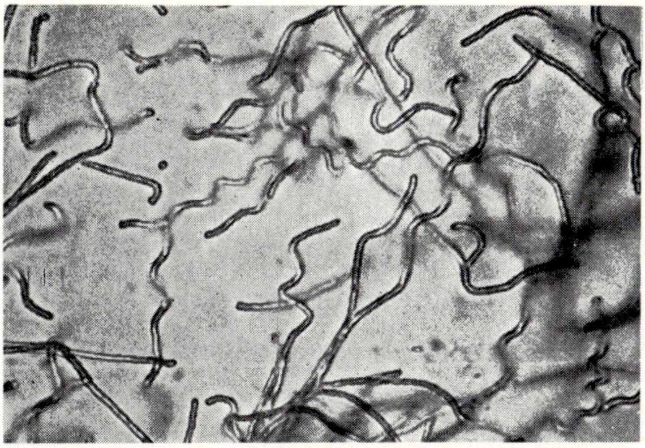

Fig. 15. Wet mount of aerial mycelia of *Streptomyces longisporoflavus* from Wheeler Valley after 14 days on starch medium. x 1000.

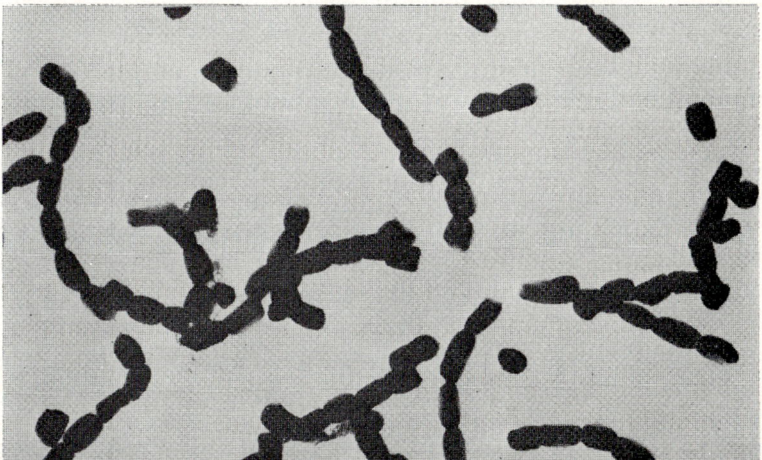

Fig. 16. Scanning electron photomicrograph of *S. longisporoflavus* showing smooth spores in chains after 15 days on starch medium. x 6,545.

has a worldwide distribution, not only in soils of the Antarctic, but also in the Arctic (Kobayasi and Sugiyama, 1969). *C. verrucosum* was first described from West Ongul Island (Tubaki, 1961) and may be more widespread in Antarctica than is realized. *Chaetomium, Cladosporium,* and *Phoma* are more prominent in soils associated with mosses and lichens (Llano, 1965; Meyer *et al.*, 1967).

Detailed reports of soil and aquatic yeast distribution have been presented previously (di Menna, 1960, 1966; Goto *et al.*, 1969; Sugiyama *et al.*, 1967). Species of *Candida, Cryptococcus, Rhodotorula,* and *Torulopsis* appeared to be the most frequently isolated. For soils from the McMurdo area and Wright Valley, *Cryptococcus* spp. were the most frequently isolated (di Menna, 1960). *Torulopsis* and *Candida* are characteristic yeast flora of mosses and penguin dung (Goto *et al.*, 1969). *Rhodotorula* and *Cryptococcus* spp. were found at many locations near Mirnyy (Meyer *et al.*, 1967) and were also the predominant yeasts isolated from our soils (di Menna, personal communication). Temperatures approaching 30°C were generally inhibitory for the isolation of yeasts (Sugiyama, 1969). It has been noted previously that some antarctic yeasts are psychrophilic and grow best at 20°C or lower. Yeasts are not generally as prevalent in soils from hotter arid areas, but they are more abundant in soil algal crusts.

The soil algae include coccoid and filamentous blue-greens and coccoid greens, with some diatoms occurring as the habitat becomes more favorable. Details of the ecology of antarctic soil algae, especially with reference to the blue-greens, has been given previously (Cameron, In press). Many algae have been listed as occurring in the Antarctic (Hirano, 1965) but, because of taxonomic difficulties (Koob, 1968), there are probably fewer species. For the McMurdo region and dry valleys, additional investigations have substantiated the evidence for approximately 10 genera (Llano, 1962). Also, all of these algae appear to be typical of similar forms found in arid soils of temperate zones (Llano, 1962).

The oscillatorioid forms are the most common (Drouet, 1962), especially the small, filamentous blue-green, *Schizothrix calcicola,* which has a number of ecophenes (Drouet, 1963). As in other desert soils receiving a sufficient quality and quantity of available water, it can exist as a single population, or in association with other algae, such as nitrogen-fixing strains of *Nostoc commune* (Holm-Hansen, 1963b). The coccoid green species may be more numerous than is realized, depending upon taxonomic criteria (especially physiology) accepted for their delineation (Bold and Parker, 1962). Sporeforming algae are rarely found or do not occur, which is typical of habitats in other desert regions receiving an insufficient or infrequent supply of moisture to support higher plants. Physiological variants undoubtedly occur, and although active algal growth is frequently obtained at 20°C or "room temperature" of approximately 20° ± 8°C, they can photosynthesize at lower temperatures or below 0°C (W. Becker, personal communication).

The antarctic protozoa, except from relatively rich coastal environments (Dillon *et al.*, 1968; Thompson and Croom, 1969), have not received much attention. In our cultures of soil samples which were positive for algal growth, the protozoa were often present, especially in the surface few centimeters, but in lesser abundance than the algae (Table 4). They were not detected as frequently as the fungi. They appeared in the algal cultures several days to several weeks after the appearance of algae. Some were transitory and few in abundance, others were more hardy and persisted for longer time periods. Only a few species were observed to contain algae. All were holozoic. Protozoa were usually flagellated or amoeboid forms, for example, species of *Bodo* and *Amoeba*. Ciliated protozoa were not found, and it would be expected that these latter forms would be more prevalent in such aqueous environments as meltwater ponds and habitats subjected to organic contamination from birds. More protozoa may be present than were found in our samples. Different culture methods and frequent examination of cultures are essential (Dillon *et al.*, 1968). Phase as well as light microscopy should be used. A more intense study is needed to determine the protozoa in antarctic soils, their functions, and their relationships to other microorganisms in the ecosystems.

CONCLUSIONS

A number of ecological factors is important for determining the presence or absence, abundance, distribution, and kinds of microorganisms in antarctic soils. For dry valley areas and similar environments, as in exposed areas in the Transantarctic Mountains, these factors have been summarized as "favorable" and "unfavorable" in Table 7. Some of these factors are measurable but others need additional details. These factors (modified from Cameron *et al.*, 1970a) have proved useful in predicting which sites would or would not contain microorganisms, and it would be possible to

Table 7. Ecological factors determining distribution of life in antarctic dry valleys.

Favorable	*Unfavorable*
N-S orientation	E-W orientation
Northern exposure and gentle north-facing slopes	Southern exposure and flat or south-facing slopes
High solar radiation	Low solar radiation
Protected habitat; microclimate above freezing	Exposed habitat; microclimate below freezing
Absence of wind (low evaporation rate, negligible abrasion)	High winds (high desiccation rate and abrasion of surface)
Northerly winds	Southerly winds
High humidities	Low humidities
Slow or impeded drainage	Rapid drainage and leaching
Lengthy duration of available, good quality H_2O (presence of glaciers, lakes, streams, meltwater pools, snow and ice fields)	Short duration of available, good quality H_2O (absence of glaciers, lakes, streams, meltwater pools, snow and ice fields)
Translucent pebbles ("micro green-houses")	Opaque pebbles
	Negligible or slow soil formation
Weathered geologic materials	Salty soils, unbalanced ionic composition, soluble toxic ions
Non-salty soils, balanced ionic composition	High (or low) pH
Approx. neutral pH	No organic contamination or accumulation (no large increments of organic matter by plants or animals; O.M. $< 0.1\%$)
Organic contamination and accumulation (skuas, seals, penguins, man, etc.)	

make rough estimates as to abundances and kinds (Cameron *et al.*, 1970a).

There is a definite sequence of microorganisms found in antarctic soils (Fig. 17) which is dependent on environmental factors. In the harshest (usually the driest) soils, we have found no detectable microorganisms, but as conditions gradually become more favorable, a single population (usually a diphtheroid) gives way to a more and more complex community of microorganisms. This sequence can be compared with recent evolutionary theory, whereby a heterotrophic ancestral bacterial or blue-green algal organism (prokaryote) may have developed following chemical evolution (Olson, 1970). Other processes and organisms followed accordingly, some of which show similarities to the sequence and processes of organisms in the Antarctic.

Some supposedly favorable niches were investigated for micro-

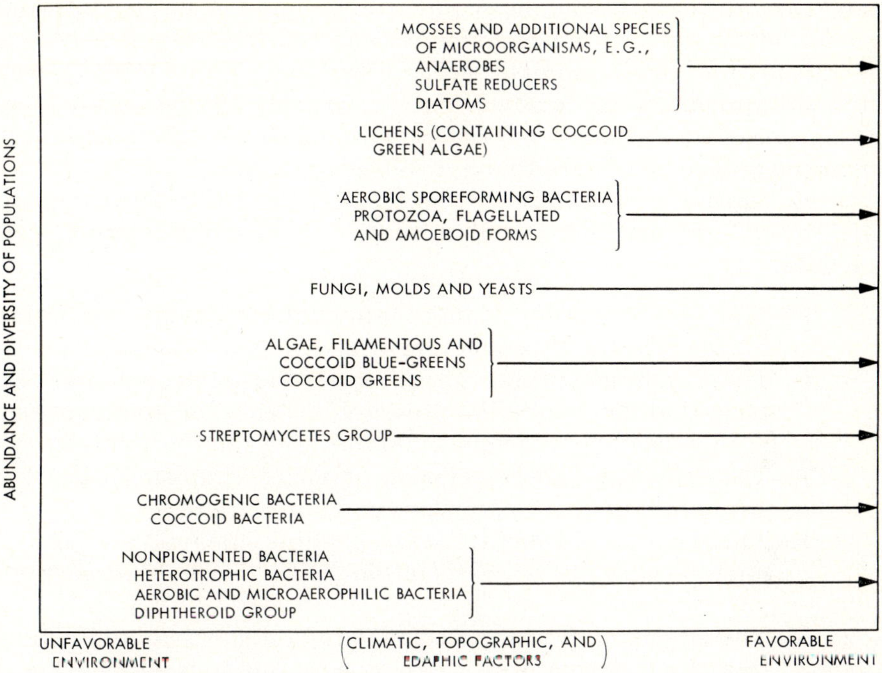

Fig. 17. Variability of population density and diversity with ecological factors in antarctic dry valleys.

organisms and yielded disappointing results. In the vicinity of north-facing slopes below and west of Coalsack Bluff, moist soil was collected at the periphery of perennial snowbanks as soon as melt was observed. Soil temperatures of these sites at time of collection ranged from 0° to +25°C. Using various cultural techniques, as well as heat shock, only one of ten soil samples was positive for growth and diphtheroid bacteria were recovered. These snowbanks can be centuries old (Berg and Black, 1966), and as they recede an outline of salt evaporite shows the historical extent of the snow deposit. Either bacteria never became established as the snow melted, or else they were inhibited by the salt deposits and could not follow the fringe of melt formed on the soil as the snowbank retreated.

Frost-crack polygons can provide evidence for life. In general, the more recent polygons, and especially those with ice wedges rather than sand wedges, are more apt to support microorganisms. However, sand wedge polygons near lakes, including Lake Vida in Victoria Valley, can support an extensive growth of algae following melt around the lake and subsequent diffusion of moisture into the surrounding soil. In general, the absence of frost-crack polygons is indicative of older and drier areas (McKelvey Valley), and fewer microorganisms were detected, except possibly in the subsurface, from these areas than from areas with more abundant and pronounced polygons as were found in Wheeler Valley.

Investigation of antarctic soil microbial ecology is not complete and more information is still needed. These investigations can include:

1. The determination of optimum and minimum conditions for growth and reproduction of endemic microorganisms.
2. The measurement and interpretation of environmental criteria that determine the presence, absence, or abundance of various populations and communities of microorganisms.
3. The influence and association of microorganisms with dry sites in transition to polygons and aquatic sites.
4. The study of subsurface relationships, survival, and age of microorganisms in association with hard, ice-cemented permafrost.
5. The effects of freezing and thawing on survival and activities of microorganisms, both *in situ* and as isolants.
6. The osmophilic tolerance and mechanisms.
7. The viability and adaptability of microorganisms from various sources of contamination.
8. Microbial fallout and survival rate.
9. Phenology.
10. A thorough physiological and taxonomic study of antarctic soil microorganisms in comparison with soil microorganisms from other regions.

The soil ecosystem of the antarctic cold desert is a relatively simple one as compared to those encountered in other areas where it has been made more complex by higher plants, animals, and man (Benoit and Hall, 1970; Cameron *et al.*, 1970a). The antarctic cold desert therefore provides an opportunity for studying soil microbial ecology at its simplest level before attempting to gain knowledge and understanding of more complex temperate, tropical, and arctic regions. But care must be taken not to disturb or destroy the antarctic ecosystem because the simplest ecosystems usually have the least stability. The antarctic cold desert not only serves a useful purpose in the study of harsh terrestrial ecological and limiting environmental factors for life, but it also provides a useful model in preparation for the search for extraterrestrial life and establishment of manned bases in an extraterrestrial environment.

Author's Note: This paper presents the results of one phase of research carried out by the Jet Propulsion Laboratory, California Institute of Technology, under contract NAS 7-100, sponsored by the National Aeronautics and Space Administration. Logistic support and facilities for the investigations in Antarctica and additional laboratory support at JPL were provided under contract CO-585-000-00 to the Office of Polar Programs, National Science Foundation.

Dr. N. Horowitz, Bioscience Section Manager, first suggested and encouraged studies in the antarctic dry valleys because of their value to extraterrestrial life detection. Dr. G. Llano, Biology Program Director, Office of Polar Programs, has further encouraged, advised, and supported microbial and ecological investigations in the Antarctic. Prof. R. Benoit, Department of Biology, Virginia Polytechnic Institute, was a fellow investigator during three austral summer's field studies in the Antarctic, and is owed a debt of gratitude for his assistance, suggestions, and use of data, as well as his companionship. Other team members in the Antarctic, including those who were with Virginia Polytechnic Institute, were G. Blank, H. Conrow, C. David, C. J. Hall, R. Hanson, J. King, G. Lacy, H. Lowman, III, and F. Morelli Mrs. D. Gensel performed most of the microbial analyses done at JPL. The assistance of many others, including U. S. Navy Task Force 43, is also gratefully acknowledged.

References

Adie, R. J., 1970. Past environments and climates of Antarctica. In *Antarctic Ecology,* edited by M. W. Holdgate; vol. 1, pp. 7–14. Academic Press, London.

Ahmadjian, V., 1970. Adaptations of antarctic terrestrial plants. In *Antarctic Ecology,* edited by M. W. Holdgate; vol. 2, pp. 801–811. Academic Press, London.

Allen, O. N., 1957. *Experiments in Soil Bacteriology;* Third Edition, Revised. Burgess Publ. Co., Minneapolis.

Barghoorn, E. S., and R. L. Nichols, 1961. Sulfate-reducing bacteria and pyritic sediments in Antarctica. *Science, 134:* 190–191.

Benoit, R. E., and C. L. Hall, Jr., 1970. The microbiology of some dry valley soils of Victoria Land, Antarctica. In *Antarctic Ecology,* edited by M. Holdgate; vol. 2, pp. 697–701. Academic Press, London.

Benoit, R. E., and R. E. Cameron, 1967. Microbial ecology of some dry valley soils of Antarctica. *Bacteriol. Proc. 1967, Abstracts;* p. 3.

Berg, T. E., and R. F. Black, 1966. Preliminary measurements of growth of nonsorted polygons, Victoria Land, Antarctica. In *Antarctic Research Series 8, Antarctic Soils and Soil Forming Processes,* edited by J. C. F. Tedrow; pp. 61–108. Am. Geophys. Union, Washington, D.C.

Black, R. F., and T. E. Berg, 1963. Patterned ground in Antarctica. *Proc. Intern. Conf. Permafrost, Publ. 1287;* pp. 121–127. Purdue Univ., Lafayette, Ind.

Bold, H. C. and B. C. Parker, 1962. Some supplementary attributes in the classification of *Chlorococcum* species. *Arch. Mikrobiol., 42:* 267–288.

Bollen, W. B. and S. Nishikawa, 1968. *Systematic Description and Key to Streptomyces Isolants from Chile, Mexico, and Arizona Desert Soils. Progress Report, Microorganism Study.* JPL Contract No. 950783. Aug. 19, 1968. Jet Propulsion Laboratory, Calif. Inst. Technol., Pasadena.

Bollen, W. B., and S. Nishkawa, 1969. *Systematic Description and Key to Streptomyces Isolants from Chile, Arizona, and Antarctica Desert Soils. Progress Report, Microorganism Study.* JPL Contract No. 950783, Feb. 18, 1969. Jet Propulsion Laboratory, Calif. Inst. Technol., Pasadena.

Boyd, W. L., 1967. Ecology and physiology of soil microorganisms in polar regions. JARE Scientific Reports. *Proc. Symp. Pacific-Antarctic Sci., Special Issue No. 1:* 265–275. Dept. of Polar Research, Nat. Sci. Museum, Ueno Park, Tokyo.

Boyd, W. L., and J. W. Boyd, 1962. Viability of thermophiles and coliform bacteria in arctic soils and water. *Can. J. Microbiol., 8:* 189–192.

Boyd, W. L., and J. W. Boyd, 1963a. Soil microorganisms of the McMurdo Sound area, Antarctica. *Appl. Microbiol., 11:* 116–121.

Boyd, W. L., and J. W. Boyd, 1963b. Viability of coliform bacteria in antarctic soil. *J. Bacteriol., 85:* 1121–1123.

Boyd, W. L., J. T. Staley, and J. W. Boyd, 1966. Ecology of soil microorganisms of Antarctica. In *Antarctic Research Series 8, Antarctic Soils and Soil Forming Processes,* edited by J. C. F. Tedrow; pp. 125–159. Am. Geophys. Union, Washington, D.C.

Buckman, H. O., and N. C. Brady, 1960. *The Nature and Properties of Soils,* Sixth Edition. MacMillan, New York.

Calkin, P. E., 1964. Geomorphology and glacial geology of the Victoria Valley System, Southern Victoria Land, Antarctica. *Inst. Polar Studies, Rept. No. 10.* Ohio State Univ., Columbus.

Cameron, R. E., 1963. The role of soil science in space exploration. *Space Sci. Rev., 2:* 297–312.

Cameron, R. E., 1966. Soil sampling parameters for extraterrestrial life detection. *J. Arizona Acad. Sci., 4:* 3–27.

Cameron, R. E., 1967. Soil studies—desert microflora. XIV. Soil properties and abundance of microflora from a soil profile in McKelvey Valley, Antarctica. *Space Programs Summary No. 37–44;* vol. IV, pp. 224–236; 239–240. Jet Propulsion Laboratory, Calif. Inst. Technol., Pasadena.

Cameron, R. E., 1969a. *Abundance of Microflora in Soils of Desert Regions. Technical Report 32–1378.* Jet Propulsion Laboratory, Calif. Inst. Technol., Pasadena.

Cameron, R. E., 1969b. Cold desert problems and characteristics relevant to other arid lands. In *Arid Lands in Perspective,* edited by W. McGinnies and B. Goldman; pp. 167–205. Univ. Arizona Press, Tucson.

Cameron, R. E., 1970. Soil microbial ecology of Valley of 10,000 Smokes, Alaska. *J. Arizona Acad. Sci., 6:* 11-40.

Cameron, R. E., In press. *Ecology of Blue-Green Algae in Antarctic Soils.* First International Symposium on Taxonomy and Biology of Blue-Green Algae. Centre for Advanced Studies in Botany, Univ. Madras, India.

Cameron, R. E., and R. E. Benoit, 1970. Microbial and ecological investigations of recent cinder cones, Deception Island, Antarctica—a preliminary report. *Ecology, 51:* 802–809.

Cameron, R. E., and G. B. Blank, 1963. *Soil Organic Matter (In Desert Soils). Technical Report 32–443.* Jet Propulsion Laboratory, Calif. Inst. Technol., Pasadena.

Cameron, R. E., and G. B. Blank, 1966. *Desert Algae: Soil Crusts and Diaphanous Substrata as Algal Habitats. Technical Report 32–971.* Jet Propulsion Laboratory, Calif. Inst. Technol., Pasadena.

Cameron, R. E., and G. B. Blank, 1967. Desert soil algae survival at extremely low temperatures. *Cryogenic Technol., 3:* 151–156.

Cameron, R. E., and H. P. Conrow, 1968. Antarctic simulator for soil storage and processing. *Antarctic. J. U.S., 3:* 219–221.

Cameron, R. E., and H. P. Conrow, 1969a. Soil moisture, relative humidity, and microbial abundance in dry valleys of Southern Victoria Land. *Antarctic J. U.S., 4:* 23–28.

Cameron, R. E., and H. P. Conrow, 1969b. Antarctic dry valley soil microbial incubation and gas composition. *Antarctic J. U.S., 4:* 28–33.

Cameron, R. E., and J. R. Devaney, 1970. Antarctic soil algal crusts: scanning electron and optical microscope study. *Trans. Am. Microscop. Soc., 89:* 264–273.

Cameron, R. E., G. B. Blank, and D. R. Gensel, 1966. *Sampling and Handling of Desert Soils. Technical Report 32–908.* Jet Propulsion Laboratory, Calif. Inst. Technol., Pasadena.

Cameron, R. E., G. B. Blank, and N. H. Horowitz, 1969, 1970. Bacterial growth in agar subjected to freezing and thawing. *Cryogenic Technol., 5:* 253–255 and *6:* 16–18.

Cameron, R. E., C. N. David, and J. King, 1968a. Soil toxicity in antarctic dry valleys. *Antarctic J. U.S., 3:* 164–166.

Cameron, R. E., J. King, and C. N. David, 1968b. Soil microbial and ecological studies in Southern Victoria Land. *Antarctic J. U.S., 3:* 121–123.

Cameron, R. E., D. D. Lawson, and C. Pazaree, 1969. Thermoluminescence characterization of antarctic dry valley soils. *Agron. Abstr., 5–5:* 106.

Cameron, R. E., J. King, and C. N. David, 1970a. Microbiology, ecology and microclimatology of soil sites in dry valleys of Southern Victoria Land, Antarctica. In *Antarctic Ecology,* edited by M. Holdgate; vol. 2, pp. 702–716. Academic Press, London.

Cameron, R. E., J. King, and C. N. David, 1970b. Soil microbial ecology of Wheeler Valley, Antarctica. *Soil Sci., 109:* 110–120.

Cameron, R. E., F. A. Morelli, and H. P. Conrow, 1970c. *Survival of Microorganisms in Desert Soil Exposed to Five Years of Continuous Very High Vacuum. Technical Report 32–1454.* Jet Propulsion Laboratory, Calif. Inst. Technology, Pasadena.

Campbell, I. B., and G. G. C. Claridge, 1969. A classification of frigic soils—the zonal soils of the Antarctic continent. *Soil Sci., 107:* 75–85.

Claridge, G. G. C., 1965. The clay mineralogy and chemistry of some soils from the Ross Dependency, Antarctica. *New Zealand J. Geol. Geophys., 8:* 186–220.

Claridge, G. G. C., and I. B. Campbell, 1968. Origin of nitrate deposits. *Nature, 217:* 428–430.

Cowan, S. T. (Chairman), 1968. The taxonomy of soil bacteria—Discussion. In *The Ecology of Soil Bacteria, An International Symposium,* edited by T. R. G. Gray and D. Parkinson; pp. 370–376. Univ. Toronto Press, Toronto.

Dillon, R. D., G. L. Walsh, and D. A. Bierle, 1968. A preliminary survey of antarctic meltwater and soil amoeba. *Trans. Am. Microscop. Soc., 87:* 486–492.

di Menna, M. E., 1960. Yeasts from Antarctica. *J. General Microbiol., 23:* 295–300.

di Menna, M. E., 1966. Yeasts in antarctic soils. *Antonie van Leeuwenhoek J. Microbiol. Serol., 32:* 29–39.

Doumani, G. A., and W. E. Long, 1962. The ancient life of the Antarctic. *Sci. Am., 207:* 168–184.

Drouet, F., 1962. The Oscillatoriaceae and their distribution in Antarctica. *Polar Record, 11:* 320–321.

Drouet, F., 1963. Ecophenes of *Schizothrix calcicola. Proc. Acad. Nat. Sci. Philadelphia, 115:* 261–281.

Drouet, F., 1968. *Revision of the Classification of the Oscillatoriaceae.* Monograph 15. The Acad. Natural Sci. Philadelphia. Fulton Press, Lancaster, Pennsylvania.

Drouet, F., and W. A. Daily, 1956. Revision of the coccoid Myxophyceae. *Butler Univ. Botan. Studies, 12:* 1–218.

Flint, E. A., and J. D. Stout, 1960. Microbiology of some soils from Antarctica. *Nature, 188:* 767–768.

Fritsch, F. E., 1912. Freshwater Algae. National Antarctic Expedition 1901–1904. *Nat. Hist. Zool. Bot., 6:* 1–60.

Gannutz, T. P., 1967. Effects of environmental extremes on lichens. Colloque sur les Lichens, Paris, 1967. *Bull. Soc. Botan. France,* 169–179.

Goto, S., J. Sugiyama, and H. Iizuka, 1969. A taxonomic study of antarctic yeasts. *Mycologia, 61:* 748–774.

Hagen, C. A., and E. J. Hawrylewicz, 1969. *Life in Extraterrestrial Environments. Report No. IITRI-L6023-16 (Quarterly Status Report).* IIT Res. Inst., Chicago, Illinois.

Hall, C. L., Jr., 1968. *Isolation of Psychophilic Halophiles from the Antarctic Polar Desert.* M.S. Thesis, unpublished. Dept. Biology, Virginia Polytechnic Inst., Blacksburg.

Hall, C. L., and R. E. Benoit, 1968. Isolation of halophilic bacteria in the antarctic polar desert. *Bacteriol. Proc., 1968, Abstr.,* p. 4.

Hawrylewicz, E. J., C. A. Hagen, and R. Ehrlich, 1965. Response to a simulated Martian environment. *Life Sci. Space Res., 3:* 64–73.

Hirano, M., 1965. Freshwater algae in the Antarctic regions. In *Biogeography and Ecology in Antarctica,* edited by J. Van Mieghem and P. Van Oye; pp. 127–193. Junk, The Hague.

Holm-Hansen, O., 1963a. Viability of blue-green and green algae after freezing. *Physiol. Plantarum, 16:* 530–540.

Holm-Hansen, O., 1963b. Algae: nitrogen fixation by antarctic species. *Science, 139:* 1059–1060.

Holm-Hansen, O., 1967. Recent advances in the physiology of blue-green algae. In *Environmental Requirements of Blue-green Algae;* pp. 87–96. Proceedings of a symposium, Sept. 23–24, 1966, Federal Water Pollution Control Administration, Northwest Region, Corvallis, Oregon, and Univ. Washington, Seattle.

Horowitz, N. H., A. J. Bauman, R. E. Cameron, P. J. Geiger, J. S. Hubbard, G. P. Shulman, P. G. Simmonds, and K. Westberg, 1969. Sterile soil from Antarctica: organic analysis. *Science, 164:* 1054–1056.

Hubbard, J. S., R. E. Cameron, and A. B. Miller, 1968. Soil studies—desert microflora. XV. In *Analysis of Antarctic Dry Valley Soils by Cultural and Radiorespirometric Methods. Space Programs Summary No. 37-52;* vol. III, pp. 172–175. Jet Propulsion Laboratory, Calif. Inst. Technol., Pasadena.

Hubbard, J. S., G. L. Hobby, N. H. Horowitz, P. J. Geiger, and F. A. Morelli, 1970. Measurement of $^{14}CO_2$ assimilation in soils: an experiment for the biological exploration of Mars. *Appl. Microbiol., 19:* 32–38.

Ingram, M., 1957. Microorganisms resisting high concentrations of sugars or salts. In *Microbial Ecology;* pp. 90–133. Seventh Symposium of the Society for General Microbiology, Cambridge. Univ. Press, Cambridge, Mass.

Jacobs, M. B., M. J. Gerstein, and W. G. Walter, 1957. *Dictionary of Microbiology.* Van Nostrand, Princeton, N. J.

Janetschek, H., 1967. Arthropod ecology of South Victoria Land. In *Antarctic Research Series 10, Entomology of Antarctica,* edited by J. L. Gressitt; pp. 205–293. Am. Geophys. Union, Washington, D. C.

Johnson, R. M., 1970. Physiology of desert bacteria. *Bacteriol. Proc. 1970, Abst.;* p. 41.

Johnson, R. W., and P. M. Smith, 1970. Antarctic research and lunar exploration. *Advan. Space Sci. Technol., 10:* 1–44.

Kobayasi, V., and J. Sugiyama, 1969. *Report on Fungus Cultures from Point Barrow, Alaska. Tokyo.* Unpublished report. Submitted to Jet Propulsion Laboratory, Calif. Inst. Tech., Pasadena.

Koob, D., 1968. Algae distribution. In *Antarctic Map Folio Series, Folio 5,* edited by V. C. Bushnell; pp. 13–15. Am. Geograph. Soc., New York.

Lamb, I. M., 1970. Antarctic terrestrial plants and their ecology. In *Antarctic Ecology,* edited by M. W. Holdgate; vol. 2, pp. 733–751. Academic Press, London.

Llano, G. A., 1962. The terrestrial life of the Antarctic. *Sci. Am., 207:* 212–230.

Llano, G. A., 1965. The flora of Antarctica. In *Antarctica,* edited by T. Hatherton; pp. 331–350. Praeger, New York.

Lochhead, A. G., 1924. Microbiological investigations of frozen soil. *Proc. Trans. Roy. Soc. Canada, 18:* 75–96 .

Matthews, S. W., and R. W. Madden, 1968. Antarctica: icy testing ground for space. *Nat. Geograph., 134:* 568–592.

McCraw, J. D., 1967. Soils of Taylor dry valley, Victoria Land, Antarctica, with notes on soils from other localities in Victoria Land. *New Zealand J. Geol. Geophys., 10:* 498–539.

Metson, A. J., 1961. *Methods of Chemical Analysis for Soil Survey Samples. Soil Bureau Bulletin 12.* New Zealand Dept. Sci. Ind. Res., Wellington.

Meyer, G. H., 1962. Microbiological populations of antarctic air, soil, snow and melt pools. *Polar Record, 11:* 317–318.

Meyer, G. H., M. B. Morrow, and O. Wyss, 1967. Bacteria, fungi, and other biota in the vicinity of Mirnyy Observatory. *Antarctic J. U. S., 2:* 248–251.

Meyer, G. H., O. Wyss, and M. B. Morrow, 1963. Incidence of soil microorganisms in Antarctica. *Ecol. Soc. Am. Bull., 44:* 38–39.

Mitchell, R. J., 1964. Trace elements in soils. In *Chemistry of the Soil, Second Edition,* edited by F. E. Bear; pp. 320–368. Reinhold, New York.

Nishita, H., and M. Hamilton, 1968. Some thermoluminescent characteristics of gamma irradiated soils. *Soil Sci., 106:* 76–84.

Olson, J. M., 1970. The evolution of photosynthesis. *Science, 168:* 438–446.

Richards, L. A. (Editor), 1954. *Diagnosis and Improvement of Saline and Alkali Soils. Agriculture Handbook No. 60.* U.S.D.A., U.S. Government Printing Office, Washington, D. C.

Rudolph, E. D., 1966. Terrestrial vegetation of Antarctica: past and present studies. In *Antarctic Research Series 8, Antarctic Soils and Soil Forming Processes,* edited by J. C. F. Tedrow; 109–124. Am. Geophys. Union, Washington, D. C.

Rudolph, E. D., 1970. Local dissemination of plant propagules in Antarctica. In *Antarctic Ecology,* edited by M. W. Holdgate; vol. 2, pp. 812–817. Academic Press, London.

Saunders, J. F., 1969. A cryobiologist's conjecture of planetary life. *Cryobiology, 6:* 151–159.

Sinclair, N. A. and J. L. Stokes, 1965. Obligately psychrophilic yeasts from the polar regions. *Canadian J. Microbiol., 11:* 259–269.

Staffeldt, E., 1969. *Microorganism Study, Desert Fungi. Final Technical Report. July 10. JPL Contract No. 951602.* New Mexico State Univ., Las Cruces, N. M.

Stevenson, I. L., 1964. Biochemistry of soil. In *Chemistry of the Soil, Second Edition,* edited by F. E. Bear; pp. 242–291. Reinhold, New York.

Straka, R. P., and J. L. Stokes, 1960. Psychrophilic bacteria from Antarctica. *J. Bacteriol., 80:* 622–625.

Stuhlinger, E., 1969. Antarctic research, a prelude to space research. *Antarctic J. U.S., 4:* 5–11.

Sugiyama, J., 1969. Polar mycology in Antarctica II. The world's last frontier. *Polar News (Japan), 5:* 37–47.

Sugiyama, J., S. Sugiyama, H. Iizuka, and H. Fukushima, 1967. Mycological studies of the antarctic fungi. 2. Mycoflora of Lake Vanda, an ice-free lake. *Antarctic Record (Tokyo), 28:* 23–31.

Tedrow, J. C. F., 1968. *Soil Investigations in Inglefield Land, Greenland.* Arctic Inst. North America, Montreal.

Tedrow, J. C. F., and F. C. Ugolini, 1966. Antarctic soils. In *Antarctic Research Series 8, Antarctic Soils and Soil Forming Processes,* edited by J. C. F. Tedrow; pp. 161–177. Am. Geophys. Union, Washington, D.C.

Thompson, J. C. and J. M. Croom, 1969. Systematic survey of ciliated protozoa from the Antarctic Peninsula. *Antarctic J. U.S., 4:* 108–109.

Tubaki, K., 1961. *On Some Fungi Isolated from Antarctic Materials. Biological Results of JARE, No. 14.* Seto Marine Biol. Lab., Nagao Inst., Sirahama, Wakayama-Ken, Japan.

Ugolini, F., 1963. Soil investigations in the Lower Wright Valley, Antarctica. *Proc. Intern. Conf. Permafrost, Publ. 1287;* pp. 55–61. Purdue Univ., Lafayette, Ind.

Ugolini, F. C., 1965. *Ornithogenic Soils of Antarctica.* Agronomy Abstr. Annual Meeting, Columbus, Ohio. Am. Soc. Agron., Madison, Wis.

Ugolini, F. C. and C. Bull, 1965. Soil development and glacial events in Antarctica. *Quaternaria, 7:* 251–269.

Ugolini, F. C., and C. C. Grier, 1969. Biological weathering in Antarctica. *Antarctic J. U.S., 4:* 110–111.

Young, R. S., P. Deal, J. Bell, and J. Allen, 1963. Effects of diurnal freezing-thawing on survival and growth of selected bacteria. *Nature, 199:* 1078–1079.

Waksman, S. A., 1967. *The Actinomycetes. A Summary of Current Knowledge.* Ronald Press, New York.

Wilson, A. T., 1970. The McMurdo Dry Valleys. In *Antarctic Ecology,* edited by M. W. Holdgate; vol. 1, pp. 21–30. Academic Press, London.

Wilson, A. T., and D. A. House, 1965. Chemical composition of South Polar snow. *J. Geophys. Res., 70:* 5515–5518.

Wise, K. A., and J. L. Gressitt, 1965. Far southern animals and plants. *Nature, 207:* 101–102.

Ecology of Land Plants in Antarctica

EMANUEL D. RUDOLPH

Institute of Polar Studies, The Ohio State University, Columbus

Why go to Antarctica to study plants when there are so few plants to be found there? Upon reflection, there are several good reasons for devoting time, effort, and money to study the vegetation of that continent.

First, antarctic terrestrial vegetation is sparse with only about 800 plant species, only two of which are flowering plants and the remainder are mosses, lichens, algae, and fungi. The vegetation, composed of a single layer at ground level, provides a unique opportunity to study a relatively uncomplex ecosystem where organisms exist in marginal environmental conditions. In a world becoming increasingly polluted, and thus more unfavorable for most living organisms, it is important to understand the survival mechanisms of organisms living under marginal conditions.

Second, their ecosystem is very vulnerable to slight physical changes. We need to have information about the reproductive potential of plants and the recolonization time for plant communities in the Antarctic. By studying antarctic situations where man has had an effect on the vegetation, we can hope to understand some of these problems and use comparisons with the many undisturbed antarctic areas. The marginal existence of the plants also charges us with the added responsibility of protecting their sensitive ecosystem from disturbance until we fully realize the effects of disturbances.

Third, the absence of large resident land animals presents a unique situation. What are the food webs of the microscopic fauna and macroscopic arthropods there? How productive is the vegetation? What is the relationship between the fauna and the primary producers?

Fourth, how do the plants living far inland, away from the organic and inorganic nutrient replenishment of coastal visiting birds, obtain nutrients necessary for growth and reproduction?

Fifth, what are the environmental conditions under which the low-growing plants exist? Which environmental constituents are most limiting for growth and reproduction? Knowing them may help us to evaluate the possibility of life in outer space where conditions could be similar.

Sixth, what is the composition of the ecosystem? What kinds of plants and animals compose it and in what numbers?

Finally, what is the relationship of the vegetation to the nearest land masses, the subantarctic islands, and the southern hemispheric islands and continents? How long has the present vegetation been in Antarctica? Where did it come from? Is it changing?

As anyone can see, there is no lack of questions that can be asked about antarctic vegetation. Many of the answers to these questions would help us to understand better our whole biosphere and even our universe. And so it is well worth while for a terrestrial biologist and botanist to be concerned with antarctic vegetation and to go to the far southern part of the earth to study it.

Not surprisingly, in the approximately 70 years that man has sporadically studied vegetation at first hand in Antarctica, answers to the many ecological questions posed above are just now beginning to be found. Not until the last ten years, as a result of the international antarctic scientific program, have botanists been able to make detailed observations and experiments in the field and laboratory.

ANTARCTIC TERRESTRIAL ECOSYSTEMS

The vegetation of Antarctica is at best a poorly developed tundra. In the maritime area of Antarctica, which includes the South Shetland Islands, South Orkney Islands, Palmer Archipelago, and the west coast of the Antarctic Peninsula (Holdgate, 1964), a somewhat oceanic climate exists which supports a polar-alpine tundra formation (Longton, 1967). It is here that the two flowering plants, a grass *Deschampsia antarctica* Desv. and a flowering herb *Colobanthus crassifolius* (D'Urv.) Hook. f., are to be found on the Peninsula as far south as about 68°S, together with some liverworts and larger fungi (Greene *et al.*, 1967). Lush moss and lichen growths are common here (Fig. 1). By contrast, on the remainder of Antarctica, the continental area of Holdgate (1964), where monthly mean temperatures never reach above freezing and where winter monthly means usually fall below −20°C, the macroscopic

Fig. 1. Tundra composed mostly of *Usnea* lichens several centimeters high on Livingston Island in the South Shetland Islands (Photograph taken by Dr. K. R. Everett).

vegetation is very sparse, consisting of lichens, mosses, and algae, often extremely patchy in appearance (Fig. 2). At best this vegetation could be called an antarctic cold desert cryptogamic tundra, the bryosystem of Janetschek (1963). Antarctica has a very limited variety and number of sites available for vegetation. These consist of coastal rocks; moraines of boulders, gravels, and sand; rock outcrops and scoria slopes; permanent lakes, some with continuous ice cover; temporary ponds and puddles; and some more unusual sites such as volcanic fumaroles and snow-free valleys (dry valleys) (Figs. 3, 4). The ground-level single-layered vegetation, seldom over a few centimeters in height, sometimes with its associated small animals (springtails, mites, protozoans, rotifers, tardigrades, and nematodes), provides the simplest ecosystems to be found on earth. Simplicity is a relative term and the ecosystems in themselves are complex and difficult to understand. Compared with the multilayered vegetation of other regions, with its numerous and varied kinds of animals, the Antarctic does indeed seem simple. We can anticipate that these "simple" ecosystems may lend themselves to analyses more easily than others. The ecology of antarctic terrestrial ecosystems is being studied and some of the questions are beginning to be answered.

Fig. 2. Antarctic cold desert cryptogamic tundra consisting of mosses, lichens, and algae at the base of Cape Hallett in the Ross Sea area. Vegetation is inconspicuous, Adélie penguins are about 50 cm high.

Fig. 3. Mountain peaks protruding above ice plateau in the Ford Ranges, Marie Byrd Land.

Fig. 4. The Barwick Valley, a dry valley in southern Victoria Land with glacier and frozen lake.

REPRODUCTIVE POTENTIAL AND RECOLONIZATION

Antarctic plants characteristically exhibit little sexual reproduction. The two flowering plants bloom throughout their antarctic ranges, but rarely set seed (Skottsberg, 1954; Corte, 1961; Holtom and Greene, 1967). Under field conditions and in the laboratory, the viability of their naturally produced seeds is usually less than ten percent (Corte, 1961). The mosses likewise rarely produce sporophytes under natural conditions (Fig. 5). It has been shown for several species that fertility is reduced with increasing altitude and latitude in the maritime antarctic area (Greene, 1966; Longton, 1966b). The algae and lichens exhibit similar reduced sexuality. Asexual reproductive mechanisms must be operative and the biological danger of reduced variability results.

With disturbance by man, well illustrated on the subantarctic islands, alien organisms may become established and disrupt the delicate balance in a marginal ecosystem. Two grasses, *Poa annua* L. and *P. pratensis* L., have already become established locally in several areas on the South Shetland Islands and Antarctic Peninsula (Greene and Greene, 1963; Longton, 1966a; Greene *et al.*,

Fig. 5. *Bryum argenteum* moss at Cape Hallett. The typical non-sporophyte condition of antarctic mosses. Round white spike head is about 3 cm across.

1967). It is more difficult to assess the possibility of introduction of microorganisms, some of which may be harmful to native plants and animals. Bacteria and fungi have already been introduced by man, some remaining viable for over fifty years (Boyd and Boyd, 1963a, b; Meyer *et al.*, 1963; Tubaki and Asano, 1965; Boyd *et al.*, 1966). Although these bacteria may not normally have psychrophilic metabolism, it has been shown that this type of metabolism may be induced with little difficulty (Olsen and Metcalf, 1968). Microscopic molds and yeasts are also probably being introduced locally (Wicklow, 1968; Rudolph, 1970), and perhaps some beetles as well (Tilbrook, 1967). The elimination of introduced organisms may not be possible. The reestablishment of native vegetation is a long-term process and this is especially so where the reproductive potential is low in native plants. The alien plants on Macquarie Island, one of the subantarctic islands, for example, are first to recolonize disturbed areas (Gillham, 1961).

Any student of antarctic vegetation knows that as he goes inland from the Antarctic Peninsula or coastal sectors of the continent, the vegetation becomes progressively sparser and less structured. If we hope to preserve the simple antarctic ecosystems for further study, it is important that the recommendations for conservation made by the signators of the Antarctic Treaty be diligently followed. We do not know if the vegetation of Antarctica will re-establish itself once destroyed. It is the duty of every person visiting this unique continent to take it upon himself to do all he can to preserve its ecosystems. Our survival in the future may depend upon the understanding of such "simple" ecosystems existing under hostile environmental conditions.

PRODUCTIVITY AND FOOD WEBS

For an understanding of the dynamics of any ecosystem, it is necessary to know about its energy balance, including its primary productivity and energy transfer through the links in the food chains. It is also interesting to know how any ecosystem compares with similar ones in other places. For the tundra vegetation in the maritime antarctic, the productivity when compared with temperate vegetation is very low. Holdgate (1967) gives a figure of 100 grams dry weight per square meter per year as the standing crop for lush mosses on Signy Island. This is a low figure when compared with those given for arctic and alpine vegetation by Billings and Mooney (1968). Longton (1970) indicates that the moss *Polytrichum alpestre* Hoppe produces 2.5 times greater dry weight per shoot per year in the Falkland Islands (52°S) than in the Argentine Islands farther south (65°S). Several investigators are gathering information about primary productivity in other parts of Antarctica where figures will probably be lower. Caution must be used when generalizing, because in local situations higher rates of productivity may be found. For example, on the subantarctic Macquarie Island (54°S) grassland vegetation is two to three times as productive as comparable vegetation is in Australia and about equivalent to that of vegetation in northern Britain (Jenkin and Ashton, 1970). It has also been shown that nitrogen fixation by a blue-green alga in the maritime antarctic is within the range of a similar alga on the coast of Scotland (Fogg and Stewart, 1968).

Primary productivity of antarctic lakes seems to be comparable to some arctic ones of low productivity (Goldman, 1964; D. D. Koob, personal communication), but only 0.5 to 3 percent of that of most temperate lakes. Snow algae fix 10 milligrams of carbon per day per square meter of snow surface in the South Orkney Islands (Fogg, 1967). This is a very low value for primary productivity corresponding to 0.1 to 0.5 percent of that of extremely oligotrophic lakes in Swedish Lapland. By any measure, the primary productivity of antarctic algae is low compared with other areas.

The transfer of energy in antarctic terrestrial food chains appears to be simpler than in most other regions. The chains go no farther than the first carnivore level (Gless, 1967; Greene *et al.*, 1967; Gressitt and Shoup, 1967; Heywood, 1967; Janetschek, 1967; Strong, 1967; Tilbrook, 1967). From all the evidence available, primary producers are green plants and perhaps bacteria. These, mostly the microscopic algae, are eaten by the animals or they are used as food sources for the fungi and bacteria which, in turn, are eaten by the animals. A few of the free-living mites are carnivorous. Lichens are food sources used by a few animals. It appears that living mosses are not eaten but are used for shelter by animals. The presence of arthropods away from sites of macroscopic vegetation indicates that they can feed solely upon microscopic algae, fungi, and bacteria. Covarrubias (1965) has shown that numbers of invertebrates vary considerably from one type of habitat to another and that in some sites the numbers may be great even though generally they are low when compared with other parts of the world. We have no figures for energy loss through the food web. What is significant is that these webs are so abbreviated that there are not even zooplankton in some continuously ice-covered lakes (D. D. Koob, personal communication). Holdgate (1967) has estimated standing crops of vegetation and fauna for the maritime antarctic of 10^7 milligrams per square meter of surface and 0 to 5.2×10^3 milligrams per square meter of surface respectively.

NUTRIENT AND MINERAL CYCLING

All organisms, including autotrophs, require certain mineral elements for their continued metabolism. In noncoastal parts of Antarctica, the availability of nitrogen in usable form for plants is a critical requirement. Organic nitrogen can be provided by nitrogen-fixing bacteria (Boyd and Boyd, 1962; Boyd *et al.*, 1966) or blue-green algae (Holm-Hansen, 1963; Fogg and Stewart, 1968). However, sites where these organisms are present are probably quite limited. On the coast and for some kilometers inland the provision of nitrogen salts by nesting birds or by seals is important (Fig. 6). Dry guano fragments may be blown inland for distances. Flying birds may fertilize inland snow and ice and the minerals

Fig. 6. Adélie penguin rookery at Cape Hallett illustrating large accumulations of guano.

may later be found in the meltwater where plants grow. There is evidence of the presence of salts of nitrogen in precipitation far from the coast (Claridge and Campbell, 1968; Mueller, 1968). Nitrogen dioxide gas has also been found in the atmosphere far from human habitation (Fischer *et al.*, 1968).

Sea water is probably a source of mineral elements near the coast in the form of spray as well as in precipitation (Allen *et al.*, 1967). The atmosphere must also contain trace amounts of mineral ions, for example, from volcanic eruptions at some distance, as indicated by the evidence from strontium-90 findings in antarctic snow (Wilgain *et al.*, 1965). Sulfur in the form of sulfur dioxide is known to be present in the atmosphere (Fischer *et al.*, 1968) and sulfur-reducing bacteria are found in the soil (Barghoorn and Nichols, 1961). The primary source of mineral salts, however, is probably the native rocks from which they are released as a result of physical and chemical weathering taking place at very slow rates (Ugolini, 1966; Tedrow and Ugolini, 1966; Allen *et al.*, 1967). A winter increase in extractable phosphorus, and perhaps nitrogen similar to that known in temperate regions, has been reported in the maritime antarctic (Northover and Allen, 1967).

Where there is an abundance of mosses or algae, peat formation occurs. This peat acts as a reservoir for nitrogen and phosphorus as well as for organic carbon (Heal *et al.*, 1967; Holdgate *et al.*, 1967). Live mosses and perhaps other plants adsorb sodium, calcium, and magnesium in addition to phosphorus (Allen *et al.*, 1967). In one study, penguin guano had a carbon to nitrate ratio of one, while old guano in abandoned rookeries had ratios of seven, as compared with 21 for nonrookery soils (Campbell and Claridge, 1966). The organic content showed a decided decrease of from 57 percent for guano, to 8 percent for abandoned rookery soils, to 0.8 percent for nonrookery soils. Similar decreases have been noted for nitrogen and phosphorus. The activity of such marine-feeding animals as penguins can play a significant role in introducing minerals into the ecosystem. On the other hand, such animals accumulate quantities of salts in rookeries that are toxic to most plants. Studies of mineral cycling now in progress in Antarctica may well provide some of the answers to problems of availability of nutrients for organisms, particularly for those far inland.

ENVIRONMENTAL FACTORS

It is difficult to select the most critical factor which limits the growth of plants among the many extreme factors in the antarctic environment. This is especially true because we lack needed experimental data. The absence of moisture, the frequent freeze-thaw cycles particularly in the summer, the short growing seasons, the frequent occurrence of toxic salinity, the paucity of some essential mineral ions, and the presence of strong desiccating winds sometimes carrying abrasive sand and snow crystals are all important limiting factors for plant growth and reproduction. Many of the biologists who have visited Antarctica have noted the decided influence of liquid water on plant distribution (Rudolph, 1963, 1966b; Wise and Gressitt, 1965; Cameron, 1966; Gimingham, 1967; Longton, 1967; Fukushima, 1968) (Figs. 7, 8). Whereas liquid water is a distinct limiting factor on a continent in which frozen water is abundant, low temperatures are not necessarily limiting. Most of the organisms that have been studied in laboratory conditions are not psychrophiles, but rather are cold tolerant or cold adapted (di Menna, 1960, 1966; Lange, 1965, 1969; Holdgate, 1967; Tilbrook, 1967; Stanley and Rose, 1967; Sugiyama *et al.*, 1967). Documentation is available to show that the microclimate at ground level or on rocks where plants grow is at times quite temperate

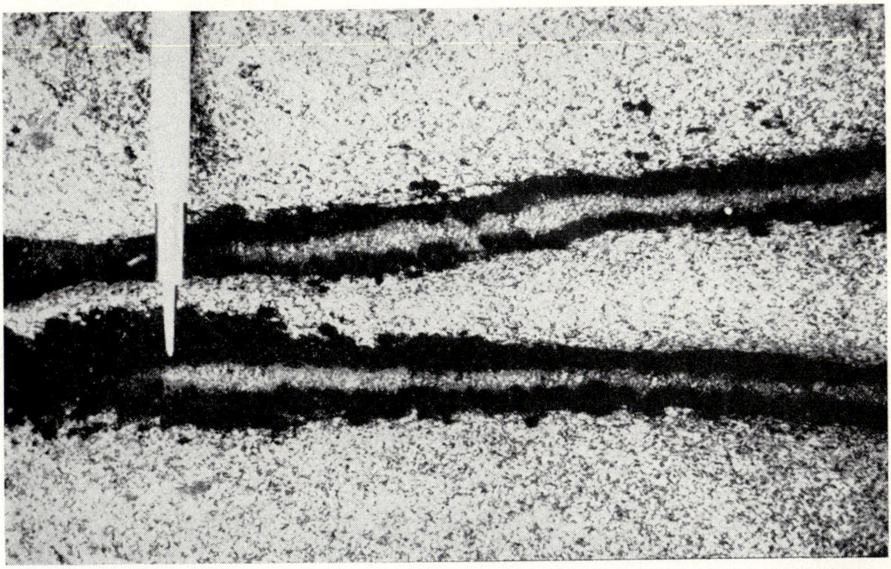

Fig. 7. Watercourse channels on boulder outlined by *Usnea* lichens in Marie Byrd Land. Ice axe tip at left (Photograph taken by Mr. Geoffrey Leister).

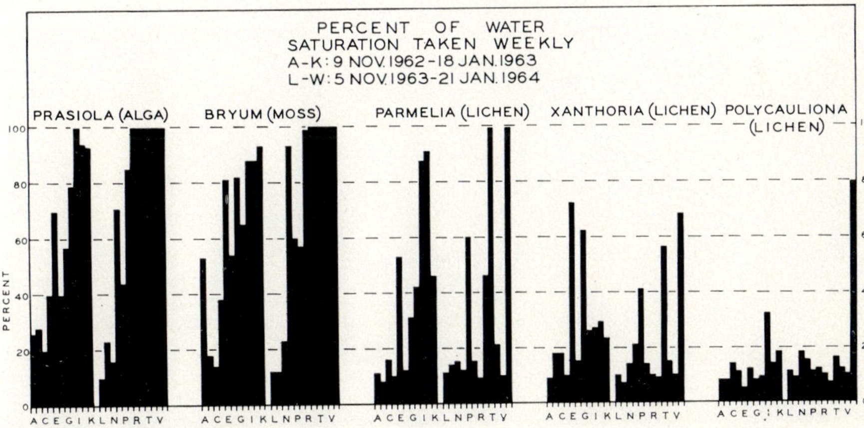

Fig. 8. Data for base of Cape Hallett illustrating differences in moisture content of various vegetational components.

(Rudolph, 1963, 1966b; Matsuda, 1964; Llano, 1965; Janetschek, 1967; Longton and Holdgate, 1967); however, the total of these periods adds up to a very short growing season. *Poa pratensis* germinated and grew when planted at Cape Hallett in the continental area (Rudolph, 1966a) (Fig. 9). Several workers have reported mosses being kept frozen for three and five years and reviving readily when the temperature was raised (Horikawa and Ando, 1967; Longton and Holdgate, 1967).

A few organisms can grow in places of high salt concentrations, either in rookeries or evaporitic ponds. These may be the green alga *Prasiola crispa* (Lightf.) Menegh., or other algae, fungi, mosses, lichens, and various invertebrates (Meyer *et al.*, 1962; Follmann, 1965; Llano, 1965; Allen *et al.*, 1967; Horikawa and Ando, 1967; Sugiyama *et al.*, 1967; Goodman, 1969; Goto *et al.*, 1969; Schofield and Rudolph, 1969). The paucity of minerals, particularly nitrogen salts, may also be limiting (Likens, 1964), although direct evidence is lacking.

Individual environmental factors may be important, but it is the combination of them that makes the total environment and determines which organisms will survive. Cameron *et al.* (1970)

Fig. 9. *Poa pratensis* two weeks after germination at the base of Cape Hallett. Individual plants having one or two leaves were approximately 2.5 cm high.

in their study of the microflora of the Victoria Dry Valley system have emphasized this multiple-factor approach (Table 1; Fig. 10).

POPULATION DENSITY AND COMPOSITION

Although the kinds (species) of plants in Antarctica are becoming better known every year, the relative numbers and frequencies of each in various formations remain little known. Lichens, for example, are the most widespread group of macroscopic plants, but in some coastal habitats they are minor constituents of the formations. In one study area at Cape Hallett (72°S on the Ross Sea), where algae, mostly *Prasiola crispa,* comprise 83 percent of the vegetation, mosses, mostly *Bryum argenteum* Hedwig, comprise 15 percent and the lichens only 2 percent. The situation inland, with reduced moisture, favors lichens which make up a high percentage of the vegetation (Ugolini, 1964; author's observations). Microorganisms are often cosmopolitan, and in favorable sites are present in numbers comparable to temperate localities (di Menna, 1960; Flint and Stout, 1960; Toriumi and Katô, 1962; Corte and Daglio, 1963; di Menna, 1966; Ugolini and Starkey, 1966; Heal *et al.,* 1967). In places where mosses and algae form peat, other

Table 1. Ecological factors determining distribution of life in antarctic dry valleys (From Cameron *et al.,* 1968).

Favorable	*Unfavorable*
N-S orientation	E-W orientation
Northern exposure	Southern exposure
Gentle, north-facing slopes	Flat or south-facing slopes
High solar radiation	Low solar radiation
Microclimate above freezing	Microclimate below freezing
Absence of wind	High winds
Northerly winds	Southerly winds
High humidities	Low humidities
Slow or impeded drainage	Rapid drainage
Lengthy duration of available H_2O (presence of glaciers, lakes, streams, snow and ice fields)	Short duration of available H_2O (absence of glaciers, lakes, streams, snow and ice fields)
Translucent pebbles	Opaque pebbles
Non-salty soils, balanced ionic composition	Salty soils, unbalanced ionic composition
Approx. neutral pH	High (or low) pH
Organic contamination (skuas, seals, etc.)	No organic contamination (no large increments of organic matter)

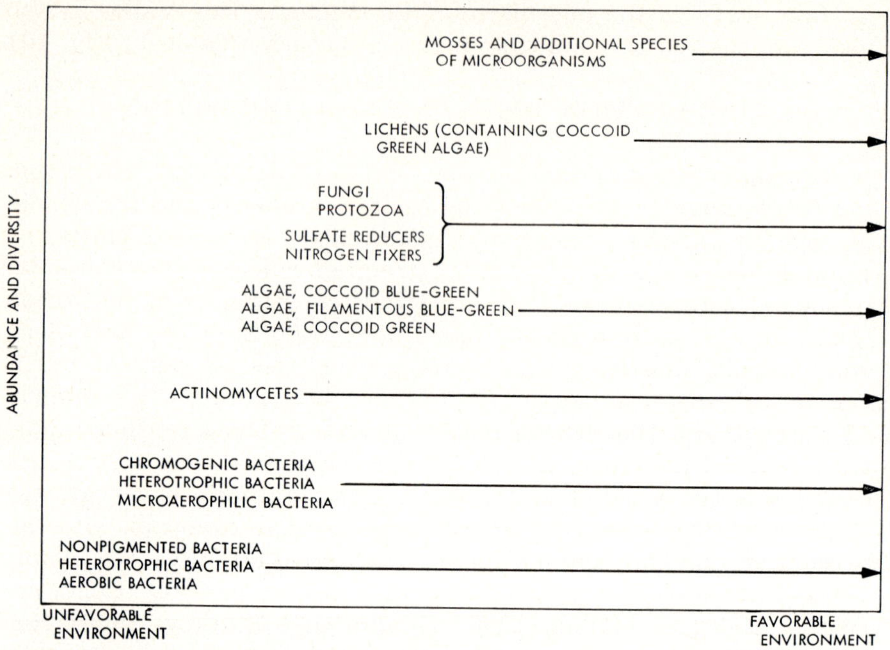

Fig. 10. Schematic summary of variation in diversity and succession of organisms as related to ecological factors, favorable and unfavorable (See Table 1) in antarctic dry valleys of Victoria Land. The arrowheads on the right indicate that all the groups of organisms can grow in favorable environments. The distance from the arrowhead to the start of the names of the organisms on the left indicates their relative tolerances of the totality of unfavorable conditions (From Cameron *et al.*, 1968).

organisms occur in fair numbers (Armitage and House, 1962; Holm-Hansen, 1963; Covarrubias, 1965; Longton, 1967; Tilbrook, 1967). What strikes one most about antarctic vegetation is its opportunistic nature. Wherever conditions are at all favorable, plants can be found in patches surrounded by large areas of no visible vegetation. Frequently, only one macroscopic species may be present in a particular patch, and even in the most favorable localities the total number of species is small. More statistics are needed about populations before antarctic ecosystems can be thoroughly interpreted.

COLONIZATION AND PHYTOGEOGRAPHY

The geologically recent history of antarctic vegetation remains an unknown quantity. What is its age, its invasion route, its establishment time, and its rate of spread? There is evidence from the Antarctic Peninsula that Tertiary floras contained a preponderance of southern beech (*Nothofagus* spp.) along with other tree species (Cranwell *et al.*, 1960; Wace, 1965). The more recent extensive glaciation of Antarctica could have eliminated all of the plants on the continent, or else reduced their occupancy to a few isolated mountain refugia. If the first hypothesis be true, all of the plants now found must have invaded from distant land masses since glacial retreat. If the second hypothesis be true, islands of vegetation must have readily been at hand for recolonization of land exposed by glacial retreat. Evidence is lacking for validation of either hypothesis or a combination of the two.

At present, plants have been found in almost all explored ice-free areas of Antarctica (Greene *et al.*, 1967). The southernmost records for the various visible components of the vegetation are: lichens 86°09′S at 1,980 meters, macroscopic algae 85°09′S at 1,737 meters, mosses 84°37′S at 760 meters, liverworts 72°S at sea level, flowering plants 68°12′S at sea level, and larger fungi 64°09′S at sea level (Wise and Gressitt, 1965; Greene *et al.*, 1967) (Fig. 11). The vegetation in the maritime antarctic is more extensively developed than that in the continental antarctic and thus has been classified into several formations with subformations (Holdgate, 1964; Longton, 1967). Moss peat on Signy Island in the maritime antarctic has been dated at 1900 B.P. (Holdgate, 1967). This record, together with its extensive development, would indicate that the Peninsula vegetation has been established for some time. Many of the plants composing the maritime antarctic vegetation are cosmopolitan or are also found on adjacent subantarctic islands and continents (Skottsberg, 1954; Corte and Daglio, 1963; Hirano, 1965; Greene *et al.*, 1967), thus favoring the hypothesis of post-glacial invasion from adjacent land masses. On the other hand, the evidence is not so strong for the continental area where vegetation is poorly developed and where endemic species are more abundant (Cailleux, 1961; Greene *et al.*, 1967).

Actual dispersal of plants in Antarctica where reproductive potential is low warrants considerable interest. Long-distance transport has been suggested and Taylor (1954) has claimed such a mechanism for Macquarie Island, but there is no direct evidence for this in continental Antarctica. Local dispersal has been shown to be operative for microfungi (Corte and Daglio, 1963; Heal *et al.*, 1967; Rudolph, 1970) and for algae, mosses, and lichens (Rudolph, 1970). The establishment of individual species in communities in

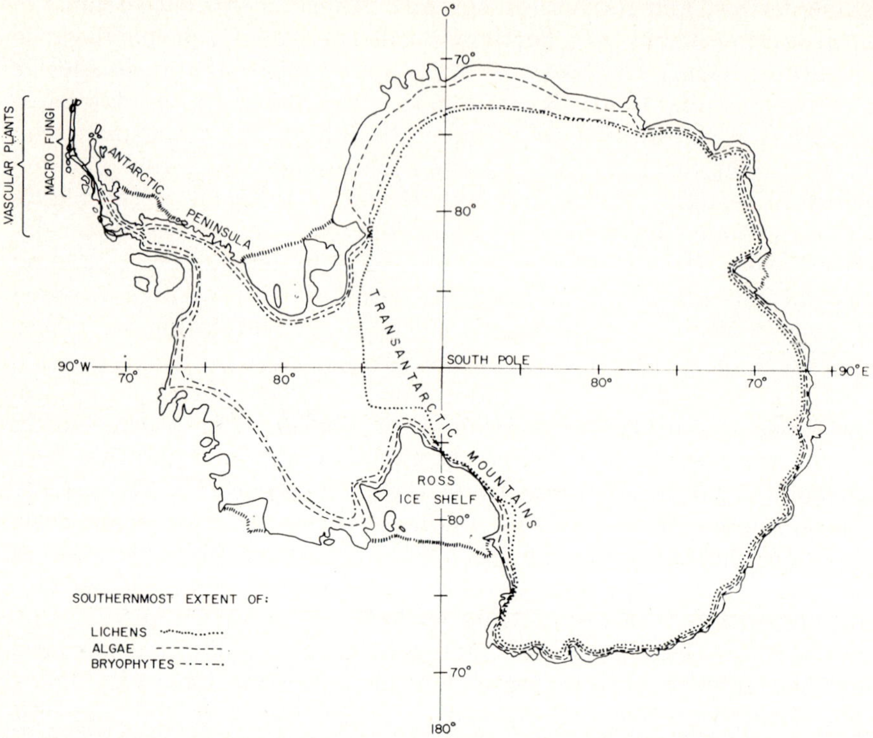

Fig. 11. Distribution of antarctic vegetational components showing southern limits (Based mostly on data in Greene *et al.*, 1967).

new localities is possible. Llano (1965) has indicated an ecological succession in deglaciated areas beginning with algae and soil microorganisms and leading up to mosses or lichens. Mosses sometimes become covered with blue-green algae or lichens (Rudolph, 1966a; Horikawa and Ando, 1967). Succession in such simple ecosystems is limited in extent and controlled by environmental conditions.

If we were to obtain spore and pollen analyses of peat samples from the continent and subantarctic islands, some of the problems of the history of the antarctic vegetation might be resolved. Searching for plant propagules on migratory birds would also be worth studying.

The understanding of the apparently simple terrestrial ecosystem in Antarctica eludes the biologists. However, as the many challenging problems are studied and as new answers appear each year, we can hope that some of the elusiveness will disappear. We have already begun to understand some ecological aspects of the vegetation, and as a result of the activities of many able biologists from many countries the understanding will continue to increase.

Author's Notes: This paper is based on data obtained under grants G-19586, GA-52, GA-496, GA-840, and GA-1039, U. S. Antarctic Research Programs, Office of Polar Programs, National Science Foundation. The author gratefully acknowledges this assistance.

This paper is Contribution No. 147 of the Institute of Polar Studies, The Ohio State University, Columbus.

References

Allen, S. E., H. M. Grimshaw, and M. W. Holdgate, 1967. Factors affecting the availability of plant nutrients on an antarctic island. *J. Ecol., 55:* 381–396.

Armitage, K. B., and H. B. House, 1962. A limnological reconnaissance in the area of McMurdo Sound, Antarctica. *Limnol. Oceanog., 7:* 36–41.

Barghoorn, E. S., and R. L. Nichols, 1961. Sulfate-reducing bacteria and pyritic sediments in Antarctica. *Science, 134:* 190.

Billings, W. D., and H. A. Mooney, 1968. The ecology of arctic and alpine plants. *Biol. Rev. Cambridge Phil. Soc., 43:* 481–529.

Boyd, W. L., and J. W. Boyd, 1962. Presence of *Azotobacter* species in polar regions. *J. Bacteriol., 83:* 429–430.

Boyd, W. L., and J. W. Boyd, 1963a. Soil microorganisms of the McMurdo Sound area, Antarctica. *Appl. Microbiol., 11:* 116–121.

Boyd, W. L., and J. W. Boyd, 1963b. Viability of coliform bacteria in antarctic soil. *J. Bacteriol., 85:* 1121–1123.

Boyd, W. L., J. T. Staley, and J. W. Boyd, 1966. Ecology of soil microorganisms of Antarctica. In *Antarctic Research Series 8, Antarctic Soils and Soil Forming Processes,* edited by J. C. F. Tedrow; pp. 125–159. Am. Geophys. Union, Washington, D. C.

Cailleux, A., 1961. Endémicité actuelle et passée de l'Antarctique. *Compt. Rend. Soc. Biogéographie, Paris, 334:* 65–71.

Cameron, R. E., 1966. B. Soil studies—desert microflora. XIII. Identification of some algae from Antarctica. *NASA Space Programs Sum. No. 37-40, 4:* 123–133.

Cameron, R., J. King, and C. David, 1968. Soil microbial and ecological studies in southern Victoria Land. *Antarctic J. U.S., 3:* 121–123.

Cameron, R. E., J. King, and C. N. David, 1970. Microbiology, ecology, and microclimatology of soil sites in dry valleys of southern Victoria Land, Antarctica. In *Antarctic Ecology,* edited by M. W. Holdgate; vol. 2, pp. 702–716. Academic Press, New York.

Campbell, I. B., and G. G. C. Claridge, 1966. A sequence of soils from a penguin rookery, Inexpressible Island, Antarctica. *New Zealand J. Sci., 9:* 361–372.

Claridge, G. G. C., and I. B. Campbell, 1968. Origin of nitrate deposits. *Nature, 217:* 428–430.

Corte, A., 1961. Fertilidad de las semillas en fanerogamas que crecen en Cabo Primavera (Costa de Danco), Peninsula Antártica. *Contrib. Inst. Antártico Argentino,* No. *65,* 16 p.

Corte, A., and C. A. N. Daglio, 1963. Micromicetes aislados en el Antártico. *Contrib. Inst. Antártico Argentino*, No. *74*, 27 p.

Covarrubias, R., 1965. Observaciones cuantitativas sobre los invertebrados terrestres Antárticos y preantarticos. *Inst. Antártico Chileno, Publ.*, *9*: 1–62. (printed 1967)

Cranwell, L. M., H. J. Harrington, and I. G. Speden, 1960. Lower Tertiary microfossils from McMurdo Sound, Antarctica. *Nature*, *186*: 700–702.

di Menna, M. E., 1960. Yeasts from Antarctica. *J. Gen. Microbiol.*, *23*: 295–300.

di Menna, M. E., 1966. Yeasts in antarctic soils. *Antonie van Leeuwenhoek, J. Microbiol. Serol*, 32: 29–39.

Fischer, W. H., J. P. Lodge, Jr., A. F. Wartburg, and J. B. Pate, 1968. Estimation of some atmospheric trace gases in Antarctica. *Environ. Sci. Technol.*, *2*: 464–466.

Flint, E. A., and J. D. Stout, 1960. Microbiology of some soils from Antarctica. *Nature*, *188*: 767–768.

Fogg, G. E., 1967. Observations on the snow algae of the South Orkney Islands. *Phil. Trans. Roy. Soc., London, Ser. B*, *252*: 279–287.

Fogg, G. E., and W. D. P. Stewart, 1968. *In situ* determinations of biological nitrogen fixation in Antarctica. *Brit. Antarctic Surv. Bull.*, *15*: 39–46.

Follmann, G., 1965. Una asociación nitrófila de líquenes epipétricos de la Antártica Occidental con *Ramalina terebrata* Tayl. et Hook. como especie caracterizante. *Inst. Antártico Chileno, Publ.*, *4*: 1–18.

Fukushima, H., 1968. Notes on mosses on Ongul Islands, Antarctica. *Antarctic Record (Tokyo)*, *31*: 66–72.

Gillham, M. E., 1961. Modification of sub-Antarctic flora on Macquarie Island by sea birds and sea elephants. *Proc. Roy. Soc. Victoria*, *74*: 1–12.

Gimingham, C. H., 1967. Quantitative community analysis and bryophyte ecology on Signy Island. *Phil. Trans. Roy. Soc., London, Ser. B*, *252*: 251–259.

Gless, E. E., 1967. Notes on the biology of *Coccorhagidia gressitti* Womersley and Strandtmann. In *Antarctic Research Series 10, Entomology of Antarctica*, edited by J. L. Gressitt; pp. 321–323. Am. Geophys. Union, Washington, D. C.

Goldman, C. R., 1964. Primary productivity studies in antarctic lakes. In *Biologie Antarctique;* pp. 291–299. Hermann, Paris.

Goodman, B. J. A., 1969. A physical, chemical and biological investigation of some fresh-water pools on Signy Island, South Orkney Islands. *Brit. Antarctic Surv. Bull.*, *20*: 1–31.

Goto, S., J. Sugiyama, and H. Iizuka, 1969. A taxonomic study of antarctic yeasts. *Mycologia*, *61*: 748–774.

Greene, S. W., 1966. The changing pattern of Antarctic botanical studies. *Misc. Bryolog. Lichenolog.*, *4*: 61–62.

Greene, S. W., and K. M. Greene, 1963. Check list of the subantarctic and antarctic vascular flora. *Polar Record*, *11*: 411–418.

Greene, S. W., J. L. Gressitt, D. Koob, G. A. Llano, E. D. Rudolph, R. Singer, W. C. Steere, and F. C. Ugolini, 1967. Terrestrial Life of Antarctica. In *Antarctic Map Folio Series, Folio 5;* pp. 1–24. Am. Geograph. Soc., New York.

Gressitt, J. L., and J. Shoup, 1967. Ecological notes on free-living mites in north Victoria Land. In *Antarctic Research Series 10, Entomology of Antarctica,* edited by J. L. Gressitt; pp. 307–320. Am. Geophys. Union, Washington, D. C.

Heal, O. W., A. D. Bailey, and P. M. Latter, 1967. Bacteria, fungi and protozoa in Signy Island soils compared with those from a temperate moorland. *Phil. Trans. Roy. Soc., London, Ser. B, 252:* 191–197.

Heywood, R. B., 1967. The freshwater lakes of Signy Island and their fauna. *Phil. Trans. Roy. Soc., London, Ser. B, 252:* 347–362.

Hirano, M., 1965. Freshwater algae in the antarctic regions. In *Biogeography and Ecology in Antarctica,* edited by P. van Oye and J. van Mieghem; pp. 127–193. Monographiae Biologicae, 15, Junk, The Hague.

Holdgate, M. W., 1964. Terrestrial ecology in the Maritime Antarctic. In *Biologie Antarctique;* pp. 181–194. Hermann, Paris.

Holdgate, M. W., 1967. The antarctic ecosystem. *Phil. Trans. Roy. Soc., London, Ser. B, 252:* 363–383.

Holdgate, M. W., S. E. Allen, and M. J. G. Chambers, 1967. A preliminary investigation of the soils of Signy Island, South Orkney Islands. *Brit. Antarctic Surv. Bull., 12:* 53–71.

Holm-Hansen, O., 1963. Algae: nitrogen fixation by antarctic species. *Science, 139:* 1059–1060.

Holtom, A., and S. W. Greene, 1967. The growth and reproduction of antarctic flowering plants. *Phil. Trans. Roy. Soc., London, Ser. B, 252:* 323–341.

Horikawa, Y., and H. Ando, 1967. The mosses of the Ongul Islands and adjoining coastal areas of the Antarctic continent. In *Japanese Antarctic Research Expedition Scientific Reports;* Special Issue No. 1, pp. 245–252. National Science Museum, Tokyo.

Janetschek, H., 1963. Ueber die wirbellose Landfauna des Rossmeergebietes (Antarktika). *Vorlaeufige Mitteilung Anz-Schaedlingsk, 36:* 8–12.

Janetschek, H., 1967. Arthropod ecology of South Victoria Land. In *Antarctic Research Series 10, Entomology of Antarctica,* edited by J. L. Gressitt; pp. 205–293. Am. Geophys. Union, Washington, D. C.

Jenkin, J. F., and D. H. Ashton, 1970. Productivity studies on Macquarie Island vegetation. In *Antarctic Ecology,* edited by M. W. Holdgate; vol. 2, pp. 851–863. Academic Press, New York.

Lange, O. L., 1965. Der CO_2-Gaswechsel von Flechten bei tiefen Temperaturen. *Planta, 64:* 1–19.

Lange, O. L., 1969. Die funktionellen Anpassungen der Flechten an die ökologischen Bedingungen arider Gebiete. *Ber. Dtsch. Bot. Ges., 82:* 3–22.

Likens, G. E., 1964. An unusual distribution of algae in an antarctic lake. *Bull. Torrey Botan. Club, 91:* 213–217.

Llano, G. A., 1965. The flora of Antarctica. In *Antarctica,* edited by T. Hatherton; pp. 331–350. Methuen, London.

Longton, R. E., 1966a. Alien vascular plants on Deception Island, South Shetland Islands. *Brit. Antarctic Surv. Bull., 9:* 55–60.

Longton, R. E., 1966b. Botanical studies in the Antarctic during the 1963–64 seasons. *Brit. Antarctic Surv. Bull., 10:* 85–95.

Longton, R. E., 1967. Vegetation in the Maritime Antarctic. *Phil. Trans. Roy. Soc., London, Ser. B, 252:* 213–235.

Longton, R. E., 1970. Growth and productivity of the moss *Polytrichum alpestre* Hoppe in antarctic regions. In *Antarctic Ecology,* edited by M. W. Holdgate; vol. 2, pp. 818–837. Academic Press, New York.

Longton, R. E., and M. W. Holdgate, 1967. Temperature relationships of antarctic vegetation. *Phil. Trans. Roy. Soc., London, Ser. B, 252:* 237–250.

Matsuda, T., 1964. Microclimate in the community of mosses near Syowa Base at East Ongul Island, Antarctica. *Antarctic Record (Tokyo), 21:* 12–24.

Meyer, G. H., M. B. Morrow, and O. Wyss, 1963. Viable organisms from feces and food stuffs from early antarctic expeditions. *Can. J. Microbiol., 9:* 163–167.

Meyer, G. H., M. B. Morrow, O. Wyss, T. E. Berg, and J. L. Littlepage, 1962. Antarctica: The microbiology of an unfrozen saline pond. *Science, 138:* 1103–1104.

Mueller, G., 1968. Genetic histories of nitrate deposits from Antarctica and Chile. *Nature, 219:* 1131–1134.

Northover, M. J., and S. E. Allen, 1967. Seasonal availability of chemical nutrients on Signy Island. *Phil. Trans. Roy. Soc., London, Ser. B, 252:* 187–189.

Olsen, R. H., and E. S. Metcalf, 1968. Conversion of mesophilic to psychrophilic bacteria. *Science, 162:* 1288–1289.

Rudolph, E. D., 1963. Vegetation of Hallett Station area, Victoria Land, Antarctica. *Ecology, 44:* 585–586.

Rudolph, E. D., 1966a. Terrestrial vegetation of Antarctica: Past and present studies. In *Antarctic Research Series 8, Antarctic Soils and Soil Forming Processes,* edited by J. C. F. Tedrow; pp. 109–124. Am. Geophys. Union, Washington, D. C.

Rudolph, E. D., 1966b. Lichen ecology and microclimate studies at Cape Hallett, Antarctica. In *Proc. Third Internat. Biometeorol. Congr. (1–7 Sept. 1963), Biometeorol. 2;* pp. 900–910. Pergamon, Oxford.

Rudolph, E. D., 1970. Local dissemination of plant propagules in Antarctica. In *Antarctic Ecology,* edited by M. W. Holdgate; vol. 2, pp. 812–817. Academic Press, New York.

Schofield, E. and E. D. Rudolph, 1969. Ecophysiology of some macroscopic antarctic terrestrial cryptogams. *Bull. Ecol. Soc. Amr., 50:* 159–160.

Skottsberg, C., 1954. Antarctic flowering plants. *Botan. Tidsskr., 51:* 330–338.

Stanley, S. O., and A. H. Rose, 1967. Bacteria and yeasts from lakes on Deception Island. *Phil. Trans. Roy. Soc., London, Ser. B, 252:* 199–207.

Strong, J., 1967. Ecology of terrestrial arthropods at Palmer Station, Antarctica. In *Antarctic Research Series 10, Entomology of Antarctica,* edited by J. L. Gressitt; pp. 357–371. Am. Geophys. Union, Washington, D. C.

Sugiyama, J., Y. Sugiyama, H. Iizuka, and T. Torii, 1967. Report of the Japanese summer parties in dry valleys, Victoria Land, 1963–1965. IV. Mycological studies of the antarctic fungi. Pt. 2. Mycoflora of Lake Vanda, an ice-free lake. *Antarctic Record (Tokyo), 28:* 23–32.

Taylor, B. W., 1954. An example of long distance dispersal. *Ecology, 35:* 569–572.

Tedrow, J. C. F., and F. C. Ugolini, 1966. Antarctic soils. In *Antarctic Research Series 8, Antarctic Soils and Soil Forming Processes,* edited by J. C. F. Tedrow; pp. 161–177. Am. Geophys. Union, Washington, D. C.

Tilbrook, P. J., 1967. The terrestrial invertebrate fauna of the Maritime Antarctic. *Phil. Trans. Roy. Soc., London, Ser. B, 252:* 261–278.

Toriumi, M., and M. Katô, 1962. Preliminary report on the microfauna and flora among the mosses come from Ongul Islands. *Bull. Marine Biol. Stat. Asamushi, Tohoku Univ., 10:* 231–236.

Tubaki, K., and I. Asano, 1965. Additional species of fungi isolated from antarctic materials. *Japanese Antarctic Research Expedition, 1956–1962, Scientific Reports, Ser. E, No. 27.* National Science Museum, Tokyo.

Ugolini, F. C., 1964. A study of pedologic processes in Antarctica. In *Final Report to the National Science Foundation.* Rutgers University, New Brunswick, N. J.

Ugolini, F. C., 1966. Soil investigations in the Lower Wright Valley, Antarctica. *Proc. Intern. Conf. Permafrost, Publ. 1287;* pp. 55–61. National Academy of Sciences—National Research Council, Washington, D. C.

Ugolini, F. C., and R. L. Starkey, 1966. Soils and micro-organisms from Mount Erebus, Antarctica. *Nature, 211:* 440–441.

Wace, N. M., 1965. Vascular plants. In *Biogeography and Ecology in Antarctica,* edited by P. van Oye and J. van Mieghem; pp. 201–266. Monographiae Biologicae, 15. Junk, The Hague.

Wicklow, D. T., 1968. *Aspergillus fumigatus* Fresenius isolated from ornithogenic soil collected at Hallett Station, Antarctica. *Can. J. Microbiol., 14:* 717–719.

Wilgain, S., E. Picciotto, and W. De Breuck, 1965. Strontium 90 fallout in Antarctica. *J. Geophys. Res., 70:* 6023–6032.

Wise, K. A. J., and J. L. Gressitt, 1965. Far southern animals and plants. *Nature, 207:* 101–102.

Ecodynamics of Lichen Communities in Antarctica

T. P. GANNUTZ

Department of Biology, Clark University, Worcester, Massachusetts

Antarctica, characterized by high winds, extremes of temperature, and extended periods of darkness, drought, and light, presents a unique environmental complex to terrestrial organisms. Terrestrial plants inhabiting this continent are subjected to only short periods during which environmental conditions are favorable for optimal metabolism (Gannutz, 1970). Changes from environmental stress conditions to conditions favorable for metabolism are not gradual. Consequently, a plant inhabiting this area must be able to take advantage of any favorable environmental complex almost instantaneously. Antarctic plants must also be able to survive extended periods of inactivity during environmental stress conditions. These severe stress conditions would be encountered during winter months when low temperatures, darkness, and heavy snow cover prevail. Few groups of plants can survive these conditions and consequently be represented in Antarctica. The groups that do (algae, fungi, mosses, and lichens), however, are similar to organisms inhabiting alpine, arctic, and other climatic regions with a rigorous environment. In the less climatically severe areas of the Antarctic Peninsular region, two species of higher plants, *Colobanthus crassifolius* (d'Urv.) Hook f. and *Deschampsia antarctica* Desv., are present in limited numbers, in addition to a great abundance of the aforementioned organisms.

It has been sufficiently established (Rudolph, 1963; Dodge, 1964; Lamb, 1964; Llano, 1965) that lichens are present in great abundance in some antarctic regions. Although it is relatively simple to propose and substantiate generalized statements explaining the distribution of these organisms, it is quite difficult to provide concrete scientific data to explain the distribution and density of lichens in any one region of the world. Collection of large amounts of data on many variables is necessary. For my own research to determine the critical factors which control the establishment and growth of lichens in Antarctica, I have selected two methods: evidence by distribution of plants in an area and evidence by plant physiology.

DETERMINING LICHEN ECOLOGY BY PLANT DISTRIBUTION

Examination of the lichens present in an area, in relation to various physical factors of the measured and assumed environment, is one of the more convenient and feasible methods of determining lichen ecology. This method is relatively effective in determining the specificity of the plants for certain environmental complexes. Lichens, being a delicate symbiosis, will not inhabit an area where substrate, temperature, and other physical conditions do not provide an optimal combination of variables. The slow growth of lichens (Hale, 1970) and consequently slow metabolism (Gannutz, 1967) makes this type of investigation highly significant when considering variables which are stable for long periods of time. However, the basic difficulty in this approach is the slow responses of lichens to environmental extremes (Brodo, 1962; Gannutz, 1967). Several months are necessary for a lichen to demonstrate damage from an environmental extreme, whether it be the application of pollution or a drastic change in the environment or microenvironment, for example, removal of a forest canopy or shrub layer.

Antarctica provides an ideal field laboratory for this type of investigation because there is relatively little disturbance of the environment by man and because the lower plant community is not affected by the more dominant members of the higher plant community. There are no higher plant successions or seasonal fluctuations, caused by a forest canopy for instance, as there are in more moderate regions of the world. These factors greatly complicate the general environment for less substantial members of the ecosystem. In addition, the ability to set aside Specially Protected Areas reserved for future research activities provides undisturbed areas for accurate long-range studies of growth rates and successional patterns.

The talus slopes on the western side of Cape Hallett (72° 18′ S, 170° 18′ E) provided an ideal location for study of distributional patterns of lichens in relation to a limited number of environmental factors. The slopes which were considered in this experiment were approximately 2,000 feet high and 6,000 feet long, oriented north to south. The lichen species were representative of those found within a 60-mile radius of Cape Hallett (Rudolph, 1963). The entire area received uniform sunlight exposure and snowfall and was generally composed of basaltic rock. There were no higher plants in the area to affect the ecology of this lower plant community. A distinct variation in the distribution of lichens was noticed along these slopes in spite of the apparently uniform and stable physical conditions. The two variables examined in an attempt to explain the distribution of lichens were substrate stability and snow cover persistence.

Substrate Stability

The area studied for the stability of possible lichen substrata is a talus slope composed of loose rocks of varying sizes on slopes of varying inclinations. The rocks of which these slopes are composed are not in any way connected or held together by plant material. Substrate stability was determined by recording the slope angle, rock diameter, and percentage of lichen coverage of rocks at 50 randomly selected sites on this talus slope during the 1967 austral summer.

The results of this study of the abundance of lichens in relation to substrate stability are presented in Figure 1 where rock size is plotted against slope angle. All data are not represented in this figure, but only those points where there is a distinction between the presence or absence of the lichens, providing a representation of those degrees of stability which are critical for the establishment and growth of the lichens. The initial establishment of lichens on rock surfaces in the Antarctic is important. If stability is sufficient, temperature, light, and other environmental variables can be taken into consideration. It is generally difficult to consider temperature and water condition to be of prime importance if the lichens are initially unable to grow on a substrate.

Rocks larger than one inch in diameter were more stable on the steeper slopes than small rocks and were therefore able to support lichen growth. At slope angles greater than 37°, almost all rocks were unstable and did not support lichen growth, regardless of their size. Consequently, although slope stability might seem of primary importance in the establishment of the lichens, the size of the rock is a critical factor.

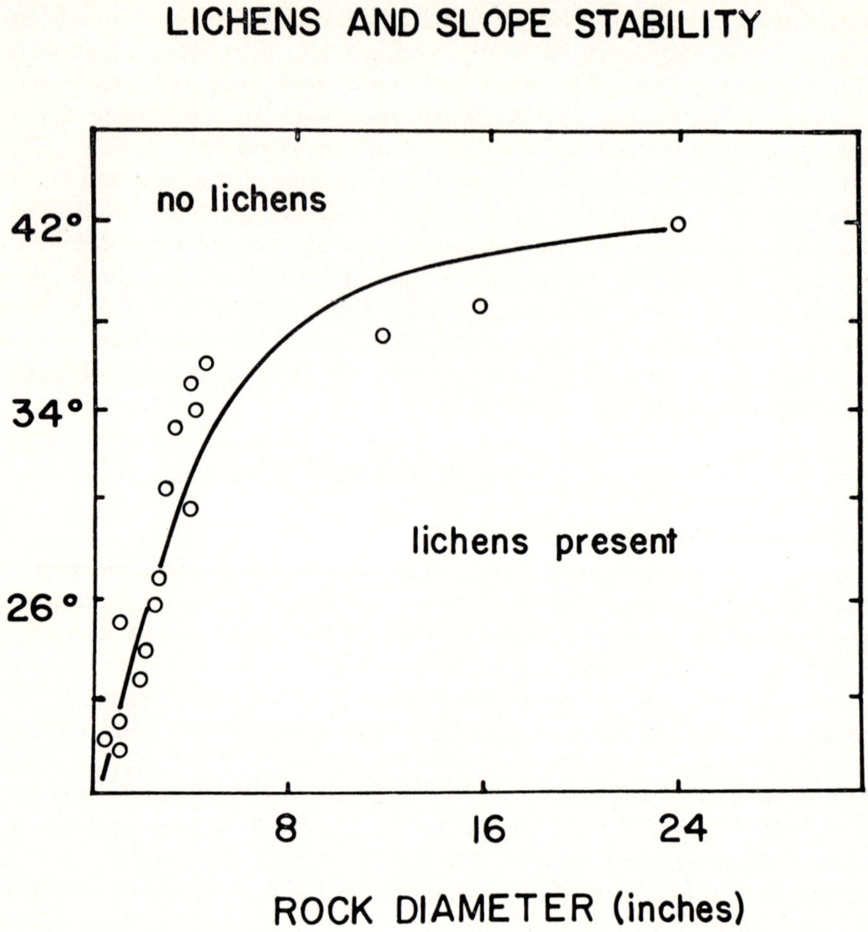

Fig. 1. Rock diameter in inches is plotted against slope angle in degrees from horizontal as a determination of stability of slope necessary for lichen inhabitance.

Snow Cover Persistence

This experiment was designed to determine the importance of a snow or ice cover to the distribution of lichens on rock surfaces in Antarctica. The density of lichens beneath a snowfield was examined, although the snowfield did not melt completely during the course of the summer, but some part of it remained throughout the year.

Precipitation in the form of snow during both summer and

winter months does not accumulate uniformly at Cape Hallett. The microtopography of the area provides for accumulation of more snow in certain areas because the prevailing wind is along the lateral axis of the slope. Raised surfaces remain snow-free while depressions are filled with snow. Some snow melts rapidly and becomes available to plants very soon after falling during the summer months; when exposed, rock temperatures are above freezing much of the time. During the winter months, however, snow accumulates, filling low areas, and when summer months arrive, melting lasts for a considerable time sometimes throughout the entire summer. Some of these snow-filled areas never melt completely from one year to the next. To determine the effects of snow cover on lichen distribution, a large semipermanent snowfield (Fig. 2) was selected and studied as it decreased in size throughout the summer of 1967. Outlines of the snowfield were marked by string four times during the summer. Early in January, 1967, the density of lichens on rocks was determined at several locations up to 25 feet from the melting edge. Fifteen measurements were made at each

Fig. 2. The semipermanent snowfield (A) which was examined to determine the importance of snow cover and meltwater to lichen inhabitance.

distance from the melting edge on all sides of the snowfield. The percentage of lichen cover was determined at each location. Slope angle and rock size were generally uniform within the study area.

The importance of melting snow to lichen density is presented in Table 1. The results of measurements conducted on January 2, 1967, indicate a decrease in lichen density as the distance from the melting edge increased. Points close to the melting edge at the time of measurement were covered with snow longer during the summer than those farther from the melting edge. There is a definite gradation in lichen density in relation to the exposure of the plant material from beneath the snow cover.

Discussion

It is obvious from this ecological study that stable substrate and snow cover are important for lichen survival in Antarctica. Substrate stability appears to be a prime factor in determining initial establishment of lichens. If the surface is not stable, the initial establishment of the symbiosis cannot occur. Several different types of possible antarctic lichen substrates were examined including relatively solid outcrops which protrude from the talus. Vertical or nearly vertical surfaces generally will not support lichen growth, because of the constant fracturing and falling away of the rock. On the top or uphill side of outcrops, slope angles are negligible and, consequently, the lichen population is dense. This type of outcrop provides an additional effect on lichen distribution. Figure 3 illustrates an icefall, the size of which decreased substantially in coverage within the last 100 years. Point A indicates an outcrop which has been sufficiently prominent to inhibit ice flow into the area below it at a time when the icefall was more extensive in land coverage. At one time, however, the ice covered area

Table 1. Density of lichens in relation to snow melt.

Feet from edge	% Coverage	Date exposed
0	100	— 1/ 2/67
2	94	— 12/ 7/66
4	73	
6	68	— 11/15/66
8	70	
12	54	— 10/ 1/66
20	20	
25	10	

Fig. 3. An icefall which has receded in coverage at Cape Hallett. Point A marks the location of a large outcrop below which lichens are present. Point B indicates where the icefall was previously and where there are no lichens growing.

B. Rocks in the entire area are sufficiently stable to warrant a high degree of lichen coverage, but area B is devoid of lichens.

The significance of the above observation is that more than a hundred years is necessary for lichen establishment in Antarctica. Personal communication with people who were at Hallett Station in 1962 indicated that the coverage and size of this icefall has not changed noticeably in the past five years. Although the substrates below this icefall show stability, availability of water, and the type of rock material comprising the slope, there are no lichens. Johnsen (1959) and Robinson (1959) established that the initiation of lichen succession in more moderate climates normally requires seven years. Hawksworth (1969) indicated that a species of crustose lichen provided 85 percent coverage of a concrete wall within five years. Gannutz (1968) demonstrated that succession in an oak-pine forest under the influence of chronic gamma radiation underwent a change in successional patterns in less than five years. Therefore, lichen succession in the Antarctic is extremely slow when compared to other areas where the environmental complexes are more moderate and the substrates are of a different nature.

The above investigation indicates that snow cover persistence during the summer is important to lichens. It is true that water from snowmelt is useful in metabolism (Gannutz, 1967, 1970), but our results do not necessarily indicate that meltwater should be a prime consideration. A snow cover of 1 to 15 inches can moderate the temperatures and light intensities that the lichens beneath it receive (Rudolph, 1966). In addition, there would be sufficient water to carry on active metabolism. These are conditions important for optimal photosynthesis of antarctic lichens (Gannutz, 1967, 1970). Contrary to popular belief, the warm antarctic summer days with high rock surface temperatures are not favorable to lichens but actually detrimental. Rudolph (1966) and Gannutz have found that temperatures approach 100°F on rock surfaces at Cape Hallett and are accompanied by high light intensities. These conditions, in addition to rapid air circulation, dry lichens rapidly, reducing photosynthetic rates considerably. The longer the duration of the snow cover during the summer months, the longer the periods persist which are favorable for lichen metabolism.

Surface erosion, by ice crystals and sand, is also one of the environmental factors necessary for lichen establishment and growth. This is quite common in Antarctica but was not a factor in our study area. Another factor is the presence of a large penguin rookery in the area. Some lichens and many of the antarctic plants can utilize penguin guano or some component thereof (Rudolph, 1967) as a source of some essential nutrients. However, effects of penguin guano on lichen distribution in this study area were limited since the rookery was located on the extreme northern end with the prevailing wind from the south. In addition, guano distribution would tend to be uniform over such a limited area. Microclimatic temperatures and water uptake of lichens have been examined by Rudolph (1966), but the characteristics of the study area indicate that these are not critical for primary lichen establishment. There seem to be some physical factors of greater importance in determining the distribution of lichens here, and among them may be the persistence of snow cover through the summer and the stability of substrate. When these factors exist, other environmental variables must be studied.

ECOPHYSIOLOGY VIA METABOLISM MEASUREMENTS

An effective method to study the immediate responses of plants to their environment is measuring a portion of their metabolism. The most convenient method is to determine photosynthesis and respiration of plants by means of infrared carbon dioxide analysis. The most advantageous feature of measuring the carbon dioxide exchange is that both photosynthesis and respiration rates can be measured simultaneously by examining change in carbon dioxide level in the air of the plant chamber (Fig. 4). The amount of carbon dioxide in the air is determined by infrared absorption and does not necessitate removal of the carbon dioxide from the air. In this manner, plants which are exposed to optimal conditions and thus metabolizing rapidly can be studied, as well as plants which

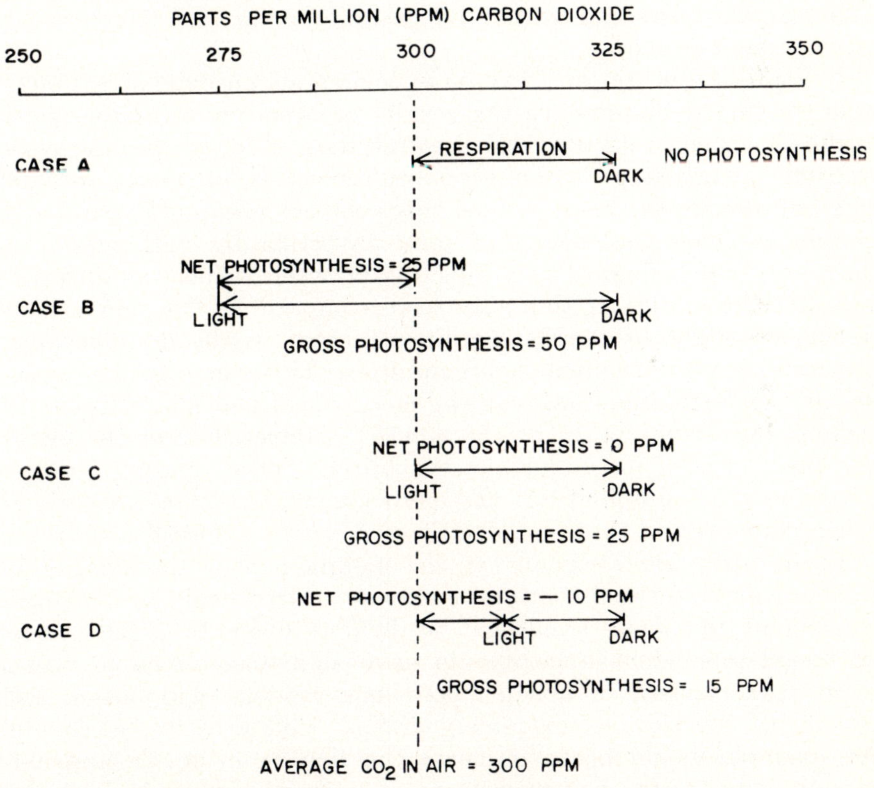

Fig. 4. Measurement of metabolism by measuring the change in carbon dioxide levels around lichens.

are being subjected to environmental stress and are not metabolizing at a rapid rate. Advantages of using this technique are that the plants can be immersed in the same air for several hours, if necessary, without altering the environment to which they are being subjected, and as long a time as necessary can be utilized to achieve significant changes in the carbon dioxide levels.

A major difficulty encountered when working with lichens in this type of study is that the lichens are very specific for the microclimate in which they developed (Brodo, 1962). This is especially true in Antarctica, where lichens are not subjected to drastic seasonal environmental changes which would be brought about by the changes in the state of a more dominant higher plant community. In temperate communities many lichens grow on the ground beneath a higher plant canopy which changes in coverage seasonally. Change in carbon dioxide level as an index of metabolism can be measured while the plants remain in their original environmental niche.

Prior to the initiation of these experiments, an extensive survey was conducted to compare the results of other investigators with results I hoped to derive from these studies. I found the literature extremely confusing. Although many ecologists, physiologists, and microclimatologists have studied this problem (Gannutz, 1967) one cannot compare the results of some investigators with others to determine physiological relationships between lichens in different parts of the world. If this data were comparable, one might have a better insight of the determining factors in the distributional characteristics of the lichen communities. This was a primary reason for undertaking studies in the metabolism and microclimate of lichens in various parts of the world. Antarctica was chosen as the ideal location to undertake the initial studies mainly because of the relative simplicity of the environmental complex, especially when compared to that of a deciduous hardwood forest.

Preliminary examinations of the metabolism of the lichens in a laboratory indicated that any response desired could be obtained, contingent upon the treatment of lichens prior to experiments. Although laboratory experiments have significance, the pretreatment characteristic of lichen metabolism renders distribution and specificity correlations extremely difficult and grossly inaccurate. An example would be to immerse the lichens in water approximately one hour prior to measurement, after they have been stored in a deep-freeze for several months. The warm pretreatment is sufficient to activate the plants and have them demonstrate exaggerated metabolism not normally occurring in the field. Another example of an exaggerated response would be to keep lichens at 20°C in the laboratory for a week and then reduce the temperature to −20°C. Therefore, it was decided that field metabolism experiments of several months' duration, would have to be enacted with measurement of the complete environmental complex. By measuring the complete energy budget of the antarctic environment in one location, the nature of the growth and survival of the antarctic lichens could be determined.

Energy Relationships of the Plant Community

In order to study completely the energy budget of the plant community, several phases of the energy chain have to be examined. The amount of energy bound up in each plant has to be determined first, and this is done by calorimetry. Then the biomass of the standing crop of the plant community and all its components has to be determined. Then the amount of energy which a plant receives from the microclimate has to be determined. Finally, the energy conversion (metabolism) rates for plants have to be determined (Fig. 5). It is possible to do this type of study for a few days, but to achieve the best results, it is necessary to conduct the study over an entire year, examining a plant each season and determining what it is doing at any one time of the year. The total

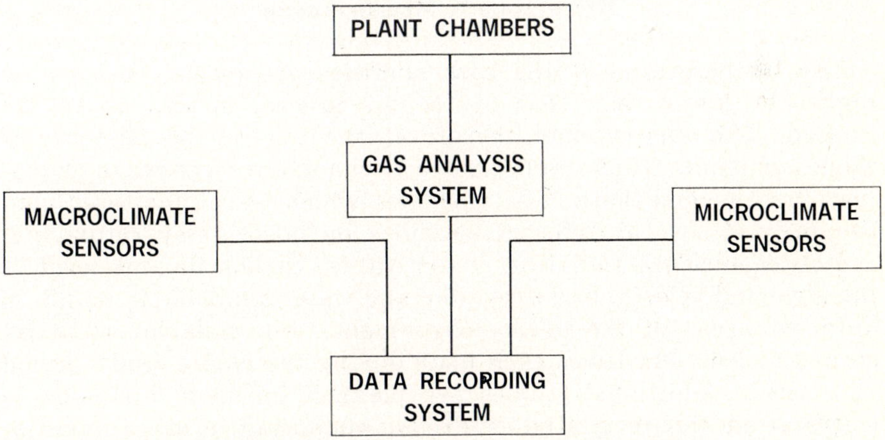

Fig. 5. Block diagram of instrumentation system.

energy balance of the plants and the environment can then be calculated.

This was accomplished during 1968 at Palmer Station and is to be tied in with work that has been completed with the same instrumentation system at Hallett Station, New Zealand, Florida, and Massachusetts. Some of the environmental specificity and the dynamics of the lichen community will be determined by using this method of measurement.

The elaborate measurement system consists of infrared gas analyzers which are linked via tubing and an elaborate switching system to each of 12 metabolism chambers. The air in each of these systems can remain isolated though circulating indefinitely. The air is sampled and the carbon dioxide levels determined at various times, contingent upon the rate of metabolism of plants in the chambers. It is necessary, at times, to allow the plants to remain in the chambers with the air undisturbed for several hours in order to determine their metabolism (closed system). At other times, due to rapid plant carbon dioxide exchange, it is necessary to bring in fresh air continuously (open system) to prevent the levels of carbon dioxide from being too high or low within the chamber. Regardless of the type of system, open or closed, that is used, the exact responses of the plants to their environment can be determined rapidly and easily. This is then correlated to the climatic factors of the environment and many implications of the metabolism of these organisms can be explored.

Microclimatic Measurements

The temperatures of the rock surfaces are often considerably higher or lower than that of the air several meters above the ground. The microclimate, therefore, is critical to the existence of the lower plants which cannot move or change in response to changing climatic conditions. The variables which were monitored continuously at several different locations included: temperature, net radiation, incident radiation, water vapor, carbon dioxide level of the air, wind velocity and direction, and water available to plants in different areas of the microenvironment. All variables were recorded at least six times each hour during the entire study period of a year. Additional studies are planned for long durations to augment shorter-term studies already conducted in other environmental areas by other investigators.

Meteorological Conditions

To compare the microclimate with the meteorological conditions of each area, and to have a direct correlation of microclimatic and metabolic studies, a complete weather station was maintained in each of the study areas. Air temperatures, wind direction, wind speed, barometric pressure, relative humidity, cloud cover, precipitation, water equivalent of the precipitation, water vapor in the air, and carbon dioxide levels were all measured and recorded at the same intervals as the microclimatic variables.

Compilation

When these data are finally recorded, a computer analysis will be made to give the entire energy relationship of the plant community and to determine the important environmental factors affecting the metabolisms of these plants. This data collection and analysis system will provide detailed evidence to substantiate or negate theories on the distributional patterns of the lichen communities in various climatic areas of the world. Examples of the significance and importance of these results have been provided by Gannutz (1967, 1970). The conditions under which the plants carry on their optimal metabolism can be determined and, through microclimatic and meteorological records, the amount of time lichens are subjected to various conditions in the environment can be determined. I have found that the lichens are unique in not being able to survive in an area unless a specific sequence of conditions and combination of environmental variables are present. The problems of lichen distribution are not of dissemination but of the environment. The lichen thallus has a delicate symbiosis, so certain series of conditions combining both environmental stress and optimal conditions for metabolism are necessary to develop and maintain the thallus. For these reasons, it is extremely difficult to transplant the lichens into other areas, even though the transplant sites might be within feet of the area. When one compares the entire lichen communities in some areas of the world with those found in other areas, one finds that, although the lichens can resist environmental extremes and stress for a considerable time, it seriously alters their nature. This is the major drawback to moving the plant specimens into the laboratory and freezing them for several months prior to experimentation. Long-term and complete field studies, considering all possible factors affecting metabolism, are consequently necessary to determine the ecodynamics of lichen communities.

Author's Note: This paper is based on data obtained under grants GA-227, GA-651, and GA-13295, U.S. Antarctic Research Programs, Office of Polar Programs, National Science Foundation.

References

Brodo, L. M., 1962. Transplant experiments with corticolous lichens using a new technique. *Ecology, 42:* 838–842.

Dodge, C. W., 1964. Ecology and geographical distribution of antarctic lichens. In *Biologie Antarctique,* edited by R. Carrick, M. Holdgate, and J. Prevost; pp. 165–171. Hermann, Paris.

Gannutz, T. P., 1968. Effects of chronic gamma irradiation on lichens in the field. *Nuclear Sci. Abstracts, No. 24766, 23* (13) : 2525.

Gannutz, T. P., 1969. Effects of environmental extremes on lichens. *Colloque sur les lichens;* pp. 169–179. Societé Botanique de France, Paris.

Gannutz, T. P., 1970. Photosynthesis and respiration of plants in the Antarctic Peninsula area. *Antarctic J. U. S., 5:* 49–52.

Hale, M. E., 1970. Single-lobe growth-rates patterns in the lichen *Parmelia caperata. Bryologist, 73:* 72–81.

Hawksworth, D. L., 1969. The lichen flora of Derbyshire. *The Lichenologist, 4:* 105–193.

Johnsen, I. N., 1959. Terrestrial cryptogams in a pine woodland with and without litter. *Bryologist, 62:* 35–41.

Lamb, I. M., 1964. Antarctic lichens. I. The genera *Usnea, Ramalina, Himantormia, Alectoria, Cornicularia. Brit. Antarctic Surv. Sci. Rept., 38:* 1–34.

Llano, G. A., 1965. The flora of Antarctica. In *Antarctica, a New Zealand Antarctic Society Survey,* edited by T. Hatherton; pp. 331–350. Methuen, London.

Robinson, H., 1959. Lichen succession in abandoned fields in the piedmont of North Carolina. *Bryologist, 62:* 254–259.

Rudolph, E. D., 1963. Vegetation of Hallett Station area, Victoria Land. *Ecology, 44:* 585–586.

Rudolph, E. D., 1966. Lichen ecology and microclimate studies at Cape Hallett. *Biometeorology, 2:* 900–910.

Rudolph, E. D., 1967. Environmental features: Biotic factors. In *Antarctic Map Folio Series, Folio 5,* edited by V. Bushnell; p. 7. Am. Geograph. Soc., New York.

Blood Proteins and Muscle Enzymes of Cold-Adapted Antarctic Fishes

Robert E. Feeney and David T. Osuga

College of Agricultural and Environmental Sciences, University of California, Davis

The water temperature in McMurdo Sound, Antarctica, is at freezing or near freezing temperature throughout the year. The average temperature is −1.9°C, with variations of no more than 0.1°C (Wohlschlag, 1964). This large area of marine waters at nearly constant and very cold temperature has provided unique opportunities for studying the physiology and biochemistry of cold adaptation. Many of the introductory quantitative measurements were made by Professor Donald E. Wohlschlag, and the work was continued by several of his students. An excellent report on respiratory metabolism and ecological characteristics of some of these fishes has been published by Wohlschlag (1964). Two general advantages of ecological studies of McMurdo Sound fishes adapted to a uniformly cold environment were described as follows:

1. Physical and biological variables associated with influences on diurnal or seasonal cycles can be evaluated in relation to cold adaptation and thermal acclimation, without the confounding effects of temperature on the variables themselves.
2. Unlike most temperate-zone fishes, which are exposed to normal fluctuating thermal conditions, McMurdo Sound fishes need not be physiologically altered for experimental procedures at constant temperatures.

Two students of Wohlschlag, Somero and DeVries (1967), showed that some of these antarctic fishes studied by Wohlschlag were truly cold adapted. The lethal temperature data (Table 1) indicated that all three species studied by Somero and DeVries

Table 1. Median resistance times for three antarctic fishes. Time is given in minutes (1 week = 10,080 minutes). Numbers in parentheses represent numbers of specimens (Adapted from Somero and DeVries, 1967).

Species	Median time of death		
	15°C	10°C	5°C
T. bernacchii	6 (6)	140 (12)	12,960 (6)
T. hansoni	8 (18)	60 (10)	15,840 (6)
T. borchgrevinki	7 (12)	81 (14)	

had a markedly low tolerance to higher temperature. *In vitro* studies of the metabolism of gill tissue of one species, *Trematomus bernacchii,* did not indicate such a sharp sensitivity to temperature (G. N. Somero, unpublished data). But Somero and DeVries (1967) found that brain tissue was sensitive. This sensitivity was expressed as a decrease in oxygen consumption at 5 to 10°C and physical disintegration of the tissue at these temperatures. Somero and co-workers (1968) continued the studies at the tissue metabolism level with *T. bernacchii* and found that the characteristics of the enzyme succinic dehydrogenase in gill tissue were indicative of cold adaptation. The activation energy of this enzyme was markedly low, and the authors considered this as an indication that adaptation to sub-zero temperatures had resulted in the development of highly efficient enzymes in this species. Hochachka and Somero (1968) and Somero and Hochachka (1968) reported evidence for low-temperature adaptation of two muscle enzymes, lactate dehydrogenase (LDH) and pyruvate kinase. They found that the affinity of both enzymes for their respective substrates was highest at the habitat temperatures of the fish. A high affinity of the enzyme for the substrate at physiological concentrations usually results in higher apparent enzyme activity, and hence allows for more efficient functioning.

A related subject of great interest has been the oxygen requirement and metabolism of the antarctic fishes of the family Chaenichthydae (popularly called "bloodless" fishes) which, unlike other vertebrates, lack hemoglobin as well as erythrocytes (Ruud, 1954). The obvious questions are: how do these fishes transport oxygen to the tissues, and do the tissues have a reduced oxygen requirement? The lower requirement might seem necessary because of the reduced availability of oxygen resulting from the lack of a specialized transport substance like hemoglobin. The blood from these hemoglobinless fishes has an oxygen capacity only one-tenth that of blood in fishes with hemoglobin (Ruud, 1954; Scholander and Van Dam, 1957). In contrast to this very low oxygen capacity, however, the metabolism and oxygen utilization in the tissues are as high as in antarctic species with hemoglobin (Ralph and Everson, 1968; Hemmingsen *et al.*, 1969). The problem of how enough oxygen gets to the tissues apparently is not yet solved, but there is an indication that substantial cutaneous respiration may take place and some species of the family have well-vascularized skin and fins (Walvig, 1960).

The blood and blood proteins of antarctic fishes offer as many challenges as do the general problems of metabolism and enzymes of the physically active muscle tissues. One of the more obvious is whether, in cold-adapted fishes, there are any unique constituents in the blood to allow it to function at the low sub-freezing temperatures. Two very important functional differences have been found. One is a rapid clotting of the blood at 0°C. The other concerns the presence and action of a particular substance which lowers the freezing point of the blood (DeVries and Wohlschlag, 1969).

The possibility of the presence of a substance in the blood which lowers the freezing point was raised by Scholander and co-workers (1953). They found that the blood serums of cold arctic fishes had lower freezing points than the blood serums of non-cold-adapted fishes. In extending this work, Scholander's group (Gordon *et al.*, 1962) reported that the serums of these cold-adapted species contained more "nonprotein nitrogen" than did those of non-cold-adapted species and that the difference in freezing-point depression could not be accounted for by any increases in sodium chloride content. There thus appeared to be something in the blood serum which was adaptably produced and which helped to lower the freezing point. DeVries and Wohlschlag (1969) then examined this problem in detail, using three different antarctic species. Measurements of serum freezing points in *T. borchgrevinki, T. hansoni,* and *T. bernacchii* indicated that the reason these fishes do not freeze in the −1.9°C sea water is not because their blood is isosmotic to sea water. Concentrations of sodium chloride, urea, and free amino acids in the serum accounted for only part of the freezing-point depression. Proteins containing carbohydrate were isolated which accounted for 30 percent of the freezing-point depression of the serum. When freezing points of aqueous solutions of the glycoproteins, sodium chloride, or dextrose were measured at several concentrations, the glycoprotein was as efficient at low concentrations as sodium chloride in depressing the freezing point of water. The depression by the glycoprotein was much greater than could be accounted for by its molecular weight. Analyses indicated that only two amino acids, alanine and threonine, were present in the glycoprotein and that the glycoprotein contained 34 to 50 percent carbohydrate. The glycoprotein was soluble in most protein-precipitating agents. No comparisons were possible with the earlier material of Scholander's group, but the solubility of the glycoprotein in protein-precipitating agents indicates that the glycoprotein of DeVries and Wohlschlag (1969) may be similar to the nonprotein nitrogen constituent of Scholander's group (Gordon *et al.*, 1962).

The erythrocytes and their oxygen-hemoglobin equilibriums in several antarctic fishes have been investigated by Grigg (1967). An increase in temperature was found to have a marked effect on the affinity of blood for oxygen. When this effect was compared with data from other fishes, it was found to be extreme in the antarctic species. The magnitude of the effect on the oxygen-hemoglobin equilibrium was assessed with whole blood of *T. bernacchii* and *T. borchgrevinki.* The absolute oxygen capacity of the blood in *T. bernacchii* decreased considerably with absolute temperature. At 5.4°C it became only 70 percent saturated, even at atmospheric pressure. The magnitude of the effect of temperature on the oxygen equilibrium curve was expressed as the change in the partial pressure of oxygen when the whole blood has reached 50 percent saturation (P_{50}) with temperature (Fig. 1). When these were compared with P_{50} values given in the literature for other fishes, it was apparent that the two antarctic forms were much more sensitive to temperature. Unfortunately, further studies of these interesting observations and, more particularly, with purified preparations of the hemoglobin itself, have apparently not been done.

OBJECTIVES AND RESEARCH PROGRAM WITH COLD-ADAPTED ANTARCTIC FISHES

The principal programs in our laboratory are concerned with the relationship of the structure of proteins to their properties and, in particular, to any biological or biochemical function they may have. To achieve these objectives, it is necessary to purify the proteins and to study both the functions and properties of the proteins,

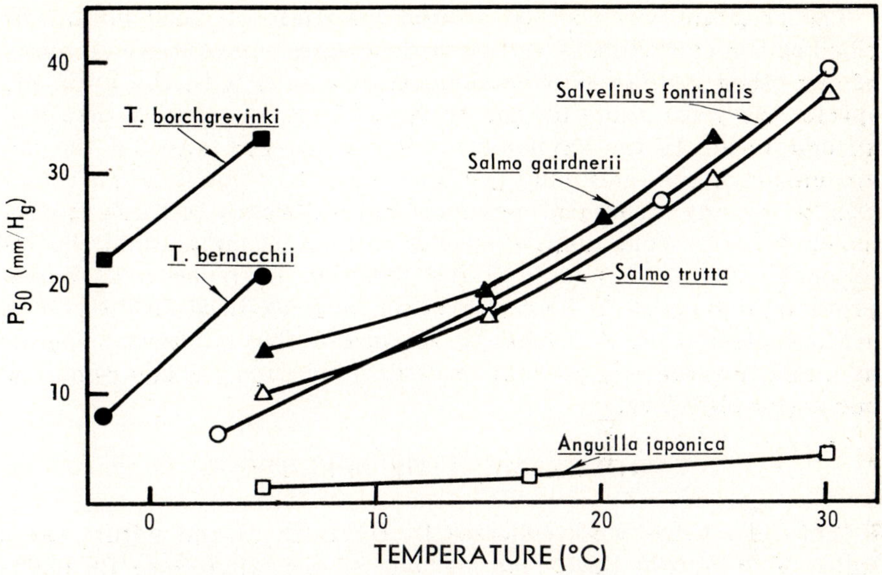

Fig. 1. *T. bernacchii* and *T. borchgrevinki.* Magnitude of change in P_{50} with temperature compared with that in trout (Irving *et al.*, 1941) and *Anguilla japonica* (Kawamoto, 1929) (From Grigg, 1967).

including their physical and chemical structures. One of the main tools that we have used is the comparison of the properties and functions of homologous proteins from different species. In this kind of approach, the hope is that the differences in structure and function of similar proteins from different species will be such that equating these differences will give valuable information on the importance, and even the actual participation, of different parts of the protein molecule in its functions and properties. Sometimes a useful protein for such purposes can be found by examining proteins from closely related species, or from species with no particular difference in adaptation to their environments. Such has been the case with our studies of the egg-white proteins of different avian species (Feeney and Allison, 1969). The extension of this avian egg-white program in 1964 to include the proteins of the Adélie penguin on Ross Island (Feeney *et al.*, 1968) was directly responsible for the program on cold-adapted fishes. After observing the laboratory facilities at McMurdo, and noting the comparative ease with which cold-adapted fishes could be obtained in the nearby McMurdo Sound, we started a program in the antarctic summer of 1965.

The program was planned around the study of blood plasma or blood serum constituents and muscle enzymes. In contrast to many of our other studies with homologous proteins, with the antarctic species we were studying constituents from the species that had an adaptation to the environment which directly affected the environment of the individual protein molecules. Our original intent was to use any structural or functional difference in these macromolecules from cold-adapted species to help us understand the relationship between structure and function of blood and muscle proteins in general. We soon, however, also acquired an interest in cold adaptation *per se,* although the use of these antarctic species as a tool for studying protein structure and function has remained our major objective.

PROCUREMENT OF SPECIMENS

Antarctic fishes were collected in McMurdo Sound within three miles of McMurdo Base. The periods of collection were from October through December or October through January from 1965 to 1969. *T. bernacchii* and several other species were caught in traps through ice holes in fish houses during the first part of the antarctic spring, usually at depths between 250 and 500 meters. Later in the summer, *T. bernacchii* were also caught by hook and line near the shore. *T. borchgrevinki* were all caught by hook and line at the water surface in the ice holes, usually during November. These fishes run in large schools, and as many as 100 may appear in and directly under a fish hole at one time. Usually, large numbers of *T. borchgrevinki* could be lured up to the surface of the water in the fish hole (usually 8 to 10 feet deep) by dangling a large shiny lure 10 to 25 feet below the bottom of the hole and then slowly pulling the lure up into the hole. The fishes, which were 6 to 12 inches long, were then caught on small hooks baited with seal meat.

Dissostichus mawsoni were captured alive from seals who surfaced, carrying the fish, in the fishing holes inside the fish house. They were caught in two of the four years in which an attempt was made to obtain them, always at the end of the antarctic spring. Of the 16 caught in 1966, ten of these were alive and in perfect shape for chemical studies. In 1968, five of the eight caught were also in excellent shape. The *D. mawsoni* varied in length from three to five feet and weighed 35 to 70 lbs. During each of the years when the seals brought up the *D. mawsoni,* the fish hole was visited frequently by the seal several weeks before it began to bring up the large fish. Any seal that appeared in the fish hole early in November was usually discouraged from remaining at the hole by pushing it down into the water with a pole, because at that time the large schools of *T. borchgrevinki* were surfacing in the hole and the small fish were frightened away by the seals. But, as the season progressed, and the schools of *T. borchgrevinki* were disappearing, we were careful to avoid frightening the seals. It seemed that usually only one seal was the primary occupant of a hole and attempts were made to condition the seal to the presence of the fishermen. During the 1966 season, two New Zealand investigators used our facilities to observe our capturing of the *D. mawsoni* from the seals, and have written a more detailed report on this (Calhaem and Christoffel, 1969).

BLOOD AND BLOOD PLASMA PROTEINS

Rates of Blood Clotting

One of the first things we noted in studying the blood of several antarctic fishes was the relatively rapid rate of clotting at or near 0°C. Clotting time was measured by the relatively simple method of coagulation in capillary tubes. This simple procedure facilitated comparisons of rates of clotting in Antarctica, and again at the University of California at Davis, where bloods of other species were available. Human blood from the same individual was used as a control in all determinations and the same experimenter made the determinations both in Antarctica and California. Blood was obtained from the caudal artery of the fishes, the ear of the rabbit, and the finger of the man. Temperatures were controlled by immersing the blood-filled capillary tube in a water bath within a few seconds after the blood was taken. Clotting times were usually based on the first appearance of the thread of the clot when the tubes were broken.

When the clotting times of several species were compared at different temperatures, extensive differences were noted (Fig. 2). Bloods of the two fishes capable of living at or near 0°C, *T. borchgrevinki* and trout, clotted rapidly at low temperature. But they either did not clot, or clotted only very slowly, at higher temperatures at which the bloods of the warm-blooded species, rabbit and man, clotted rapidly. The bloods of carp and sucker (not shown in the figure) had clotting times intermediate between those of the cold-adapted fishes and those of the mammals.

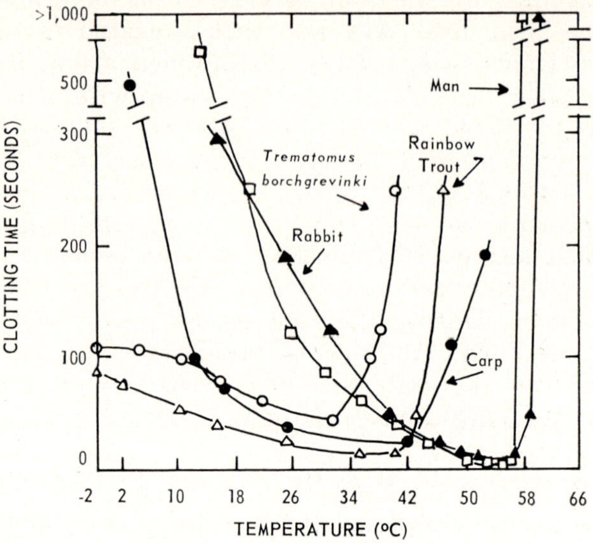

Fig. 2. Effect of temperature on blood clotting times of different species. The clotting times of human blood found in this study compare favorably with those obtained by others. Times of 3 to 5 minutes are reported for room temperature (Tocantins and Kazal, 1964) (From Komatsu *et al.*, 1970b).

A heat-labile constituent required for the clotting mechanism of *T. borchgrevinki* was found. When the blood of this species was quickly warmed to 38°C, incubated at that temperature for 30 seconds, and then incubated at 25°C, no clotting occurred in 6 minutes. The cold-water species thus showed a lability of one or more components when incubated for 30 seconds at 38°C and a rapidity of clotting at low temperatures, neither of which were seen in the warm-blooded species.

General Comparisons of Proteins in Blood Serum

The disc gel electrophoretic patterns of blood serums from several antarctic and non-antarctic species of fishes and of man differ in many respects (Fig. 3a,b). The principal fraction in all instances was apparently the serum albumin. Examination of blood serum from 30 individual *T. borchgrevinki* revealed only one difference. This difference was that the females always had two distinct components near the origin, which were missing from the pattern of males. This constancy of *T. borchgrevinki* serum was not found, however, in *T. bernacchii* (Fig. 3b). The patterns of blood serums from six *D. mawsoni* were all different from one another. Thus, the *T. borchgrevinki* appeared to be a relatively homogeneous and less radiating population than the other two antarctic species. The near identity of the patterns of *T. borchgrevinki* instilled confidence in our use of quick-frozen pooled samples of blood from this species for chemical studies of several problems. In the case of *D. mawsoni*, however, the variation within the species was not a serious problem, because material from one individual provided sufficient material so that pooling of blood or muscle was unnecessary.

The blood serums of *T. borchgrevinki* and *D. mawsoni* were fractionated by ion-exchange chromatography, molecular exclusion (Sephadex filtration), and salt precipitation. With the exception of the freezing-point-depressing glycoproteins, no unique properties which indicated an important adaptation to low temperature were found in the proteins.

The blood serums were also examined for the presence of the serum protein transferrin by radioautography of samples to which ^{59}Fe had been added. This protein binds the metal ion, iron, and serves in vertebrates as the main, or only, iron-transporting agent in the blood. One of its main functions has been considered to be transportation of iron for synthesis of hemoglobin in red blood cells. The transferrin was identified in a blood sample of *Chinodraco kathleenae*, a member of the family Chaenichthydae, the "bloodless" fishes, which contain no hemoglobin. Therefore, at least in this species, the transport of iron for the production of hemoglobin in red blood cells is not a major function of this protein.

Studies on the Freezing-Point-Depressing Glycoprotein

Investigation of the chemical nature of the freezing-point-depressing glycoprotein from antarctic fishes was instituted in our laboratory in 1968 when Dr. A. L. DeVries finished his graduate work at Stanford and joined our laboratory to continue work on the chemistry of this protein. One of the main objectives in our recent activities in Antarctica has been to obtain relatively large quantities of serum and plasma from *T. borchgrevinki* and *D. mawsoni*. These have been employed for preparing the glycoproteins to use in these studies (DeVries *et al.*, 1970; Komatsu *et al.*, 1970a). Active glycoproteins with very similar properties were obtained from both species, indicating close identity in the structures of the antifreeze in the two species.

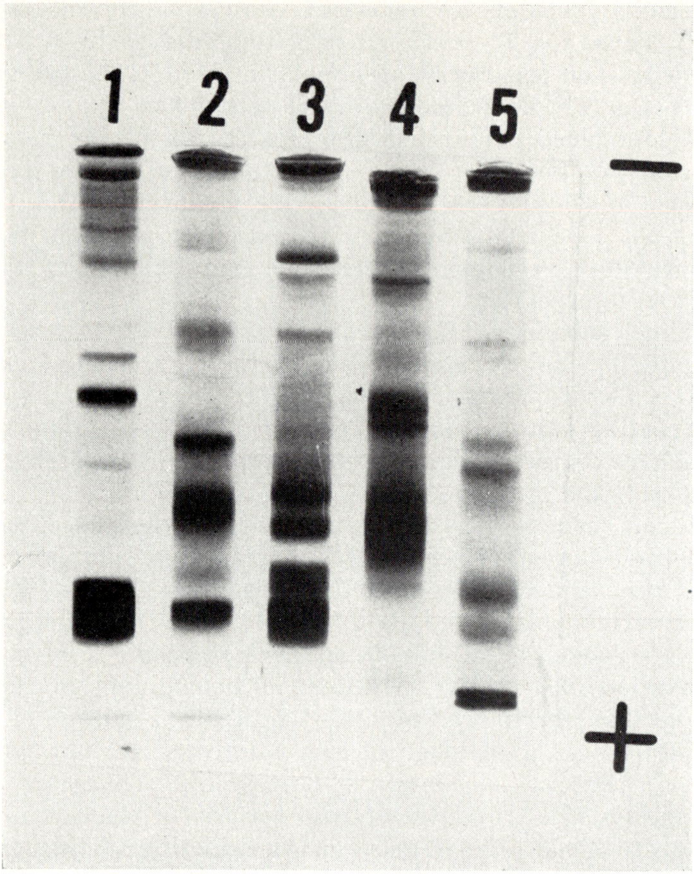

Fig. 3a. Disc electrophoretic patterns of blood sera. (1) Man; (2) king salmon; (3) rainbow trout; (4) *T. borchgrevinki;* (5) *D. mawsoni.* For *D. mawsoni* the most acidic component is the albumin, the next two bands the transferrins, and the freezing-point-depressing glycoproteins appear between the origin and the first band when the gel is stained for carbohydrate (From Komatsu *et al.*, 1970b).

Preparations of freezing-point-depressing glycoprotein were found to exist in groups or families with different molecular sizes. The active glycoproteins were separated into three distinct groups, based on results with ion-exchange chromatography and acrylamide gel electrophoresis. The groups occur in about equal amounts in the blood serums and have closely similar compositions on a weight basis, but differ in molecular weights (10,500, 17,000, and 21,500 g). Physical studies using viscosity, circular dichroism, and dialy-

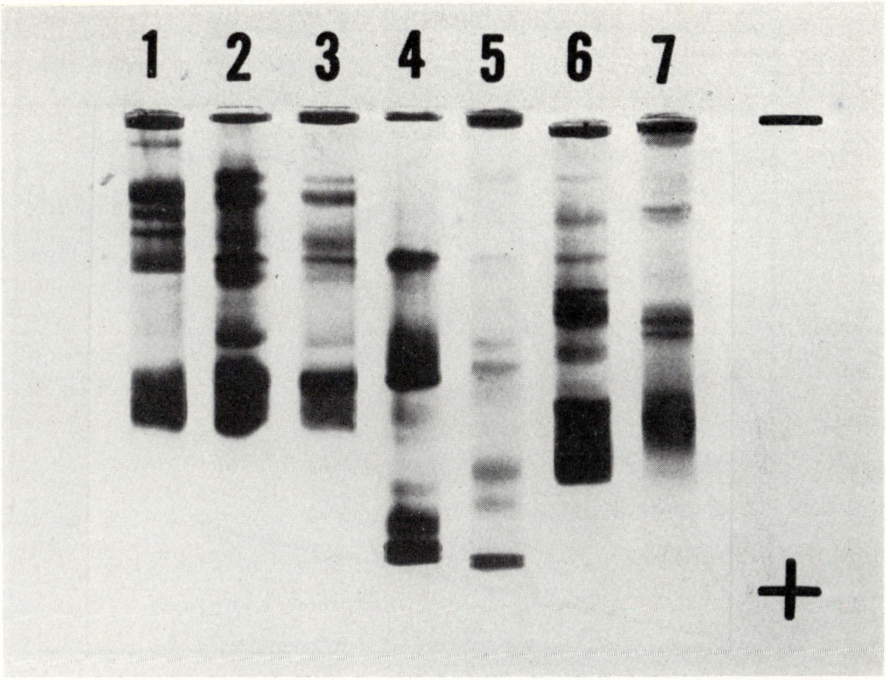

Fig. 3b. Disc electrophoretic patterns of blood sera of antarctic fishes: (1) *Gymnodraco acuticeps;* (2) *T. bernacchii;* (3) *T. bernacchii* (3 spotted); (4) *T. bernacchii* (1 solid spot); (5) *D. mawsoni;* (6) *T. hansoni;* (7) *T. borchgrevinki* (From Komatsu *et al.*, 1970b).

sis rates indicate that the active glycoproteins are expanded molecules, which may have an important bearing on the function. In confirming and extending the previous observations of DeVries and Wohlschlag (1969), DeVries *et al.* (1970) found that the active glycoproteins depressed the freezing point of water many more times (>200×) than two other proteins tested, and that the glycoprotein was even more active than a comparable weight of sodium chloride (Fig. 4). At higher concentrations of the glycoprotein, a saturation phenomenon was observed. Mixtures of the glycoproteins with sodium chloride gave strictly additive effects.

As initially reported by DeVries and Wohlschlag (1969), there are only two amino acids, alanine and threonine, in the glycoprotein. The chemical composition of the active glycoproteins was found to be: threonine (16 percent), alanine (23 percent), N-acetyl galactosamine (29 percent), and galactose (28 percent). The intact structure of the glycoprotein appears to be essential for its

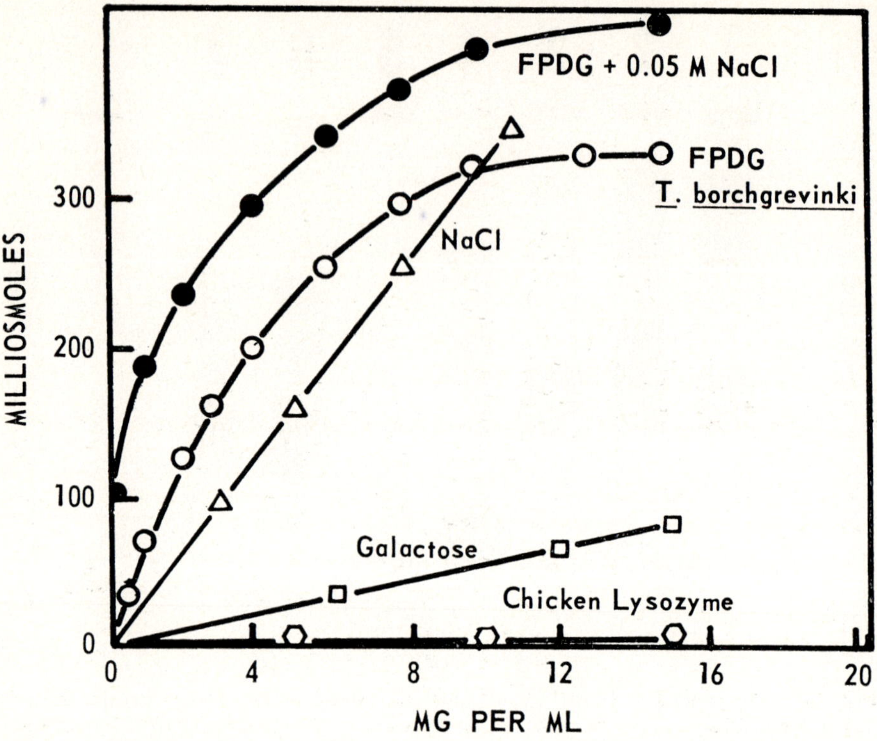

Fig. 4. Freezing points of various solutions compared with freezing-point-depressing glycoprotein (FPDG) from *T. borchgrevinki.* A milliosmolar solution has a freezing point of —0.00186° (From DeVries *et al.,* 1970).

freezing-point-depressing activity (Komatsu *et al.,* 1970a). When only a few peptide bonds were enzymatically cleaved by either the bacterial proteinase subtilisin or a fungal proteinase, the activity was lost. Similarly, modification of the hydroxy groups of the carbohydrate side chain or removal of the carbohydrate from the protein backbone by alkali elimination destroyed the freezing-point-depressing activity. The importance of the hydroxy groups of the carbohydrates was clearly demonstrated by a reversible chemical modification in which an inactive derivative was prepared and then the modifying agent was removed to reform the active glycoprotein. This was accomplished by acetylation of the hydroxy groups and subsequent removal of the 0-acyl groups with hydroxylamine. The carbohydrate exists as disaccharides of galactosyl-N-acetyl galactosamine, and each one of these is joined by a glycosyl linkage to the hydroxy group of each of the threonines in the molecule. Sequential degradation of the peptide structure showed that the amino acid sequence was repeating units of alanine-alanine-threonine to give a total average chain length of fifty amino acid residues (DeVries *et al.*, 1971). The probable structure of the molecule is given in Figure 5.

A poorly understood facet of the problem is the presence of inactive glycoproteins in the blood serum. These inactive glycoproteins appear similar to the active glycoproteins with the exception that they contain an additional amino acid, proline, and appear to be of smaller molecular weight.

STUDIES OF MUSCLE ENZYMES

Five different muscle enzymes have been studied from the tissues of *T. borchgrevinki* and, in some cases, from those of *D. mawsoni*. Five were obtained from the general body musculature and one

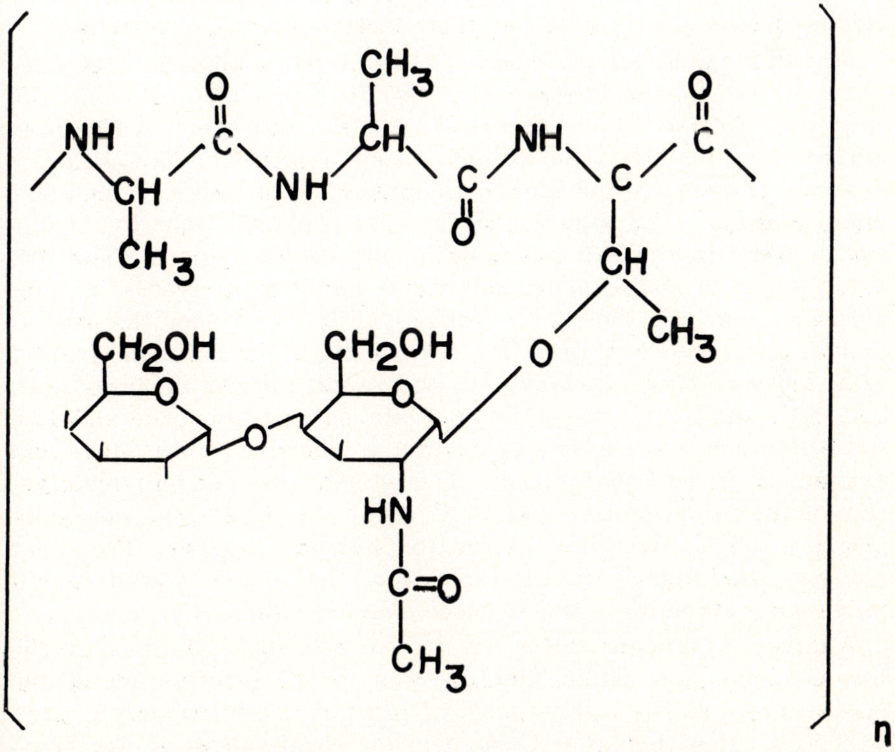

Fig. 5. Presumptive formula for antifreeze (From DeVries *et al.*, 1970).

was from the heart of *T. borchgrevinki.* The five from the general musculature were: fructose-1,6-diphosphate aldolase, glyceraldehyde-3-phosphate dehydrogenase (GAPD), LDH, glycogen phosphorylase, and phosphofructokinase. The heart muscle enzyme was LDH.

Fructose-1,6-Diphosphate Aldolase

Muscle aldolases from *T. borchgrevinki* and *D. mawsoni* were purified by $(NH_4)_2SO_4$ precipitation, by ion-exchange chromatography on DEAE- and CM-cellulose, and by fractionation on Sephadex G-200. Both of the fish aldolases had many properties which were similar to those of the rabbit aldolase. The molecular weights of the aldolases from *T. borchgrevinki, D. mawsoni,* and rabbit were 169,000, 162,000, and 160,000 g, respectively. These values must be considered as nearly identical, because they are within the limits of the sedimentation equilibrium methods. The three aldolases were also similar in their electrophoretic properties.

The amino acid compositions of the two fish aldolases (Table 2) were similar to one another and also to the published value for sturgeon aldolase (Anderson *et al.,* 1969). But the fish aldolases differed significantly from rabbit muscle aldolase in having lower amounts of cysteine and higher amounts of methionine, valine, and phenylalanine. The significance of this comparatively low value for cysteine in the fish aldolases is not yet recognized. The fish aldolases were also considerably more labile to increases in temperature than was the rabbit aldolase (Fig. 6). Under the experimental conditions employed, the temperatures for half inactivation of *T. borchgrevinki, D. mawsoni,* and rabbit muscle aldolases were 29°, 38°, and 55°C, respectively. Data on rainbow trout aldolase were obtained with muscle extracts and compared with data from extracts of *D. mawsoni* muscle. The temperature for half inactivation of the trout aldolase was 44°C, while that of *D. mawsoni* aldolase was 38°C, the same as for the purified enzyme. The trout aldolase was slightly more stable than that of *D. mawsoni,* but much more stable than the *T. borchgrevinki* aldolase.

Another significant difference in the relative stabilities of the fish aldolases and rabbit aldolase was in the inactivation of the enzymes by a sulfhydryl reagent, 5,5′-dithiobis(2-nitrobenzoic acid) (DTNB). Reaction at 0°C led to slow inactivation of the enzymatic activity of the fish aldolases and complete loss occurred when

Table 2. Amino acid composition of aldolases (From Komatsu and Feeney, 1970). Rabbit data, Riordan and Christen (1968); *T. borchgrevinki* and *D. mawsoni* values were the average or best values from duplicate 22-, 48-, and 72-hour hydrolysis in 6*N* HCl at 110°C; except serine, threonine, tyrosine, and CySH which were determined by extrapolation to zero hydrolysis time, and tryptophan which was by the method of Goodwin and Morton (1946); sturgeon data, Anderson *et al.* (1969).

	Aldolases Residues per 160,000 g			
Constituents	Rabbit	*T. borchgrevinki*	*D. mawsoni*	Sturgeon
Aspartic acid	115	106	107	115
Threonine	82	91	94	98
Serine	79	66	67	77
Glutamic acid	152	171	167	152
Proline	88	80	79	69
Glycine	123	108	109	111
Alanine	165	161	164	158
Valine	61	91	85	90
CySH	28	16	15	22
Methionine	13	23	24	22
Isoleucine	57	65	70	81
Leucine	131	117	119	114
Tyrosine	41	46	47	54
Phenylalanine	27	45	46	42
Lysine	105	107	110	121
Histidine	43	44	44	26
Arginine	61	64	64	60
Tryptophan	12	12	10	12

only about nine sulfhydryl groups were reacted (Fig. 7). In contrast, rabbit aldolase retained almost all of its activity after nine of its sulfhydryl groups were reacted. Reaction with the reagent at 25°C caused rapid inactivation of both fish aldolases but not of the rabbit enzyme. Thus, reactions of the fish enzymes and the rabbit enzyme with the sulfhydryl reagent were in agreement with the inactivations by temperature. However, it has not been determined whether the temperature lability is directly due to lability of the sulfhydryls. It appears more than coincidental, however, that the relative inactivations of the two antarctic fish enzymes and the rabbit enzyme are similar by heat and by the sulfhydryl reagent.

The fish and rabbit aldolases also were similar in two other important parameters related to temperature. These were the activa-

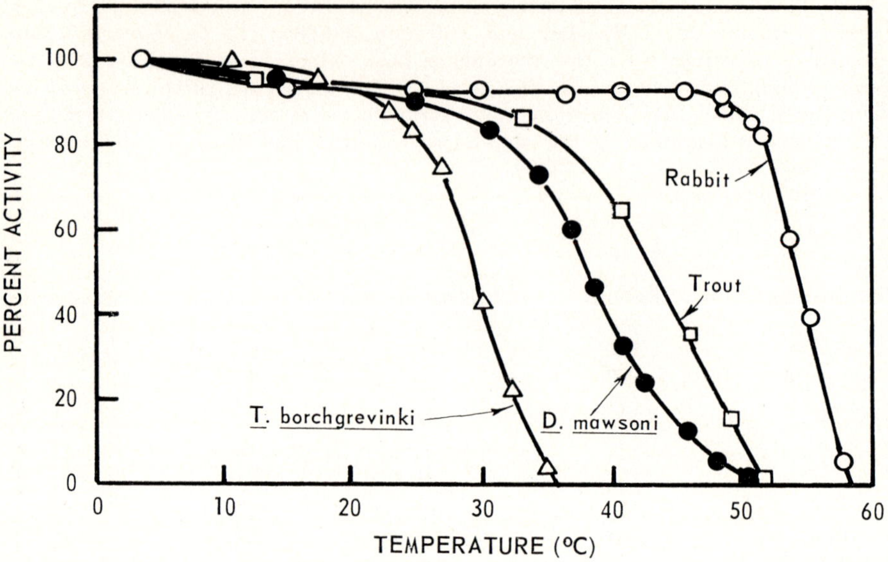

Fig. 6. Temperature stability of different aldolases. Incubations were done at the indicated temperatures for 30 minutes. The buffer used was 0.2 *M* Tris-HCl, 0.002 *M* β-mercaptoethylamine, 0.001 *M* EDTA (pH 6.8). Data were obtained with purified enzymes except with the trout enzyme, which was done with a muscle extract (From Komatsu and Feeney, 1970).

tion energies and the Michaelis constants (K_m). Values for the activation energies of rabbit, *D. mawsoni,* and *T. borchgrevinki* aldolases were 16,800, 15,600, and 15,000 calories per mole, respectively. All three aldolases responded to changes in temperature with small changes in K_m, and there was a probable minimum K_m at about 14°C for all the aldolases under the conditions of the study (Table 3). This latter observation has significant import. Somero and Hochachka (1968) and Hochachka and Somero (1968) showed that pyruvate kinases from *T. bernacchii* and rainbow trout, and LDH from rainbow trout and *T. borchgrevinki* have a minimum K_m at the environmental temperature of the fish. They suggested that this is advantageous for efficient operation at this temperature. This does not, however, seem to be the case insofar as the aldolase is concerned.

Glyceraldehyde-3-Phosphate Dehydrogenase

GAPD was prepared from *D. mawsoni* muscle by a method similar to that used for the preparation of aldolase, but with variations

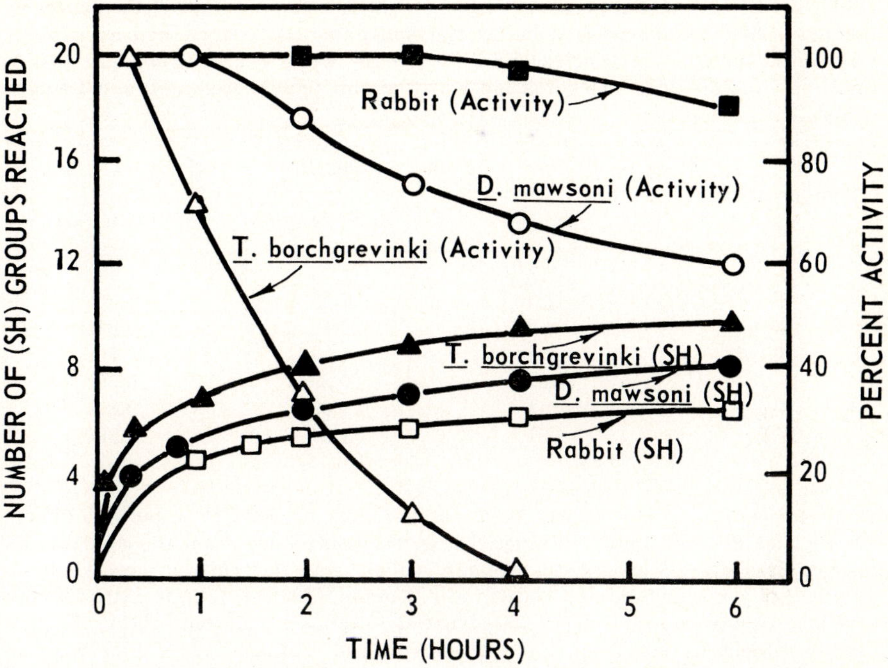

Fig. 7. Reactions of the sulfhydryl groups (SH) of different aldolases with DTNB at 0°C and the concomitant losses of enzymatic activity. Concentrations of aldolase and DTNB were 0.167 mg per ml and 0.067 mM, respectively. Buffer was 0.01 M sodium phosphate (pH 8.0) (From Komatsu and Feeney, 1970).

requisite for GAPD (Greene and Feeney, 1970). The specific activity of the GAPD preparations was similar to that of rabbit muscle GAPD.

In most respects the fish GAPD was found to be similar to rabbit muscle GAPD. The molecular weights for *D. mawsoni* and rabbit GAPD were 142,000 and 145,000 g, respectively. The amino acid compositions of *D. mawsoni* and rabbit GAPD were quite similar (Table 4), in contrast to the differences between the fish and the rabbit aldolases. The fish GAPD had a small, but significant, lower activation energy than did the rabbit GAPD. The values were 14,500 ± 1,700 calories per mole for *D. mawsoni* and 18,100 ± 1,200 calories per mole for rabbit GAPD. The lower activation energy gave the fish GAPD a slightly higher specific activity at 0°C than that of the rabbit, and a relatively lower specific activity at higher temperatures. But the higher activity at lower temperatures was

Table 3. Effect of temperature on the K_m for fructose-1,6-diphosphate by aldolases. The assays were done by the hydrazine-coupled method at pH 6.8. The concentrations of fructose-1,6-diphosphate were varied from 120 μM to 4 mM and the aldolase concentration was 3 μg/ml (From Komatsu and Feeney, 1970).

Temperature °C	K_m (moles/liter) $\times 10^4$		
	Rabbit	*T. borchgrevinki*	*D. mawsoni*
−2	1.8	1.66	1.83
0	2.4	1.45	1.36
4	4.9	2.1	0.835
8	2.1	1.13	0.599
14	0.9	0.89	0.555
21	1.1	1.39	0.800
27.5	2.1	1.5	0.890

Table 4. Approximate amino acid composition of GAPD subunits (From Greene and Feeney, 1970). Values for *D. mawsoni* were from the analysis on 24-hour hydrolysis, except tryptophan which was determined spectrophotometrically by the method of Goodwin and Morton (1946); halibut data, Kaplan (1965); rabbit data, Velick and Furfine (1963); sturgeon data, Kaplan (1965), except CySH which is from Allison and Kaplan (1964); lobster and pig data, Harris and Perham (1968).

	GAPD Residues per 36,250 g					
Constituents	*D. mawsoni*	Halibut	Rabbit	Sturgeon	Lobster	Pig
Aspartic acid	39	44	38	39	32	36
Threonine	21–22	18	24	20	20	22
Serine	19–20	22	21	18	25	19
Glutamic acid	20	23	20	20	24	18
Proline	13–14	13	13	13	12	12
Glycine	30	29	34	29	30	32
Alanine	35–36	32	32	34	32	32
Valine	30–31	32	34	36	38	32
CySH	4	—	4	3	5	4
Methionine	9	9	9	9	10	9
Isoleucine	19	22	18	20	18	19
Leucine	17	19	19	19	18	17
Tyrosine	10	10	9	12	9	9
Phenylalanine	13–14	15	14	14	15	12
Lysine	28	26	26	29	28	25
Histidine	11	13	11	6	5	11
Arginine	11	11	11	11	9	10
Tryptophan	4	4	4	4	3	3

not greater than 30 percent, and insufficient to give an important relative advantage to the fish metabolism at low temperature. However, at higher temperatures, as 37°C, the environmental temperature in the rabbit, there was a pronounced advantage to the activity of the rabbit enzyme, which was over twice that of the fish enzyme at this temperature. The fish and rabbit enzymes also had K_m values of similar magnitude. These were similar in temperature dependence, reflecting the gradual increase with increasing temperatures expected in most association phenomena. Again, these values do not support the suggestion by Hochachka and Somero (1968) and Somero and Hochachka (1968) that enzymes have a minimal K_m at the environmental temperature of the organism.

The rabbit and the *D. mawsoni* GAPD also experienced similar decreases in molecular weight with decreases in concentration (Fig. 8). Hoagland and Teller (1969) have interpreted such results with rabbit GAPD to indicate dissociation equilibrium among subpolymer units. Subunit equilibrium must also be the case with the *D. mawsoni* enzyme. The low temperature dissociation of rabbit GAPD might be interpreted as a reversible inactivation of the enzyme at temperatures much lower than the environmental temperature of the organism, conditions where enzymatic activity is unnecessary. This obviously cannot be the case with the *D. mawsoni* GAPD. It is therefore doubtful that the dissociation of the rabbit GAPD at low temperature is significant in terms of the environmental temperature of the rabbit.

In contrast, *D. mawsoni* GAPD was much less sensitive to ATP in the cold than was rabbit GAPD. Incubation of rabbit GAPD at 0°C in the presence of ATP caused extensive loss of activity, while similar treatment of *D. mawsoni* GAPD was without significant effect. Preliminary results by ultracentrifugation indicated that only the rabbit GAPD was dissociated into subunits by this treatment.

The rabbit and *D. mawsoni* enzymes had nearly identical temperature stability curves (Fig. 9). There thus appears to be no loss of temperature stability in the fish GAPD, which is in contrast to the loss of stability in the fish aldolase.

Lactic Dehydrogenase

LDH was prepared from *D. mawsoni* and *T. borchgrevinki* by modifications of methods used for the above two enzymes (Osuga and Feeney, In preparation). In addition to studies of the purified

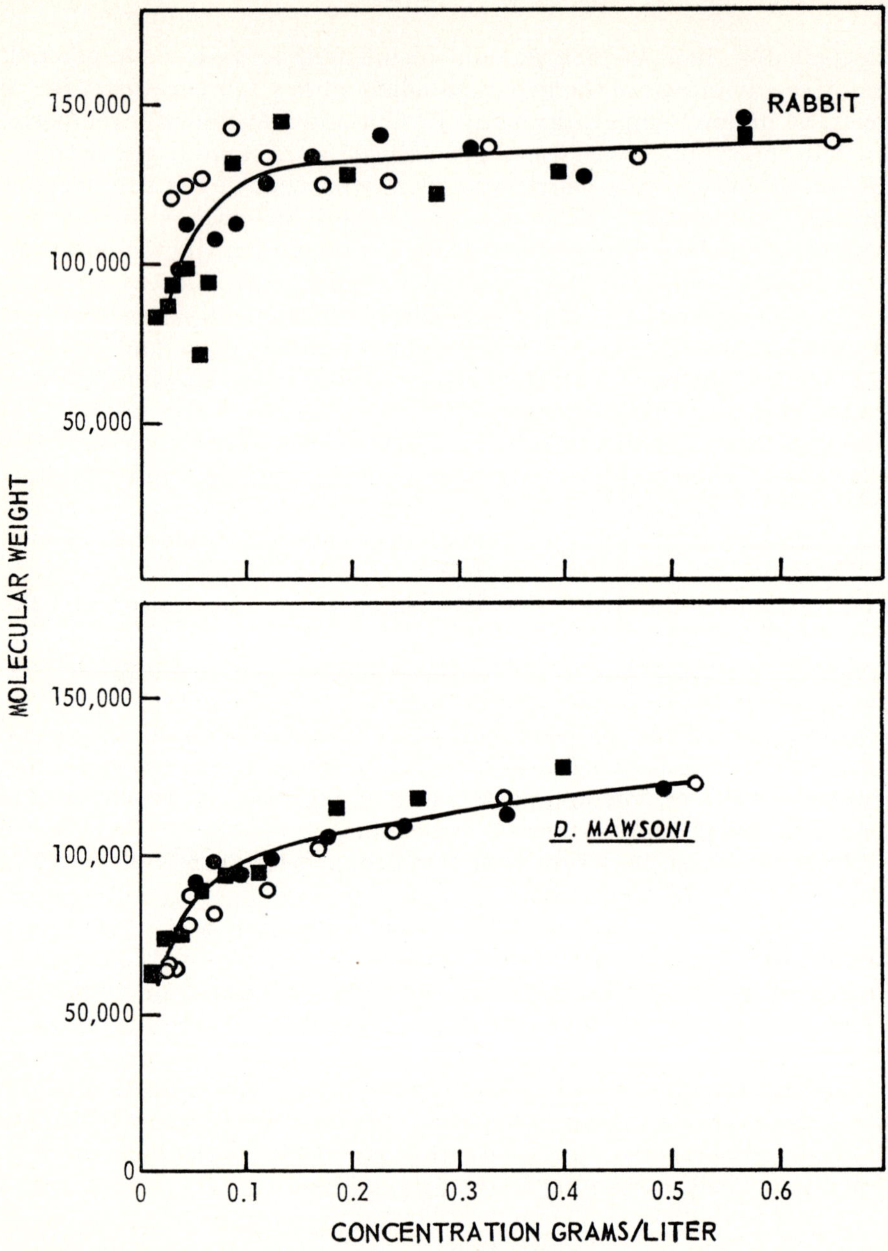

Fig. 8. Concentration dependence of GAPD molecular weight. (Top) Rabbit muscle GAPD with 1.8 NAD^+/mole. (Bottom) *D. mawsoni* muscle GAPD with 1.5 NAD^+/mole. Buffer, 0.1 *M* Tris-0.001*M* EDTA pH 7.0; temperature, 4°. Initial protein concentrations were: (●) 0.75 g/liter; (○) 0.50 g/liter; (■) 0.25 g/liter (From Greene and Feeney, 1970).

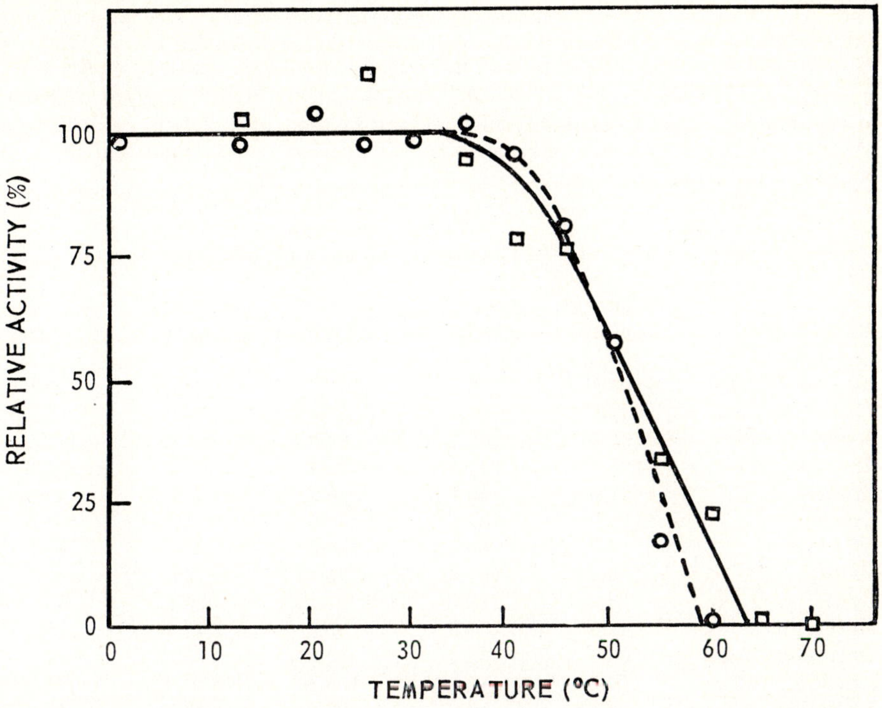

Fig. 9. Heat stability of rabbit and *D. mawsoni* GAPD. 4.5 μg enzyme was incubated for 30 min. at indicated temperature. In the presence of 0.0006 *M* DPN, 0.4 *M* $NaHAsO_4$ (total volume 0.1 ml) immediately cooled to 0°, and assayed at 15°C. (□) Rabbit; (○) *D. mawsoni* (From Greene and Feeney, 1970).

enzyme and the usual assays for enzymatic activities in test tubes, assays of enzymatic activity in various extracts, as well as of purified preparations, were made by the "enzyme staining" of acrylamide and starch gels after electrophoresis of the sample in the gel. Comparisons were made of the properties of the LDH preparations from the antarctic fishes, the king salmon, and the rabbit.

The general physical properties of the muscle LDH from the antarctic fishes were similar to those from the other species. The molecular weights of LDH from *T. borchgrevinki, D. mawsoni,* and rabbit were 135,000, 135,000, and 134,000 g, respectively. In general, the LDH of the antarctic fishes had properties similar to those of LDH from non-cold-adapted species. There appeared to be no particularly advantageous properties of the cold-adapted LDH over the non-cold-adapted LDH. Only small differences in amino acid content were found (Table 5).

Table 5. Amino acid composition of lactic dehydrogenase. Average or best values for *D. mawsoni* and *T. borchgrevinki* from the analysis of 22- and 72-hour hydrolysis at 110°C in 6*N* HCl, except threonine, serine, CySH, and tyrosine which were corrected for destruction during hydrolysis; in addition to tryptophan, which was determined by the method of Goodwin and Morton (1946) (From Osuga and Feeney, In preparation). Halibut, dogfish, and lamprey data taken from Pesce *et al.* (1967).

	Lactic dehydrogenase Residues per 140,000 g				
Constituents	*D. mawsoni*	*T. borchgrevinki*	Halibut	Dogfish	Lamprey
Aspartic acid	108.2	115.8	109.4	132.6	123.8
Threonine	49.6	48.7	59.7	55.9	54.4
Serine	93.1	105.7	94.3	100.9	103.0
Glutamic acid	138.2	141.4	129.3	97.0	114.8
Proline	41.6	40.8	48.7	39.8	49.9
Glycine	108.2	109.4	104.9	94.1	107.5
Alanine	60.3	60.3	65.2	76.4	83.8
Valine	168.4	161.6	135.4	124.2	143.7
CySH	14.6	19.6	—	20.8	—
Methionine	43.5	43.6	50.1	41.4	18.8
Isoleucine	69.0	64.4	54.6	78.5	70.2
Leucine	112.5	115.7	119.8	130.3	133.5
Tyrosine	18.3	19.6	20.8	25.7	23.0
Phenylalanine	22.6	22.7	28.9	25.7	24.5
Lysine	97.4	97.5	110.5	119.7	88.2
Histidine	46.1	42.4	48.9	42.3	40.8
Arginine	30.5	30.2	33.1	29.6	47.4
Tryptophan	33.2	35.7	18	22	—

The starch gel electrophoretic patterns of various muscle extracts from antarctic fishes showed identical patterns on staining for LDH activity. However, LDH from the antarctic fishes differed in one important respect from those of other species. This was the absence of the distinctive differences in electrophoretic patterns of the heart and muscle forms. In the antarctic fishes, they were identical (Fig. 10). Both heart and muscle LDH were present in multiple molecular forms but the patterns from the two sources were similar to one another. All antarctic fishes studied gave similar results. In contrast, there was a distinct difference between the muscle and heart LDH spots of salmon. Thus, as indicated by starch gels, the LDH from the antarctic fishes existed predominantly in one type. This is quite unlike the LDH found in other fishes and higher vertebrates.

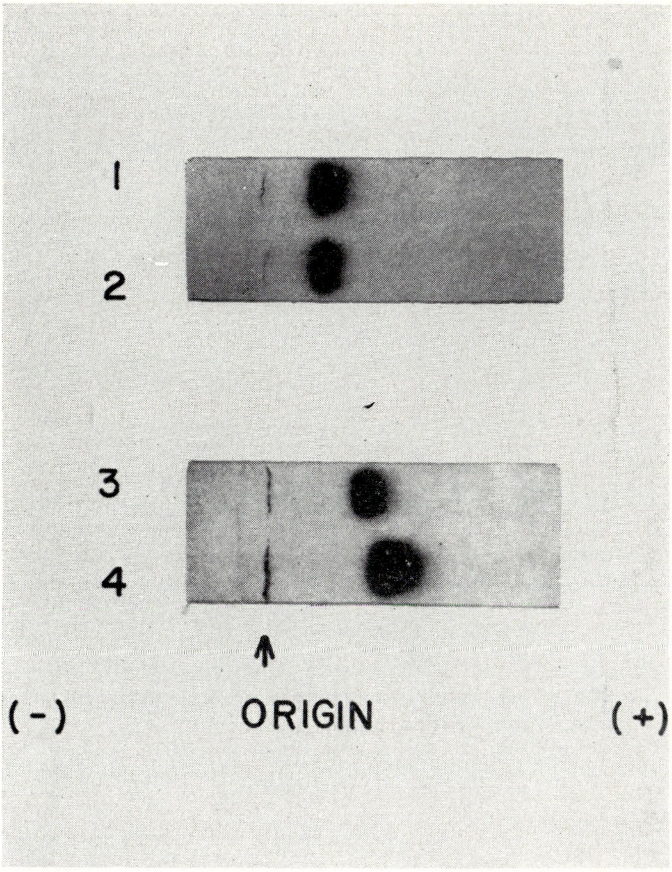

Fig. 10. Starch gel electrophoretic patterns of samples stained for LDH: (1) *T. bernacchii* muscle; (2) *T. bernacchii* heart; (3) salmon muscle; (4) salmon heart (From Osuga and Feeney, In preparation).

Another characteristic of the heart and muscle LDH in these antarctic fishes was unusual. The LDH from the muscle and heart from *D. mawsoni* (Fig. 11) and *T. borchgrevinki* had almost identical inhibitory profiles with changes in pyruvate concentrations. Trout heart was similar to LDH of other vertebrates and was markedly influenced by higher levels of pyruvate.

Temperature stabilities of the heart and muscle LDH of the antarctic fishes also indicated similarities. Rabbit, salmon, and trout had the usual preferential temperature stability of the heart type LDH over the muscle type (Table 6). However, the LDH of carp and sucker, comparatively warm-water fishes, had similar stability

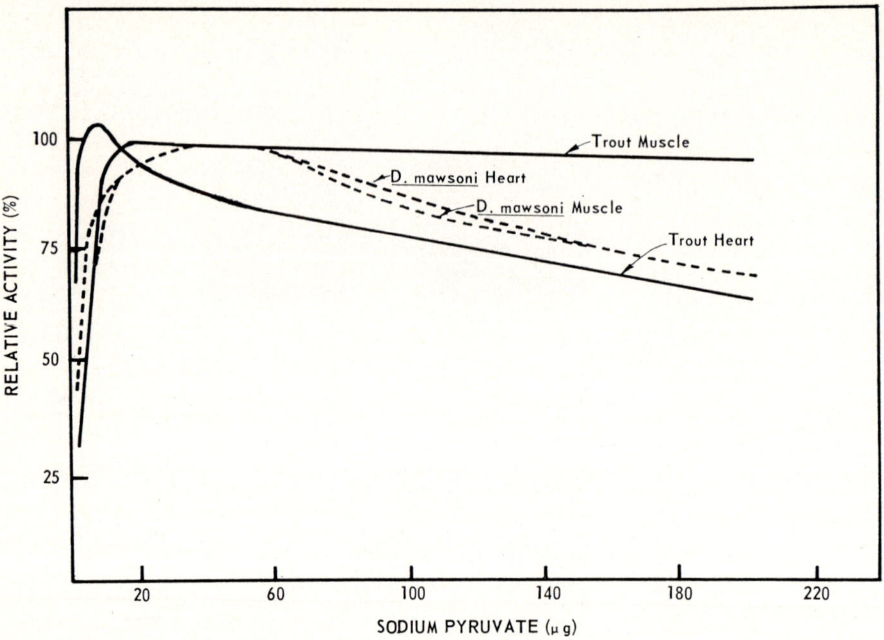

Fig. 11. Relative activity of LDH extracts from trout and *D. mawsoni* muscle and heart at 26°C with varying concentrations of sodium pyruvate (From Osuga and Feeney, In preparation).

Table 6. Temperature stability of LDH. Values are the temperature at which 50 percent of the enzymatic activities were lost after the incubation of the extracts for 20 minutes (From Osuga and Feeney, In preparation).

Extracts	Muscle (°C)	Heart (°C)
Rabbit	51	65
Carp	63	61
Sucker	68	65
Salmon	53	68
Trout	51	70
D. mawsoni	57	58
T. borchgrevinki	50	49

between their respective muscle and heart enzyme like the antarctic fishes.

Bailey and Wilson (1969) have reported that the trout muscle and heart LDH are homologous to the LDH from the respective sources in higher vertebrates. In trout, the heart and muscle LDH have different thermal stabilities, electrophoretic patterns, and differential sensitivity to pyruvate concentration. Thus it appears as though the LDH from the heart and muscle of antarctic fishes is unique in having several very similar properties.

Phosphofructokinase

Phosphofructokinase was extracted from fresh *T. borchgrevinki* muscle and studies made of its lability to temperature. In these crude extracts, the phosphofructokinase showed no unusual temperature lability or substrate affinity (F. C. Greene and R. E. Feeney, unpublished data).

Glycogen Phosphorylase

Studies on this enzyme were begun in 1968 in cooperation with Dr. Jerry L. Hedrick, and are not complete as yet (Osuga *et al.*, In preparation). The enzyme exists both as phosphorylase *a* and phosphorylase *b*, as it does in other species.

The pH optima of the enzymes from *D. mawsoni, T. borchgrevinki*, rabbit, trout, and salmon were essentially identical, approximately 6.5, and their Arrhenius plots were very similar. All appeared to have a higher activation energy value at an approximate temperature range of from 2° to 15°C and a somewhat lower value from 15° to 30°C.

Temperature stabilities of the enzymes were studied by incubating the samples for 20 minutes at various temperatures and assaying them. The temperature at which 50 percent of the enzymatic activity was lost indicated no striking differences, ranging from 42° to 48°C.

The various phosphorylases migrated differently in disc gel electrophoresis, indicating that they all had a different net charge. This difference was also noted during chromatography. Using different gel concentrations in the manner described by Hedrick and Smith (1968), the plot of the log of the migration rates of the samples to that of the gel concentrations produced almost parallel lines. Thus the size of the enzymes was similar. Similarities in size were also found by Sephadex G-200 separations and analytical ultracentrifugation experiments.

Kent *et al.* (1958) studied the effect of temperature on the dimerization of rabbit phosphorylase *b*. They found that the enzyme aggregated at lower temperatures, approximately 80 percent at 20°C. Salmon phosphorylase had some aggregated components at 20°C, whereas *D. mawsoni* and trout did not indicate the presence of any aggregation at 20°C.

DISCUSSION AND SUMMARY

In considering the effect of temperature on biological reactions, it is first necessary to remember that biological reactions are restricted to the temperatures at which water is a liquid and that this is a small fraction of the absolute temperature scale as compared to most chemical reactions. When the problem is viewed on this basis, it is apparent that the internal environmental temperature of most homeothermic animals (310°A) is not very much higher than the internal temperature of poikilothermic animals in ice water (271–273°A). A general discussion of the effects of temperature on biochemical mechanisms has been given by Precht *et al.* (1955).

The question that is usually asked is how poikilothermic organisms are able to grow at low temperatures. Ingraham and Maaloe (1967), however, have obtained data with microorganisms suggesting that the more appropriate question is why non-poikilotherms are not able to grow at low temperatures. These authors found that a cold-sensitive mutant of *E. coli* was sensitive to feedback inhibition (allosteric control) in the cold. The amount of inhibition was greater at lower temperatures. In other words, in many cases the problem may resolve itself into a question of efficiency of function at the environmental temperature of the organism. There may be, of course, drastic differences in the properties of enzymes at different temperatures. There may be loss of the structure (denaturation) of enzyme molecules from a cold-adapted organism at temperatures well below where the enzymes from warm-blooded mammalian species are not affected. Enzymes are large complex molecules and may undergo large structural changes over rather narrow temperature ranges and hence will have very high activation energies over these ranges. A short discussion of these phenomena has been recently presented (Feeney, 1970).

The studies of our laboratory on the blood constituents have concerned two elements of the blood, both of which show biochemical cold adaptation. One, the blood-clotting mechanism, has two different characteristics related to cold adaptation: (1) high efficiency of function at low temperature, and (2) lability at higher temperatures. The other biochemical adaptation is the presence of the "antifreeze protein," the freezing-point-depressing glycoprotein of DeVries and Wohlschlag (1969), in the serum of the antarctic fish living in icy waters. The antifreeze protein is a result of adaptation to living in icy waters and not an adaptation in the usual sense of a constituent functioning at different temperatures. It is thus a very special case of molecular adaptation.

The physical chemical mechanism whereby the antifreeze protein lowers the freezing point is one of the most provocative questions yet unanswered. Proteins are recognized to have a variety of quite different functions such as catalytic (enzymes), structural (skin and tendons), transport (hemoglobin), permeases (cell membrane proteins), and messenger control (hormones). The antifreeze protein may be a new type of classification. Since it does not have the general properties of a substance affecting water by colligative action, the physical mechanism whereby the freezing point of water is depressed could be a kinetic process rather than a thermodynamic one. The antifreeze protein may therefore function as an inhibitor of ice crystal formation by direct action on microcrystals or on the structure of water so that its crystallization temperature is lowered.

In considering cold adaptation at the molecular level, the two among several possibilities (Feeney, 1970) are that there are novel enzyme systems; or that the enzymes in tissues would not be unusual or novel ones, but the tissue would have a much higher catalytic activity than corresponding tissues of non-cold-adapted species. This greatly increased activity in the cold-adapted species could be accomplished in several ways:

1. There could simply be many more individual molecules of each enzyme in the tissues, i.e., a higher level of enzymes. This does not seem to be the case from our studies.
2. The enzymes could be "hyperactive" enzymes, although not possessing any particular novel structures. Our studies would indicate that some of the enzymes may be slightly more active (as much as twice) but this does not seem to be the general rule.

3. The enzymes are similar in most respects to those found in non-cold-adapted species but are controlled in such a way that they function at a rate satisfactory for the requirements of the organism.

In some cases, a lowered activity as compared to the activity found in warm tissues might be satisfactory to the organism. In other cases there might be an overall increased activity caused by special activators or the absence of inhibitory effects (allosteric effects). Our results would seem to support this last category. The antarctic fish glyceraldehyde-3-phosphate dehydrogenase and ATP relationships show a definite resistance of the enzyme to inhibition and loss of activity at low temperatures.

The study of five different enzymes involved in the metabolism, however, indicates that the enzymes usually show significant differences from their counterparts in warm-blooded species, but that there is no characteristic difference common to all. In some cases, there is a general physical-chemical property which is in favor of low temperature function. One of these is the decrease in K_m at low temperature which should favor enzyme catalytic efficiency at substrate concentrations found in tissues and at low temperatures. This, however, is a general property common to most enzymes from both poikilotherms and warm-blooded species, and our studies have not shown any special adaptation in this property, although, of course, some instances might occur. A decrease in K_m with lowering of the temperature was reported for the enzyme formyltetrahydrofolate synthetase from the bacterium, *Clostridium cylindrosporum* (Himes and Wilder, 1968) and for two enzymes from fish, lactate dehydrogenase and pyruvate kinase (Hochachka and Somero, 1968; Somero and Hochachka, 1968). The observations of Somero and Hochachka (1968), however, showing that the K_m of an enzyme was lowest at the environmental temperature of the fish, probably should be reexamined with purified enzymes.

One generality can be drawn from our studies. In every instance when there is a difference in the effect of temperature on the properties of the enzyme from cold *versus* warm species, the difference is in agreement with properties that might be expected for an enzyme which must function at low temperatures but not at higher temperatures.

Authors' Notes: The authors appreciate the advice and assistance of Mrs. Kathy Else, Dr. F. C. Greene, Dr. S. K. Komatsu, and

Mrs. Judith Tweedie and helpful criticisms from Dr. Allan C. Wilson. The researches were supported, in part, by Grant GA-12607 under the United States Antarctic Research Program, Office of Polar Programs, National Science Foundation.

References

Allison, W. S., and N. O. Kaplan, 1964. Effect of tetrathionate on the stability and immunological properties of muscle triosephosphate dehydrogenases. *Biochemistry, 3:* 1792–1800.

Anderson, P. J., I. Gibbons, and R. N. Perham, 1969. A comparative study of the structure of muscle fructose 1,6-diphosphate aldolases. *European J. Biochem., 11:* 503–509.

Bailey, G. S., and A. C. Wilson, 1969. Homologies between isoenzymes of fishes and those of higher vertebrates. *J. Biol. Chem., 243:* 5843–5853.

Calhaem, I., and D. A. Christoffel, 1969. Some observations of the feeding habits of a Weddell seal, and measurements of its prey, *Dissostichus mawsoni,* at McMurdo Sound, Antarctica. *New Zealand J. Marine Fresh Water Res., 3:* 181–190.

DeVries, A. L., S. K. Komatsu, and R. E. Feeney, 1970. Chemical and physical properties of freezing-point-depressing glycoproteins from antarctic fishes. *J. Biol. Chem., 245:* 2901–2908.

DeVries, A. L., J. Vandenheede, and R. E. Feeney, 1971. Primary structure of freezing-point-depressing glycoproteins from antarctic fishes. *J. Biol. Chem., 245:* pp. not available.

DeVries, A. L., and D. E. Wohlschlag, 1969. Freezing resistance in some antarctic fishes. *Science, 163:* 1073–1075.

Feeney, R. E., 1970. Biochemistry of proteins and enzymes of antarctic fish. In *Antarctic Ecology,* edited by M. W. Holdgate; vol. 1, pp. 344–351. Academic Press, New York.

Feeney, R. E., and R. G. Allison, 1969. *Evolutionary Biochemistry of Proteins. Homologous and Analogous Proteins from Avian Egg Whites, Blood Sera, Milk and Other Substances.* Wiley-Interscience, New York.

Feeney, R. E., R. G. Allison, D. T. Osuga, J. C. Bigler, and H. T. Miller, 1968. Biochemistry of the Adelie penguin: Studies on egg and blood serum proteins. In *Antarctic Research Series 12, Antarctic Bird Studies,* edited by O. L. Austin, Jr.; pp. 151–165. Am. Geophys. Union, Washington, D.C.

Goodwin, T. W., and R. A. Morton, 1946. The spectrophotometric determination of tyrosine and tryptophan in proteins. *Biochem. J., 40:* 628–632.

Gordon, M. S., B. H. Amdur, and P. F. Scholander, 1962. Freezing resistance in some northern fishes. *Biol. Bull., 122:* 52–62.

Greene, F. C., and R. E. Feeney, 1970. Properties of muscle glyceraldehyde-3-phosphate dehydrogenase from the cold-adapted antarctic fish *Dissostichus mawsoni. Biochim. Biophys. Acta, 220:* 430–442.

Grigg, G. C., 1967. Some respiratory properties of the blood of four species of antarctic fishes. *Comp. Biochem. Physiol., 23:* 139–148.

Harris, J. I., and R. N. Perham, 1968. Glyceraldehyde-3-phosphate dehydrogenase from pig muscle. *Nature, 219:* 1025–1028.

Hedrick, J. L., and A. J. Smith, 1968. Size and charge isomer separation and estimation of molecular weights of proteins by disc gel electrophoresis. *Arch. Biochem. Biophys., 126:* 155–164.

Hemmingsen, E. A., E. L. Douglas, and G. C. Grigg, 1969. Oxygen consumption in an antarctic hemoglobin-free fish, *Pagetopsis macropterus,* and in three species of *Notothenia. Comp. Biochim. Physiol., 29:* 467–470.

Himes, R. H., and T. Wilder, 1968. Formyltetrahydrofolate synthetase. Effect of pH and temperature on the reaction. *Arch. Biochem. Biophys., 124:* 230–237.

Hoagland, V. D., Jr. and D. C. Teller, 1969. Influences of substrates on the dissociation of rabbit muscle D-glyceraldehyde-3-phosphate dehydrogenase. *Biochemistry, 8:* 594–602.

Hochachka, P. W., and G. N. Somero, 1968. The adaptation of enzymes to temperature. *Comp. Biochem. Physiol., 27:* 659–668.

Ingraham, J. L., and O. Maaloe, 1967. Cold sensitive mutants and the minimum temperature of growth of bacteria. In *Molecular Mechanisms of Temperature Adaptation,* edited by C. L. Prosser; pp. 297–309. Am. Assoc. Advan. Sci., Washington, D.C.

Irving, L., E. C. Black, and V. Safford, 1941. The influence of temperature on the combination of oxygen with the blood of trout. *Biol. Bull., 80:* 1–17.

Kaplan, N. O., 1965. Evolution of dehydrogenases. In *Evolving Genes and Proteins,* edited by V. Bryson and H. J. Vogel; pp. 243–277. Academic Press, New York.

Kawamoto, N., 1929. Physiological studies on the eel. II. The influence of temperature and of relative volume of the red corpuscles and plasma upon the haemoglobin dissociation curve. *Tohiuku Univ. Sci. Rep. Biology, 4:* 643–659.

Kent, A. B., E. G. Krebs, and E. H. Fischer, 1958. Properties of crystalline phosphorylase b. *J. Biol. Chem., 232:* 549–558.

Komatsu, S. K., and R. E. Feeney, 1970. A heat labile aldolase from cold-adapted antarctic fishes. *Biochim. Biophys. Acta, 206:* 305–315.

Komatsu, S. K., A. L. DeVries, and R. E. Feeney, 1970a. Studies of the structure of freezing-point-depressing glycoproteins from an antarctic fish. *J. Biol. Chem., 245:* 2909–2913.

Komatsu, S. K., H. T. Miller, A. L. DeVries, D. T. Osuga, and R. E. Feeney, 1970b. Blood plasma proteins of cold-adapted antarctic fishes. *Comp. Biochem. Physiol., 32:* 519–527.

Pesce, A., T. P. Fondy, F. Stolzenbach, F. Castillo, and N. O. Kaplan, 1967. The comparative enzymology of lactic dehydrogenases. *J. Biol. Chem., 242:* 2151–2167.

Precht, H., J. Christophersen, and H. Hensel, 1955. *Temperatur und Leben.* Springer-Verlag, Berlin.

Ralph, R., and I. Everson, 1968. The respiratory metabolism of some antarctic fish. *Comp. Biochem. Physiol., 27:* 299–307.

Riordan, J. F., and P. Christen, 1968. Reaction of tetranitromethane with protein sulfhydryl groups. Inactivation of aldolase. *Biochemistry, 7:* 1525–1530.

Ruud, J. T., 1954. Vertebrates without erythrocytes and blood pigment. *Nature, 173:* 848–850.

Scholander, P. F., W. Flagg, V. Walters, and L. Irving, 1953. Climatic adaptation in arctic and tropical poikilotherms. *Physiol. Zool., 26:* 67–92.

Scholander, P. F., and L. Van Dam, 1957. The concentration of hemoglobin in some cold-water arctic fishes. *J. Cell. Comp. Physiol., 49:* 1–4.

Somero, G. N., and A. L. DeVries, 1967. Temperature tolerance of some antarctic fishes. *Science, 156:* 257–258.

Somero, G. N., A. C. Giese, and D. E. Wohlschlag, 1968. Cold adaptation of the antarctic fish *Trematomus bernacchii. Comp. Biochem. Physiol., 26:* 223–233.

Somero, G. N., and P. W. Hochachka, 1968. The effect of temperature on catalytic and regulatory functions of pyruvate kinases of the rainbow trout and the antarctic fish *Trematomus bernacchii. Biochem. J., 110:* 395–400.

Tocantins, L. M., and L. A. Kazal, 1964. *Blood Coagulation, Hemorrhage, and Thrombosis.* Gruen and Stratton, New York.

Velick, S. F., and C. Furfine, 1963. Glyceraldehyde 3-phosphate dehydrogenase. In *The Enzymes,* edited by P. D. Boyer, H. Lardy, and K. Myrback; vol. 7, 2nd edition, pp. 243–273. Academic Press, New York.

Walvig, F., 1960. The integument of the ice fish, *Chaenocethalus aceratus* (Lönnberg). *Nytt Mag. Zool., 9:* 31–36.

Wohlschlag, D. E., 1964. Respiratory metabolism and ecological characteristics of some fishes in McMurdo Sound, Antarctica. In *Antarctic Research Series 1, Biology of the Antarctic Seas,* edited by M. O. Lee; pp. 33–62. Am. Geophys. Union, Washington, D.C.

Behavior of Antarctic Penguins and Seals

DIETLAND MÜLLER-SCHWARZE
Department of Wildlife Resources, Utah State University, Logan

This paper reviews primarily the progress made during post-1964 studies of the behavior of antarctic penguins and seals. The basic breeding cycle and the more conspicuous displays of Adélie penguins *(Pygoscelis adeliae)* have been decribed by Sladen (1958) and Sapin-Jaloustre (1960), while those of the emperor penguin *(Aptenodytes forsteri)* were reported by Wilson (1907), Stonehouse (1952, 1953), and Prévost (1961).

THE BASIC BREEDING CYCLE AND BEHAVIOR OF ANTARCTIC PENGUINS

Adélie Penguins

Adélie penguins start to arrive at their rookeries on the coasts and offshore islands of Antarctica in mid-October. The males immediately start to display (ecstatic display) and to collect stones for their nests, and upon arrival of the females pairs are formed. The two eggs are laid by early November. After egg-laying the female leaves the rookery for the ocean, and the male incubates for two weeks. Including the prelaying courtship phase the male then has been ashore and without food for five weeks.

Upon the female's return she incubates for another two weeks while the male goes off to seek food. After his return the male again takes over incubation duties for a few days until the chicks hatch (Fig. 1).

Once the chicks are hatched, nest reliefs are more frequent, first occurring every two days and then every day after the chicks are about a week old (Penney, 1968). The parents start to leave the chicks when they reach the age of about three weeks. During this period the chicks stay together in "crèches". At Hallett, the author observed the first hatched chick on December 5, and the first crèche

Fig. 1. Adélie penguin on nest with eggs, snowed in during a severe blizzard.

on December 27. On December 30, each crèche included up to 12 or 13 chicks; on December 31, the numbers were 16 to 20 chicks per crèche.

On January 9 the chicks started to molt into their waterproof plumage with a white belly and dark back. The chicks do not have the black throat and white eye-ring of the adults. The first fully molted chick was observed on January 23, and by February 3 the exodus of birds from the colony had reached its climax. The young swim and drift on ice flows northward, largely independent of the adults. The birds then spend approximately eight months at sea and in the pack ice, awaiting the next breeding season.

Emperor Penguins

The emperor penguin holds several records among the birds: it breeds under the most adverse conditions on earth, during the polar night with its furious blizzards and temperatures reaching −60°C. The males of this species also incubate the single egg without interruption for two months. With the preceding courtship phase this means that the males go without food for three or four months. Finally, there is no phase in the life cycle of these birds that requires solid land, not even for reproduction.

According to Prévos (1961), in colonies at 66–67°S, the birds arrive in March and April at their breeding site on the sea ice. Courtship takes place from March through May. The egg is laid in May; the male incubates for two months, and the females start to return at the end of June. The chicks begin to hatch during the first days of July. Nine weeks later, early in September, the chicks are gathering in crèches. In late December, after about ten months, the ice of the colony breaks up, and old and young birds leave the breeding site.

At the extremely southern rookery at Cape Crozier (77°29′S), the birds arrive in May and all phases of the breeding cycle are delayed by about one month relative to the more northerly populations. At Cape Crozier, the coldest months are July (average temperature −27°C in 1902) and August (average temperature −29.5°C in 1903). The average minimum temperature for August, 1902, was −44.5° and for July, 1903, −48.4°C (Prévost, 1961). This means that the chicks hatch during the most extreme conditions any bird is known to experience. It has not been determined yet at what age the emperor penguin starts to reproduce. Among Adélie penguins observed in 1970, only 8 percent of the 3-year-old birds bred, 57 percent of the 5-year-olds, 86 percent of the 7-year-olds, and all (5) of the 8-year-olds (Wood *et al.*, 1970).

BEHAVIOR IN RELATION TO THE PHYSICAL ENVIRONMENT

Behavior in Relation to Space

In 1964 Emlen and Penney reported results of distance navigation experiments involving Adélie penguins. Male penguins were taken from rookeries at Cape Crozier and Cape Hallett. These birds were released on featureless ice plains on the Ross Ice Shelf near Byrd Station in Marie Byrd Land, and on the Victoria Land plateau. The birds headed in a general NNE direction, but not toward their home rookery. The birds showed directional but not goal orientation. They used the sun as an orientation cue; when the sun was obscured, the direction orientation broke down. Although the penguins compensated for the movement of 15° per hour by the sun, they did not correct for the variation in sun azimuth speed due to the tilt of the earth's axis.

In further experiments (Penney and Emlen, 1967) Adélie penguins were released at the South Pole and on offshore pack ice. Again, the departure direction was NNE, meaning that the birds in the pack ice would travel away from the coast and their rookery. Juveniles also headed NNE.

Penney and Riker (1969) brought Adélie penguins from Cape Crozier to the Northern Hemisphere and released them on partially snow-covered fields in South Dakota. The same birds were released twice within an interval of several hours. While compensating for the 15° per hour movement of the sun, these penguins were actually deviating 30 degrees per hour from their chosen direction because in North Dakota the sun "moves" in the opposite direction to what it does at Cape Crozier.

Behavior in Relation to Time

At Hallett Station Müller-Schwarze (1968) observed the behavior of Adélie penguins throughout 24-hour cycles at different times of the breeding season. The observations indicated 24-hour cycles of intensity for most of the behavior patterns examined. The fluctuations correlated with a light intensity amplitude between 300 lux at midnight and 60,000 lux at noon during midsummer.

At the start of the incubation period the following activities were observed: turning eggs over, preening, gathering pebbles, walking, nest building, vocalizing, and courtship displays. After the hatching of the chicks in mid-December, notations were made of the number of adults walking over the sea ice in search of food, and after the breaking up of the ice, the numbers of birds swimming out for food were recorded. The activities of the chicks while they were in crèches, such as running, preening, or demanding and consuming food, were investigated for rhythmicities. All activities showed a mid-day minimum. This was observed particularly in the ecstatic display of the males, the numbers of birds walking over the sea ice, and the birds swimming out for food.

When experimentally confined in a hut at a constant light intensity of 100 lux, two males showed a "free running" activity rhythm with a period shorter than 24 hours. In two experiments the activity peaks were spaced 20.3 and 20.5 hours apart, respectively. At an intensity of 100 lux, many diurnal species of birds and plants show a period shorter than 24 hours, while nocturnal animal species, such as mice, increase their period to about 25 hours. Therefore, the Adélie penguin with its unusually short period of 20.5 hours has to be considered a diurnal species.

The activity pattern over 24 hours of the Weddell seal *(Leptonychotes weddelli)* is the reverse of that of the penguin. The seals at Hallett were most active, i.e. swimming in the water, at about 0200 hrs, after the light intensity minimum had occurred 1 to 2 hours earlier (Müller-Schwarze, 1965). The largest numbers of animals resting on the ice occurred around 1400 hrs. Knowledge of these circadian activity rhythms is essential in designing significant census methods. Past discrepancies between different population estimates may have been because counts were taken at different times of the day.

Social Behavior

Ever since the large aggregations of penguins were first described, biologists have argued about the survival functions of living and reproducing in a densely packed rookery. A mutual stimulation and synchronization of breeding has been assumed to be a function of colonial breeding in sea birds. When only a small number of predators are active, synchronization of breeding reduces the number of eggs and chicks taken, as has been shown for the black-headed gull *(Larus ridibundus)* by Tinbergen (1967) and for the wideawake *(Sterna fuscata)* by Ashmole (1963). The short summer season is an additional cause of the highly synchronized breeding cycle of antarctic penguins.

An entire breeding area is called a "rookery," the isolated groups within it "colonies" (Fig. 2). The spatial arrangement of the dense penguin colonies facilitates protection of the offspring and the collective defense by the adult Adélie penguins makes it very difficult for South Polar skuas (often the only predator in the rookery) to seize eggs or chicks (Fig. 3). At the periphery of a colony the nests are more exposed to predation by skuas, which typically sit only 1 to 5 meters from a penguin nest. But there are also disadvantages inherent in living in the center of a colony: penguins nesting there have to "run a gauntlet" every time they

Fig. 2. Part of the Adélie penguin rookery at Cape Crozier. Note the various colonies separated by "neutral areas." Fresh snow as shown in the picture is rare.

Fig. 3. Adélie penguin attacks and drives away a South Polar skua.

leave or come back to their territory. Owners of the other territories peck at them, and often deter them from their goal, so that they have to try to pass through later (Penney, 1968).

Penney also noted that he never saw a colony larger than 24 m in diameter. On level ground, the birds sometimes vacate the center, so that a ring-shaped colony results. In rookeries on steep slopes, such as at Cape Crozier, the colonies are rows running downhill on narrow ridges.

Adélie penguins return in most cases to the same colony. Penney (1968) found that 99 percent of 428 banded birds returned in the following season to the same colony. Ninety-three percent of the experienced breeding males and 62 percent of the experienced breeding females returned to the same territory.

The Displays

Upon arrival at the prospective breeding territory, the males perform the *ecstatic display* which attracts females and the *bill-to-axilla* display. Displays usually involving more than one individual include the *mutual display,* the *oblique stare bow,* the *alternate stare,* and the *direct stare.*

In the *ecstatic display,* which was first observed and named by Wilson (1907), a male within his territory thrusts out his breast and raises his head slowly until the bill points up vertically. During the righting of the body the flippers are waved back and forth and the bird utters rhythmical clacking sounds ("pumping": Penney, 1968). The eye is turned so that its white sclera is visible. Finally, with the bill pointing skyward, loud explosive guttural sounds mark the climax of the display. During the climax the bill is slightly opened, but may be fully open. The ecstatic display is contagious. Often one displaying bird induces groups of 5 to 15 males to follow suit. Penney (1968) described an outburst of displays that lasted one hour and 40 minutes without interruption.

The *bill-to-axilla display* of the males was reported first and named by Sladen (1953, 1958). The body is held forward at an angle of 45° to the ground. The closed bill points to the base of the flipper (axilla) while the head is turned back and forth around its longitudinal axis. The white sclera of the eye is visible. Through the turning of the head the bill performs "boring" movements, accompanied by a slow growling which sounds like "orr-orr-orr." The function of the bill-to-axilla display has not been determined. Penney (1968) noted that males accompanied by females did not show this display. It was most often exhibited by lone males without eggs or chicks and by incubating or chick-guarding males, often when being disturbed by another penguin. Penney, therefore, concluded that the bill-to-axilla display may serve as "threat display functional in territorial declaration and defense."

The *mutual display* is so called because it is characteristically performed by two birds of opposite sex who are facing each other (Fig. 4). Both point their bills upwards and vocalize together. There are two forms of this display: the *loud* and the *quiet*. During the loud mutual display the bill is open and the birds utter loud cawing calls. During the quiet mutual display the bills are closed, and only a soft humming sound can be heard. In both forms the heads are waved from side to side into opposite directions, the flippers are pressed to the sides, and the feather crest on the nape is erected. In agreement with Penney's (1968) observations, the author saw the loud mutual display in the following situations: 1. Between male and female: when they know each other and meet again at the start of the breeding season; during nest relief; after a fight with an outsider; after a disturbance or trespassing by penguins or people; when the pair meets at the nest during the collection of pebbles for their nest; and after the laying of an egg by the female. 2. By lone birds: when arriving at its nest-site at the

Fig. 4. Loud mutual display, performed by a breeding pair.

beginning of the breeding season; towards the egg(s) or chick(s); after jumping ashore (seen only once); as reaction to a nearby loud mutual display involving one or more pairs; and while chasing another bird. 3. Between parent and young: before and during feeding; towards chicks before and after hatching; and by adults (not parents) towards chicks in crèches.

Since the loud mutual display occurs after fighting and during chases, it seems to possess aggressive components. The display shows remarkable situational and functional similarities with the "triumph ceremony" of the grey-lag goose *(Anser anser)*, as analyzed by H. Fischer (1965). In the triumph ceremony a pair of geese cross their necks and wave them back and forth under accompanying vocalizations of two types after an intruder has been driven away by the male.

Sladen (1958) found that penguin parents feed only their own chicks in the crèches of up to 30 young birds. Penney (1968) has shown that the loud mutual display of parents toward their young during the crèche stage provides for an auditory recognition. In Penney's words: "In the early crèche stage a food-laden parent on reaching the colony approaches the site of its former nest and gives the loud mutual call toward the ground or sometimes in the air if a crèche occupies the site. Almost immediately its chicks and often one or two others run up and begin begging for food." The chicks may respond to the parental call over distances of 25 to 30 meters. The parent runs away from the begging chicks, which follow. In breaks during this "feeding chase" the chicks are fed with regurgitated food. As long as the parent is silent the chicks do not respond to its presence. Chicks often beg from birds other than their parents but they are not fed.

When Penney played back tape recordings of a loud mutual display by parent birds, their own young "stood up, looked around the colony, and then moved to the edge of the crèche in an alert posture." The chicks then ambled to their natal territory and remained there for 3 to 9 minutes. Penney identified three important points: a chick recognizes the voice of its parents, the chicks remember the exact location of their natal territory, and they respond to their parents' voices as if they expect to meet their parents on the natal territory. According to Thompson and Emlen (1968) the parent's ability to discriminate between their own and strange young develops when the chicks are between eight and 17 days old.

In the quiet mutual display the birds face each other and wave their heads back and forth in opposite directions as in the loud mutual display. But the bill remains closed and the sound uttered is a humming, best described as "mmmm." Quiet mutual displays occur mostly between paired birds; females do it in response to an ecstatic display by their mates. Penney assumes that the quiet mutual display serves primarily to ensure established pair bonds. The author's preliminary observations showed that the quiet mutual display of a female or a pair does inhibit the ecstatic display in the male *of that pair* as Penney (1968) stated. But in *neighboring males* it often stimulated ecstatic and bill-to-axilla displays.

The *oblique stare bow* is a sexual display, while *alternate stare* and *direct stare* serve in territory defense. In the oblique stare bow, the head is bent down slowly and turned to one side in the presence of a bird of the opposite sex. This display occurs regularly when two birds of opposite sex meet at the male's territory at the beginning of the breeding season. Penney (1968) assumed that the oblique stare bow primarily signals mutual acceptance and appeasement. After a disturbance, the oblique stare bow often alternates with quiet mutual displays. The alternate stare may be performed by birds that are standing, lying prone, or crouching. The bird lowers his bill and arches the neck up. The bill is closed and the eyes are turned down so that the white sclerae are exposed. The flippers are spread from the body and moved slowly. The bird faces the intruder (penguin, skua, or human) and turns his head from side to side (Fig. 5). Sometimes the birds growl during this display. The alternate stare is a threat; if the intruder approaches further, he will be attacked. The direct stare consists in a forward pointing of the closed bill. The bill is held upward when the opponent is a tall human or a flying skua. The direct stare may be accompanied by a harsh growl and often precedes attack.

PAIR FORMATION

When two birds of opposite sex meet at the prospective breeding territory, the ceremonies leading to a pair bond may take one of two different forms depending on whether the birds know each other from the previous season or not. Birds familiar with each other greet one another with a loud mutual display. Previously unacquainted penguins go through a sequence of slow movements: the female is attracted to a male by his ecstatic display; the female

Fig. 5. South Polar skuas scavenge in an emperor penguin colony. The chicks are about two months old.

bows (oblique stare bow); the male also often bows; then he may lie down and scrape the nest or nest site with one foot; the female often then starts to collect stones for the nest and drops them near the male; the male puts the stones in place; again there may be mutual bowing and stone collecting. Finally copulation occurs.

Depending on the outcome of the sexual association, Penney (1968) distinguished between two different types of pairing: *trial pairing* and *true pairing.* Trial pairing does not lead to egg production and is only temporary, while true pairing results in the laying of eggs and lasts at least a whole breeding season. A third type, *recurrent pairing,* may be considered a form of true pairing.

In trial pairing the nest is defended, stones are gathered, and mutual displays and copulations occur, but the pair does not stay together. Penney (1968) reported that females which had not bred the previous year associated on the average with 3.2 different males before they established a permanent pair bond leading to egg production. Males which had not bred in the previous season stayed together with 2.6 females on the average before they paired with a female that laid eggs. Of the penguins pairing with the same partner in two subsequent years, 61 percent associated temporarily with other birds of the opposite sex before they met their mate again.

True pairing starts with the same behavior patterns as trial pairing (ecstatic display, bowing, etc.), but the intensity is higher. The birds stay together and eggs are produced.

Interspecific Relationships

Both the emperor and Adélie penguins interact with a small number of other vertebrate species in their antarctic environment. These are primarily the leopard seal *(Hydrurga leptonyx)* and Weddell seal *(Leptonychotes weddelli)* among the mammals, and the South Polar skua *(Catharacta maccormicki),* the giant petrel *(Macronectes gigantea),* and the wattled sheathbill *(Chionis alba).* Kooyman (1966) established that Weddell seals *(Leptonychotes weddelli)* dive as deep as 600 meters, and can stay under water as long as 43 minutes. Of particular importance are the predator-prey relationships between the leopard seal and the penguins (Fig. 6), and between the South Polar skua and the Adélie penguin. As an example, the interactions between the leopard seals and Adélie penguins at Cape Crozier are described here in detail.

The leopard seal is found along the coasts of Antarctica during

Fig. 6. Young leopard seal pursuing Adélie penguins on an ice floe.

the austral summer. During winter and spring (May through October) leopard seals are found farther north on subantarctic islands, such as South Georgia, Heard, and Macquarie Islands. From June to September 300 to 600 seals were reported at Heard Island (Brown, 1957). But neither reproductive behavior nor parturitions have been observed at either of the two ends of the annual migration route. Apparently the young are born in the pack-ice belt.

During the austral summer of 1969–1970 we observed up to six leopard seals working the beaches of Cape Crozier simultaneously. The leopard seal is a solitary hunter and patrols up and down the beaches at a distance of 5 to 100 meters from the shoreline (Fig. 7). Swimming penguins are attacked under water. The success rate of the seal depends on environmental factors such as ice conditions or tide. More penguins are captured at low tide than at high because when attacked, penguins cannot jump to safety on the 2–3 m high and overhanging icefoot. Early in the summer season (October to early November) when heavy and continuous ice covers the coastal waters, the leopard seal has to push through the ice from below in order to attack. Under these conditions he is less successful (Müller-Schwarze and Müller-Schwarze, 1970).

Fig. 7. Leopard seal emerging out of water while cruising along the beach.

Table 1 summarizes some of the 1969 study results. The kill rates are similar to those found by Penney and Lowry (1967) for approximately the same area off the Adélie rookery.

Adélie penguins possess a number of built-in precautions and countermeasures against predation by the leopard seal. During their march over the frozen ocean they avoid thin ice, which a seal could break through from beneath (Fig. 8). When they encounter an open channel in the ice, they are reluctant to cross it; they tend to wait until it is frozen again overnight. On partly ice-covered coastal waters they prefer to walk from ice floe to ice floe, even if this deflects them temporarily from their general travel direction. On ice floes they stay away from the edges, along which the leopard seal could reach up out of the water. Their travelling in groups may also be an anti-predator measure impeding the focussing on one individual. When a penguin is actually attacked in the water, it is often able to escape from the leopard seal by quick and frequent changes of direction. Dispersed from a

Table 1. Frequency of attacks and kills by leopard seals at Cape Crozier in 1969.

Time period	Sea conditions	Attack/ hr.	Kill/ hr.	% Success	Observ. time (hr)
Oct-Nov	Heavy ice cover	4.9	0.37	7.5	24
Dec	Med. & high tide	1.3	0.47	35	15
Dec	Low tide	2.3	1.0	40	6

Fig. 8. On their march over the sea ice, Adélie penguins stop at the edge of thin ice (dark grey) and cross it only reluctantly. In foreground five holes made by leopard seals when attacking penguins from underneath can be seen.

group on the sea ice by an attack, a single penguin remains motionless for a long time, but turns its head an average of 11 times per minute, while birds in groups turn their heads only six times per minute.

There are peculiar temporal relationships between the activity times of the predator and the prey. The largest number of penguins swimming back to the rookery at Cape Crozier was seen between 0700 and 1100 hrs., but at that time only 50 to 65 percent of the observed leopard seals were active (Fig. 9). The remainder rested on ice floes. The numbers of penguins in the water were

Fig. 9. Leopard seal swimming along the beach.

minimal between 1700 and 0300 hrs., yet 65 to 100 percent of all leopard seals near the shore were active during that period (Table 2).

The tendency to "nocturnal" activity had been shown earlier for the Weddell seal (Müller-Schwarze, 1965). It was later confirmed for a Weddell seal population in McMurdo Sound (Stirling, 1967).

However, when the number of surfacing seals is recorded, the opposite tendency is found. The number of surfacing seals is highest between 1200 and 1600 hrs. This apparent paradox can perhaps be interpreted as a different dispersion pattern for seals in the ocean, possibly in relation to dispersion of penguins. At any rate, it shows how misleading any one parameter may be, if used alone.

This survey is not intended to be complete. It merely points out some of the ethological and ecological problems encountered by antarctic species of birds and mammals, as currently investigated by animal behaviorists.

Many behavioral phenomena apply to birds and mammals in general; but the peculiar and extreme polar environment requires special adaptations and aggravates problems existing elsewhere.

On the one hand, the short summer season and the inclemency

Table. 2. Relations between the activity levels of leopard seals and Adélie penguins at Cape Crozier in 1969. Extreme values are in italics.

LEOPARD SEAL				PENGUINS
Time of day	Number of seals active	Number of seals resting	% Active	% of numbers in water above the common median
0 – 4	20	0	*100*	25
4 – 8	17	3	85	87
8 – 12	24	22	*52*	*100*
12 – 16	38	22	63	59
16 – 20	31	12	72	19
20 – 24	28	3	90	*7*

of the weather permit only slow progress of field studies. On the other hand, the large number of scientific and support personnel and the excellent facilities in antarctic stations have greatly facilitated systematic and sophisticated research.

If one relates the large number of biologists active in Antarctica to the small area of livable terrestrial habitat, or to the number of animal species occurring there, the *terra australis incognita* may currently be the most intensively investigated continent.

References

Ashmole, N. P., 1963. The biology of the wideawake or sooty tern (*Sterna fusscata*) on Ascension Island. *Ibis, 103 b:* 297–364.

Brown, K. G., 1957. The leopard seal at Heard Island, 1951–54. *Austral. National Antarctic Research Expeditions, Interim Rept. 16.*

Emlen, J. T., and R. L. Penney, 1964. Distance navigation in the Adélie penguin. *Ibis, 106:* 417–431.

Fischer, H., 1965. Das Triumphgeschrei der Graugans (Anser anser). *Z. Tierpsychol., 22:* 247–304.

Kooyman, G. L., 1966. Maximum diving capacities of the Weddell seal, *Leptonychotes weddelli. Science, 151:* 1553–1554.

Müller-Schwarze, D., 1965. Zur Tagesperiodik der allgemeinen Aktivität der Weddell-Robbe *(Leptonychotes weddelli)* in Hallett, Antarktika. *Z. Morph. Ökol. Tiere, 55:* 796–803.

Müller-Schwarze, D., 1968. Circadian rhythms of activity in the Adélie penguin (Pygoscelis adeliae) during the austral summer. *Antarctic Research Series 12, Antarctic Bird Studies,* edited by O. L. Austin, Jr.; pp. 133–149. Am. Geophys. Union, Washington, D.C.

Müller-Schwarze, D., and C. Müller-Schwarze, 1970. Anti-predator behavior in Adélie penguins. *Antarctic J. U.S., 5:* 124–126.

Penney, R. L., 1968. Territorial and social behavior in the Adélie penguin. *Antarctic Research Series 12, Antarctic Bird Studies,* edited by O. L. Austin, Jr.; pp. 83–131. Am. Geophys. Union, Washington, D.C.

Penney, R. L., and J. T. Emlen, 1967. Further experiments on distance navigation in the Adélie penguin, *Pygoscelis adeliae. Ibis, 109:* 99–109.

Penney, R. L., and G. Lowry, 1967. Leopard seal predation on Adélie penguins. *Ecology, 48:* 878–882.

Penney, R. L., and D. K. Riker, 1969. Adélie penguin orientation under the northern sun. *Antarctic J. U.S., 4:* 116–117.

Prévost, J., 1961. Écologie du Manchot Empereur, *Aptenodytes forsteri* Gray. *Exped. Pol. Franç. Publ. 222.* Hermann, Paris.

Sapin-Jaloustre, J., 1960. Écologie du manchot Adélie. *Exped. Pol. Franç. Publ. 208.* Hermann, Paris.

Sladen, W. J. L., 1953. The Adélie penguin. *Nature, 171:* 953–955.

Sladen, W. J. L., 1958. The Pygoscelid penguins. *Falkland Islands Dependency Sur., Sci. Rept.* No. 17.

Stirling, I., 1967. Population studies on the Weddell seal. *Tuatara, 15:* 133–141.

Stonehouse, B., 1952. Breeding behavior of the emperor penguins. *Nature, 169:* 760.

Stonehouse, B., 1953. The emperor penguin (*Aptenodytes forsteri* Gray). I. Breeding behavior and development. *Falkland Islands Dependency Surv., Sci. Rept. 17.*

Tinbergen, N., 1967. Adaptive features of the black-headed gull *Larvs ridibundus* L. *Proc. Int. Orn. Cong., 14:* 43–59. (Blackwell Scientific Publications, Oxford).

Thompson, D. H., and J. T. Emlen, 1968. Parent-chick individual recognition in the Adélie penguin. *Antarctic J. U.S., 3:* 132.

Wilson, E. A., 1907. Aves. *Brit. Nat. Antarctic Exped., 1901–04;* Vol. 2, Zoology. (Blandford Press, London, 1966)

Wood, R. C., D. G. Ainley, and W. J. L. Sladen, 1970. Antarctic avian population studies 1969–1970. *Antarctic J. U.S., 5:* 126–128.

New Directions in Antarctic Biomedical Research

JAY T. SHURLEY

Veterans Administration, Oklahoma City; University of Oklahoma School of Medicine, Oklahoma City

A fresh look at the impact of the challenge to urban-dwelling, Temperate Zone personnel wintering over at the United States Amundsen-Scott South Pole Station (90°S) has been taken recently by a team of medical research scientists from the University of Oklahoma with support from the National Science Foundation's Office of Polar Programs. A broadly based, comprehensive survey, centering on a highly detailed quantitative and qualitative psychophysiological study of sleeping and dreaming behavior of approximately ten winter-over party volunteers on each of two consecutive years (1967 and 1968) was made, utilizing, as far as practicable, the conceptual and laboratory tools common to a modern American university medical center. Baseline and follow-up studies on the same individual volunteers were made prior to departure for Antarctica and following return to the continental United States. With one exception, this period constituted each man's first experience in polar living, and each came as a stranger to all the others in the group as it formed at Davisville (Rhode Island), Skyland (Virginia), Christchurch (New Zealand), and South Pole.

Lewis and Masterson (1963), in their review of British contributions to polar physiology, concluded with the statement, "Our studies have now entered a phase where we have perhaps come to the end of using relatively crude methods: we can now offer facilities to specialists who wish to apply their own advanced techniques to the unique opportunities of the Antarctic." The Oklahoma project entered the field at Davisville in July, 1966, to begin one such application by medical research specialists to the antarctic scientific arena. Formidable technical and logistical problems had yet to be overcome; nevertheless, a large body of detailed and systematic data on behavior, psychophysiology of sleep and dreaming, and the functioning of the hematological, cardiopulmonary, and central nervous system was obtained. The facilities were found to be superb.

OBJECTIVES

An objective of the Oklahoma project was to apply, systematically and persistently, advanced technology and specialized knowledge of the psychophysiology of human adaptation, in both base and field laboratories, to the documentation of some of the more accessible physiological, psychophysiological, psychological, and social responses of men performing their normal job functions during a year spent at 90°S. Repeated all-night polygraphic studies of sleep and dreaming physiology, augmented by selected, detailed hematological, cardiopulmonary, psychological, and behavioral measures, were the main vehicles chosen for study. From these data, a fuller scientific picture of man's response patterns while engaged in pioneer efforts at continuous, year-round occupation of this particular and unique ecological niche was constructed. The results are being viewed in the framework of an eclectic and comprehensive modern biomedical and biobehavioral science as a fluid, multilevel process of adaptation and adjustment in the lives of particular young, healthy men, seen as proceeding from certain genetic and sociocultural origins—by way of this period of antarctic service—toward specific social, occupational, and individual life goals within this segment of their lives, and in this global theater of action. Incomplete, inadequate, and imperfect approximations would no doubt result from this somewhat global concept, with a possible reward of enduring heuristic value for the effort.

Personal discussion with Newell Berry, Paul Nelson, Eric Gunderson, and John Rasmussen, of the United States Navy Medical Neuropsychiatric Unit, San Diego, and the reading of Wilson's (1965) masterful review, and other polar literature, led to the conclusion that the traditional problems heretofore attacked in polar biomedical research—those of cold adaptation, nutrition and metabolic factors, darkness, low relative humidity, infectious diseases, and the like—were easily gotten around by modern technology in clothing, shelter, nutrition, and public health measures, and offered small opportunity for new contributions at this time. Injuries and accidents were by far the leading causes of morbidity and death, as in any frontier, and dental trouble far outweighed mental trouble as a reason for consulting a physician. Therefore, the important problems of life support and survival presented less challenge than those common to many other military and industrial operations, where personal motivation, social compatibility, and job performance are paramount considerations for the individual; and leadership, communication, and morale are most significant for the group. From experience, it was felt that a direct, frontal attack on these latter problems would not be particularly productive in this setting; therefore, we chose to approach the situation through the avenue of adjustment as revealed in the psychophysiology of sleep and dreaming. The "polar big eye" (insomnia) was the principal medical problem we would attempt to solve.

DAILY ACTIVITY SURVEY

Building on the work of Kleitman and Kleitman (1953), and Lewis and Masterson (1957), we began our survey of polar sleep with an instrument (Fig. 1) with which we were able to obtain records of the daily allocation of time to sleep and waking activity by each man at South Pole and other Antarctic stations. Using a brief time sample period of seven or eight days, we were able to obtain fair approximations of each man's global activity at appropriate intervals during his entire duty cycle from a Temperate Zone residence, through the antarctic year, and his return to the Temperate Zone. A preliminary test of the method in the field (Shurley *et al.*, 1970) gave results in good agreement with previously published studies and allowed us to construct a hypothetical picture of the composite South Polar resident man. Incidentally, it also documented the markedly reduced and simplified scope of a man's activities in antarctic station life, compared with that found in the urban culture from which he originated. Briefly, it was found that our subjects spent 31.5 percent, or 7.55 hours per 24-hour day in sleep during the very busy early antarctic summer season, with a range of 5.6 to 10.5 hours mean sleep averaged over a seven-day period for the shortest- and longest-sleeping individuals. As in the Temperate Zone environment from which they came, the majority of sleep was taken between 0200 and 0500 hours, in the strictly arbitrary clock-time used for the station,

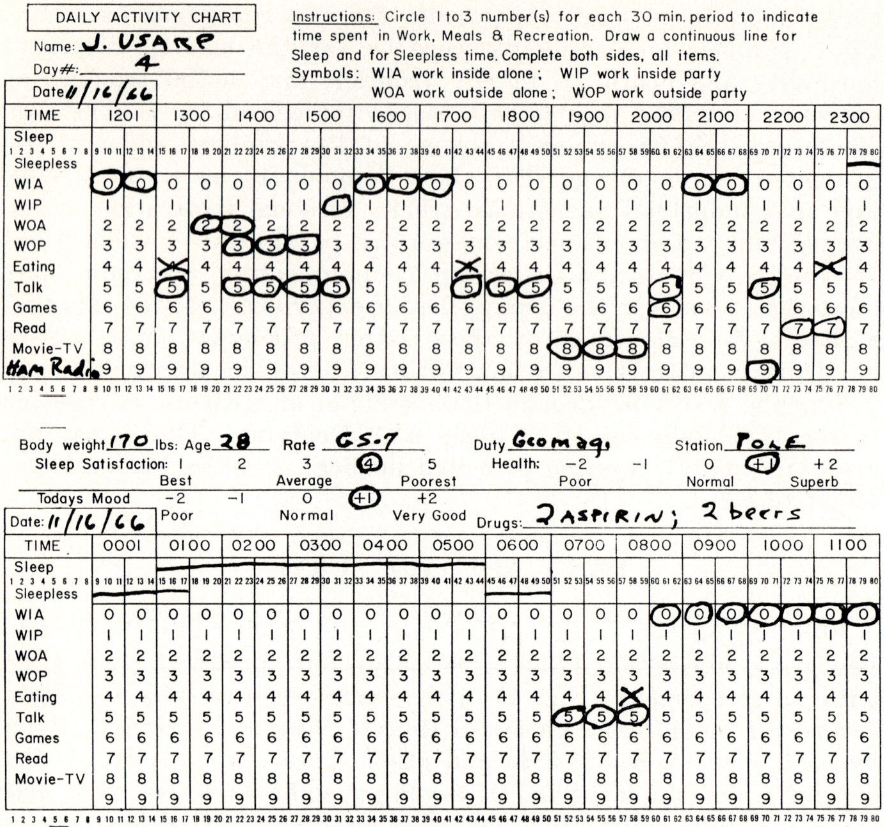
DAILY ACTIVITY CHART
Name: J. USARP
Day#: 4
Date 11/16/66
Instructions: Circle 1 to 3 number(s) for each 30 min. period to indicate time spent in Work, Meals & Recreation. Draw a continuous line for Sleep and for Sleepless time. Complete both sides, all items.
Symbols: WIA work inside alone; WIP work inside party
WOA work outside alone; WOP work outside party
TIME 1201 1300 1400 1500 1600 1700 1800 1900 2000 2100 2200 2300
Sleep
Sleepless
WIA
WIP
WOA
WOP
Eating
Talk
Games
Read
Movie-TV
Ham Radio
IBM M59421
PLE - BIO - OKLA
Body weight 170 lbs: Age 28 Rate GS-7 Duty Geomag. Station Pole
Sleep Satisfaction: 1 Best 2 3 Average 4 5 Poorest
Health: −2 Poor −1 0 Normal +1 +2 Superb
Todays Mood −2 Poor −1 0 Normal +1 +2 Very Good
Date: 11/16/66
Drugs: 2 ASPIRIN; 2 beers
TIME 0001 0100 0200 0300 0400 0500 0600 0700 0800 0900 1000 1100
Sleep
Sleepless
WIA
WIP
WOA
WOP
Eating
Talk
Games
Read
Movie-TV
IBM M59422

Fig. 1. Front and back of a foldable keypunch card served for the self-report of daily sleep and waking activity in half-hour increments, as well as for subjective global ratings of sleep satisfaction, health, and mood. Carried in a shirt pocket, filled in frequently, and collected daily, it attained high reliability with minimal training and cooperation.

corresponding to Greenwich Mean Time plus 12 hours. In this particular week, with one holiday, work output averaged 56.8 hours per man, with a range of 18.5 to 101.5 hours in different individuals, despite no illnesses. The remainder of the time accounted for (36 percent) was spent primarily in recreational activities and eating, with a mean of 4½ hours per day per man (19 percent) of social conversation overlapping all other categories except sleep.

The same method of accounting for activities was used by each subject for the days immediately preceding and succeeding his three-night stint on the sleep recorder, so that the picture of his sleep physiology and dream reports could, we hoped, be tied in with his waking activity somewhat closer than otherwise.

PSYCHOPHYSIOLOGY OF SLEEP

The core of the project, however, was the collection of seven channels of continuously recorded electrophysiological information (Table 1) covering the complete daily sleeping period of each of a selected sample of 20 volunteers on 18 nights each. These 18 nights were aggregated in increments of three consecutive nights each, taken at six periods in time, covering the period from base line, two to three months prior to departure for Antarctica, over four quarters of the year at South Pole Station; then a final recording from three to eleven months following return to the continental United States. From these approximately 360 complete nights of polygraphically recorded sleep, the second nights of each period of three were selected for "calibration nights." The signals recorded over these approximately 120 calibration nights of sleep

Table 1. Psychophysiology of human sleep at South Pole: signal acquisition array.*

Channel allocation	Anatomical derivation	Time constants	Signal designation**
1	L & R outer canthi	1.0 sec.	electro-oculogram (EOG)
2	LP-LO	0.3 sec.	electroencephalogram (EEG)
3	LF-LP	0.3 sec.	electroencephalogram (EEG)
4	L-R hyoid region	0.03 sec.	electromyogram (EMG)
5	RF-RP	0.3 sec.	electroencephalogram (EEG)
6	L arm – R arm	0.03 sec.	electrocardiogram (ECG)
7	Left 3rd finger, palmar surface	1.0 sec.	electrodermal response (EDR)

* Bioelectric physiological signal processing by Beckman Biomedical Data Recording and Display System.

** Data recorded on ½-inch magnetic tape by Ampex SP-300 Instrumentation Recorder at 3¾ ips tape transport speed.

were written out on strip charts in our laboratory in Oklahoma City from the magnetic tapes returned from the Antarctic. These charts, each approximately 1,500 feet in length, were divided into 20-second epochs, and "scored" by the standard visuo-manual method common to electroencephalographers, using the manual of Rechtschaffen and Kales (1968). By this means, some 24 indices of sleep physiology were derived for each night's sleep, which could then be subjected to sophisticated statistical analytic techniques using a digital computer, as well as studied individually by the case method for each man.

The first night's data from each period was held in reserve and not used in this analysis, because of the greater variability commonly seen, and referred to by Agnew *et al.* (1966) as the "first night effect." The third nights were interrupted nights, owing to attempts to obtain verbal reports of dreams from rapid-eye movement (REM) wakening. These dream reports were tape-recorded, transcribed into typescript, and are being subjected to study by the several methods now coming into use for content analysis and interpretation of dreams. Approximately a hundred dreams collected in this way are now available for this study.

A preliminary analysis of the detailed records of the calibration (second) nights of four subjects across all time periods has been the subject of a preliminary report by Natani *et al.* (1970). This report reveals objective evidence of the ubiquitous tendency to periodic, as well as general, insomnia attributed to residents at the highest latitudes. It also reveals significant fluctuations in the amount of REM-stage sleep, with lower amounts in mid-winter (23 percent as compared with 27 percent for base-line mean values). Quite unpredicted and unexpectedly, it also revealed that the amount and percentage of slow-wave sleep (SWS) was markedly lowered by the end of the wintering-over period, with one component (Stage Four, or "purest" delta sleep) virtually abolished. Even more surprising, there was no recovery of this type of sleep on return to the United States.

EFFECTS OF HYPOBARIC HYPOXIA

With C. A. Guenter, a colleague from the University of Oklahoma who specializes in pulmonary physiology and pathology, we proceeded in our second field year to perform a survey of the hypobaric hypoxia effects. We utilized a well-equipped pulmonary function laboratory. Guenter *et al.* (1970) reported that the forced vital capacity (FVC) was not significantly altered throughout the year, but the forced expiratory volume (FEV), the forced expiratory flow rate (FEF), and the maximum voluntary ventilation (MVV) all increased while at the South Pole and returned to base line upon return to the United States. The mean FEF, however, unexpectedly increased progressively throughout the year at the South Pole. Spirometry of nine subjects after work at −95°F revealed no significant changes in any of the determinations, even after 30 minutes' exposure.

A study of the blood-gas exchanges revealed that the mean alveolar PO_2 decreased from a mean of 108 mm Hg to 67 mm Hg for samples of 5 to 11 volunteers. This was associated with a decrease in mean arterial PO_2 from 87 to 53 mm Hg. The mean blood pH increased from 7.40 to 7.46 and remained alkalotic throughout the year. The mean arterial PCO_2 decreased from 34 to 27 mm Hg and remained in the hypocapnic range. Expected increases in the hematocrit and blood hemoglobin level proportional to the altitude and at the usual time were observed. Interestingly, it was also found that the mean oral temperature decreased progressively during the stay at South Pole from a mean of 98.3°F (36.8°C) on arrival, to a mean of 96.6°F (35.8°C) at the end of the winter. Thus this study was able to document the important role which altitude and hypoxia with its accompanying alkalosis and hypothermia may play in the functioning of wintering-over personnel.

In the same year, with the collaboration of another colleague, W. H. Whitcomb, a classic study (Whitcomb *et al.*, 1970) of the effects of the low oxygen environment upon plasma and urine erythropoietin levels was carried out which revealed increased activity on the second, third, and fourth day after arrival at altitude, in both plasma and urine levels of erythrocyte stimulating factor (ESF). An unexplained variability in the levels of erythropoietin activity in the urine samples from the different subjects was found.

Finally, direct measurements were made of the pulmonary function and the sleep-stage patterns of two of the investigators immediately after arrival at the South Pole Station from sea level. Documented by Joern *et al.* (1970) this first study attempted to correlate these factors in two subjects, only one of whom suffered the symptoms of acute mountain sickness. A complete loss of delta sleep throughout the first week was recorded in both. Both showed a tendency to insomnia with shortened sleep times, and showed other, more striking variations of their sleep patterns. A hypothesis was proposed that the striking curtailment of Stages Three and Four sleep might well be the outcome of an adaptive attempt to avoid the physiological depression of the carbon dioxide drive of respiration associated with the deepest stage of sleep, thus guarding the brain against a more profound hypoxia.

PSYCHOSOCIAL OBSERVATIONS

In addition to the physiological data outlined and discussed above, we were also able to record a considerable amount of psychosocial data in each of the two years. This was designed to augment the psychiatric screening data and sociometric and other questionnaire data which have regularly been obtained by the Navy Medical Neuropsychiatric Research Unit investigators at San Diego over the past ten years. We feel that these data nicely fill the gap in time, and add a new dimension to the available information. Systematic collection of psychological response data, using standard instruments such as the Minnesota Multiphasic Personality Index and the Cattell 16 Personality Factor Test, was postponed until an adequate level of rapport between the investigators and the subjects was reached. These instruments were then administered to each man of the sleep sample during his sojourn at South Pole Station, and again following his return to the continental United States and the Oklahoma sleep laboratory for his follow-up sleep recordings. A detailed psychiatric exit interview was conducted by the principal investigator immediately upon his arrival on the first (relief) plane into the South Pole at the end of each of the two consecutive winters. A second, structured exit interview was conducted at the end of the follow-up period with each of the sleep subjects. This material was collected in an effort to establish the broadest and deepest possible consistent understanding of the basic personality variables brought into play by the adaptive efforts of each man faced by the stress of this novel hostile environment, and of the joy and (sometimes) distress of the return and readaptation to his accustomed habitat and society.

The overt sources of stress so far identified by Shurley and his co-workers (Shurley, 1970a) were identified as extreme cold and dryness, altitude, markedly different light-dark cycles, novelty, monotony, and eight months of unbroken group social isolation and close confinement. Most of these factors, individually and collectively, were sometimes found to be viewed as stimulating and gratifying, rather than stressful deprivations, depending on the value system of the man and his group at the time questioned. In a comment upon Sir Raymond Priestley's article (1969), "Inexpressible Island" (in which Sir Raymond gave, for the first time, a classic first-person account of the survival against incredible odds of Scott's Northern Party in the antarctic winter of 1912), Shurley (1970b) elaborated seven factors—in addition to the obvious ones of personal courage and self-discipline of extraordinary, heroic men—which might help explain their survival. To a degree, this commentary propounds a modern psychiatric view of the role of certain psychosocial factors, as reflected in their dreams, which help understand successful survival of explorers who are "caught out," as Priestley and his group were. The extremes described in this account, however, depict graphically, by contrast, the long way modern technology and exploration methods have taken us, so that factors involved in adaptation to modern antarctic conditions are of a different order of magnitude, and may be subtle indeed.

In addition, pilot studies were made using several other types of instruments to measure responses to such things as the personal use of space in this confined environment, and the placement of each individual upon a sensation-seeking scale in an attempt to get at factors in the personality which may be correlated with willingness to volunteer for antarctic duty.

AD HOC INVESTIGATIONS

Ad hoc investigations of two kinds grew out of on-the-spot associations with other scientists in the Antarctic; first, with Lt. A. B. Blackburn (MC) (USN), the Navy doctor who commanded the Plateau Station during the 1967 season. This resulted in the collection of data documenting the striking neutropenia occurring in healthy men under conditions of extreme isolation at Plateau Station (See Muchmore *et al.*, 1970). A hypothesis was advanced in this report that the virtual gnotobiotic environment in which the South Polar Plateau man lives in splendid isolation during the winter months produces a situation conceived as the "mirror image" of the neutrophilic response to the mixture of benign and pathogenic organisms which are a normal accompaniment of average social contact. This phenomenon could be of considerable practical importance in prolonged space travel and in other situations of extreme social isolation.

A second ad hoc investigation was launched in the Antarctic, utilizing the sleep and activity cards, referred to above, due to opportunities to contact personally the station leaders at Scott Base (New Zealand), and the physician at Vostok (U.S.S.R.) in December, 1966. The subsequent collection of similar data to those collected at the South Pole Station at similar periods in time makes possible a number of interesting comparisons in the way in which men from different cultures program their time in the unique international scientific culture of the Antarctic.

It is our belief that the studies outlined above have initiated a new era in antarctic biomedical and biobehavioral research efforts, and have demonstrated that the facilities now available make possible an entry into exciting new problems in the ecology of man in the polar zones.

Author's Notes: The investigations upon which this article is based were supported in part by National Science Foundation Grants Numbers GA274, GA683, GA1226, GA10455, and GA18698 to the Oklahoma Medical Research Foundation, and in part by Medical Research (8200) Funds of the Department of Medicine and Surgery, Veterans Administration.

Grateful acknowledgment is made to the unpaid volunteers, officers, men, and scientific technicians of Operations Deepfreeze 1967 and 1968, and the United States Antarctic Research Programs for 1967 and 1968 without whose splendid cooperation this study could not have been accomplished. Special acknowledgment is due Dr. G. A. Llano, Program Director for Antarctic Biology, National Science Foundation, whose administrative skill and support made this project possible, and to the extraordinary logistical support furnished by Operations Division, the Office of Polar Programs, National Science Foundation, headed by Mr. Philip Smith, and by the United States Navy Task Force 43 at many levels of command.

Chester M. Pierce, M.D., was my co-investigator throughout, and Kirmach Natani, Albert T. Joern, and Robert E. Brooks carried the brunt of the field work in Antarctica and in Oklahoma City.

References

Agnew, H. W., Jr., W. B. Webb, and R. L. Williams, 1966. The first night effect: An EEG study of sleep. *Psychophysiology, 2:* 263–266.

Guenter, C. A., A. T. Joern, J. T. Shurley, and C. M. Pierce, 1970. Cardiorespiratory and metabolic effects in men on the South Polar plateau. *Arch. Internal Med., 125:* 630–637.

Joern, A. T., J. T. Shurley, R. E. Brooks, C. A. Guenter, and C. M. Pierce, 1970. Short-term changes in sleep patterns on arrival at the South Polar plateau. *Arch. Internal Med., 125:* 649–654.

Kleitman, N., and H. Kleitman, 1953. The sleep-wakefulness pattern in the Arctic. *Sci. Monthly, 76:* 349–356.

Lewis, H. E., and J. P. Masterson, 1957. Sleep and wakefulness in the Arctic. *Lancet, 1:* 1262–1266.

Lewis, H. E., and J. P. Masterson, 1963. Polar physiology: Its development in Britain. *Lancet, 1* (7289) : 1009–1014.

Muchmore, H. G., A. B. Blackburn, J. T. Shurley, C. M. Pierce, and B. A. McKown, 1970. Neutropenia in healthy men at the South Polar plateau. *Arch. Internal Med., 125:* 646–648.

Natani, K., J. T. Shurley, C. M. Pierce, and R. E. Brooks, 1970. Long-term changes in sleep patterns in men on the South Polar plateau. *Arch. Internal Med., 125:* 655–659.

Priestley, R., 1969. Inexpressible island. *Nutrition Today, 4:* 18–27.

Rechtschaffen, A., and A. Kales (Editors), 1968. A manual of standardized terminology, techniques and scoring system for sleep stages of human subjects. *Nat. Inst. Health Publ., No. 204.* U.S. Government Printing Office, Washington, D.C.

Shurley, J. T., 1970a. Man on the South Polar plateau: Guest editorial to symposium: Man on the South Polar plateau. *Arch. Internal Med., 125:* 625–629.

Shurley, J. T., 1970b. Dreams good and bad. *Nutrition Today, 5:* 30–31.

Shurley, J. T., C. M. Pierce, K. Natani, and R. E. Brooks, 1970. Sleep and activity patterns at South Pole Station. *Arch. Gen. Psychiat., 22:* 385–389.

Whitcomb, W. H., A. T. Joern, C. A. Guenter, M. Moore, J. T. Shurley, and C. M. Pierce, 1970. Effect of the South Polar plateau on plasma and urine erythropoietin levels. *Arch. Internal Med., 125:* 638–645.

Wilson, O., 1965. Human adaptation to life in Antarctica. In *Biogeography and Ecology in Antarctica*, edited by J. Van Meighem, P. Van Oye, and J. Schell; vol. 15, pp. 690–752. W. Junk, publisher, Monographiae Biologicae, The Hague.

PART III

Glaciology

PART III

Glaciology

In this brief section we review four glaciological problems which have occupied scientists for nearly a decade in an extensive study of the characteristics of the Antarctic Ice Sheet. How much ice is there? How much snow is accumulating annually? What is our progress in obtaining and interpreting ice samples from great depths within the ice sheet? What have we learned of the history of the ice sheet from evidence available in the few ice-free areas of Antarctica?

Dr. Bull covers in some depth the painstaking though routine work of the scores of people who have been involved in obtaining values for the annual snow accumulation, which varies from practically zero on the high plateau to over a meter in a few areas near the coast. Our friends from Belgium have been foremost in reducing this tedious task to a scientific level with the use of radioisotopes and in particular the identification of the first radioactive debris, left by the nuclear bomb test in 1954.

In a brief article, I describe the efforts of geophysics to determine the ice thickness. Most of this has been done with the seismic method of the oil prospectors. We see this method now superseded by airborne radar sounding which is done more quickly, in greater density coverage, and, to say the least, in greater comfort.

Dr. Langway describes the long efforts that have been put on the deep drilling program that has allowed us to retrieve ice cores that represent snow deposited several thousand years ago. Drilling deeply into this visco-plastic material has required the solution to unique problems which have used nearly a decade of effort. Many of the studies of the future can now be built on these proven techniques.

Dr. Nichols brings several decades of experience to bear on the subject of glacial geology. Here once again, as in the other studies, new technological advances, permitting scientists to determine the absolute dating, have led to a better understanding of the scattered evidence that the ice sheet has left in these few ice-free areas.

It might be instructive at this time to outline some of the major items of the future—those that are not covered in this review, principally because the knowledge is too sparse. Although some work may still continue on annual accumulation and ice thickness, more detail is really not needed except perhaps in special areas. The present ice budget of Antarctica will not be adequately known until we can determine bottom melting values, and until we can amass great efforts to determine ice flow around the complete periphery of the continent. The history of the present ice sheet will remain an unresolved question until extensive drilling can be done in many parts of the continent.

The history of glaciated Antarctica will probably always remain somewhat of a mystery, as much of the evidence has long ago been assembled and reassembled repeatedly, then pushed out to sea. We really would like to know what the effect is of the great weight of the Antarctic Ice Sheet on the crust and the mantle. What is the story of the last few millions of years in Antarctica, and what is happening at the ice-rock interface at present? These are all immensely difficult problems. The Antarctic Ice Sheet is a lengthy, intriguing book and we are now opening only the first few pages.

A. P. Crary

Division of Environmental Sciences
National Science Foundation
Washington, D.C.

Glacial Geology of the Wright Valley McMurdo Sound

Robert L. Nichols

Department of Geology, Tufts University, Medford, Massachusetts

Several valleys approximately 40 miles (64 km) long extend from the Antarctic Ice Plateau on the west down to McMurdo Sound or the Wilson Piedmont Glacier on the east. Some, such as the Ferrar and MacKay Valleys, are filled with large outlet glaciers; others, such as the Taylor and Victoria Valleys, are in part nearly ice-free due to deglaciation (Péwé, 1960; Calkin, 1964a). These deglaciated valleys are locally called "dry valleys."

The Wright Valley is a dry valley (Fig. 1). It is aligned west to east and lies between the Ferrar Glacier to the south and the MacKay Glacier to the north at approximately 77°30′S and between 160°45′ E and 162°30′ E.

The Wright Upper Glacier, at the western end of the Wright Valley, is an outlet glacier which moves eastward down the valley from the Antarctic Ice Sheet. The Wright Lower Glacier, at the eastern end of the valley, separates the valley from McMurdo Sound by approximately 12 miles (19 km). It is a channel glacier, the western part of which moves westward up the valley. The Wright Lower Glacier is continuous with the Wilson Piedmont Glacier, which extends from Granite Harbor on the north almost to Cape Bernacchi on the south and from which it is differentiated only by more rapid movement. The Wright Lower Glacier is fed by valley glaciers from the coastal mountains and by snow that falls directly on it. The deglaciated part of the Wright Valley is approximately 30 miles (48 km) long and 4 miles (6 km) wide; some of the peaks immediately north and south of the valley stand about a mile (1,525 m) above the valley floor.

"Wright Lake" is a perennially frozen proglacial lake a few miles (3 km) long and less than a mile (1,600 m) wide, located just

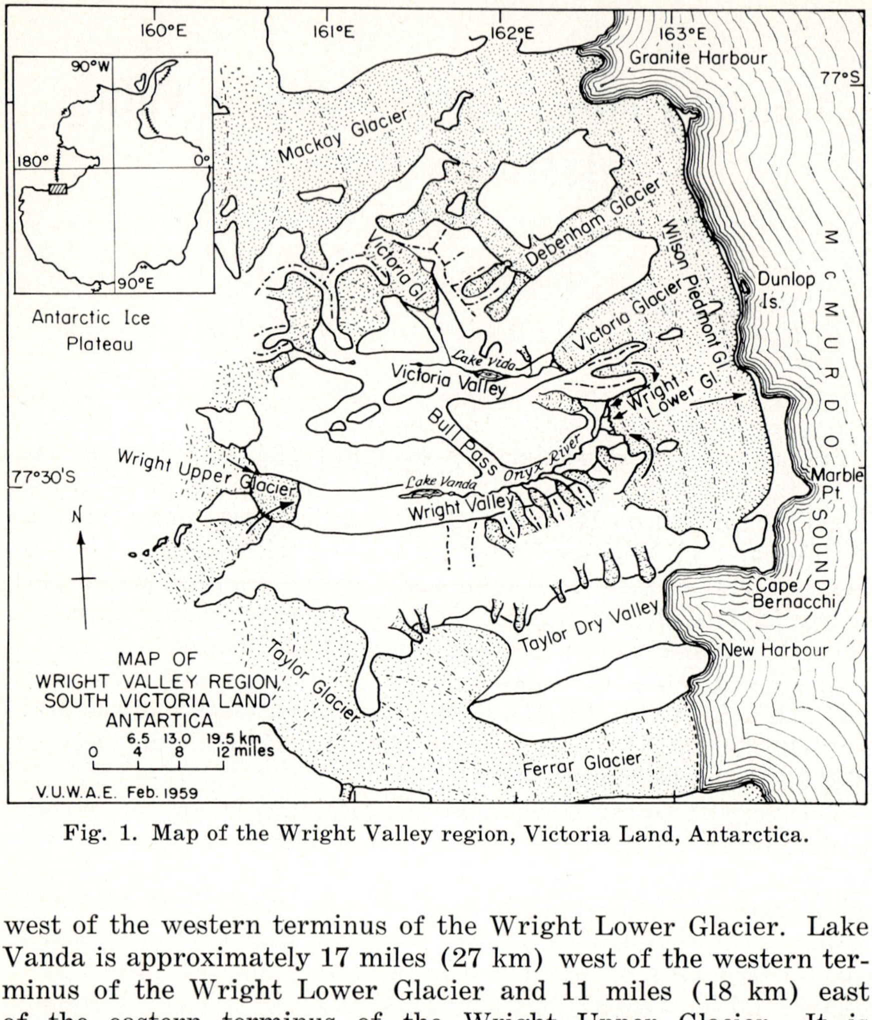

Fig. 1. Map of the Wright Valley region, Victoria Land, Antarctica.

west of the western terminus of the Wright Lower Glacier. Lake Vanda is approximately 17 miles (27 km) west of the western terminus of the Wright Lower Glacier and 11 miles (18 km) east of the eastern terminus of the Wright Upper Glacier. It is approximately 4 miles (6 km) long, averages less than a mile (1,600 m) wide, and is more than 217 feet (66 m) deep. Except for a narrow marginal zone of varying width, Lake Vanda is perennially frozen. It occupies an undrained bedrock basin. The Onyx River, a meltwater stream that runs approximately 15 miles (24 km) up the Wright Valley and in so doing drops about 500 feet (152 m), flows from the "Wright Lake" into Lake Vanda. During the warmest part of the summer the river is is a few feet (1 m) deep in some places so that a dry crossing on foot is difficult.

Small cirque glaciers are found along the sides of the valley,

Fig. 2. An aerial photograph (U. S. Navy) looking eastward down the Wright Valley. The Wright Lower Glacier is in the distance; beyond it, the sea ice and open water in McMurdo Sound. Five alpine glaciers are seen on the south wall of the valley. The locality where the shells were found is indicated by the letter S.

and small glaciers from hanging valleys extend down the valley walls and almost reach the floor (Fig. 2). The valley is veneered with moraines of different ages, glaciofluvial deposits, small patches of windblown sand, and other deposits. Several small volcanic cones are present on the valley floor and walls (Nichols, 1962, 1965).

The mean annual temperature of the Wright Valley must be close to 0°F (−18°C) (Nichols and Ball, 1964) and several kinds of geologic evidence prove that the valley is very arid (Nichols, 1963). During the summer months the deglaciated part of the valley is essentially snow-free, and in the eastern part, at least, the winds almost continually blow from the east up the valley. In winter the winds are much stronger, and geologic evidence indicates that they blow from the west down the valley.

MULTIPLE GLACIATION IN THE WRIGHT VALLEY

Evidence for four glacial episodes is found in the eastern end of the Wright Valley. During the oldest glacial episode (which may have included more than one), the Vanda, ice moved from the Antarctic Ice Plateau eastward down the Wright Valley and out into McMurdo Sound. During the three younger glacial episodes (Pecten, Loop, and Trilogy) ice moved from McMurdo Sound and/or the coastal mountains westward up the valley (Nichols, 1961). Péwé (1960), Bull *et al.* (1962, 1964), Bull (1962), McGregor (1963), Gunn (1963), Calkin (1964 a, b), Armstrong *et al.* (1968), Mercer (1968), Denton and Armstrong (1968), and others have written on multiple glaciation in the McMurdo Sound area and elsewhere in Antarctica.

VANDA GLACIAL EPISODE

Evidence for Vanda Glacial Episode

A longitudinal profile of the Wright Valley made by Bull (1960) shows the most important geomorphic characteristics of the valley (Fig. 3). Lake Vanda occupies a glacially formed bedrock basin whose bottom is approximately 200 feet (61 m) above sea level. From Lake Vanda westward, the bedrock bottom of the valley rises rapidly, reaching an elevation of approximately 2,500 feet (762 m) in 8 miles (13 km) (Fig. 4). The valley also rises from Lake Vanda eastward, so that at the western terminus of the Wright Lower Glacier the valley has an elevation of about 1,000 feet (305

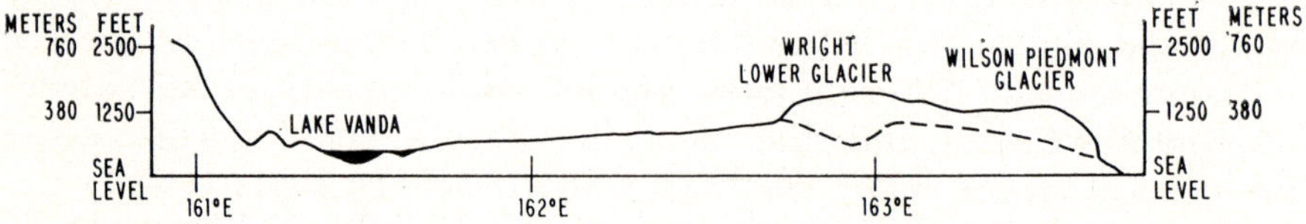

Fig. 3. Longitudinal profile of the Wright Valley and the Wilson Piedmont Glacier, showing the undrained bedrock basin in which Lake Vanda is located and the threshold near the terminus of the Wright Lower Glacier. Vertical exaggeration about 14 times. (Profile made by C. Bull.)

m). A threshold is located beneath the Wright Lower and Wilson Piedmont Glaciers. From the top of the threshold, the bedrock slopes eastward down to sea level, westward down to Lake Vanda. The bedrock basin up-valley from the threshold is approximately 800 feet (244 m) deep. The threshold is probably composed mainly of bedrock, but glacial deposits and even volcanic material may be present. The presence of the threshold and basin is responsible for the fact that the Onyx River runs up the valley for approximately 17 miles (27 km) (Fig. 5).

Fig. 4. An aerial photograph (U. S. Navy) looking westward showing Lake Vanda, which occupies a glacially formed bedrock basin cut during the Vanda glacial episode.

The fjord-like longitudinal profile of the Wright Valley (Flint, 1947) owes its origin to the Vanda glacial episode, the ice of which moved from the Antarctic Ice Plateau eastward down the Wright Valley and out into McMurdo Sound. The Vanda is the oldest glacial episode recognized by the writer. The fjord-like longitudinal profile is due mainly to greater glacial bedrock erosion up-valley where the ice was presumably thicker and faster moving, and to the deposition of a greater thickness of moraine down-valley in the area where the threshold is now found. The work of McKelvey and Webb (1962) indicates that differential resistance of the bedrock to glacial erosion was not a factor. Truncated spurs are found between the Goodspeed and Hart Glaciers, the Hart and Meserve Glaciers, the Meserve and Bartley Glaciers, and elsewhere (Fig. 5). Their location in areas not reached by the younger glacial episodes proves that they were formed during the Vanda glacial episode. The Wright Valley is essentially an asymmetrical U-shaped valley which attained its shape during the Vanda glacial epi-

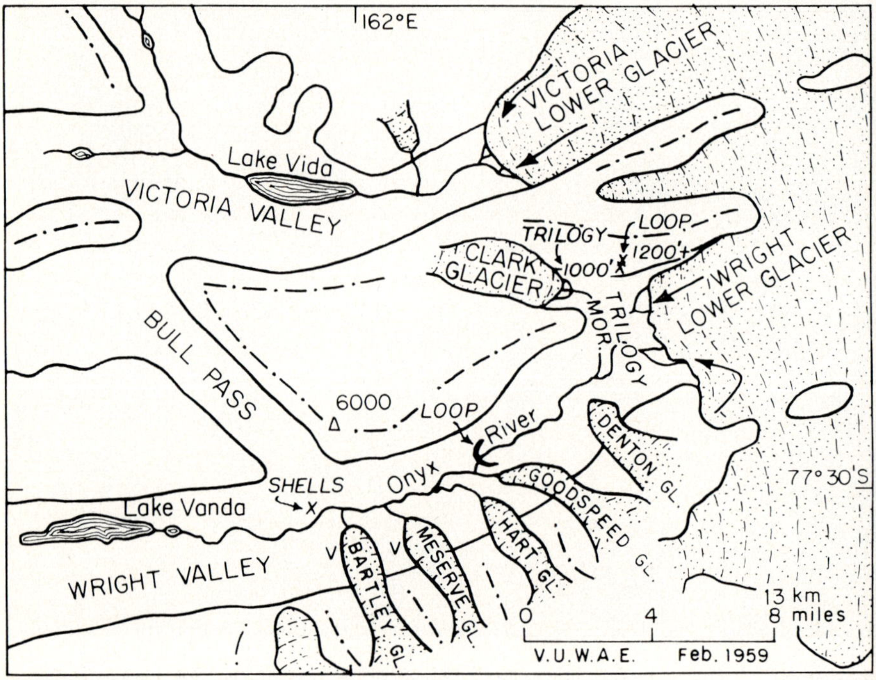

Fig. 5. Map of the eastern end of the Wright Valley, showing the locations of the Trilogy deposits, the Loop moraine, and the pecten shells.

sode. The Bartley, Meserve, Hart, Goodspeed, Denton, and other glaciers are located in hanging valleys. The Bartley Glacier occupies a hanging valley whose lip is approximately 2,500 feet (762 m) above the floor of the Wright Valley. Although it is certain that some of this difference in elevation is due to differential glacial erosion during the Vanda glacial episode, it is not certain that all of it is. If a fluvial cycle preceded the Vanda glacial episode (Nichols, 1966), fluvial hanging valleys might have been formed if the tectonic history of the area favored erosion of the Wright Valley rather than of its tributary valleys (Matthes, 1930).

In summary, the evidence for the Vanda glacial episode consists of the fjord-like longitudinal profile of the valley, the U-shaped transverse cross section, the truncated spurs, and perhaps the hanging valleys.

Amount of Erosion and Thickness of Ice

A very rough reconstruction of the pre-Vanda bedrock long profile of the Wright Valley, based on the assumption that a fluvial cycle preceded glaciation, suggests that perhaps more than 1,500 feet (457 m) of bedrock was removed in the Lake Vanda area by the Vanda glacial episode. Glacial deposits, roughly equivalent in volume to the material excavated from the Wright Valley during the Vanda glacial episode, are not now present in the valley or beneath the Wright Lower Glacier. The ice of this glaciation presumably went out into McMurdo Sound and deposited its moraines there. Echo sounding might locate them. Their location deserves investigation.

The height of the truncated spurs above the bottom of the valley, the present thickness of the Wilson Piedmont Glacier (Fig. 3), the depth of the glacially formed bedrock basin occupied by Lake Vanda, and the thickness of the Wright Lower Glacier during Loop and Trilogy time suggest that the Wright Glacier during the full-bodied stage of the Vanda glacial episode could have been more than 3,000 feet (914 m) thick.

It is not known from field work in the Wright Valley whether the Vanda glacial episode involved one or more glacial advances and retreats. Field work in the uplands both north and south of the Wright Valley on terrain not buried or eroded by post-Vanda processes might yield information. Field work in the Taylor Valley, however, indicates that at least three glacial invasions occurred in the Wright Valley during Vanda time (Denton and Armstrong, 1968).

Rock Bastions

Two rock bastions which project from the south wall out into the Wright Valley are found immediately below the Goodspeed and Denton Glaciers (Figs. 5, 6). From a distance they look like morainal deposits because bedrock is not readily discernible. However, on the bastion immediately below the Goodspeed Glacier an outcrop of diorite more than 100 feet (30 m) long was seen, 50 feet (15 m) of continuous rock was found close by, and in the same area a dike was traced for 36 feet (11 m). All of this rock was flush with the ground. Moreover, an area of gneiss approximately 40 feet (12 m) long and 25 feet (8 m) wide was seen on the bastion below the Denton Glacier. The writer has never seen boulders of this size in

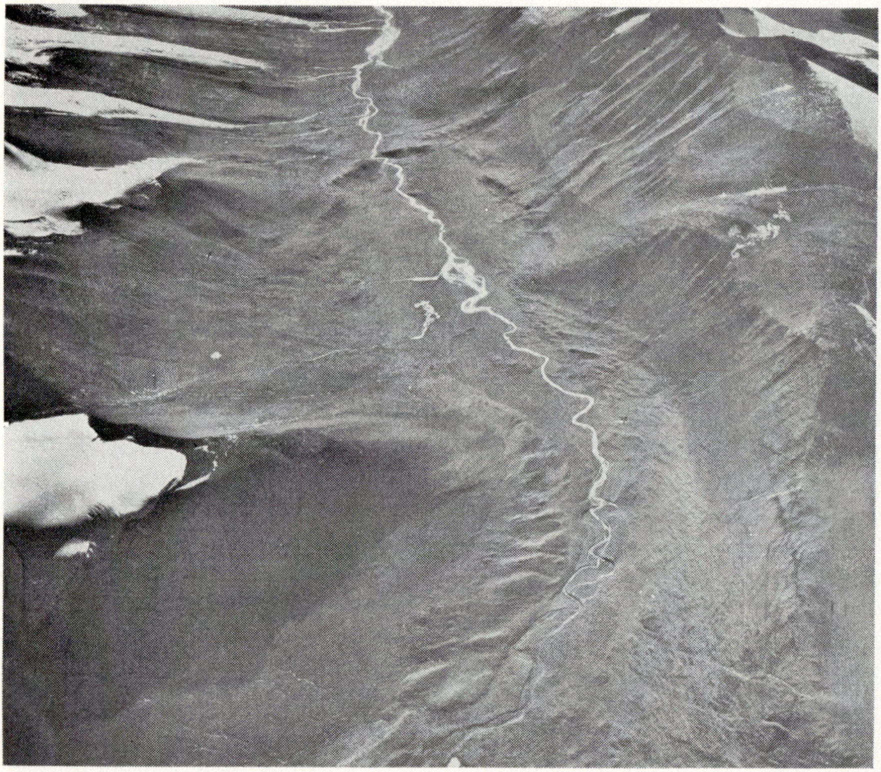

Fig. 6. An aerial photograph (U. S. Navy) looking westward up the Wright Valley. The rock bastions below the Denton and Goodspeed Glaciers are shown, and also the concavity and very steep valley wall opposite the Denton rock bastion.

the Wright Valley and therefore concludes that these features are not morainal deposits but rock bastions thinly veneered with till. Only the front and side slopes of these bastions are visible, as the upper surfaces are buried by the Denton and Goodspeed Glaciers. The bastion below the Denton Glacier, which is the larger, projects for more than a mile (1,610 m) into the valley and has a relief of approximately 1,500 feet (457 m) as it extends from a point somewhat above the floor of the valley up to the Denton Glacier. The side wall of the Wright Valley opposite the Denton Glacier is concave and very steep.

Rock bastions have been described by Flückiger (1934). They are found in the Alps, in Alaska (von Engeln, 1937), in Norway (Cotton, 1942), and in Colorado (Ives, 1946). Rock bastions project into the main glacial valley in front of a glacial hanging valley. They owe their origin to the fact that erosion by the main glacier is weakened by the interference of the tributary glacier. Apparently the northward thrust of the Denton Glacier diverted the Wright Glacier so that glacial erosion of the north wall of the Wright Valley was intensified. The Hart, Meserve, and Bartley Glaciers, located farther up the valley than the Denton and Goodspeed Glaciers (Fig. 5), have no rock bastions below them. The reason for the absence of bastions here is not known. Perhaps the tributary glaciers were not strong enough to divert the Wright Glacier significantly because here the glacier was farther up the valley and presumably thicker. The loop lateral moraines wrap around the Denton bastion; it is, therefore, pre-Loop.

All of the major features of the Wright Valley were formed by the end of Vanda time. Younger glacial, glaciofluvial, eolian, and lacustrine landforms, avalanche chutes, felsenmeers, and other geologic features were formed later, but these constitute only minor alterations of the valley.

Age

A moraine in the upper part of the Wright Valley whose precise age is not known was found to be ice-free to a depth of 25 feet (8 m) (Bell, 1966). Using this depth and making several assumptions, Bell calculated that at least 7.5×10^4 years were necessary for the moraine to dry to this depth by the diffusion of water vapor. This moraine if present would have been removed by Vanda ice; hence the Vanda glacial episode must have occurred more than 7.5×10^4 years ago.

A consideration of the total salt content of Lake Vanda (Angino and Armitage, 1963) and of the rates at which the Onyx River has added salt to the lake suggests that a minimum of about 6×10^4 years was necessary for the accumulation of the salts and that the Vanda glacial episode is probably over 6×10^4 years old (Bell, 1966).

Two small basaltic volcanic cones are located on the south wall of the Wright Valley a few hundred yards (230 m) above the prominent steep-sided end moraine which is approximately 7 miles (11 km) west of the Wright Lower Glacier (Fig. 5). These cones were built on a bedrock surface which in general slopes downward up-valley. They therefore postdate the Vanda glacial episode (Nichols, 1965). Professor Richard L. Armstrong, Department of Geology, Yale University, and Dr. George H. Denton, American Geographical Society, wrote (personal communication, 1968), "A K-Ar measurement of the easternmost of these two cones indicates that it is $3.7 \pm 0.3 \times 10^6$ years old." This measurement gives, therefore, a minimum age for the Vanda glacial episode. Three very small, closely spaced areas which contain small unglaciated volcanic cones are found on the west side of the Bartley Glacier. They rest on deposits that were laid down on a bedrock surface cut by the Vanda glacial episode. They therefore postdate the Vanda glacial espisode. Professor Armstrong and Dr. Denton wrote, "A K-Ar measurement of the northernmost of these 3 volcanic areas indicates that it is $3.9 \pm 0.3 \times 10^6$ years old." These measurements indicate that the Vanda glacial episode is more than $3.9 \pm 0.3 \times 10^6$ years old.

The demonstration of the great antiquity of the Vanda glacial episode in the Wright Valley and also of glaciation in the nearby Taylor Valley (Armstrong *et al.*, 1968; Denton and Armstrong, 1968) is one of the important milestones in antarctic glacial geology. This demonstration is in agreement with the findings in other parts of the world of Craddock *et al.* (1964), Opdyke *et al.* (1966), Bandy (1966), Curry (1966), Einarsson *et al.* (1967) and Goodell and Watkins (1968), all of whom have shown that in the areas they have investigated, glaciation started in the Tertiary.

PECTEN GLACIAL EPISODE

Fossiliferous Gravels

A stratified layer of sand and gravel which appears to be essentially horizontal is found on the floor of the Wright Valley. It is approximately 25 miles (40 km) from McMurdo Sound and 14 miles (23 km) from the western terminus of the Wright Lower Glacier, between 100 and 200 yards (90–180 m) from the Onyx River in a gully cut by a meltwater stream that came from Bull Pass (Figs. 2, 5). The layer is a foot (0.3 m) thick and 20 feet (6 m) long, has been weathered yellow, with unweathered till immediately beneath it. It was buried by approximately 20 feet (6 m) of glacial drift and has been exhumed and eroded by a meltwater stream. The deposit contains a high percentage of pecten shells (Fig. 2). Only a single, extinct species first described by Turner (1967) is present *(Chlamys (Zygochlamys) tuftsensis)* (Fig. 7). Most of the shells consist of broken fragments although a few unbroken valves have been found. A carbon-14 analysis (L-645) indicates

Fig. 7. *Chlamys (Zygochlamys) tuftsensis,* a new species of pecten found in glaciofluvial deposits in the Wright Valley.

that the shells are more than 3.5×10^4 years old, and radium-uranium measurements suggest that they are more than 8×10^5 years old (personal communication from David Thurber).

Origin of Fossiliferous Gravels

There is no evidence known to the writer that the shells have been transported to their present location by wind or birds. Because the layer contains marine shells and is similar to a beach deposit, one might think that it is an elevated beach formed on the margin of a fjord which occupied the Wright Valley in late Vanda time when the area was still isostatically depressed. If the depression was great enough, water from McMurdo Sound might have crossed the threshold at the eastern end of the Wright Valley and converted the valley into a fjord, or, depending upon the topography, McMurdo Sound might have invaded the Wright Valley by way of the Victoria Valley and Bull Pass (Figs. 1, 5). Although the depth of water in which *Chlamys (Zygochlamys) tuftsensis* lived is not known, Dr. Ruth D. Turner, Harvard University (personal communication), believes that it did not live in water so deep that it could not have been washed up onto a beach. Indeed, Beu (1965) has collected numerous specimens of the same genus *(Chlamys dieffenbachi)* on the beaches around Port Nicholson Bay, at Wellington, New Zealand.

The threshold buried by the Wright Lower Glacier at the eastern end of the valley is about 1,000 feet (305 m) above sea level (Fig. 3), and the threshold at the eastern end of the Victoria Valley probably has a similar altitude. Water from McMurdo Sound would have to cross one of these thresholds to convert the Wright Valley into a fjord.

The volume of glacial ice in the Wright Valley was much greater immediately after the Wright Glacier of Vanda time had retreated westward of the threshold than it was in Trilogy time. It may have been great enough to have depressed the area isostatically so that the waters of McMurdo Sound could have invaded the Wright Valley if the Wilson Piedmont Glacier did not then exist. By the time that the Wright Glacier of late Vanda time had retreated westward of the Pecten layer, however, there could not have been much more ice in the valley than in late Trilogy time. The marine limit on the west side of McMurdo Sound is now only about 67 feet (20 m) above sea level (Nichols, 1968). This uplift was due to the deglaciation which followed late Trilogy time; therefore the isostatic depression of the area in late Trilogy time was not great. If the delay in isostatic rebound was not great, it seems unlikely that the isostatic depression of the area by the late Vanda ice, after it had retreated westward of the Pecten locality, would have been sufficient to allow the waters of McMurdo Sound to invade the Wright Valley.

Even if the Wright Valley had been converted into a fjord, however, it seems likely that the area where the fossiliferous layer is found would have been covered by deep water at this time, and fine-grained offshore marine sediments rather than sand and gravel would presumably have been deposited here. With the disappearance of the fjord because of isostatic rebound, the nearshore marine sediments might have been reworked by meltwater streams and a deposit similar to the fossiliferous layer might have been formed here. Moreover, when this hypothetical fjord was replaced by a relict lake (McLeod, 1963) deposits similar to the fossiliferous layer but related to the lake might have been formed.

The apparent absence in the Wright Valley of marine deltas, shoreline features, and widespread fine-grained marine deposits makes it very unlikely that either a fjord or a relict lake ever occupied the valley.

The writer believes that the shells are in glaciofluvial deposits, that they were initially transported by glacial ice from the floor of McMurdo Sound up into the Wright Valley, and that they were later picked up and redeposited by meltwater streams. The presence of unweathered till below the fossiliferous sand and gravel is what might be expected if this interpretation is correct. Fossiliferous till and also glaciofluvial deposits containing marine fossils are found near Boston, Massachusetts (Crosby and Ballard, 1894; Nichols and Lord, 1938) and similar deposits are found in England and Ireland near the coast (Wright, 1914). Moreover, fossiliferous till containing marine organisms which was plowed up from the bottom of McMurdo Sound is also found on Ross Island (David and Priestley, 1914).

This fossiliferous glaciofluvial layer is the type locality of the Pecten glacial episode (Nichols, 1961), the oldest of the glacial episodes during which ice moved westward up the Wright Valley. No other deposits which can be definitely assigned to this glacial episode were found by the writer in the Wright Valley, with the exception of the unweathered till beneath the Pecten layer; and it is not known, therefore, how much farther up the valley the

Pecten ice went. The apparent absence of a Pecten end moraine is of interest. It may have been deposited in the western end of the valley and later destroyed by the Wright Upper Glacier.

Distribution of Pecten Ice

In order for glacial ice to carry marine shells from McMurdo Sound up into the Wright Valley, the ice, in part at least, must have been resting on the bottom of the sound. The depth of McMurdo Sound (U. S. Navy Hydrographic Office, 1958), the height of the threshold and of the Wright Lower Glacier near the eastern end of the Wright Valley (Fig. 3), the distance of the Pecten deposits from the eastern end of the valley, and an estimate of the gradient of the Wright Lower Glacier at the time the shells were being deposited in the Wright Valley indicate that there must have been more than 3,500 feet (1,070 m) of glacial ice in parts of McMurdo Sound at this time. It seems probable that the ice which filled the sound during Pecten time resulted from an enlargement of the Ross Ice Shelf and the Koettlitz, Ferrar, MacKay, and other outlet glaciers. Moreover, unless the surface of the Antarctic Ice Sheet was lower near the Wright Upper Glacier during the Pecten than during the Vanda, the ice sheet would have spilled across the threshold at the western end of the Wright Valley and filled the valley with eastward-moving ice. However, the surface of the ice sheet was presumably higher than it is now, for the outlet glaciers in the McMurdo Sound area in general were larger and more extensive than at present. The Wright Upper Glacier, therefore, was probably more extensive in Pecten time and moved farther eastward down the valley than it does now.

If true, this would mean that during the full-bodied stage of Pecten time most of the Wright Valley was filled with either eastward- or westward-moving ice and that there was at most only a small ice-free area. If an ice-dammed lake existed between the eastward- and westward-moving glaciers, no evidence of its existence has been positively identified (Nichols, 1965). It is not known whether the unweathered till immediately below the Pecten gravels was deposited by the Wright Upper Glacier, by the Wright Lower Glacier, or by ice which came from Bull Pass.

The location of the shells near Bull Pass raises the question of whether the ice that transported the shells moved from McMurdo Sound directly up into the Wright Valley or whether it moved first up the Victoria Valley and then over into the Wright Valley by way of Bull Pass (Fig. 1). The distance from McMurdo Sound to the Pecten deposits is approximately 15 miles (24 km) farther by way of the Victoria Valley and Bull Pass than directly by way of the Wright Valley. The divide in Bull Pass between the Victoria and Wright Valleys is many hundreds of feet (hundreds of meters) above the Pecten deposits. It is concluded, therefore, that the shells were transported from McMurdo Sound directly up the Wright Valley.

That glacial ice moved up into the Wright Valley from McMurdo Sound in Pecten time is not surprising because there is considerable evidence that McMurdo Sound was at one or more times filled with glacial ice. The studies Taylor (1922) made in Granite Harbor at Mount Suess indicate that at one time the MacKay Glacier was more than 1,000 feet (305 m) thicker than it is now and extended far out into McMurdo Sound. Granite, gneiss, schist, porphyry, and sandstone erratics, all foreign to Ross Island, are found at Cape Royds on Ross Island (David and Priestly, 1914). The location of these erratics proves that when they were deposited McMurdo Sound was filled with ice which at Cape Royds extended at least 1,000 feet (305 m) above the present sea level. Granite erratics are found at least 650 feet (198 m) above sea level on Beaufort Island (Péwé, 1960). A lake 1,000 feet (305 m) deep was located in the Taylor Valley, which was then dammed by ice that filled the sound (Péwé, 1960). The presence of till containing marine organisms on Ross Island proves that the sound was filled with ice that extended more than 160 feet (49 m) above the present sea level (David and Priestley, 1914). Calkin (1964b) envisions an invasion of ice from McMurdo Sound into the Mount Gran area during his second glaciation, and he believes that there was about 4,000 feet (1,220 m) of ice in the McMurdo Sound–Ross Sea area at that time.

The distribution of glacial ice during the full-bodied stage of the Pecten glacial episode differed greatly from that during the Vanda glacial episode and from that at present. In an attempt to explain this difference, Bull (1962) wrote: "Hollin (1962) has shown that the extent of the grounded ice mass of Antarctica is determined almost entirely by the position of sea-level. A decrease in the sea-level of 150 m. [492 feet] would result in the seaward extension of the continental ice by about 100 km. [62 miles] and an increase in the ice thickness at the present edge of the continent of about 1,200 m. [3,940 feet]. However, near the centre of the ice sheet (for example, inland from the western end of the Wright Valley) the increase in thickness would be very much smaller, 50 m. [164 feet] in a calculation made with one particular set of simplifying assumptions and about 200 m. [656 feet] in Hollin's calculation. The second effect of such a decrease in sea-level would be the grounding of ice in the area at present occupied by the Ross Ice Shelf. Once the ice was grounded, the area would accumulate the ice flowing from western Antarctica and from the southern parts of eastern Antarctica until its surface attained a nearly parabolic profile. With a drop in sea-level of 150 m. [492 feet] the northern limit of the grounded ice in the Ross Sea area would be at about lat. 76°30′S. and the elevation of the surface east of the Wright Valley would be about 1,200 m. [3,940 feet]. In such circumstances the transport of pectens from an area previously occupied by sea into the Wright Valley would have been possible, while the extent of the glaciers flowing eastwards from the inland ice plateau was not greatly different from now."

The writer has no new data on why glacial ice was thousands of feet (1,000 m) thick in McMurdo Sound during Pecten time. It may have been because:

1. Sea level was lower than now and the glaciers were therefore more extensive, as suggested by Hollin (1962).
2. A glacial surge occurred at this time (Wilson, 1964). An area somewhat south of the Wright Valley might be favored for the location of surges, since the geothermal gradient was presumably steeper here than elsewhere because of the concentration of pre-Pleistocene and Pleistocene volcanic activity (Nichols, 1965).
3. The ice thickness was related to climate and to the control of the heights of thresholds by tectonic activity.
4. It was the result of a combination of these factors.

The Pecten glacial episode is younger than the Vanda glacial episode, since the fossiliferous layer was deposited on bedrock topography cut during Vanda time. The fossiliferous layer cannot be older than the Vanda glacial episode, because if it had been it would have been removed by Vanda ice. It seems likely that considerable time elapsed between the Vanda and Pecten glacial episodes, for during Vanda time a vigorous glacier moved eastward down the valley while in Pecten time a glacier moved westward from McMurdo Sound up into the Wright Valley.

If the pectens were alive when they were picked up from McMurdo Sound by Pecten ice, the advancing hemicycle of Pecten time occurred more than 8×10^5 years ago. If, however, they had long been dead, the advancing hemicycle of Pecten time is younger and might have occurred less than 8×10^5 years ago. The full-bodied stage of the Pecten glacial episode is younger than the shells, but how much younger is not known.

The possibility was considered that the Pecten glacial episode did not occur, since the Pecten gravels might have been deposited by the Loop glacial episode (see below) (Bull, 1962). That this is apparently not the case is suggested by the following:

1. The coarseness of the Pecten gravels suggests that the ice from which they were derived could not have been very distant. The terminal moraine of the Wright Lower Glacier of Loop time, however, is about 6 miles (10 km) east of the Pecten gravels.
2. The Pecten gravels appear to be too high topographically to have been deposited by meltwater streams from the Wright Lower Glacier of Loop time.
3. The magnitude of erosion following the deposition of the glacial drift that buried the Pecten gravels suggests that this drift is too old to be Trilogy and therefore must be Loop or older. Since the Pecten gravels were weathered before their burial, it would appear that they are pre-Loop.
4. The glacial drift deposited on the Pecten gravels is more profoundly weathered than Loop deposits (personal communication from P. E. Calkin). The weathered Pecten gravels must, therefore, be pre-Loop.

Thus all the available evidence favors the idea that the Pecten gravels were deposited during a glacial episode younger than the Vanda and older than the Loop.

LOOP GLACIAL EPISODE

Type Deposit

A prominent, steep-sided, horseshoe end moraine about 250 feet (76 m) high which is concave eastward down-valley is found on the floor of the valley approximately 8 miles (13 km) west of the western terminus of the Wright Lower Glacier (Figs. 5, 8, 9). The Onyx River has cut a notch through the moraine, and in places the

Fig. 8. An aerial photograph (U. S. Navy) looking westward up the Wright Valley. On the floor of the valley are the prominent horseshoe end moraine, which is the type locality of the Loop glacial episode, and the lateral moraines attached to it. Denton bastion is in the foreground.

Fig. 9. The prominent, looped, steep-sided end moraine about 250 feet (76 m) high, which is the type locality of the Loop glacial episode.

moraine is veneered with eolian sand sheets and alluvium. A large compound alluvial fan, most of which is interglacial and older than the moraine (Nichols, 1965), is located close by on the north side of the valley. With the possible exception of the deposits immediately below Bull Pass where the type locality of the Pecten glacial episode is located, and of deposits on the bottom of the valley less than a mile (1.6 km) west of the Wright Lower Glacier, the moraine and fan constitute the most prominent deposit in the eastern end of the valley. This end moraine is the type deposit of the Loop glacial episode, the second oldest of the glacial episodes whose features were formed by ice that moved westward up the Wright Valley.

Extent of Wright Lower Glacier

The end moraine is continuous with large lateral moraines on both sides of the valley (Fig. 8). These lateral moraines extend higher and higher above the valley floor as they are traced eastward down the valley. Several small, indistinct lateral moraines which extend a few hundred feet (100 m) above the large end moraine are located on the south side of the valley (Fig. 9). These small lateral moraines are weathered about as much as the type deposit and were therefore formed during Loop time. When traced westward up the valley they get closer and closer to the bottom of the valley and apparently merge into small, indistinct end moraines about a mile (1.6 km) west of the type locality. The Wright Lower Glacier extended approximately 9 miles (14 km) farther westward up the Wright Valley than at present during the full-bodied stage of the Loop glacial episode when the uppermost of these lateral moraines and its associated end moraine were being formed. Moreover, as shown by the distribution of Loop deposits at the extreme eastern end of the valley, the Wright Lower Glacier was approximately 1,200 feet (366 m) thick at its present terminus during the full-bodied stage of the Loop glacial episode.

Characteristics of Loop Deposits

The deposits of the Loop glacial episode show considerable antiquity. They are characterized as follows:

1. Many of the fragments at the surface have been weathered and eroded down to ground level (Fig. 10). The surfaces of these fragments are so shattered that a geologic hammer

Fig. 10. Loop deposits which contain fragments weathered and eroded down to ground level.

can be driven almost an inch (2.5 cm) into them. Some of these fragments are more than 3 feet (1 + m) in diameter, and at least a few feet (1 m) of material must have been removed. It is usually the coarse-grained igneous and metamorphic rocks which are weathered to such an extent; the fine-grained doleritic fragments (McKelvey and Webb, 1962), which are rather common in the Wright Valley, are not weathered in this way. In places, more than a score of these truncated fragments can be found in an area of several thousand square feet (1,000 sq m). For this reason the Loop deposits are much less bouldery than the younger glacial deposits in the valley. The work of Kelly and Zumberge (1961) has shown that in this part of the Antarctic, weathering is due mainly to physical rather than chemical changes. It seems likely, therefore, that the weathering and erosion of these fragments result in part at least from frost action and deflation.

2. Cavernously weathered fragments composed of coarse-grained igneous and metamorphic rocks, which project

Fig. 11. A pitted cavernous fragment with soft, crumbly, weathered surfaces, resting on Loop deposits.

above ground level, are common on Loop deposits (Fig. 11) (Calkin and Cailleux, 1962). The pits and hollows indicate that more than 3 feet (1 m) of rock has been removed from some of them. Small caves large enough to hold a man are found between the ground and the bottom of some fragments. The surfaces of these fragments are flaky, scaly, and punky; more than 1/8 inch (0.3 cm) can commonly be removed with an ice axe. The pits and hollows are therefore not due to wind cutting. Since there is no apron of grains and flakes on the ground below the pits and hollows, it seems likely that they are formed by frost action (Kelly and Zumberge, 1961), perhaps in a minor way by other kinds of weathering, and by deflation.

3. Ventifacts are unusually well developed and numerous on Loop deposits. Commonly more than a foot (0.3 m) of rock has been removed from the larger ventifacts, and wind cutting has taken place as much as 3 to 4 feet (1 m) above ground level. Strong winds are indicated by the fact that abrasion took place at this height. In a 3-foot-square (1 sq m) area, 53 ventifacts 1 to 5 inches long were counted. Scores of ventifacts smaller than an inch (2.5 cm) in diameter are also present, and wind-polished stones are still more abundant. In many places thousands of shining ventifacts can be seen between the sun and the observer. They vary in size from a fraction of an inch (2.5 cm) up to a few feet (1 m) in diameter, and einkanters and dreikanters are common. The ventifacts are best preserved on the fine-grained dolerites, which are not rapidly weathered and eroded by other processes. Ventifacts are found in general only near the bottom of the valley, either because of a lack of sand in the upper slopes of the valley or because the winds are katabatic and have, therefore, no great vertical extent.

The larger ventifacts have on their western side a hard, shiny, polished and wind-cut surface which rings when tapped with a geologic hammer, and on their eastern side a soft, flaky, crumbly, weathered surface which gives a dull thud when tapped with a geologic hammer (Fig. 12). During the two summer field seasons (1959–1960, 1960–1961) spent by the writer in the Wright Valley, the winds were not strong enough either to polish or to cut rock (Ugolini and Bull, 1965). Strong winds moving from the ice plateau

Fig. 12. A large ventifact on Loop deposits. Hard, shiny, wind-cut surface on the right; soft, flaky, crumbly weathered surface on the left; wind blew from right to left (black field notebook gives scale).

eastward down the valley during the winter months were therefore responsible for this unusual development of ventifacts. Their formation was also favored because: (1) the area is devoid of vegetation; (2) the deposits on which the ventifacts are found are old; (3) the snowfall is light; (4) the winds are strong; and (5) there is enough sand to do the cutting but not enough to bury the terrain.

4. The Loop deposits are also characterized by a pronounced yellow stain.

Kame-and-Kettle Topography

An area of well-developed kame-and-kettle topography is located immediately eastward down-valley from the end moraine and between the large lateral moraines (Fig. 13). The knobs are steep and several feet (1 + m) high; those investigated were composed of stratified sand and gravel. The steepness of the knobs and the stratification of the deposit preclude the possibility that it is lodge moraine. The absence of any alignment of the knobs suggests that

Fig. 13. The prominent end moraine and lateral moraines attached to it. An area of kame-and-kettle topography is found between the moraines. The sand and gravel of which the kames are composed was initially deposited on the Wright Lower Glacier and finally let down onto the valley floor when the wastage of the ice was completed.

they were not formed in front of and next to the margin of the Wright Lower Glacier. It seems likely that the sand and gravel were initially deposited when meltwater was abundant in the hollows and depressions on the surface of the stagnant or nearly stagnant Wright Lower Glacier, and were finally let down onto the floor of the valley when the wastage of the ice was completed. There is no evidence that the deposit is ice-cored; ventifacts are uncommonly numerous on the deposit and their presence results, no doubt, from the abundant supply of sand.

Age and Source of Loop Ice

Volcanic activity in the Wright Valley in pre-Loop time is indicated by two small basaltic volcanic cones on the south side of the valley above the end moraine. These cones have been glacially eroded; material from them is incorporated in the Loop deposits (Nichols, 1965); and they are therefore older than the Loop glaciation. The easternmost of these cones is $3.7 \pm 0.3 \times 10^6$ years old (Denton, personal communication); the Loop is therefore younger.

The Wright Lower Glacier is fed today by glaciers from the coastal mountains and by the snow that falls on it and on the Wilson Piedmont Glacier. During Pecten time, however, the immediate source of the Wright Lower Glacier was the thousands of feet (1,000 m) of glacial ice which occupied McMurdo Sound. The writer is not certain what the sources of the Wright Lower Glacier were during Loop time.

TRILOGY GLACIAL EPISODE

Characteristics of Deposits

Deposits of the Trilogy glacial episode are best developed at the extreme eastern end of the Wright Valley (Fig. 14). They consist

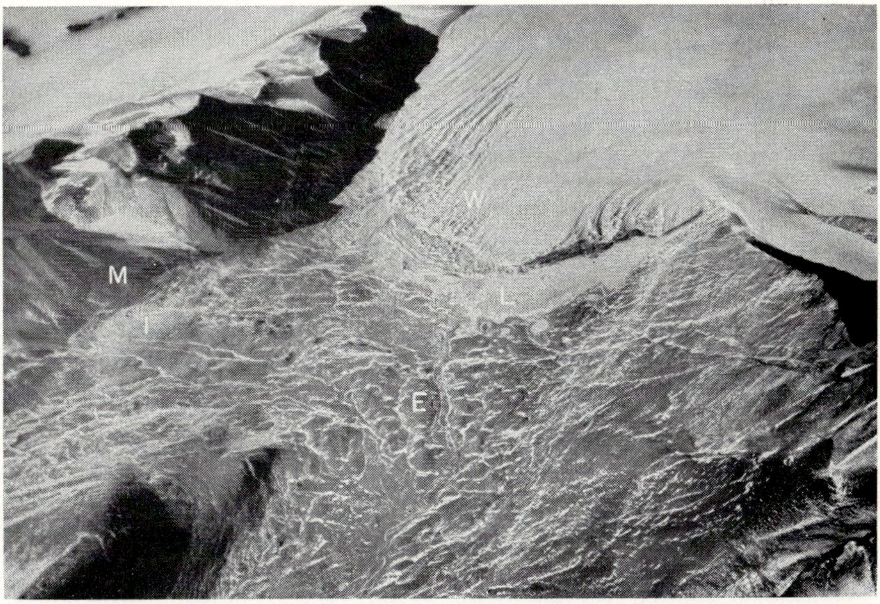

Fig. 14. An aerial photograph of the eastern end of the Wright Valley, showing the Wright Lower Glacier (W), the "Wright Lake" (L), the position of the lateral moraine deposited during the full-bodied stage of the Trilogy (M), the Trilogy end moraine on the floor of the Wright Valley (E), and the ice-cored moraine on the north side of the valley (I). (U. S. Navy aerial photograph.)

of high-level lateral moraines, an end moraine with an associated valley train on the floor of the valley, and ice-cored moraines.

In general Trilogy deposits are characterized by:

1. A smaller amount of wind-cutting than on Loop deposits.
2. An absence of cavernously weathered fragments. In general less than an inch (2.5 cm) of material has been removed from the edges and corners of fragments and little or nothing from the faces.
3. An absence of fragments eroded to ground level. This makes the Trilogy deposits much more bouldery than Loop deposits.
4. Only minor staining.

A comparison of the weathering of Trilogy and Loop deposits proves that the Loop deposits are very much older.

In some places Trilogy deposits are contaminated with weathered Loop material. This contamination occurred when (1) weathered Loop deposits were thinly veneered with Trilogy deposits, (2) thin Trilogy ice picked up and incorporated weathered Loop deposits with unweathered deposits, and (3) weathered Loop material fell onto Trilogy glaciers and was deposited at their termini with unweathered material.

Oldest Trilogy Deposits

A series of indistinct lateral moraines is found on the north side of the eastern end of the valley close to the terminus of the Wright Lower Glacier and just east of the easternmost cirque glacier, near the terminus of the "Clark Valley" (Fig. 14). The highest well-developed lateral moraine is approximately 1,000 feet (305 m) above the valley floor. It can be traced westward up the valley where it becomes lower and lower and finally merges into a small, poorly developed end moraine approximately 5 miles (8 km) west of the present terminus of the Wright Lower Glacier. These moraines represent the oldest and most extensive stage of the Wright Lower Glacier during the Trilogy. The Wright Lower Glacier then extended approximately 5 miles (8 km) farther up the valley than now and was about 1,000 feet (305 m) thick at its present terminus. It was neither as extensive nor as thick at that time, however, as during its most advanced position in the Loop. During Late Trilogy time a series of small recessional moraines was built on the floor of the valley as the glacier retreated eastward down the valley.

End Moraine

A prominent end moraine of Trilogy age, formed after the full-bodied stage of the Trilogy glacial episode, is found on the valley floor between the terminus of the Wright Lower Glacier and the junction of the Clark Glacier and Onyx Rivers (Fig. 14). This end moraine is about 3 miles (5 km) east of the small, indistinct end moraine deposited by the Wright Lower Glacier during the full-bodied stage of the Trilogy glacial episode. It is bounded on its western, up-valley side by a valley train and on its eastern side by flattish topography that slopes gradually downward to the "Wright Lake." The moraine extends lengthwise across the valley in roughly a north-south direction for over a mile (1.6 km); its maximum width measured approximately parallel to the axis of the valley is also about a mile (1.6 km); and its maximum relief is a little over 60 feet (18 m). The Onyx River crosses the moraine, and here the river valley is, in places, approximately 60 feet (18 m) deep. The moraine is characterized by gentle slopes. It is composed of ridges and swales which are oriented nearly in the same direction as the valley and extend across the total width of the moraine. The ridges are divided by transverse trenches into low, rounded, smooth, gentle hills (Fig. 15). One ridge is 30 feet (9 m) high. The moraine is very bouldery; boulders 1 to 2 feet (0.3–0.6 m) in diameter are common and the largest are 10 feet (3 m) across. Some of the moraine is composed of stratified sand and gravel, as was shown by digging. Frost cracks are found on the moraine, wind-polished and wind-cut fragments are common, and travertine is found on the bottom of some fragments (Nichols, 1963).

The moraine appears gray when the observer looks east, yellowish when he looks west, because the west sides of the fragments are wind-cut whereas the east sides are weathered. Over considerable areas there is a desert pavement; eolian sand sheets are also present. The upper 1 to 3 inches (2.5–7.5 cm) of the morainal deposit is gray because of eolian abrasion and frost stirring but beneath this zone the deposit is stained yellow; eolian abrasion, therefore, helps to keep the moraine young looking. Poorly developed cavernous boulders and fragments weathered down to ground level are present but not common; they were probably derived from Loop deposits.

The writer does not think that the end moraine is ice-cored. No ice was seen at the surface or exposed by digging, and no

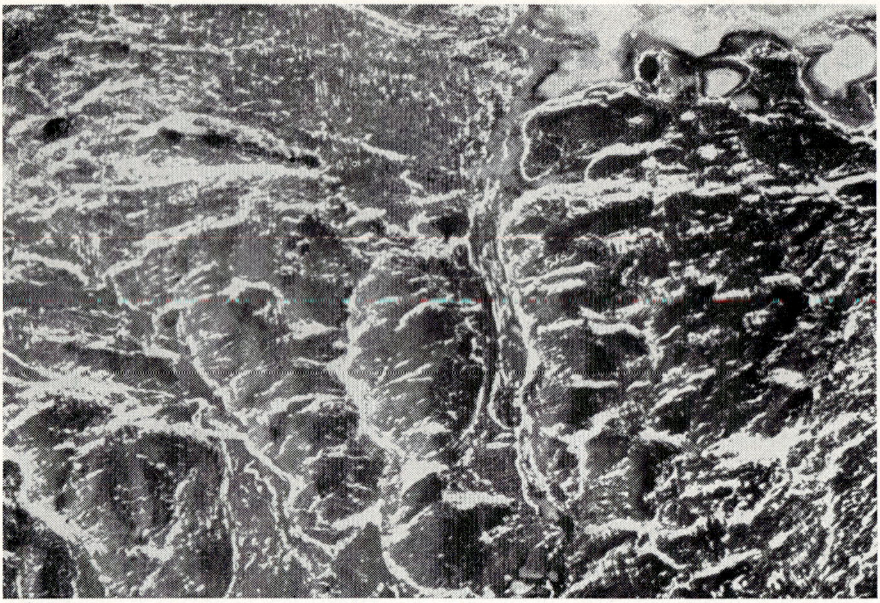

Fig. 15. The end moraine of Trilogy age at the eastern end of the Wright Valley.

wetted areas resulting from the melting of buried ice were seen.

Because the stratified sand and gravel is water-laid and the large boulders were deposited directly from the Wright Lower Glacier, the moraine is partly a kame and partly a till moraine. The exact mechanism of formation is not known . The ridges may have been formed in reentrants in the ice front and the swales may be essentially constructional, or the swales may have resulted from the presence of large meltwater streams along which less deposition took place than elsewhere. It is not known how the valley occupied by the Onyx River was formed. Perhaps it is an original feature of the moraine somewhat widened and deepened by the river. Perhaps it was formed entirely by the Onyx River, which established itself where the moraine was low when the lake was higher than it is now. The absence of elevated shorelines around the lake, however, makes this most unlikely.

A ridge between the lake and the northeast side of the end moraine is an anomalous feature. It is steep, stands approximately 100 feet (30 m) above the surrounding area, and is about 2,000 feet (610 m) long. The ridge is oriented north-south and is roughly parallel to the terminus of the Wright Lower Glacier. Its steepness contrasts sharply with the gentle slopes of the end moraine. Its orientation suggests that it is a terminal feature of the Wright Lower Glacier rather than of the Clark or cirque glaciers on the north side of the valley. Whether the ridge is a kame moraine with its ice-contact slope on the east, or a push moraine made by a readvance, is not known. Perhaps it correlates with the ice-cored moraines (see below) at the eastern end of the valley, which are younger than the gentle end moraine. The ridge is less than a mile (1.6 km) from them, but it has no wetted surfaces from the melting of buried ice, and digging did not uncover any ice.

Valley Train

Irregular topography on the valley floor extends for a few miles (3 km) westward up-valley from the end moraine. Not enough time was available for a detailed study of this area, but the following observations and interpretations were made. In general this topography slopes downward westward up the valley. It is characterized by numerous pits, kettles, and hillocks. A cut made by the Onyx River shows that the deposits immediately below the surface are stratified and cross-bedded, slope downward up-valley, are parallel to the surface and nearly horizontal, and are composed essentially of sand and a few pebble layers. A thickness of 8 feet (2.4 m) of these deposits, extending 33 feet (10 m) along the river, was exposed in one cut; here the surface was approximately 20 feet (6 m) above the river. The area is therefore a pitted valley train. Some of the kettles on the north side of the valley are 200 to 300 yards (180–275 m) long, 100 yards (90 m) wide, and 10 to 15 feet (3–5 m) deep. The kettles are so large that they must have resulted from the wastage of buried stagnant blocks of ice rather than from the melting of rafted blocks of ice. That the kettles owe their origin to stagnant glacial ice is not surprising, as buried stagnant ice is now found immediately in front of the Wright Lower Glacier, in the "Clark Valley," and elsewhere in the eastern end of the Wright Valley. Kettle holes are not common in the upstream, western part of the valley train, where it is generally flat and smooth, but they are common in the downstream, eastern part, where its surface is irregular. A kettle hole containing fine-grained lacustrine silt is located close to the junction of the Onyx and Clark Glacier Rivers. The absence of silt in other kettle holes and the proximity of this kettle to the Onyx River make it certain that the deposit resulted from the flooding of the kettle by the river, not from the meltwater streams that built the valley train. The valley train seems to be higher near the valley walls and lower in the center of the valley near the Onyx River, as would be expected if it were deposited on stagnant ice. Although the valley train is not as bouldery as the Trilogy end moraine, large boulders several feet (2 + m) long are nevertheless found on it. They decrease in number, however, and finally disappear with increasing distance from the end moraine. These boulders are much too large to have been transported by meltwater. It is not known whether they fell onto the valley train from stagnant blocks of glacial ice that protruded above its surface or whether they are part of the till immediately below, which was not buried by the valley train. Unfortunately, no time was available to determine the location of the boulders in relation to the kettles. If they are without exception marginal to kettles, they probably fell from stagnant blocks. In places the hillocks may be till highs not buried by the valley train; in other places they may have resulted from the burial of ice which was thinner here than elsewhere. It is not thought that the valley train is at present ice-cored, since no buried ice was seen in the cuts made by the Onyx River and there was no water or even dampness in any of the kettles.

In places, a sharp break in slope occurs where the flat surface of the valley train meets the steep surface of the end moraine. This suggests that the valley train buries the lower part of the end moraine and is an independent geologic unit formed under different conditions from those of the end moraine. Its geographic relation to the end moraine, however, and its degree of weathering prove that both are approximately the same age.

Thermal contraction cracks commonly filled with windblown sand are abundant on the valley train; a deflation pavement is found at the surface, and wind-cut fragments are also present.

No ridges transverse to the valley train are present. It is not, therefore, a series of coalescing kettled kame moraines formed during a succession of stillstands of the terminus of the Wright Lower Glacier as it retreated eastward.

No abandoned channels or other features characteristic of valley-train surfaces were seen. Presumably they were initially poorly developed and were later destroyed by collapse, deflation, and the formation of ice-wedge furrows and levees.

The Onyx River in places has formed four non-paired terraces below the valley-train surface. One of these terraces is 15 to 20 feet (4–6 m) below that surface. Meander scars and cusps are common. The largest ice-wedge furrows and levees the writer has seen in the Antarctic are found on these terraces. The levees on one terrace were approximately 3 feet (1 m) high and the wedge measured from the outside edges of levees was approximately 21 feet (6.4 m) wide. The terraces are kettled in places. Larger kettles are found on the higher terraces than on the lower. The surfaces of the terraces are less bouldery, in places, than the surface of the valley train. Terraces cut in valley-train deposits, however, should in general be more bouldery than the valley train, and the lower terraces should be more bouldery than the upper. It is not known for certain whether these terraces were cut in the valley-train deposits or in a younger fill inset in these deposits, or whether they had a more complex origin. The solution of this problem has considerable significance in tracing the history of the Trilogy glacial episode.

Ice-Cored Moraines

Ice-cored moraines are found in many places in the Wright Valley. The largest is located on the north side of the eastern end of the valley about a mile (1.6 km) southeast of the Clark Glacier (Fig. 14). Its surface slopes gently and has an average relief of less than 5 feet (1.5 m). It is characterized by hillocks, kettles, and furrows. The hillocks are commonly less than 5 feet (1.5 m) high and 40 feet (12 m) across; the kettles are up to 4 feet (1.2 m) deep and 30 feet (9 m) across and are commonly connected by furrows so that undrained depressions, if present, are not common (Fig. 16). The moraine is covered by more furrows than any other deposit the writer has studied in the Antarctic. Large rock blocks, some 10 feet (3 m) in diameter, are abundant. Stratified sand and gravel is found at the surface, and in places large rocks derived from adjacent hillocks rest on the sand and gravel. At no time during the two field seasons when the writer studied this deposit was there enough meltwater from any source to have deposited the sand and gravel. This was not because the 1959–1960 and 1960–1961 summers may have been colder than usual, nor because the writer left the valley before the melt season was completed. The necessary meltwater was available, however, when ablation was more rapid because the moraine was thinner. Ice does not crop out at the surface and there is no significant wetting of the surface indicating ice melting at depth. Digging showed, however, that ice is present beneath 1 to 2 feet (0.3–0.6 m) of moraine

Fig. 16. The ice-cored moraine of Trilogy age, which is located at the north-eastern end of the Wright Valley. Ventifacts, weathered fragments, and the yellow stain at the surface indicate that the deposit has some antiquity.

Fig. 17. The ice-cored moraine. Shovel and ice-axe give scale.

(Fig. 17). In general the ice is clean, although some is sandy and contain scattered pebbles and cobbles. Its widespread distribution, cleanness, and considerable thickness prove that it is glacial rather than ice-wedge ice or the ice found in lenses near the top of the permafrost. These ice lenses are usually less than a foot (0.3 m) thick, have little continuity, and are commonly dirty. The ice-wedge ice commonly has continuity in two directions but not in the third, and it too tends to be dirty. The small amount of meltwater, the scarcity of wet moraine, the absence of ice at the surface, and the thickness of the moraine suggest that most of the ice is in the permafrost zone and that wastage is very slow. A steep-sided, V-shaped ravine 15 to 20 feet (4.5–6.0 m) deep has been cut into the ice-cored moraine; the absence of an alluvial fan below the ravine proves that it was mainly ice which was removed. In places the moraine terminates in a steep slope over 50 feet (15 m) high, which suggests that in places 50 feet (15 m) of ice is still present beneath the moraine. This thickness of ice and the flatness of the slope on which it rests suggest that the ice is stagnant (Matthes, 1899–1900). The absence of significant quantities of morainal material at the terminus of the ice-cored moraine indicates that it was not active for very long. The presence of tens of feet (15 m) of ice and only a few feet (0.6 m) of moraine proves that these features are essentially shrunken glaciers and that their steep marginal slopes owe their existence mainly to the presence of glacial ice, not to the moraine. Several steep-sided cone-shaped kames are found near the margin of the ice-cored moraine; two are more than 50 feet (15 m) high. They are easily identified by their steep slopes and shapes, which are in sharp contrast to the extensive, gentle, subdued topography of the end moraine and the large flattish areas of the ice-cored moraine. Their height, and the absence of significant relief on the ice-cored moraine, suggest that they were formed in front of the glacier from which the ice-cored moraine was derived. They indicate that tens of feet ($>$ 15 m) of ablation has taken place since their formation. Moreover, the thickness of the moraine and the cleanness of the ice from which it was derived indicate that many feet (many meters) of ice have been lost by ablation. The surface of the moraine is in general covered with fresh, unweathered fragments; but this loss of ice, the yellow color of the surface of the moraine, the veneer of travertine on the bottoms of fragments (Nichols, 1963), and the crumbly, weathered surfaces of some fragments all suggest that the ice-cored moraine has some antiquity.

The ice-cored moraine is younger than the lateral moraine formed during the most extensive stage of the Trilogy, as it is topographically below the lateral moraine. Hundreds of feet (hundreds of meters) of glacial ice that existed during the most extensive stage of the Trilogy had to be wasted away before the ice-cored moraine was formed.

Moreover, the ice-cored moraine has a longitudinal profile like that of an active glacier. If the ice-cored moraine had been formed by the down-wastage of the glacier that built the lateral moraine, it would probably not have this kind of profile. This suggests that the ice-cored moraine is derived from glacial ice that accumulated after the complete destruction of the glacier which deposited the lateral moraine during the full-bodied stage of the Trilogy.

The writer found it impossible to determine the relative age of the ice-cored moraine and the end moraine by a comparison of the degree of weathering and wind-cutting on the two deposits. The difference in weathering is small. Although wind-cutting in places is more common on the end moraine, sand appears to be more abundant there and consequently the amount of wind-cutting is not a good criterion of age.

The presence of glacial ice only a foot (0.3 m) or so beneath the surface of the ice-cored moraine, and its absence or presence at depths too great to be reached by digging in the end moraine suggest that the ice-cored moraine is younger. The ice-cored moraine is closer to active glacial ice than the end moraine; this also suggests that it is younger.

The presence in one area of smooth, gently sloping topography 200 to 300 yards (180–275 m) wide that separates the ice-cored moraine from the end moraine and is about 20 feet (6 m) lower than both deposits, is probably better explained by a readvance to form the ice-cored moraine than by continuous retreat of the ice front from the end moraine to the present position of the ice-cored moraine. In addition, alluvium which may correlate with the ice-cored stage was deposited near the junction of the "Clark Valley" and Onyx River on an erosion surface cut on the Trilogy valley-train deposits. This suggests that the ice-cored moraine and valley-train stages are separated by a time interval.

Several kame terraces are found in the "Clark Valley." The best developed and preserved is on the east side of the river only a few hundred yards ($>$ 200 m) from the steep 50-foot (15 m) slope of the ice-cored moraine. This kame terrace appears to have been deposited on an ice-cored moraine. The kame terraces, ice-cored moraines, and morainal ridges found in the "Clark Valley" may have a more complex glacial history than suggested. The area deserves further study.

Relation to the Loop Glacial Episode

The writer believes that following the full-bodied stage of the Loop glacial episode the Wright Lower Glacier retreated eastward in the Wright Valley at least as far as its present position and later readvanced to the position it occupied during the full-bodied stage of the Trilogy—in other words, that the Loop and Trilogy glacial episodes are distinct events, separated by an interglacial episode. Evidence for this can perhaps be seen in Figure 18 which shows deposits laid down by one of the hanging glaciers (Fig. 5). Badly weathered Loop deposits, with very few boulders which project above ground level, can be seen in the middle left of the photo; only slightly weathered Trilogy deposits, with numerous boulders lying on the ground, can be seen in the foreground and middle right. A small moraine separates the Loop deposits from the Trilogy deposits.

Fig. 18. A part of Wright Valley, showing badly weathered Loop deposits and only slightly weathered Trilogy deposits, separated by a small moraine.

It might be thought that these features and relations can be explained by the following sequence: (1) deposition of the Loop deposits; (2) retreat of the ice front to the position of the small moraine; (3) a long-continued stillstand of the ice at the position of the moraine, during which the Loop deposits were profoundly weathered; (4) a retreat which completely deglaciated the area and occurred so recently that the bouldery Trilogy deposits are only slightly weathered. Such a sequence, however, would result in the formation of a large moraine rather than the existing small one (Nichols and Miller, 1951).

The small moraine and the other glacial features in the area can be explained, however, as follows: (1) deposition of the Loop deposits; (2) deglaciation of all of the area, during which time the Loop deposits were profoundly weathered; (3) readvance of glacial ice in the Trilogy to the position of the small moraine; (4) a stillstand at this position so brief that only a small moraine could be formed; and (5) a retreat which occurred so recently that the bouldery Trilogy deposits are only slightly weathered.

Evidence for a Trilogy readvance is also found in the "Clark Valley." Trilogy deposits are found on the floor of the "Clark Valley" less than a mile from the Clark Glacier. As they are traced from the floor upward on the valley wall on the west, they finally terminate against Loop deposits. No topographic break is found where they meet. Here the Trilogy ice advanced over Loop deposits and at its most advanced position halted for such a short time that no moraine was formed. Following a short halt, the Trilogy ice retreated and its deposits were exposed.

A lateral moraine composed of many ridges and swales transverse to its alignment is found on the south side of the valley near the floor just eastward from the bastion at the foot of the Denton Glacier (Fig. 6). It appears to be a washboard moraine (Flint, 1957). It is badly weathered and dates, therefore, from the Loop. Its position near the floor of the valley proves that it was formed during a retreatal stage, not during the most extensive stage of the Loop. Farther eastward the ridges and swales disappear and still farther eastward the material at the surface of the moraine appears younger and may be of Trilogy age. Perhaps here we have an example of a Loop moraine overrun by readvancing Trilogy ice. In any event the moraine proves that at the time of its formation, as at present, the Wright Lower Glacier was transporting more material along its southern margin than on its center.

Still further proof of a readvance in the Trilogy is shown by the presence of weathered Loop material in Trilogy deposits and by the fact that in places it appears that thin Trilogy deposits rest on Loop deposits.

Moreover, alluvial deposits presumably of Trilogy age, as indicated by their degree of weathering, are found on the floor of the valley eastward from the type locality of the Loop. They appear to have been deposited in a shallow valley cut in Loop deposits and therefore suggest a time interval between the two glacial episodes.

In addition, Loop deposits are found both above and below the highest Trilogy lateral moraine at the eastern end of the valley, a fact which also indicates the existence of a time interval between the Loop and Trilogy glacial episodes.

Age

The end moraine at the present terminus of the Wright Lower Glacier has been observed for approximately 10 years. In the writer's opinion, no significant change in size has occurred. The Trilogy end moraine, even if ice-cored, is many times as large as the moraine at the present terminus of the Wright Lower Glacier. This suggests that hundreds, perhaps thousands, of years were required to build the Trilogy end moraine.

No careful measurements were made of the volume of the end moraines deposited by the Wright Lower Glacier during Loop and Trilogy time. It seems likely that the Loop end moraines are larger than those of the Trilogy, but we cannot conclude from this that the Loop glacial episode was longer than the Trilogy. The Wright Lower Glacier extended farther up the valley in Loop than in Trilogy time. For more of its length, therefore, high cliffs extended above it, more material fell onto it, and the end moraine was thus formed more rapidly in Loop than in Trilogy time.

Excellently developed elevated beaches are found just north of Marble Point on the west side of McMurdo Sound (Nichols, 1966). A radiocarbon measurement of an elephant seal (L-594) buried in an elevated beach about 44 feet (13 m) above sea level at Marble Point indicates that this beach is $4.6 \times 10^3 \pm 200$ years old. The highest beaches at Marble Point, approximately 66 feet (20 m) above sea level, are therefore perhaps 6.0 to 7.0×10^3 years old. The highest beaches at Marble Point roughly correlate on the basis of their degree of weathering with the deposits laid down during the Trilogy glacial episode. During the full-bodied stage of the

Trilogy glacial episode, the Wright Lower Glacier extended approximately 5 miles (8 km) farther up the Wright Valley than at present and was about 1,000 feet (305 m) thick at its present terminus. Because the Wright Lower Glacier had a greater extent in the Wright Valley during Trilogy time than now, and because of the present proximity of the highest elevated beaches and the terminal positions of the glaciers around McMurdo Sound, it is certain that in many places these glaciers must have extended out into McMurdo Sound beyond the positions of the highest elevated beaches during the most extensive stage of Trilogy time. Thus the highest beaches around McMurdo Sound were not formed until the Trilogy glaciers had retreated considerably from their most advanced positions. The full-bodied stage of the Trilogy glacial episode occurred, therefore, more than 6.0 to 7.0×10^3 years ago. It seems likely that the Loop deposits are many tens of thousands of years old and are, therefore, pre-Wisconsin in age (Flint, 1957).

FEATURES ASSOCIATED WITH HANGING GLACIERS

Lateral and terminal moraines, solifluction lobes and sheets, alluvial fans, torrential boulder deposits, and bastions are associated with the hanging glaciers on the south wall of the valley.

Small ice-cored lateral moraines composed of unweathered material commonly occur close to the glaciers; larger moraines composed of material which is somewhat weathered are found farther away; and still farther away are moraines composed of badly weathered material with fragments eroded to ground level. Most of these moraines are located within a few hundred yards (few hundred meters) of the glaciers (Fig. 19). They indicate that for a very long time the glaciers have not been much more extensive than at present. These moraines presumably correlate with the Loop and Trilogy deposits laid down by the Wright Lower Glacier.

Solifluction lobes and sheets are commonly found close to the glaciers. It is the writer's impression that solifluction is more active close to glaciers than elsewhere. The low humidity that characterizes the valley tends to produce ice-free soils (Bell, 1966). Since the snowfall in the valley is small and most of it evaporates, it adds little moisture to the soils (Nichols, 1963). The soil moisture necessary for solifluction is therefore found only near snowdrifts and glaciers.

Small intermittent streams run from most of the hanging gla-

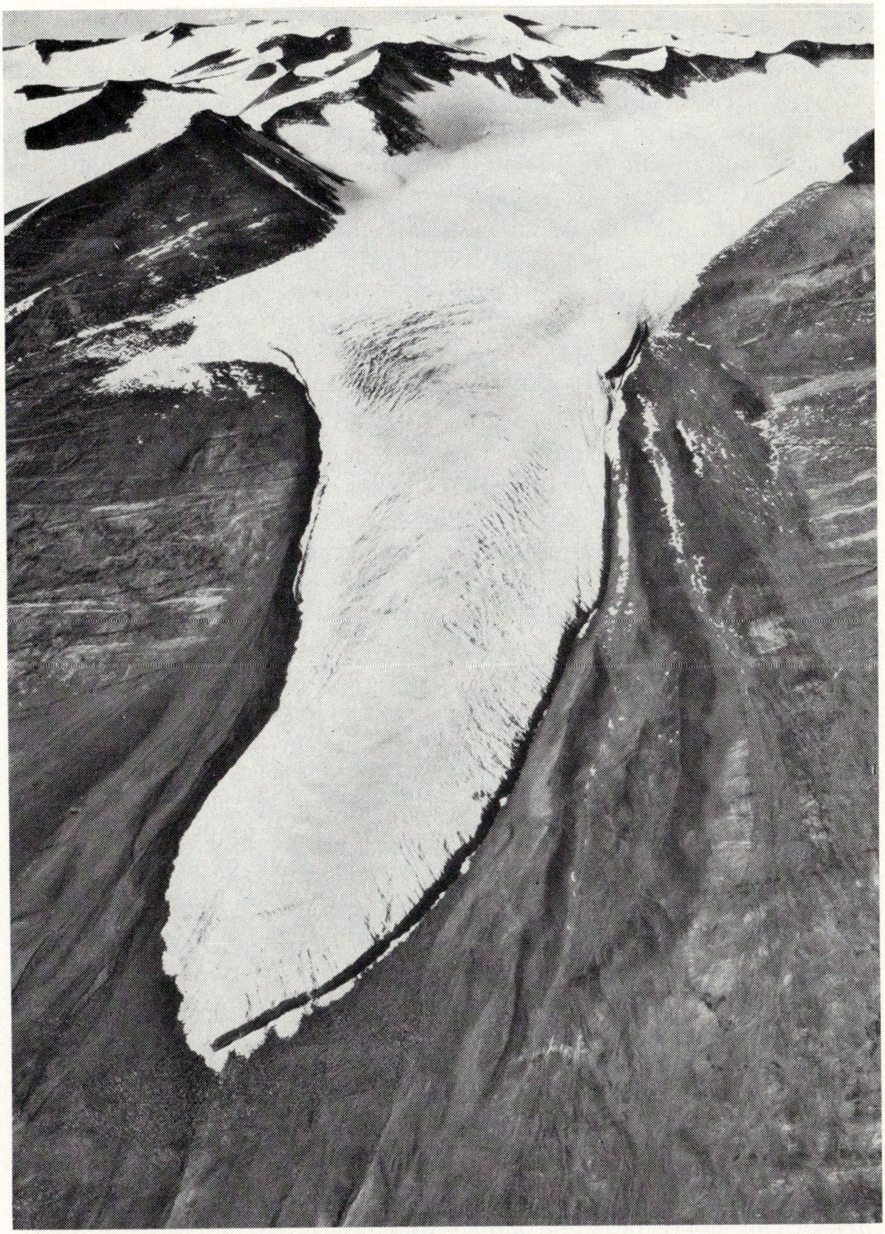

Fig. 19. An aerial photograph (U. S. Navy) showing the prominent lateral moraines on the west side of the Meserve Glacier in the Wright Valley.

ciers, and it is thus not surprising that sizable fans are found below them.

Fluvial torrential boulder deposits associated with the hanging glaciers are found at the southeast end of Bull Pass, on the north side of the valley some distance above the prominent horseshoe moraine, and on the west side of the Meserve Glacier. The boulders are somewhat rounded; some are a few feet (1 m) in diameter; and they are distributed in thin elongated threads. Because the boulders are not appreciably weathered, these deposits are among the youngest in the valley. It is not known whether these coarse deposits were formed (1) by the periodic drainage of ice-dammed lakes, (2) during a climate warmer than that at present when water was more abundant than now, (3) by larger meltwater streams formed from larger glaciers, (4) by meltwater streams formed by volcanic heat, or (5) whether, which seems most unlikely, the 1959–1961 field seasons were unusually cold (Nichols, 1966).

Two deposits are found, below a hanging valley, on the fan on the north wall of the Wright Valley near the prominent horseshoe end moraine about 8 miles (13 km) west of the Wright Lower Glacier (Nichols, 1965). The older and lower of these deposits is approximately 600 feet (183 m) wide and 1,000 feet (305 m) long. The lower end terminates in a steep slope 50 to 60 feet (15–18 m) high. Angular fragments eroded to ground level occur, and from a distance the deposit appears yellow. Mudflows with levees and channels are found on it. One flow about 75 feet (23 m) wide has levees 2 feet (< 1 m) high and 4 feet (> 1 m) wide. The younger of the two deposits is found higher up on the fan. It is covered with unweathered fragments, terminates in a 20° slope about 35 feet (11 m) high, and from a distance looks gray. A similar deposit is found on the north side of the valley just east of Bull Pass. It too has steep sides and associated mudflows and is located beneath a hanging valley.

These deposits are not paired and not ridgelike. They are short and wide and have flat, mesa-like upper surfaces. It seems unlikely, therefore, that they are lateral moraines. It is not known whether they are mudflows, ice-cored moraines, or deposits formed from ice-cored moraines; topographically they are similar to all three. The steep marginal slopes and flat upper surfaces suggest that they may be mudflows, but the absence of marginal levees and a medial channel suggests either that they are not or that, if mudflows, they were made of very viscous material. As far as is known, they contain no ice or wetted areas indicating ice at depth. Whatever their origin, they are undoubtedly related to the hanging valleys immediately above them. The cliffs above these deposits and below the hanging valleys are so steep that one wonders if the deposits are not related to reconstructed glaciers.

THE TERMINUS OF THE WRIGHT LOWER GLACIER

During the retreat of the Wright Lower Glacier from the prominent end moraine of Trilogy time to its present terminus, the following occurred:

1. Alluvial fans continued to grow below hanging glaciers.
2. Solifluction was active primarily below glaciers.
3. Trilogy and pre-Trilogy deposits were weathered.
4. The Onyx River cut a series of non-paired terraces in the Trilogy valley train.
5. The surface of Lake Vanda was lowered approximately 185 feet (56 m) (Nichols, 1965).
6. The Wright Lower and other glaciers retreated, readvanced, and again retreated, forming the ice-cored moraine, kames, and other features.
7. A short time ago small volcanic cones (Nichols, 1962) and "Wright Lake" were formed in the extreme eastern end of the valley.
8. The Wright Lower Glacier reached its present terminal position a very short time ago, as indicated by the size of the end moraine now found there.

An ice-cored kame moraine is being formed at the north end of the present terminus of the Wright Lower Glacier. In places it is being built out into "Wright Lake"; elsewhere it is bounded by a marginal meltwater stream that runs into the lake. It extends for more than half a mile (.8 km) along the terminus of the glacier. In places, where the meltwater streams that build it are small and overloaded, the kame moraine is a series of steep alluvial cones (Fig. 20). Where the streams are larger and not so heavily loaded, it is an alluvial apron composed of coalescing fans (Fig. 21). The stratified, cross-bedded sand of which it is composed rests on ice (Fig. 22). In one place the sand is about 8 feet (> 2 m) thick. The active zone in this area is less than 3 feet (1 m) thick. Wastage of ice buried by 8 feet (> 2 m) of sand takes place only by the diffusion of water vapor and must, therefore, be slow. The ice core

Fig. 20. The active ice-cored kame moraine at the northern end of the terminus of the Wright Lower Glacier. Here it is an alluvial cone which rests on ice. The perennially frozen "Wright Lake" is in the foreground and the Wright Lower Glacier in the background.

is thin and must be stagnant. A small fosse and an ice-contact slope are present where the ice front has recently retreated a short distance. Rocks fall onto the outwash from the glacier, and also roll from small detached knobs of ice, protected by ablation moraine, onto the outwash that surrounds them. Channels up to 6 feet (< 2 m) deep, eroded into unfrozen sand, frozen sand, and ice, are common. Swiftly moving streams flow in the channels at the height of the melt season. Kettle holes up to 30 feet (9 m) in diameter are present. At one place immediately adjacent to the glacier, a layer of frozen sand was tilted up by a minor glacial readvance so that it dipped at an angle of 50° toward the glacier. A series of ridges and valleys essentially parallel to the ice front could be traced for scores of feet (many meters). The ridges were only a few feet (1 m) apart and the valleys only a few feet (1 m) deep. This topography resulted from the thrust of the glacier into frozen outwash sand.

The sand in the kame moraine is very well rounded and was formed by the mechanical breakup of the Beacon Sandstone that

Fig. 21. The active ice-cored kame moraine at the northern end of the terminus of the Wright Lower Glacier. Here it consists of an alluvial apron, is composed of stratified cross-bedded sand, and rests on ice.

crops out in the upper part of the Wright Valley (McKelvey and Webb, 1962; Shaw, 1962; Harrington and Speden, 1962). The winter winds, which blow eastward, carry the sand down the valley and up onto the Wright Lower Glacier. The kame moraine was formed during the summer season when this sand was washed off the glacier by meltwater streams.

A series of small, ice-cored, ridgelike end moraines, parallel to and a few hundred yards (few hundred meters) in front of the terminus of the Wright Lower Glacier, is found in "Wright Lake" southwest of the kame moraine. These represent minor halts in the retreat of the glacier. One moraine was 25 feet (8 m) high. Fans, deltas, sand flows, alluvial aprons, and solifluction deposits are associated with these moraines. Blocks 10 feet (3 m) in diameter are found on them.

An ice-cored till moraine is found at the south end of the terminus of the Wright Lower Glacier (Fig. 23). A minor amount of glaciofluvial deposits are associated with it. The till is in places a foot (0.3 m) thick, below which there is ice. Perennially frozen ponds are found in kettles on the moraine. The moraine is com-

Fig. 22. The stratified, cross-bedded sand of which the ice-cored kame moraine is composed, seen on the wall of a channel cut into the moraine by a meltwater stream. Channel was not deep enough to reach glacial ice. Ice-axe gives indication of size.

posed of crude ridges parallel to the ice front. One ridge was 37 feet (11 m) high and its sides were at the angle of repose. It is not known whether the ridges resulted from: (1) the accumulation, in crevasses parallel to the terminus of the glacier, of moraine which protected the ice beneath it from ablation so that a ridge was formed where a crevasse had been; (2) the folding of the glacier near its terminus; (3) the formation of shear-plane moraines on the surface of the glacier followed by differential ablation; or (4) the accumulation of moraine on the toe of the glacier followed by retreat, ablation, and a stillstand. The moraine owes its origin to material which fell from cliffs onto that part of the glacier above this part of the terminus.

The end moraine is much smaller near the center of the glacier between the ice-cored till moraine on the south and the ice-cored kame moraine on the north. This is because apparently less wind-blown sand is deposited on the center of the glacier and no nunataks or bedrock cliffs occur up-glacier from this part of the terminus. Only a cursory examination was made of the deposits at the terminus of the Wright Lower Glacier. More detailed studies should prove profitable.

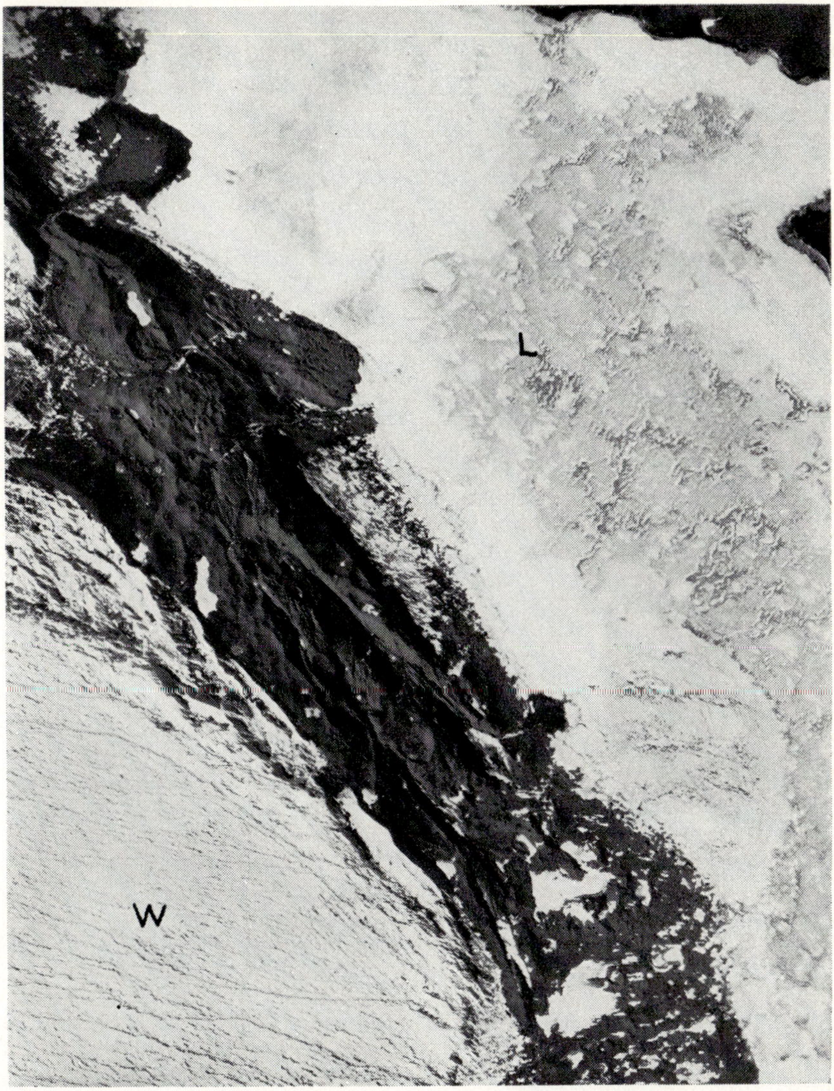

Fig. 23. An aerial photograph (U. S. Navy) of the ice-cored till moraine at the southern end of the terminus of the Wright Lower Glacier. An alluvial fan associated with it can be seen in the upper left-hand corner. Glacier is labeled W, the perennially frozen "Wright Lake" L.

The composition and dimensions of the end moraine which will be formed at the present terminus of the Wright Lower Glacier on the deglaciation of the area will therefore vary from place to place because the conditions under which deposition and accumulation now take place vary. In general the moraines deposited by the North American continental ice sheet do not vary so markedly from place to place because the ice front regime was more uniform than in the Wright Valley.

Author's Notes: I made reconnaissance geomorphic studies in the lower part of the Wright Valley, McMurdo Sound, during the interval between December 19, 1959, and January 5, 1960, and between December 10, 1960, and January 10, 1961. I was ably assisted by Professor Harold W. Borns, Jr., University of Maine, and by George H. Denton, Robert M. Goodspeed, Roger A. Hart, and William G. Meserve, at that time students at Tufts University.

The work was sponsored by the Office of Polar Programs of the National Science Foundation, and logistic support was furnished by the VX-6 squadron of the U. S. Navy.

I thank the National Science Foundation for support under the U. S. Antarctic Research Program and all of the members of the Antarctic Research Program for encouragement and courtesies too numerous to mention. Professor P. E. Calkin, State University of New York at Buffalo, and Dr. G. H. Denton, American Geographical Society, made many helpful suggestions for which I am appreciative.

References

Angino, E. E., and K. B. Armitage, 1963. A geochemical study of Lakes Bonney and Vanda, Victoria Land, Antarctica. *J. Geol., 71* (1) : 89–95.

Armstrong, R. L., W. Hamilton, and G. H. Denton, 1968. Glaciation in Taylor Valley, Anarctica, older than 2.7 million years. *Science, 159:* 187–188.

Bandy, O. L., 1966. Faunal evidence of Miocene-to-Recent paleoclimatology in Antarctic. *Bull. Am. Assoc. Petrol. Geologists, 50* (part 1) : 643–644.

Bell, R. A. I., 1966. A seismic reconnaissance in the McMurdo Sound region, Antarctica. *J. Glaciol., 6* (44) : 209–221.

Beu, A. G., 1965. Ecological variation of *Chlamys dieffenbachi* (Reeve) (Mollusca, Lamellibranchiata). *Trans. Roy. Soc. New Zealand, Zool., 7* (5) : 93–96.

Bull, C., 1960. Gravity observations in the Wright Valley area, Victoria Land, Antarctica. *New Zealand J. Geol. Geophys., 3:* 543–552.

Bull, C., 1962. Quaternary glaciations in southern Victoria Land, Antarctica. *J. Glaciol., 4* (32) : 240–241.

Bull, C., B. C. McKelvey, and P. N. Webb, 1962. Quaternary glaciations in southern Victoria Land, Antarctica. *J. Glaciol., 4* (31) : 63–78.

Bull, C., B. C. McKelvey, and P. N. Webb, 1964. Glacial benches in South Victoria Land. *J. Glaciol., 5* (37) : 131–133.

Calkin, P. E., 1964a. Geomorphology and glacial geology of the Victoria Valley system, southern Victoria Land, Antarctica. *Ohio State Univ. Inst. Polar Studies Rept. 10.* Ohio State Univ., Columbus, Ohio.

Calkin, P. E., 1964b. Glacial geology of the Mount Gran area, southern Victoria Land, Antarctica. *Bull. Geol. Soc. Am., 75* (10) : 1031–1036.

Calkin, P. E., and A. Cailleux, 1962. A quantitative study of cavernous weathering (taffonis) and its application to glacial chronology in Victoria Valley, Antarctica. *Z. Geomorphologie, N. F., 6:* 317–324.

Cotton, C. A., 1942. *Climatic Accidents.* Whitcombe and Tombs Ltd., Christchurch, New Zealand.

Craddock, C., T. W. Bastien, and R. H. Rutford, 1964. Geology of the Jones Mountains area. In *Antarctic Geology,* edited by R. J. Adie; pp. 171–187. North-Holland Publishing Co., Amsterdam.

Crosby, W. O., and H. O. Ballard, 1894. Distribution and probable age of the fossil shells in the drumlins of the Boston Basin. *Am. J. Sci., 48:* 486–496.

Curry, R. R., 1966. Glaciation about 3,000,000 years ago in the Sierra Nevada. *Science, 154:* 770–771.

David, T. W. E., and R. E. Priestley, 1914. *Reports on the Scientific Investigations, Glaciology, Physiography, Stratigraphy, and Tectonic Geology of South Victoria Land, British Antarctic Expedition, 1907–1909;* vol. 1. Heinemann, London.

Denton, G. H., and R. L. Armstrong, 1968. Glacial geology and chronology of the McMurdo Sound region. *Antarctic J. U.S., 3* (4): 99–101.

Einarsson, T., D. M. Hopkins, and R. R. Doell, 1967. The stratigraphy of Tjörnes, northern Iceland, and the history of the Bering Land Bridge. In *The Bering Land Bridge,* edited by D. M. Hopkins; pp. 312–325. Stanford Univ. Press, Stanford, California.

Flint, R. F., 1947. *Glacial Geology and the Pleistocene Epoch.* John Wiley and Sons, New York.

Flint, R. F., 1957. *Glacial and Pleistocene Geology.* John Wiley and Sons, New York.

Flückiger, O., 1934. Glaziale Felsformen. *Petermanns Geograph. Mitt. Ergänzungsheft, 218:* 7–55.

Goodell, H. G., and N. D. Watkins, 1968. The paleomagnetic stratigraphy of the Southern Ocean; 20° west to 160° east longitude. *Deep-Sea Res., 15* (1): 89–112.

Gunn, B. M., 1963. Quaternary glaciations in Victoria Land. *J. Glaciol., 4* (36): 829–830.

Harrington, H. J., and I. G. Speden, 1962. Section through the Beacon Sandstone at Beacon Height West, Antarctica. *New Zealand J. Geol. Geophys., 5* (5): 707–717.

Hollin, J. T., 1962. On the glacial history of Antarctica. *J. Glaciol., 4* (32): 173–195.

Ives, R. L., 1946. Glacial bastions in northern Colorado. *J. Geol., 54:* 391–397.

Kelly, W. C., and J. H. Zumberge, 1961. Weathering of a quartz diorite at Marble Point, McMurdo Sound, Antarctica. *J. Geol., 69* (4): 433–446.

Matthes, F. E., 1899–1900. Glacial sculpture of the Bighorn Mountains, Wyoming. *U. S. Geol. Surv. Ann. Rept., 21* (2): 167–190.

Matthes, F. E., 1930. Geologic History of the Yosemite Valley. *U.S. Geol. Surv. Prof. Paper 160.*

McGregor, V. R., 1963. Structural or glacial benches? *J. Glaciol., 4* (34): 494–495 (letter).

McKelvey, B. C., and P. N. Webb, 1962. Geological investigations in southern Victoria Land, Antarctica—Geology of Wright Valley. *New Zealand J. Geol. Geophys., 5* (1): 143–162.

McLeod, I. R., 1963. The saline lakes of the Vestfold Hills, Princess Elizabeth Land. *Polar Record, 11* (75) : 750.

Mercer, J. H., 1968. Glacial geology of the Reedy Glacier area, Antarctica. *Bull. Geol. Soc. Am., 79* (4) : 471–485.

Nichols, R. L., 1961. Multiple glaciation in the Wright Valley, McMurdo Sound, Antarctica (abstract). In *Tenth Pacific Science Congress of the Pacific Science Association;* p. 317. Honolulu, Hawaii.

Nichols, R. L., 1962. Geology of Lake Vanda, Wright Valley, South Victoria Land, Antarctica. *Antarctic Research, Geophysical Monograph 7;* pp. 47–52. Am. Geophys. Union, Washington, D.C.

Nichols, R. L., 1963. Geologic features demonstrating aridity of McMurdo Sound area, Antarctica. *Am. J. Sci., 261:* 20–31.

Nichols, R. L., 1965. Antarctic interglacial features. *J. Glaciol., 5* (40) : 433–449.

Nichols, R. L., 1966. Geomorphology of Antarctica. *Antarctic Research Series 8, Antarctic Soils and Soil Forming Processes,* edited by J. C. F. Tedrow; pp. 1–46. Am. Geophys. Union, Washington, D.C.

Nichols, R. L., 1968. Coastal geomorphology, McMurdo Sound, Antarctica. *J. Glaciol., 7* (51) : 449–478.

Nichols, R. L., and D. G. Ball, 1964. Four-fold check on mean annual temperature, McMurdo Sound, Antarctica. *J. Glaciol., 5* (39) : 353–355.

Nichols, R. L., and G. S. Lord, 1938. Fossiliferous eskers and outwash plains. *Geol. Soc. Am. Proc. 1937:* 324–325.

Nichols, R. L., and M. M. Miller, 1951. Glacial geology of Ameghino Valley, Lago Argentino, Patagonia. *Geograph. Rev., 41:* 274–294.

Opdyke, N. D., B. Glass, J. D. Hays, and J. Foster, 1966. Paleomagnetic study of antarctic deep-sea cores. *Science, 154:* 349–357.

Péwé, T. L., 1960. Multiple glaciation in the McMurdo Sound region, Antarctica—A progress report. *J. Geol., 68:* 498–514.

Shaw, S. E., 1962. Petrography of Beacon Sandstone samples from Beacon Height West, Upper Taylor Glacier, Antarctica. *New Zealand J. Geol. Geophys., 5* (5) : 733–739.

Taylor, G., 1922. *The Physiography of the McMurdo Sound and Granite Harbour Region, British Antarctic (Terra Nova) Expedition, 1910–1913.* Harrison and Sons, Ltd., London.

Turner, R. D., 1967. A new species of fossil *Chlamys* from Wright Valley, McMurdo Sound, Antarctica. *New Zealand J. Geol. Geophys., 10* (2) : 446–455.

Ugolini, F. C., and C. Bull, 1965. Soil development and glacial events in Antarctica. *Quaternaria Roma, 7:* 251–269.

U.S. Navy Hydrographic Office, 1958. New Harbor and Marble Point Vicinity. *H. O. 6635.* Washington, D.C.

von Engeln, O. D., 1937. Rock sculpture by glaciers: A review. *Geograph. Rev., 27:* 478–482.

Wilson, A. T., 1964. Origin of ice ages: An ice shelf theory for Pleistocene glaciation. *Nature, 201* (4915) : 147–149.

Wright, W. B., 1914. *The Quaternary Ice Age.* Macmillan and Co., London.

Thickness of Ice and Isostatic Adjustments of Ice-Rock Interface

A. P. CRARY

Division of Environmental Sciences, National Science Foundation, Washington, D.C.

Information on ice thickness in the polar ice caps must be found by indirect means since the high cost of drilling deters frequent direct observations. In Antarctica, Byrd Station is the only inland direct observation site. Even along the coasts the only two major drilling operations have been just south of Mirnyy Station and at the abandoned Little America Station.

METHODS OF FINDING ICE THICKNESS

Indirect methods of finding ice thickness include seismic reflections, radio echoes, and gravity observations. The traditional method of obtaining ice thickness values has been by seismic reflections, using equipment and techniques that have been standard since the early 1930's in petroleum exploration. This method has had widespread use in Greenland and Antarctica and has usually worked very well. In the Norwegian-British-Swedish Antarctic Expedition, however, Robin (1958) found that results on the inland plateau were poor. Bull (1956) had the same experience during the British North Greenland Expedition in 1952–1954. The seasonal variation in quality of records was recognized during the IGY by Bentley and Crary at Byrd and Little America Stations when winter observations were unsuccessful where satisfactory results had been obtained in the summer season. The poor quality of the results was caused by the high surface-noise level following the detonation of explosives when the temperature of the surface snows was below about −25°C. This reduced the signal-to-noise ratios below acceptable levels. The high noise level results from the rapid increase in the viscosity of the snow with decreases in temperatures (Nakaya, 1958). The surface temperatures in East Antarctica are rarely above −25°C even in the summer, so seismic results in that area have not been acceptable unless holes are drilled 40 to 60 meters deep for the explosives, a rather slow and expensive undertaking.

The seismic refraction method, where long distances are involved between source and receiver, is the only known practical method that will give indications of the seismic velocity of the rock below the ice. However, ice has a seismic velocity of about 3,850 to 3,950 m/sec, a value not far below the 4,000 to 4,500 m/sec values usually assigned to sedimentary rocks, such as sandstones. Because of this small difference in velocities and the thick ice layer, distances of 20 or 30 km between shot and recorder are required. Explosives in drill holes in the surface snows cannot be tamped efficiently as they are in land shooting with a large head of water; therefore, seismic refraction over long distances in the inland of Antarctica is difficult. Also, seismic refraction profiles will not locate low-velocity layers below high-velocity layers, such as soil or glacial moraine beneath the ice. Only about a dozen refraction profiles have been made in the inland of Antarctica, a number that is insignificant considering the size of the area.

The seismic reflection method can give good information over the extensive ice shelves of Antarctica where ice thickness and water depth below the ice may be significant. The shear wave has been used in some cases to obtain ice thickness over water, but there is no easy method of generating the shear impulses.

The radio echo method, using frequencies of 20 to 100 megahertz, is a recent development for measuring ice thickness. This procedure originated with U. S. Army experiments on electromagnetic propagation across the ice caps and, later, United Kingdom studies of an anomalous wave generated by ionosonde equipment on the ice shelves at Halley Bay, identified as the reflected impulse from the ice-water interface. The radio echo method has overwhelming advantages over the seismic method in the inland areas of Antarctica. First, the signals can be repeated at extremely close intervals, permitting continuous operations in a traveling vehicle or an aircraft much like measurements by a fathometer on a ship. A further advantage of the radio echo method for most of Antarctica lies in the favorable dielectric properties of cold, dry ice. The high plateaus of Antarctica, the most difficult areas for using the seismic method, are particularly well suited for the radio echo technique. Though high attenuation in the warmer ice in West Antarctica poses a problem, sufficient power will soon be applied to the units to overcome this difficulty. Recent successful flights with the radiosounder in a Constellation aircraft in Greenland (Walker *et al.*, 1968) and in Antarctica (Robin *et al.*, 1970) have demonstrated that these will be the ice-thickness measuring methods of the future. Radio sounding equipment is not suitable for determining water depths below the ice shelves, nor can it be used to ascertain the characteristics of rock below the ice.

In the seismic and radio sounding methods of measuring ice thickness, the accuracy is limited by our uncertain knowledge of the wave velocity which is a function of the elastic and electric properties of the ice. These inaccuracies, however, represent only a small percentage of total ice thickness. Drill holes now can penetrate the ice sheet and hole-logging velocity data will provide more precise information.

Gravity values have been used extensively for measuring ice thickness, especially over valley glaciers where rock outcrops are nearby and interpolation is minimal. Gravity value is the sum of the effects of the vertical component of gravitational attraction of all mass in the vicinity, the latitude, and the elevation. Such changes as tidal effects, are negligible for ice-thickness problems. Inasmuch as the density of ice is only about one-third the density of the rock immediately below, changes in ice thickness are the principal causes of gravity changes over ice sheets. Where some ice thicknesses are known by seismic methods, interpolation by gravity measurements between sites is a big improvement over having no values at all. Much of the apparent success of the gravity method, I believe, results from the lack of direct checks on the thickness values. Fortunately, the radiosounder will eliminate the requirement for interpolations by providing continuous records. A major contribution to knowledge of the gravity field is the establishment of a rational basis for determining whether isostatic adjustments have been made for the heavy load of ice on the crustal and mantle material.

In the years since the Norwegian-British-Swedish Expedition made the first extensive measurements of ice thickness in Antarctica, over 50,000 km have been covered by the inland oversnow traverses. These measurements have been made principally by United States, U.S.S.R., Australian, British, and Japanese scientists. In total number of traverses and total number of thickness measurements, the United States has greatly exceeded all others. In West Antarctica, including the Ross, Ronne, and Filchner Ice Shelves, United States scientists have covered a total of 18,400 km, with about 400 observed values of seismic thickness. In this area the surface temperatures are usually between $-10°$ and $-20°C$ during the summer months, and the seismic results have been unquestioned. In East Antarctica, the number of unquestioned results has not been satisfactorily resolved internationally, but fortunately, with the use of the radiosounder, the arguments will be decided.

THE LAND BENEATH THE ANTARCTIC ICE

The ice-rock interface, the land beneath the antarctic ice, shows that West Antarctica is an archipelago and that East Antarctica is the main body of the continent. The old continental remnant is about the size of the United States, and with the exception of mountain ranges, much of its surface is near sea level. The principal areas above sea level are the Transantarctic Mountains, the subglacial Gamburtsev-Vernadskiy Mountains*, and the Queen Maud Land Massif. Now that the theories of sea-floor spreading and continental drift are becoming accepted, it will be interesting to see how the pieces of the non-volcanic West Antarctica archipelago fit into the East Antarctic block. The time scale of sea-floor spreading, 1 to 5 cm per year, would amount to from 50 to 250 km in the five million years that we might consider as a tentative age for antarctic ice.

The many gravity surveys over Antarctica show a computed free-air anomaly that averages close to zero although individual values vary from -100 to $+100$ milligals. The average implies that isostasy is approximated, that is, that the crust and mantle have adjusted to the heavy load of ice. For illustration, if the crust and mantle were not adjusted at all for a thickness of 2,000 m of ice on Antarctica, the average free-air gravity anomaly would be about $+77$ milligals. There is, however, a considerable chance of error in the gravity readings because of the lack of well-established gravity bases in Antarctica, because of inherent drift problems of the portable meters, and because of possible errors in determining elevations in the interior. Although most writers on antarctic isostasy tend to believe the continent has adjusted to the ice, some even in complete isostatic adjustment, there are areas of

* Name not yet approved by U. S. Board on Geographic Names.

Antarctica of normally positive free-air anomalies such as the mountainous areas of the coast in East Antarctica (Kapitsa, 1966). Values in the interior will vary with thickness of local ice, and Bentley (1964) has noted that the average change in the free-air gravity anomaly in the interior is about .05 milligals per meter difference in rock elevation. This implies that local areas, whether ice is thin or thick, are not in complete isostatic adjustment. I believe that there are too few gravity values to permit conclusions about the percentage of total adjustment.

Any attempt to portray the present ice-rock interface configuration of Antarctica is meaningless and deceiving. We are, however, interested in what Antarctica might have looked like before the load of ice settled on it, or even what it might look like if all the ice were removed and the land were allowed enough time to re-establish equilibrium. The effect of the load on the crust and mantle is a fascinating problem, one that is relevant to many areas of the world around us. The Mississippi Delta, for example, builds up each year but, unlike the antarctic annual snowfall, it is not balanced by outflow. The great artificial lakes behind dams we are constructing are also loading our crust and mantle by sizable amounts.

Our objective is to find the properties of the crust and the mantle of the earth that would match the known reaction of the earth to excess loads. Fortunately, the ice caps of the north, which disappeared about 10,000 years ago except for Greenland and other smaller ice sheets, have provided some ideas of the reverse process, the reaction of the earth to the removal of excess loads. Details of the Fennoscandia and North America rebound that has taken place in the past 10,000 years have been studied for over a century by means of strand lines, tilted beaches, mudflats, etc. Professor Daly summarized most of this in his book, *The Changing World of the Ice Age,* in 1934. An early use of the Fennoscandia uplift to determine the viscosity of the crust and mantle was made by Haskell in his classic paper of 1935, in which a viscosity value of 10^{22} stokes was found, assuming a homogenous earth and relaxation time, the time required for any deviation to diminish to 1/e or .37 of its value, of about 10,000 years.

More recently, new techniques have contributed to this information. Carbon-14 observations have increased the accuracy of the dating of shorelines, and with the aid of computers multilayered models of the properties of the earth can be tested. McConnell (1965) recently extended the Fennoscandia uplift data using layered earth models to fit the variation of relaxation time with wavelength. Satisfactory agreement was found with an elastic crust to about 120 km, then a viscous region between 120 and 400 km of 3×10^{21} stokes, below which the mantle viscosity increased to nearly 10^{23} stokes at 1,250 km.

The study of the deformation of the earth received new impetus when the earth's gravitational potential was found from satellite motion showing that the earth had a pear-shaped appearance (O'Keefe *et al.*, 1966). This departure from the hydrostatic rotational ellipsoid had been discussed by various authors, including Wang (1966) and McKenzie (1966); but the viscosity required, over 10^{25} stokes, was inconsistent with values derived from postglacial uplift. However, McConnell (1958) produced a model of the earth which indicates that the Pleistocene glacial loading is indeed responsible for the earth's nonhydrostatic bulge.

For this latest model to be consistent, the viscosity must increase from 10^{21} stokes near the top of the mantle to 10^{25} stokes near 1,000 km. This requires a relaxation time of about 300,000 years for wavelengths of 2,000 km. Since the original viscosity values for the lower mantle were derived from the Fennoscandia uplift information on the assumption that the hinge line of no deformation was near Leningrad, about 450 km from the center of glaciation, this assumption had to be abandoned. The new model also explains the historical nontidal increase in the length of the day over the past 2,000 years, discussed by Munk and MacDonald (1960).

The acceptance of very long relaxation times for long wavelengths, in order to satisfy higher viscosity values in the lower mantle, would also explain why the antarctic continental shelves can average about 600 m around Antarctica while 150 m is nearer the world average. It had been generally accepted by many writers that the ice load was responsible, but proof heretofore had been lacking. The way seems clear now for an application of this latest earth's model, consistent with deglaciation in the north, to the Antarctic Continent.

Broecker (1962) made an estimate of the possible magnitude of land surface depression that might result from phase changes produced by continental glaciation. Using an assumed Mohorovicic discontinuity of eclogite to basalt, and an ice sheet 2,000 m thick, he found that from this cause alone about 100 m of land surface depression would result. He concluded, however, that this would not change by any significant amount estimates of crust and mantle character calculated on adjustment evidence.

There are two other equally difficult problems still to be resolved before we can be certain of the character of the preglacial land beneath the antarctic ice. Around the fringes of the ice sheet of Antarctica, trenches as deep as 2,000 m running parallel to the coastline have been located. These are delineated best off the coasts of East Antarctica and under the ice shelves. Guilcher (1963) has summarized evidences of these longitudinal depressions within the continental shelf areas. Such troughs are also common in the once-glaciated areas of Labrador, Alaska, and Norway. Similar trenches, now filled with sediments, also occur in such areas as the Gulf of Maine and off the coast of the northwestern states. Woollard (1967) compared the antarctic depressions to fractures around a punch when a compressive stress is applied to a plate. In this case the Antarctic Ice Sheet has acted as the punch which has induced crustal failure at its boundary. However, if this is the explanation, we would expect to see parallel trenches representing different stands of the ice front, and we would also expect to find these trenches in the once-glaciated areas of the northern United States. Crary (1966) has attributed the deep inner waters of fjords to natural flow characteristics of floating ice that cause them to thicken inland. Possibly when the ice shelves reached their maximum extent in glaciated times, the thickest floating ice was located over the trenches. Floating ice of thicknesses of up to 2,000 m are not uncommon in Antarctica.

The final process that I shall deal with very briefly is the erosion of Antarctica by the ice sheet in the past few million years. The northern areas of North America and Europe furnish evidence of the quantitative aspects of glacial erosion (Flint, 1957). The large areas of the Canadian shield and similar areas in Finland probably lost only about 20 m. These are areas where there have been several glacial and interglacial periods, and they may therefore be more eroded than the shield area of Antarctica. On the other hand, extensive mountainous areas of Scandanavia and Alaska may have lost over 500 m, and certainly we would expect as much in similar areas in Antarctica. At the deep drill hole at Camp Century in northern Greenland, discussed by Hansen and Langway (1966), glacial moraine was found beneath the ice, with the ice-rock interface at a temperature of −13°C. It is becoming apparent that erosion takes place principally when the ice at the bottom is at melting temperatures, a condition that must have been prevalent at the beginning of glacial periods when the new ice sheet was beginning to form.

Evidence for ice-rafted glacial detritus material in 159 piston cores in the South Pacific Ocean and Scotia Sea between 60° and 70°S has recently been given by Goodell and Watkins (1968) in their study of sediment rates basing the dating on the magnetic reversal events at 0.7 and 2.35 million years. Though the deposition was quite variable and obviously subject to bottom currents, the rate per million years averaged less than 10 m; and even if this were all glacial detritus, we would hardly expect more than a few tens of meters to have been eroded from this area of Antarctica.

In this brief summary, I have attempted to indicate a few of the recent results which I think will have considerable impact on future studies. Certainly there will be a vast improvement in ice thickness information with the new techniques of airborne radio soundings. Better knowledge of the character of the earth's crust and mantle, increased information on Pleistocene history, and more studies of sediment cores in the southern oceans will soon enable scientists to construct a realistic picture of the pre-glaciated Antarctic Continent. With this information, the most favorable sites for life can be located, and perhaps the continent will be host at some time in the near future to a new, different kind of scientist, the archaeologist.

References

Bentley, C. R., 1964. The structure of Antarctica and its ice cover. Chapter 14. In *Research in Geophysics, Solid Earth and Interface Phenomena*, edited by H. Odishaw; vol. 2, ch. 2, pp. 335–389. M.I.T. Press, Cambridge, Mass.

Broecker, W. S., 1962. The contribution of pressure-induced phase charges to glacial rebound. *J. Geophys. Res.*, *67*, (12) : 4837–4842.

Bull, C., 1956. Seismic investigations on the northern part of the Greenland Ice-Sheet, *Geograph. J.*, *122* (2) : 219–225.

Crary, A. P., 1966. Mechanism for fiord formation indicated by studies of an ice-covered inlet, *Geol. Soc. Am. Bull.*, *77:* 911–930.

Daly, R. A., 1934. *The Changing World of the Ice Age.* Yale Univ. Press, New Haven, Conn.

Flint, R. F., 1957. *Glacial and Pleistocene Geology.* John Wiley and Sons, New York.

Goodell, H. G., and R. D. Watkins, 1968. The paleomagnetic stratigraphy of the southern oceans: 20° West to 160° East Longitude. *Deep-Sea Res.*, *15:* 89–112.

Guilcher, A., 1963. Continental shelf and slope (Continental margin), In *The Sea*, edited by, M. N. Hill; vol. 3, ch. 13. Interscience, John Wiley and Sons, New York.

Hansen, B. L., and C. C. Langway, Jr., 1966. Deep core drilling in ice and core analysis at Camp Century, Greenland, 1961–1966. *Antarctic J. U.S., 1* (5): 207–208.

Haskell, N. A., 1935. The motion of a viscous fluid under a surface load. *Physics, 6:* 265–269.

Kapitsa, A. P., 1966. Glacial and subglacial relief of Antarctica. *Soviet Antarctic Exped. Inform. Bull., No. 5:* 5–12. (Translation by Scripta Technica, Inc. for the *Am. Geophys. Union, Issue 2, 6:* 143–150).

McConnell, K., 1958. Viscosity of the mantle from relaxation time spectra of isostatic adjustment. *J. Geophys. Res., 73* (22): 7089–7105.

McConnell, R. K., 1965. Isostatic adjustment in a layered earth. *J. Geophys. Res., 70,* (20): 5171–5189.

McKenzie, D. P., 1966. The viscosity of the lower mantle. *J. Geophys. Res., 71,* (16): 3995–4010.

Munk, W. H., and G. J. F. MacDonald, 1960. *The Rotation of the Earth.* Cambridge Univ. Press, New York.

Nakaya, U., 1958. Visco-elastic properties of snow and ice in Greenland Ice Cap. In *Physics of the Movement of the Ice, Symposium of Chamonix;* No. 47, pp. 199–212. Intern. Assoc. Sci. Hydrol., Gentbrugge, Belgium.

O'Keefe, J. A., A. Eckels, and R. K. Squires, 1966. The gravitational field of the earth. *Astron. J., 64:* 245–253.

Robin, G. de Q., 1958. Seismic shooting and related investigations. In *Norwegian-British-Swedish Antarctic Expedition, 1949–52, Scientific Results;* vol. 5 (Glaciology III). Norsk Polar Institutt, Oslo.

Robin, G. deQ., C. W. M. Swithinbank, and B. M. E. Smith, 1970. Radio echo exploration of the Antarctic Ice Sheet. In *International Symposium on Antarctic Glaciological Exploration (ISAGE), Hanover, N.H., Sept. 3–7, 1968;* No. 86, pp. 97–115. Intern. Assoc. Sci. Hydrol., Gentbrugge, Belgium.

Walker, J. W., D. C. Pearce, and A. H. Zanella, 1968. Airborne radar soundings of the Greenland Ice Cap. Flight 1. *Geol. Soc. Am. Bull., 79,* (11): 1639–1646.

Wang, C. Y., 1966. Earth's zonal deformations. *J. Geophys. Res., 71:* 1713–1720.

Woollard, G. P., 1967. Continental structure of Antarctica. *Annals Intern. Geophys. Year, 44:* 122–143.

Deep Drilling into Polar Ice Sheets for Continuous Cores

C. C. LANGWAY, JR., A. J. GOW, AND B. LYLE HANSEN

U. S. Army Cold Regions Research and Engineering Laboratory, Hanover, New Hampshire

One of the major objectives of the recent Antarctic International Geophysical Year (IGY) Programs was to obtain a better understanding of the nature, properties, and inner structure of large ice masses (Bader, 1958; Crary *et al.*, 1962). Earlier glaciological investigations (e.g., Schytt, 1958) had shown the necessity for analyzing deep continuous ice cores and for obtaining precise temperature and deformation measurements by using boreholes. The Greenland and Antarctic Ice Sheets are similar to the oceans of the world in that they act as temporary reservoirs for solid, soluble, and gaseous materials of terrestrial and extraterrestrial origin. Some minerals and organic substances undergo changes in structure and composition while settling to the ocean bed, but because of the cold temperatures on the high polar inland ice little chemical reaction takes place there and substances remain more or less as they were when encapsulated during snowfall. Ice sheets are among the few places where we can observe how climate has changed in the past and obtain clues to how it might change in the future.

A program of deep-core drilling in ice was initiated in Greenland by the U.S. Army Cold Regions Research and Engineering Laboratory (USACRREL) during pre-IGY activities (Langway, 1958a,b; Hansen and Landauer, 1958; Lange *et al.*, 1959), in Antarctica during the IGY (Patenaude *et al.*, 1959; Ragle *et al.*, 1960; Bender and Gow, 1961; Gow, 1961, 1968a), and is being continued in Antarctica. The drilling program has produced eight deep ice cores (Table 1). Both the 1966 and 1968 cores penetrated through the ice sheets. During the 1966 Greenland operation 3.5 m

Table 1. Deep-core drilling in Greenland and Antarctica.

Year	Depth (m)	Location
1956	305	Site 2, Greenland
1957	411	Site 2, Greenland
1958	308	Byrd Station, Antarctica
1959	256	Little America V, Antarctica
1961	185	Camp Century, Greenland
1962	235	Camp Century, Greenland
1966	1,375	Camp Century, Greenland
1968	2,164	Byrd Station, Antarctica

of sub-ice material was recovered and the ice/sub-ice interface temperature was found to be −13°C (Hansen and Langway, 1966; Garfield and Ueda, 1967). The interface temperature at Byrd Station was at the pressure melting point of −1.6°C and no sub-ice material has yet been recovered (Gow *et al.*, 1968; Ueda and Garfield, 1969).

METHODS OF CORE DRILLING

Three basic drilling methods are used to obtain ice cores of 10 to 12.5 cm in diameter: (1) a conventional rotary system using a drill pipe to advance the tool and recover the core; (2) a thermal coring device using a hoist and an armored cable to transmit power and to lower and raise the tool; and (3) an electromechanical boring tool which also uses the hoist-cable concept for delivery and power transmission. A variety of drilling tools, bits, and systems to recover chips and cores were developed or modified before the present techniques were perfected. Dry-bored holes are feasible to depths of about 400 m below the surface of ice sheets, but for greater depths it is necessary to fill the borehole with fluids to prevent the hole from closing. Chip recovery is accomplished with the rotary drill to depths of about 400 m by using cooled compressed air as the activator. With the thermal coring device the meltwater is pumped and recovered in a heated compartment of the boring tool.

The electromechanical system utilizes a unique glycol-dilution technique to put the ice chips into solution and will be discussed in greater detail since it was the method used successfully to core through both ice sheets.

Fig. 1. Electrohydraulic hoist with 12,000 feet of cable in position at Byrd Station, January, 1968.

In 1964, a reconditioned Electrodrill (Sutton and Arutunoff, 1954) was purchased and modified for use in ice (Fig. 1). The final version was 87 ft long and weighed 2,650 lb. (Ueda and Garfield, 1969). It consisted of six main sections (Fig. 2) : an inclinometer housing, a torque reaction section, a bailer, an electric motor, a pump and gear reducer section, and a core barrel with attached cutting bit.

The inclinometer housing was made of No. 304 stainless steel and was designed to permit rapid installation and removal of the inclinometer, thus permitting hole deviation measurements to be made on any coring run. A Parsons Survey single-shot inclinometer, sealed in a pressure-tight container and electrically triggered from the surface, measured the direction and magnitude of the hole inclination from the vertical.

The reaction torque section consisted of four sets of hinged friction blades designed to swing freely out against the hole wall when the drill motor was started. This restrained the rotation

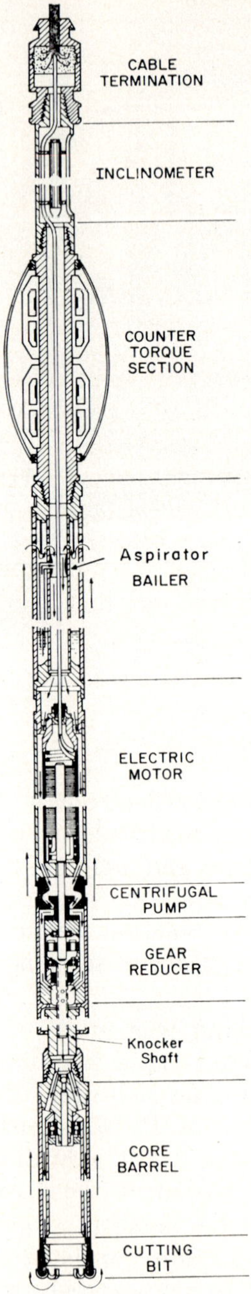

Fig. 2. Details of Electrodrill.

of all drill sections except the core barrel and cutting bit. Additional restraint was provided by two leaf springs and by the inherent torsional rigidity in the suspension cable.

The bailer was located just below the torque section and was modified for drilling in ice. In the original design the cuttings were deposited in the bottom of the bailer after being removed from the path of fluid flow. Since the density of the fluid in the hole was essentially equal to the density of ice chips, the ice chips were dissolved in an aqueous ethylene glycol solution. This technique depends on a knowledge of the freezing points of aqueous ethylene glycol solutions and of the ice temperature and depth profile for the location. A volume of concentrated glycol, the amount depending upon the downhole ice temperature and the volume of chips formed, is sent down in the bailer on each run. An aspirator assembly ensures mixing of the concentrated solution into the pump flow. This glycol dissolves the chips and dilutes itself to the equilibrium concentration for the downhole temperature. A bailer full of dilute solution is removed on each return trip with the core. Any solution remaining downhole will stay downhole since it is denser than, and immiscible with, the hole fluid. It will not melt any ice since it is at the equilibrium concentration.

Below the bailer was a 17½-hp, three-phase submersible induction motor, operated at 2,300 v at a nominal speed of 3,600 rpm. The glycol flowed through an annular space between the motor and its cylindrical housing. Heat from the motor, transferred to the glycol, provided the heat to dissolve the ice chips.

Beneath the motor was a gear section which included a pump and gear reducer. The centrifugal pump was operated at 3,600 rpm and rated at 80 gal/min with a 120-ft head. Below the pump, a planetary gear reducer dropped the shaft speed from 3,600 rpm to 225 rpm, the speed of rotation of the core barrel and cutter.

Power was transmitted from the gear reducer to the core barrel through a splined hollow driveshaft. An 18-inch axial movement of the shaft allowed the core to be broken by impact if necessary. The core barrel was a double-tube, swivel-head type capable of holding a 20-ft core.

Two types of cutting bits with similar configurations were used, a steel bit with eight vertical mild steel inserts and a diamond bit with eight sintered tungsten carbide inserts. Diamonds were distributed around the outer face of each tungsten carbide insert with approximately 0.22–0.28 karats per stone and eight karats per insert. Outer dimensions of the bits were 6⅛ inches and the inner dimensions were 4½ inches. Core diameters averaged 4¼ inches or slightly less.

Each method of core drilling has certain advantages and disadvantages in the quality of recovered core and the depth of penetration. A fluid-filled hole presents a contamination problem for certain core analyses. Because of the heat, the thermally bored cores are physically and chemically altered over the depth of porous firn (surface to about 70 m). Except for some fracturing between 200 and 900 m, core recovery and quality using the electromechanical rig is good to excellent at greater depths.

SCOPE OF ICE-CORE STUDIES

Ice sheets are vast storehouses of geochemical information which contain, within the annual accumulation layers, atmospheric gases and entrapped foreign material that fell upon the snow surface or served as snow crystal nuclei (Bader, 1962). The recovery of the deep ice cores offered research opportunities that had not existed before (Langway, 1962). Never had the firn-ice mantle of glaciers been so deeply penetrated nor had the entire third dimension of polar continental-type glaciers been exposed. In a dry snow zone, where summer surface temperatures never exceed the melting point, each year the new snowfall buries the previous accumulation deeper, densifies the underlying snow by compaction, and gradually, with depth, the firn transforms into ice. Ice cores are, in essence, vertical profiles of polar history contained in layered sequence (Fig. 3). It is now possible to examine systematically the physical (Langway, 1962; Gow, 1963a, 1968b,c; Bader, 1964) and chemical (Langway, 1962; Crozaz *et al.*, 1966; Crozaz and Langway, 1966; Gow, 1968a) nature of a glacier as a continuous function of depth. It is also possible, once the depth-age relationship (Dansgaard and Johnsen, 1969) has been established, to investigate any climatological trends (Dansgaard *et al.*, 1970) and significant meteorological variations that affected the world's atmosphere, such as volcanic disturbances. The time scale fills a gap in our knowledge of earth history, overlapping dendrochronological and carbon-dating studies, and some of the information extracted from ice cores cannot be obtained from any other source on earth.

Of initial and prime importance in the core investigations was establishing methods of estimating the yearly accumulation. The dating of the upper 100 m of the snow-firn-ice mantle was done in much the same manner as surface pit studies are accomplished:

Fig. 3. Twenty-foot core from 6,500-ft depth at Byrd Station.

(1) by observing visible stratigraphic features (wind crusts, discrete summer melt crusts, grain size variations) by placing the core on a light table and transmitting light through the core, and (2) by seasonal density variations (where summer snows are less dense than those in winter). These relative seasonal relationships were found to be the same to depths of about 100 m. Below this depth, megascopic features become obscure and the annual layers must be investigated by other physical and chemical techniques. A comprehensive and detailed core study program is being conducted at USACRREL in cooperation with scientists from other United States and foreign universities and institutes (Langway, 1968a,b).

CORE STUDIES

The most successful physical approach for determining seasonal variations from deep cores is by measuring the stable oxygen isotope (0^{18}:0^{16}) ratio (Langway, 1962, 1967). Summer snows contain more 0^{18} than do winter snows. Tritium and deuterium analyses have also been measured. Deuterium is a temperature indicator and parallels the 0^{18}:0^{16} ratio data; the natural tritium balance has been affected by atmospheric thermonuclear testing since 1954, and hence is of less value for determining annual accumulation since then. Other natural and artificial radioactive isotope studies on the cores have provided measurements of the average annual accumulation over larger vertical profiles. Lead-210 (Crozaz and Langway, 1966), with a half-life of 21.6 years, allows us to obtain the average accumulation at a location for the last 100 to 150 years (60–80 m depths). Silicon-32 with about a 500-year half-life is still being tested. Fission product fallout (primarily strontium-90) from thermonuclear tests provides several excellent index horizons from 1954 to date (Crozaz *et al.*, 1966). The levels of these index horizons differ for the Greenland and Antarctic Ice Sheets owing to the proximity of the testing sites and atmospheric residence times. Studies of the dissolved ionic constituents in melted ice-core samples show that very little material is present (averaging about 1 to 2 mg/liter) and that winter snows contain more dissolved materials than summer snows (Langway, 1967; Gow, 1968a). The same seasonal distribution is found in the submicroscopic solid particles (0.3 to 5 μ in diameter) (Hamilton and Langway, 1967; Bader *et al*, 1965). Examination of microscopic insoluble materials (larger than 0.5 μ in diameter) contained in the core shows that the residue contains mineral fragments, glassy shards, magnetic particles, and spherical micrometeorites (Langway, 1962). Investigations of the composition and distribution of the black spherules (Hodge *et al.*, 1966; Wright *et al.*, 1967; Langway, 1967) show that they are mainly iron-rich (magnetite), that nickel is present but rare, and that greater spherule concentrations occur in the summer snow deposits. Rare gases and cosmic ray-induced radioactivities have been measured at the Smithsonian Astrophysical Observatory in bulk dust collections gathered from millions of liters of glacier meltwater at Camp Century, Greenland (Fireman and Langway, 1965; Fireman *et al.*, 1967; McCorkell *et al.*, 1967, Fireman *et al.*, 1968). Deep ice cores from Byrd Station show several prominent volcanic ash layers which will be studied in an attempt to date the age of the ice and establish deep-seated index horizons (Gow, 1968d; Gow et al., 1968). The volcanic eruptions of Katmai in 1912 and Krakatoa in 1883 will be investigated in all the deep cores.

A new down-borehole gas extraction device is being perfected and tested in the deep borehole at Byrd Station (Oeschger *et al.*, 1969). The device was developed by the University of Bern and USACRREL for boreholes in Greenland (Langway *et al.*, 1965; Oeschger et al., 1966; Oeschger *et al.*, 1967), and is designed to melt a volume of ice, in situ, and to separate with an ion exchange column the CO_2 component from the atmospheric gases in the air bubbles trapped in the ice. The exchange column is then brought to the surface. The carbon-14 is measured at the University of Bern (Oeschger *et al.*, 1967).

The seasonal variations of the oxygen isotope ratio (0^{18}:0^{16}) gradually dampen with depth (age) by molecular diffusion, but long-term variations in the isotope ratios remain practically undisturbed for much greater lengths of time and depict climatic changes. Recent measurements made at the University of Copenhagen (Dansgaard *et al.*, 1970) on nearly 7,000 core samples, taken over the entire vertical profile of the Camp Century core, revealed that climatic (temperature) maxima existed 40 years ago and about 6,000 years ago. The cores indicated a minor temperature minimum 200 to 300 years ago and an extreme temperature minimum about 15,000 years ago. This temperature chronology extends continuously from the present back approximately 1,000 centuries and allows climatic prediction curves to be drawn for the future (Johnson *et al.*, 1970).

Deep-core drilling at Byrd Station (Fig. 4) has proved particularly interesting (Ueda and Garfield, 1968; Gow *et al.*, 1968; Gow, 1970). Horizontally banded debris, including layers of clay, sand, pebbles, and some large fragments of granite, was present in the basal ice. Liquid water, indicative of pressure melting, was encountered at the bed. A temperature minimum of $-28.8°C$ was recorded at 800 m depth and the heat flow through the base of the ice sheet is estimated at 1.8 cal/cm^2 per sec. Several thin layers of dirt (up to 0.5 mm thick) were observed between 1,300 and 1,700 m depth. Tentatively identified as volcanic ash, these layers are estimated to have been deposited from nearby volcanoes, for example, Executive Committee Range, between 15,000 and 25,000 years ago. No trace of air bubbles (Gow *et al.*, 1968; Gow, 1970) was observed in freshly cored ice from below 1,200 m at which

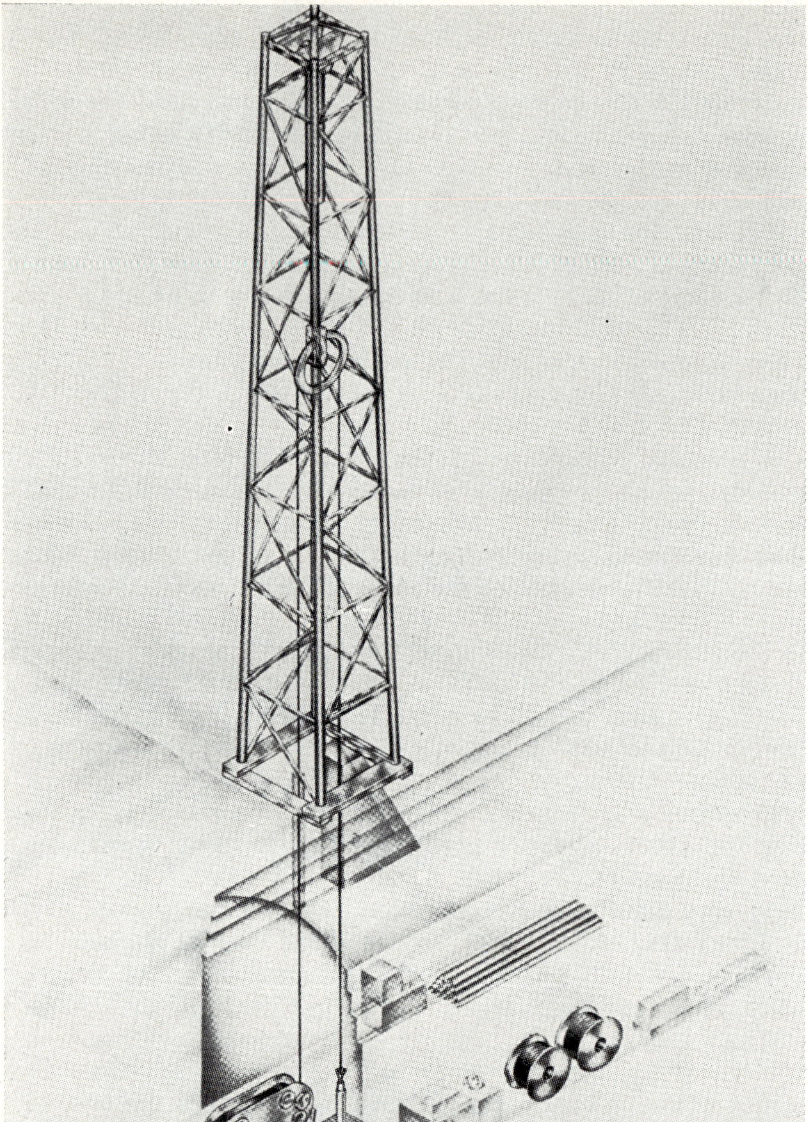

Fig. 4. Core drilling through the Antarctic Ice Sheet. Equipment layout at Byrd Station.

depth the *c*-axes of crystals had become substantially vertically oriented. This zone of oriented ice crystals, which also contained numerous cloudy bands composed of very small crystals that might be attributed to shear, persisted to about 1,800 m depth. Below 1,800 m this deformed ice structure gave way to the growth of large annealed crystals measuring as much as 30 cm^2 in cross section. Measurements of electrolytic conductivity of melted samples (Gow, 1970) showed very low levels of dissolved solids at all depths in the ice sheet. Preliminary studies of the oxygen and hydrogen isotope profiles indicate that major climatic changes in Antarctica during the Wisconsin were essentially synchronous with those of the Northern Hemisphere (Epstein *et al.*, 1970).

BOREHOLE STUDIES

Direct measurements made over the entire borehole profile include the diameter changes with time, the inclination and drift patterns with time, and the temperature variations as a function of depth. New borehole instruments are being developed, such as an electrical property measuring probe, a camera to observe bottom bed-slip, and remotely operated collection devices for solids, liquid, or gases. The boreholes make available larger deep glacier ice samples necessary for some investigations or allow other parameter determinations, such as temperature, hole closure, etc., that supplement or are not possible to measure on the ice cores (Hansen and Landauer, 1958; Gow, 1963b).

CONCLUSION

In view of the summary of results presented above it is seen that the value of investigating deep ice cores and boreholes is far reaching and has considerable scientific value. The results of the investigations have a bearing on many scientific disciplines—glaciology, meteorology, atmospheric chemistry, geochronology, hydrology, paleoclimatology, geothermometry, physical dynamics, ceramics, and rheology. From core and borehole investigations one is able to study transporting processes of the atmosphere and the interaction between the hemispheres, to date ancient atmospheres, to study the change in precipitation chemistry during historical times, to make compositional analyses of fossil atmospheric gases, to investigate high-latitude pollution and the effect of industrial wastes, to study the distribution of volcanic and cosmic dust as a function of time, and to make climatological inferences from the resultant data. The current studies by no means exhaust the avenues of search or the potential information that is sealed within the ice cores.

The United States program for deep-core drilling in ice is continuing in Antarctica. Considerable scientific interest has developed in this program and discussions are being held regarding an international cooperative program using United States drilling rigs to bore intermediate and deep holes at selected sites over the entire Antarctic Continent and in southern Greenland. The Canadians, Australians, Japanese, French, and a group from the Ohio State University are boring or have bored into glaciers in the arctic and antarctic regions using a thermal coring rig of USACRREL design capable of penetrating to 400 m depths. Several other countries in Europe and Africa are now planning ice-core drilling projects in Antarctica.

References

Bader, H., 1958. United States polar ice and snow studies in the International Geophysical Year. *Am. Geophys. Union, Geophys. Monograph 2:* 177–181.

Bader, H., 1962. Scope, problems, and potential value of deep core drilling in ice sheets. *U.S. Army Cold Regions Res. Eng. Lab., Spec. Rept., 58.* Hanover, N.H.

Bader, H., 1964. Criteria for measurement of strain rates in deep bore holes in polar glaciers. *U.S. Army Cold Regions Res. Eng. Lab. Res. Rept., 127.* Hanover, N.H.

Bader, H., W. L. Hamilton, and P. L. Brown, 1965. Measurement of natural particulate fallout onto high polar ice sheets, Part I, Laboratory Techniques and First Results. *U.S. Army Cold Regions Res. Eng. Lab. Res. Rept., 139.* Hanover, N.H.

Bender, J. A., and A. J. Gow, 1961. Deep drilling in Antarctica. *Colloque sur la Glaciologie Antarctique, Assoc. Internat. Hydrol. Sci., Publ. No. 55;* pp. 132–141.

Crary, A. P., W. O. Field, and M. F. Meier, 1962. The United States glaciological researches during the International Geophysical Year. *J. Glaciol., 4:* 5–24.

Crozaz, G., C. C. Langway, Jr., and E. Picciotto, 1966. Artificial radioactivity reference horizons in Greenland firn. *Earth Planetary Sci. Letters, 1:* 42–48 (and *U.S. Army Cold Regions Res. Eng. Lab. Res. Rept., 208.* Hanover, N. H.),

Crozaz, G., and C. C. Langway, Jr., 1966. Dating Greenland firn-ice cores with Pb-210. *Earth Planetary Sci. Letters, 1:* 194-196 (and *U.S. Army Cold Regions Res. Eng. Lab. Tech. Note, May 1966.* Hanover, N.H.).

Dansgaard, W., and S. J. Johnsen, 1969. A flow model and a time scale for the ice core from Camp Century, Greenland. *J. Glaciol., 8:* 215–223.

Dansgaard, W., S. J. Johnsen, J. Møller, and C. C. Langway, Jr., 1969. One thousand centuries of climatic record from Camp Century on the Greenland ice sheet. *Science, 166:* 377–381.

Epstein, S., R. P. Sharp, and A. J. Gow, 1970. Antarctic Ice Sheet: Stable isotope analyses of Byrd Station cores and interhemispheric climatic implications. *Science, 168:* 1570–1572.

Fireman, E. L., and C. C. Langway, Jr., 1965. Search for aluminum-26 in dust from the Greenland ice sheet. *Geochim. Cosmochim. Acta, 29:* 21–27.

Fireman, E. L., J. DeFelice, and C. C. Langway, Jr., 1967. Helium-3 released at low temperature from Greenland dust (Abstract). *Trans. Am. Geophys. Union, 48:* 158.

Fireman, E. L., R. H. McCorkell, and C. C. Langway, Jr., 1968. Ni^{63} and Ni^{59} in Greenland ice (Abstract). *Trans. Am. Geophys. Union, 49:* 245.

Garfield, D. E., and H. Ueda, 1967. Drilling through the Greenland ice sheet. *U.S. Army Cold Regions Res. Eng. Lab. Tech. Note, September, 1967.* Hanover, N.H.

Gow, A. J., 1961. Drill-hole measurements and snow studies at Byrd Station, Antarctica. *U.S. Army Cold Regions Res. Eng. Lab. Tech. Rept., 78.* Hanover, N.H.

Gow, A. J., 1963a. The inner structure of the Ross Ice Shelf at Little America V, Antarctica, as revealed by deep core drilling. *Assemblee Generale de Berkeley, Assoc. Internal. Hydrol. Sci., Publ. No. 61:* pp. 262–284.

Gow, A. J., 1963b. Results of measurements in the 309 meter bore hole at Byrd Station, Antarctica. *J. Glaciol., 4:* 771–784.

Gow, A. J., 1968a. Electrical conductivity of antarctic snow and glacier ice. *J. Geophys. Res., 73:* 3643-3649 (and *U. S. Army Cold Regions Res. Eng. Lab. Res. Rept., 248.* Hanover, N.H.

Gow, A. J., 1968b. Bubbles and bubble pressures in antarctic glacier ice. *J. Glaciol., 7:* 167–182 (and *U.S. Army Cold Regions Res. Eng. Lab. Res. Rept., 249.* Hanover, N.H.).

Gow, A. J., 1968c. Deep core studies of the accumulation and densification of snow at Byrd Station and Little America V, Antarctica. *U.S. Army Cold Regions Res. Eng. Lab. Res. Rept., 197.* Hanover, N.H.

Gow, A. J., 1968d. Preliminary analyses of ice core from Byrd Station, Antarctica. *Antarctic J. U. S., 3:* 113–114.

Gow, A. J., 1970. Preliminary results of studies of ice cores from the 2164 m deep drill hole, Byrd Station, Antarctica. In *International Symposium on Antarctic Glaciological Exploration, (ISAGE), Hanover, New Hampshire, Sept. 1968*, edited by A. J. Gow *et. al.;* pp. 78–90. (Pub. No. 86 of IASH) Cambridge, Mass.

Gow, A. J., H. T. Ueda, and D. E. Garfield, 1968. The Antarctic Ice Sheet. Preliminary results of core drilling to bedrock. *Science, 161:* 1011–1013.

Hamilton, W. L., and C. C. Langway, Jr., 1967. A correlation of microparticle concentrations with oxygen isotope ratios in 700 year old Greenland ice. *Earth Planetary Sci. Letters,* 3: 363–366.

Hansen, B. L., and J. K. Landauer, 1958. Some results of ice cap drill hole measurements. *Symposium de Chamonix; Assoc. Internat. Hydrol. Sci., Publ. No. 47;* p. 313–317.

Hansen, B. L., and C. C. Langway, Jr., 1966. Deep core drilling in ice and core analyses at Camp Century, Greenland, 1961–1966. *Antarctic J. U. S., 1:* 207–208 (and *U.S. Army Cold Regions Res. Eng. Lab. Tech. Note, July, 1966.* Hanover, N.H.).

Hodge, P. W., F. W. Wright, and C. C. Langway, Jr., 1966. Studies of particles for extraterrestrial origin, 5. Compositions of the interior of spherules from arctic and antarctic ice deposits. *J. Geophys. Res., 72:* 1404–1406.

Johnsen, S. J., W. Dansgaard, H. B. Clausen, and C. C. Langway, Jr., 1970. Climatic oscillations 1200–2000 AD. *Nature, 227:* 482–483.

Lange, G. R., C. C. Langway, Jr., and B. L. Hansen, 1959. Deep core drilling in glaciers. *Proc. 1959, U.S. Army Sci. Conf., West Point, New York;* vol. 2, pp. 97–107. Available at USACRREL Library, Hanover, N.H.

Langway, C. C., Jr., 1958a. A 400 meter deep ice core in Greenland. *J. Glaciol., 3:* 216–217.

Langway, C. C., Jr., 1958b. Bubble pressures in Greenland glacier ice. *Symposium de Chamonix; Assoc. Internat. Hydrol. Sci., Publ. No. 47;* pp. 336–349.

Langway, C. C., Jr., 1962. Some physical and chemical investigations of a 411 meter deep Greenland ice core and their relationship to accumulations. *Colloque d' Obergurgl; Assoc. Internat. Hydrol. Sci., Publ. No. 58;* pp. 101–118.

Langway, C. C., Jr., 1967. Stratigraphic analysis of a deep ice core from Greenland. *U.S. Army Cold Regions Res. Eng. Lab. Res. Rept., 77.* Hanover, N.H.

Langway, C. C., Jr., 1968a. Outlines on the investigations of the deep ice and sub-ice cores from Site 2, Greenland 1956–57 and Camp Century, Greenland 1961–66. *U.S. Army Cold Regions Res. Eng. Lab. Tech. Note, February 1968 (revised August 1968).* Hanover, N.H.

Langway, C. C., Jr., 1968b. Deep ice core study program Greenland, 1967–68. *Antarctic J. U. S., 3:* 184–185.

Langway, C. C., Jr., H. Oeschger, A. Renaud, and B. Alder, 1965. Sampling polar ice for radiocarbon dating. *Nature, 206:* 500–501.

McCorkell, R., E. C. Fireman, and C. C. Langway, Jr., 1967. Dissolved iron, nickel and cobalt in Greenland ice (Abstract). *Trans. Am. Geophys. Union, 48:* 158.

Oeschger, H., B. Alder, H. Loosli, and C. C. Langway, Jr., 1966. Radiocarbon dating of ice. *Earth Planetary Sci. Letters, 1:* 49–54.

Oeschger, H., C. C. Langway, Jr., and B. Alder, 1967. An in situ gas extraction system for radiocarbon dating glacier ice. *J. Glaciol., 6:* 939–942 (and *U.S. Army Cold Regions Res. Eng. Lab. Res. Rept., 236, 1967.* Hanover, N.H.).

Oeschger, H., B. Stauffer, C. C. Langway, Jr., and B. L. Hansen, 1969. *Deep bore-hole carbon dating at Byrd Station, Antarctica (Abstract). INQUA Congress, Paris, August, 1969.* INQUA Proceedings, Paris.

Patenaude, R. W., E. W. Marshall, and A. J. Gow, 1959. Deep core drilling in ice, Byrd Station, Antarctica. *U.S. Army Snow, Ice and Permafrost Res. Estab., Tech. Rept., 60.* Hanover, N.H.

Ragle, R. H., B. L. Hansen, A. J. Gow, and R. W. Patenaude, 1960. Deep core drilling in the Ross Ice Shelf, Little America V, Antarctica. *U.S. Army Snow, Ice and Permafrost Res. Estab., Tech. Rept., 70.* Hanover, N.H.

Schytt, V., 1958. Scientific Results of the Norwegian-British-Swedish Antarctic Expedition, 1949–52. *Glaciology II;* vol. 4, pp. 7–148. Norsk Polar Institut, Oslo.

Sutton, B., and A. Arutunoff, 1954. *Use of electrodrill for oil coring and drilling.* Report prepared for presentation at the Petroleum Industry Electrical Conference of the American Institute of Electrical Engineering.

Ueda, H. T., and D. E. Garfield, 1968. Deep core drilling program at Byrd Station, (1967–68). *Antarctic J. U. S.,* 3: 111–112.

Ueda, H. T., and D. E. Garfield, 1969. Core drilling through the Antarctic Ice Sheet. *U.S. Army Cold Regions Res. Eng. Lab. Tech. Rept., 231.* Hanover, N.H.

Wright, F. W., F. A. Franklin, P. W. Hodge, and C. C. Langway, Jr., 1967. Determination of the densities of individual meteoritic glacial and volcanic spherules. *J. Geophys. Res., 72:* 2543–2546.

Snow Accumulation in Antarctica

Colin Bull

Institute of Polar Studies and Department of Geology, The Ohio State University, Columbus

The Antarctic Continent, with the exception of the northern part of the Antarctic Peninsula and small peripheral parts south of the Indian Ocean, lies entirely south of the Antarctic Circle. Excluding the offshore islands and ice shelves that extend seaward around much of the continent, the area of the Antarctic is about 12,393,000 km². The ice shelves and the islands and ice rises within them add another 1,582,000 km² (Bardin and Suyetova, 1967). Of this area more than 98 percent (13,779,000 km²) is permanently covered with ice (Shumskiy, 1967). Excluding the ice shelves, the mean elevation of this, the highest continent, is about 2,300 m.

Estimates of the total volume of ice on the continent and in the floating ice shelves still vary widely, reflecting our inadequate knowledge of the ice thickness, especially in East Antarctica. Recent estimates range from 24,031,000 km³ (Bardin and Suyetova, 1967), which includes 418,000 km³ for the ice shelves, to 30,000,000 km³ (Gow, 1965a). Thus the Antarctic Continent contains about 90 percent of the glacier mass on earth (Hoinkes, 1968; Loewe, 1967).

Most of our knowledge of the Antarctic Ice Sheet has been gained since the beginning of the International Geophysical Year, 1957–1958. Gould (1957) estimated that in 1955 at least half of inland Antarctica had never been seen. Since then oversnow and airborne traverses undertaken by scientists from twelve or more countries have enabled geophysicists and glaciologists to obtain a "good reconnaissance" knowledge of the surface and subsurface features of the inland ice, so that it is now unlikely that any large subglacial mountain ranges or troughs remain to be discovered (Bentley, 1962, 1964; Kapitza, 1967).

In addition to determinations of surface elevations and ice thicknesses, most of these traverse parties have undertaken measurements of annual snow accumulation, by a variety of methods, and the estimation of mean annual air temperature, by measuring temperatures in the firn at depths below that of significant fluctuations resulting from the annual temperature variations at the surface (Bull, 1964). These measurements, supplementing year-round meteorological recordings at eight or more inland stations, have allowed Dalrymple (1966) to present a regional climatic classification for inland Antarctica. In this he delimits four climatic regions: Cold Central Core (mean annual temperature, less than $-50°C$; mean annual wind speed, 3 to 5 m/sec, mean annual precipitation, 0 to 15 g/cm^2), Cold Interior ($-40°$ to $-50°C$; 5 to 7 m/sec; 0 to 30 g/cm^2), Cold Katabatic ($-30°$ to $-40°C$; 9 to 12 m/sec; 0 to 45 g/cm^2), and Cold Transitional ($-25°$ to $-40°C$; 7 to 10 m/sec; 10 to 35 g/cm^2). In this way Dalrymple has been able to extend the earlier classifications (e.g., Dolgushin, 1961; Sabbagh, 1962) in which no subdivisions were made of the high parts of the Antarctic Ice Sheet.

Some of the reasons for undertaking studies of snow accumulation and other glaciological parameters have been well summarized by Meier (1967). To choose one reason, it may be pointed out that as the melting of the Antarctic Ice Sheet would raise sea level by 50 to 60 m, a knowledge of the present mass balance is of some economic significance. Oceanographers and dynamic meteorologists have their own, equally valid, interests in the results of the studies.

It is estimated that more than 99 percent of the area of the Antarctic Ice Sheet is a region of positive balance in which snow accumulation exceeds ablation (Giovinetto, 1964a). Only around the coasts (especially in the Antarctic Peninsula), in isolated areas in the inland mountains, and perhaps intermittently in the highest parts of East Antarctica does the ablation exceed the snow accumulation. Almost all of the ice loss from the continent is by calving of glaciers and ice shelves into the open ocean. In these circumstances the lateral extent of the ice sheets is controlled mainly by sea level (Hollin, 1962) and the elevation of the "grounding-line" where the peripheral glacier cliffs and ice shelves begin to float. Special attention must be paid to the ice sheet in West Antarctica, much of which is below sea level. This ice sheet may only exist while the air temperatures and other parameters allow ice shelves to exist around the coast (Mercer, 1968a,b, 1970).

METHODS OF MEASURING SNOW BALANCE

Strictly, the term "accumulation" refers to all of the processes by which material is added to the glacier, ice sheet, or ice shelf, and is distinguished from "ablation" which refers to all of the processes by which mass is lost (Meier, 1962; Anon., 1969). On the Antarctic Ice Sheet, and elsewhere, the quantity of material ablating from the upper surface frequently cannot be determined accurately, and rates of accumulation or ablation that may be occurring at the bottom of the ice sheet and the ice shelves are not known. In glaciological studies on traverses, and at inland stations, the quantity measured is almost invariably the positive balance at the upper surface. Similarly, in the small ablation zone at the edge of the continent, the quantity measured is usually the negative balance, rather than the true ablation.

The methods available for estimating local balance that have been used in Antarctica are (See foldout map):

1. Direct measurement of precipitation with snow gauges.
2. Direct measurements of balance, using stakes and other markers.
3. Interpretation of snow stratigraphy revealed in walls of pits and in snow and ice cores.
4. Stable and radioactive isotope studies.
5. Studies of microparticle concentrations.

Balance measurements might also be made from the detection of marker horizons of known age, such as worldwide fallout from major volcanic eruptions, but except for those horizons relating to nuclear bombs, this method has been used only twice, once using a buried vehicle of known date of deposition (Vickers, 1959) and once with the 1963 eruption of Mt. Agung in Bali (Hamilton, 1969).

Precipitation Gauges

Although measurements of falling snow are made at many antarctic stations, with modified or with standard snow gauges, it is generally appreciated that, except in unusual meteorological conditions, these do not give accurate measurements of the true precipitation (Aver'ianov, 1963; Black, 1954; Swithinbank, 1957). Most of the troubles are due to the wind: under different conditions snow may be blown from or deposited in the gauge. Additional errors arise from the collection of hoarfrost, preferentially deposited on the gauge. An accurate measurement of the precipitation at a particular place is of great value to the meteorologist, but in the Antarctic probably most of the snow originally deposited in one place is moved a greater or lesser distance by drifting, and the glaciologist is more concerned with the quantity of snow that settles at a given place. Consequently the few quoted values of precipitation may be disregarded.

Stake Measurements

The simplest and probably the most reliable method of measuring balance at a repeatedly or continuously occupied station, or along a route repeatedly traversed, is by measurements on stakes implanted in areas free from abnormal snow drifting or ablation. Even in these circumstances, however, many precautions must be taken. In an ablation zone, in general the emergence of the stake is not equal to the negative balance; corrections should be made for the vertical strain of the ice between the surface and the depth at which the stake is anchored (Nye, 1968; Vallon, 1968). In an accumulation zone the same kind of error may arise, but of greater importance is the settling of snow that normally occurs around the pole. If the stake were anchored relative to the surrounding snow at a known depth, the settling could be accounted for by repeated measurements of snow density to this depth, but a more satisfactory method in areas where melting is slight is to place markers (usually squares of plywood) at, or just under, the snow surface (Benson, 1962). In only a few of the antarctic studies have the necessary measurements been made to allow the settling correction to be applied.

Even if allowances are made for these factors, measurements at a single stake may not be representative of the balance in that area. In the ablation zone Schytt (1962) recommended a concentration of 10 to 20 stakes per km^2, to avoid errors produced by surface irregularities and thermal effects around the stakes. At individual stakes, measurements of the annual surface lowering show large departures from the mean even in small areas; for example, Keeler (1964) reported departures of 26 percent.

In the accumulation zone even larger variations in the balance are observed over small areas, especially where the accumulation is low and the winds are strong. On small glaciers the variations may be extreme, with annual balances ranging from −4 to +10

g/cm^2 at different points at the same elevation only a few tens of meters apart (Bull and Carnein, 1970).

In this discussion we deal mainly with ice sheets and ice shelves, where, in general, such extreme variations do not occur. Nevertheless, the local studies in Antarctica referred to below show that, even in a generally flat area, the presence of a small undulation near the stake can double or halve the balance at that stake, compared with the mean value in the area.

It is convenient to consider separately the temporal and areal variations (Giovinetto, 1964b; Giovinetto and Schwerdtfeger, 1966) that contribute to the total variability in a small area. On the ice sheets a few square kilometers, the area covered by the networks of stakes laid out at many stations, may be considered a small area. The areal variations that occur are well shown in the continuing studies at Byrd Station, West Antarctica, and at Pole Station. At Old Byrd Station, 100 bamboo stakes, spaced 100 m apart in a square grid 1 km on a side, were measured regularly during the period 1957–1962 (Benson, 1970; Cameron, In press; Long, 1961; Shimizu, 1964). Long and Shimizu have illustrated with contour maps the microrelief that can appear and disappear in periods of about a month. The annual positive balance in this area is about 40 cm of snow (14 g/cm^2), but in different parts of the grid the accumulation over a one-month period may differ by more than 30 cm.

The positive balance at these 100 stakes was obtained from measurements on December 27, 1959, and approximately monthly thereafter. Snow depths given by Benson (1970) have been converted to loads, assuming a density of 0.35 g/cm^3 (Table 1).

The microrelief produced by variations in accumulation lessens in importance as the period of observation increases, but even in an area of relatively high balance with stakes observed for a year, the ratio of the standard deviation to the mean positive balance does not fall much below one-quarter.

A second 100-stake square array has been laid out near New Byrd Station, about 10 km from that at Old Byrd Station. In this 1 km^2 area the surface slopes to the southeast, dropping in elevation by about 5 m. For the two-year period of December 17, 1963, to December 17, 1965, the mean annual balance was 10.3 g/cm^2, but different values were obtained for the 25 stakes in the four quadrants, as shown in Table 2 (Cameron, In press).

Cameron pointed out that there is a 90 percent probability that the sampling in Quadrants II and III represent different values

Table 1. Balance at 100 stakes near Old Byrd Station. Datum is the surface level on December 27, 1959 (After Benson, 1970).

Date (1960)	Mean positive balance, A (g/cm²)	Range (g/cm²)	Standard deviation, σ (g/cm²)	$\frac{\sigma}{\bar{A}}$ (%)
Jan 30	−0.39	6.3	1.16	300
Mar 5	0.56	9.1	1.37	244
Mar 12	1.26	9.1	1.61	124
Mar 22	1.30	9.1	1.58	122
Apr 5	1.68	8.4	1.47	88
Apr 30	2.63	8.8	1.61	61
June 30	5.29	8.1	2.14	40
Aug 31	7.95	13.3	2.38	30
Sept 30	8.44	11.2	2.10	25
Oct 27	8.89	9.5	2.17	24

Table 2. Values at New Byrd Station, 25 stakes in the four quadrants, for the two-year period 1963–1965.

Quadrant	Mean positive balance (g/cm²/yr)	Standard deviation (g/cm²/yr)
I	10.4	1.52
II	11.4	0.71
III	9.1	2.77
IV	10.1	1.35

of balance. In Quadrants I, II, and IV the prevailing wind is normal to the slope; in Quadrant III it is parallel. The lower accumulation is related to the slightly higher wind velocity. Thus, even extremely small slopes, as present in this area, may have significant effects on the accumulation. A similar relationship between high wind speed and low accumulation, on slopes inland from Maudheim, has been found by Schytt (1958); and Swithinbank (1957), on the Maudheim Ice Shelf, also found that the accumulation is greatest where the slope is least.

In other studies of snow accumulation near New Byrd Station, Gow (1965b) set out stakes in two lines, each 10 km long. In his east-west line, which traversed prominent troughs with 30 m of relief, the positive balance was higher in the troughs. At two places in his north-south line the positive balance was higher on the ridges and less on the slopes immediately downwind. Black and Budd (1964), on the Wilkes Ice Dome, also observed accumulation minimums downwind from topographic highs, and maximums downwind from troughs, but Cronk (1968), in the same area, found that accumulation was greater in the troughs. Barkov and Ivanov (1967), working inland from Mirnyy, found that the accumulation was largest on the steeper slopes, presumably because these were north-facing and in the lee from the strong katabatic winds.

At South Pole Station observations on stake farms have been continued since 1958. Giovinetto and Schwerdtfeger (1966), in analyzing data from 33 poles for the six years 1958–1963, gave the results shown in Table 3.

Giovinetto (1964b) has listed the local areal variability determined with stake networks at seven other sites in Antarctica, over periods of 9 to 14 months. At two sites, with annual positive balances of about 10 and 40 g/cm^2, the variability was 7 g/cm^2 per year, but elsewhere the variability was between 1.9 and 3.7 g/cm^2 per year, although the positive balance ranged from little more than 2 to 40 g/cm^2 per year.

On the 350-km traverse inland in Antarctica from Byrd Station to the Whitmore Mountains, first made in late 1962, single stakes were set at about 3-km intervals, and six arrays of 10 to 15 stakes were set at intervals of 60 km. The stakes were remeasured in late 1965 and again late in 1966 (Brecher, 1967a,b). In the three years 1962–1965, the positive balance measured at the stakes in the first 300 km from Byrd Station, including the first five arrays of stakes, was scattered irregularly around 16.1 g/cm^2 per year (standard deviation, 0.4 g/cm^2 per year) with no obvious

Table 3. Local total variability of annual positive balance values measured at 33 stakes at South Pole for period 1958–1963 (Giovinetto and Schwerdtfeger, 1966).

	Mean balance	Total variability	
	($\bar{A}$ g/cm^2/yr)	(g/cm^2/yr)	σ ($\bar{A}$ %)
Minimum accumulation	5.3	2.9	55
Maximum accumulation	7.8	2.7	35
Minimum variability	6.9	1.5	22
Maximum variability	7.1	6.4	90
For 33 stakes	(6.5)	(3.6)	(51)

relationship between the variations and topography. Over the 50 km nearest the Whitmore Mountains the balance was 21.3 g/cm² per year (standard deviation 0.8). At the sixth array, 5 km from Mt. Chapman, the positive balance was 42.3 g/cm² per year (standard deviation 4.4) but areal variability here is very large and at other points in the neighborhood the balance was much less. Brecher estimated that the standard deviation of one observation from the mean positive balance for the three years was about 10 percent; the largest deviation of one observation was about 20 percent.

For the year 1965–1966, however, the positive balance at the stakes in the first 300 km was greatly reduced, 11.5 compared with 16.1 g/cm² per year for the three previous years. The annual balance between 300 and 350 km remained unchanged. The variations in balance along the line for the two periods are closely related (correlation coefficient, 0.926). Similar variabilities have been recorded in other repeated measurements of stakes along traverses (e.g., Heap and Rundle, 1964).

This temporal variation of positive balance is also demonstrated by stake measurements near Byrd Station, shown in Table 4.

For a given year the balance in small areas at Old and New Byrd Stations (10 km apart) may be different because the two areas may be differently related to the topographic highs of the long wavelength surface undulations, referred to above. However, it seems unlikely that this cause can account for all of the variations shown in Table 4.

Table 4. Variation with time of annual balance near Byrd Station.

Time period	No. of stakes	Annual balance (g/cm²)	Reference
Location: *Old Byrd Station*			
Mar, 1957–Jan, 1958	7	16.5	Anderson, 1958
Mar, 1957–Dec, 1958	120	17.8	Long, 1961
Feb, 1959–Oct, 1959	100	21.8	Pirrit and Doumani, 1961
Nov, 1960–Oct, 1961	100	13.6	Shimizu, 1964
Location: *New Byrd Station*			
Feb, 1962–Jan, 1963	43	10.7	Gow, 1965b, and pers. comm.
Jan, 1963–Jan, 1964	43	9.3	Gow, 1965b, and pers. comm.
Jan, 1964–Jan, 1965	43	12.8	Gow, 1965b, and pers. comm.
Jan, 1965–Jan, 1966	43	11.0	Gow, 1965b, and pers. comm.
Dec, 1963–Dec, 1965	100	10.3	Cameron (in press)

It is apparent from the foregoing discussion that the accurate estimation of annual positive balance is difficult even with such a simple technique as stake measurements. Areal variability over distances up to 5 km may easily be as much as 20 percent, and temporal variability over five-year periods may greatly exceed this.

Additional information on both sources of error in estimates of balance obtained from limited numbers of stakes measured over short periods is obtained from the longer time sequences observed in pits and in cores. A very detailed treatment of the errors is given by Giovinetto (1964b). The long sequences are discussed later.

Snow Stratigraphy

The earliest work on the identification of annual layers in the dry snow facies of the accumulation zones of ice sheets (Benson, 1962; Giovinetto, 1964a) was carried out in south-central Greenland by Sorge (1935). Here, where the annual balance is about 35 g/cm^2 and the mean wind speed is low, it is usually possible to detect the annual layering. This is done from differences in grain size (the winter snow being finer-grained than the summer), from radiation crusts, ice lenses, and partial melting and rounding of the grains during the summer, and by the presence of low density layers frequently called "depth-hoar" layers that are due to the migration of ice molecules from the layer immediately beneath the surface when there are large temperature gradients at the beginning of winter. The same techniques have been used, with some difficulty, in areas of lower accumulation in Greenland (Benson, 1962; Lister, 1961) and in some parts of Antarctica, especially the coastal areas (e.g., Cameron, 1964a; Schytt, 1958). At S-2 Station (annual balance 13.3 g/cm^2, mean annual temperature $-19.4°C$), Cameron (1964a) found that grain-size changes and attendant changes in hardness are the most useful criteria for distinguishing annual units. From a depth of 4 to 35 m, melt crusts and layers were used to indicate summer horizons. In this way Cameron was able to determine the positive balance each year from 1783 to 1956.

Shimizu (1964) used the same techniques for determining annual units in 2- and 3-m pits on two traverses in the northern parts of West Antarctica. Positive balances and annual temperatures here are high (15 to 60 g/cm^2 per year; $-14°$ to $-30°C$), and Shimizu considered the stratigraphic method not very reliable, especially in areas of very high snowfall, near the coast. He felt that the determination of annual layers is too subjective to be valuable, since different observers obtain widely differing estimates of the balance.

At New Byrd Station (annual balance about 14 g/cm^2; mean annual temperature −28°C), much greater success has been obtained. Benson (1970) in 1961–1962 examined the stratigraphy exposed in long trenches up to 6 m deep and supplemented the techniques given above with estimates of mean accumulation based on the variation of density with depth. From these studies Benson determined the positive annual balance as about 20 g/cm^2 between 1947 and 1954, and about 14 g/cm^2 from 1955 to 1961. These values are in general agreement with those from the stake measurements. Cameron (In press) also examined snow stratigraphy at New Byrd Station in the walls of a trench 14 m long, 2 m wide, and 2 m deep. About half of the depth-hoar layers (grain size 3 to 4 mm) and hard-packed winter snow layers (grain size 1 mm or less) could be traced along the entire 14-m wall, and a further one-third for half the length of the wall. His estimates of annual accumulation from the stratigraphy at three points along the wall are shown in Table 5.

The variations from year to year do not correspond with those shown by the nearby stake measurements. However, the increase from west to east of 12.7 to 14.4 g/cm^2 for the mean balance for the four-year period does appear to be real. The prominent summer horizon of 1958–1959 appeared at increasing depths, 175, 189, and 198 cm in the three studied sections, from west to east.

Koerner (1964a) studied snow stratigraphy at New Byrd Station in late 1962 to establish criteria for identifying annual layers (by comparison with the stake measurements) which could be used

Table 5. Annual balance, g/cm^2, in 14-m-long pit at New Byrd Station (Modified from Cameron, In press).

	West end	Midline	East end	Mean
1963	9.2	11.6	13.8	11.5
1962	15.1	9.4	13.8	12.8
1961	8.3	17.1	11.8	12.4
1960	15.2	19.9	20.0	18.4
1959	15.6	12.4	12.8	13.6
Mean	12.7	14.1	14.4	13.7

on the Byrd Station-Whitmore Mountains traverse. Again he was able to use variations in grain size and hardness, layers of sublimation crystals (depth-hoar), and radiation crusts to distinguish annual units, but in some pits no evidence was found for winter accumulation in particular years, and in others a summer layer was probably missing.

These observations are consistent with the stake measurements of balance. During about half of the winter and summer periods observed, up to 5 percent of the stakes showed no positive balance. At the time of the first Byrd Station-Whitmore Mountains traverse the only control that Koerner had was the stake measurement balance at Byrd Station. Using the stratigraphic method in a pit and on cores drilled from below the pit level Koerner obtained 14.7 g/cm^2 as the mean annual balance for the period 1930–1960, compared with 13.9 g/cm^2 obtained by Gow (1961) using the same techniques on the Old Byrd Station deep core, and stake measurement values varying between 9 and 22 g/cm^2 in different years.

On the Byrd Station-Whitmore Mountains traverse Koerner used the same stratigraphic criteria to determine annual units, paying particular attention to the cyclic pattern of grain size and the occurrence of radiation crusts.

The values of positive balance at seven points by the stratigraphic method are compared in Table 6 with the measurements at stake arrays subsequently obtained by Brecher (1967a,b, and In preparation).

It is apparent that except at Station VI the difference between the stratigraphically determined annual positive balance and the direct stake measurement is less than the difference in the direct stake measurements in different years. At Station VI the areal variability in accumulation is extremely large.

An even more closely controlled set of stake measurements and pit-stratigraphy estimates of balance, on the Ross Ice Shelf (Heap and Rundle, 1964), was initiated by Swithinbank following his earlier work at Maudheim (Swithinbank, 1957, 1959). Excellent agreement was obtained between the estimates of balance by the two methods.

These results give confidence in the stratigraphic method when used by experienced observers in areas of moderately high balance, but the difficulties of its use, or of the short-period stake measurements, in determining mean balance are clear.

In West Antarctica, Vickers (1966) attempted a more precise

Table 6. Comparison of values of positive balance by stakes and the stratigraphic method. Balance in g/cm².

Station	Koerner's pit stratigraphy		Stakes	
	Annual balance	Period	Annual balance	Period
Byrd	14.2	1958–62	14.2	1957–62
I	13.7	1958–62	14.2	1962–65
			8.0	1965–66
II	12.0	1957–62	16.2	1962–65
			11.0	1965–66
III	13.1	1956–62	18.5	1962–65
			14.6	1965–66
IV	13.7	1957–62	16.1	1962–65
			11.4	1965–66
V	13.5	1957–62	16.8	1962–65
			16.3	1965–66
VI	13.0	1957–62	42.3	1962–65
			48.7	1965–66

statistical analysis of grain size in an attempt to follow individual layers over great distances. Although his methods and interpretations are open to criticism he was able to identify over large distances layers associated with particular storms, and hence to obtain estimates of the annual balance.

In areas where mean annual temperatures are lower than −40°C and balance is less than about 8 g/cm², which includes much of East Antarctica, the stratigraphic method is much more difficult to apply than in West Antarctica and on the major ice shelves. Because air temperatures do not rise much above −20°C, the easily discernible summer radiation and partial-melting crusts are often absent, and in low accumulation areas no snow at all may be deposited at the pit site in a particular year.

At the Amundsen-Scott South Pole Station (mean annual air temperature −51°C, mean balance about 7 g/cm²), stratigraphic studies have been carried out by Lister (1960), Giovinetto (1960, 1963), Picciotto *et al.* (1964), Gow (1965c), Taylor (1965), and Koerner (In press). Giovinetto's interpretation was based on seasonal changes in density, hardness, and grain size. Taylor relied mainly on density variations between winter and summer. Gow found an annual depth-hoar layer, but Koerner found that such a layer was present in only 70 percent of the years. Furthermore, he found that the macroscopic textural variations revealed in a pit wall were very difficult to interpret. Despite these and other difficulties, all of the observers have reported annual positive balance values between 5 and 9 g/cm², comparable with stake-measured values.

In areas of lower accumulation, high on the East Antarctic plateau, difficulties have been experienced in interpreting snow stratigraphy. Kotliakov (1961a,b,c, 1966) and other Soviet glaciologists have attempted to distinguish winter and summer layers by density, hardness, grain size, height of capillary rise, maximum waterholding capacity, and air permeability. Overall, they have been quite successful in using the method, but significant differences exist between Kotliakov's stratigraphic estimates and stake measurements (Giovinetto, 1964b). The problems are illustrated by the published values for the balance at Vostok, which range from 3.4 to 7.6 g/cm² per year (Battye, 1965; Kotliakov, 1962; Kotliakov *et al.*, 1966; Ukhov, 1963; Zotikov *et al.*, 1965).

At the U.S.S.R. Pole of Inaccessibility Station, mean annual air temperature is −57°C, the annual positive balance, by measurements on 19 stakes, is 3.1 ± 0.5 g/cm² (Picciotto *et al.*, 1968). The upper few meters of snow show some abrupt changes in grain size and hardness, but the layering is due mainly to depth-hoar layers, 0.2 to 2.0 m thick, associated iced crusts up to 0.1 cm thick, thin continuous crusts of hard bonded grains, and very hard, dense, and fine-grained layers of variable thickness between 0.5 and 15 cm thickness. Picciotto *et al.* found it impossible to recognize annual units, but, assuming that the depth-hoar layers were annual, obtained maximum values of annual balance of 8 and 12 g/cm² in two neighboring pits.

At Plateau Station (annual air temperature −54°C, positive annual balance 2 to 3 g/cm²), Koerner (In press) developed a stratigraphic method that appears to be reliable. From examinations of the strata exposed in 66 shallow pits dug early in December, 1966, before the summer's "warmth" had affected the surface, and in 50 shallow pits dug in late January, 1967 (after the summer), Koerner was able to determine the effects of the summer. The grain size of the previous winter's snow doubled to 0.04 cm, with considerable rounding of the grains and a sixfold hardening of the surface. In December the upper annual unit was remarkably homogeneous; by late January hard fine-grained, sintered layers were present near the surface and a loose, coarser-grained layer beneath, quite unlike the sequence in West Antarctica, where the winter layers are usually much harder than the summer layers.

In deeper pits Koerner was able to distinguish a repetition of these summer features, and his main difficulties in estimating annual positive balance were in not knowing how many years are missing from the pit-wall stratigraphy. About 10 percent of the stakes in the area showed no accumulation in the 1966–1967 year, and probably the same percentage of annual layers is missing in the pits. A few other years of very small accumulation may also be missed in the pits. From 60 shallow pits Koerner obtained a value for the annual balance of 2.45 g/cm^2 with a standard deviation of 1.58, compared with 2.29 g/cm^2 and a standard deviation of 2.06 determined at 99 stakes.

Applying the same techniques at points on the traverse from the Pole of Inaccessibility to Plateau Station, Koerner (In press) obtained values ranging between 2 and 4.3 g/cm^2 per year which compare well with values obtained by other methods. At the Pole of Inaccessibility Koerner's stratigraphic value is 2.9 g/cm^2 per year, while the stakes give 3.1 g/cm^2.

On the 1967–1968 traverse from Plateau Station toward the Queen Maud Land coast, Rundle (1968; In press) attempted to use the criteria of summer features established by Koerner (In press) at Plateau Station, but found them increasingly difficult to apply as he went farther away from the station. In ten shallow pits at Plateau Station in late November, 1967, Rundle found a surface layer of hard, fine-grained snow with a density of 0.364 g/cm^3 extending to an average depth of 6.5 cm. According to Koerner's criteria this layer should represent a summer horizon, but Rundle considers that it is largely the result of the strong winds, averaging 32 km/hr and with a maximum of 80 km/hr, that persisted from November 13 through 15, 1967.

Underlying this hard surface layer in late November, 1967, was a softer layer, and, at an average depth of 14.7 cm, a second hard layer. The direct interpretation that this second layer represents the 1966–1967 summer surface gives annual accumulation values around 5 g/cm^2, almost twice that from stake measurements. At this site, where adequate control is available, it is possible to reinterpret the stratigraphy, so that the second layer is taken as the 1965–1966 summer surface, and the storms of mid-November, 1967, are assumed to have redistributed all of the 1967 and part of the 1966 accumulation. The difficulties of the stratigraphic method, without controls from stake measurements, are apparent.

On the 1967–1968 traverse from Plateau Station toward the Queen Maud Land coast, Rundle (1968; In press) found that the stratigraphy, always complex, changed a great deal over distances of 100 km; and only by studying many shallow profiles at each site was Rundle able to make apparently reliable interpretations. At a number of sites the interpretation appears to be unambiguous, and Rundle believes that the probability of missing years in the profiles decreases toward the coast.

On the first leg of this traverse, Rundle's (1968) preliminary estimates of the positive balance show an irregular increase toward the coast, from about 2.7 g/cm^2 per year near Plateau Station to 7.1 g/cm^2 per year near the turning point of 75°56′S, 7°13′E. Along the same leg Picciotto *et al.* (1970), from measurements of total β-particle activity, gave values varying from 2.7 g/cm^2 per year at Plateau Station to 5.1 g/cm^2 at the turning point. As Rundle's values refer to two years of snow accumulation, while Picciotto *et al.* gave the average positive balance since 1955, the two sets of results may not be in conflict.

On the other hand, Rundle's preliminary estimates of positive balance on the second leg of the traverse, from the turning point to 78°42′S, 6°52′W, average about 9 g/cm^2 per year, ranging from 7 to 14 g/cm^2, while Picciotto *et al.* obtained values ranging from 4.2 to 5.9 g/cm^2 per year. Although not impossible, it seems unlikely that the positive balance for the two years from 1966 to 1968 was twice the average value over the 13 years from 1955 to 1968, the period used in the Picciotto *et al.* study. In summary, it may be stated that in areas of very low balance the uncontrolled stratigraphic method often tends to underestimate the number of annual units exposed in a profile.

Long Series of Accumulation Data from Deep Pits and Cores

At most of the semipermanent stations established inland in Antarctica, attempts have been made to determine the annual positive balance over relatively long periods from an examination of the stratigraphy revealed in deep pits and ice cores. The difficulties experienced in interpreting surface stratigraphy increase with depth, because seasonal markers tend to be lost during diagenesis and the ice becomes more homogeneous. Nevertheless, observers have been able to discern annual layers to considerable depths. A partial list of the results obtained is given in Table 7. Some other results, covering shorter periods, are given by Giovinetto (1964b) and by Barkov and Petrov (1966).

Table 7. Long sequences of annual positive balance measurements, from stratigraphy of deep pits and ice cores (Partly after Giovinetto, 1964b).

Station	Depth (m)	Years	Annual balance (g/cm^2)	Variability and trend ($g/cm^2/yr$)	Reference
South Pole	27	1760–1957	(5.4 1760–1825) (6.8 1826–1891) (7.5 1892–1957)	2.6 increasing	Giovinetto and Schwerdtfeger, 1966
Wilkes S-2	27–50 35	1550–1760 1783–1956	10 to 6 13.3	decreasing? 4.6 no trend	Cameron, 1964a
Little America	39	1855–1958	22.1	6.4 no trend	Gow, 1963
Plateau	10.2	1840–1967	2.78	1.48 no trend	Koerner, in press, a
Byrd	18.7	1893–1960	14.4	3.2	Gow, 1961
South Ice	15.1	1895–1957	11.2	4.2	Lister, 1959
McMurdo Sound	14.7	1913–1958	17.6	5.0	Stuart and Bull, 1963
Lazarev		1924–1960	22.2	9.7	Kruchinin, 1962

The most thorough analysis of long-term data is that from South Pole (Giovinetto and Schwerdtfeger, 1966). They recognized a statistically significant increase in accumulation in three successive 66-year periods, as shown in Table 7, and a less well-substantiated trend in the previous 200 years. At the other stations no significant trends were noted by the original observers, but Petrov *et al.* (1966) re-analyzed most of the data and believed that they could detect significant variations with periods of 3–4, 5–7, 10–11, and 18–20 years. At the sites with the longest runs, South Pole and Wilkes S-2, Petrov *et al.* detected two longer-period variations, of 30 and 44 years. They claimed that the probability of a random variation in the annual positive balance giving these periodic variations is quite small for all the series. It is not apparent, however, that Petrov *et al.* have paid due attention to the areal variability of accumulation at a given station, that may easily amount to 20 percent of the mean balance (at South Pole and Plateau Stations it is more than 50 percent) and must necessarily be periodic at a given point, or to the errors in counting annual layers that exist in all the series. For example, at South Ice, Lister (1960) gave ± 10 years as the safe estimate in dating annual layers over a 50-year sequence, and, for the South Pole, Giovinetto and Schwerdtfeger (1966) gave an estimated error of ± 13 years in their 198-year series. Giovinetto and Schwerdtfeger concluded, after comparing data from Wilkes S-2 and Little America where any long-term changes in annual balance are definitely insignificant, with data from South Pole, where the change in the last 200 years is significant, that the South Pole increase cannot be generalized for other parts of Antarctica. Petrov *et al.* (1966) gave the contrary view "that similar variations in snow accumulation exist over the entire territory of Antarctica," and Barkov and Petrov (1966) considered that they were able to relate the changes in accumulation to changes in worldwide atmospheric circulation patterns. The period from 1901 to 1936 was one of dominantly meridional circulation, while that since 1937 has shown dominant zonal circulation.

Isotope Studies

During the last few years methods have been developed for dating ice or determining the temperature of deposition, and therefore of determining values of the annual balance, which depend on measurements of stable and radioactive isotopes. A brief review of some of these methods has been given by Picciotto *et al.* (1968). These methods are particularly applicable to the dry-snow facies where melting is absent, so that little vertical mixing occurs after deposition.

Oxygen and Hydrogen Isotope Variations

Simply stated, the ratio of the two most common stable isotopes of oxygen, O^{16} and O^{18}, and of the two stable hydrogen isotopes, H^1 and H^2, depends on the temperature at which the snow condenses. (The ratios also depend on the distance from the source of the vapor and on the precipitation history along the track, but the effects are relatively small.) Consequently, at a given location it should be possible to distinguish between winter and summer precipitation and to determine annual positive balance from profiles of the $O^{18}:O^{16}$ or $H^2:H^1$ ratios.

A number of other factors tend to distort this simple model: the temperature in the cloud where the snow condenses may not be simply related to the surface air temperature where the snow is precipitated; the snow may drift along the surface for considerable distances after precipitation, before finally settling; and changes in the isotope ratios occur by vertical diffusion between the various strata after the snow has accumulated. Nevertheless, as long as the original depositional sequence is maintained, it has proved possible to follow the variations in the isotope ratios to considerable depths, below the level to which the original snow stratigraphy is discernible.

In Greenland, Epstein's early work (Benson, 1962) showed excellent agreement between variations of $O^{18}:O^{16}$ ratios and Benson's near-surface stratigraphy, giving confidence in both methods of determining annual positive balance. In Antarctica the oxygen isotope method has now been applied at many locations. Gonfiantini *et al.* (1963a) showed that the oxygen ratios in samples averaging a complete year's accumulation are closely related to elevation, and thus to mean annual air temperature. The same workers (Gonfiantini *et al.*, 1963b) measured the oxygen isotope ratios to a depth of 16 m at Roi Baudouin Station and, although they felt that the interpretation of the oxygen-ratio profile involved a similar degree of uncertainty to that in the stratigraphic method, found good agreement between the average annual balances deduced from the two methods.

At South Pole the early oxygen isotope work of Epstein *et al.*

(1963) suggested an annual positive balance of 15.0 g/cm^2, compared with 7 or 8 g/cm^2 from surface stake measurements. Later oxygen isotope work, perhaps with more careful collecting procedures, has given values of 7 g/cm^2 (Epstein *et al.*, 1965).

Epstein and Sharp (1967) measured oxygen- and hydrogen-isotope ratios in a core from Eights Station that had been examined stratigraphically by Shimizu (1964). The variations with depth of both isotope ratios are very similar, but both profiles are difficult to interpret. Epstein and Sharp picked ten summer layers in the 7-m core, giving a mean annual positive balance of 39 or 40 g/cm^2, but there is a strong possibility that eleven annual units were present, reducing the balance to about 36 g/cm^2. Two other maximums in the oxygen ratio profiles and one in the hydrogen ratio profile could also be interpreted as summer horizons.

In the area of Eights Station, Shimizu (1964) had some difficulty in interpreting the stratigraphy, and in his initial interpretation the average value for the four upper annual units, 15.3 g/cm^2, does not seem to be compatible with Epstein and Sharp's isotopically determined value, nor with that obtained from studies of the microparticulate content of the core.

At the Pole of Relative Inaccessibility, where stake measurements gave balance values of about 3 g/cm^2 per year, the oxygen-isotope ratio profile gave 8.6 ± 0.9 g/cm^2 (Picciotto *et al.*, 1968). At this site Picciotto *et al.* had great difficulty in picking annual units from the stratigraphy, and could only say that the balance was probably less than 12 g/cm^2 per year, but Koerner's reinterpretation (Koerner, In press) gave about 3 g/cm^2 per year.

A large number of oxygen- and hydrogen-isotope ratio profiles have now been made on antarctic snow and ice samples. While the ratio measurements themselves are completely objective, the interpretation of the variations is still to some extent subjective, especially in areas of low accumulation; and, as the examples show, wide ranges can be obtained in the estimates of balance.

Giovinetto (1964b) and Lorius (1963) have given valuable comparisons of the annual balance determined by stake measurements, stratigraphic methods, and measurements of stable isotopes, at nine sites. In general, the oxygen- or hydrogen-isotope method results, then available, gave results consistent with stake measurements at sites where the annual positive balance was 20 g/cm^2 or more, but elsewhere values from the isotope ratio profiles were greater than those from the direct measurements. At that time Giovinetto considered the stratigraphic method to be more reliable than the stable isotope method in areas of low and moderate balance, like South Pole and Byrd Stations.

The variation of the annual average of $O^{18}:O^{16}$ and $H^2:H^1$ ratios with depth have been used to determine long-period variations of the mean annual temperature. Epstein *et al.* (1963) concluded from their studies of oxygen-isotope ratios at the surface and at 288-m depth at Byrd Station that the mean temperature has increased 2° to 4°C in the last 200 years. Lorius *et al.* (1968), studying the hydrogen-isotope ratios in the coastal part of Adélie Coast, concluded that the temperature change there in the last two centuries is not significant (0.3° ± 0.3°C). Such studies can also give valuable information on the temperature at the initial site of deposition of the ice now found at great depth near the coast of Antarctica, and hence on the large-scale mechanics of flow of the ice sheet. A first attempt at this, for Greenland, was made by Dansgaard (1961), and for part of Antarctica by Lorius *et al.* (1968). More recently Dansgaard *et al.* (1969) have made oxygen-isotope analyses at intervals on the complete 1,373-m core through the Greenland Ice Sheet at Camp Century, and from it have inferred temperature changes over the last 70,000 or more years. Similar work on the core obtained through the Antarctic Ice Sheet at Byrd Station (Gow, 1970) has now been carried out (Epstein *et al.*, 1970) ; the information that has been obtained on climatic changes over long periods is of direct importance in many fields of study besides glaciology.

Strontium-90 and Gross β-particle Activity

During March to May, 1954, the "Castle" series of high-altitude nuclear tests produced a considerable increase in the stratospheric inventory of fission products. Some of this material was deposited on the Greenland and Antarctic Ice Sheets, and, in areas where little melting or mixing of the deposited snow occurs, produced a very simple and unambiguous reference horizon in pit and core studies. Libby (1956) first reported results of measurements for radioactivity on an ice core from Admiral Byrd Bay. Vicker's (1966) assessment of the stratigraphy indicates that the fission products started to be deposited in about October, 1954, and reached a maximum at the beginning of 1955. Thus the travel time from the test site to the Antarctic was about six months, compared with Martell's (1959) estimate of nine months for travel to Greenland (Crozaz *et al.*, 1966).

A detailed study of Sr^{90} and gross β-activity at Roi Baudouin Station was made by Picciotto and Wilgain (1963), and at Roi Baudouin, Scott Base, and South Pole Stations by Wilgain *et al.* (1965). At Roi Baudouin Station, where firn cores have been dated by stake measurements, stratigraphic studies, and oxygen-isotope studies, the deepest level showing a discernible increase in gross β-activity is at the end of 1953 (the "Ivy" series of tests). The prominent horizon of late 1954- early 1955, from the "Castle" test series, shows an increase in both Sr^{90} and gross β-activity; and a third horizon, late in 1962, is marked by a sudden increase in gross β-activity but not in the Sr^{90} content.

A comparison of the annual balance at these three sites and at the Pole of Relative Inaccessibility (Picciotto *et al.*, 1968), determined by different methods, is given in Table 8.

Wilgain *et al.* (1965) pointed out that the 1953 level, associated with the "Ivy" series of tests, cannot readily be determined from gross β-activity, because the activity is little more than the background, and that the Sr^{90} activity is so low that large samples (several kg) and very sensitive techniques are required for its detection. The early 1955 level, on the other hand, shows large changes both in Sr^{90} and in gross β-activity, which increases from 1 to 2 to 20–50 disintegrations per kg/min. The β-activity can be detected in 100-g samples. The jump in activity in 1962 resulted from fission productions of relatively short half-life, so that the 1962 horizon, with an increase in β-activity but not in Sr^{90}, will be detectable for only a few years. The half-life of Sr^{90}, however, is about 28 years, so that the 1955 horizon will serve as a very useful reference level for several decades to come.

Tritium Methods

Tritium, H^3, is produced in the atmosphere by cosmic-radiation-induced spallations of N^{14} and O^{16}. Accordingly, the rate of production suffers the same variations with time and place as the other radionuclides produced by cosmic rays. Begemann (1959) and Renaud *et al.* (1963) suggested that the rate of tritium production is inversely related to sunspot activity. Since the beginning of nuclear bomb testing, the quantity of H^3 in the atmosphere has greatly increased, and as the half-life is only 12.4 years and the measurements of activity are difficult, little use has been made of this isotope in dating ice.

Oeschger *et al.* (1962) have used the method with success in

Table 8. Comparison of annual positive balance at four sites.

Station	Method	Period	Annual Positive Balance (g/cm^2)	Reference
Roi Baudouin	$O^{18}:O^{16}$	1933–57	36.7	Gonfiantini *et al.*, 1963b
	Stratigraphy	1933–58	19	Picciotto, 1961
	Stratigraphy	1955–61	39.5	Gonfiantini *et al.*, 1968b
	Stakes	1959–61	32.8	Gonfiantini *et al.*, 1968b
	Stakes	1960	45.5	DeBreuck, 1961
	Sr^{90} and gross β	1955–64	40	Wilgain *et al.*, 1965
	Pb^{210}	1887–1961	45.0 ± 3	Crozaz, 1967
Scott Base	$H^2:H^1$	1957–61	46.0	Lorius, 1963
	Stratigraphy	1913–58	17.6	Stuart and Bull, 1963
	Stratigraphy	1958–62	13.5	Heap and Rundle, 1964
	Stakes	1959–60	13.6	Stuart and Bull, 1963
	Gross β	1955–61	11.4 ± 1	Wilgain *et al.*, 1965
South Pole	$O^{18}:O^{16}$	1954–58	15	Sharp and Epstein, 1962
	$O^{18}:O^{16}$	1958–63	7	Epstein *et al.*, 1965
	Stratigraphy	1850–1950	7.4	Giovinetto and Schwerdtfeger, 1966
	Stakes	1958–63	6.5	Giovinetto and Schwerdtfeger, 1966
	Sr^{90} and gross β	1953–62	6.8 ± 0.5	Wilgain *et al.*, 1965
	Pb^{210}	1850–1963	6 ± 1	Crozaz *et al.*, 1964
Pole of Relative Inaccessibility	$O^{18}:O^{16}$	1955–65	8.6 ± 0.9	Picciotto *et al.*, 1968
	Stratigraphy	? –65	<12	Picciotto *et al.*, 1968
	Stratigraphy	1962–65	2.9	Koerner, In press
	Stakes	1965	3.1	Picciotto *et al.*, 1968
	Gross β	1955–65	3.0 ± 0.1	Picciotto *et al.*, 1968
	Pb^{210} (Bi^{210})	1890–1965	3.5 ± 0.5	Picciotto *et al.*, 1968
	Pb^{210} (Po^{210})	1890–1965	2.9 ± 0.3	Picciotto *et al.*, 1968

Switzerland, and Renaud *et al.* (1963) in Greenland. Other experiments on alpine glaciers, more concerned with the use of tritium as a tracer for measuring water movements than for balance measurements, have been carried out by Ambach *et al.* (1968).

In Antarctica, tritium has been little used in dating ice. At Little America III, Libby (1956) deduced an annual positive balance, from tritium concentrations, of 19.8 g/cm^2, in good agreement with the 16 g/cm^2 per year in the same area found by Vickers (1966).

The Lead-210 Method

Lead-210 (radon D) is produced in the atmosphere by the decay of radon-222, which itself is produced from naturally occurring uranium-238. The Pb^{210} decays by β-emission with a half-life of 22 years. Although Pb^{210} occurs in only minute amounts in precipitations from the atmosphere, sensitive chemical and counting techniques are available for detecting and measuring not only the Pb^{210}, but also two of its daughters, bismuth-210, a β-emitter with a half-life of five days, and polonium-210, an α-emitter of 138-day half-life.

The concentration of radon and hence of Pb^{210} in the air at ground level varies from place to place by more than 1,000 (Crozaz *et al.*, 1964; Picciotto, 1961) and with the season (Lockhart *et al.*, 1965). It also decreases with increasing altitude (Wexler *et al.*, 1956). Furthermore, the daughter elements of radon are electrically charged and may be preferentially adsorbed onto aerosols, and some Pb^{210} has been produced by nuclear explosions. Nevertheless, the quantity of Pb^{210} precipitated onto the ground at a given place, averaged over a year or more, appears to be constant and not to have changed significantly since the advent of H-bombs.

In these circumstances it is possible to determine the activity of Pb^{210} from a given depth in an accumulating ice sheet, and by comparing it with the Pb^{210} activity in surface layers, calculate the time of burial, and hence the average positive balance. The first use of the Pb^{210} method to measure positive balance was by Goldberg (1963), using firn cores from south-central Greenland. The method has now been refined considerably; Pb^{210} concentrations may be measured by counting β-emissions of Bi^{210} (Crozaz *et al.*, 1964) or α-emissions of Po^{210} (Crozaz and Fabri, 1966). A full description of the chemical and counting techniques for both methods has been given by Crozaz (1967).

The Pb^{210} method has been used in Antarctica at Roi Baudouin, South Pole, and Pole of Relative Inaccessibility by Picciotto and his co-workers. These results, all in good agreement with direct measurements and those from the position of the 1955 layer, are given in Table 8. Determinations of positive balance by the Pb^{210} method have been made at a few other points in Antarctica by Nezami *et al.* (1964) and by Picciotto's group; in Greenland by Crozaz and Langway (1966); and with partial success on a temperate glacier by Crozaz (1967).

Carbon-14 Methods

The most reliable of the geochemical methods of determining accumulation rates are the Pb^{210} method and the detection of the 1955 level by measurement of the gross β-activity. The gross β-particle method allows only the determination of the mean positive balance since 1955, and the Pb^{210} method is not sufficiently accurate to indicate temporal variations, the accuracy of the balance rate determinations being only about 15 percent (Crozaz, 1967). Furthermore, the half-life of Pb^{210} is 22 years, and the initial Pb^{210} concentration is so small that the period over which the method may be applied is limited to the last 100 years.

Consequently, attempts have been made in the last few years to detect and measure the activity of longer-lived naturally produced radioisotopes which could be used for dating very much older ice, for example that obtained from near the bottom of the Greenland Ice Sheet at Camp Century and the Antarctic Ice Sheet at Byrd Station.

Carbon-14 is produced in the atmosphere from the capture by nitrogen nuclei of fast neutrons resulting from cosmic radiation. The $C^{14}:C^{12}$ ratio in the atmosphere remains approximately constant, the ratio being controlled by the half-life of C^{14} (about 5,600 years) and its rate of production. Appreciable variations of the atmospheric C^{14} content have occurred in the past (Suess, 1965); these include short-term variations of a few percent lasting for a few centuries, and a long-term increase of about 14 percent from 6,000 to 2,500 years ago. Variations in the cosmic-ray flux may result from changes in the earth's magnetic field or changes in the primary flux from the sun (Stuiver, 1967). Changes in the primary flux would probably be associated with changes in the solar constant, which may well be the cause of the major variations in the earth's climate in the past.

In addition to these longer-term variations in atmospheric C^{14} content, the industrial revolution, H-bomb explosions in the last two decades, and perhaps changes in worldwide vegetation patterns have caused the $C^{14}:C^{12}$ ratio to vary. These changes are becoming well documented, however, so that measures of the $C^{14}:C^{12}$ ratio on the CO_2 contained in the air bubbles in glacier ice can be used to determine the age of the ice. The difficulty with the method until recently was that with old ice, several tons of ice free from carbon contamination were required for a single age determination. The method has been used on a temperate glacier in Norway (Coachman *et al.,* 1958). Other experiments have been carried out in Greenland, the more recent ones involving new counting techniques requiring about one ton of ice (Langway *et al.,* 1965; Oeschger *et al.,* 1966; Scholander *et al.,* 1962). Ages of up to 3,100 ± 150 years have been obtained for ice from icebergs and up to 6,000 ±700 years for samples cut from a tunnel wall near Thule, Greenland. However, it is apparent that there are severe difficulties, mainly in obtaining a sufficiently large sample of CO_2 free from carbon contamination, in using the method for determining the age of ice at the bottom of a borehole through an ice sheet.

Proposals have also been made to measure the age of ice in ice-cored moraines in South Victoria Land and elsewhere, as an aid to determining the chronology of the glacial variations. With old ice exposed near the surface there is some possibility that C^{14} may be produced at a rate comparable with the natural decay by the bombardment of O^{16} by μ-mesons in cosmic radiation.

Silicon-32 Dating Methods

Silicon-32 is produced continuously in the atmosphere by cosmic-ray-induced spallations of Ar^{40}. It decays by β-emission with a half-life of about 500 years, and hence would be useful in determining the age of ice specimens intermediate in age between those datable by Pb^{210} and C^{14} methods. The rate of precipitation of Si^{32} is low, 1.6×10^{-4} atoms/cm^2 per second (Lal and Peters, 1962), and rate varies with geomagnetic latitude and with time. Si^{32} has also been produced by nuclear bomb tests (Dansgaard *et al.,* 1966a). In spite of these difficulties, which necessitate the use of very large samples of ice and reference samples predating the nuclear tests, encouraging preliminary results have been obtained on glaciers in Norway (Dansgaard *et al.,* 1966b) and in the Alps (Clausen *et al.,* 1968). The Si^{32} method on ice from Antarctica has not yet been carried out.

Studies of Microparticles

For many years it has been known that dust particles of terrestrial origin can be wind-carried for great distances before deposition. In temperate glaciated regions and in polar regions adjacent to ice-free areas a visible layer of dust may be deposited on the ice every summer (Wright and Priestley, 1922), which may readily be used for the measurement of annual positive balance. In the last century Nordenskiöld (1874) recognized that dust also falls on the interior of the Greenland Ice Sheet; he attributed at least part of the dust to an extraterrestrial source.

The first attempt to detect periodicity in the rate of microparticle fallout on an ice sheet, and to use the variations stratigraphically, was made in 1956 by Marshall (1962) with samples from Greenland. He filtered known volumes of melted firn samples through Millipore filters and counted particles by microscope. For the first work in Antarctica, Marshall (1959, 1962) refined the counting techniques, using an electronic (Coulter) counter, with which particles between about 0.6 and 200 μ may be measured and counted. Marshall found that at Byrd Station a layer of summer snow contained about 20 times as many particles in the 0.7- to 5-μ range as did a winter layer, and suggested that the variation in particle concentration could be used to determine the annual increments of snow accumulation.

Schmidt (1963) made a regional survey of microscopic particles in ice cores from the Antarctic Peninsula traverse area, but found no correlations of particle abundance in snow layers representing the same year at different stations. Consequently he thought that Marshall's suggestion of their use as a stratigraphic parameter "appears to be a forlorn hope" (Schmidt, 1965).

Considerable improvements in the Coulter counting technique have been made in the past few years (Bader *et al.*, 1965; Hamilton, 1967, 1969). Cyclic variations in the particle concentrations have been found in cores from many parts of Antarctica and in Greenland. Assuming that the prominent peaks in the vertical profiles of particle concentration each represents an annual maximum of particle accumulation, the distance between peaks is equivalent to the annual snow balance. Examples are given in Table 9.

Taylor and Gliozzi (1964) initially interpreted their particle variations at Eights Station in terms of Shimizu's original (1964) stratigraphically determined annual balance, and suggested that

Table 9. Comparison of estimates of annual balance, g/cm^2, by microparticle studies and other methods.

Site (depth)	Particle concentration	Stakes	Surface stratigraphy	$O^{18}:O^{16}$	References
Byrd Station (246 m)	11–16.5	10–15 (7 yr)	14	10–15	Hamilton, 1967; this paper
Byrd Station (96 m)	18	10–15 (7 yr)	14	10–15	Hamilton, 1967; this paper
Little America V (148 m)	13.6	22 (2 yr)	13.6 (13 yr)		Hamilton, 1967; Vickers, 1966
Eights Station	25 or 40	40	10–20 (4 yr)	40	Taylor and Gliozzi, 1964; Epstein and Sharp, 1967; Shimizu, 1964; Gliozzi, 1966

there might be a two-year period to the particle concentration cycle. Epstein and Sharp's (1967) $O^{18}:O^{16}$ work on the same core gave an annual accumulation of about 40 g/cm^2, approximately twice Shimizu's value. Accepting Epstein and Sharp's value, which coincides with the one-year surface stake measurement (Gliozzi, 1966), Taylor and Gliozzi's cycle again becomes annual.

In areas of low accumulation, such as South Pole, the microparticle concentration profile becomes more difficult to interpret (Hamilton and O'Kelley, In press). The simple, annual cycle gives way to an essentially semiannual cyclic pattern. Some annual layers contain three or even four concentration maximums, others only one. Originally it was presumed that this was for the same reason, mixing of the surface layers (which may represent a whole year's accumulation) during storms, that the snow stratigraphic pattern tends to be destroyed. However, Hamilton (1969) showed that the microparticle size distribution varied directly with the particle concentration in vertical profiles at the South Pole. This strongly suggests that the complex pattern is not the result of mixing (which would tend to diminish differences in particle size distribution) but is rather the original depositional pattern. Hamilton argued that seasonal patterns of temperature, relative humidity, and precipitation rate (which controls the rate of depletion of atmospheric dust) could lead to the observed patterns of microparticle deposition with snow. It appears that a detailed study of microparticle size distribution in samples from the deep ice cores may give valuable information on atmospheric conditions in the distant past.

In areas of higher or very low annual accumulation (even at the Pole of Relative Inaccessibility where the annual accumulation is only about 3 g/cm^2), the variations of microparticle concentration with depth can be used directly in determining annual accumulation. The microparticle method has the merit that, like the $O^{18}:O^{16}$ and $H^2:H^1$ ratio methods, the variations can be detected to depths at which the normal stratigraphic parameters are no longer discernible. The microparticle method also has the advantage that the particles probably do not diffuse, so that the only limit to the depth at which the method can be used is the level at which the annual layers become comparable with the sample size.

A very convincing example of the use of the microparticle method is given by Hamilton and Langway (1967). On a 1.3-m core from 300 m depth at Site 2, Greenland, completely independent studies were made of the $O^{18}:O^{16}$ ratios and of the microparticle concentration. Four maximums (summer) and three minimums (winter) occurred in the oxygen profile, giving an annual positive balance of 33 g/cm^2, in good agreement with present values. The maximums of the microparticle profile were each displaced upward about 4 cm from the minimums of the oxygen profile, showing that the maximum particle fallout occurred in February or March.

Other recent studies (Brocas and Picciotto, 1967; Hamilton and Bull, 1966; Schmidt, 1963, 1965; Tilles, 1965, 1966, 1967) suggest that some, and possibly most, of the microparticles falling on Antarctica and Greenland are of extraterrestrial origin. This conflicts with the results from other studies (Fireman *et al.*, 1965; McCorkell *et al.*, 1970; Wright and Hodge, 1970), which indicate that terrestrial sources are predominantly responsible for the fallout. Hanappe *et al.* (1968) have concluded from their chemical studies of firn samples from South Pole, Plateau, and Roi Baudouin Stations, that nickel concentrations reported by Brocas and Picciotto were erroneously high, but that 80 percent of the nickel at Plateau Station may be of cosmic origin. Their upper limit for the influx of extraterrestrial matter over the earth, 10^5 tons per year, is much less than in most previous studies.

From studies of deep cores from Greenland and the Antarctic, the variation of fallout rate of microparticles may be determined over many thousands of years (Hamilton and O'Kelley, In press), and from the deep antarctic cores it may be possible to evaluate theories that glacier fluctuations in the Northern Hemisphere are related to the abundance of microparticles, acting as nucleating agents for snow precipitation.

Summary of Snow Accumulation Measurement Methods

The reliability and applicability of the various methods available for measuring balance are listed in Table 10. Necessarily the assessment of the reliability is subjective, and is given on a scale from 10 (most reliable) to 1 (least reliable). A guess of the relative cost of an individual determination of balance is also given, on a scale from 9 (most expensive) to 1 (least expensive). It must be borne in mind that the cost of the associated field logistics far exceeds that of the positive balance measurements.

THE DATA

The first worthwhile attempts in Antarctica at measuring the balance at points away from permanent stations were those of

Table 10. Reliability and applicability of balance methods.

Method	Applicability	Relative reliability	Cost
Gross β-activity	Dry-snow facies; little mixing. Mean balance since 1955.	10	3
Sr^{90}	Dry-snow facies; little mixing. Mean balance since 1955.	10?	7
Pb^{210}	Dry-snow facies; little mixing. Usually mean balance over ~ 50-year period.	8	8
Stakes	Everywhere; require repeated visits. ± 20 percent with single stake, well placed. Areal variability.	6–10	2
Stratigraphy	Dry-snow and percolation facies. Reliability depends on observer. Most useful with balance between 10 and 40 g/cm^2 per year.	0–6	1
$O^{18}:O^{16}$	Dry-snow and percolation facies. Interpretation depends on observer. Most useful with balance between 10 and 40 g/cm^2 per year. Extendable below visible stratigraphy.	2–6	5
$H^2:H^1$	As with $O^{18}:O^{16}$.	1–5	6
Microparticles	As with $O^{18}:O^{16}$, but potentially extendable through ice sheet.	1–6	4
C^{14}	Not in areas with excessive melting. Large samples required. Averages balance over very long period. Contamination?	?	9

the Norwegian-British-Swedish (Maudheim) Expedition, 1949–1952 (Schytt, 1958; Swithinbank, 1957, 1959). Their work included detailed examinations of the variations of balance over small areas of the ice shelf, using stakes, and estimates of the balance at isolated points on journeys through the coastal mountains and onto the ice sheet, using both stakes and stratigraphic techniques.

Since the beginning of the International Geophysical Year estimates have been made at points on most of the major oversnow traverses, studies have been carried out near several of the inland stations, and detailed surveys have been made of distinct areas. Some of these surveys have yielded results that are of value with other glaciological problems, for example, the dynamics of small ice caps (McLaren, 1968; Rundle, 1970) and of ice shelves (Budd, 1966a,b; Budd *et al.*, 1967; Crary *et al.*, 1962a,b), and with the flow law of cold ice in small mountain glaciers (Bull and Carnein, 1970; Holdsworth and Bull, 1970). Other detailed local studies have been more concerned with the relationship between atmospheric processes and snow precipitation, for example, those near Mirnyy (Barkov and Ivanov, 1967; Kotliakov, 1963; Voskresenskiy, 1967) and on the Lazarev Ice Shelf (Aver'ianov, 1966; Simonov, 1964). Nearly all of these detailed studies have given reliable estimates of the balance, for the stratigraphic studies have been controlled by extensive use of stakes, but, being concentrated in small areas, the individual values usually cannot be plotted on a large-scale map.

The reliability of the estimates of the balance at points on the longer oversnow traverses is highly variable. On some of them the estimates are completely reliable. For example, on the three parts of the South Pole-Queen Maud Land traverse, Picciotto *et al.* (1970) used radioisotope methods to determine the mean balance over about 12-year periods at 74 locations and could quote a standard error of estimate (usually 0.2 g/cm^2) in the annual balance. Along a 600-km line near the northern edge of the Ross Ice Shelf, Swithinbank used almost 2,000 stakes to measure the balance over 2- and 3-year periods (Heap and Rundle, 1964). Although the balance for those years may be different from the long-term average, there can be no reasonable doubt that the quoted values are accurate estimates of the balance for those years.

On the other hand, some of the estimates based on pit stratigraphy are very much open to question. Some of the observers on the early United States traverses were quite inexperienced. At that time reliable criteria for distinguishing annual layers had not been developed, especially in low balance areas, even at the inland stations and few people had realized the extent of the variations that can exist in the layering in two pits a short distance apart. In the reports of some of these traverses (e.g., Goodwin, 1959), the observers recorded the stratigraphy as carefully as possible, but declined to interpret it in terms of annual units. On others (e.g., Stuart and Heine, 1961) the difficulties of interpretation were appreciated ("It should be emphasized that the accumulation figures derived from these pits are only approximate. The interpretations given here are those which appear best to the senior author. Other possible interpretations . . .") and a "best guess" of the balance was given.

From their earlier work near Scott Base, Stuart and Heine had realized that stake measurements were much more reliable than stratigraphic techniques, and erected stake networks at several points on their traverse of Victoria Land. Unfortunately this traverse was not repeated before the stakes were buried, so that the stratigraphic estimates of balance are still open to doubt, but the value of leaving stakes on traverses, even when there appears no possibility that the route will be repeated, is demonstrated in other cases. For example, on the Byrd Station-South Pole traverse, 1960–1961, Brecher (1964), after a few days' training at Byrd Station, attempted to interpret the stratigraphy in pits at about 45-km intervals, but also set out measured stakes at 8-km intervals. Two years later, during the South Pole traverse, the 27 stakes between latitude 88°S and the South Pole were remeasured. They gave values for the balance almost identical with those from the pit stratigraphy, in the interpretation of which no one, least of all Brecher and the present author, had very much confidence until that time.

During the 1957–1958 Ross Ice Shelf traverse, Crary set out stakes near the foot of the Beardmore Glacier where Boyd estimated the annual balance from stratigraphy as 19 g/cm^2 (Crary *et al.,* 1962b). The stakes were remeasured by Swithinbank in 1961 and 1962. They gave a mean balance over these years of 19 g/cm^2 (Swithinbank, personal communication), which gives authenticity to Boyd's stratigraphic interpretations in this area. Without this support his interpretations, and the recognition that a part of the neighboring small area has a balance greater than 20 g/cm^2 per year, which is based on this stratigraphy, might have been questioned, because on the northern edge of the ice shelf and on parts of the eastern side Boyd's estimates are considerably higher than the stake-controlled values of Heap and Rundle (1964).

In some areas two or more experienced observers have obtained quite different estimates for the balance from pit stratigraphy. The large range of the estimates at Vostok Station has already been mentioned. An extensive stake array erected there and along the repeatedly traversed routes from the coastal stations would, if measured regularly over several years, have given completely reliable values. In the area between 87°S, 150°E and the upper Skelton Glacier, Lister (1960) obtained annual balances averaging about 8 g/cm^2, while Giovinetto's (1963) averaged only half of that. If stakes had been erected by the first traverse party, some of them could have been measured by the second, and removed all ambiguity. As it is, the present author can judge only by comparing these values with the unsubstantiated stratigraphically determined balances on Ukhov's (1963) traverse from Vostok to the South Pole, 300 km away, and by examining Giovinetto's published stratigraphic records (Lister's have not been published). In this case the author slightly favors Giovinetto's values. What then does he do with Lister's values between South Ice and South Pole, most of which lie in areas not visited by other parties, but which are based on reliable values at the two end points, and all of which do look reasonable?

In compiling the present map an attempt has been made to review all of the published estimates of balance and the diagrams of the stratigraphy on which some of them are based, especially where large differences exist in the estimates based on different methods. In some cases where the original observer did not pick annual units or estimate the balance, the author has felt that the stratigraphy was sufficiently unambiguous to allow him to guess the annual layering, and with some sets of values he has had the temerity to reinterpret the published diagrams. All of these new interpretations are marked with a query on the map, and the original estimates are also given.

On several of the traverse routes two or more sets of estimates of the balance have been published. In general only the more reliable set has been plotted on the map. Thus, on the South Pole-Queen Maud Land traverses, only Picciotto *et al.'s* (1970) values from radioisotope methods are given and the very careful stratigraphic work of Koerner (In press) and Rundle (In press) has been ignored, although this stratigraphic work is probably the best that has been done in low positive balance areas, and their values are very similar to those from the β-activity measurements. Although Rundle (In press) may be correct in concluding that "accumulation rates on the Antarctic Plateau appear to be below the limit which permits a straightforward analysis, without information from stake and radiochemical measurements," his work, and Koerner's (In press) at Plateau Station, does give valuable new information on the snow metamorphic process under conditions of very low temperature and positive balance.

Similarly, on the southward traverses from Wilkes (S-2) and Dumont d'Urville Stations, the balances from stake measurements (Battye, 1965; Black and Budd, 1964; Lorius, 1964) are preferred to the pit stratigraphic estimates, although the balances from the stakes refer to only one or two years.

For the two very close traverses along the northern edge of the Ross Ice Shelf (Crary *et al.*, 1962a,b; Heap and Rundle, 1964), both the stratigraphic estimates (for the five or so years to 1958) are given on the map to illustrate other difficulties. Heap and Rundle's mean positive balance from the stakes is 14.4 g/cm^2 per year; Crary *et al.* obtained about 18.5 g/cm^2. Ignoring a possible 5 percent underestimate in the balance from the stakes, because no account was taken of snow settlement, Heap and Rundle's values, which are the most detailed yet obtained from stake measurements, may still underestimate the "climatic average" by 10 to 30 percent.

Reference has already been made to the apparent cyclic variation of balance at Byrd Station; detailed continuous measurements elsewhere would probably reveal similar patterns. Obviously the balance map for the continent should present either the long-term average values or those for a given short period, preferably one year. In 1964 this was not possible (Cameron, 1964b) and, although some additional information on the periodicity of balance has been gained, the data are still not sufficient to distinguish between true temporal variations and those associated with changes of surface conditions, especially surface slope at the measurement sites. As data from any one year are still too sparse to make a worthwhile map, the author has attempted to use all the data available in the libraries of the Institute of Polar Studies, Columbus, and the Scott Polar Research Institute, Cambridge. He has tried to remember in the overall interpretation that the balance in one area in one year may differ from the long-term average by a factor of three or more, and that balances from single stakes or isolated uncontrolled pits may be grossly in error (See foldout map).

THE MAP AND THE BALANCE PATTERN

In the early stages of data compilation a computer program was developed by P. J. Morgan in which the balance in squares with 50-km sides was calculated from all the estimates in that area, weighing the estimates according to method. First attempts at machine-contouring lines of equal balance were based on linear interpolation among the nearest three non-collinear points at which estimates can be made, limiting the interpolation to a few hundred kilometers. For the interior of West Antarctica, and for parts of interior East Antarctica, the method works well, but in the large interior areas where no data exist it will be necessary to control the contours of equal balance, probably by functions based on the mean annual air temperature (Loewe, 1967), and in the coastal areas a much more sophisticated approach is necessary.

Faced with a time-consuming but necessary data review and a submission deadline, the author has temporarily abandoned the automatic plotting method in favor of hand contouring. In drawing the contours, weight approaching 100 percent has been given, in the areas where they are available, to reliable stake and radiochemical measurements. These values are underlined on the map. Elsewhere, particularly where only estimates based on stratigraphy are available, some subjective judgment has been necessary so that, as Cameron (1964b) pointed out while drawing an earlier map, "others may have drawn the lines of equal accumulation somewhat differently." The number of data points is now in the unfortunate state of being too large to allow uninhibited broad generalizations, and too small to permit completely objective contouring. For example, in the area between Mirnyy and Mawson, including the Amery Ice Shelf and Lambert Glacier, several interpretations are possible. Does the 20-g contour from a few kilometers inland of Mirnyy follow approximately along the elevation contour, inland of the Lambert Glacier? Does it join Budd's well-established 20-g contour on the Amery Ice Shelf, or does it run out to sea somewhere west of Mirnyy?

The major deficiencies of the map at present are:

1. Except for values on local glaciers and ice shelves (e.g., Bryan, 1965; Koerner, 1964b) and on the Anvers Island ice cap (Rundle, 1970), no estimates of balance are available for the Antarctic Peninsula.
2. In interior East Antarctica the contouring could be great-

ly improved by determinations of balance by β-activity methods at as few as ten well-selected points, for example, near 73°S at longitudes 150°E, 125°E, 80°E, and 55°E; near 78°S at longitudes 140°E, 65°E, and 20°W; and near 85°S near 150°E, 90°E, and 45°W.

3. In interior West Antarctica no worthwhile control exists in the areas 82°S, 140°W; 82°S, 80°W; 77°S, 75°W, and on the western part of the Filchner Ice Shelf.
4. Around the coasts the balance varies enormously from place to place. Far too few data are available to allow the production of an accurate balance map of the coast.

The map presented appears to be a significant improvement on the two best maps that preceded it, namely those by Cameron (1964b) and in the Soviet *Atlas Antarktiki* (Bakayev, 1966). The area of the continent in which the annual balance is less than 10 g/cm^2 is substantially greater in this map than in the earlier ones, and the new data near the coasts of East Antarctica are quite inconsistent with the generalizations of these earlier maps.

Despite the deficiencies mentioned above, the general characteristics of the balance pattern are well established. The single most obvious feature is that over almost all of East Antarctica above 2,000-m surface elevation, the annual balance is less than 10 g/cm^2. Within this region is an area of 2 million km^2 in which the balance is less than 5 g/cm^2. For comparison, the parts of the Sahara and Gobi Deserts that have annual rainfall less than 5 cm have the following areas *(The Times Atlas of the World, 1958):*

Sahara	$\sim 6 \times 10^6$ km^2
Gobi	$< 1.5 \times 10^6$ km^2
Antarctic "technical desert"	2×10^6 km^2

The data of Picciotto *et al.* (1970) suggest that within this 5 g/cm^2 per year contour, near 25°E, is an elongate area of about 4×10^4 km^2 in which the average annual balance between 1955 and 1967 was less than 2 g/cm^2. This extremely arid region, underlain by several thousand meters of frozen water, has anomalous 10-m ice temperatures (Kane, 1970) and is obviously worthy of much more attention.

Around the coasts of East Antarctica, the pattern of snow annual balance is complex and not yet well defined. Apart from the large range of local values expected in mountainous areas, the conditions around the coastal stations vary greatly. Mawson is in the ablation zone, and the ice surface nearby, at 75-m elevation, loses 40 g/cm^2 annually (McLeod, 1967). Near Mirnyy, at the same elevation and latitude, the annual balance is positive, at about 60 g/cm^2 (Barkov and Ivanov, 1967). Inland from Mawson the positive balance increases quite regularly with elevation and distance (Crohn, 1959; Mellor, 1967), reaching about 20 g/cm^2 per year at about 1,800 m, 300 km from the coast.

Inland from Mirnyy the annual balance decreases over the first 20 km, from 60 to about 30 g/cm^2. A maximum, 35 g/cm^2, occurs about 35 km inland, and a minimum, 18 g/cm^2, 45 km inland. Over the next 60 km the balance increases to about 30 g/cm^2 (Kotliakov, 1963; Voskresenskiy, 1967). Over the whole distance elevations increase inland.

Inland from the coast near Wilkes Station the pattern is different again (Battye, 1965; Budd *et al.*, 1967; McLaren, 1968). From an ablation zone near the coast the annual balance increases to 13 g/cm^2 at 1,166 m (S-2) and to 60 g/cm^2 near the top of the Wilkes Ice Dome, at 1,400 m. South of S-2 the surface elevation decreases over 100 km to about 800 m, and then increases onto the main part of the East Antarctic plateau. The balance increases from S-2 southward, reaching about 60 g/cm^2 near the bottom of the depression and then decreases regularly to about 12 g/cm^2 over the next 400 km.

The pattern immediately inland from Mirnyy, where the balance is a maximum some distance from the coast, is repeated, in part, near Halley Bay (Ardus, 1965; Hollas, 1965), Roi Baudouin (Autenboer, 1964; De Breuck, 1961) and Dumont d'Urville (Lorius, 1964). The elevation at which the maximum balance occurs varies from place to place, however, being about 1,200 m, 250 m, and 800 m at the last three named sites, compared with 600 m at Mirnyy, where the level coincides with the base height of nimbostratus clouds (Voskresenskiy, 1967).

Across most of the relatively small ice shelves around East Antarctica that have been examined, similar balance patterns are found. On the Maudheim (Schytt, 1958; Swithinbank, 1959), Fimbul (Lunde, 1961; Neethling, 1970), Amery (Budd *et al.*, 1967), and Lazarev (Aver'ianov, 1966; Simonov, 1964), the positive balance is greatest at the seaward edge of the shelf, and decreases inland. Ablation areas exist on the Lazarev and Amery Ice Shelves. On all of these shelves except the Amery Ice Shelf, the balance increases again at the inland edge, where the ice surface rises onto the inland ice.

The same pattern probably exists on the Ross Ice Shelf. The balance decreases southward from the edge (Crary *et al.*, 1962a; Heap and Rundle, 1964) and increases again near 79°S, near the Transantarctic Mountains. On the Filchner Ice Shelf the data are too sparse to give a clear pattern.

On the Brunt Ice Shelf (Ardus, 1965; MacDowall *et al.*, 1964; Thomas and Coslett, 1970) the balance is distinctly lower near the seaward edge, but is almost constant over most of the width of the shelf. Local effects are large at the inland edge of the shelf, but inland the balance decreases rapidly with increasing elevation.

In the interior of West Antarctica, south of 77°S, the balance is surprisingly uniform, being between 10 and 20 g/cm^2 per year everywhere except on the Hollick-Kenyon Plateau. Here, and farther toward the coast, the annual balance increases to 25 or 30 g/cm^2 in northern Marie Byrd Land, and to more than 60 g/cm^2 on the Eights Coast, but at present the available data from the coast are insufficient to allow the lines of equal balance there to be drawn with any confidence.

The explanation of the balance pattern over the Antarctic Continent is primarily the concern of the meteorologists. Since the first weather and sea-ice observations were made in Antarctica, attempts have been made to determine the predominant storm tracks (e.g., Scott, 1873), but even those plotted in Astapenko's (1964) and Weyant's (1967) comprehensive accounts of atmospheric processes on the continental scale do not fully explain the balance pattern. Similarly, initial attempts have been made to explain the temporal and areal variability of balance in particular areas, the effects of local topography, and the relationships between precipitation, drifting snow, and deposition (e.g., Budd *et al.*, 1964).

THE MASS BALANCE OF ANTARCTICA

The total balance on the Antarctic Continent and the adjoining ice shelves, excluding the Antarctic Peninsula north of 73°S, has been determined by planimetry, using the American Geographical Society's 1:5,000,000 (1965) map of Antarctica. The results are given in Table 11.

In this assessment the ablation area of the upper surface of the ice sheet and shelves is greatly underestimated, no account having been taken of the innumerable ablation areas in the mountains, especially in southern Victoria Land (Bull and Carnein, 1970),

Table 11. Positive annual balance on the Antarctic Ice Sheet and ice shelves.

Contour interval (g/cm^2)	Area (10^5 km^2)	Mean balance (g/cm^2)	Total (10^{16} g per year)
<0	0.19	−10	−0.19
0–5	20.92	3	6.28
5–10	39.70	7.5	29.77
10–20	41.49	15	62.24
20–30	18.45	25	46.12
30–40	6.51	35	22.78
40–60	6.07	50	30.37
>60	1.63	70	11.41
Totals	134.96		208.78

Table 12. Estimates of mean annual balance on the Antarctic Continent and ice shelves. References to other estimates are given in Wexler (1961) and Losev (1963).

Author	Mean annual balance (g/cm^2)
Meinardus, 1938	7.0
Kidson, 1946	9.0
Kosack, 1954	20.1
Mellor, 1959	14.0
Loewe, 1959	13.1
Rubin, 1960 (In Wexler, 1961)	7.0
Kotliakov, 1961c	19.0
Cameron and Goldthwait, 1961	14.0
Rubin, 1962	14.5
Giovinetto, 1964b	15 ± 3
Cameron, 1964b	17.2
Loewe, 1967	13–14
This paper	15.5 ± 2.0

and on some of the ice shelves (Aver'ianov, 1966). The total area of the upper surface ablation zone probably exceeds 70,000 km^2, but this is still much less than one percent of the total area considered.

The present estimate of the mean annual balance is compared with some previous estimates in Table 12. Of the investigators only Giovinetto has attempted a realistic assessment of the accuracy of his estimate. His method is based mainly on a consideration of the areal and temporal variabilities of balance at the sites where sufficient information is available for these to be calculated accurately. He realized that these sites may not be representative of the whole continent, but was unable to estimate variabilities in other areas from the scant meteorological data available.

The present author believes that the main sources of error in the estimate of the mean annual balance lie in the subjective assessment of the reliability of the stratigraphic interpretations of the original investigators (most of the available data are still from this method), in drawing lines of equal balance, and in estimating the mean balance in the areas between neighboring contours. Accordingly two other maps have been prepared, based on the same data points as on the map presented, in which the interpretations have been stretched as far as the author deemed prudent, to give maximum and minimum total values. The maximum corresponds to a mean annual balance of 17.2 g/cm^2 (which is identical with Cameron's (1964b) estimate based on about half of the same data points) and the minimum to a mean balance of 13.7 g/cm^2. Thus quoting the mean annual balance as 15.5 $\pm$ 2.0 g/cm^2 seems to be safe, and as good as the present data will allow. The author, however, is prepared to give only a vague name, like "guessed probable error of estimate," to the $\pm$ 2.0.

The pattern of the balance over the continent is of interest to meteorologists. The estimate of the mean balance will probably be used by others in assessments of the state of equilibrium of the ice mass. The present author is not able to improve significantly on Loewe's (1967) estimates for the ablation terms. According to him, the factors in the total balance equation are as given in Table 13.

This gain, if real, distributed over the area of ice sheet and ice shelves considered, would give an annual increase of about 3 g/cm^2.

Table 13. Annual mass balance of Antarctic Ice Sheet and ice shelves (Partly from Loewe, 1967).

	10^{16} g
Accumulation zone (as Table 11)	+208
Ablation zone, melting and evaporation	− 1
Calving, ice sheet	− 5
Calving, glaciers	− 52
Calving, ice shelves	− 88
Bottom melting	− 20
Total	+ 42

Loewe considered that his estimates of all the ablation terms are on the high side and concluded that although some of the terms are uncertain, so that a case can be made for an equilibrium state, at first sight the Antarctic Ice Sheet seems to have an overall positive mass balance. The present estimate of the mean annual balance in the accumulation zone, 15.5 g/cm^2, is higher than that used by Loewe (13–14 g/cm^2), which would reinforce Loew's conclusion.

Nevertheless a great deal of caution must be exercised before any conclusion is drawn about the overall mass balance. The figures in Table 12 show that since 1959 the estimates of the balance in the accumulation facies have all, except one, been within 25 percent of the average value, 15.5 g/cm^2 per year. On the other hand the estimates of the ablation terms vary enormously; for example, the estimates of the loss by bottom melting of the ice shelves range from 5 to 68 $\times$ 10^{16} g per year, and for the loss by calving from 54 to 174 $\times$ 10^{16} g per year (Losev, 1963; Lorius, 1965).

In some of the calculations of the balance of the Antarctic, allowance has been made for the loss of snow by wind transport, and for the annual loss by evaporation in the accumulation zone. Although both of these factors are important in the complete consideration of water mass transfer in the Antarctic (e.g., Loewe, 1970), neither enters the present calculations, because the measured values of balance at points in the accumulation facies are net values.

Most of the other recent estimates of the total mass balance of the Antarctic have also been positive. Losev (1963) and Lorius (1965) have listed positive estimates that range from 33 to 149 $\times$ 10^6 g per year, with only one negative value, 41 $\times$ 10^{16} g per year (Loewe's (1967) value and the present one, both positive, are 24 and 42 $\times$ 10^{16} g per year, respectively). It is apparent, however, that the possible errors in the ablation terms are far larger than the magnitude of the assessed mass balance, so that at present no conclusion at all may be drawn on whether the ice sheet is decreasing or increasing in size. Similarly the state of the Antarctic Ice Sheet cannot be satisfactorily inferred from the annual rise of sea level of about 1 mm that has been observed over the last 100 years or so (Fairbridge, 1961). While the rise could be associated with a negative balance for Antarctica (of about 30 $\times$ 10^{16} g per year), it may equally well be explained in terms of a rise in oceanic temperatures and the melting of land-based ice in other parts of the world.

On the other hand, assessments of the mass balance of various specific parts of the Antarctic may be much more meaningful. For example, in the western part of the Ross Ice Shelf drainage system (Giovinetto and Robinson, 1966), the total annual gain of mass exceeds the total loss by 4.8×10^{16} g, an amount large enough, relative to the estimated errors, to indicate a probable positive balance for the whole area. Dolgushin *et al.* (1962) and Giovinetto (1970) have extended these ideas by considering separately the "interior province" and the "peripheral province" of the continent. Giovinetto considers that the "interior province" has a positive mass balance of 30 or 40×10^{16} g per year but that the "peripheral province" probably has a negative balance. These may be the conditions necessary to produce, eventually, a surge of a major part of the Antarctic Ice Sheet, a rapid rise of sea level of perhaps 20 m, and the initiation of a major Northern Hemisphere glaciation (Hollin, 1965; Wilson, 1964).

Some deficiencies exist in our present knowledge of the annual gain of mass in the accumulation facies, but they are small compared with the serious limitations to our knowledge of the loss by melting on the lower surface of the ice shelves and by calving of icebergs into the surrounding oceans. Both of these are difficult problems to tackle. The indirect methods of assessing the melting of the ice shelves have given widely varying results so far and reliable estimates will only be obtained by the type of repeated accurate leveling now being done on the Brunt Ice Shelf, or perhaps by direct experiment, using submarine vessels. The reliable assessment of the loss by calving requires either the measurement of ice velocity and thickness around an appreciable part of the antarctic coastline, a prodigious task, or the use of photographs from satellites. At present these photographs can be used for following the course of large icebergs (Swithinbank, 1969), but an increase in resolution is necessary before they can be used for the smaller icebergs that constitute the bulk of the loss by calving.

Author's Notes: Most of this paper has been written while the author enjoyed a Quarter of Assigned Research Duty from the College of Mathematics and Physical Sciences, The Ohio State University; and the hospitality and library facilities of the Scott Polar Research Institute, University of Cambridge. I am very grateful to many colleagues in the Institute of Polar Studies and the Scott Polar Research Institute for access to their unpublished work, and for lively discussions on many points. Mr. P. J. Morgan did most of the work on the computer program and Mr. M. J. McSaveney helped with the initial compilation of data.

All of the data collected for use in this paper are filed in the

Institute of Polar Studies. We shall be pleased to know of any material that has been overlooked and of new data produced, so that our file can be kept up-to-date and periodic new editions of the map produced.

This paper is Contribution No. 156 of the Institute of Polar Studies, The Ohio State University.

References

(Asterisk (*) indicates data references not specifically mentioned in text)

Ambach, W., H. Eisner, and L. L. Thatcher, 1968. Tritium content in the firn layer of an alpine glacier. *Intern. Assoc. Sci. Hydrol., Publ. 79;* pp. 126–134.

Anderson, V. H., 1958. Byrd Station glaciological data, 1957–1958. *Ohio State Univ. Res. Found. Rept. 825–1; Part II.*

Anonymous, 1969. Mass-balance terms. *J. Glaciol., 8:* 3–7.

Ardus, D. A., 1965. Morphology and regime of the Brunt Ice Shelf and the adjacent inland ice, 1960–61. *Brit. Antarctic Surv. Bull., 5:* 13–42.

Astapenko, P. D., 1964. *Atmospheric Processes in the High Latitudes of the Southern Hemisphere.* Israel Program for Scientific Translations, Jerusalem.

*Aughenbaugh, N., H. Neuburg, and P. Walker, 1958. Ellsworth Station glaciological and geological data, 1957–1958. *Ohio State Univ. Res. Found. Rept. 825–1, Part I:* 1–232.

Autenboer, T. Van, 1964. The geomorphology and glacial geology of the Sør-Rondane, Dronning Maud Land, Antarctica. *Mededel. Koninkl. Vlaam. Acad. Wetenschap. Belg. Kl. Wetenschap., XXVI, 8.*

Aver'ianov, V. G., 1963. On the methods of precipitation measurements in the central Antarctica. *Acad. Sci. U.S.S.R., Glaciol. Res., Section 9 I.G.Y. Program;* pp. 195–197.

Aver'ianov, V. G., 1966. Snow accumulation and the reasons for the existence of a melting area on the Lazarev Ice Shelf. *Soviet Antarctic Exped. Inform. Bull., 56* (Translated as vol. 6, pp. 43–45, by Am. Geophys. Union, Washington, D.C.)

Bader, H., W. L. Hamilton, and P. L. Brown, 1965. Measurements of natural particulate fallout onto high polar ice sheets, Part 1. *U. S. Army Cold Regions Res. Eng. Lab. Res. Rept. 139, Part 1.* Hanover, N. H.

Bakayev, V. G. (Editor), 1966. *Atlas Antarktikii;* vol. 1, pp. 1–22. Main Administration of Geodesy and Cartography, Ministry of Geology, Moscow. [Text and legend matter publ. in English as a *Special Issue of Soviet Geography,* review and translation; vol. 7, nos. 5–6, pp. 261–507. Am. Geograph. Soc., New York.]

Bardin, V. I., and I. A. Suyetova, 1967. Basic morphometric characteristics for Antarctica and budget of the Antarctic ice cover. *Proc. Symp. Pacific-Antarctic Sci.,* edited by T. Nagata; pp. 92–100. Eleventh Pacific Sci. Congr., Tokyo, 1966; National Science Museum, Tokyo.

Barkov, N. I., and G. B. Ivanov, 1967. Snow accumulation on the ice slope and sea ice in the Mirnyy region in 1960. *Soviet Antarctic Exped. Inform. Bull., 63* (Translated as vol. 6, pp. 391–393, by Am. Geophys. Union, Washington, D. C.)

Barkov, N. I., and V. N. Petrov, 1966. Snow accumulation variability and some characteristics of the climate and atmospheric circulation in Antarctica. *Soviet Antarctic Exped. Inform. Bull., 59* (Translated as vol. 6, pp. 197–203, by Am. Geophys. Union, Washington, D. C.)

Battye, A., 1965. *Glaciological Studies Made at Wilkes Station, 1962.* M.Sc. thesis. Meteorology Department, Univ. Melbourne.

Begemann, F., 1959. Neubestimmung der natürlichen irdischen Tritiumzerfallsrate und die Frage der Herkunft des "natürlichen" Tritium. *Z. Naturforschung, 14A:* 334–342.

Benson, C. S., 1962. Stratigraphic studies in the snow and firn of the Greenland Ice Sheet. *U. S. Army Snow, Ice and Permafrost Res. Estab. Res. Rept. 70.*

Benson, C. S., 1970. Comparative snow studies on the Antarctic and Greenland Ice Sheets. *Intern. Assoc. Sci. Hydrol., Publ. 86;* pp. 242–253.

Bentley, C. R., 1962. Glacial and subglacial geography of Antarctica. In *Antarctic Research,* edited by H. Wexler, M. J. Rubin, and J. E. Caskey; pp. 11–25. *Geophys. Monograph Ser. No. 7.* Am. Geophys. Union, Washington, D. C.

Bentley, C. R., 1964. The structure of Antarctica and its ice cover. In *Research in Geophysics, Solid Earth and Interface Phenomena;* vol. 2, pp. 335–389. Mass. Inst. Tech. Press, Cambridge.

Black, H. P., and W. Budd, 1964. Accumulation in the region of Wilkes, Wilkes Land, Antarctica. *J. Glaciol., 5:* 3–15.

Black, R. F., 1954. Precipitation at Barrow, Alaska, greater than recorded. *Trans. Am. Geophys. Union, 35:* 203–207.

Brecher, H. H., 1964. Glaciological observations on the "Byrd" Station-South Pole Traverse, 1960–61. *J. Glaciol., 5:* 339–343.

Brecher, H. H., 1967a. Accumulation between Mount Chapman and "Byrd" Station, Antarctica. *J. Glaciol., 6:* 573–577.

Brecher, H. H., 1967b. Accumulation between Mount Chapman and "Byrd" Station, Antarctica. *J. Glaciol., 6:* 959–960.

Brocas, J., and E. Picciotto, 1967. Nickel content of Antarctic snow, implications on the influx rate of extraterrestrial dust. *J. Geophys. Res., 72:* 2229–2236.

Bryan, R., 1965. Observations on snow accumulation patterns at Adelaide Island. *Brit. Antarctic Surv. Bull., 6:* 51–62.

Budd, W., 1966a. The dynamics of the Amery Ice Shelf. *J. Glaciol., 6:* 335–358.

Budd, W., 1966b. Glaciological studies in the region of Wilkes, Eastern Antarctica, 1961. *Australian National Antarctic Res. Expeditions Sci. Rept., Series A (IV), Publ. 88.* Dept. External Affairs, Melbourne.

Budd, W., R. Dingle, and U. Radok, 1964. Byrd Snow Drift Project. *Univ. Melbourne, Meteorol. Dept., Publ. 6.*

Budd, W., I. Langdon Smith, and E. Wishart, 1967. The Amery Ice Shelf. In *Physics of Snow and Ice,* edited by H. Ôura; pp. 447–469. *Proc. Intern. Conf. Low Temperature Sci., Japan, August, 1966, Vol. 1.* The Institute of Low Temperature Science, Hokkaido Univ., Japan.

Bull, C., 1964. Mean annual surface temperature. Physical characteristics of the Antarctic Ice Sheet. In *Antarctic Map Folio Series, Folio 2,* edited by V. C. Bushnell. Am. Geograph. Soc., New York.

Bull, C., and C. R. Carnein, 1970. The mass balance of a cold glacier: Meserve Glacier, South Victoria Land, Antarctica. *Intern. Assoc. Sci. Hydrol., Publ. 86;* pp. 429–446.

*Cameron, R. L., 1964a. Glaciological studies at Wilkes Station, Budd Coast, Antarctica. In *Antarctic Research Series 2, Antarctic Snow and Ice Studies,* edited by M. Mellor; pp. 1–36. Am. Geophys. Union, Washington, D.C.

Cameron, R. L., 1964b. Snow accumulation. Physical characteristics of the Antarctic Ice Sheet. *Antarctic Map Folio Series, Folio 2,* edited by V. C. Bushnell. Am. Geograph. Soc., New York.

Cameron, R. L., (In press). Glaciological studies at Byrd Station, Antarctica, 1963–1965. In *Antarctic Research Series 17, Antarctic Snow and Ice Studies II,* edited by A. P. Crary. Am. Geophys. Union, Washington, D.C.

Cameron, R. L., and R. P. Goldthwait, 1961. The US-IGY contribution to antarctic glaciology. Symposium on Antarctic Glaciology. *Intern. Assoc. Sci. Hydrol., Publ. 55;* pp. 7–13.

Clausen, H. B., B. Buchman, and W. Ambach, 1968. Si^{32} dating of an alpine glacier. *Intern. Assoc. Sci. Hydrol. Publ. 79;* pp. 135–140.

Coachman, L. K., E. Hemmingsen, P. F. Scholander, T. Enns, and H. deVries, 1958. Gases in glaciers. *Science, 127:* 1288.

Crary, A. P., E. S. Robinson, H. F. Bennett, and W. W. Boyd, 1962a. Glaciological regime of the Ross Ice Shelf. *J. Geophys. Res., 67:* 2791–2807.

Crary, A. P., E. S. Robinson, H. F. Bennett, and W. W. Boyd, 1962b. Glaciological studies of the Ross Ice Shelf, Antarctica, 1957–1960. *IGY Rept. Ser., No. 6.* IGY World Data Center A: Glaciology, Am. Geograph. Soc., New York.

Crohn, P. W., 1959. A contribution to the geology and glaciology of the western part of Australian Antarctic Territory. *Australian Natl. Antarctic Res. Expeditions Rept., Ser. A, No. 3.* Dept. External Affairs, Melbourne.

Cronk, C., 1968. *Glaciological Investigations Near the Ice Sheet Margin, Wilkes Station, Antarctica.* Ph.D. dissertation, Ohio State Univ., Columbus, Ohio.

Crozaz, G., 1967. *Mise au Point d'une Méthod de Datation des Glaciers Basée sur la Radioactivité du Plomb-210.* Thesis, Université Libre de Bruxelles.

Crozaz, G., and P. Fabri, 1966. Mesure du Polonium á l'échelle de 10^{-13} Curie, tracage par le Po-208 et application à la chronologie des glaces. *Earth Planetary Sci. Letters, 1:* 446–448.

Crozaz, G., and C. C. Langway, 1966. Dating Greenland firn-ice cores with Pb-210. *Earth Planetary Sci. Letters, 1:* 194–196.

Crozaz, G., C. C. Langway, and E. Picciotto, 1966. Artificial radioactivity reference horizons in Greenland firn. *Earth Planetary Sci. Letters, 1:* 42–48.

Crozaz, G., E. Picciotto, and W. DeBreuck, 1964. Antarctic snow chronology with Pb-210. *J. Geophys. Res.*, 69: 2597–2604.

Dalrymple, P. C., 1966. A physical climatology of the Antarctic Plateau. In *Antarctic Research Series 9, Studies in Antarctic Meteorology,* edited by M. J. Rubin; pp. 195–231. Am. Geophys. Union, Washington, D. C.

Dansgaard, W., 1961. The isotopic composition of natural waters, with special reference to the Greenland Ice Cap. *Medd. Grønland, 165,* (2) : 1–120.

Dansgaard, W., H. B. Clausen, and A. Aarkrog, 1966a. Evidence for bomb-produced silicon-32. *J. Geophys. Res., 71:* 5474–5477.

Dansgaard, W., H. B. Clausen, and A. Aarkrog, 1966b. The Si^{32} fallout in Scandinavia, a new method for ice-dating. *Tellus, 18:* 187–191.

Dansgaard, W., S. J. Johnsen, J. Møller, and C. C. Langway, 1969. One thousand centuries of climatic record from Camp Century on the Greenland Ice Sheet. *Science, 166:* 377–381.

DeBreuck, W., 1961. Glaciology in Eastern Queen Maud Land, Preliminary report, Third Belgian Antarctic Expedition, 1960. *Mededel. Koninkl. Vlaam. Acad. Wetenschap., Belg., K. Wetenschap., XXIII, 6.*

*Den Hartog, S. L., 1961. Snow pit work in Little America—Victoria Land traverse, 1958–1959. *Ohio State Univ. Res. Found. Rept. 825–2, Part II:* 1–107.

Dolgushin, L. D., 1961. Zones of snow accumulation in eastern Antarctica. *Intern. Assoc. Sci. Hydrol., Publ. 55:* 63–70.

Dolgushin, L. D., S. A. Evteev, and V. M. Kotliakov, 1962. Current changes in the Antarctic ice sheet. *Intern. Assoc. Sci. Hydrol. Publ. 58:* 286–294.

Epstein, S., and R. P. Sharp, 1967. Oxygen- and hydrogen-isotope variations in a firn core, Eights Station, Western Antarctica. *J. Geophys. Res., 72:* 5595–5598.

Epstein, S., R. P. Sharp, and I. Goddard, 1963. Oxygen-isotope ratios in antarctic snow, firn and ice. *J. Geol., 71:* 698–720.

Epstein, S., R. P. Sharp, and A. J. Gow, 1965. Six-year record of oxygen and hydrogen isotope variations in South Pole firn. *J. Geophys. Res., 70:* 1809–1814.

Epstein, S., R. P. Sharp, and A. J. Gow, 1970. Antarctic Ice Sheet: Stable isotope analyses of Byrd Station cores and interhemispheric climatic implications. *Science, 168:* 1570–1572.

Fairbridge, R. W., 1961. Eustatic changes in sea level. In *Physics and Chemistry of the Earth, Vol. 4,* edited by L. H. Ahrens, W. Rankama, and S. K. Runcorn; pp. 9–185. Pergamon Press, New York.

Fireman, E. L., J. Defelice, and C. C. Langway, 1965. Greenland dust: radioactivity studies. *Trans. Am. Geophys. Union, 46:* 177.

Giovinetto, M. B., 1960. Glaciology report for 1958, South Pole Station. *Ohio State Univ. Res. Found. Rept. 825–2, Part IV.*

Giovinetto, M. B., 1963. Glaciological studies on the McMurdo-South Pole traverse, 1960–1961. *Ohio State Univ. Inst. Polar Studies Rept. 7.*

Giovinetto, M. B., 1964a. Distribution of diagenetic snow facies in Antarctica and in Greenland. *Arctic, 17:* 32–40.

Giovinetto, M. B., 1964b. The drainage systems of Antarctica: accumulation. In *Antarctic Research Series 2, Antarctic Snow and Ice Studies,* edited by M. Mellor; pp. 127–156. Am. Geophys. Union, Washington, D. C.

Giovinetto, M. B., 1970. The Antarctic Ice Sheet and its probable bimodal response to climate. *Intern. Assoc. Sci. Hydrol., Publ. 86;* pp. 347–358.

Giovinetto, M. B., and E. S. Robinson, 1966. The regime of the western part of the Ross Ice Shelf drainage system. *J. Glaciol., 6:* 55–68.

Giovinetto, M. B., and W. Schwerdtfeger, 1966. Analysis of a 200 year snow accumulation series from the South Pole. *Arch. Meteorol. Geophys. Bioklimatol., Ser. A, 15:* 227–250.

Gliozzi, J., 1966. Quantitative analysis of microparticles in two antarctic firn cores. *J. Geophys. Res., 71:* 1993–1998.

Goldberg, E. D., 1963. Geochronology with lead-210. *Symposium on Radioactive Dating, International Atomic Energy Agency, Athens, November 1962;* pp. 121–130. Vienna.

Gonfiantini, R., V. Togliatti, W. DeBreuck, E. Picciotto, and E. Tongiorgi, 1963a. Geographical variations of oxygen-18/oxygen-16 ratio in surface snow and ice from Queen Maud Land, Antarctica. *Nature, 197:* 1096–1098.

Gonfiantini, R., V. Togliatti, E. Tongiorgi, W. DeBreuck, and E. Picciotto, 1963b. Snow stratigraphy and oxygen isotope variations in the glaciological pit of King Baudouin Station, Queen Maud Land, Antarctica. *J. Geophys. Res., 68:* 3791–3798.

Goodwin, R., 1959. Ellsworth Station glaciological observations, 1958–1959. *Ohio State Univ. Res. Found. Rept. 825-2, Part III.*.

Gould, L. M., 1957. Antarctic prospect. *Geograph. Rev., 47:* 1–28.

Gow, A. J., 1961. Drill-hole measurements and snow studies at Byrd Station, Antarctica. *U. S. Army Cold Regions Res. Eng. Lab., Tech. Rept. 78.*

*Gow, A. J., 1963. The inner structure of the Ross Ice Shelf at Little America V, as revealed by deep core drilling. *Intern. Assoc. Sci. Hydrol., Publ. 61:* 272–284.

Gow, A. J., 1965a. The ice sheet. In *Antarctica,* edited by T. Hatherton; pp. 221–258. New Zealand Antarctic Soc., Methuen, London.

Gow, A. J., 1965b. Snow studies in Antarctica. *U. S. Army Cold Regions Res. Eng. Lab. Res. Rept. 177.*

Gow, A. J., 1965c. On the accumulation and seasonal stratification of snow at the South Pole. *J. Glaciol., 5:* 467–478.

Gow, A. J., 1970. Preliminary results of studies of ice cores from the 2164 m deep drill hole, Byrd Station, Antarctica. *Intern. Assoc. Sci. Hydrol. Publ. 86;* pp. 78–90.

*Gow, A. J., and R. Rowland, 1965. On the relationship of snow accumulation to surface topography at "Byrd Station". *J. Glaciol., 5:* 843–847.

Hamilton, W. L., 1967. Measurements of natural particulate fallout onto high polar ice sheets, Part II. Antarctic and Greenland cores. *U. S. Army Cold Regions Res. Eng. Lab. Res. Rept. 139, Part II.*

Hamilton, W. L., 1969. *Microparticle deposition on polar ice sheets.* Ph.D. dissertation, Ohio State Univ., Columbus, Ohio.

Hamilton, W. L., and C. Bull, 1966. A comparison of the dust flux in the upper atmosphere and on the polar ice sheets. *J. Geophys. Res., 71:* 2679–2683.

Hamilton, W. L., and C. C. Langway, 1967. A correlation of microparticle concentrations with oxygen isotope ratios in 700 year old Greenland ice. *Earth Planetary Sci. Letters, 3:* 363–366.

Hamilton, W., and M. O'Kelley, (In press). Investigations of particulate matter in antarctic firn. *Antarctic Research Series 17, Antarctic Snow and Ice Studies II,* edited by A. P. Crary. Am. Geophys. Union, Washington, D. C.

Hanappe, F., M. Vosters, E. Picciotto, and S. Deutsch, 1968. Chimie des neige Antarctique et taux de déposition de matière extra-terrestre—deuxieme article. *Earth Planetary Sci. Letters, 4:* 487–496.

Heap, J. A., and A. S. Rundle, 1964. Snow accumulation on the Ross Ice Shelf, Antarctica. In *Antarctic Research Series 2, Antarctic Snow and Ice Studies,* edited by M. Mellor; pp. 119–125. Am. Geophys. Union, Washington, D. C.

Hoinkes, H., 1968. Glaciology in the International Hydrological Decade. *Intern. Assoc. Sci. Hydrol., Publ. 79:* 7–16.

Holdsworth, G., and C. Bull, 1970. The flow law of cold ice: investigations on Meserve Glacier, Antarctica. *Intern. Assoc. Sci. Hydrol., Publ. 86;* pp. 204–216.

Hollas, D., 1965. *Glaciology Report, Halley Bay 1964.* Unpublished internal report of British Antarctic Survey, Reference G.8/1964/Z. (On file in World Data Center, Glaciology, C; Scott Polar Research Institute, Cambridge)

Hollin, J. T., 1962. On the glacial history of Antarctica. *J. Glaciol., 4:* 173–195.

Hollin, J. T., 1965. Wilson's theory of ice ages. *Nature, 208:* 12–16.

Kane, H. S., 1970. A study of 10-meter firn temperatures in central east Antarctica. *Intern. Assoc. Sci. Hydrol., Publ. 86;* pp. 165–174.

Kapitza, A. P., 1967. Antarctic glacial and subglacial topography. *Proceedings of the Symposium on Pacific-Antarctic Sciences,* edited by T. Nagata; pp. 82–91. Eleventh Pacific Science Congress, Tokyo, 1966. National Science Museum, Tokyo.

Keeler, C. M., 1964. Relationship between climate, ablation, and run-off on the Sverdrup Glacier, 1963, Devon Island, N.W.T. *Arctic Inst. N. Am., Res. Paper 27.*

Kidson, E., 1946. Meteorology. Discussions of observations at Adélie Land, Queen Mary Land and Macquarie Island. *Australian Antarctic Expedition, 1911–1914, Sci. Rept., Ser. B, Vol. 6.*

Koerner, R. M., 1964a. Firn stratigraphy studies on the Byrd-Whitmore Mountains traverse, 1962–1963. In *Antarctic Research Series 2, Antarctic Snow and Ice Studies,* edited by M. Mellor; pp. 219–236. Am. Geophys. Union, Washington, D. C.

Koerner, R. M., 1964b. Glaciological observations in Trinity Peninsula and the islands in Prince Gustav Channel, Graham Land, 1958–60. *Brit. Antarctic Surv. Sci. Rept. 42.*

Koerner, R. M., In press. A stratigraphic method of determining the snow accumulation rate at Plateau Station, Antarctica, and application to South Pole-Queen Maud Land Traverse 2, 1965–1966. *Antarctic Research Series 17, Antarctic Snow and Ice Studies II,* edited by A. P. Crary. Am. Geophys. Union, Washington, D. C.

*Kojima, K., 1964. Densification of snow in Antarctica. In *Antarctic Research Series 2, Antarctic Snow and Ice Studies,* edited by M. Mellor; pp. 157–218. Am. Geophys. Union, Washington, D. C.

Kosack, H. P., 1954. Zur Frage des Wasserhaushalts in der Antarktis. *Polarforsch., 3 (1/2):* 286–294.

Kotliakov, V. M., 1961a. Indications of seasonal snow deposits in the central regions of Antarctica. *Soviet Antarctic Exped. Inform. Bull., No. 26.* (Translated as vol. 3; pp. 220–223, by Am. Geophys. Union, Washington, D. C.)

Kotliakov, V. M., 1961b. Results of a study of the processes of formation and structure of the upper layer of the ice sheet in eastern Antarctica. *Intern. Assoc. Sci. Hydrol., Publ. No. 55:* 88–99.

Kotliakov, V. M., 1961c. The intensity of nourishment of the Antarctic Ice Sheet. *Intern. Assoc. Sci. Hydrol., Publ. No. 55:* 100–110.

Kotliakov, V. M., 1962. Changes in snow accumulation in Antarctica in the last ten years. *Soviet Antarctic Exped. Inform. Bull., No. 35.* (Translated as vol. 4, pp. 140–143, by Am. Geophys. Union, Washington, D. C.)

Kotliakov, V. M., 1963. Snow accumulation in the coastal belt of East Antarctica from 1957–61. *Soviet Antarctic Exped. Inform. Bull., No. 44.* (Translated as vol. 5, pp. 64–66, by Am. Geophys. Union, Washington, D. C.)

Kotliakov, V. M., 1966. *The Snow Cover of the Antarctic and Its Role in the Present-Day Glaciation of the Continent.* U.S.S.R. Glaciology Research, Section 9 of the IGY program, Israel Program for Scientific Translations, Jerusalem.

Kotliakov, V. M., G. E. Lazarev, and M. M. Liubarets, 1966. New data on the snow accumulation regime in the interior of East Antarctica. *Soviet Antarctic Exped. Inform. Bull., No. 57.* (Translated as vol. 6, pp. 116–124, by Am. Geophys. Union, Washington, D. C.)

*Kruchinin, I., 1962. Stratigraphic study of the upper layers of the snow-firn thickness of the Lazarev ice shelf. *Soviet Antarctic Exped. Inform. Bull., No. 32.* (Translated as vol. 4, pp. 41–44, by Am. Geophys. Union, Washington, D. C.)

Lal, D., and B. Peters, 1962. Cosmic ray produced isotopes and their application to problems in geophysics. In *Progress in Cosmic Ray and Elementary Particle Physics;* vol. 6, pp. 3–74. North Holland Publishing Co., Amsterdam.

Langway, C. C., H. Oeschger, B. Alder, and A. Renaud, 1965. Sampling polar ice for radiocarbon dating. *Nature,* 206: 500–501.

Libby, W. F., 1956. Radioactive strontium fallout. *Proc. Natl. Acad. Sci. U. S., 42:* 365–390.

*Limbert, D. W. S., 1963. The snow accumulation budget at Halley Bay in 1959, and associated meteorological factors. *Brit. Antarctic Surv. Bull., 2:* 73–92.

*Lister, H., 1959. Geophysical investigations of the Commonwealth Trans-Antarctic Expedition. *Geograph. J., 125:* 343–351.

Lister, H., 1960. Solid precipitation and snow drift, Glaciology 1. *Trans-Antarctic Expedition, 1958–59, Sci. Rept. 5.*

Lister, H., 1961. Accumulation and firnification in north Greenland. *Folia Geograph. Danica, 9:* 163–174.

Lockhart, L. B., R. L. Patterson, and A. W. Saunders, 1965. Atmospheric radioactivity in Antarctica 1956–1963. *U. S. Naval Res. Lab. Rept. 6341.*

*Loewe, F., 1956. Études de glaciologie en Terre Adélie, 1951–1952. In *Expéditions Polaires Françaises.* Herman, Paris.

Loewe, F., 1959. Notes concerning the mass budget of the Antarctic inland ice. In *Antarctic Meteorology,* edited by L. J. Dwyer; pp. 361–369. Proceedings of a symposium in Melbourne, 1959, Pergamon Press, New York.

Loewe, F., 1967. The water budget in Antarctica. *Proceedings of the Symposium on Pacific-Antarctic Sciences,* edited by T. Nagata; pp. 101–110. Eleventh Pacific Science Congress, Tokyo, 1966. National Science Museum, Tokyo.

Loewe, F., 1970. The transport of snow on ice sheets by the wind. In *Studies on Drifting Snow,* Univ. Melbourne, Dept. Meteorology, Publ. 13, 69 pp.

Long, W. E., 1961. Glaciology, Byrd Station and Marie Byrd Land Traverse, 1958–1959. *Ohio State Univ. Res. Found. Rept., 825-2,* Part XI.

*Lorius, C., 1962. Contribution to the knowledge of the Antarctic Ice Sheet: a synthesis of glaciological measurements in Terre Adélie. *J. Glaciol., 4:* 79–92.

Lorius, C., 1963. *Le Deuterium.* Publication No. 8 of the Comité National Français des Recherches Antarctiques. Paris.

Lorius, C., 1964. Contribution à la connaissance de l'Antarctique glaciologie en Terre Adélie (1956–1959). *Centre Natl. Rech. Sci., Année Geophys. Intern., Particip. Franc., Ser. IX, Fasc. 1.*

Lorius, C., 1965. Bilan de masse des calottes polaires. In *Territoire des Terres Australes et Antarctiques Françaises (TAAF);* No. 30, pp. 28–41. Paris.

*Lorius, C., 1968. A physical and chemical study of the coastal ice sampled from a core drilling in Antarctica. *Intern. Assoc. Sci. Hydrol., Publ. 79;* pp. 141–148.

Lorius, C., R. Hagemann, G. Nief, and E. Roth, 1968. Teneurs en deuterium le long d'un profile de 106 m dans le névé Antarctique. Application à l'étude des variations climatiques. *Earth Planetary Sci. Letters, 4:* 237–244.

Losev, K. S., 1963. Computations of the mass balance of the antarctic ice cap. *Soviet Antarctic Exped. Inform. Bull., No. 44.* (Translated as vol. 5, pp. 60–63, by Am. Geophys. Union, Washington, D. C.)

*Lunde, T., 1961. On the snow accumulation in Dronning Maud Land: Den Norske Antarktiske Spedisjonen, 1959/60, Scientific Results No. 1. *Norsk Polarinst. Skrift., 123:* 1–48.

*MacDowall, J., 1964. Glaciological Observations, Part I, Glaciological observations at the Base. In *The Royal Society International Geophysical Year Antarctic Expedition, Halley Bay, Coats Land, Falkland Islands Dependencies, 1955–59,* edited by D. Brunt; vol. 4, pp. 269–313. Royal Soc., London.

MacDowall, J., L. W. Barclay, and J. M. C. Burton, 1964. Glaciological Observations, Part II, Glaciological observations during sledging journeys. *The Royal Society International Geophysical Year Antarctic Expedition, Halley Bay, Coats Land, Falkland Islands Dependencies, 1955–59;* vol. IV, pp. 314–328. Royal Soc., London.

Marshall, E. W., 1959. Stratigraphic use of particulates in polar ice caps. *Bull. Geol. Soc. Am., 70:* 1643.

Marshall, E. W., 1962. The stratigraphic distribution of particulate matter in the firn at Byrd Station, Antarctica. In *Antarctic Research,* edited by H. Wexler, M. J. Rubin, and J. E. Caskey; pp. 185–196. *Geophys. Monograph Ser., No. 7.* Am. Geophys. Union, Washington, D. C.

Martell, E. A., 1959. Atmospheric aspects of strontium 90 fallout. *Science, 129:* 1197–1206.

McCorkell, R. H., W. H. Pinson, E. L. Fireman, and C. C. Langway, 1970. A search for cosmic dust in a large collection of particulate and dissolved material from polar ice. *Intern. Assoc. Sci. Hydrol., Publ. 86;* pp. 25–30.

McLaren, W. A., 1968. A study of the local ice cap near Wilkes, Antarctica. *Australian Natl. Antarctic Res. Expeditions Sci. Repts., Ser. A (IV), Publ. 103.* Dept. External Affairs, Melbourne.

McLeod, I. R., 1967. Glaciological observations in Enderby, Kemp and Mac-Robertson Lands, Antarctica. *Australian Natl. Antarctic Res. Expeditions Interim Rept., Ser. A (IV), Publ. 90.* Dept. External Affairs, Melbourne.

Meier, M. F., 1962. Proposed definitions for glacier mass budget terms. *J. Glaciol., 4:* 252–263.

Meier, M. F., 1967. Why study glaciers? In the context of water resources. *Trans. Am. Geophys. Union, 48:* 798–802.

Meinardus, W., 1938. Klimakunde der Antarktis. *Handbuch der Klimatologie;* vol. 4, pt. U. Gerbrüder Borntraeger, Berlin.

Mellor, M., 1959. Mass balance studies in Antarctica. *J. Glaciol., 3:* 522–533.

Mellor, M., 1967. Mass economy of Antarctica: measurements at Mawson, 1957. *Australian Natl. Antarctic Res. Expeditions Sci. Repts., Ser. A (IV), Publ. 97.* Dept. External Affairs, Melbourne.

Mercer, J. H., 1968a. The discontinuous glacio-eustatic fall in Tertiary sea level. *Palaeogeograph. Palaeoclimatol. Palaeoecol., 5:* 77–85.

Mercer, J. H., 1968b. Antarctic ice and Sangamon sea level. *Intern. Assoc. Sci. Hydrol., Publ. 79:* 217–225.

Mercer, J. H., 1970. Former ice sheet in the Arctic Ocean? *Paleogeograph. Paleoclimatol. Paleoecol., 8:* 19–27.

*Neethling, D. C., 1970. Snow accumulation on the Fimbul Ice Shelf, Western Dronning Maud Land, Antarctica. *Intern. Assoc. Sci. Hydrol., Publ. 86;* pp. 390–404.

*Neuburg, H., 1959. IGY airborne traverse glaciological report, 1958–1959. *Ohio State Univ. Res. Found. Rept., 825-2, Part I.*

Nezami, M., G. Lambert, C. Lorius, and J. Labeyrie, 1964. Mesure du taux d'accumulation de la neige au bord du continent Antarctique par la méthode du plomb 210. *Compt. Rend. Hebdomadaires Séances;* tome 259, pp. 3319–3322. Acad. Sci., Paris.

Nordenskiöld, N. A. E., 1874. On the cosmic dust which falls on the surface of the earth with the atmospheric precipitation. *Phil. Mag., Ser. 4, 48:* 546.

Nye, J. F., 1968. Errors in the determination of ablation using stakes: comments on Dr. Vallon's letter. *J. Glaciol., 7:* 133.

Oeschger, H., B. Alder, H. Loosli, C. C. Langway, and A. Renaud, 1966. Radiocarbon dating of ice. *Earth Planetary Sci. Letters, 1:* 49–54.

Oeschger, H., A. Renaud, and E. Schumacher, 1962. Essai de datation par le tritium des couches de névé du Jungfraufirn et détermination de l'accumulation annuelle. *Bull. Soc. Vaudoise Sci. Nat., 68:* 49–56.

Petrov, V. N., N. P. Smirnov, and N. I. Barkov, 1966. Snow accumulation periodicity in Antarctica. *Soviet Antarctic Exped. Inform. Bull., No. 57.* (Translated as vol. 6, pp. 124–128, by Am. Geophys. Union, Washington, D. C.)

Picciotto, E., 1961. Quelques résultats scientifiques de l'Expédition Antarctique Belge 1957–1958. *Ciel Terre, 77:* 126–166.

Picciotto, E., R. Cameron, G. Crozaz, S. Deutsch, and S. Wilgain, 1968. Determination of the rate of snow accumulation at the Pole of Relative Inaccessibility, East Antarctica: a comparison of glaciological and isotopic methods. *J. Glaciol., 7:* 273–287.

Picciotto, E., G. Crozaz, and W. DeBreuck, 1964. Rate of accumulation of snow at South Pole as determined by radioactive measurements. *Nature, 203:* 393–394.

Picciotto, E., W. DeBreuck, and G. Crozaz, 1970. Snow accumulation along the South Pole—Queen Maud Land Traverse. *Intern. Assoc. Sci. Hydrol., Publ. 86;* pp. 18–22.

Picciotto, E., and S. Wilgain, 1963. Fission products in antarctic snow, a reference level for measuring accumulation. *J. Geophys. Res., 68:* 5965–5972.

Pirrit, J., and G. A. Doumani, 1961. Glaciology, Byrd Station and Marie Byrd Land Traverse, 1959–1960. *Ohio State Univ. Res. Found. Rept. 968–2.*

Renaud, A., E. Schumacher, B. Hughes, H. Oeschger, and C. Mühlemann, 1963. Tritium variations in Greenland ice. *J. Geophys. Res., 68:* 3783.

Rubin, M. J., 1962. Atmospheric advection and the Antarctic mass and heat budget. In *Antarctic Research,* edited by H. Wexler, M. J. Rubin, and J. E. Caskey; pp. 149–159. *Geophys. Monograph Ser. No. 7.* Am. Geophys. Union, Washington, D. C.

Rundle, A. S., 1968. Snow stratigraphy and accumulation (SPQMLT III). *Antarctic J. U.S., 3* (4): 95–96.

Rundle, A. S., 1970. Snow accumulation and ice movement on the Anvers Island ice cap, Antarctica: a study of mass balance. *Intern. Assoc. Sci. Hydrol., Publ. 86;* pp. 377–390.

Rundle, A. S., (In press). Snow accumulation and firn stratigraphy on the East Antarctica Plateau. *Antarctic Research Series 17, Antarctic Snow and Ice Studies II,* edited by A. P. Crary. Am. Geophys. Union, Washington, D. C.

Sabbagh, M. E., 1962. A preliminary regional dynamic climatology of the Antarctic continent. *Erdkunde, 16:* 94–111.

Schmidt, R. A., 1963. Microscopic extraterrestrial particles from the Antarctic Peninsula. *Geophys. Polar Res. Center, Univ. Wisconsin, Res. Rept., 63-2.*

Schmidt, R. A., 1965. A survey of data on microscopic extraterrestrial particles. *National Aeronautics and Space Administration, Tech. Note D-2719.* Washington, D. C.

Scholander, P. F., W. Dansgaard, D. C. Nutt, H. de Vries, L. K. Coachman, and E. Hemmingsen, 1962. Radiocarbon age and oxygen-18 content of Greenland icebergs. *Medd. Grønland, 165* (1): 1–26.

Schytt, V., 1958. Glaciology II. A. Snow studies at Maudheim; B. Snow studies inland; C. The inner structure of the ice shelf at Maudheim as shown by core drilling. *Norwegian-British-Swedish Antarctic Expedition 1949–1952, Scientific Results, 4.* Norsk Polarinstitutt. Oslo.

Schytt, V., 1962. Mass balance studies in Kebnekajse. *J. Glaciol., 4:* 281–286.

Scott, R. H., 1873. *Contributions to Our Knowledge of the Meteorology of the Antarctic Regions.* Published for the Meteorological Committee by E. Stanford, London.

Sharp, R. P., and S. Epstein, 1962. Comments on annual rates of accumulation in West Antarctica. *Intern. Assoc. Sci. Hydrol., Publ. 58;* pp. 273–285.

Shimizu, H., 1964. Glaciological studies in west Antarctica, 1960–1962. In *Antarctic Research Series 2, Antarctic Snow and Ice Studies,* edited by M. Mellor; pp. 37–64. Am. Geophys. Union, Washington, D. C.

Shumskiy, P. A., 1967. The Antarctic Ice Sheet. In *General Results of Research in Antarctica During 10 Years;* pp. 27–75. Academy of Sciences of the U.S.S.R., National Committee for Antarctic Research. (Read in translation prepared by U. Radok and V. J. Vinocuroff, September 1968, for International Symposium on Antarctic Glaciological Exploration, Hanover, N. H.

Simonov, I. M., 1964. Snow accumulation on ice shelves in the vicinity of Lazarev and Novolazarevskaya stations in 1962. *Soviet Antarctic Exped. Inform. Bull., No. 49.* (Translated as vol. 5, pp. 229–232, by Am. Geophys. Union, Washington, D.C.)

Sorge, E., 1935. Glaziologische Untersuchungen in Eismitte. In *Wissenschaft Ergebnisse Deutsch Grönland-Expedition Alfred Wegener 1929 und 1930/31;* vol. 3, pp. 62–720. F. A. Brockhaus, Leipzig.

Stuart, A. W., and C. Bull, 1963. Glaciological observations on the Ross Ice Shelf near Scott Base, Antarctica. *J. Glaciol., 4:* 399–414.

Stuart, A. W., and A. J. Heine, 1961. Glaciology, Victoria Land Traverse, 1959–60. *Ohio State Univ. Res. Found. Rept., 968-1.*

Stuiver, M., 1967. *Origin and Extent of Atmospheric C^{14} Variations During the Past 10,000 Years.* (Reprint of paper presented March, 1967, at International Atomic Energy Agency Conference, Monaco.)

Suess, H. E., 1965. Secular variations of the cosmic-ray-produced carbon-14 in the atmosphere and their interpretations. *J. Geophys. Res., 70:* 5937–5952.

Swithinbank, C., 1957. Glaciology I. The regime of the ice shelves at Maudheim as shown by stake measurements. *Norwegian-British-Swedish Antarctic Expedition, 1949–1952, Scientific Results, 3 (B);* pp. 41–75. Norsk Polarinstitutt, Oslo.

Swithinbank, C., 1959. Glaciology I. The regime of the ice sheet of western Dronning Maud Land as shown by stake measurements. *Norwegian-British-Swedish Antarctic Expedition, 1949–1952, Sci. Results, 3 (E);* pp. 121–144. Norsk Polarinstitutt, Oslo.

*Swithinbank, C., 1962. Maudheim revisited: the morphology and regime of the ice shelf, 1950–1960. *Norsk Polarinstitutt Årbok 1960;* pp. 28–31. Oslo.

Swithinbank, C., 1969. Giant icebergs in the Weddell Sea, 1967–68. *Polar Record, 14:* 477–478.

Taylor, L. D., 1965. Glaciological studies on the South Pole traverse. *Ohio State Univ. Inst. Polar Studies Rept. 17.*

Taylor, L. D., and J. Gliozzi, 1964. Distribution of particulate matter in a firn core from Eights Station, Antarctica. In *Antarctic Research Series 2, Antarctic Snow and Ice Studies,* edited by M. Mellor; pp. 267–277. Am. Geophys. Union, Washington, D. C.

Thomas, R. H., and P. H. Coslett, 1970. Bottom melting of ice shelves and the mass balance of Antarctica. *Nature, 228:* 47–49.

Tilles, D., 1965. Anomalous argon isotope ratios in particles from Greenland ice and Pacific Ocean sediments. *Trans. Am. Geophys. Union, 46:* 117.

Tilles, D., 1966. Implantation in interplanetary dust of rare gas ions from solar flares. *Science, 153:* 981–984.

Tilles, D., 1967. Some studies of separated fractions of low accumulation rate "dust". Smithsonian Institution Contributions, *Astrophysics, 11:* 399–412.

The Times Atlas of the World, 1958. Vol. 1. The Times Publishing Co. Ltd., London.

Ukhov, S. B., 1963. Engineering investigations of snow cover between Komsomolskaya and Amundsen-Scott stations. *Soviet Antarctic Exped. Inform. Bull., No. 44.* (Translated as vol. 5, pp. 69–73, by Am. Geophys. Union, Washington, D. C.)

Vallon, M., 1968. Errors in the determination of ablation using stakes. *J. Glaciol., 7:* 132–133.

*Vickers, W. W., 1958. Glaciological report of the USNC-IGY airborne traverse unit, 1957–58. *Ohio State Univ. Res. Found. Rept., 825-1, Part I:* 234–279.

Vickers, W. W., 1959. Antarctic snow stratigraphy. *Trans. Am. Geophys. Union, 40:* 181–184.

Vickers, W. W., 1966. A study of ice accumulation and tropospheric circulation in western Antarctica. In *Antarctic Research Series 9, Studies in Antarctic Meteorology,* edited by M. J. Rubin; pp. 135–176. Am. Geophys. Union, Washington, D. C.

Voskresenskiy, A. I., 1967. Snow accumulation on the ice slope from Mirnyy to the one-hundredth kilometer. *Soviet Antarctic Exped. Inform. Bull., No. 63.* (Translated as vol. 6, pp. 393–395, by Am. Geophys. Union, Washington, D. C.)

Wexler, H., 1961. Ice budget for Antarctica and changes in sea-level. *J. Glaciol., 3:* 867–872.

Wexler, H., L. Machta, D. H. Pack, and F. D. White, 1956. Atomic energy and meteorology. *Proc. Intern. Conf. Peaceful Uses of Atomic Energy, 13:* 333–344. Geneva.

Weyant, W. S., 1967. The antarctic atmosphere: Climatology of the surface environment. *Antarctic Map Folio Series, Folio 8,* edited by V. C. Bushnell. Am. Geograph. Soc., New York.

Wilgain, S., E. Picciotto, and W. DeBreuck, 1965. Strontium 90 fallout in Antarctica. *J. Geophys. Res., 70:* 6023–6032.

Wilson, A. T., 1964. Origin of ice ages: an ice shelf theory for Pleistocene glaciation. *Nature, 201:* 147–149.

Wright, C. S., and R. E. Priestley, 1922. Glaciology. In *British (Terra-Nova) Antarctic Expedition 1910–1913.* Harrison and Sons, Ltd., London.

Wright, F. W., and P. W. Hodge, 1970. The question of the origin of the magnetic spherules found in antarctic ice. *Intern. Assoc. Sci. Hydrol., Publ. 86;* pp. 42–47.

Zotikov, I. A., A. P. Kapitza, and O. G. Sorokhtin, 1965. Thermal regime of the ice cover of central Antarctica. *Soviet Antarctic Exped. Inform. Bull., No. 51.* (Translated as vol. 5, pp. 304–308, by Am. Geophys. Union, Washington, D. C.)

PART IV

Cold Poles and Heat Balances

PART IV

Cold Poles and Heat Balances

The somewhat cryptic title for this section of the volume was meant to stimulate the imagination and evoke the concept that the polar regions play an important role in the heat budget of the earth. For the planet, and for any area on the surface, an annual heat balance must exist if the mean temperature is to remain essentially the same from year to year. Because of differences in types of surface, amounts of cloudiness, atmospheric transmissivity, and particularly latitudinal differences in solar energy received, imbalances in radiational energy exist at most points on the earth's surface. This is particularly true for the polar regions. Heat storage, loss from snow and ice depths, and energy transformations in melting and freezing are also elements of the heat budget.

Slightly more than eight percent of the earth's surface is strictly polar, i.e., poleward of the polar circles. Slightly more than thirteen percent lies poleward of 60° latitude. These are not significant percentages in terms of the entire planet, but since the polar regions form the principal heat sink of the atmospheric system, their importance in the system far outweighs their area. Furthermore, these are the regions on earth least cluttered with atmospheric variables such as carbon dioxide, dust, and water vapor. Because these important variables in atmospheric radiative power transfer are minimized, the polar regions offer the possibility of a better understanding of the radiative processes. Since it is these processes which serve to a large extent as the "forcing function" for atmospheric circulation, the polar regions are an important factor in understanding the global circulation. One of the principal aims of meteorology is to explain the whole atmospheric thermodynamic system, and thereby to develop predictions of the global circulation for extended periods of time. This involves knowing accurately the distribution of the net radiative flux, i.e., the solar radiation minus the emitted long-ray radiation. The largest values of net outgoing flux are in the region of the polar night. This flux must be accurately known if extended prediction models are to portray correctly the major large-scale energy transformations.

The maximum extent of the ice cover over the Antarctic Ocean in September, which is the Southern Hemisphere spring season, is about 18.8 million sq km. The Antarctic Continent itself, at sea level, only covers 13.9 million sq km and the addition of the minimum sea ice in March, which is the Southern Hemisphere fall season, adds only 2.6 million sq km to that amount. We see, then, that this minimum total of 16.5 million sq km is just about half of the total ice cover. There is an effective doubling of the continent from fall to spring. This is a significant factor in the heat budget, since the reflection power or the albedo of the ice is very high, up to as much as 80 percent or more, while the albedo of the sea surface is as low as 4 percent, depending on the roughness of the sea or the elevation angle of the sun. In addition, the melting of the ice takes considerable heat either from the ocean or the atmosphere and may be a significant factor in the seasonal heat budget.

The carbon dioxide content of the atmosphere has been increasing at the rate of about 0.2 percent per year in recent years. Because carbon dioxide is an excellent absorber and back radiator of infrared radiation, it causes temperatures near the earth's surface to increase more than they would with a lesser carbon dioxide concentration. Estimates have been made that indicate that a doubling of the carbon dioxide concentration would increase the average temperature near the earth's surface by about 2°C, while temperature at 40 km above the earth surface would decrease by 15°C. Such a rise in temperature near ground level might trigger the melting of polar ice caps, while lower temperatures in the stratosphere might contribute to climate change by altering stratospheric air mass flow patterns. Unlike carbon dioxide which influences the weather and climate through its infrared radiative and absorptive properties, atmospheric ozone does so by functioning as an excellent absorber of ultraviolet radiation. While comprising less than .00005 percent of the atmosphere, it prevents much of the sun's ultraviolet radiation from reaching the earth's surface and thereby enabling plant and animal life, as we know it, to survive. As an absorber of ultraviolet and to a lesser extent of visible and infrared radiation, ozone serves as a heat source within the stratosphere, thereby contributing to convective air mass movements and affecting the radiation balance at the tropopause. The bulk of the atmospheric ozone is at about 22 km, which is the altitude at which supersonic transports are designed to cruise.

In the papers which follow, a number of the unique characteristics of Antarctica and its potentials as a meteorological laboratory are brought out. Dalrymple discusses the climate of the interior, its effects on man and operations there, the microclimate, and the great antarctic temperature inversion; Van Loon considers meteorological interactions between Antarctica and middle latitudes and discusses the causes of the seasonal variations of pressure and winds; and Lettau looks at Antarctica as a laboratory for testing meteorological theory involving solar energy at the snow-air interface, micro-meteorological phenomena, wind systems, and other kinds of studies in this unique environment.

MORTON J. RUBIN

Office of Special Studies
National Oceanic and Atmospheric Administration
Rockville, Maryland

Some Aspects of the Climate of Interior Antarctica

PAUL C. DALRYMPLE and THOMAS O. FROSTMAN*

Earth Sciences Laboratory, U. S. Army Natick Laboratories, Natick, Massachusetts

Antarctica is the fastest growing continent on earth. The areal extent of the Antarctic has expanded northward as oceanographic research vessels, such as the U.S. *Eltanin* and the U.S.S.R.'s *Professor Vize,* and even full oceanographic expeditions, such as the IWSOE (International Weddell Sea Oceanographic Expedition), have pushed the realm of Antarctica far from the coastline. Thirty-seven scientific stations are operated year-round by Argentina, Australia, Chile, France, Japan, New Zealand, South Africa, the United Kingdom, the United States, and the U.S.S.R. Scientists continue to probe into the atmosphere of the continent and to core deeper and deeper into its ice cover. Even though its weather has been studied in some detail since the earliest exploration, there are still some meteorological problems associated with understanding Antarctica, and one could say that the continent today is in a youthful stage of scientific exploration.

Satellites and computers are proving extremely useful and powerful tools for scientific investigation, with video satellite output being more dramatic and computer capabilities more complex and with greater potential for theoretical applications. Digitized video output from ESSA satellites, for example, is used to produce maps distinguishing antarctic snow, ice, and water on average brightness charts (Fig. 1). The breakup of the ice in the Ross Sea, the disappearance of most of the ice along the coast of East Antarctica, and the persistency of the ice in the Weddell Sea are clearly shown in the average brightness map for mid-December to mid-January.

---

* Thomas O. Frostman is now with the Science Department, Wausau High School, Wausau, Wisconsin.

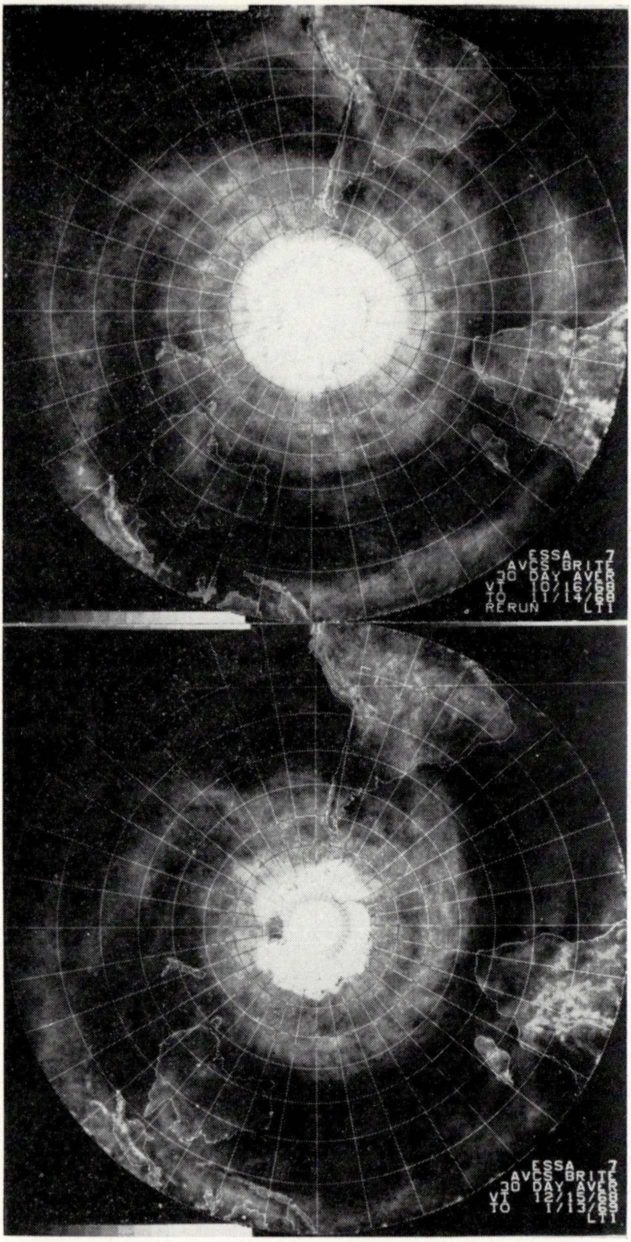

Fig. 1. Thirty-day average brightness charts for Antarctica, prepared from ESSA-7 satellites. Top chart, October 16-November 14, 1968; bottom chart, December 15, 1968–January 13, 1969 (National Environmental Satellite Center, ESSA).

Such maps not only provide useful climatological information on snow and ice conditions, but also on cloud cover and storms. In recent years satellites have confirmed or revealed for the first time major changes which are occurring in the geographical outline of the continent. Noticeable recent alterations in the face of Antarctica include: recession of the West Ice Shelf along Leopold and Astrid Coast; shearing off of the Fimbul Ice Shelf near its base; recession of the outer margin of the Amery Ice Shelf (around 100 km in recent years); the near disappearance of the Ninnis and Mertz glacier tongues; and a calving and detachment in the western end of the Ronne Ice Shelf.

As antarctic researchers, we all have our ideas of what constitutes Antarctica. Even though its interior is a vast expanse of snow, a seemingly never-ending desert plain, it is a continent of many faces. Its periphery, and especially that of the Antarctic Peninsula, is a geomorphological complex of snow, land, and mountains, and sites and exposures are often overriding factors in determining local climates. As these are atypical of Antarctica as a whole, they are being omitted from this report. What makes Antarctica unique is its extreme cold temperatures; nowhere else on earth are they colder than on the Antarctic Plateau. Because of this, we will devote most of our attention to this theme and to this area.

CLIMATIC CLASSIFICATIONS

Climatic classifications for Antarctica cannot be correlated to vegetation criteria because of the simple fact that the continent is basically snow covered. However, some sort of climatic classification can be devised showing mankind's adaptability to stress regions which would be more meaningful as one is more interested in the response of the individual and his equipment and vehicles. The environment becomes increasingly important at the snow-air interface where the most profound changes take place. With one common surface predominating, consisting of extensive "flatlands" with no great discontinuities of physical features, the horizontal differences are minimized. The same features contribute to significant vertical changes in the environment above the snow surface.

One could characterize the interior of the continent as a region of great stability and the coastal areas as regions subject to rapid changes. Climatic means may mask most significant extremes. For example, though the mean wind speed along the coast of Wilkes

Land in East Antarctica is low, extremely high winds well over a hundred knots occur periodically at stations such as Wilkes, Mawson, Mirnyy, and Dumont d'Urville. Such phenomena have been the curse of mankind in Antarctica since early exploration, as they not only bring a halt to all human activity outside, but they also increase the fire hazard inside camp and call for the exercise of extreme caution. At the Russian station at Mirnyy, a fire which broke out in the meteorological building when winds were about 55 meters per second and the temperature was around −45°C resulted in the death of eight meteorologists and the loss of their data. High winds on the polar plateau are most unusual, the maximums at Vostok and Plateau being 25 meters per second; at the South Pole, 23 meters per second. The strongest winds of Antarctica are the katabatic winds flowing off the interior of West Antarctica. They are confined to the height of the inversion, are extremely gusty, show a diurnal effect, are stronger and more frequent in winter than in summer and at night than in the day (during periods with both sunlight and darkness), and are often accelerated or dampened by the passage of storms off the coast.

In contrast to the coastal region, the cold, dry interior of Antarctica can be a most pleasant habitational environment. As soon as one goes onto the polar plateau, he is removed from a great unpleasantness for both man and vehicles, that of thawing snow. The sensible midsummer temperature over snow, with its high albedo, is tens of degrees higher than the ambient temperature. Also, in the interior of Antarctica, storms are most infrequent. Stable conditions develop and the surface temperature inversion persists throughout the winter. On the polar plateau winds have a small standard deviation and there is an exceedingly large concentration of speeds around the norm. The same applies to wind directions, as winds blow almost consistently from the same directions in all seasons, reflecting terrain and thermal conditions.

Temperatures in the high latitudes are not subject to the diurnal cycling of the mid to low latitudes; consequently, the temperature trace is more or less an orderly cooling off in late summer, followed by a long coreless winter, a slow rising of temperatures in early summer, and then a short summer with small diurnal ranges. On the polar plateau, summer lasts at best for two months, winter for at least eight months, with two short one-month transitional periods. The coreless winter results in the mean annual temperature being warmer than the mean monthly temperature for seven or eight months of the year. The coldest month can occur as early as April or as late as September but, on the average, over a period of several years, the months of July and August are found to have the lowest mean temperatures. It is not uncommon at the interior stations such as Vostok, South Pole, and Plateau, to have the low temperature for the year occur near or shortly after the return of the sun above the horizon. On the whole, the interior of Antarctica is controlled by a giant thermostat which does not favor extremes.

Based on the premise that climatic criteria for the Antarctic which are not based on the physiology of man are not truly indicative of the severity of the climate, the cooling power of the atmosphere must be considered. Probably the best instrument available for sensing cooling power is the frigorimeter, an instrument which has been used by some Europeans since the 1920's. It measures the amount of current necessary to maintain a copper sphere at a temperature comparable to that of man's skin. It is sensitive to temperature, wind speed, solar radiation, and water vapor, and is an improvement upon the wind chill computation which is based solely on temperature and wind speed. Unfortunately, only the United States (South Pole) and Russia (Mirnyy) have used frigorimeters, and the extreme low values at the South Pole were beyond the range of the instrument. Near the edge of the continent, where warmer temperatures prevail, the strong katabatic winds probably result in high values of cooling power comparable to those experienced in the interior where the extreme low temperatures exist with much lower wind speeds. The cooling power, consequently, is a uniting factor for much of interior Antarctica, tending to create one large conterminous region.

WEATHER AND OPERATIONAL PROBLEMS

What is the limiting temperature for operation? Vehicles and aircraft seem to function quite well at temperatures down to −45°C and cold-acclimatized men work well in temperatures down to −55°C. Vehicles and aircraft can be considered as marginally operable at temperatures below −50°C. Man can dress for the most extreme cold temperatures, although his productivity and efficiency will be lowered by the necessity of his having to wear numerous layers of protective clothing. As long as a person can move and exercise, he can be kept relatively comfortable at the lowest of observed temperatures. Heated gloves were shunned by the observers at Plateau Station who had to climb a 32-meter tower to maintain instrumentation at temperatures lower than −80°C, because their regular clothing was sufficient and the wearing of multiple layers of clothing is physically restricting. In addition, because of the high elevation of interior Antarctica, with its thin atmosphere, manual labor is more difficult and machinery functions at a lower efficiency rate.

High winds are probably a limiting factor more than low temperatures. Regardless of the temperature, and irrespective of the surface, the snow-covered areas become a virtual mixing bowl of snow when winds are over 25 meters per second. Under these conditions, and with visibility near zero, one experiences what is probably the most unpleasant weather in the dry part of Antarctica. Threshold wind speeds for drifting snow depend upon the availability of loose snow on the surface. With an ample supply, drifting will commence over the surface when speeds at ten meters above the surface are around five meters per second; with a hard, wind-packed surface extending for tens of miles there may be no drifting with speeds as high as ten meters per second. Blizzards result both from falling snow and from snow picked up from the surface, and are usually associated with winds in excess of twenty meters per second. Fortunately, much of interior plateau Antarctica has a relatively hard snow surface and blizzards are infrequent because of the low frequency of high winds. Certainly, the frequency of blizzards in interior Antarctica is much lower than on the ice cap of Greenland where a greater supply of loose surface snow results in a more favorable environment for blizzards.

Clouds can have a somewhat supernatural affect on personnel in the Antarctic. With a thick low overcast, whiteouts can exist where the horizon blends into the snow surface, objects appear to float in space, depth perception is lost, and footing becomes uncertain. It is the plague of pilots, and some have landed at full speeds thinking they were still well above the surface. The fair-weather low-overcast whiteout is less dangerous near open water, because from the snow surface the clouds above the open water will appear a darkish blue, the so-called "water sky." There are various types of whiteouts, but all have the same "inside of a milk bottle" effect. This is certainly the most feared and respected of all atmospheric phenomena encountered by pilots in the Antarctic; extreme safety precautions are taken to minimize accidents.

ANTARCTIC MICROCLIMATE

Antarctic meteorology is more interesting from a "micro" than from a "macro" point of view. Micrometeorological programs have been conducted by the authors at the most extreme cold high-altitude interior station of Plateau (40°30′E, 79°15′S) in East Antarctica (1967–1968), at the less extreme cold station at the Geographical South Pole (1958), and at a marine modified coastal station on the Ross Ice Shelf at Little America (1957). Data from these three stations are the primary basis in this paper for assumptions made on the microclimate of Antarctica. This is not intended to detract in any way from the outstanding work of Liljequist at Maudheim on the Norwegian-British-Swedish Expedition (1949–1952), as that program will remain the premier micrometeorological study conducted in the Antarctic (Liljequist, 1957).

Of major interest to those investigating the microclimate of the Antarctic is the great inversion and its variation across the continent. The inversion exists at all stations throughout the winter and generally throughout the whole year at the high interior stations. The inversions in the higher elevations of East Antarctica are about twice as strong and high as those in the central part of West Antarctica. The gradient in the first ten meters is greater, however, at some of the coastal stations than it is in the interior. Liljequist had an inversion at Maudheim of 19°C, and an inversion of 15°C was observed at Little America in 1957 (Lettau *et al.*, 1967), while the largest inversion at South Pole in 1958 was 10°C (Dalrymple *et al.*, 1963).

During the winter months of 1966–1968, Sponholz of the University of Wisconsin and ESSA initiated a special program to study the great inversion at Plateau Station. Radiometersondes attached to balloons of slow ascension rate were released, as the synoptic situation warranted, to obtain profiles of temperature (Fig. 2), net longwave radiation, and upper winds through the inversion and several miles above the inversion. A July, 1968, flight showed the following: surface, pressure 597 millibars and temperature −73°C (a temperature not reached again until 170 mb); top of the inversion, pressure 550 millibars and temperature −47°C; loss of signal at 122 millibars and −79°C; no tropopause detected. Data from a series of releases made July 28, 1966, revealed an inversion of over 33°C with the steepness of the inversion close to the surface particularly noticeable, approximately 26°C in less than 40 meters.

Perhaps the most comprehensive microclimate investigation done recently in Antarctica was the three-year study at Plateau Station (1966–1968). Located on the high plateau of East Antarctica, some 1,100 kilometers from the Geographical South Pole, Plateau Station (elevation 3,625 m) provided a unique opportunity for probing one

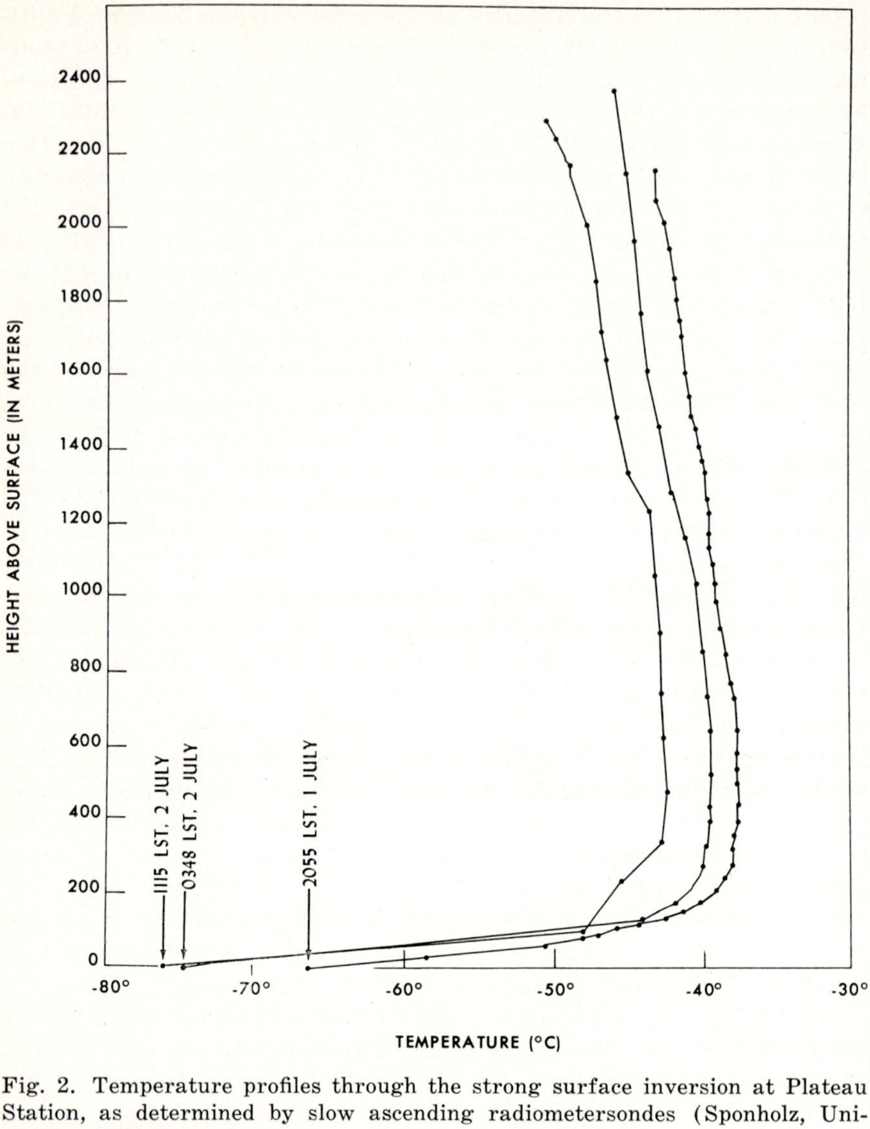

Fig. 2. Temperature profiles through the strong surface inversion at Plateau Station, as determined by slow ascending radiometersondes (Sponholz, University of Wisconsin).

of the extreme microclimates of the world. Plateau's average temperature of −57°C makes it the coldest "inhabited" spot on earth; the temperature ranged from −18.5° to −86.2°C. The latter is the lowest temperature recorded by the United States and was reached in July of 1968; the average temperature for that month was

−73.2°C. Despite the fact that ice crystal precipitation occurs on over 300 days a year, the annual net accumulation from all sources is only about ten centimeters. Winds at this site, lacking in gustiness, average about five meters per second and blow almost constantly from the northern sector. Final analysis of Plateau Station's three years of surface observations reveals that 70 percent of the observed daily prevailing wind direction cases fall in the northwest-north-northeast sector.

In an attempt to resolve in some detail the characteristics of the lower portion of the great inversion in this part of the continent, the U.S. Army Natick Laboratories erected and instrumented a 32-meter tower at Plateau Station (Fig. 3). Wind speed, wind direction, and temperature data were obtained from sensors at 32, 24, 20, 16, 12, 8, 4, 2, 1, and ½ meters. Additional temperature probes were located at ¼ meter, surface, and minus ⅛, ¼, ½, 1, 2, and 10 meters.

Generally speaking, analysis shows that the inversion is very persistent throughout the year with some rather remarkable cases noted during winter months following extended periods of radiation cooling. In June, 1967, an inversion of 36.5°C was observed in the 32-meter layer. Inversions as large as 15°C persisted for as long as 24 hours between four and eight meters. Summertime inversions are generally 5°C or less over the height of the tower. Temperature reversals in the lowest four meters appear periodically in summer, indicating alternating layers of warmer and cooler air.

Corresponding wind profiles for a typical summer day show negative upward shear averaging about 25 degrees. Winter profiles are more dramatic with several observed cases with shears of 90 degrees or more. A most unusual situation, documented on film by Kuhn (Fig. 4), was observed for a half-hour period in August, 1967, when calm conditions existed at the two-meter level with a 1.3 meters per second south wind at four meters, and a 1.1 meters per second north wind at the half-meter level. During the brief spring and autumn transition periods, daily variations in the inversion are strongest in the lower layers, and maximum winds are usually found at the height of the strongest negative gradient (Fig. 5).

Another technique by which the low-level lapse rate was determined at Plateau Station employed an optical method developed by Sparkman (1962). A reflex camera, with a 400-millimeter telephoto lens positioned near the snow surface, was used to take sev-

Fig. 3. Thirty-two-meter micrometeorological tower at Plateau Station measured wind speed, wind direction, and temperature at ten levels. Photo shows tower at time of erection in January, 1967, when instrumentation was in process of being installed and calibrated (Stroschein, U.S. Army Natick Laboratories).

eral hundred photos of three vertical triangular targets each 300 meters apart, with the first about 400 meters from the camera. The targets were strung with colored lights and the resulting distortion

Fig. 4. Wind shear of 180 degrees between 0.5 and 4.0 meters on Plateau Station micrometerological tower, August, 1967 (Kuhn, University of Innsbruck).

of the light rays through the kilometer-long horizontal path was analyzed geometrically on the prints to obtain a line-average of lapse rate close to the surface over a nearly linear path. The theory supporting this optical technique, geometrically analyzing the bending of light rays in a vertical plane, is based on the fact that the

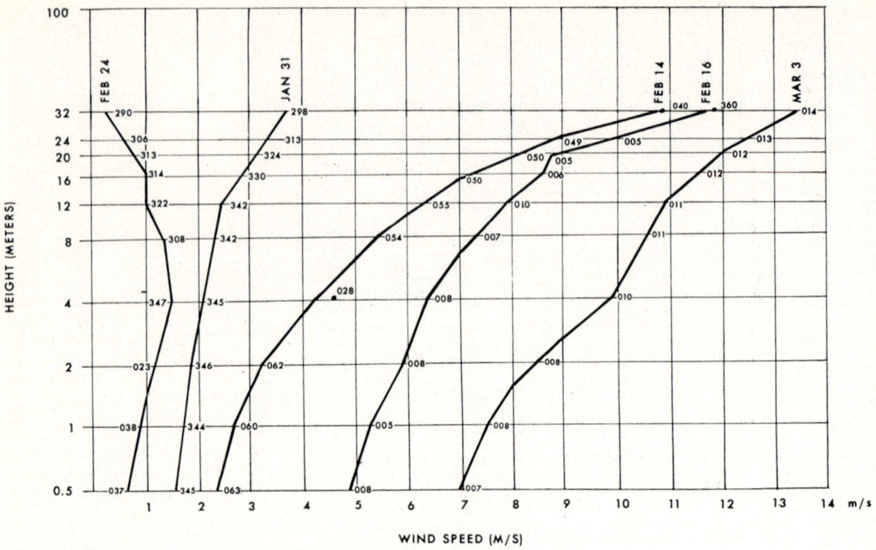

Fig. 5. Wind speed profiles, Plateau Station, 1967. Wind shears shown by direction of winds being placed adjacent to wind speeds. Strong backing of wind direction characterizes wind profiles with greatest amount associated with low surface winds (U.S. Army Natick Laboratories).

refractive index of light is a function of air density, that is, of temperature gradient. Usually only the gross structure of the temperature profiles as revealed by the refraction technique could be verified by the micrometeorological tower temperature probes which were spaced at relatively wide intervals.

In a 1966 publication, Lettau showed that air motion in the lower atmosphere at the South Pole is controlled by surface friction and by the geostrophic motion in the free atmosphere above the inversion layer, modified by the thermal wind caused by the horizontal temperature gradient which results from the general slope of the terrain. Expanding on Lettau's work, and employing a geometric technique to determine the thermal wind, knowing the surface and upper winds, Schwerdtfeger and Mahrt (1969) have examined the wind regimes at other interior stations and compared the results to coastal flow. They noted that the thermal stability of the lower layers is of prime importance in explaining the nature of the surface winds. While upper winds over the interior are quite variable in speed and direction, surface winds are characterized by directional constancy and low speed; the relationship between surface and upper wind direction is a function of the thermal wind induced by the sloped inversion (the inversion over the sloped terrain of the plateau). It is shown that the thermal wind is parallel to the terrain contours, with higher ground to the right, and is proportional to the strength of the inversion and to the slope of the terrain. In cases with strong inversions, the assumption of balanced flow at the surface seems to be valid. With weak inversions, two other components of the total thermal wind are of relatively greater importance: (1) the component caused by climatic temperature gradient (horizontal temperature variation between the cold interior and warmer ocean or between cold West Antarctica and colder East Antarctica); and (2) the component caused by a synoptic scale temperature gradient (the result of cyclonic disturbances intruding into the continent). Compared to coastal slopes, where the time scale of typical katabatic flow is considerably smaller than that of strong surface conditions over the plateau, Coriolis-induced deflection of flow from the fall line is greater over the plateau.

RADIATION PROGRAM

Radiation instruments used at Plateau Station included: one CSIRO pyrradiometer to measure incoming visible and infrared, another for net radiation; one Kipp solarimeter for global and one for reflected shortwave; one Linke-Feussner pyrheliometer with quartz, OG1, RG2, and RG8 filters; one Eppley UV photometer (0.29 to 0.38μ); four Eppley pyranometers equipped with OG1, RG2, RG8, and WG7 spectral domes. During the 1968–1969 summer season, illumination and albedo measurements were also attempted. Plateau was the first station in the world to use the four-component radiation balance meter designed and constructed by the radiation experts at the Davos Observatory in Switzerland. The instrument was used in 1967 and 1968 to measure the upward and downward fluxes in the visible and infrared, and simultaneous records were run for one year with other instruments so that comparisons could be made.

Kuhn (1969) has reached certain conclusions from preliminary analysis of the 1967 Plateau Station data. These include a maximum direct solar radiation intensity of 1.6 langleys per minute when the solar elevation angle is at 30 degrees. Net flux ranged between zero and −0.02 langleys per minute for typical wintertime conditions—low vapor pressure and snow temperatures around −80°C. Positive net flux is observed during the initial stages of precipitation or drifting snow, following which time cooling occurs accompanied by net losses of up to −0.05 langleys per minute. More frequent periods of positive flux are to be expected in November when the snow surface is still very cold and the solar elevation approaches summertime levels. Albedo readings taken throughout the summer range from 80 to 90, partly dependent on instrument response.

Authors' Notes: For those who may be interested in a more recent and broader treatment on the climatology of Antarctica, attention is directed to Dr. Schwerdtfeger's chapter on "The Climate of the Antarctic" in *World Survey of Climatology,* Volume 14, H. E. Landsberg (Editor-in-Chief); pp. 253–354. Elsevier Publishing Co., Amsterdam, 1970.

Both authors would like to express deep thanks to one and all who had anything to do with their selection for antarctic service, and to the National Science Foundation for the support of analysis of micrometeorological data collected in the Antarctic.

References

Dalrymple, P. C., H. H. Lettau, and S. H. Wollaston, 1963. *South Pole Micrometeorology Program, Part II: Data Analysis. Tech. Rept., ES-7.* Quartermaster Research and Engineering Center, Natick, Mass.

Kuhn, M., 1969. *Preliminary Report on Meteorological Studies at Plateau Station, Antarctica, 1967.* Preliminary report for ESSA Grant E-22-67 (G). Meteorol. Dept., Univ. Melbourne, Australia.

Lettau, H. H., 1966. A case study of katabatic flow on the South Polar Plateau. In *Antarctic Research Series 9, Studies in Antarctic Meteorology,* edited by M. J. Rubin; pp. 1–11. Am. Geophys. Union, Washington, D.C.

Lettau, H. H., S. H. Wollaston, and P. C. Dalrymple, 1967. *Little American Micrometeorology Program, Data and Analysis. Technical Report ES-29.* U.S. Army Natick Laboratories, Natick, Mass.

Liljequist, G. H., 1957. *Energy Exchange of an Antarctic Snow-Field,* Part A: Short-Wave Radiation; Part B: Long-Wave Radiation and Radiation Balance; Part C: Wind Structure in the Low Layer; Part D: Surface Inversions and Turbulent Heat Transfer. Norsk Polarinstitutt, Oslo.

Schwerdtfeger, W., and L. J. Mahrt, 1969. The relation between the antarctic temperature inversion in the surface layer and the wind regime. *Proceedings of the Symposium on Antarctic Glaciological Exploration, September 1968.* Dartmouth, N. H.

Sparkman, J. K., 1962. Preliminary report on an optical method for low-level lapse rate determination. *Final Report: Studies of the Three Dimensional Structure of the Planetary Boundary Layer,* edited by H. H. Lettau; pp. 69–79. Dept. Meteorol., Univ. Wisconsin, Madison.

Antarctic Atmosphere as a Test Tube for Meteorological Theories

HEINZ LETTAU

Department of Meteorology, University of Wisconsin, Madison

Nowhere else on earth are external geophysical-meteorological environments as test-tube-like or clear-cut and well defined as in the Antarctic. I will restrict the discussion of "meteorological theories" to those which refer specifically to mathematical models of thermodynamic and dynamic consequences of solar energy supplies at the snow-air interface. The natural processes involved are of primary significance to a host of scientific fields, including micro- and macrometeorology, physical meteorology, climatology, glaciology, etc. There are three important principal factors: the exceptional uniformity of the physical structure of the antarctic snow surface, the large horizontal scale of the topographical gradients of the continental ice-dome, and the relative paucity of short-time disturbances of the dominant long-period (seasonal) variation of insolation. These factors justify a comparison of atmospheric structure with laboratory results, such as testings in a gigantic wind tunnel, or in a rotating dishpan, or a coldchamber, or the unusual combination of a cold-air wind-tunnel which is whirling around. The same three factors stimulate the further development of existing theoretical models. For example, the snow-air interface energy budget invites theoretical deductions and predictions which can be tested most readily by observations from previous and future antarctic programs.

Poleward of around 60°S lies a huge continent, 98 percent of which is covered with ice and snow. With an average meridional radius of about 3,500 km, this mass rises to more than 3,500 m above the level of the surrounding sea which is covered by fields and belts of floating ice. The vertical and horizontal dimensions correspond to a characteristic terrain slope of 1:1,000. Such a slope

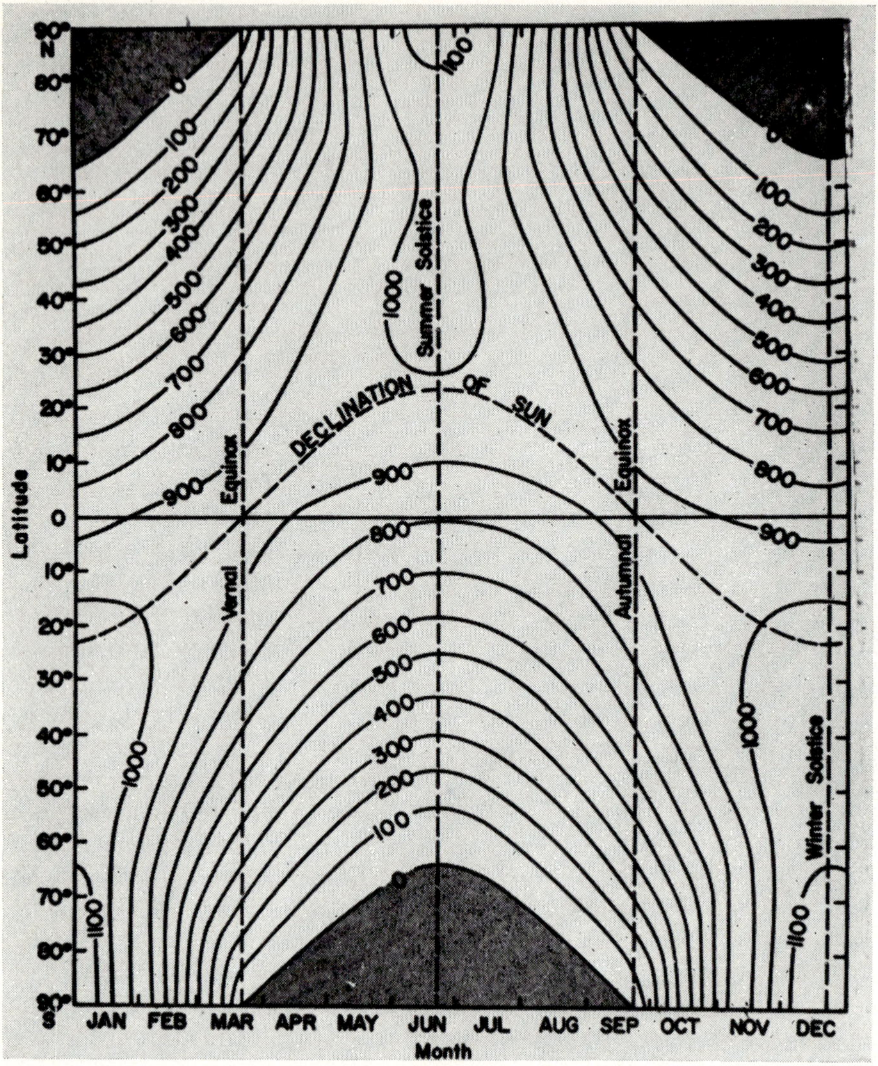

Fig. 1. The annual variation of solar radiation, in langleys per day, at the top of the atmosphere at indicated geographic latitudes; latitudinal variation of potential insolation from pole to pole (Sellers, 1965).

is uninteresting to a skier. Meteorologically, however, it is highly significant for two reasons: (1) its vast, truly continent-wide horizontal extent, and (2) its intermediate position between a typical slope of the order of 1:10,000 for isobaric surfaces, and that of about 1:100 for temperature discontinuities in the free troposphere.

From an overall viewpoint it is also important to note certain similarities in horizontal dimension and curvature structure between characteristic meteorological surfaces (like those in semipermanent anticyclones) and the antarctic snow-air interface. This ice-dome is extraordinarily simple or uniform in topographical detail. There appear to be hardly any significant spectral peaks in the spectral variance of height as a function of topographical wave numbers for the huge range (approximately 10^9) between the macrometeorological or continent-wide scale (one cycle per Mm) to the micrometeorological scale of aerodynamic roughness elements (one cycle per mm).

Anywhere on earth, as on any planetary surface, the primary source of energy is solar radiation. At the geographic pole the sun's elevation angle always equals the declination angle. Thus, after six months of darkness, the sun appears and circles around the horizon, gradually spiraling up for three months and, after reaching a solstice maximum (23.5° on earth), spirals down again to the horizon for the following three months. The polar extreme together with the worldwide seasonal distribution of daily totals of "potential" solar radiation is illustrated in Figure 1. ("Potential" means radiation intercepted by a horizontal area, in absence of atmospheric attenuation.) The seasonal variations between about 60° and 90° latitude are relevant for the following discussion of the relationship between antarctic temperature and insolation. At the South Pole, the annual variation of potential insolation from September to March is correctly described by a truncated cosine-arc (from the argument-value of $-\pi/2$ to $+\pi/2$), with a peak value of about 1,000 langleys per day (ly/day), and a flat zero-value from March to September. At the rim of the Antarctic Continent, that is to say near the Antarctic Circle, the annual variation of potential insolation is similar to a complete cosine-arc, ranging nearly harmonically from a near-zero minimum at the June solstice, through averages of about 400 ly/day in September and March, to a maximum of nearly 1,000 ly/day at the December solstice.

Fourier's theorem states that any odd-shaped but periodic function can be expressed as a finite sum of higher harmonics added to the basic cycle. As a direct consequence of the application of this theorem to the annual period of potential insolation, the amplitude ratio of second to first harmonic can be predicted. While at the rim of the Antarctic Continent this ratio is practically zero, it increases systematically to 0.42 at the Pole, certainly a significant value. As shall be demonstrated later, the superposition of first plus second harmonic variation determines satisfactorily (with 95 percent accuracy) the seasonal or monthly departures from the annual mean value. Since in Antarctica the maximum of the first harmonic occurs at the December solstice, while the two maximums of the second harmonic coincide with the December as well as June solstices, a basic ratio of potential amplitudes $A_2/A_1 = 0.42/1.00$ implies that the departure from the annual mean peaks at $1.00 + 0.42$, or 1.42 relative units in December, but is reduced to $-1.00 + 0.42 = -0.58$, or 0.58 relative units in June. However, near the Antarctic Circle the same theoretical argumentation yields peak departures of +1.0 in December and −1.0 in June, because, here, the first harmonic dominates the annual cycle without significant contribution from the second or higher harmonics.

It is self-suggestive to speculate that any meteorological element which undergoes annual variations, in direct or quasi-direct relationship to potential insolation, should exhibit similar departures from the annual average as a function of latitude within the antarctic range. That is to say, a close to perfectly harmonic annual trend near the rim of the Antarctic Continent should gradually change with increasing latitude into a specifically polar type of annual variation with a flattened broad region of moderately negative departures, lasting from at least one-half month before to at least one-half month after the dark season (a total duration of at least seven months), followed by a strongly peaked narrow region (of less than five months duration) of positive departure during the sunlit season. This speculation amounts to a theoretical explanation of the feature of polar climates known as the "kernlose" or "coreless" winter (Dalrymple, 1966). This new theory will be tested with the aid of snow temperatures in the following section.

SNOW TEMPERATURE TRENDS IN ANTARCTICA

The uppermost layers of antarctic snow remain generally below freezing temperatures and react like any semi-infinite conductor to harmonic heating pulses generated near the surface. Conduction theory predicts that the downward propagation of a harmonic heat pulse occurs under reduction of amplitude as well as retardation of phase angle with increasing depth; higher harmonics are attenuated more (for example, in the case of a uniform conductor, in proportion to the square root of cycle frequency) than the basic frequency. Via the surface energy budget, the heating pulse at the

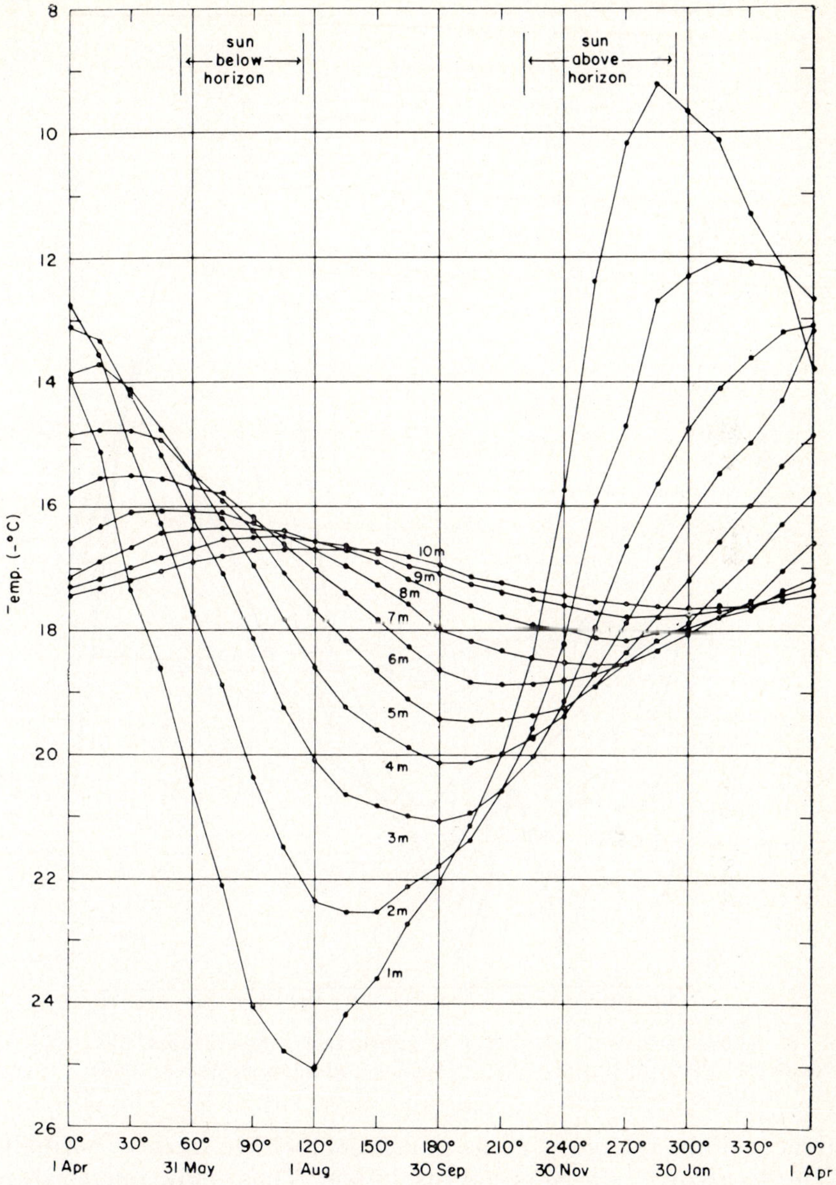

Fig. 2. Annual trends (1950–1951) of subsurface temperatures (°C) at indicated depth, Maudheim, 71.0°S (Dalrymple *et al.*, 1966).

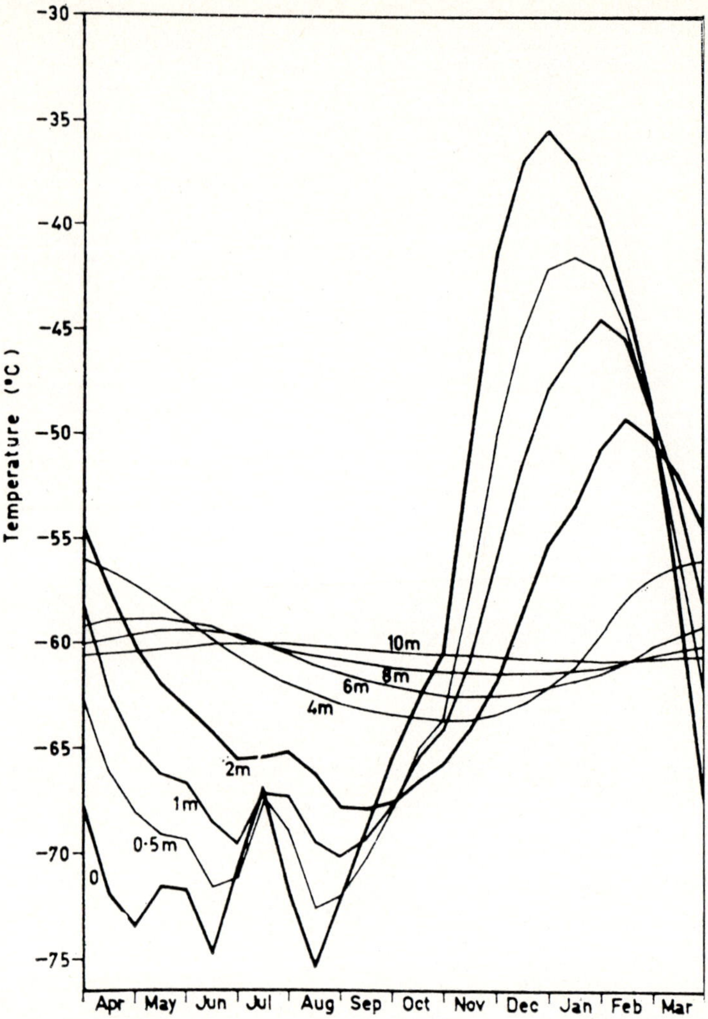

Fig. 3. Annual trends (1966–1967) of subsurface temperatures (°C) at indicated depth, Plateau Station, 79.2°S (Weller and Schwerdtfeger, 1968).

surface will be related to actual insolation, which, in turn, normally varies in accord with potential insolation. Thus, snow temperature will exhibit annual and semiannual variations causing amplitudes to depend characteristically on antarctic latitude. Figures 2 to 4 show annual trends of snow temperatures between the surface and several meters depth. Figure 2 refers to Maudheim at 71°S, relatively close to the Antarctic Circle; Figure 3 to Plateau Station

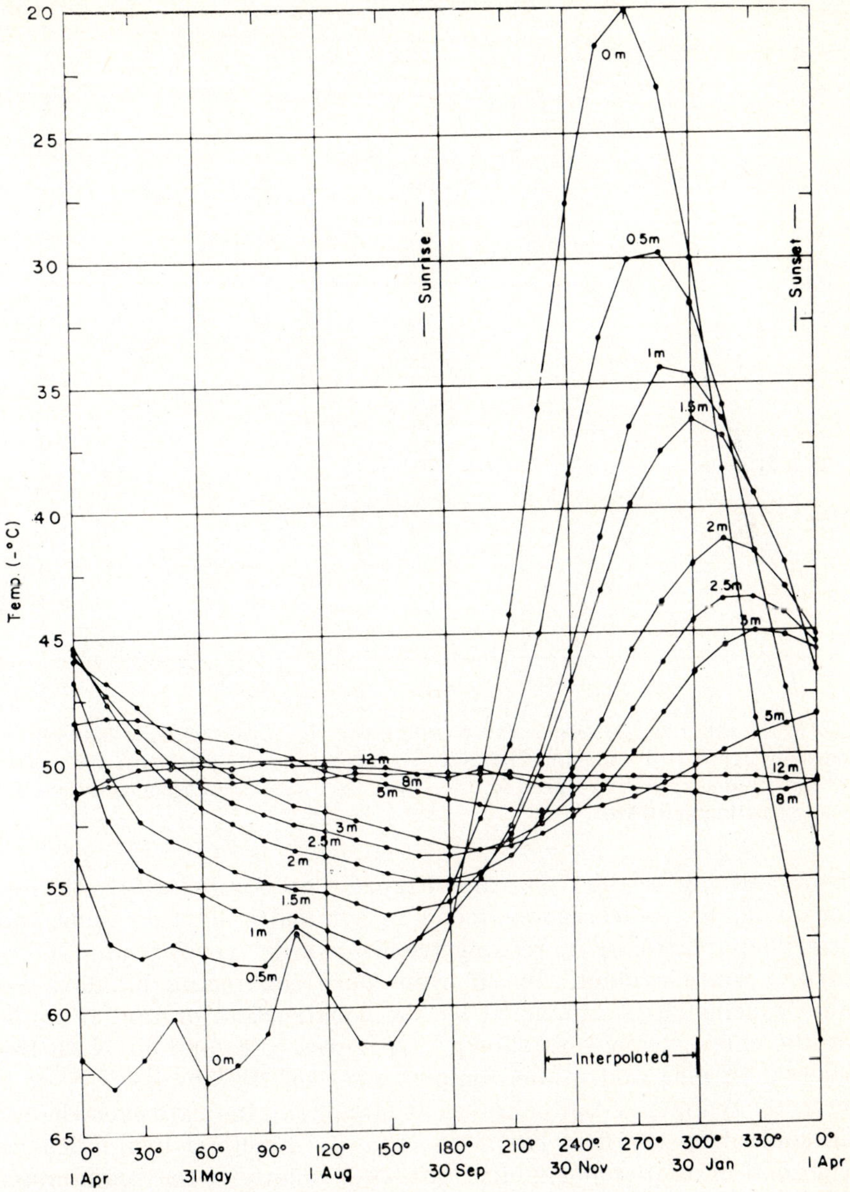

Fig. 4. Annual trends (1957–1958) of subsurface temperatures (°C) at indicated depth, Amundsen-Scott Station, 90.0°S (Dalrymple *et al.*, 1966). Note how "corelessness," especially evidenced by the 0-m trend-curve, has systematically increased polewards, in comparison with Figures 2 and 3.

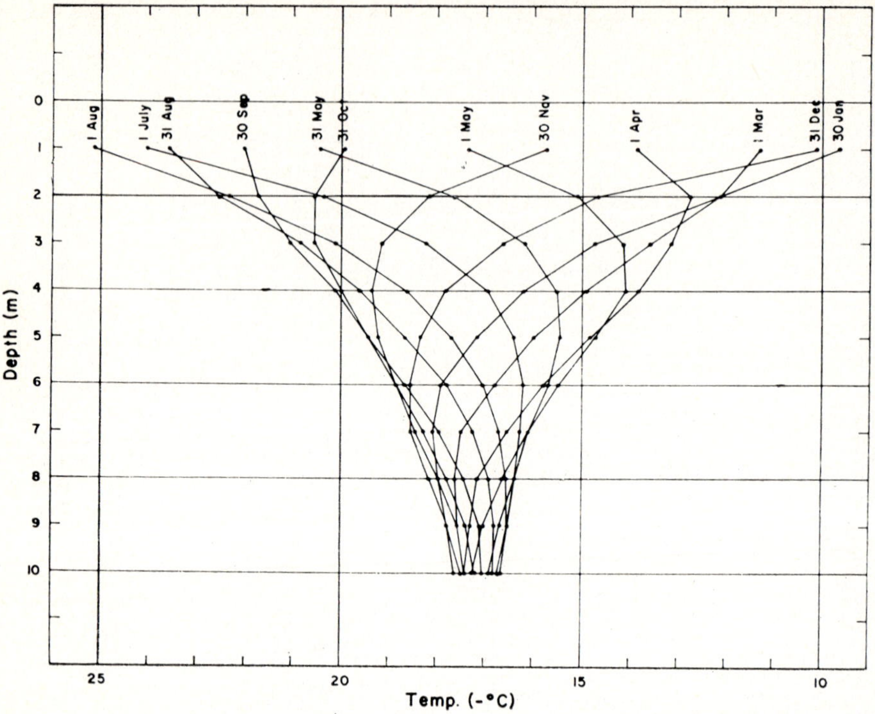

Fig. 5. Monthly tautochrones (1950–1951) for the layer of snow between 1- and 10-m depth at Maudheim, 71.0°S (Dalrymple *et al.*, 1966). Note the nearly perfect symmetry with respect to a vertical line which corresponds to annual mean snow temperature.

about halfway to the Pole; and Figure 4 to Amundsen-Scott Station at 90°S. A decreasing trend to symmetry between plus and minus departures, or increasing trend towards "corelessness" poleward is quite evident. In an even more convincing manner the same conclusion is supported by the construction of tautochrones for the three stations as shown in Figures 5, 6, and 7. Note the reversal of plus and minus temperatures on the abscissa. Nearly perfectly symmetric tautochrones at Maudheim indicate overwhelming control by the first harmonic, that is, practical insignificance of second or higher harmonics. Farther poleward the semiannual variation begins to appear and produces pronounced asymmetry which culminates at the Pole. The more rapid attenuation of the second harmonic with increasing snow depth enhances tautochrone asymmetry in the uppermost snow layers at Amundsen-Scott Sta-

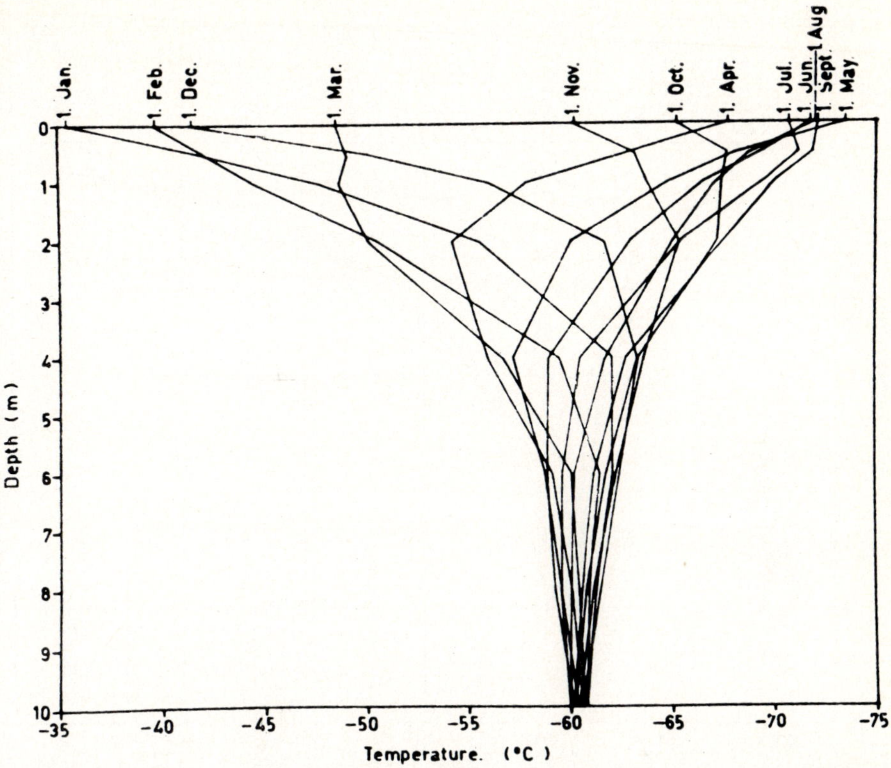

Fig. 6. Monthly tautochrones (1966–1967) for the layer of snow between surface and 10-m depth at Plateau Station, 79.2°S (Weller and Schwerdtfeger, 1968). In comparison with Figure 5, note pronounced asymmetry with respect to vertical line which corresponds to annual mean snow temperature.

tion. It may be concluded that these station data have passed the test with positive results and imply that a significant coupling between potential or actual insolation and snow temperature exists.

The theoretical structure of annual insolation trends at the Pole, and its demonstrated correlation with snow temperature variations, clarifies a puzzle which was vividly described by one of our most distinguished antarctic pioneers, the late Paul Siple (1959). In his book, *90 Degrees South,* he described his exceptionally active study of snow temperatures just after his arrival at the Pole in December of 1956:

> That first day of digging I removed about five tons of snow, and in four days I had created a pit 18 feet deep.

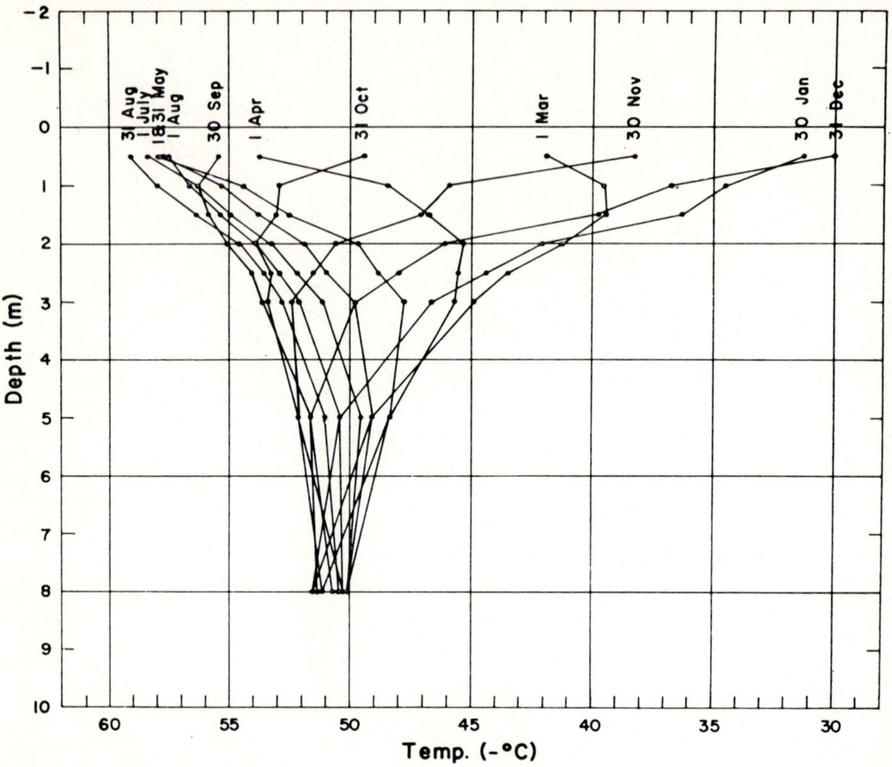

Fig. 7. Monthly tautochrones (1957–1958) for the layer of snow between 0.5- and 8-m depth at Amundsen-Scott Station, 90.0°S (Dalrymple *et al.*, 1966). Note extreme asymmetry (considering that tautochrone construction was ended at 0.5 m but could have been easily extrapolated to the surface) in comparison with Figures 5 and 6.

My thermometers showed −62°F, or what I believed to be a close estimate of the Pole's annual mean temperature. Similar diggings on earlier expeditions to Little America had produced a comparable −10°F. Thus I reasoned that we could look forward to a temperature 50°F colder than Little America. Since the winter night at Little America got down to −70°F, then −120°F was a reasonable guess for the coldest winter temperature we might expect at the Pole. I checked my conclusions by another line of reasoning. If −60°F was the mean temperature and 0°F the highest summer temperature, then, if the South Pole was like most other places, the coldest winter temperature

> would be displaced equally below the mean. Again the answer was −120°F.

Toward the end of the 1957 dark season, Paul Siple commented:

> One of the most puzzling things about our winter was that we did not hit the −120°F temperature I had earlier predicted. Our average temperature curve, which I had expected to round normally at the bottom as it did elsewhere on the globe, instead flattened out in the minus nineties Fahrenheit, save for a brief dip below this level at the beginning and end of the winter night. We could only hypothecate that the normal curve was flattened by the mixing action of the winds which were considerably stronger than we had anticipated, and without the winds the temperature curve would have dropped as predicted.

From hindsight it is now relatively easy to state that antarctic snow temperatures must respond at all latitudes to the annual variations of radiation and insolation. The difference between symmetry, "rounded at the botton," and asymmetry, "flattened at the bottom" (or "corelessness"), of the annual temperature curve, as between antarctic stations at moderate and extreme geographic latitudes, is explained by the truncation of the annual cycle of potential insolation and the important role of the second annual harmonic, and specifically by the polar-day feature that the second-harmonic amplitude grows systematically from practically zero at and near the Antarctic Circle to 42 percent of the annual amplitude at the Pole. With this fact established there is no need to search for other and undoubtedly spurious causes of the "coreless" polar winter such as a mixing action of the wind. It would have been possible to predict the winter departure of snow surface temperature at the South Pole in 1956–1957 as −0.58/1.42 or approximately −0.41 of the peak value of summer temperature departures from the annual mean. Thus, using Paul Siple's measurements obtained in December of 1956 (0°F as summer peak versus an estimated annual mean of −62°F) the winter departure from the mean at South Pole Station would be −25°F, resulting in an average minimum of −87°F, as roughly confirmed by actual data. The more harmonic nature of annual insolation trends near the rim of the Antarctic Continent explains also why Siple's method of predicting winter minimum temperatures had worked reasonably well at Little America.

NON-CONDUCTIVE MODES OF HEAT TRANSFER IN THE SNOW

If insolation is the primary cause of snow temperature variations it is imperative to investigate the possibility of vertical transfer of heat in the uppermost snow layer by other modes than ordinary molecular conduction. Figure 8 summarizes a possible variety of such processes: (1) genuine or molecular conduction which by definition occurs in the direction of and is proportional to the gradient of temperature, (2) radiation penetration and absorption, (3) heat

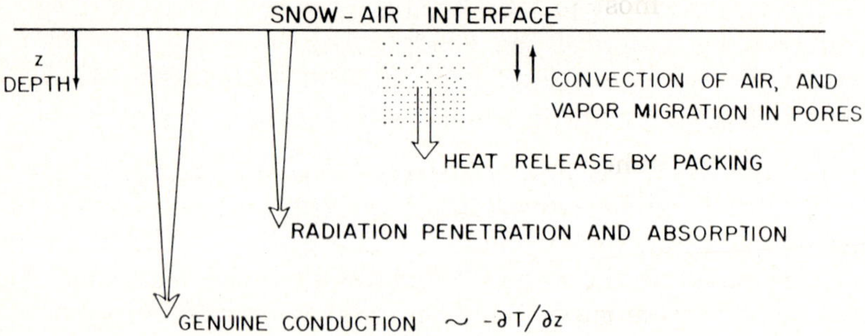

Fig. 8. Variety of processes possibly involved in vertical transfer of heat in a layer of snow, with solar radiation intercepted at the surface as the source of energy.

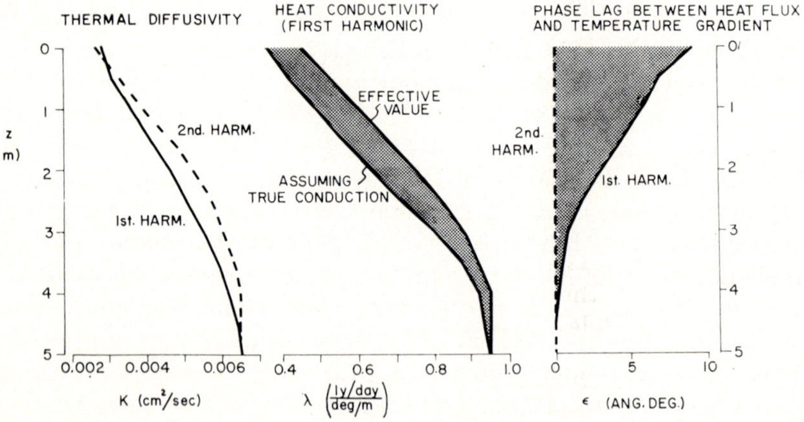

Fig. 9. Results of analysis of snow temperature, observed at Amundsen-Scott Station (1958), based on annual and semi-annual cycles in snow layer between 0 and 5 m.

release by packing which like (2) will be largely independent of a temperature gradient, and (4) convection of air in pores and water vapor migration possibly dependent on absolute temperature as well as vertical gradients. Figure 9 summarizes results of data analysis of South Pole observations as reported by Dalrymple *et al.* (1963, 1966). Among the three different items shown for comparison on Figure 9, the third, that is, the phase lag between vertical heat flux (derived from vertical integration of local time derivatives of snow temperature with specific heat per unit volume as a parameter) and vertical temperature gradient, appears to demonstrate most conclusively the role of non-conductive processes. It is suggested that their effects decrease gradually with depth, to become practically insignificant at and below 3 m. However, the method depicted in Figure 9 will work satisfactorily only when the second harmonic is relatively large. Direct measurements and evaluation were reported by Weller and Schwerdtfeger (1968). More work of this nature is desirable. But again, it can be stated that the test-tube potential of antarctic snow layers appears to be remarkable.

MICROMETEOROLOGICAL STRATIFICATION OF AIR TEMPERATURE AND WIND SPEED

During the years prior to the International Geophysical Year I was engaged in micrometeorological field research at the U.S. Air Force Cambridge Research Directorate. At this organization I found understanding and support for my proposal of a multi-institutional field program and was entrusted with the organization of a sizable out-of-doors experiment known as the "Great Plains Turbulence Field Program of 1953" (Lettau and Davidson, 1957). One year later, upon being asked for an opinion, I had decided to advise the Air Force against including a micrometeorological program in antarctic IGY activities. In view of snowdrift and extreme cold problems, I believed that in the severe climate and microclimate of Antarctica the required relatively sensitive mast profile equipment would probably function poorly, and that human observers would be handicapped greatly by cold fingers in performing the necessary fine adjustments and delicate matchings of micrometeorological sensors. Fortunately, such advice did not carry too far. Independently of the Air Force, the U.S. Army Quartermaster Corps organized a micrometeorological program, first in Little America and then at the South Pole, with Paul Dalrymple in charge. I am convinced now that detailed micrometeorological measurements in the lowest stratum of the antarctic atmosphere are not only feasible but offer exceptional opportunities for the study of low-atmospheric inversion effects and some of their disturbances occurring naturally.

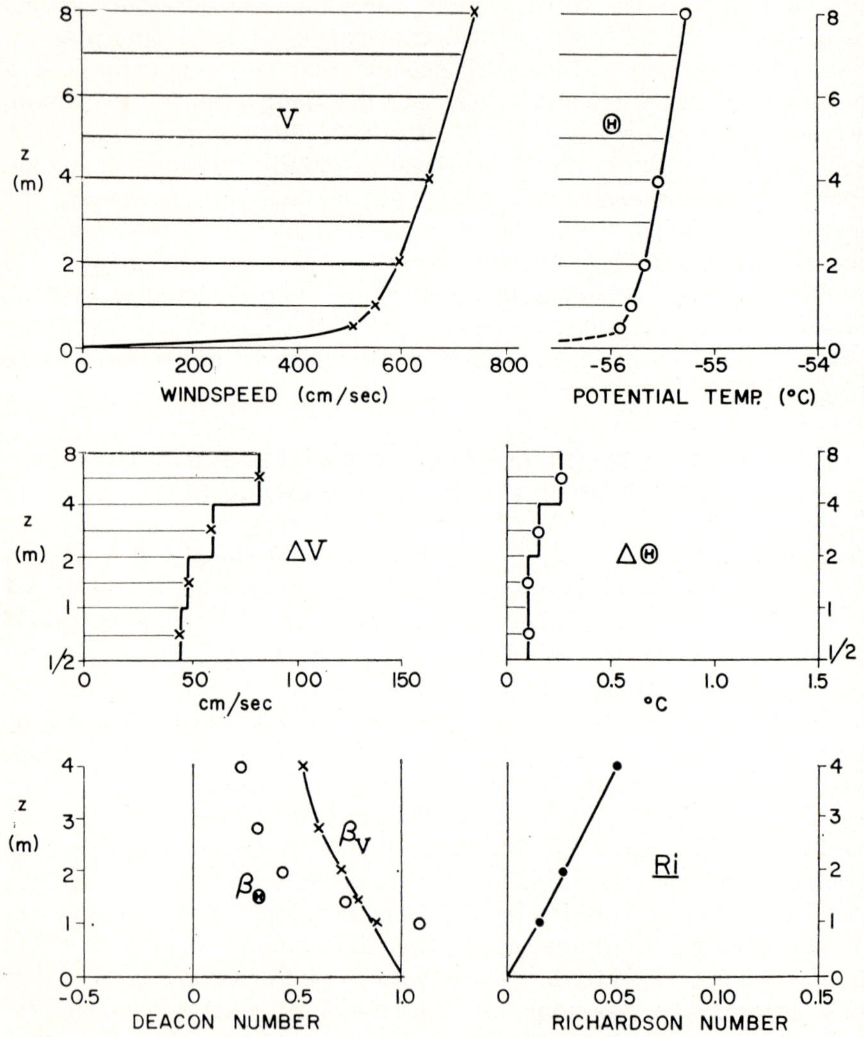

Fig. 10. Structure of vertical profiles of wind speed (V, cm/sec) and potential temperature (Θ, °C) in the lower 8 m of atmosphere at Amundsen-Scott Station. Shown are representative averages of thirty runs observed in 1958, for which the 1-m Richardson number was between 0.0134 and 0.0141.

Two composite graphs illustrate this. They show simultaneous profiles of potential temperature and wind speed in the lowest 8 m at the South Pole (Figs. 10 and 11). Average conditions for 30 hours of profile data are shown for relatively moderate Richardson numbers in Figure 10, and for relatively extreme Richardson num-

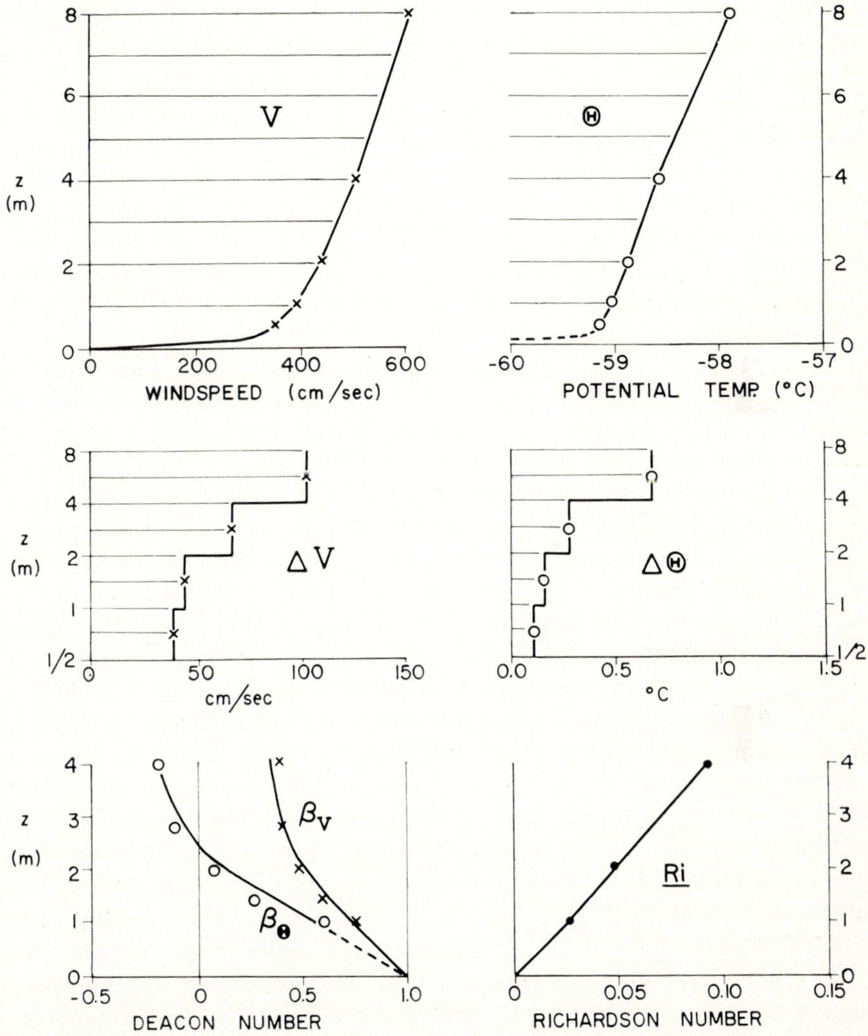

Fig. 11. Structure of vertical profiles of wind speed (V, cm/sec) and potential temperature (Θ, °C) in the lower 8 m of atmosphere at Amundsen-Scott Station. Shown are representative averages of thirty runs observed in 1958 for which the 1-m Richardson number was between 0.023 and 0.025.

bers in Figure 11. Actual Richardson numbers and their dependency on height are found on the lower right of each graph. The upper third shows profiles of wind speed and potential temperature linearly versus height; the center part the corresponding vertical differences (using a geometric rather than linear height scale) for the four adjacent pairs of "double levels" of Dalrymple's array of micrometeorological sensors; and, on the lower part of the graphs, the vertical profiles (again with a linear height scale) of such non-dimensional characteristics as the two Deacon numbers (β_v, and β_Θ) and the Richardson number (*Ri*). The Deacon number is the best and only truly objective measure of profile curvature; a value of unity corresponds exactly to a profile which is strictly logarithmic in height. Figures 10 and 11 illustrate several interesting facts: (1) Deacon numbers in general are smaller than unity, but there are trends strongly suggesting unity as an asymptotic value at height zero; (2) the profile of potential temperature departs from logarithmic curvature significantly more than the profile of wind speed; (3) for relatively extreme *Ri*-number, the Deacon number of the profile of potential temperature (β_Θ) may become negative, while the Deacon number of the wind profile (β_v) remains positive. The actual profile of potential temperature in Figure 11 shows that in case of extreme departure from logarithmic curvature there appears an "inflection point" (as can be seen near the 4-meter level of the Θ profile curve) confirming the mathematical implications of a negative Deacon number as a measure of profile curvature. Dalrymple *et al.* (1963, 1966) provided more detail concerning the statistical relationship between Richardson numbers (which represent an *independent* variable or a "scaling factor" of micrometeorological theories) and the Deacon numbers, at the same level where *Ri* is calculated. (Note that the Deacon numbers represent *dependent* variables which require the existence of an empirical or theoretical function between them and *Ri.*) The establishment of a "universally accepted" β versus *Ri* relationship for micrometeorological surface layer conditions, including extreme inversion as well as lapse cases, must be taken as the only truly objective basis for the testing of micrometeorological theories.

Another important advantage of the use of Deacon number profiles is that they permit us to derive objectively the two geometric characteristics of micrometeorological profile structure, which are the aerodynamic roughness length (z_0) of the ground surface and the zero-point displacement (D) of a mast-array of sensors, without the prerequisite of having to measure profile structure during adiabatic surface-layer conditions. Even in recent literature there appears to be confusion concerning the physical meaning of the two lengths z_0 and D; for clarification reference can be made to a discussion of the problem in Lettau (1967a, 1969a). The value of z_0 is a physical surface characteristic of the micrometeorological site; in contrast, the value of D is the vertical adjustment between the aerodynamically defined zero-level of the logarithmic or extended model of the wind profile, and the arbitrary datum from which anemometer heights are measured, which is usually the physical point where a vertical line through the string of anemometers intersects solid ground. Obviously, z_0 must be invariant with respect to arbitrary raisings and lowerings of the mast assembly as a whole, as long as the relative positions of the anemometers remain fixed, while the value of D must vary exactly by the amount by which the mast assembly is arbitrarily displaced in the vertical from one run to another. Lettau (1967a) described wind profile experiments on the ice of Lake Mendota in Madison, Wisconsin, where z_0 was artificially controlled by obstacle layout while D could be controlled independently by the above-mentioned technique.

The problem of objective distinction between z_0 and D is important for antarctic micrometeorology because snow accumulation will normally affect D for stationary mast installation at a site but not necessarily z_0 of the surroundings. It may be added that a new formula for estimating z_0 from geometrical and statistical distribution properties of the roughness elements was derived as a result of the Lake Mendota experiments (Lettau, 1969a). G. E. Weller (1968) tested the formula for sea ice as well as the typical cusped blue ice surface at Mawson Station and found relatively close agreement between predicted estimates (z_0 = 0.015 cm and 0.2 cm) and values derived from wind profile measurements (z_0 = 0.013 cm and 0.23 cm).

COMPLEXITIES OF TEMPERATURE PROFILE STRUCTURE AND OPTICAL REFRACTION PHENOMENA

Air temperatures in the micrometeorological layer show a more complex behavior than the regularity exhibited in the seasonal trends of snow temperature. This is evidenced, for example, by the isopleth pattern shown in Figure 12. While there is a pronounced tendency of orderly damping and phase-lagging of the annual wave in the snow, the mean isotherms in the air are arranged in nearly vertical lines which suggests near-zero phase lags

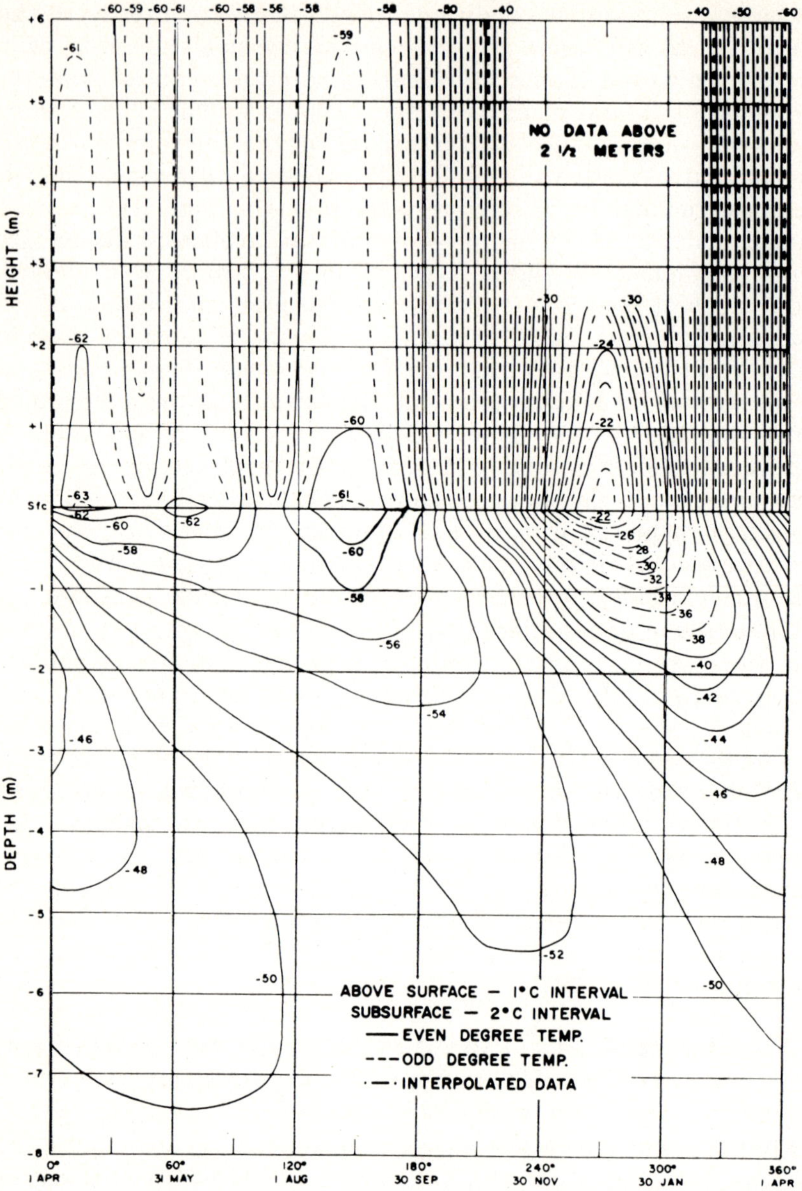

Fig. 12. Annual variation (1958) in representative temperature fields at both sides of the air-snow interface, illustrated by mean isotherms in the layer from 8 m below to 6 m above the surface at Amundsen-Scott Station (Dalrymple *et al.* 1966).

and only a small rate of amplitude reduction with height, at least within the lowest few meters. No mathematical trick could transform the isotherm structure in air into a pattern which is similar to that in the snow. Two physical reasons for this are: (1) heat conduction is essentially molecular and quasi-homogeneous in the snow, but it is turbulent in the air with a thermal diffusivity that increases significantly with increasing height from a very low surface value; (2) a few meters below the surface the snow is undisturbed by external influences, while in the air above the micrometeorological layer a great diversity of processes occurs (including advection, subsidence, and re-radiation) which affects significantly the thermal structure of the lower levels.

Figures 10 and 11 show that windspeeds at the Pole Station are relatively high. It can be said that a well-defined overall air motion is a prerequisite for some approach to "order" in the micrometeorological layer. Occasionally, however, the low-level windspeed is reduced to small value over vast antarctic regions. Then, there is a possibility that infrared radiation from relatively warm cloud bases can produce (for about a few hours at a time) surface heating even during the winter night. The directional shear of wind may also become quite extreme or even erratic, as evidenced by recordings from the 150-foot micrometeorological tower at Plateau Station.

Following my suggestion at the pre-planning phase for additional observations at Plateau Station, M. Sponholz set up during the first year of Plateau Station occupancy a horizontal array of three optical targets to document photographically day-to-day changes in the refraction of light in the lower atmosphere. Each target consisted of a rod inclined 45° toward the ground, supported by a 10-foot-tall pole, at distances of 1,000, 2,000, and 3,000 feet from the station. The inclined rods were initially marked by colored strips, and later by strings of electric lights brought to Plateau Station by M. Kuhn at the beginning of the second year. Because the index of refraction in air is a function of air density, the vertical temperature profile corresponds to density stratification in the lower atmosphere which causes a curvature of horizontal and near-horizontal optical rays. This in turn will distort the visual or photographic appearance of the target. In a mathematical "inversional" process, the vertical temperature profile may be recovered from measured ray-curvature. Many applications of this principle are reported in the literature. In comparison with previous techniques, the use of the slant-target line has the advantage

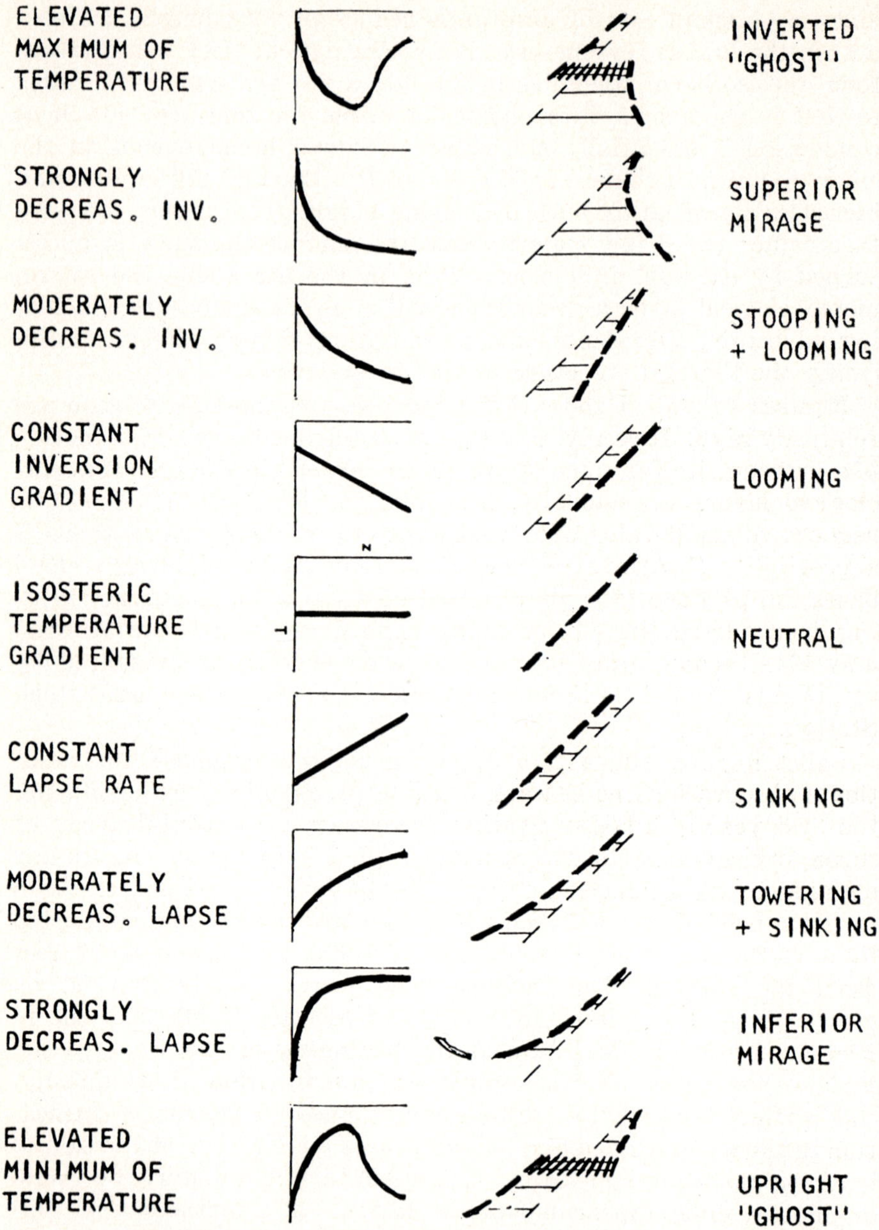

Fig. 13. Schematic illustration showing how a "slant-line target" (thin dashes in upper part) will be optically distorted (into heavy-dash configurations) by atmospheric refraction if the vertical profile of air temperature corresponds to cases as indicated in the lower part. For comparison with the text and with the photographs shown in Figure 14, turn figure by 90° so that the temperature profile curves appear below the target distortions.

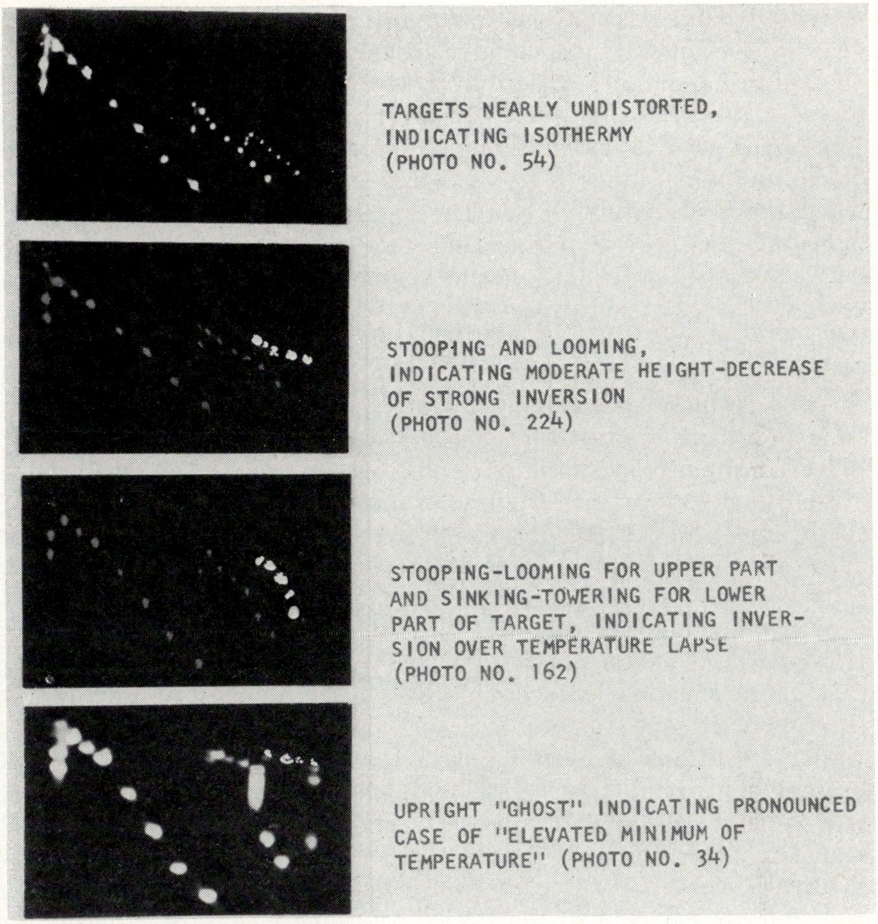

Fig. 14. Four typical examples of optical distortion, caused by refraction of light in the lower 3 m of atmosphere at Plateau Station. Three lighted "slant-line targets" were photographed with a telelens camera by M. Kuhn, 1958. Explanatory text refers to terms as defined in Figure 13.

that simultaneous refraction effects over a height range can be most readily documented photographically, provided that proper distances and target sizes are chosen. In the upper part of Figure 13 a systematic series of predicted distortions of a dashed 45° slant line is indicated, each accompanied in the lower half by a schematic sketch of the respective temperature profile within the air layer between camera and target points which could generate the indicated distortion. Note that the ordinate extends only over a few meters, whereas the abscissa ranges over several degrees centigrade. Consequently, the small (although over larger height intervals quite important) difference between isothermal and isopycnic temperature gradients (0.00°/m versus −0.03°/m) can be ignored. The terms used to describe target deformation are: "sinking" and "looming" when there is no distortion, "towering" and "stooping" when there is distortion, to the extreme cases of "mirages" and "ghosts" (See, for example, Johnson, 1954). The correspondence between target deformation and vertical structure of temperature is theoretically straightforward.

In a preliminary testing of the theory, Figure 14 shows four pictures taken by M. Kuhn during the second antarctic winter and selected from several hundred similar photographs. Tentative results of direct temperature measurements along the tower show indeed frequently elevated minimums which explain the appearance of ghosts as indicated in Figure 13 and photographed in Figure 14; for example, the temperature near the five-foot level is lower than at two feet or at ten feet. The systematic matching of photographically documented ray curvature with simultaneous direct thermal probings has not yet been achieved; it is planned for future work. However, the photographic evidence appears to be so convincing that there remains little doubt that measurements of optical refraction can serve as an accurate method of thermal probing. Under conditions of extreme stratification, especially with ghosts present, all geodetic surveying methods employing optical or electromagnetic rays will hardly be reliable without consideration of actual ray curvature. It is also likely that atmospheric conditions of erratic vertical profile structure are not uniform horizontally, and that optical rays in the lower atmosphere may be laterally as well as vertically curved. By using lamps of different colors it became evident in Mr. Kuhn's photographs taken at Plateau Station, that occasionally not only "up" and "down" but also "left" and "right" were interchanged.

LARGE- TO MESOSCALE WIND SYSTEMS OVER ANTARCTICA; GEOTRIPTIC THERMAL WINDS OF THE SLOPED INVERSION, IN CONTRAST TO KATABATIC FLOW

In the free troposphere over Antarctica, the prominent feature of the large-scale temperature field is that of approximate symmetry with respect to the South Pole. Hence, prevailing tendencies towards hydrostatic-geostrophic equilibrium cause a gigantic circumpolar vortex. At a given upper level the strength of the zonal winds reflects the temperature difference between the rim and the center of the continent. Geostrophic equilibrium implies a balance between horizontal pressure gradient force and Coriolis force. Hydrostatic equilibrium implies that the horizontal temperature gradient is rigorously coupled to the vertical shear of the geostrophic wind. Accordingly, the vector difference of geostrophic motion between an upper and an adjacent lower level is conventionally referred to as the thermal wind of the layer bounded by these two levels. Thermal winds are highly organized and significant in the troposphere over Antarctica.

The transition zone between the free troposphere and the ice is the "inversion layer," the antarctic version of a continent-wide aerodynamic boundary layer. The following four facts are important for understanding the characteristic winds in the inversion layer: (1) the dynamics of this boundary layer cannot be treated separately from that of the overlying free-tropospheric vortex; (2) in addition to pressure gradient and Coriolis forces, frictional resistance (due to both internal Reynolds stress and external ground drag) enters the balance as a third force which changes the geostrophic equilibrium into a "geotriptic" equilibrium, if the nomenclature proposed by Johnson (1966) is used; (3) climatic station data and averaged results from aerological soundings, especially when combined to form meridional cross sections, show that isothermal surfaces possess gradients and curvatures which are similar to gradients and curvature of ice-dome topography; and (4) the thickness of the inversion layer amounts normally to a few hundred meters which is necessary and sufficient to generate, over typical antarctic (large-scale) terrain slopes, thermal winds of a magnitude comparable to that of the average geostrophic wind at the top of the boundary layer (that is to say, at the first level of maximum temperature above a given point on the continent).

Items (3) and (4) imply that in a downward approach from the free atmosphere towards the icy ground, once the level of maximum temperature has been passed, a terrain-dependent thermal wind effect must be encountered which tends to turn any upper geostrophic vector into the locally fixed direction parallel to the general contour lines of the ice dome. The efficiency of such forcing increases in direct proportion to (1) the thickness of the inversion layer, (2) the inclination angle of the large-scale ice-dome topography, and (3) the total temperature drop from top to bottom of the inversion.

A series of recent publications has convincingly documented that it is the rule rather than the exception that thermal winds caused by antarctic ice-dome slopes in the adhering inversion layer overrule the dynamics of existing free tropospheric pressure disturbances and generate, here as nowhere else on earth, a typical surface wind regime. Reference can be made to work by Lettau in Dalrymple *et al.* (1963, 1966), Lettau and Schwerdtfeger (1967), or Lettau (1967b). Recently, Schwerdtfeger and Mahrt (1968) employed as a relevant statistical measure of wind variability the conventionally defined constancy; in their systematic analysis of the aerological soundings during several seasons at the three important inland stations, South Pole, Vostok, and Byrd, they find that constancy is very high with a range between 80 to 91 percent for the surface winds, and remarkably lower with a range between 27 to 55 percent for the upper winds (at the top of the local inversion layers). Schwerdtfeger and Mahrt reported that near the ground the directional alignment was clearly overruling and that the cross-contour flow or the outflow rate of the cold air of the inversion layer was relatively small.

As in any aerodynamic boundary layer, the Reynolds stresses are important for the antarctic inversion layer, in spite of relatively low turbulence intensity due to stable density stratification. Independent studies have established that the frictional effect may be additive to the thermal wind effect, at least within reasonably realistic limits of error tolerance. The simplifying assumption of a constant thermal wind (which is the same as a linearly height-varying geostrophic wind) yields interesting distortions of the Ekman spiral, as first discussed more than 50 years ago by Hesselberg and Sverdrup (Lettau, 1967b). For antarctic inversion conditions, a more realistic model is that of exponentially height-varying thermal wind, as discovered by Mahrt (Mahrt and Schwerdtfeger, 1970). Thermal wind distortions can be added not only to the Ekman spiral but also to other theoretical wind profiles, such as the "Variangular Spiral" discussed by Lettau and Dabberdt (1970). Obviously, this brief summary illustrates clearly the value of the antarctic atmosphere as a test tube for wind profile theories. The importance of providing improved observational data, especially vector wind profile data from micrometeorological tower installations, is also obvious. Excellent examples are the interesting records from Plateau Station, with detailed measurements of wind speed and direction in the lower 32 m of the inversion layer.

The main result of presently available theoretical and observational analyses can be summarized by saying that the equilibrium dynamics of the lower troposphere, including the inversion layer, over the Antarctic Continent are controlled by air motions, generated by the large-scale ice-dome contour, which must be classified as "geotriptic thermal winds." These represent a topographic modification of the basic geostrophic-thermal vortex system which exists around the South Pole and dominates the dynamics of the free troposphere. In noteworthy contrast, older concepts and studies dealt nearly exclusively with a scheme of a direct gravitational circulation known in the literature as katabatic winds. According to the *Glossary of Meteorology* of the American Meteorological Society, this term is synonymous with gravity wind and denotes in atmospheric dynamics any wind blowing down an incline. Mather and Miller (1967) have summarized literature with special emphasis on katabatic winds in Antarctica. However, genuine katabatic flow may be important only near the coastline. By its very nature a katabatic wind will rapidly exhaust a pre-existing cold-air supply and thus will tend to be unsteady. Only exceptionally will a gravity wind represent an equilibrium flow, but even then it must differ significantly from the "geotriptic" thermal wind of the sloped inversion which has been established as the characteristic flow over the major portion of the Antarctic Continent. To justify this statement, a general discourse on the physical background of atmospheric circulation theorems is helpful.

Let **i**,**j**,**k** denote the three unit vectors in space (**k** positive vertically upwards), and $\mathbf{V} = \mathbf{i}\,u + \mathbf{j}\,v + \mathbf{k}\,w$ the three-dimensional wind vector. According to Newton's law, the vector of acceleration, $d\mathbf{V}/dt$, must equal the resultant of all forces acting on the unit mass,

$$d\mathbf{V}/dt = \Sigma\, \alpha\, \mathbf{F} \tag{1}$$

where α = specific volume = $1/\rho$ (where ρ = air density) and $\mathbf{F} = \mathbf{i}\,F_1 + \mathbf{j}\,F_2 + \mathbf{k}\,F_3$ denotes the three spatial components of any among several forces, including gravitational, pressure gradient, Coriolis, Reynolds stress, viscous, and inertia. Of prime importance are forces that cause circulations of air. Relevant theorems (such as those by Kelvin or Bjerknes) are most universally derived if the vector-operator *curl* is applied to equation (1). Following general rules of vector calculus, one transforms first the right-hand side of Newton's law,

$$curl\, \Sigma\, \alpha\, \mathbf{F} = \Sigma\, curl\, \alpha\, \mathbf{F} = \Sigma\, \{(grad\, \alpha) \times \mathbf{F} + \alpha\, curl\, \mathbf{F}\} \quad (2a)$$

and then the left-hand side,

$$\begin{aligned} curl\ (\mathrm{d}\mathbf{V}/\mathrm{dt}) &= \mathrm{d}(curl\ \mathbf{V})/\mathrm{dt} + (curl\ \mathbf{V})(div\ \mathbf{V}) \\ &\quad - ((curl\ \mathbf{V})\ grad)\mathbf{V} \end{aligned} \quad (2b)$$

or, upon re-arrangement of terms,

$$\begin{aligned} \mathrm{d}(curl\ \mathbf{V})/\mathrm{dt} &= -\ (curl\ \mathbf{V})(div\ \mathbf{V}) + ((curl\ \mathbf{V})grad)\mathbf{V} \\ &\quad + curl(\mathrm{d}\mathbf{V}/\mathrm{dt}) \end{aligned} \quad (2b')$$

Let subscripts x,y,z, denote partial derivatives with respect to x,y, and z. Defining identities are:

$$div\ \mathbf{V} = u_x + v_y + w_z\ ; \qquad grad\ \alpha = \mathbf{i}\ \alpha_x + \mathbf{j}\ \alpha_y + \mathbf{k}\ \alpha_z\ ;$$
$$curl\ \mathbf{V} = \mathbf{i}(w_y - v_z) + \mathbf{j}(u_z - w_x) + \mathbf{k}(v_x - u_y) = \mathbf{i}\ \xi + \mathbf{j}\ \eta + \mathbf{k}\ \zeta\ .$$

The rectangular components of *curl* **V** represent the three vorticities, ζ about the (vertical) z-axis, η about the y-axis, and ξ about the x-axis. For each of these, Newton's law yields a rigorous equation which expresses the time-rate of vorticity change, assuming $w_z = -u_x - v_y$,

$$\mathrm{d}\zeta/\mathrm{dt} = \zeta\ w_z + (\xi\ w_x + \eta\ w_y) + \Sigma\ \{(\alpha\ F_2)_x - (\alpha\ F_1)_y\}\ , \quad (3a)$$

$$\mathrm{d}\eta/\mathrm{dt} = \eta\ v_y + (\zeta\ v_z + \xi\ v_x) + \Sigma\ \{(\alpha\ F_1)_z - (\alpha\ F_3)_x\}\ , \quad (3b)$$

$$\mathrm{d}\xi/\mathrm{dt} = \xi\ u_x + (\eta\ u_y + \zeta\ u_z) + \Sigma\ \{(\alpha\ F_3)_y - (\alpha\ F_2)_z\}\ . \quad (3c)$$

The members on the right-hand sides are conventionally named the divergence term, the twisting term, and the force terms, respectively.

As is customary, let the x-axis point towards east and the y-axis towards north so that u is the zonal or west-component, and v the meridional or south component of air motion. To emphasize the relevant feature of antarctic circulation it appears permissible to assume polar symmetry in both ice-dome topography and atmospheric variables (pressure as well as temperature). Then, truly katabatic flow would occur exclusively in meridional-vertical planes radially emerging from the South Pole. Only the wind components v and w would be involved and, correspondingly, only the rate of production of ξ-vorticity is of interest, $\xi = w_y - v_z$. If indeed u, as well as all derivatives of u, vanishes, neither divergence nor twisting terms in equation (3c) differ from zero. The force terms must include gravity ($-\mathbf{k}\ \rho\ g$), pressure gradient ($grad\ p = \mathbf{j}\ p_y + \mathbf{k}\ p_z$), and Reynolds stress ($-\mathbf{j}\ (\overline{v'w'})_z$, which may be parameterized with the aid of eddy diffusivity, K, as $\mathbf{j}(K\ v_z)_z$, if K is large in comparison with kinematic viscosity). Furthermore, there is the Coriolis force $\mathbf{i}(2\ \omega\ v\ \sin\phi - w\ \cos\phi)$, if $u = 0$ and where ω = angular speed of the earth's rotation and ϕ = geographic latitude. Hence, equation (3c) applies, and transforms into the following,

$$d\xi/dt = \partial\xi/\partial t + v\ \xi_y + w\ \xi_z = \alpha_z\ p_y - \alpha_y\ p_z + (\overline{v'w'})_{zz} \quad (4)$$

Equation (4) permits steadiness (that is, $\partial\xi/\partial t = 0$), and the resulting form, considering that $p_z = -\rho\ g$, served indeed as the basic dynamics equation in Prandtl's original theory of katabatic winds; reference may be made to the discussion in Lettau (1966). Also involved in the Prandtl model are continuity equations for mass as well as heat. However, as shown by Lettau (1966) the theoretically assumed thermal equilibrium between downslope advection of cold air and cross-slope vertical eddy diffusion of heat turns out to impose unrealistic demands on the snow-surface energy budget (including longwave radiation as well as subsurface heat flux). Lettau (1966) supported this conclusion with the discussion of the theoretical coupling between wind and temperature profiles in the surface layer, with the aid of a result of Prandtl's theory which is usually ignored but establishes a useful relationship between ground drag of katabatic winds and eddy flux of heat.

The improbability of an equilibrium nature of genuine katabatic flow over Antarctica, if described by equation (4) for $\partial\xi/\partial t = 0$, is furthermore supported by strictly dynamical facts. Suppose that for an initially quiet atmosphere with polar symmetry (in fields of air pressure and temperature), ξ-vorticity is generated according to equation (4) which will produce finite v and w components within any y,z-plane containing the polar axis. As quoted before, the Coriolis force, which acts on such v,w circulation, has strictly a zonal component, whereupon Newton's law, equation (1), yields

$$du/dt = 2\ \omega\ (v\ \sin\phi - w\ \cos\phi) \approx 2\ \omega\ v\ \sin\phi\,, \quad (5)$$

because, near 90°S, $\cos\phi$ is small in comparison with $\sin\phi$; and for average antarctic terrain slope, w is significantly smaller than v. Now, the earth's angular speed is $\omega = 2\ \pi$ per 24 hours which means in equation (5) that for any steady v-value the Coriolis acceleration generates a u-component at such a rate that u becomes equal to v within the relatively short time-increment of $\delta t = 24/4\ \pi = 1.9$ hours. Consequently, after only two hours duration of a steady v-component, the Coriolis effect will build up a u-component such that the flow direction has turned closer toward the direction of the contour line than the fall line of the slope.

Let us return to the vorticity theorem. All three equations (3a,b,c) demonstrate clearly that ξ-vorticity can exist alone only as long as three conditions are satisfied: the u-component must remain zero, the existing v- and w-components must be independent of x, and none of the forces can have zonal or vertical *curl*-components. In other words, whenever w_x or $(\alpha F_2)_x - (\alpha F_1)_z$ exists, ζ-vorticity will be generated according to equation (3a); and, correspondingly, whenever v_x or $(\alpha F_1)_z - (\alpha F_3)_x$ exists, η-vorticity will be generated according to equation (3b). Hence, it becomes necessary to consider the complete form of the Coriolis acceleration,

$$\mathbf{i}\, 2\, \omega\, (v \sin\phi - w \cos\phi) - \mathbf{j}\, 2\, \omega\, u \sin\phi + \mathbf{k}\, 2\, \omega\, u \cos\phi\, .$$

It can readily be verified that with initially generated wind-components v and w, the y-derivative of the originally zonal Coriolis force will finally lead to dominance of ζ-vorticity. This is indeed the cause of the polar vortex in the free atmosphere, while the corresponding equilibrium in the boundary layer is also dependent on ice-dome topography in the form of "geotriptic thermal" winds of the sloped inversion. The above discussion shows that "geotriptic" alignment of initially katabatic winds will be perfected within the relatively short time interval of a fraction of a day. These conclusions are even more forcefully supported by the divergence theorem which exists in analogy to the vorticity theorem and which is derived by taking the divergence of equation (1); this will be omitted here for reason of space.

Lastly, let us remark that η-vorticity may be generated according to equation (3b), either via the twisting term, if ξ-vorticity exists; or as a consequence of the divergence term (considering that $u_x \approx - v_y - w_z$). A band-like structure of helical vortices can result which may be related to the often reported horizontal nonuniformity and pulsating nature of the occasionally very strong katabatic winds of the coastal regions of Antarctica.

In summary it can be said that vorticity considerations are establishing another test-tube aspect of the antarctic atmosphere, in a verification of the classical "geodynamic paradox." As described by Hess (1959), this paradox states that on the rotating earth a particle subject to a constant force does not move parallel to the force with constant acceleration (as, to be expected according to Newton's law, equation (1), for conservative forces), but ultimately will move perpendicular to the force with constant speed (that is to say, in geostrophic equilibrium). The physical reason for this seeming contradiction is the action of the Coriolis force.

The significance of the geodynamic paradox is obvious. If it is ignored, undue emphasis will be put on direct circulations such as those represented by gravity winds. A classic example of its disregard can be seen in Hobbs' concept of the "glacial anticyclone," as propagated in the twenties of this century but later abandoned (Hare, 1951; Lettau and Schwerdtfeger, 1967). The latter authors point out that instead of Hobbs' semi-permanent glacial high-pressure center over Greenland or Antarctica, it is more realistic to expect a cold-core low-pressure center over an icedome of meso-to large-scale dimensions, with corresponding important consequences for the outflow rate of air (reduction, or even a partial reversal to cyclonic inflow).

CALCULATED CLIMATE ASSUMING THAT THE SOUTH POLE REGION WERE SNOWLESS

As a last problem let me briefly discuss an antarctic application of my recently developed theoretical model of "climatonomy" (Lettau, 1969). This scheme permits a calculation or theoretical prediction of diurnal as well as annual courses of surface temperature on any planet, if only energy supply from the central star (the sun), and physical parameters of the submedium, the interface, and the overlying atmosphere are prescribed. Application to the South Pole region means that only annual variation needs to be considered. The primary forcing function, F, is insolation absorbed at the ground surface, $F = (1-a)G$, where G = global radiation and a = surface albedo. The potential insolation as discussed earlier is received at the outer fringe of the atmosphere. It must be corrected for attenuation due to gases, cloud elements, and aerosol particles in the air, then supplemented by diffuse sky radiation. Global radiation at the South Pole has been measured, and observations of surface albedo are also available (Dalrymple, 1966; Dalrymple *et al.*, 1966). Figure 15 illustrates the seasonal trend of F for the South Pole; on the left side as presently valid, on the right side as would exist if the surface albedo were 0.20 instead of 0.85. Note that due to high snow albedo, multiple reflection between surface and air, and the so-called "back-scatterance" of the sky, b^*, the global radiation G_s observed over snow of albedo a_s will be modified into G over a surface having an albedo a, as follows:

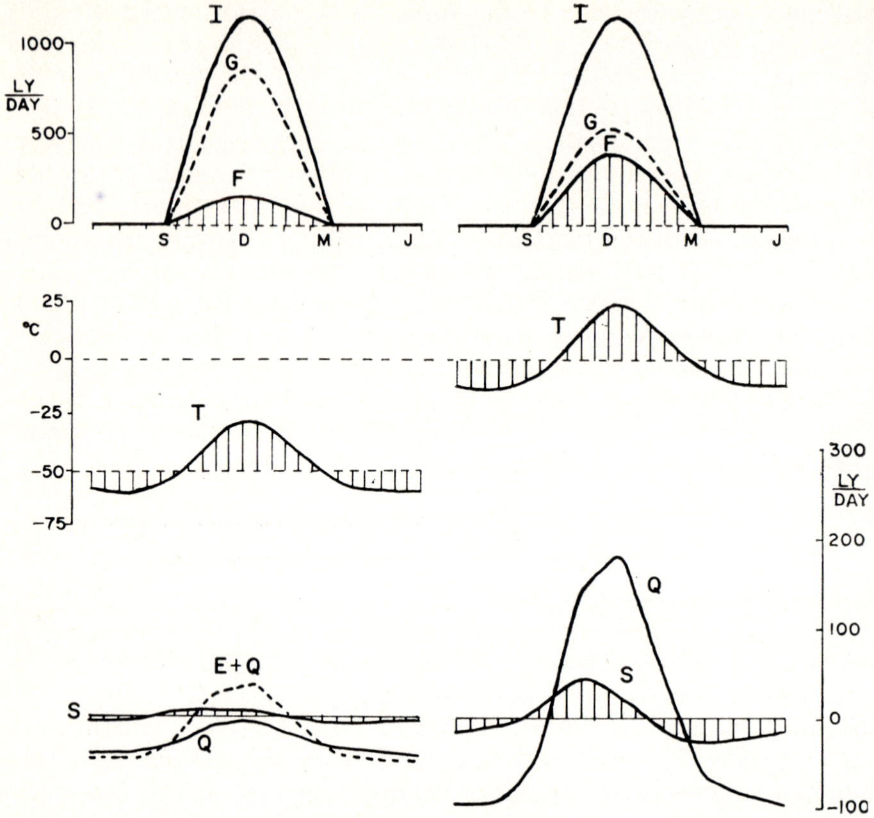

Fig. 15. Annual trends at Amundsen-Scott Station of: potential insolation; global radiation, G, and forcing function F = (1-a)G; also of air temperature T (at standard screen height), and of surface heat budget constituents (fluxes of sensible heat into snow, S, and into air, Q; and E = latent heat into the air by evaporation). On the left side, variables are shown as observed; on the right side, shown trends are calculated for conditions of an assumed rocky interface (albedo 0.20 instead of 0.85; surface roughness $z_0 = 5.0$ cm instead of 0.018 cm; thermal admittance of the submedium 45 millilangleys per (deg. $sec^{1/2}$) instead of 10; and no moisture available for evaporation, E = O).

$$G = G_s\ (1 - a_s b^*)/(1 - a\ b^*)\ , \tag{6a}$$

so that the forcing function changes as follows,

$$F = F_s\ (1-a) \cdot (1 - a_s b^*)/(1 - a_s) \cdot (1 - a\ b^*)\ . \tag{6b}$$

With an assumed b^*-value of 0.55, F/F_s will be 3.2 for the change in surface albedo from 0.85 to 0.20.

The model of surface temperature "climatonomy" will be described in detail elsewhere. It may suffice here to say that it is based on a Fourier expansion of the forcing function, under full consideration of all harmonics of a given cycle (for example, all six harmonics if the annual cycle is given by 12 monthly means). Data on Figure 15 were computed and illustrated with the aid of eight equidistant means (that is, for 8 ordinate values, on the following days: Jan. 1, Feb. 14, Apr. 1, May 15, etc.), requiring 4 harmonics, or specifically,

$$F = 1.53 + 2.37 \cos(nt+12^\circ) + 0.96 \cos(2nt+29^\circ) + 0.16 \cos(3nt+87^\circ) + 0.06 \cos(4nt+180^\circ) , \quad (7)$$

where the mean and the amplitudes are in millilangleys per second, and n is 2 π per 365 days, the annual frequency. The primary response function is surface temperature T_o. It is calculated with the aid of the predictor equation:

$$T_o(t) = \overline{T_o(F)} + \Sigma_i \, (\Delta_i F / Z_i) \cos(int - \delta_i - \zeta_i) \quad (8)$$

if the forcing function is given as

$$F(t) = \overline{F} + \Sigma_i \, \Delta_i F \cos(int - \delta_i) \; . \quad (9)$$

In equations (8) and (9) i is an integer varying from i = 1 to one-half the even number of required ordinate values. For each harmonic Z_i is the total impedance of the two-layer system (soil-interface-air) and ζ_i the phase lag of the response function. Parameterization is required to express the total impedance as a composite of partial impedances describing in detail the relationships between the constituents of the energy budget equation and surface temperature cycles,

$$F = \epsilon \, \sigma \, T_o^4 \, A^* + S_o + Q_o + E_o \quad (10)$$

where ϵ = emissivity of the surface, A^* the "Ångstrom ratio" (that is, the ratio of effective longwave radiation to emitted radiation). The other terms are as defined in the legend of Figure 15.

For each term on the right-hand side of equation (10), a series of steps is required involving numerical evaluation of the partial impedances and phase lags with the aid of pertinent parameters (such as thermal admittance of the submedium, aerodynamic roughness of the interface, eddy diffusivity of the air as estimated from geostrophic drag-coefficients, etc.). The thermal response of a hypothetically bare, rock-strewn, high South Polar plateau, under otherwise unchanged conditions, to the forcing function prescribed by equation (7) was derived as

$$T_o = 273 + 18.6\ cos(nt + 1°) + 6.7\ cos(2nt+16°) + 1.0\ cos(3nt+73°) + 0.3\ cos(4nt+165°)\ . (11)$$

Finally, a height reduction from T_o, to T at z = 180 to 200 cm (corresponding to standard level of air temperature observation at climatic stations) is made with the aid of previously determined Q_o-values and the friction velocity, under full consideration of effects of aerodynamic roughness changes as specified in the caption of Figure 15. Important for the evaluation of E_o are concepts summarized under the term "evapotranspiration climatonomy" (See Lettau, 1969).

A series of simplifying assumptions had to be made, which may ultimately be in need of revision. For example, effective longwave radiation was estimated for the modified surface using new surface temperature and emissivity but the same "Ångstrom ratio" as evaluated from present data. Also, a possible effect of shortwave radiation penetration into the snow, in contrast to the opaqueness of rocky ground, was not considered. However, it appears likely that there will be no radical change of the basic result. This suggests that with the simultaneous lowering of albedo and increase of surface roughness as well as thermal admittance, there is not only more energy input, but also more substantial carry-over of both soil-heat and air-heat storage from the sunlit to the dark season. Hence, the climate at the South Pole would be substantially warmer, accompanied by only slight increase of the seasonal difference between summer and winter temperatures. Not considered in this tentative model calculation is a feedback on the atmospheric vortex over the Antarctic Continent. Positive and relatively large Q_o values during the summer season shown on the lower right of Figure 15 will certainly eliminate the inversion layer over Antarctica. The problem is highly complex and will be taken up in future discussions.

References

Dalrymple, P. C., 1966. A physical climatology of the Antarctic Plateau. *Antarctic Research Series 9, Studies in Antarctic Meteorology,* edited by M. J. Rubin; pp. 195–231. Am. Geophys. Union, Washington, D.C.

Dalrymple, P. C., H. Lettau, and S. Wollaston, 1966. South Pole micrometeorology program (data analysis). *Antarctic Research Series 9, Studies in Antarctic Meteorology,* edited by M. J. Rubin; pp. 13–57. Am. Geophys. Union, Washington, D.C.

Hare, F. K., 1951. Some climatological problems of the Arctic and Subarctic. In *Compendium of Meteorology;* pp. 952–964. Am. Meteorol. Soc., Boston.

Hess, S. L., 1959. *Introduction to Theoretical Meteorology.* Holt, New York.

Johnson, J. E., 1954. *Physical Meteorology.* John Wiley and Sons, New York.

Johnson, W. B., Jr., 1966. The geotriptic wind, *Bull. Am. Meteorol. Soc., 47:* 982.

Lettau, H., 1966. A case study of katabatic flow on the South Polar Plateau, *Antarctic Research Series 9, Studies in Antarctic Meteorology,* edited by M. J. Rubin; pp. 1–11. Am. Geophys. Union, Washington, D.C.

Lettau, H., 1967a. Problems of micrometeorological measurements. In *The Collection and Processing of Field Data,* edited by E. F. Bradley and O. T. Denmead; sect. 1, pp 3–40. John Wiley and Sons, New York.

Lettau, H., 1967b. Small-to-large-scale features of boundary layer structure over mountain slopes. In *Proceedings of Symposium on Mountain Meteorology,* edited by E. Reiter and J. L. Rasmussen; sect. 1, pp. 1–74. Colorado State Univ., Fort Collins, Colo.

Lettau, H., 1969a. Note on aerodynamic roughness-parameter estimation on the basis of roughness element description. *J. Appl. Meteorol., 8:* 828–832.

Lettau, H., 1969b. Evapotranspiration climatonomy. *Monthly Weather Rev., 97:* 691–699.

Lettau, H., and W. Dabberdt, 1970. Variangular windspirals. *Boundary Layer Meteorol., 1:* 64–79.

Lettau, H., and B. Davidson (Editors), 1957. *Exploring the Atmosphere's First Mile;* two volumes, 578 pp. Pergamon Press, New York.

Lettau, H., and W. Schwerdtfeger, 1967. Dynamics of the surface-wind regime over the interior of Antarctica. *Antarctic J. U. S., 2:* 155–158.

Mahrt, L. J., and W. Schwerdtfeger, 1970. Ekman spirals for exponential thermal wind. *Boundary Layer Meteorol., 1:* 137–145.

Mather, K. B., and G. S. Miller, 1967. Notes of topographic factors affecting the surface wind in Antarctica, with special reference to katabatic winds. *Tech. Rept. Geophys. Inst. UAG R-189.* Univ. Alaska, College.

Schwerdtfeger, W., and L. Mahrt, 1968. The relation between the antarctic temperature inversion in the surface layer and its wind regime, *Proc. Int. Symp. Antarctic Glaciol. Explor. Dartmouth.* Hanover, N.H.

Sellers, W. D., 1965. *Physical Climatology.* Univ. Chicago Press.

Siple, P., 1959. *90 Degrees South,* (The Story of the American South Pole Conquest). G. P. Putnam's Sons, New York.

Weller, G., 1968. The heat budget and heat transfer processes in Antarctic Plateau ice and sea ice. *ANARE Sci. Repts., Ser. A (IV) Glaciology, Publ. No. 102.* Melbourne, Australia.

Weller, G., and P. Schwerdtfeger, 1968. Thermal properties and heat transfer processes of the snow of the central Antarctic Plateau. Paper No. 15, *Proc. Intern. Symp. Antarctic Glaciol. Explor. Dartmouth.* Hanover, N.H.

On the Interaction Between Antarctica and Middle Latitudes

HARRY VAN LOON

National Center for Atmospheric Research, Boulder, Colorado

Climatological data from Antarctica and the oceans in middle and high southern latitudes have revealed marked, often dominant, half-yearly components in the annual march of pressure, temperature contrasts, and wind. Schwerdtfeger and Prohaska (1956) demonstrated that neither phase nor amplitude made it likely that these half-yearly components are linked with the sun's passage twice a year across the equator. Rather, their cause should be sought in the regions where they happen.

PRESSURE

Pressure was the first atmospheric element in which the half-yearly components (second harmonics) were noted. The meager data available in the 1930's and 1940's revealed that the amplitude of the second harmonic in the surface pressure generally is large on the poleward side of the subtropics (Reuter, 1936; Wahl, 1942). But it was not till Schwerdtfeger's paper appeared in 1956 that a coherent picture emerged of the distribution of the second harmonic in the annual march of the surface pressure in middle and high southern latitudes. It turned out to be not only of comparatively large amplitude, but also of opposite phase in the two regions. As an example, the average amplitude of the second harmonic in the sea-level pressure at two parallels, representative of the two regions, is shown in Table 1. Although the amplitudes (half-ranges) may not be impressive, it should be noted that the harmonic accounts for a substantial portion of the total variance at both parallels, and that the phase reverses from one region to the other.

Table 1. Average amplitude, in millibars, of the second harmonic in the sea-level mean pressure at 50° and 70°S, its dates of maximums, and the percentage of the total variance for which it accounts.

	50°S	70°S
Amplitude	1.7	3.0
Dates	3 Apr/Oct	1 Jan/Jul
Percent	36	57

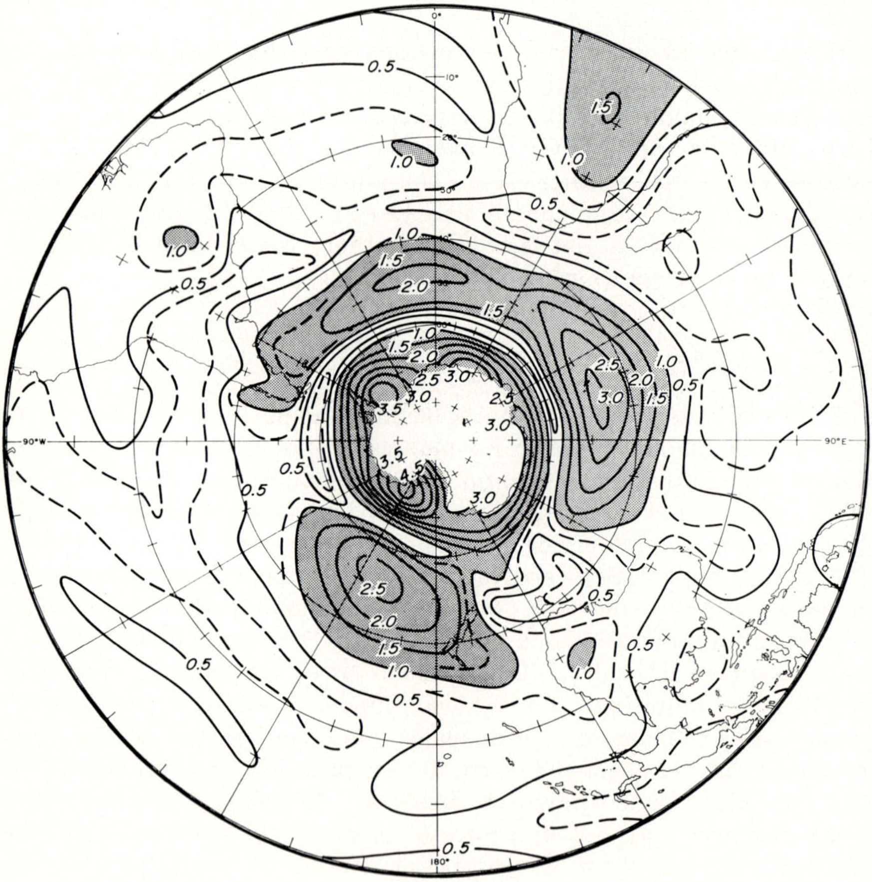

Fig. 1. Amplitude (mb) of the second harmonic in the annual march of mean sea-level pressure.

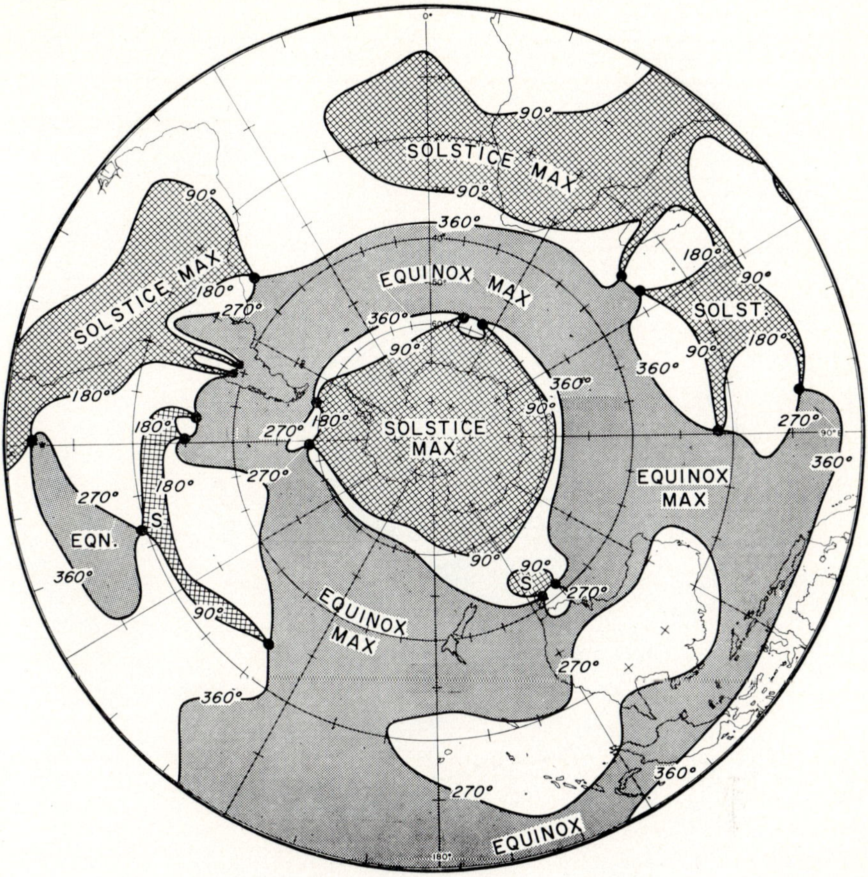

Fig. 2. Phase angle of the second harmonic in the annual march of mean sea-level pressure. On January 16 the angle = 90°.

Figures 1 to 3 show the distribution over the Southern Hemisphere of amplitude and phase angle of the second harmonic in the sea-level pressure, and the percentage of the total variance of the annual curve for which it accounts. In Figure 1 it is apparent that two of the areas where the amplitude exceeds one millibar (shaded) are systematically arranged with respect to each other: namely the ones in middle and polar latitudes. Comparison with Figure 3 shows that they are also the parts where the harmonic dominates the annual march. Figure 2 yields the further information that the phases are in complete opposition, the harmonic reaching maximums in the three weeks on either side of the equi-

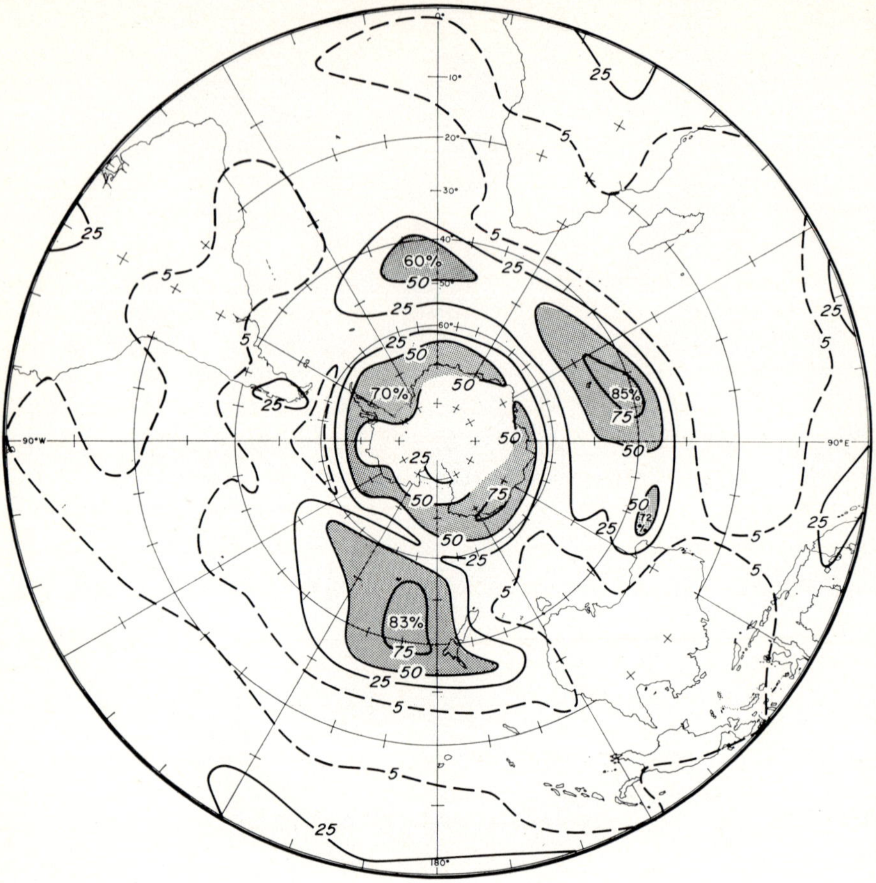

Fig. 3. The percentage of the total variance in the mean annual march of sea-level pressure which is accounted for by the second harmonic.

noxes in middle latitudes and of the solstices in the polar regions. A narrow belt along 60°S, where the amplitude tends toward zero, separates the two regions.

WIND

The fact that the second harmonic in the annual march of pressure accounts for a large share of the total variance, combined with the circumstance of phase reversal from middle to high latitudes, means that the pressure *difference* between the two regions must acquire a considerable half-yearly oscillation. Since the pressure decreases from middle to high latitudes, the latitudinal pressure difference must have maximums in the equinoctial periods. Because the size of the geostrophic wind is directly proportional to the pressure difference over a unit distance, it follows that the west-to-east (zonal) component of the wind at sea level in subpolar latitudes must have a large half-yearly oscillation with maximums in fall and spring.

That this is so may be seen in Figure 4. In the latitudes between 55° and 65°S the influence of the second harmonic on the shape of the annual curve is strong enough to create a wind maximum in each transition period.

At 50°S (Fig. 4) there is little variation during the year, but from 45° to 25°S a second harmonic again takes a hand in shaping the annual curves, though it can be seen directly that its phase must be the reverse of that at higher latitudes. The phase reversal at 50°S of the second harmonic in the *zonal wind* takes place because this is where the amplitude of the second harmonic in the sea-level *pressure* is largest. If the amplitude of the second harmonic in the *pressure* decreases along a meridian, this by itself is enough to produce a second harmonic in the pressure *difference* along the meridian, and thus also in the zonal wind. If the phase of the second harmonic in the *pressure* reverses along a meridian, as it does between 50° and 70°S, it will enhance the amplitude of the second harmonic in the meridional pressure *difference*, and in the wind.

The peak amplitude near 50°S of the second harmonic in the pressure, and the phase reversal of the harmonic from middle to high latitudes, both exist throughout the troposphere and lowest stratosphere. Second harmonics in the wind, such as those at sea level, therefore form through a considerable depth of the atmosphere. Figure 5 shows the annual march of the zonal component of the geostrophic wind at the 200-millibar level, averaged round every fifth parallel. In middle and high latitudes this level is in the lowest stratosphere. The half-yearly components visibly affect the shape of the annual curve, and it is obvious that they reverse phase in the latitudes near 45°S. In Table 2 the second harmonics in the winds at two latitudes can be compared. The one latitude is in the region of equinoctial maximums, the other where the maximums fall near the solstices. Besides the two levels illustrated in Figures 4 and 5, a level in the middle troposphere has been added. In subpolar latitudes the phase hardly changes with height, and as far into the stratosphere as the data have been analyzed (16

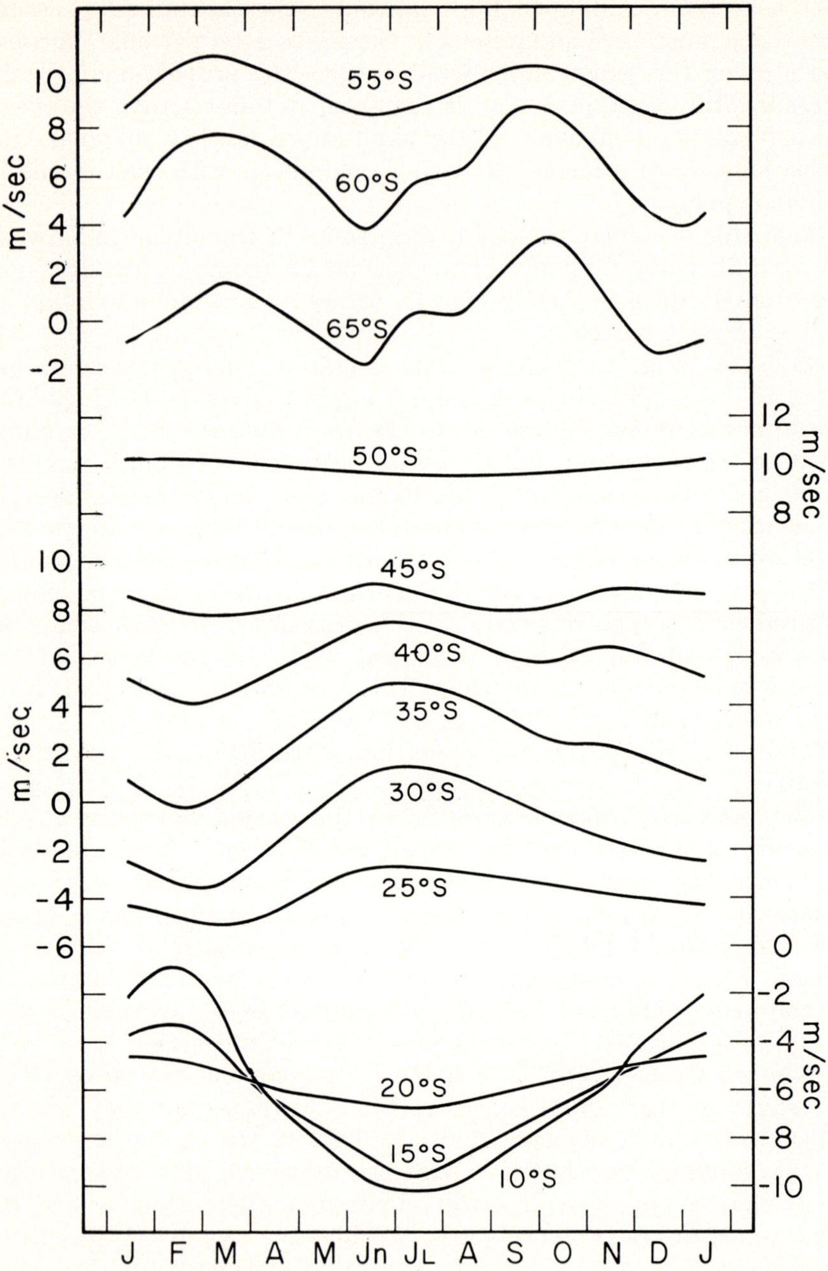

Fig. 4. Annual march of mean zonal geostrophic wind at sea level (m/sec), averaged round the hemisphere.

Table 2. Amplitude, in meters per second, of the second harmonic in the zonally averaged, zonal component of the geostrophic mean wind at three levels, its dates of maximums, and the percentage of the total variance for which it accounts.

	40°S	60°S
Sea Level		
Amplitude	0.7	2.0
Dates	9 Jun/Dec	24 Mar/Sep
Percent	29	87
500 mb		
Amplitude	0.8	2.4
Dates	6 Jun/Dec	27 Mar/Sep
Percent	40	65
200 mb		
Amplitude	1.4	3.8
Dates	3 Jan/Jul	27 Mar/Sep
Percent	40	34

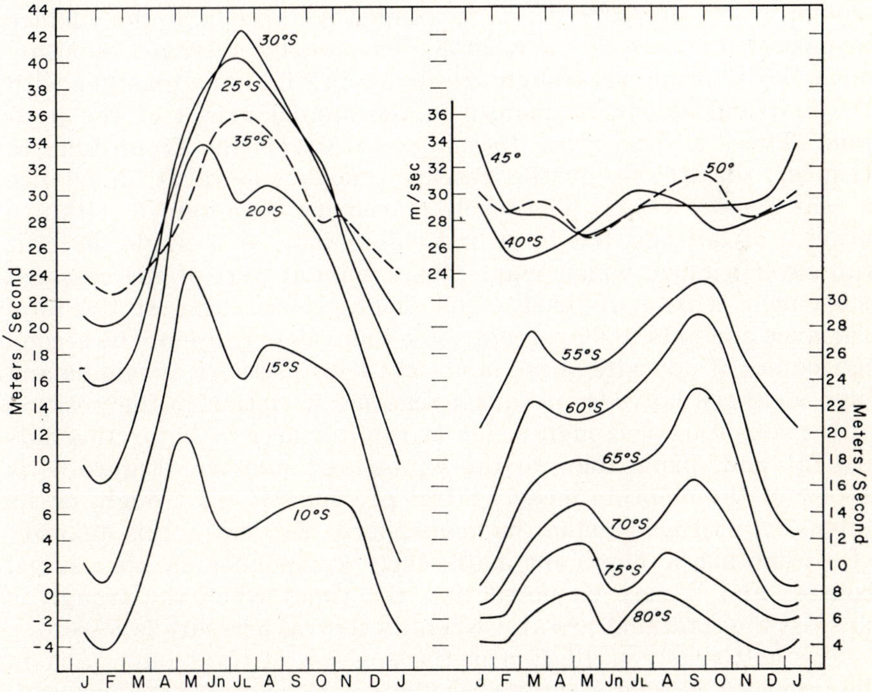

Fig. 5. The same as Figure 4 but at the 200-millibar level (about 11.5 km).

km above sea level) the phase is only a week different from that in the troposphere. In middle latitudes, however, the phase begins to slide above the tropopause, and at the 16-kilometer level it is 7 weeks out of phase with the oscillations in the troposphere. The percentage of the total variance for which the second harmonic accounts begins to drop rapidly in the stratosphere which, in middle and high latitudes, is dominated by large annual variations. It is well to remember that what is shown in Figures 4 and 5 and in Table 2 is zonal averages, and that there are large regional variations. (In the tropics (van Loon and Jenne, 1969) another half-yearly oscillation can be discerned in the annual march of the wind at the 200-millibar level (Fig. 5). Its origin is, however, different from that of the oscillations at higher latitudes, and it is thus beyond the scope of this paper.)

CAUSES

In the first approximation, the half-yearly oscillation in the sea-level pressure can be linked with the seasonal movement of the trough of low pressure which surrounds Antarctica at the surface in the belt between 60° and 70°S. The zonally averaged, monthly mean positions of this trough are shown in Figure 6a together with the first and second harmonics in the annual march of the position. Twice a year, from December to March and from June to October, the trough, on the average, moves polewards, and twice a year equatorwards. The whole movement is contained within 5 degrees of latitude, but in an individual year, at a single place, it can cover a much wider span. The dominant part of the seasonal movement is its half-yearly component, whose share of the total variance amounts to 60 percent. The immediate cause of the second harmonics of opposite phase in the sea-level pressure of middle and high southern latitudes is thus a seasonal variation in the position of the subantarctic trough which brings it nearer to Antarctica during fall and spring than during winter and summer. Figure 6c is a plot of the monthly mean central pressure of the trough, or its intensity, averaged round the hemisphere. Evidently, this quantity also contains a dominant half-yearly component in its annual course; and it may be noted that the times when the trough is nearest the continent are also when its central pressure is lowest.

The half-yearly oscillation in the position of the trough, and in its intensity, implies a similar oscillation in the most frequent position of lows and their intensity. Lows form in, and move in asso-

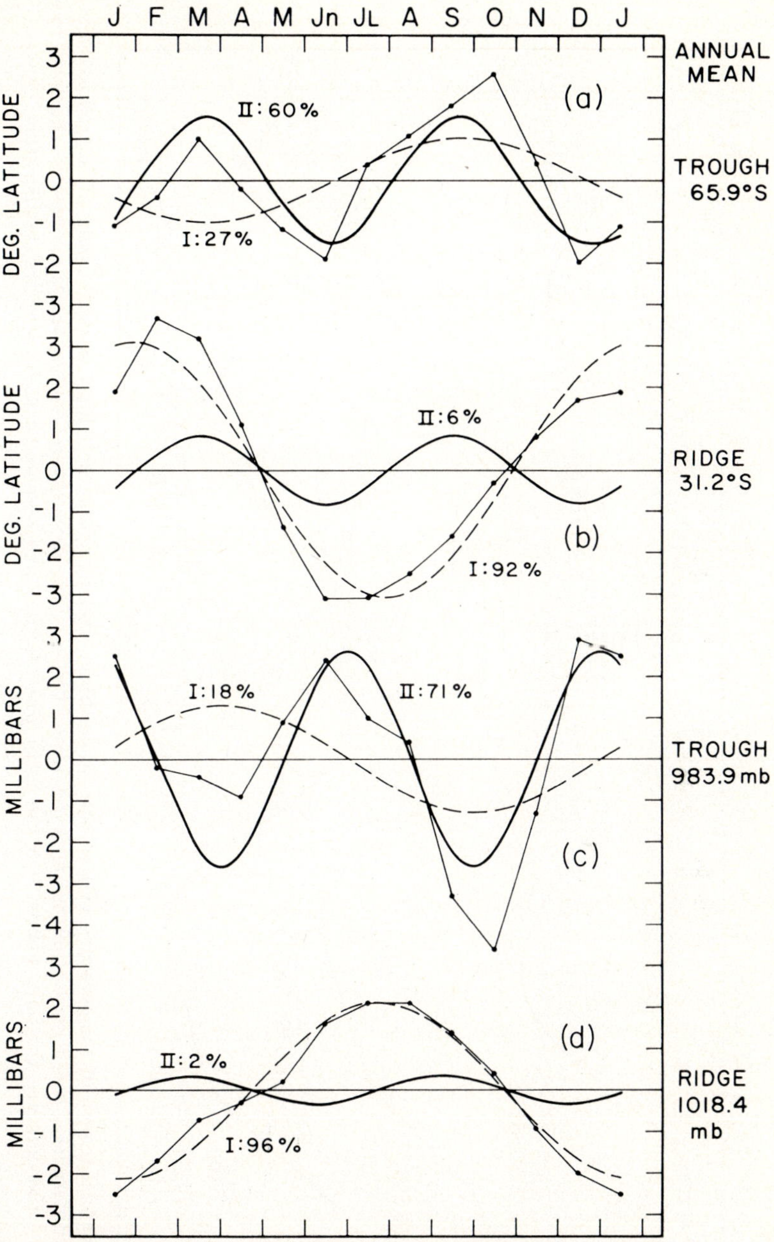

Fig. 6. Month-to-month variations of the zonally averaged positions of the subtropical ridge and subantarctic trough in the sea-level pressure and of their central pressure; and the first two harmonics of both. The percentages show the part of the total variance explained by each harmonic.

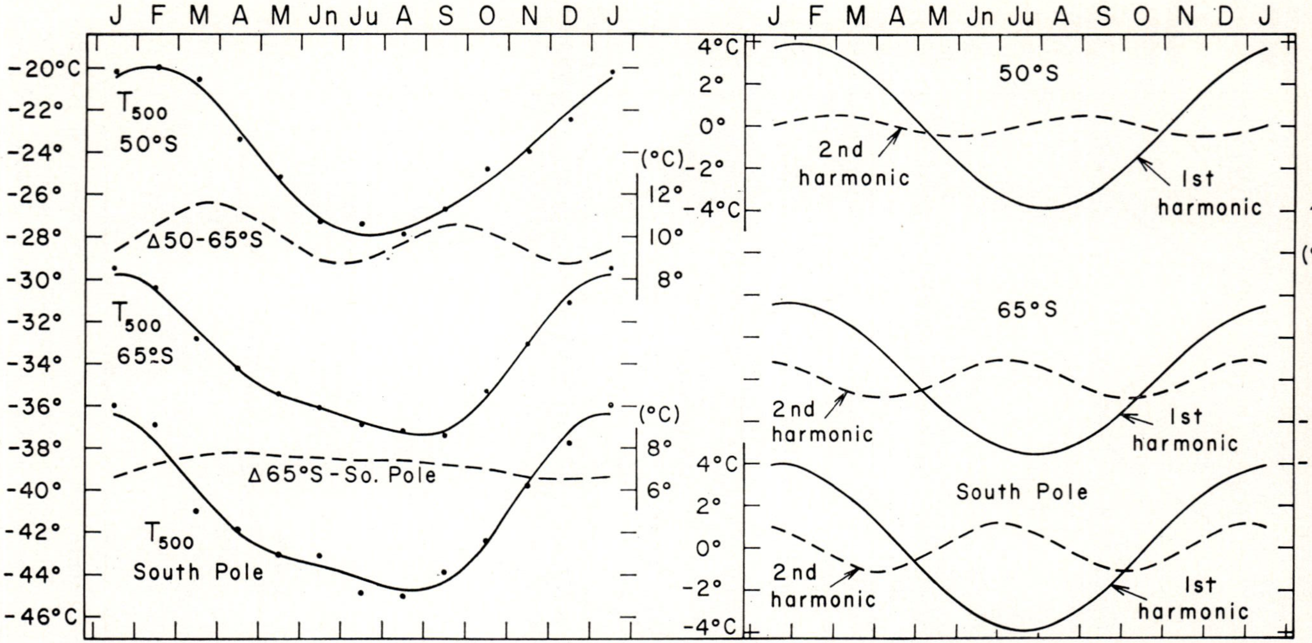

Fig. 7. Annual march of temperature (C) at the 500-millibar level in middle and high latitudes, and of latitudinal temperature differences, based on station means (van Loon, 1967). The temperature curves are the sums of the first two harmonics, the dots are the data points. On the right are the first and second harmonics of the temperature curves.

ciation with, zones of strong temperature contrast in the troposphere, and a half-yearly oscillation in their position and intensity points to a half-yearly oscillation in the temperature contrast.

In a shallow surface layer, hardly more than 1.5 kilometer thick, the radiational cooling in the antarctic winter introduces a large yearly component in the temperature, and thus also in the temperature contrasts between Antarctica and middle latitudes. Above this layer, in the rest of the troposphere, the amplitude and phase of the yearly components (first harmonics) in the temperature at middle and high latitudes approach each other. This is illustrated in Figure 7 which shows conditions in the middle troposphere. In the temperature difference between middle and high latitudes, above the layer of radiational cooling, the first harmonics will therefore cancel, and the second harmonics will come to dominate the annual march of the latitudinal temperature contrast.

The last step toward understanding the second harmonics in pressures and winds in middle and polar latitudes is to explain why the annual temperature curves have second harmonics. An important part of an explanation seems to be that the harmonics are owing to the different response of the earth's surface in the two regions to the heat budget (van Loon, 1967).

It should be stressed that the half-yearly components of the atmospheric elements, which have been described above, are not the outcome of Antarctica's one-sided influence on the outside world. They result from an interaction between two regions which amplifies the effect of otherwise insignificant quantities in the separate regions. Therefore, it is not possible to understand the problem if Antarctica's contribution is treated in isolation.

References

Reuter, F., 1936. Die synoptische Darstellung der 1/2jährigen Druckwelle. *Veröffentl. Geophys. Inst. Univ. Leipzig, 7:* 257–295.

Schwerdtfeger, W., and F. Prohaska, 1956. Der Jahresgang des Luftdrucks auf der Erde und seine halbjährige Komponente. *Meteorol. Rundschau, 9:* 33–43.

van Loon, H., 1967. The half-yearly oscillations in middle and high southern latitudes and the coreless winter. *J. Atmospheric Sci., 24*(5): 472–486.

van Loon, H., and R. L. Jenne, 1969. The half-yearly oscillations in the tropics of the Southern Hemisphere. *J. Atmospheric Sci., 26*(2): 218–232.

Wahl, E., 1942. Untersuchungen uber den jährlichen Luftdruckgang. *Veröffentl. Meteorol. Inst. Univ. Berlin, 4*(4): 4–71.

PART V

Conjugate Phenomena

PART V

Conjugate Phenomena

The next series of papers will be concerned, for the most part, with the interaction of the particles and fields from the sun with the particles and fields of earth. The measurements provide knowledge about the solar-terrestrial relationship and are most informative if made as conjugate measurements. It seems appropriate to define conjugacy and tell something about it so the reader may have some familiarity with it before beginning this section.

Think of a meridianal cross section of the earth and nearby space occupied by the popular concept of the earth's magnetic field. A particular field line emanates from one hemisphere (say, the Northern), curves around and crosses the equator, and returns to earth in the opposite hemisphere (in this case, the Southern) from which it started. If, in his thinking, one stays at low enough latitudes and doesn't consider the effect the solar wind (which carries its own magnetic field) has in distorting the earth's magnetic field, the picture is quite symmetrical about the geomagnetic equator, which is skewed some eleven degrees to the geographic equator. The two earth intercepts of the same geomagnetic field line are known as conjugate points. If the phenomenology being measured exhibits conjugacy, and this implies sufficiently low energy, then the same effect can be measured at both conjugate points.

For example, Great Whale River, Quebec, Canada, and Byrd Station, Antarctica, are a pair of conjugate points. A signal may be measured simultaneously at both points, or it may be out of phase at the two points by a measurable number of milliseconds. If the signal occurs simultaneously, and it is assumed the signal is propagating along the field line in either direction with equal velocity, it is probable that the triggering is affecting the field somewhere very near the equatorial crossing point. If, on the other hand, there is a certain time delay between the arrival of the signal at the two conjugate points and if the total path length of that particular field line is known, then some conclusions can be drawn about the nonsymmetrical position of the happening which gave rise to the signal.

The reason for trying to make conjugate measurements is that measurements at the two ends of the same line can be considerably more informative, since they are related, than two completely independent measurements, whether the two independent measurements are made both in the Northern or both in the Southern Hemisphere or in opposite hemispheres. These latter kinds of measurements, independent measurements, have their use and are made for different reasons. One of the first kind of signal in which conjugacy was detected was the VLF whistler. These signals are in the audible range and gain their name from the fact that, upon being rendered detectable, they sound like an audible note of decreasing frequency from, perhaps, 15,000 Hz to less than 1,000 Hz. Today we know that, in addition to the VLF part of the electromagnetic spectrum, the ULF and HF regions also exhibit conjugacy. Aurora measurements, too, exhibit conjugacy. The following papers will go into considerable detail in showing how conjugacy is interpreted and what we can learn about the solar-terrestrial relationship from these types of measurements.

RAY R. HEER, JR.

Atmospheric Physics Programs
Office of Polar Programs
National Science Foundation
Washington, D.C.

Very Low Frequency Magnetospheric Research in the Antarctic

R. A. HELLIWELL

Radioscience Laboratory, Stanford University, Stanford, California

The purpose of this paper is to highlight the contributions of antarctic research to the study of low frequency (100 Hz to 100 kHz) waves in the magnetosphere. Study in this area began for all practical purposes with Storey's classic paper on the origin of very low frequency (VLF) whistlers published in 1953. With the coming of the IGY in 1957 the first exploratory measurements were made in the Antarctic at Byrd Station, where the natural VLF activity was found to be very great. A continuing program of VLF observations at antarctic stations, employing investigators from several countries, has made important contributions to our knowledge of electromagnetic waves and the properties of the magnetosphere.

An interesting feature of VLF phenomena is the way they sound to the ear. Observations are made with the aid of a high-gain audio amplifier connected to a loop or long-wire antenna. Among the many remarkable sounds that may be heard are those generally known as whistlers and VLF emissions. The whistlers are long whistling tones, usually descending in frequency, and are excited by the electrical impulse from a lightning flash. The VLF emissions are less well understood but are believed to have their origin in the ionosphere and the magnetosphere. They exhibit a wide variety of sounds, ranging from hiss to musical tones. One type called the "dawn chorus" resembles the sound of birds waking in the early morning. Remarkably similar sounds are produced by seals, whales, and other seagoing mammals. During the IGY, whistlers and related phenomena were classified subjectively by trained people listening to magnetic tape recordings. This type of aural

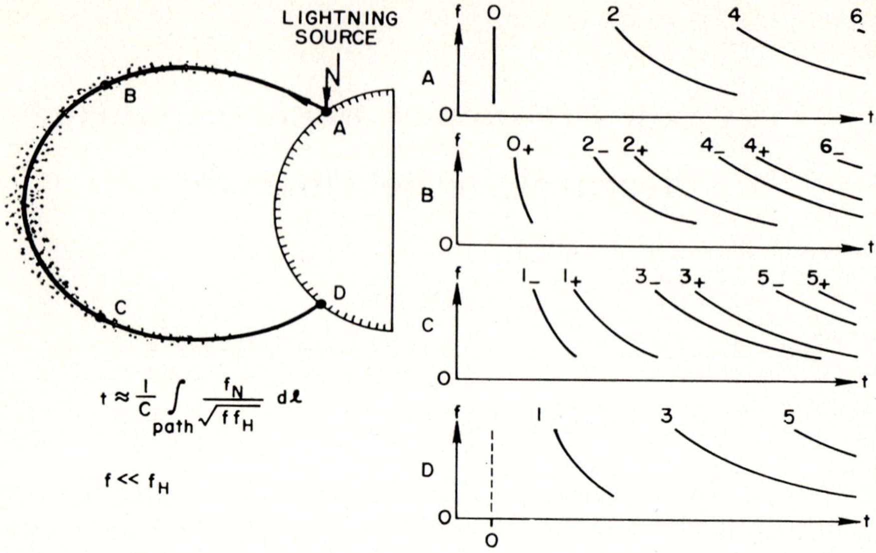

Fig. 1. Echoing ducted whistlers as observed on the ground at points A and D and in satellites at points B and C. The lighting source is located at point A, and the Eckersley approximation is used to sketch the spectra. The vertical dashed line in the lowest spectrogram represents the attenuated sferic arriving at D via the earth-ionosphere wave guide (Helliwell, 1969).

analysis has since been replaced by quantitative study of spectrograms made from the same tape recordings.

WHISTLERS

The nature of whistler propagation is illustrated in Figure 1. A single whistler duct is shown with the idealized spectra that would be observed at points A and D on the ground and at points B and C in space. The duct is a slight enhancement of electron density aligned with the earth's magnetic field within which electromagnetic waves in the audio-frequency range are trapped. Through the action of free electrons moving under the influence of the static magnetic field of the earth, the radio waves are dispersed. This effect causes a lightning impulse introduced at one end of the path to emerge at the other end as a long whistling tone. Receivers located at points A and D at the opposite ends of the duct observe the following sequence of events. First an impulse is observed at Station A, appearing as the vertical line labeled 0. Next a one-hop whistler, labeled 1, is observed at the conjugate point D. Some of this energy echoes back to point A and produces a two-hop whistler, labeled 2, and so on. Fractional-hop whistlers are observed in satellites at points B and C, as shown in Figure 1.

The time for a wave packet at the lower frequencies to travel over the path is given approximately by the equation shown in Figure 1, where f = wave frequency, f_N = plasma frequency, f_H = electron gyrofrequency (proportional to the strength of the earth's magnetic field), and c = twice the velocity of light. Since f_N is proportional to the square root of the electron density the whistler delay gives a measure of electron density. This integral is inversely proportional to the square root of wave frequency, which accounts for the falling frequency of the tone, and inversely proportional to the square root of the electron gyrofrequency. Since this latter quantity has a minimum at the top of the path, it is obvious that the time delay will be weighted toward the top of the path. This is one reason why whistlers make such good diagnostic tools for the outer magnetosphere. The low values of electron density at high altitudes are compensated by the correspondingly low values of electron gyrofrequency.

A spectrographic example of the phenomena idealized in Figure 1 is shown by the conjugate whistler echo train of Figure 2. These

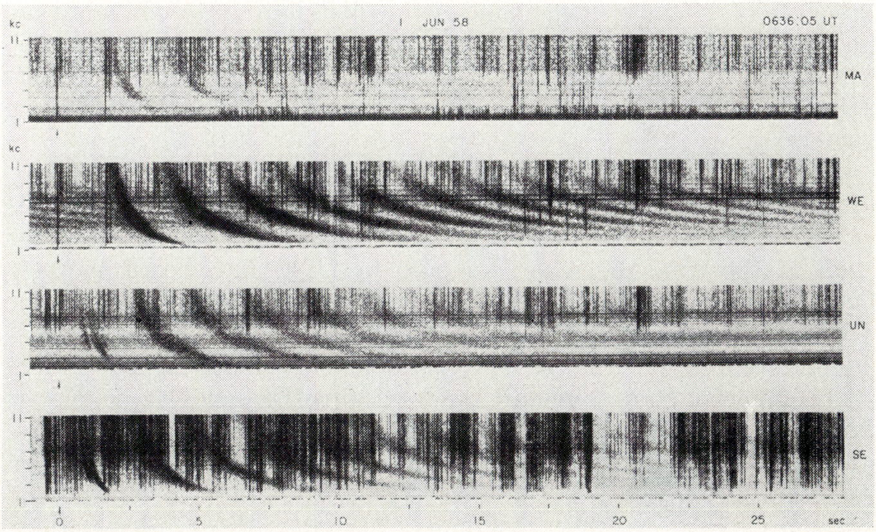

Fig. 2. Echoing whistler observed in conjugate regions. Upper two panels show even-order echo train observed at Macquarie Island and Wellington, New Zealand, in the Southern Hemisphere. Lower two panels show odd-order echo train observed at Unalaska and Seattle in the Northern Hemisphere (Helliwell, 1965).

whistlers were recorded during the IGY at Macquarie Island; Wellington, New Zealand; Unalaska; and Seattle, Washington. The lightning flash, recorded strongly at Macquarie and Wellington, is followed at Unalaska and Seattle by one-hop whistlers, exhibiting two main components corresponding to propagation in two separate ducts. The stronger component echoes between the hemispheres over a long period of time, with 12 echoes showing on the figure. It is seen that the ratio of time delays is 2, 4, 6, 8, etc., in the Southern Hemisphere and 1, 3, 5, 7, etc., in the Northern Hemisphere, in accordance with Figure 1.

As the wave frequency approaches the gyrofrequency a very interesting change occurs in the whistler spectra as compared with those shown in Figures 1 and 2. The time delay of the whistler is seen to reach a minimum at a certain frequency as illustrated by the spectra in the upper right-hand part of Figure 3. This point of minimum time delay is called the nose frequency and is labeled f_n. Two separate ducts are shown. The inner duct with the higher gyrofrequency shows a higher nose frequency and a smaller time delay. The nose frequency is closely related to the minimum gyrofrequency f_{H_0}, as indicated in the figure. By measuring this frequency the path latitude can be determined. Knowing the path latitude, the scale factor of the electron density distribution can be computed for an assumed shape of this distribution. If, in addition, several ducts are present, then a scale factor for each duct can be obtained. It is then possible by a process of curve fitting to determine the total electron distribution in the magnetosphere for simple models.

Recently it has been possible to test the duct theory of propagation using satellites. The lower right-hand spectrum shows what is observed in a satellite that happens to be situated within the lower duct at the time the whistlers pass by. The first trace shows a nose whistler which is like that seen on the ground except that the travel times are half as great. The second trace is more interesting. It represents leakage of whistler energy from the outer duct at frequencies above one-half the local gyrofrequency at which the trapping effect of an enhancement of electron density ceases. This feature of whistler transmission was discovered in the Stanford Orbiting Geophysical Observatory (OGO) 1 VLF experiment and provides strong evidence in support of the duct theory of whistlers. (The OGO 1 was an unmanned satellite sent up in 1964, number 1 of 6.)

Having considered the idealized nose whistlers of Figure 3, we can better appreciate actual examples, such as those shown in Fig-

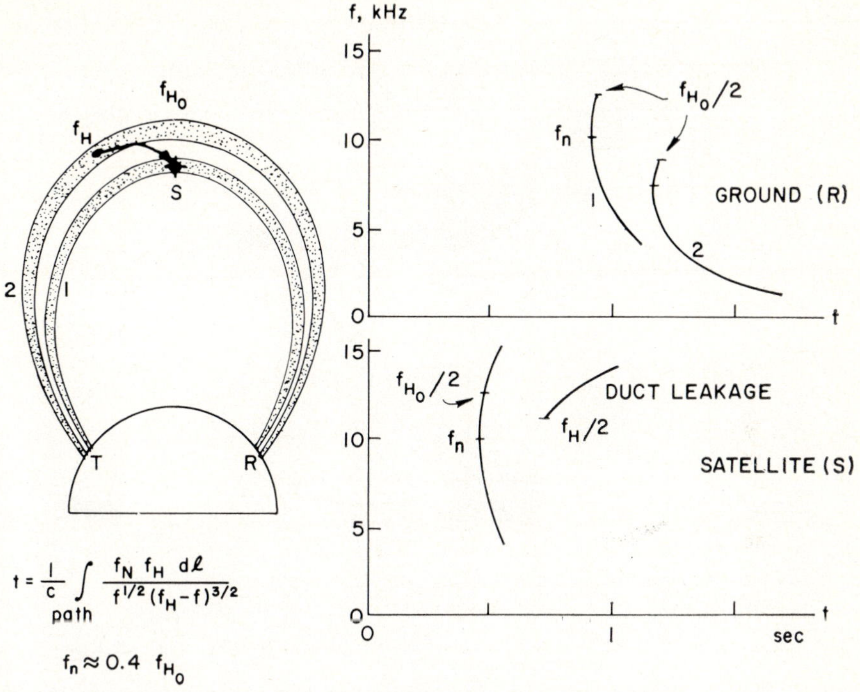

Fig. 3. Multipath ducted nose whistlers observed on ground; leakage from ducts observed on satellite for $f > f_H/2$. Nose frequency f_n gives path latitude; nose delay t_n gives electron concentration. f_H = electron gyrofrequency, f_N = electron plasma frequency, dl = element of path (l = line integral of the ray path) (Helliwell, 1969).

ure 4, recorded at Eights Station, Antarctica. In the top spectrum are many separate whistlers excited by a single impulse. The nose frequency of each trace gives the latitude of the corresponding duct, and the time delay at the nose gives a measure of the electron content in that duct. Each whistler can be scaled for its nose frequency and from this collection of data the electron density distribution can be obtained over the range of geocentric distances from 3 to 5.5 earth radii (R_E). In the lower spectrogram of Figure 4 is a train of nose whistlers obtained outside the plasmapause; each whistler is seen to have triggered a discrete VLF emission at the upper cutoff of the whistler. Artificially stimulated emissions (ASE's) triggered by station NAA on 14.7 kHz are seen in the upper panel. These emission effects are an important part of our field of study and will be discussed later.

At the conjugate point to Eights we might hope to obtain the same type of information as that shown in Figure 4. However,

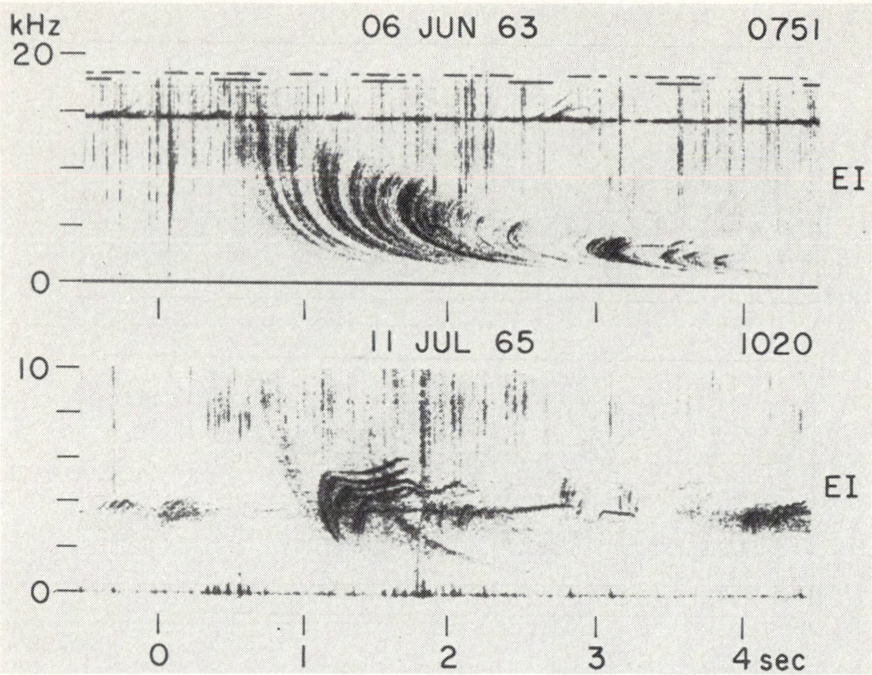

Fig. 4. Nose whistlers and triggered emissions: upper panel shows multipath nose whistler and rising tones triggered by NAA at 14.7 kHz; lower panel shows discrete emissions triggered by nose whistlers at their upper cutoff frequencies ($f_{H_0}/2$). Eights Station, June 6, 1963, 0751 UT (Helliwell, 1969).

experience shows that this is not the case, as illustrated in Figure 5. At Eights many strong one-hop whistler groups are seen in the 20-second segment of the record shown. One of these is seen to echo back to Quebec City, Canada. Much of the detail seen at Eights is missing in the Quebec City record. Thus both the quantity and quality of two-hop whistlers is low on this meridian. Few one-hop whistlers are seen at Quebec City because of the rarity of occurrence of lightning near Eights. The ideal situation is to observe one-hop whistlers from an active lightning region. Eights and other nearby stations meet this requirement and are among the best producers of usable whistlers in the world.

ELECTRON DENSITY MEASUREMENTS USING WHISTLERS

The application of whistlers to the study of electron distribution in the magnetosphere is illustrated in Figure 6. Three separate

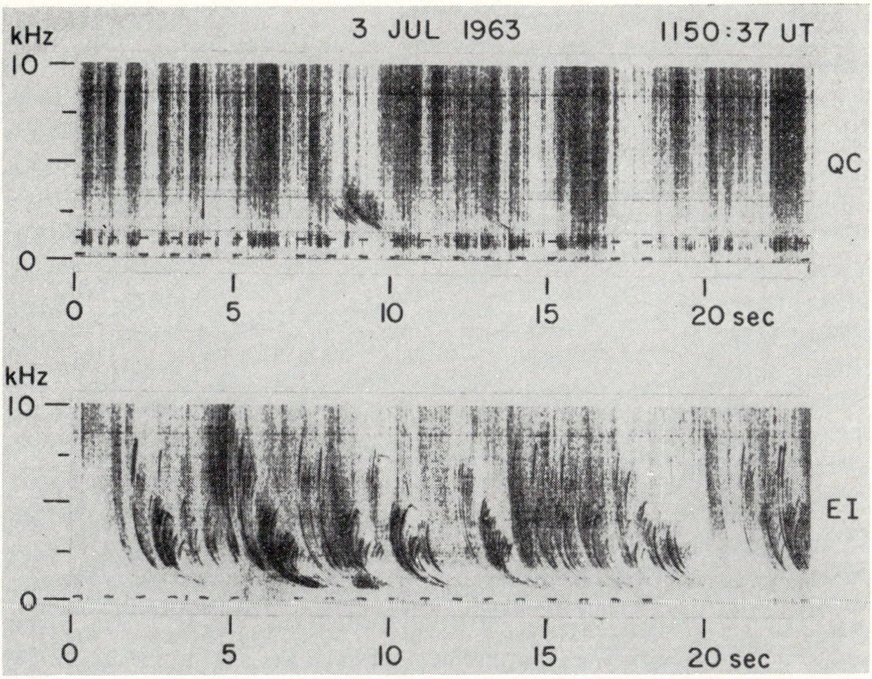

Fig. 5. Nose whistlers observed at conjugate stations Quebec City and Eights on July 3, 1963. One-hop whistlers from many sources are seen at Eights; only two relatively weak groups of echoes are seen at Quebec City. Each source excites many separate ducts.

ducts are assumed, the inner two showing greater time delays than the third. In the right-hand diagram is a meridional cross section of the magnetosphere indicating the location of the ducts corresponding to each of the whistlers. From the travel times and nose frequencies we can obtain the electron density profile in the equatorial plane shown in the lower right-hand corner. A remarkable feature exhibited by these data is the sharp drop or "knee" in electron density occurring between whistler 2 and whistler 3. This has been studied extensively using whistlers from the Antarctic and has been called the "plasmapause." The plasmapause was totally unexpected and is still not completely understood. Whistler data have demonstrated that the distribution of electrons inside the plasmapause, in a region called the plasmasphere, can be described by a diffusive equilibrium model requiring no input from sources other than the ionosphere. Outside the plasmapause, where the density tends to be very much lower, the electron distri-

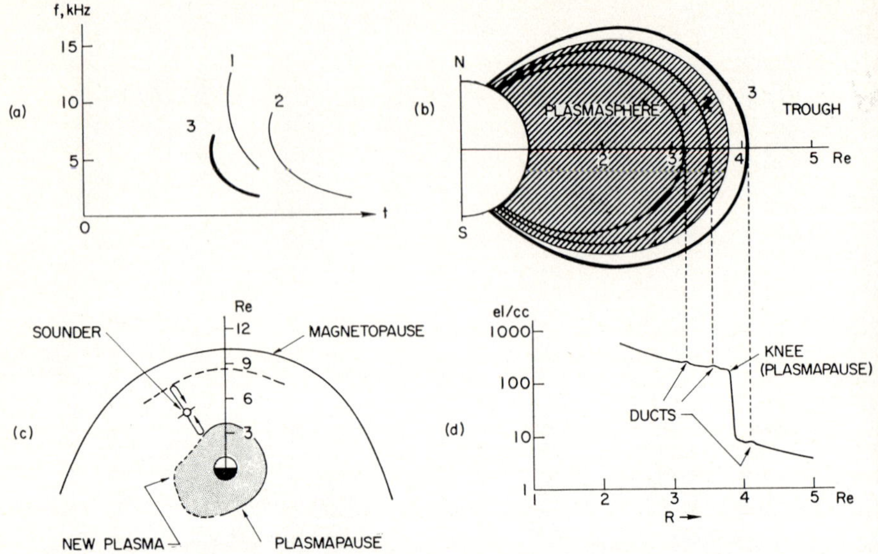

Fig. 6. (a) Nose whistler train, with knee trace; (b) meridional plane showing whistler ducts; (c) boundary of plasmasphere deduced from knee trace; possible detection of plasmapause and magnetopause by low frequency sounder located in trough; (d) equatorial profile of electron density deduced from (a) (Helliwell, 1969).

bution tends to be collisionless in form and appears to be closely connected with events in the tail of the magnetosphere and in the solar wind. The position of the boundary of the plasmasphere shown in the lower left-hand diagram varies with the local time of day, and the plasmasphere exhibits a pronounced bulge on the evening side. This is thought to be the region where high-latitude flow from the magnetospheric tail and the flow impressed by the earth's rotation are opposed. The boundary of the plasmasphere tends to move inward with magnetic disturbance, varying all the way from 6 down to less than 3 earth radii, depending upon the level of magnetic activity.

The differences in the distributions inside and outside the plasmapause are illustrated in Figure 7. Here the equatorial profile shown in Figure 6 reappears in terms of distance along the field lines to the equatorial plane beginning at 1,000 km altitude. The thin lines show the distribution of electron concentration along the lines of force terminating at the indicated radial distance from the center of the earth. It is seen that these lines have very different slopes depending on whether the line falls inside or outside the plasmapause. It is particularly interesting to note that within the

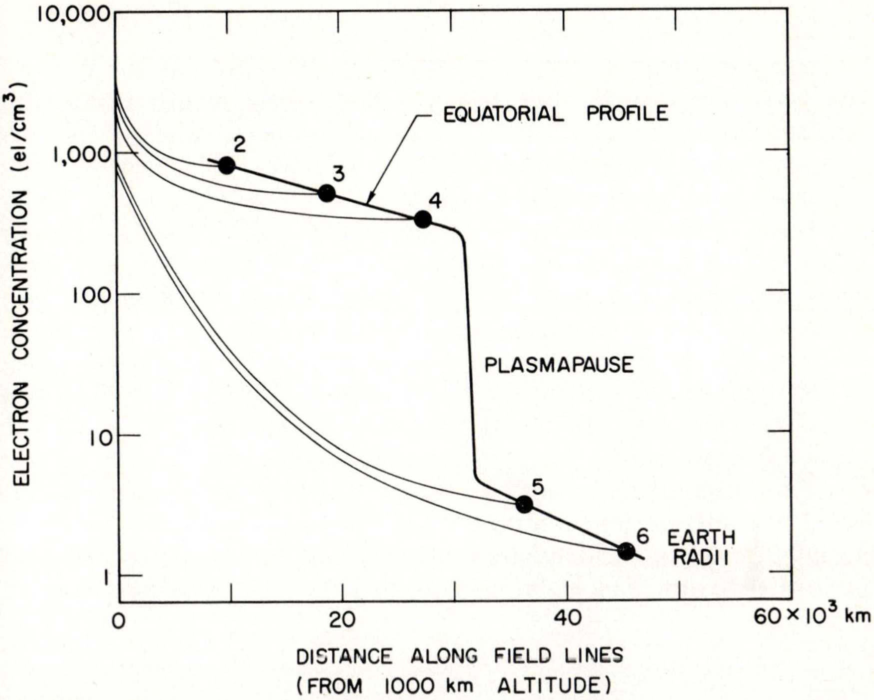

Fig. 7. Electron concentration along field lines beginning at 1,000 km altitude. Numbers indicate geocentric distance to top of field line and heavy lines indicate equatorial profile of electron density.

plasmapause, where diffusive equilibrium applies, the electron density near the equator is nearly constant. On the other hand, outside the plasmapause the variation of electron density with distance along the field line is much more rapid.

In addition to variations with local time and magnetic activity, the ionization of the plasmasphere has recently been found to drift in a systematic way. These drifts were discovered by observing systematic changes in the nose frequencies of ducted whistlers at Eights Station. Each duct drifts as a whole in response to east-west electric fields. Large portions of the magnetosphere can be observed to move inward or outward, depending on the local time at the station and the phase of the associated substorm. Drift rates as high as an earth radius per hour near 4 earth radii have been observed. The whistler has thus revealed a new feature of the magnetosphere and has introduced a new technique for measuring DC electric fields, so difficult to detect by other methods.

EMISSIONS

Closely associated with waves generated by ground sources are the wave phenomena that seem to have their origin inside the magnetosphere or ionosphere. These have been called emissions and fall roughly into two basic categories, the discrete type (chorus), and the steady type (hiss).

Figure 8 shows examples of emissions which include falling tones, rising tones, hooks, combinations of various kinds of discrete emissions and more or less steady bands of noise or hiss. Discrete emissions may be triggered by whistlers, or by man-made signals, or they may appear spontaneously. Hiss at mid-latitudes is often associated with discrete emissions. At high latitudes hiss is more often associated with the aurorae and usually occurs at higher frequencies ($>$ 4 kHz) than mid-latitude hiss.

At conjugate points, such as Great Whale River in Quebec and Byrd Station, we find that the discrete type of emission (and associated hiss) is usually seen nearly simultaneously at the two ends of the path. The example of Figure 9 shows strikingly similar

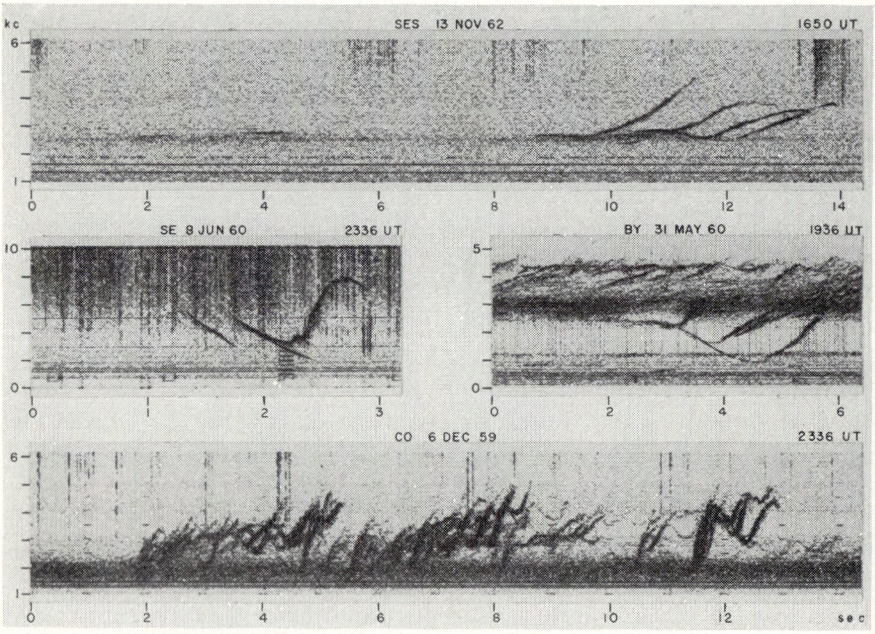

Fig. 8. Discrete emissions including rising tones, falling tones, hooks, and various combinations of these (Helliwell, 1965).

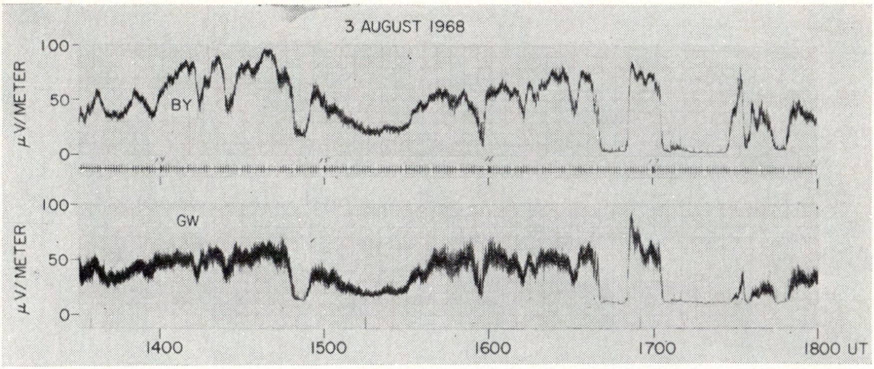

Fig. 9. Noise observed in the band of 1–2 kHz at Great Whale River, Canada, (lower trace) and Byrd Station (upper trace) on August 3, 1968.

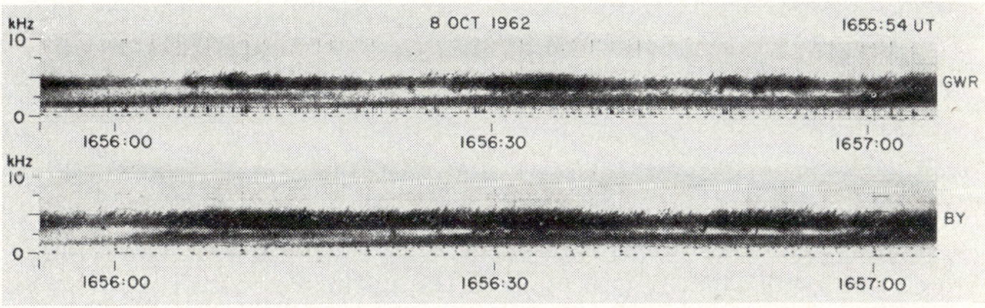

Fig. 10. Conjugate noise spectra recorded at Great Whale River, Canada, (upper panel) and Byrd Station (lower panel) (Helliwell, 1965).

intensity variations at both stations. The time scale is considerably compressed, however, covering five hours of time. When the time resolution is improved, then interesting differences appear in the conjugate noise patterns. Thus in Figure 10 we see another example of conjugate recordings covering 30 minutes of time. Here the dynamic spectrum is shown, rather than just the total field in a limited passband. Again, the gross features are the same at both stations, including the splitting of noise into two principal bands, one centered at roughly 2 kHz and the other at 4 kHz. However, close study shows differences in the fine structure of the discrete emissions appearing in the two records. Faint suggestions of periodic fluctuations can be seen in the upper band, with a period of about 3 seconds.

Detailed study of the differences in conjugate point recordings requires even better time resolution. An example of good time

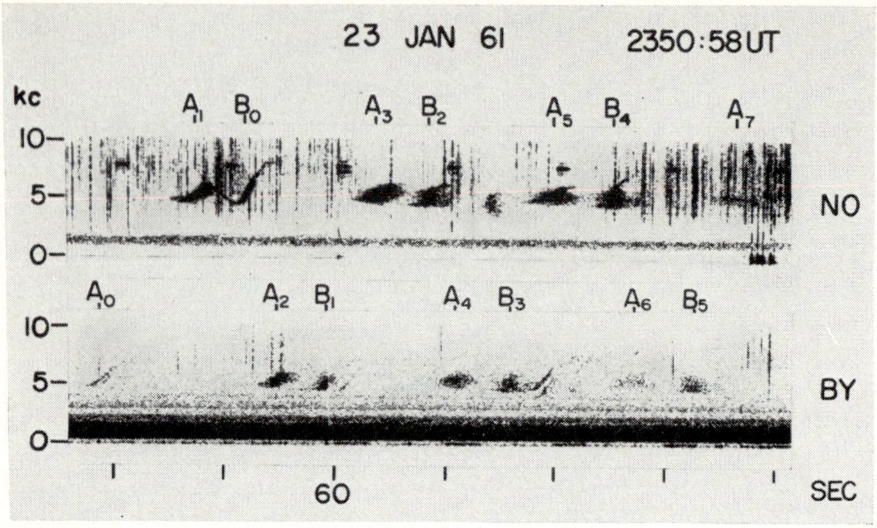

Fig. 11. Conjugate noise spectra recorded at Norwich, Vermont, (upper spectrum) and Byrd Station (lower spectrum) (Helliwell, 1965).

resolution records obtained at the roughly conjugate stations, Byrd, Antarctica, and Norwich, Vermont, is shown in Figure 11. In this series of noise bursts we see a very interesting relation between the events at the two ends of the path. First, we see a weak emission labeled A_0 at Byrd, followed about 1 second later by a stronger burst labeled A_1 at Norwich. This emission triggers a second emission labeled B_0 and both of these are seen to echo back to Byrd with a slight change in form and are labeled A_2 and B_1. This echoing process continues and, as is easily seen, produces a double sequence of periodic emissions (i.e., a two-phase emission) that are exactly 180° out of phase at the two ends of the path. It is known from other evidence that this entire sequence was started by the 9th hop of a whistler. The period between emissions was exactly equal to the echoing period of the whistler at the starting frequency of the emissions. It is deduced from data of this kind that the periodic emissions are in fact nothing more than emissions triggered by the whistler mode echo of the previous emission.

Discrete emissions triggered by man-made signals are called artificially stimulated emissions (ASE's). The example of Figure 12 shows Morse-code dashes from Station NAA located at Cutler, Maine, triggering strong discrete emissions (mainly of the rising type) that were observed on the research ship *Eltanin* near the con-

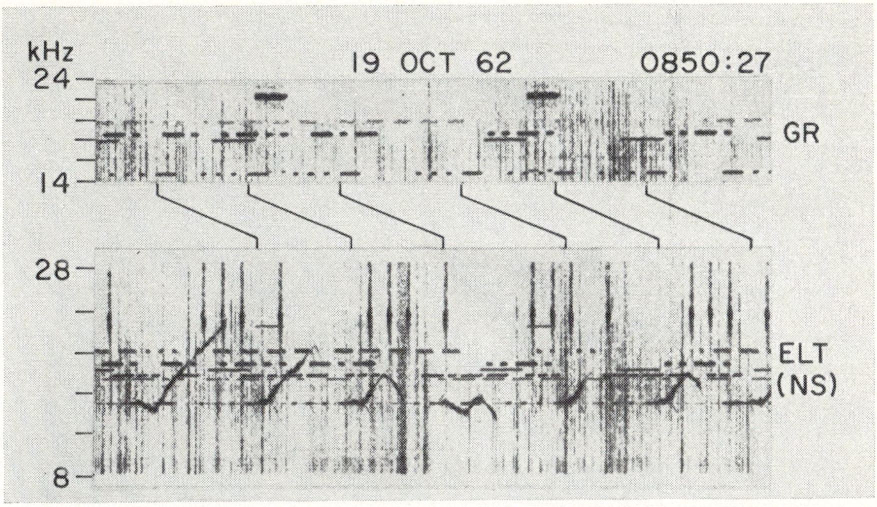

Fig. 12. Artificially stimulated emissions triggered by Morse code dashes from Station NAA. Upper spectrum shows code transmissions recorded at Great Whale River, Canada. Lower spectrum shows the emissions observed on the *Eltanin* in the Southern Hemisphere. Inclined lines connect each transmitted dash with its corresponding emission, observed 0.7 seconds later (Helliwell, 1965).

jugate point. Only the dashes (150 msec duration) produced emissions while the dots (50 msec duration) produced nothing. This result has been observed in nearly all cases of ASE's and suggests that the emission process is dependent on the duration of the triggering signal, with the critical duration being about 100 msec.

To explain the occurrence of triggered emissions, the model shown in Figure 13 has been suggested. It is supposed that the emissions are produced as a result of cyclotron resonance between energetic electrons and whistler-mode waves. The generation region is located at the top of the line of force and the emissions are triggered by an incoming wave packet interacting with electrons streaming in the opposite direction. The radiation is essentially backward-traveling cyclotron radiation which follows the same path as the whistlers. The oscillation is maintained by feedback between the incoming particles and the outgoing waves.

The magnetic field of the outgoing wave causes the electrons to be phase bunched. This phase bunching depends upon the magnitude of the output field and the transverse velocity of the electrons and occurs over a distance of several hundred kilometers. When these particles are phase bunched their radiation goes up by a very

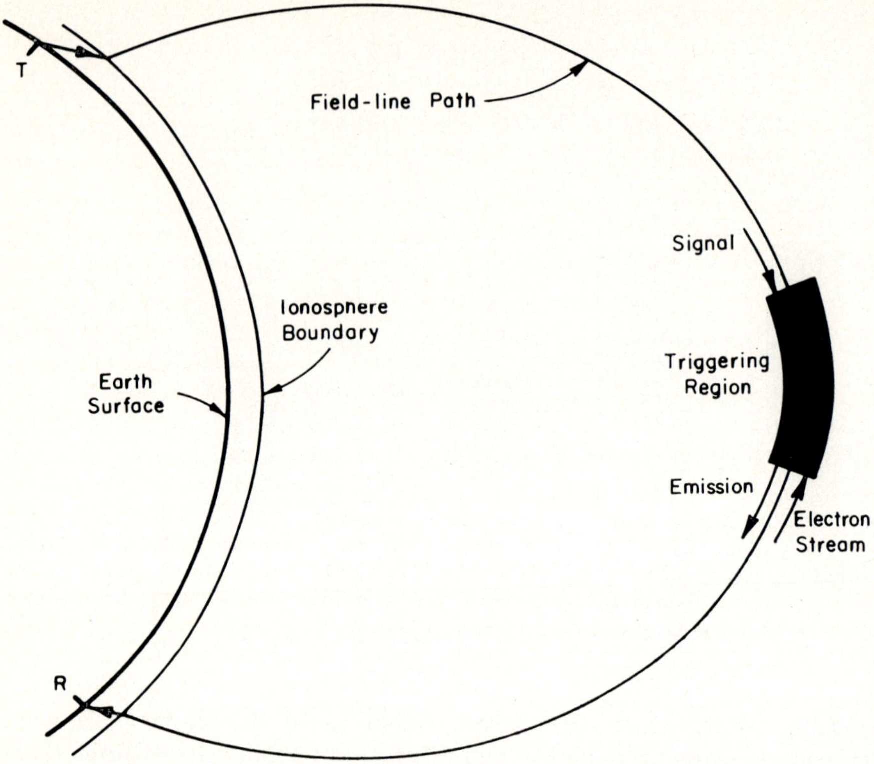

Fig. 13. Model of the generation of discrete VLF emissions based on electron cyclotron resonance (Helliwell, 1969).

large factor; it is this radiation that provides the fields in which the next entering particles are phase bunched. Thus there is established a kind of feedback loop in which the oscillation continues as long as the overall loop gain is greater than unity. Spatial inhomogeneities introduced by the earth's dipole field and the electron density distribution are thought to cause the oscillation frequency to change with time.

Although much remains to be learned about the processes of triggering and evolution of the discrete VLF emission, it appears that this phenomenon could become a powerful new tool for the study of energetic particles in the magnetosphere. Furthermore, the existence of these phenomena suggests the use of the magnetosphere as a kind of plasma laboratory that is free of the size and boundary limitations of man-made laboratories. Thus with the aid of large variable frequency transmitters on the ground or in satellites it should be possible to exercise detailed control of the emission process. In addition, it may be possible to inject energetic electrons of known characteristics that can interact with injected waves so that nearly all of the parameters of the magnetospheric laboratory could be placed under man-made control.

The other main class of emissions is the phenomenon known as auroral hiss. Observations made at Byrd Station first showed that this type of noise is closely connected with the aurora. Auroral hiss is important not only in the study of propagation and emission processes but also in the study of auroral phenomena.

The source of the hiss is not known. One theory suggests that it may be produced by incoherent Cerenkov radiation from intense streams of 1 kev electrons penetrating to the auroral zone. The experimental evidence to date suggests strongly that the mechanism of generation of auroral hiss is not connected with the generation of discrete VLF emissions and its associated hiss. However, much more research will be required to establish quantitatively the origin of auroral hiss. Interest in these relations is great because the aurora is still an enigma in science. Auroral hiss is a relatively new aspect of auroral phenomenology. Because of its quantitative nature and the ease with which it can be observed both on the ground and in satellites, it is possible that it will provide essential information from which a complete theory of auroral phenomena can ultimately be developed. Although the main thrust of this work is scientific, it has already produced a practical application. The intensity of the auroral hiss usually far exceeds the intensity of any other noise source in the Antarctic. As a result, it sets the ultimate limit on the sensitivity of a VLF receiver at high latitudes. Hence a knowledge of its occurrence both in time and space is needed for the design of high-latitude VLF communication and navigation systems as well as for VLF propagation experiments.

SUMMARY

I should like to summarize this brief review with the sketch of Figure 14, a model of the relation of VLF phenomena to the magnetosphere. The region beyond the plasmapause might be termed the polar magnetosphere since it is closely connected with high-latitude phenomena. Here are shown the polar chorus (a high-latitude form of chorus appearing near 700 Hz), auroral hiss, and other types of chorus and hiss that are not ducted and hence are

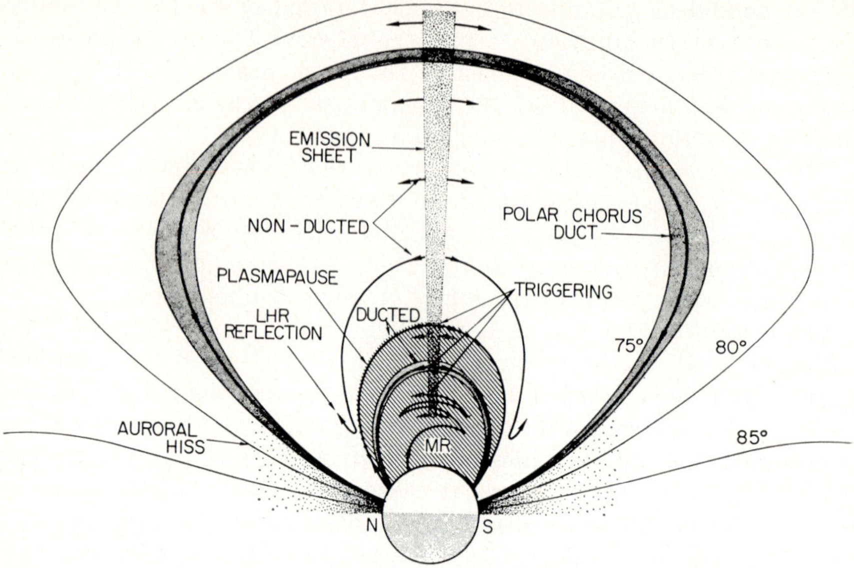

Fig. 14. Model showing distribution of low frequency waves in the geomagnetic meridional plane on the dayside of the earth (Helliwell, 1969).

seen only by satellites. Nonducted waves are thought to travel down to the lower hybrid resonance (LHR) reflection level from which they bounce back and eventually are absorbed. On the boundary of the plasmapause and within the plasmasphere are seen numerous ducts which guide whistlers and emissions. In addition, non-ducted whistler-mode signals travel to the LHR reflection region, and bounce back and forth across the equator until they are absorbed. These whistlers are never seen on the ground and can only be studied in rockets and satellites. They provide information on the properties of the magnetosphere and related wave-particle interactions.

Because the magnetic and spin axes of the earth are not parallel, the difference between geographic and geomagnetic latitude will vary with longitude. At Eights this difference is near the maximum (about 11°), and produces some useful asymmetries. Figure 15 shows two meridional views of the earth and its magnetosphere for noon and midnight on the meridian of Eights, Antarctica. They illustrate some of the advantages of stations, such as Byrd and Eights, which lie close to the magnetic meridian that passes through the geographic pole. It is seen from the figure that the tilt of the earth's magnetic field with respect to its spin axis brings the

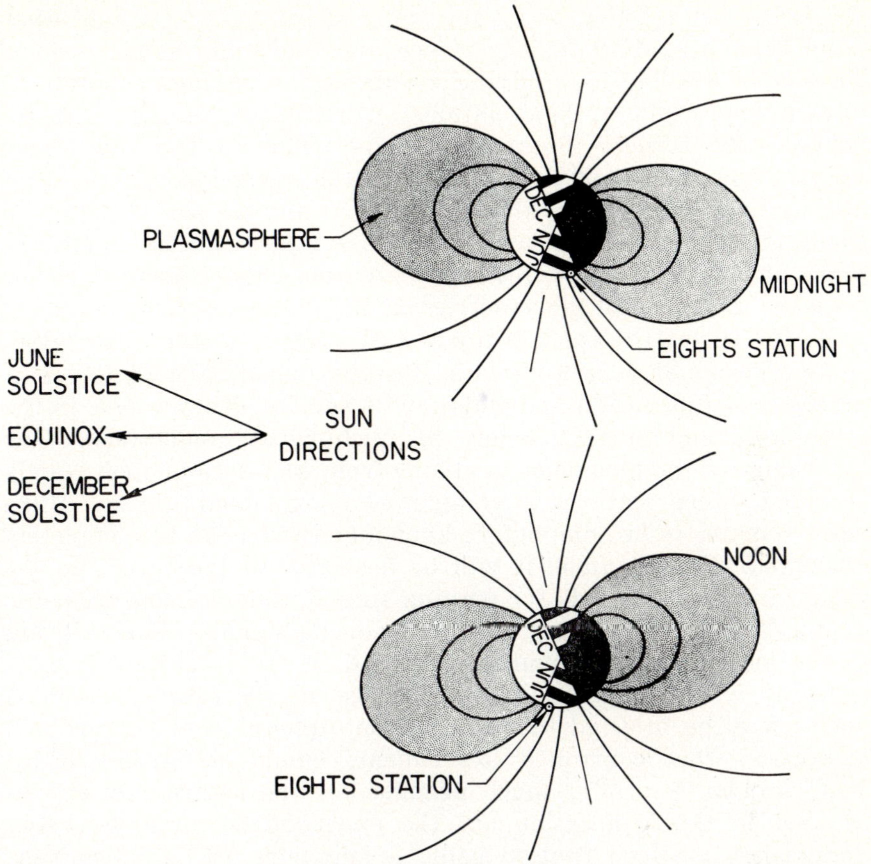

Fig. 15. Relation of the magnetosphere to direction of sun on meridian of Eights Station. Plasmapause is drawn at L = 4.0. "Noon" and "midnight" refer to local time at Eights Station. Cross hatching denotes regions in which day and night alternate seasonally. Rotation axis of earth is vertical.

conjugate point of Eights to a lower geographic latitude and hence closer to equatorial thunderstorm sources. At the same time atmospheric noise is reduced in the vicinity of Eights because of its relatively high geographic latitude. These two facts explain, to some extent at least, the relatively high rate of whistler activity at Eights and nearby stations. The tilt of the earth's field makes possible the separation of the effects of the magnetosphere and ionosphere on the phenomena being studied. Thus at the equinoxes, Eights and its conjugate point both experience day and night. Near the June solstice Eights is constantly in darkness while near the December solstice, it is constantly in sunlight. On the other hand, its conjugate point experiences day and night at all seasons. Thus it is possible by studying events at the conjugate points to have a wide range of combinations of orientation of the magnetosphere with respect to the solar wind while at the same time varying the amount of illumination on the lower ionosphere. Finally we note that the location of Eights maximizes the variation in the angle between the solar wind and the geomagnetic equatorial plane at noon and midnight. This situation should make it easier to detect north-south asymmetries in the magnetosphere resulting from the tilt of the earth's dipole with respect to the solar wind.

As a result of over ten years of study, much of it in the Antarctic, the propagation and emission of low frequency waves in the ionosphere and magnetosphere is much better understood. Our knowledge of the phenomena extends from well-documented, widely accepted interpretations to completely unexplained effects. Much work remains to be done before known questions can be completely answered. For example, it will be desirable in the future to develop improved methods for making simple, reliable measurements of the direction of arrival of whistler-mode signals. This will aid in the location of emission sources and in the tracking of ducts carrying whistler-mode signals. Because of the ease with which waves may be injected into the magnetosphere from the ground, it appears that controlled experiments employing ground-based VLF transmitters offer much promise for the future. Of special interest in this connection are the experiments currently being undertaken at Byrd Station using a long-wire VLF transmitter. While these are in the preliminary stages, available evidence suggests that with an improved antenna located at a lower geomagnetic latitude ($L \cong 4$), important contributions to the understanding of wave-particle interactions can be obtained. Closely related to the ground-based controlled experiments are those that might be conducted from satellites employing large antennas excited by very low frequency transmitters. Ultimately it is conceivable that means will be found to modify the magnetospheric environment itself through the effect of VLF waves on the concentration of energetic trapped radiation.

Back on the ground we can see an increasing need for quantitative studies of the correlation between VLF auroral effects and other auroral properties such as the light output and associated absorption and micropulsation events. Especially interesting in this connection is the possibility of coordinating VLF experiments with auroral TV experiments.

Finally, we should note the possibility that some of the research in the Antarctic might be carried on using unmanned geophysical observatories. These would be placed on the ice at appropriate locations and telemeter their data back to the home laboratory via communication satellite. This scheme would make possible the rapid analysis of data and could greatly advance the rate of research. (At present up to a year may elapse before data analysis can begin.) A "talk-back" circuit could be used to optimize experiment parameters in the light of the received data.

Author's Note: Figure 5 was prepared by John Katsufrakis; Figure 7 by Chung Park; Figure 9 by William Hudson; and Figure 15 by Jan Siren. The research was supported by the Office of Polar Programs of the National Science Foundation under Grant No. GA-1151 and Grant No. GA-1485.

References

Helliwell, R. A., 1965. *Whistlers and Related Ionospheric Phenomena.* Stanford Univ., Stanford, Calif.

Helliwell, R. A., 1969. Low-frequency waves in the magnetosphere. *Rev. Geophys., 7:* 281.

Storey, L. R. O., 1953. An investigation of whistling atmospherics. *Phil. Trans. Roy. Soc. London, Ser. A, 246:* 113.

Aurora Studies over Alaska and South of New Zealand

T. NEIL DAVIS and ALBERT E. BELON
Geophysical Institute, University of Alaska, College

NEEL W. GLASS
Los Alamos Scientific Laboratory, University of California, Los Alamos, New Mexico

Two series of observations using pairs of jet aircraft have been made over Alaska and south of New Zealand to investigate auroral conjugacy. The first series, in March, 1967, was made under magnetically undisturbed conditions. Under these conditions, the auroras in the two hemispheres were found to be identical in shape and intensity and also were located at opposite ends of geomagnetic field lines, as determined from calculations based on field sources internal to the earth (See *Authors' Notes* regarding Belon *et al.*). The second flight series was made under magnetically disturbed conditions during March, 1968. Even under disturbed conditions, the auroras occurring at the equatorward boundaries of the displays appeared to be conjugate. Though analyses are as yet incomplete, it is clear that major departures from conjugacy occurred at higher latitudes during disturbed periods. Differences in intensity, shape, and relative location were observed. In at least one instance there appeared to be a complete breakdown in conjugacy; a bright aurora was observed at high latitude in the Northern Hemisphere but no corresponding aurora could be detected in the Southern Hemisphere. One interesting finding is that there is an overall tendency for the auroras over Alaska to be brighter than those over the region south of New Zealand, even though at times the Southern Hemisphere auroras can be the brighter. At least during the disturbed evening hours, and perhaps also in the disturbed morning hours, the Southern Hemisphere auroras at high latitude tended to be displaced both equatorward and eastward of the corresponding Northern Hemisphere auroras. A search for corresponding auroral pulsations (quasi-periodic intensity variations with periods ranging from 0.1 to 100 sec) revealed several instances wherein definite correspondence was found. In these cases, the pulsations were in phase at the two ends of a geomagnetic field line.

BACKGROUND INFORMATION

There are several reasons for interest in detailed study of conjugacy of visible auroras. It is generally accepted that the visible auroral structures are the direct result of energetic electrons and protons being precipitated into the atmosphere. We are fairly certain that these charged particles undergo acceleration somewhere near the earth, perhaps quite near the atmosphere or perhaps in the outer magnetosphere at a distance of a few earth radii.

There is hope that the studies of conjugacy can contribute to the solution of the problem of where the acceleration takes place and by what mechanism it is caused. The primary auroral electrons and protons are constrained, for the most part, to move along geomagnetic field lines. Therefore these particles provide markers which can be followed for the purpose of mapping the geomagnetic field. Distortions to the geomagnetic field are expected from current sources in the Van Allen regions, in the tail of the magnetosphere, and from currents at the boundary between the magnetosphere and the solar wind. By observing relative displacements between corresponding auroras in the two hemispheres one obtains information about the magnitude and direction of geomagnetic field distortions caused by these external sources. Calculation of these effects is difficult and there is available little quantitative information regarding the configuration of the outer geomagnetic field, especially during disturbed conditions.

An analogy to the system under study is a double-ended cathode ray tube which contains phosphorescent screens at each end. In the body of the tube are one or more cathodes, and there are magnetic and electric fields which focus and accelerate the particles moving between the cathode and the two end screens. The configuration of the magnetic field within the tube is partly known; the electric field is almost unknown, as is the location of the one or more cathodes. Furthermore, not every aspect of the interaction of the charged particles with the end screen is fully understood. That is, there are still some questions regarding those interactions taking place between the auroral primaries and the earth's atmosphere which lead to the production of a visible aurora. One hopes, by simultaneous examination of both screens of this analogous system, to determine more exactly the configuration of the magnetic field and to learn something about the electric field and the location and mechanisms of particle acceleration within the system.

Various observable conjugate phenomena can be studied to determine the geomagnetic field configuration and the locations and mechanisms of particle acceleration. Choosing the visible aurora for study restricts the observations to times when there is darkness at both auroral zones; the observations can be made only on the dark side of the earth and also only near equinox (March or September). The advantage of using the aurora comes from the fact that it is highly structured so that it allows rather precise determination of position, configuration, and intensity of precipitating primary particle fluxes.

Ground-based observation of auroral conjugacy has been restricted owing to the lack of appropriately located observing stations and obscuration by cloudy skies. Using all-sky camera data obtained from the nearly conjugate station pair of Farewell, Alaska, and Campbell Island, New Zealand, DeWitt (1962) found similarities of form, intensity, and temporal variations in recorded auroras. Bond (1967) reported finding excellent examples of detailed conjugacy in all-sky camera data obtained at the nearly conjugate station pair, Kotzebue, Alaska, and Macquarie Island, Australia. Wescott and Mather (1964) utilized all-sky camera data from the conjugate station pair of Reykjavik, Iceland, and Showa, Antarctica, in an attempt to identify conjugate auroral forms and to trace their motion. They gained the impression that locational shifts from true magnetic conjugacy were occurring and that relative displacements of more than 400 km were necessary to reconcile conjugacy of the observed forms. There was indication that the southern auroras were equatorward of the northern counterparts. Watson and Spitz (1967) correlated photometric data obtained in the zeniths of the nearly conjugate station pair of Great Whale, Canada, and Byrd, Antarctica, and found a tendency toward lower correlation of auroral intensities with increasing geomagnetic activity.

OBSERVATIONS

In order to avoid the restrictive constraints of weather and observing station location, two NC-135 jet aircraft were instrumented for optical observations at conjugate locations. For the first flight series, in March, 1967, each aircraft carried an all-sky camera, several narrow-field cameras, various photometers, VLF receivers, and a magnetometer. The results presented here derive mainly from the all-sky cameras, so only these instruments are described in detail. The all-sky camera was a Fairchild 35 mm instrument with aperture of f/1.5 and a 160° field of view. It was mounted in a glass dome near the center of the aircraft so as to minimize image blurring due to vibrations. Eight-second exposures were obtained every 10 seconds, and each 5 minutes a 16-second double exposure was made. Simultaneous exposures obtained on the two aircraft were synchronized to within a few milliseconds. The Kodak 2475 film used for recording was carefully developed in Kodak K-50 developer so that recorded auroral structures and intensities could be directly compared between hemispheres.

The same all-sky cameras were used in the March, 1968, flights, except that 3-second exposures were obtained each 5 seconds. Again, double exposures were made each 5 minutes. In order to obtain better temporal and spatial resolution, an image orthicon television system was installed to observe the region within 20° of the zenith over each aircraft. Each system yielded 60 auroral images per second which were recorded on video magnetic tape.

The aircraft flights occurred over conjugate regions of Alaska and the Antarctic Ocean owing to the proximity of a major airfield, Christchurch, close to the southern auroral zone and the possibility of support from the meridian chain of observing stations in Alaska. The flight plan required the southern aircraft to go directly from Christchurch to a point on the dipole (dp) 256° meridian. (This coordinate system is based upon the configuration of the dipole approximation to the geomagnetic field; longitude is measured eastward from a meridian passing near Thule, Greenland.) From that point the flight path followed a straight course along the dp 256° meridian for a distance of 1,200 or more nautical miles. The northern aircraft was left with the task of maintaining a flight path conjugate to the southern path. The map in Figure 1 shows interconnected solid circles in each hemisphere indicating conjugate locations to be reached simultaneously by the aircraft at intervals of 15 minutes. These conjugate points (points on the two ends of a geomagnetic field line) were calculated from a model of the geomagnetic field represented by the time-dependent coefficients (Hendricks and Cain, 1966) of a spherical harmonic expansion of the geomagnetic field due to internal field sources only. The flights were planned to occur between the hours of 0800

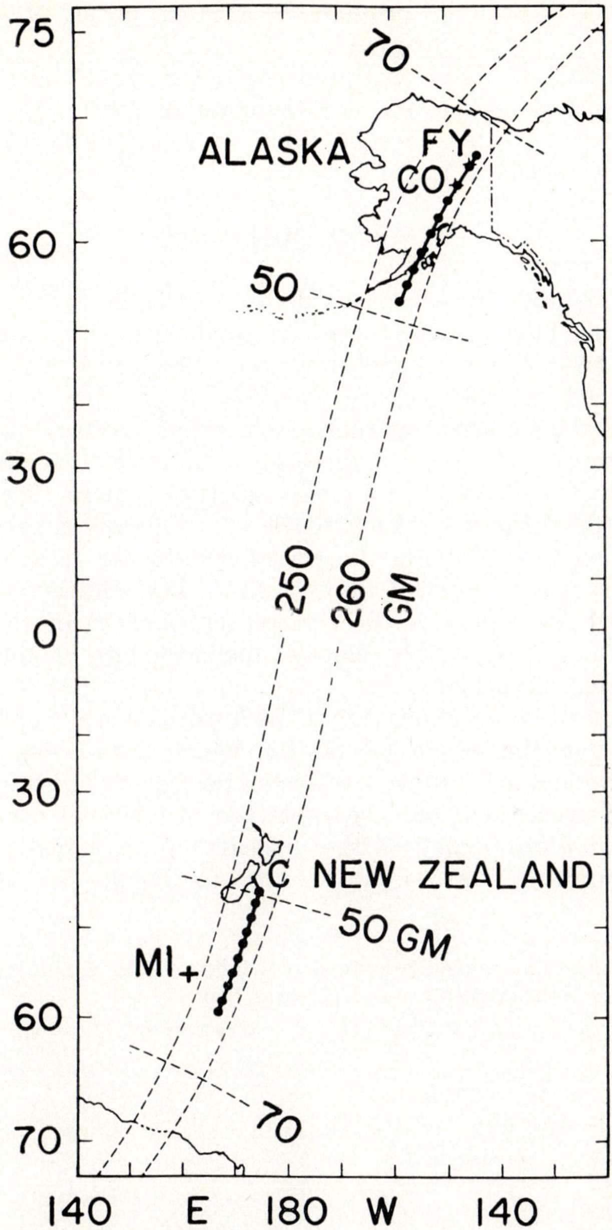

Fig. 1. Aircraft flight paths in Northern and Southern Hemispheres. Corresponding solid circles indicate conjugate locations reached simultaneously. Locations of College (CO), Fort Yukon (FY), and Macquarie Island (MI) are shown as are dipole coordinates (GM).

and 1400 UT in order to provide the greatest period of simultaneous darkness in both hemispheres.

As is shown in Table 1, quiet magnetic conditions pertained during the three conjugate flights made in 1967. Nevertheless, auroras were recorded on each flight at locations between dipole latitudes 65° and 71°.

ANALYSIS METHODS

Several methods have been used to analyze the resulting all-sky camera data. Particularly useful for qualitative examinations are composite 16-mm motion pictures assembled using all the useful data obtained in 1967. Corresponding all-sky prints from each hemisphere were placed together along with identifications of date, time, location, and cardinal directions, and the assemblage was photographed 24 times with a motion-picture camera. This process was repeated throughout each flight. At regular intervals, additional information showing the actual departures from conjugacy of the aircraft was inserted into the film. The additional information allowed evaluation of the relative appearance of the auroras in each hemisphere to the relative displacements of the aircraft from conjugate locations.

The composite films showed that the auroras were simultaneously similar during the entire period for which data were available. In general, when any differences in the positions and shapes of the aurora appeared, they could be explained in terms of displacement in the relative conjugacy of the aircraft. A principal usefulness of the composite film was its ability to display the dynamical

Table 1. College and planetary magnetic K-index during conjugate flights of 1967 and 1968. Hours shown are in Universal Time.

Date	0900–1200		1200–1500	
	K_{col}	K_p	K_{col}	K_p
March 12, 1967	2	1−	0	1−
March 14, 1967	2	1−	0	1
March 16, 1967	0	1−	1	0+
March 24, 1968	5	4−	6	4
March 26, 1968	2	4	6	3−
March 28, 1968	3	2	3	3−
March 29, 1968	4	2+	4	3
April 1, 1968	5	4	5	4−

aspects of the auroras and to show the similarity of these aspects in the two hemispheres. Although in March, 1967, the aircraft proceeded poleward only to dipole latitude 67.5°, the field of view of the all-sky camera extended to dipole latitude 71°. The composite films showed that auroras between latitudes 65° and 71° were spatially conjugate and that the dynamical characteristics in the two hemispheres were identical.

Auroras appearing on the March, 1967, composite films seemed to have the same intensity and to undergo similar intensity changes. Densitometric measurements made from the original films for selected intervals demonstrated that the intensities were indeed similar and that changes in intensity occurred at identical or nearly identical times in the two hemispheres. Figure 2 depicts an example.

Although the composite films indicated that the auroras observed in March, 1967, were conjugate, the aircraft were not always in conjugate locations, and changes in attitude of the aircraft could conceivably have hidden small deviations in conjugacy. Therefore a quantitative analysis of selected film frames was undertaken. The azimuth and elevation of points along the lower borders of selected auroral forms were scaled. A reduction pro-

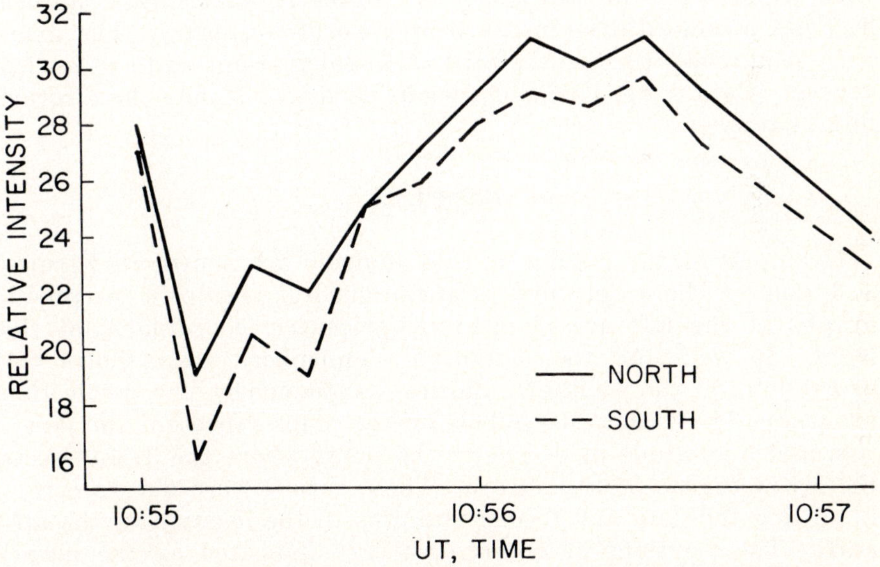

Fig. 2. Temporal variation in the intensity of conjugate auroral features. Electron-produced aurora at dp latitude 69°.

gram was then used to obtain the geocentric coordinates of each lower border. The input data to the reduction program were the position, altitude, heading, and roll and pitch of the aircraft, and the azimuth, elevation, and height of the auroral data points. An auroral height of 130 km was assumed for all the data, that height being chosen because it was measured in the Northern Hemisphere during one of the flights by using data obtained at the ground stations at College and Fort Yukon, Alaska.

In order to map the lower border of the aurora accurately the precise position and attitude of the aircraft must be known. During the flights the aircraft navigator made star fixes every 15 minutes. Instrumentation on board the aircraft recorded the speed, heading, roll, pitch, yaw, and altitude of the aircraft. These data were used in a program to make a linear interpolation of the aircraft position between the navigator's check points. In this method, the errors associated with the navigator's check point (approximately 8 nautical miles) became associated with all points along the flight path.

Once the lower border of an auroral form is mapped in geocentric coordinates, its magnetically conjugate image is found by projecting it along the geomagnetic field to the other hemisphere. A comparison of the position of a Northern Hemisphere aurora with a northern projection of a Southern Hemisphere aurora becomes a quantitative measure of auroral conjugacy. The magnetic field model used in the projection calculations is an upgraded version (Cain *et al.*, 1967) of the one used to calculate the aircraft flight paths.

RESULTS

Examples of the results of this analysis are shown in Figures 3, 4, and 5. The lower borders of the auroras shown in the photographs at the left are mapped in geocentric coordinates at the right. In addition, the Northern Hemisphere map shows the projection of the southern aurora as found by the projection program. The T-shaped symbols on the maps represent the direction and magnitude of errors at the point where the T intersects the lower border of the aurora. These errors were due to errors in scaling the data and to uncertainties in the location of the aircraft. The positions of the aircraft are indicated on the maps; note that the location of an auroral feature became more uncertain as its distance from the aircraft increased.

The examples in Figures 3, 4, and 5 are selected to show different types of auroras with various degrees of complexity. In that sense they are representative of all the data obtained in March, 1967. It is seen that, within the error limits, all the auroras observed between dipole latitudes 65° and 71° were closely conjugate according to a model of the *main* geomagnetic field. In those instances where the aircraft were in closely conjugate locations, the aspect angles to the various auroras are nearly the same and striking similarities of detail appear.

In some instances, the departures of the auroral positions from conjugate locations were slightly greater than the estimated errors. Those examples show a consistent tendency of the Southern Hemisphere aurora to be located eastward of the northern conjugate aurora.

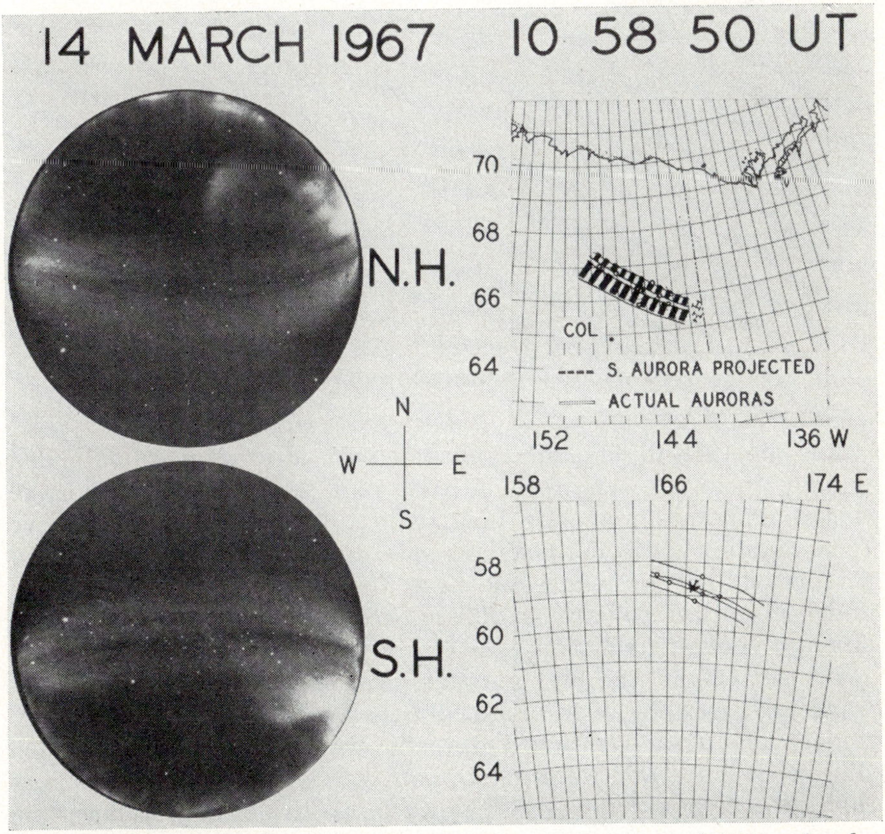

Fig. 3. Hydrogen arc near dp latitude 66°. Electron precipitation is also occurring in the arc and is responsible for its detailed structure.

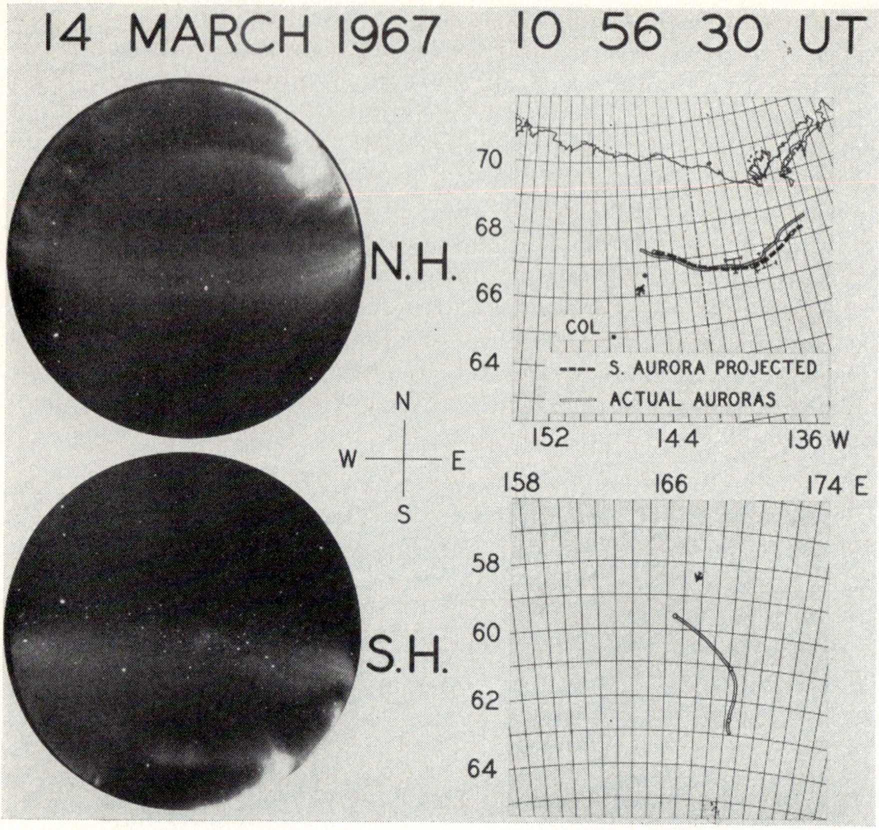

Fig. 4. Eastward loop structure at dp latitude 67° to 69°.

For the 1968 flights, the ranges of both aircraft were extended to allow them to reach dipole latitude 72°. As Table 1 shows, there was a moderate magnetic disturbance during each of the five 1968 flights. Little detailed analysis of the 1968 data has been performed, but it is already clear that the conjugate behavior under disturbed conditions differed markedly from the behavior during the quiet conditions encountered in 1967.

On each flight, the first auroral form encountered on the poleward path was the widespread, diffuse hydrogen arc. The all-sky camera photographs showed it to be closely conjugate and very similar in shape and intensity in both hemispheres, just as during the 1967 flights. However, poleward of the hydrogen arc, the electron-produced auroras exhibited differences in position and intensity, the differences tending to be greater the farther pole-

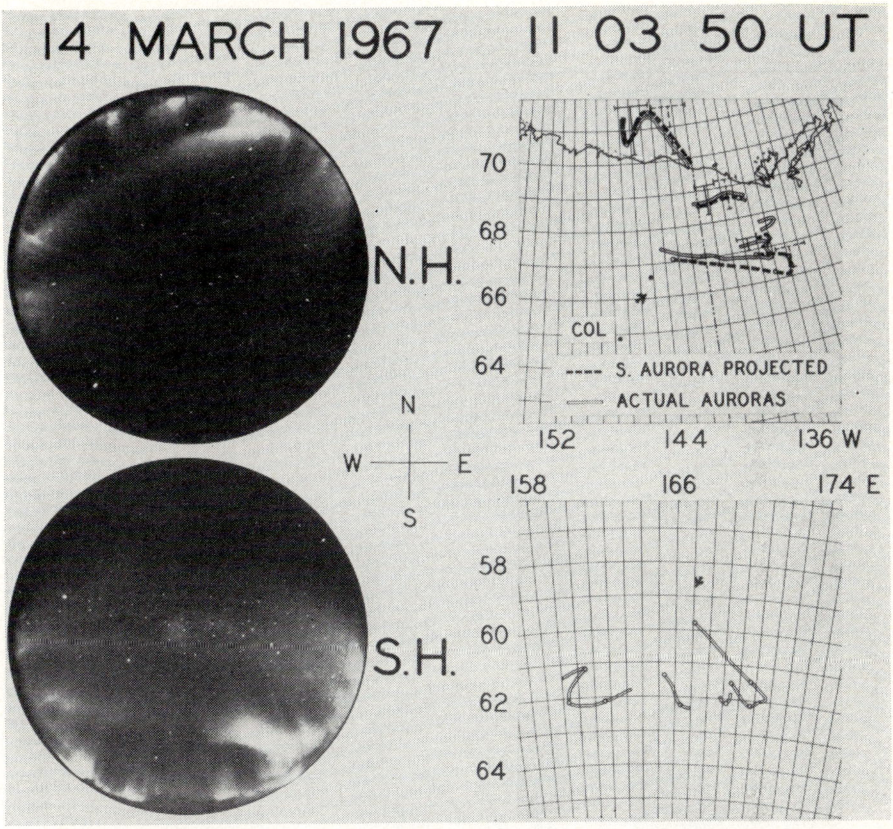

Fig. 5. Complex loops and rayed structures at dp latitudes 67° to 71°.

ward (Fig. 6). Above dipole latitude 67°, auroras exhibiting a degree of similarity were often displaced several tens of kilometers from conjugate locations calculated on the basis of an internal geomagnetic field. This displacement was not consistently in the same direction at all times and latitudes, although there is an average tendency at the higher latitudes for the southern auroras to be located equatorward and eastward relative to the conjugate northern auroras.

Another striking difference from the results of the previous year's flights is that the 1968 data show major dissimilarities in the intensities of the auroras observed poleward of the equatorward boundaries of the displays. The overall tendency was for the Northern Hemisphere auroras to be more intense; yet at times the southern aurora was more intense. At one time the aurora in one

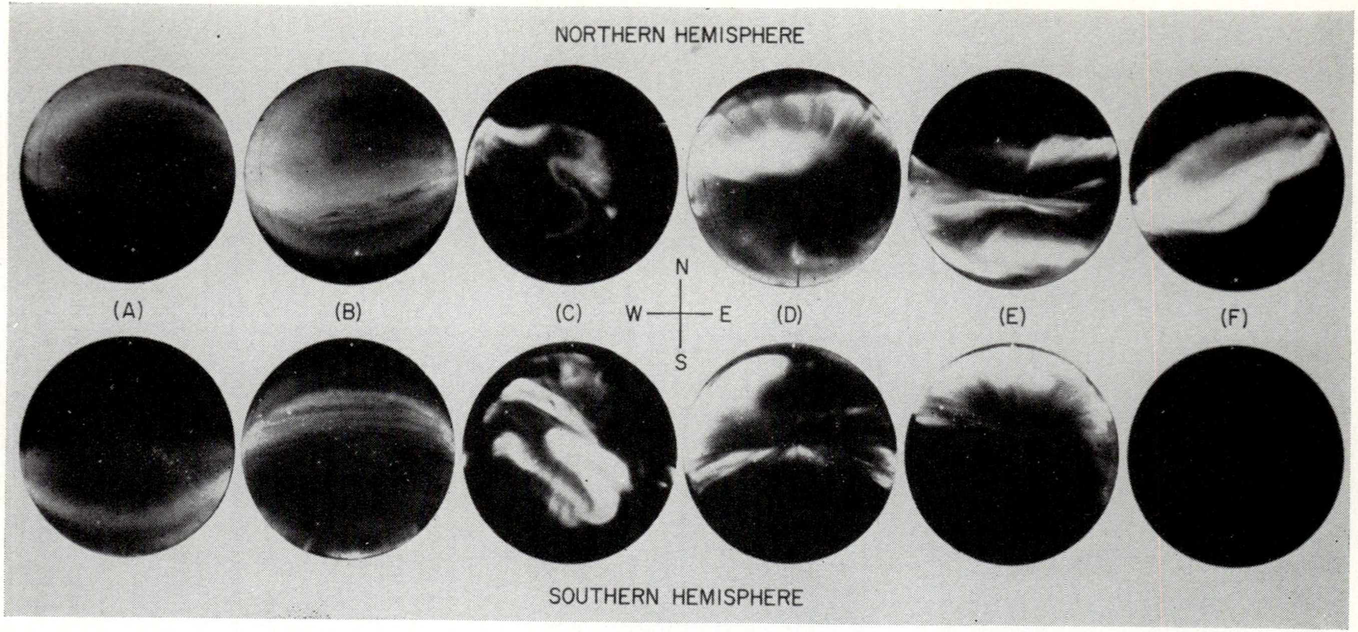

Fig. 6. Examples of all-sky camera photographs showing the degree of conjugacy of auroras in Northern and Southern Hemispheres. A. March 29, 1968, 0845 UT (dp lat 63°). Conjugate hydrogen arc (zenith) at the equatorward boundary of the auroral display. B. March 29, 1968, 0855 UT (dp lat 64.5°). Conjugate striated arcs on the poleward side of the hydrogen arc. C. March 29, 1968, 0925 UT (dp lat 67.5°). Conjugate auroral band in which the similarity of small-scale structure and brightness has greatly deteriorated. D. March 29, 1968, 0930 UT (dp lat 68°). Similar auroras which are displaced in latitude from conjugate locations calculated on the basis of an internal model of the geomagnetic field. E. March 29, 1968, 1010 UT (dp lat 67.5°). Conjugate auroral band near dp lat 65° accompanied by non-conjugate overhead auroras in the Northern Hemisphere. F. April 1, 1968, 1000 UT (dp lat 69°). Striking example of a breakdown in auroral conjugacy. As the aircraft flew from dp lat 72° to 69° there was no sign of an aurora in the Southern Hemisphere field of view (500 km).

hemisphere might be brightest, then a few minutes later the aurora in the other hemisphere became brightest, but there is no evidence of cyclic behavior in this regard.

Analysis of the 1968 data to determine if, under disturbed conditions, minor structural details were identical in the two hemispheres promises to be very difficult. This is true because both differences in auroral intensity and the differences in aspect caused by relative displacements make it difficult to ascertain the degree of detailed similarity of corresponding conjugate structures.

Similarly, it may be difficult in some cases to determine if there was a complete breakdown in conjugacy or if there were merely differences in intensity or displacements relative to the internal geomagnetic field. However, we are reasonably certain that we have observed at least one example of a complete breakdown in auroral conjugacy. During one flight a moderately bright, rayed auroral arc was observed near dipole latitude 72°N. For a period of 20 minutes at the corresponding time and conjugate location in the Southern Hemisphere, no aurora appeared in the field of view of the all-sky camera.

Analysis of the image orthicon television data obtained on the 1968 flights is still in a preliminary stage, yet several interesting results have been obtained. During the morning hours and near the equatorward boundary of the auroral display, optical pulsations were commonly observed visually and with equipment having high temporal resolution capability. Pulsating auroras were recorded concurrently in the two hemispheres on all equatorward legs of the five 1968 flights. A search for conjugate pairs of individual pulsating structures has revealed several which can be positively identified. In every case, the pulsations were exactly in phase in the two hemispheres (Fig. 7), and therefore these pulsations must be produced by a mechanism located in the equatorial plane or be in a region symmetric about the equatorial plane. By use of the television data we have located on the March 26, 1968, conjugate flight an occurrence of conjugate "fast auroral waves" (Cresswell, 1968) and also on the same night an occurrence of simultaneous "flickering auroras" (Beach *et al.*, 1968). Thus it seems that the various types of quasi-periodic phenomena in the aurora are conjugate phenomena, and we speculate that a necessary condition for the existence of the quasi-periodic behavior may be its occurrence on closed geomagnetic field lines.

The results obtained so far from the conjugate flights indicate that the aurora observed at the auroral zones is on closed and

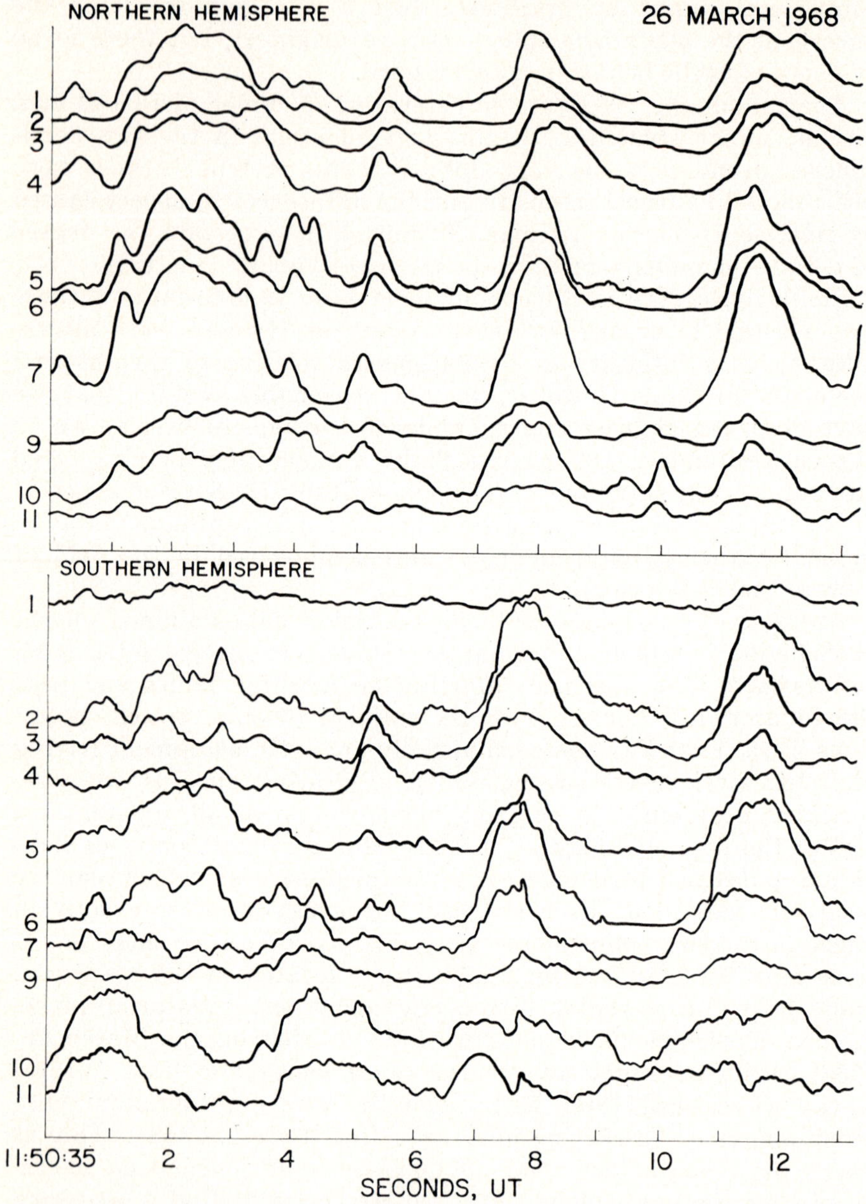

Fig. 7. Conjugate auroral pulsations observed on March 26, 1968, at dp lat 64°. Each curve represents the output of a photocell placed in front of a television monitor on which the video-taped image is displayed. Traces 1 through 4 are taken from left to right across the top (poleward) side of the screen; traces 5–7 are from the center; and traces 8–11 are taken from left to right across the bottom (equatorward) side of the screen.

relatively undistorted geomagnetic field lines during magnetically quiet times. Even under disturbed conditions, there is a class of auroral phenomena, the hydrogen arcs and the electron-produced auroras exhibiting quasi-periodic behavior, which evidently occurs on closed field lines that are not greatly distorted. But under disturbed conditions there clearly are major distortions to the geomagnetic field at the higher latitudes and marked asymmetries in the operation of the auroral acceleration mechanisms. The complete breakdown of conjugacy, as observed in at least one instance, implies that auroras can occur on geomagnetic field lines that are incapable of guiding the primary electrons across the equatorial plane.

Authors' Notes: This research project benefited greatly from the expert and splendid cooperation of many people, all of whom cannot be mentioned individually. We thank in particular Mr. Ray R. Heer, Jr., of the National Science Foundation; Messrs. William Nichparenko, Larry Sweet, Thomas Hallinan, Eldon Thompson, and Russell Beach of the Geophysical Institute; Mr. Clifton Lilliott, Mal Kennedy, Stanley Gamsby, and Ralph Armstrong at the firm of EG&G, Inc.; Drs. Harry Reynolds and Robert Donaldson of the Lawrence Radiation Laboratory; Dr. M. M. Robertson and Mr. A. F. Huters of the Sandia Corporation; Drs. Paul Rudnick and Leston Miller of the Los Alamos Scientific Laboratory; and Lt. Col. Neil Garland and his personnel on each aircraft. We also express our appreciation to Dr. Joseph Cain of NASA's Goddard Space Flight Center for providing us with the data and computer programs for the magnetic field calculations, and to the Stanford Research Institute for lending two all-sky cameras.

The Geophysical Institute participation in these projects was funded by Grants GA-798, GA-1230, and GA-1313 from the Office of Polar Programs of the National Science Foundation; by Grant GA-1306 from the Atmospheric Sciences Section of the National Science Foundation; and by NASA Contract NsR 02–001–035. The aircraft operations were funded by the Nevada Operations Office of the Atomic Energy Commission. The participation of the Los Alamos Scientific Laboratory and EG&G, Inc., occurred under the auspices of the Atomic Energy Commission.

Much of the material presented in this paper was contained in "Conjugacy of Visual Auroras During Magnetically Quiet Periods," by A. E. Belon, J. E. Maggs, T. N. Davis, K. B. Mather, N. W. Glass, and G. H. Hughes, published in the *Journal of Geophysical Research, 74* (1): 1–28, dated January 1, 1969.

References

Beach, R., G. Cresswell, T. N. Davis, T. Hallinan, and L. Sweet, 1968. Flickering, a 10-cps fluctuation within bright aurora. *Planetary Space Sci., 16* (12): 1525–1529.

Bond, F. R., 1967. *Conjugate Point Latitudes and Longitudes.* Paper presented at the XIV General Assembly of the IUGG. St. Gall, Switzerland.

Cain, J. C., S. J. Hendricks, R. A. Langel, and W. V. Hudson, 1967. A proposed model for the international geomagnetic reference field—1965. *J. Geomag. Geoelec., 19:* 335–355.

Cresswell, G., 1968. Fast temporal and spatial changes in aurora. *Sci. Rept., UAG R-206.* Univ. Alaska, College.

DeWitt, R. W., 1962. The occurrence of aurora in geomagnetically conjugate areas. *J. Geophys. Res., 67:* 1347–1352.

Hendricks, S. J., and J. C. Cain, 1966. Magnetic field data for trapped-particle evaluation. *J. Geophys. Res., 71* (1): 346–347.

Watson, M. D., and A. J. Spitz, 1967. *Photometric Observations at Auroral Zone Conjugate Points.* Paper presented at the Conjugate Point Symposium. Boulder, Colorado, June, 1967.

Wescott, E. M., and K. B. Mather, 1964. Final Report of Contract No. AF 19 (628)-2779. *Sci. Rept., UAG R-146.* Univ. Alaska, College.

Energetic Radiation over Antarctica

James R. Barcus

Department of Physics, University of Denver, Denver, Colorado

The polar atmosphere is dominated by the effects of energetic particle bombardment brought about directly or indirectly by solar activity. While the properties of the radiation environment over the polar regions are quite similar, on the average, observations over Antarctica do a great deal more than simply repeat similar observations in the Arctic. The two polar regions are probably never instantaneously exact mirror images of each other because north-south asymmetries have been established and the alternation of permanent sunlight between poles can be exploited to advantage.

This chapter is concerned with antarctic measurements of energetic solar emissions and auroral zone (or magnetospheric) phenomena, specifically those aspects for which balloon-born experiments are especially pertinent. The subject is a broad one, having close links not only with many branches of geophysics, but with astrophysics, radioastronomy, and magnetohydrodynamics as well. It is probably the astronomical features, on the small scale, which make the greatest appeal to the imagination, for in a very real sense the radiations observed can be likened to travelers who bring to us information about the nature of their origin and the regions of space through which they have passed.

Only the more energetic galactic and solar cosmic rays together with certain bands of electromagnetic waves are able to penetrate the atmospheric envelope surrounding the earth and therefore can be studied directly by apparatus located on the surface of the earth. Lower-energy charged particles and X- and γ-radiations of extra-terrestrial origin are absorbed very effectively in the upper portion of the atmosphere, requiring that direct detection apparatus be operated on space platforms at higher altitudes. Modern balloon technology offers a reliable and relatively inexpensive space vehicle from which a variety of interesting investigations may be carried out advantageously. One use of the balloon has been in studying radiations of galactic, solar, or magnetospheric origin whose energies are too feeble to penetrate the dense lower atmosphere (Winckler, 1960). Unlike the more rapidly moving space probes operating at much greater heights, experiments conducted from a balloon platform are relatively fixed in geographic coordinates and altitudes and therefore can provide unambiguous evidence for true temporal variations in the quantities under measurement.

High-altitude floating balloons have been used extensively for this purpose in the northern polar regions for some time (Anderson, 1965; Brown, 1966), although only recently has this research tool been put to use in the Antarctic (Barcus *et al.*, 1967, 1968). Owing to the notoriously unpredictable conditions of wind and weather on the surface of the continent, only rather small zero-pressure polyethylene balloons, in the 100,000 cubic foot class have been employed thus far. These balloons are convenient to launch and are capable of carrying 8 to 10 pounds of scientific apparatus and radio telemetry gear to approximately 5 to 7 g/cm^2 residual atmospheric depth.

There are at least four reasons which encouraged us to undertake this kind of research in the Antarctic:

1. The combination of geographic-geomagnetic coordinates uniquely available at U. S. stations offers opportunities for extremely long-duration flights at latitudes of interest.
2. Execution of long-duration flights would not call into play negotiations with foreign governments at the diplomatic level since there is little probability of violating territorial boundaries.
3. Observations of charge, mass, and energy discrimination with balloon-borne instruments from regions of earth relatively ignored heretofore could provide a sensitive means of testing theoretical models of the geomagnetic and interplanetary fields.
4. Balloon-borne instruments afford the opportunity to study whether point, L-shell, or area conjugacy applies in conjugate precipitation near the poleward boundary of the auroral oval, thus offering more definitive field tracing, particularly on the question of open or closed magnetic field lines during magnetospheric substorms.

All of the antarctic balloon expeditions to date have been attempted during the austral summer. At latitudes greater than about 70°, where conditions of solar illumination are almost constant, a good zero-pressure balloon will remain at a sensibly high altitude for several days. It will usually remain practically overhead as the polar stratosphere is quite calm during that time of year. The useful lifetime of the majority of experiments flown thus far has been limited by the capacity of the batteries to power the instruments continuously; the average is for only about two to three days. The use of solar cells could extend the payload lifetime substantially and will be economically feasible when large super-pressure balloons, which may float at a nearly constant pressure altitude for months, become available (Lally, 1967).

The problem areas to which the floating balloon technique has been applied in the Antarctic are primarily solar-terrestrial or magnetospheric. The character of the particle investigations carried out thus far in the southern polar region is illustrated by observations obtained during two expeditions carried out by the author and coworkers during January and February, 1967 and 1968, at Byrd Station. The observational situation has proved to be rather complex and no completely satisfactory explanation of the phenomena has yet been made. About the best that can be done with certainty is an empirical description of the particle and field environment in the vicinity of the orbit of earth. This description has proved to be of value in guiding the direction of ongoing work, when it is considered in connection with known interrelations and consequences of solar activity, and compared and interpreted with fundamental theoretical models. The study of solar emissions, the interplanetary medium, and their effects on, or coupling with, planetary atmospheres rests on the theory of magnetic plasmas (Parker, 1963) ; this is especially true of planets possessing an inherent magnetic field, such as Earth and Jupiter.

DETECTION OF THE RADIATION ENVIRONMENT

The instrumentation used in our balloon-borne experiments has been intended to detect energetic particles—protons, helium nuclei, electrons, and X- and γ-rays. The radiation encountered at balloon altitudes may be primaries of extraterrestrial origin or secondaries produced by the impact of higher-energy primaries on the atmosphere. The detectors have been rather simple, involving single Geiger counters, telescopes constructed of several counters, and scintillation devices. The properties of the detectors differ considerably (Table 1). This instrumentation is a suitable compromise between the scientific requirements and the need for lightweight,

Table 1. Typical properties of various detectors flown on high altitude balloons.

Detector	Geometry factor[1] (cm^2-steradian)	Threshold energy (Mev)[2]			Efficiency (%)[3]	
		electron	proton	photon	charged particle	photon
Single counter	10^2	0.2	4.0	0.01	100	≈1
Counter telescope	10	0.6	10	—	≈80	0
Scintillation NaI(T*l*)	10^2	0.25	5	0.010	100	90

[1] The geometry factors listed are for isotropic radiation.
[2] Typical construction and signal/noise figure.
[3] Efficiency for photons depends on energy; average values given are appropriate for the energy range 0.01 to 1 Mev.

rugged payloads capable of being launched without elaborate preparations on short notice and remaining operative for extended periods.

The Geiger counter is a thin-walled ionization chamber operated at a sufficiently large potential difference so that any initial ionization created within its active volume is greatly multiplied by an avalanche process. This multiplication is self-limiting and the counter is made "self-quenching," avoiding continuous discharge or multiple after-pulsing, by the slight addition of a halogen gas to the argon filling mixture. The counter produces a uniform pulse output, whose amplitude and duration depend only on the details of construction and operating potential, independent of the initial cause of ionization. The efficiency of the counter is high for any charged particle capable of penetrating the wall thickness although the efficiency is quite low for the detection of photons. Operation of counters in a coincidence arrangement is especially useful because a coincidence response under the conditions appropriate to our application is the unambiguous identification of penetrating charged particles as well as a directional intensity measurement.

The scintillation counter operates in an entirely different manner. Apart from complete ionization, some atoms and molecules are excited to higher-energy levels during the interaction of ionizing radiation with matter, and consequently emit light during de-excitation (fluorescence). The scintillation counter is based on the detection of this light from an optically active medium (the scintillator) by means of a high-gain photomultiplier. The primary advantage of using inorganic crystals for the scintillator, in contrast to other phosphors, is their higher density which is mainly responsible for their higher stopping power and thus greater efficiency for the detection of X- and γ-radiation. In particular, thallium-activated sodium iodide, NaI(T*l*), crystals exhibit such desirable properties as high density, high light output and transparency, fast fluorescence decay, and an index of refraction suitable for optical bonding to photomultiplier tubes. The amount of light per unit of energy absorbed produced by the scintillator depends generally on the particle species and energy, thus providing the experimenter with considerably more information about the radiation than can the Geiger counter. The fluorescence photons release a proportionate number of photoelectrons from the photocathode of the multiplier tube, and this charge pulse is collected by the first dynode and subsequently fed into the multiplier structure. At the anode of the multiplier the initial photoelectron pulse appears greatly magnified by way of secondary emission at the several intermediate dynodes. Multiplication factors as large as 10^6 are common. Typical efficiency and resolution characteristics of the scintillation detector used in our experiments for photons in the energy range of 10 to 10^3 kev are shown in Figure 1. The detector has 100 percent efficiency for counting all penetrating charged particles. After electronic amplification the pulses were sorted into integral or differential energy channels. The channel outputs were scaled in digital or analogue fashion and telemetered to the ground receiving station along with the telescopic data and certain "housekeeping" information.

Because of the frequency and the severity of solar-controlled radiation increases in the polar regions it is somewhat difficult to define a "normal" radiation environment. In the absence of such solar effects, however, the environment is due almost entirely to galactic cosmic rays and their secondaries, and this level of radiation provides a virtually constant reference which is called the "background." At the lowest range of energies to which our instrumentation responds the composition of this background is roughly 20 percent penetrating charged particles and 80 percent photonic.

Our ability to detect, directly, radiation above background level from an extraterrestrial source is restricted by the amount of residual atmosphere above the balloon. This limits the observed spectrum of charged particles to that portion for which the initial

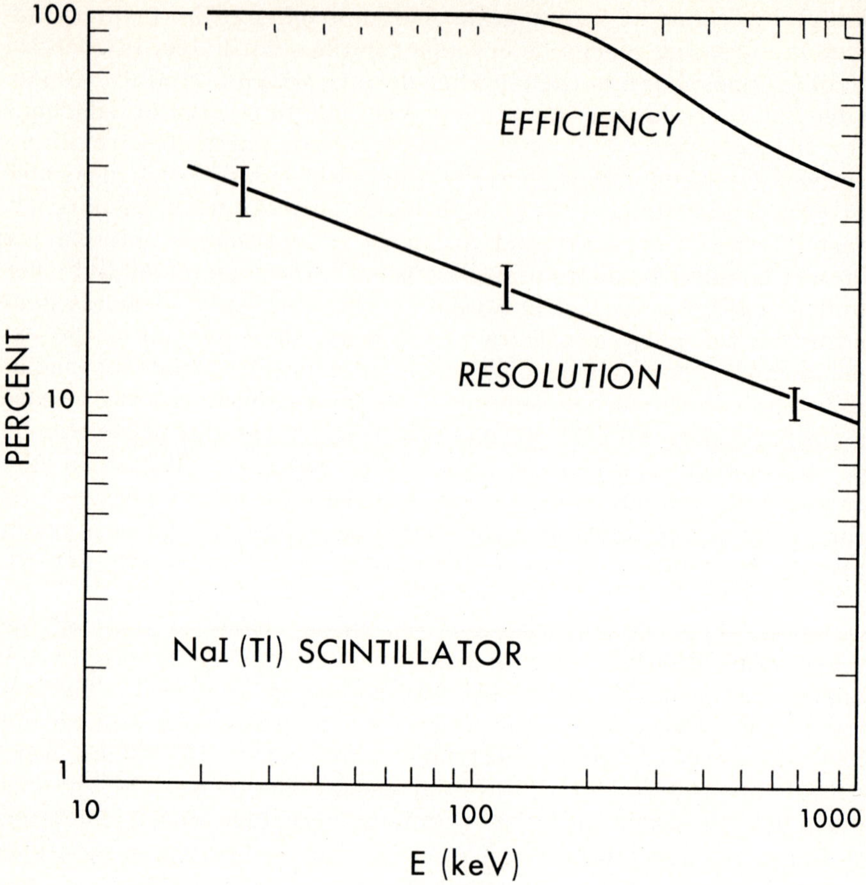

Fig. 1. Efficiency and resolution for measurement of X- and γ-rays by a NaI(T*l*) scintillation detector.

energy exceeds the ionization loss in air (Table 2). Unlike that for heavily charged particles, the range for electrons is not so sharply defined since these lighter particles can exhibit considerable straggling. The influx of lower-energy charged particles may be known indirectly by the detection of the more penetrating photonic radiation which is bremsstrahlung X-rays in the case of electron bombardment and γ-radiation from nuclear reactions in the case of proton bombardment. Table 3 gives the mass absorption coefficients for photonic radiation in air. It is clear that low-energy photons ($\leqslant$ 50 kev) may be severely attenuated by photoelectric absorption in traversing the residual atmosphere above the

Table 2. Range and penetration depths of charged particles in the atmosphere.

Height (km)	Depth (g/cm²)	Energy (Mev) electron	proton	alpha
100	4.5×10^{-4}	0.01	0.3	1.2
80	1.2×10^{-2}	0.07	2	8
60	2.4×10^{-1}	0.55	10	40
45	1.5	3.0	39	156
40	3.0	5.5	57	230
35	5.0	9.5	75	300
30	12.0	30	125	500

Table 3. Photoelectric and Compton-scattering coefficients in air.

Photon energy (kev)	Photoelectric (cm²/g)	Compton (cm²/g)
10	4.2	0.190
20	0.5	0.175
30	0.13	0.165
40	0.050	0.160
50	0.025	0.155
60	0.013	0.150
80	0.005	0.135
100	0.0025	0.125

balloon. Actually, the situation is extremely complex as higher-energy photons may be predominantly scattered, rather than absorbed, and thus Compton-degraded down to lower energies. This difficult diffusion problem has not been solved, but with some simplifying assumptions M. H. Rees, who has performed greatly improved calculations soon to be published, has obtained machine solutions for some useful cases (Bailey *et al.*, 1970).

PROTONS FROM A "BACKSIDE" SOLAR FLARE REACH EARTH

Solar cosmic rays are nuclei and electrons generated most spectacularly in great solar flares. On occasion, the energies of the particles may extend beyond upwards of 10^4 mev. The total energy flux carried by flare particles can exceed the galactic cosmic ray background in the vicinity of earth by many orders of magnitude for some days following the flare (McDonald, 1963).

Although the history of energetic radiations from solar flares dates back more than 25 years (Forbush, 1946), detailed particle measurements on such events began only a little more than a decade ago (Meyer *et al.*, 1956). As a result of continuing efforts, the concept of rare solar particle outbursts has given way to a description in which the time interval between major radiation events is to be reckoned in months rather than years, and the particle energies are typically well below the 10^3 mev range needed to penetrate to the surface of the earth. It is suspected that the sun emits weak fluxes of low-energy particles more or less continuously.

Near-earth observations on the main features of solar cosmic ray events have a direct bearing on the propagation of charged particles through the interplanetary medium and thus give information on the nature of that medium. The observations suggest that the particles diffuse anisotropically, being strongly influenced by the solar magnetic fields embedded in the ever-expanding solar corona which dominates the interplanetary medium. The diffusive action is most probably caused by irregularities in the solar magnetic field and the constants characterizing the diffusion process may be quantitatively related to the power spectrum of magnetic fluctuations.

The transport of solar protons in the space between sun and earth was studied during an unusual solar particle event observed at Byrd Station during the austral summer of 1967 (Barcus, 1969a). Commencing at about 0830 UT on January 28, a large and prolonged increase in the intensity of penetrating charged particles was observed by balloon-borne counter-telescopes. A peak intensity was recorded of approximately 60 protons/cm^2/sec/steradian with $E \geqslant 100$ mev. The event was under observation almost continuously over a period of about 100 hours until the intensity decayed below the cosmic ray background on February 1. At the same time, increases in counting rate were detected for particle detectors at sea level not only in polar regions but also down to latitudes of 30°. Unfortunately, our balloon observations were the only direct measurements made in the atmosphere below satellite altitudes, precluding therefore any possibility of studying hemispheric asymmetries in the 100 mev range. Besides being one of the most energetic solar outbursts of the present cycle, the event was unusual in that apparently it had its origin in a major solar eruption on the far side of the sun. No optical or radio features to which the event could be linked existed on the visible disk at an appropriate time; therefore the particles must have reached earth only after undergoing considerable scattering and diffusion, even at the very highest energies.

Results pertaining to the time-intensity profile and a fit to Burlaga's (1967) model of anisotropic diffusion with absorbing boundary are shown in Figure 2. Comparison with theory leads to estimates of the diffusion coefficients along and perpendicular to the mean interplanetary magnetic field of about 3×10^{21} cm^2/sec for 100 mev protons. The characteristic exponential decay late in the event, only the early part of which is shown in Figure 4, suggests that the boundary of the diffusing region, beyond which particles find relatively easy escape from the inner solar system, is located at some 2.3 astronomical units (AU) (1 AU is the mean distance from sun to earth).

In this particular event, the diffusion appears to have been velocity-dependent (Bryant *et al.*, 1965) over a large range of energy (5 mev to 5 bev), suggesting that all particles traversed essentially the same path length, or $\approx$ 10 to 15 AU, before reaching earth. Information concerning the structure of the interplanetary medium may be obtained by assuming that the scattering took place in the interplanetary medium by way of small-angle scattering from magnetic irregularities and by the random walk of magnetic lines of force. Velocity-dependent diffusion may be understood on the basis of the statistical theories of Jokipii (1966, 1967, 1968) and Parker (1968), if the distribution in the size of magnetic irregularities in interplanetary space varies in an appro-

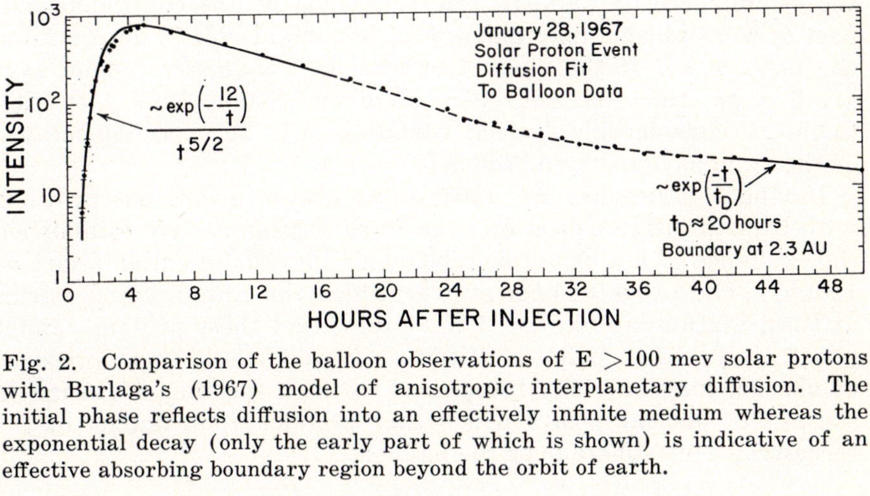

Fig. 2. Comparison of the balloon observations of E >100 mev solar protons with Burlaga's (1967) model of anisotropic interplanetary diffusion. The initial phase reflects diffusion into an effectively infinite medium whereas the exponential decay (only the early part of which is shown) is indicative of an effective absorbing boundary region beyond the orbit of earth.

priate manner. However, the scattering mean free path so deduced turns out to be about 5×10^{11} cm, which is close to the satellite-measured correlation length of the fluctuating field at the orbit of earth. Thus, application of a statistical theory is somewhat marginal in this case, and the diffusion may have appeared velocity-dependent only because of this limitation by the correlation length.

A STRONG DAILY VARIATION IN PROTON INTENSITY

As charged particles approach earth from interplanetary space, their trajectories are determined in the absence of collisions solely by the geomagnetic field. Today we know the field is contained in a finite volume of space, the magnetosphere, within the stream of solar plasma. Some years ago Störmer (1955) had worked out the minimum (cutoff) magnetic rigidity P_c (product of the radius of curvature with magnetic field strength) which a charged particle must possess in the earth's dipole field to reach the surface at a given geomagnetic latitude Θ; his result is $P_c = 14.9 \cos^4 \Theta$ where P_c is measured in units of 10^9 volts. This simple expression agrees with observation quite satisfactorily at low latitudes, say $\Theta \leqslant 40°$; however, cosmic ray cutoffs are known to exhibit anomalously low values, in comparison with Störmer's theory, at medium and high geomagnetic latitudes. Early attempts to explain this behavior suggested the existence of a variety of external sources of distant field structures in addition to the dipole-like internal field contribution which Störmer had used. Recently, it has been recognized that the geomagnetic tail (Ness, 1965), formed by the continuous impact of solar plasma may play an all-important role in determining the penetration of the magnetosphere by low-energy cosmic rays (Gall *et al.*, 1968; Michel, 1965; Reid and Sauer, 1967). In particular, a considerable diurnal variation is to be expected because of the axial asymmetry of the field.

During the January 28, 1967, solar proton event, observations with balloon instrumentation over Byrd Station clearly established the existence of a diurnal modulation of the proton cutoff (Barcus, 1969b). The range of energy over which the proton cutoff varies at Byrd Station is so low, $\approx$ 1 to 20 mev, that these protons cannot penetrate down to balloon altitudes. Nevertheless, their presence or absence may be easily recognized through the time variation in the flux of nuclear γ-rays which they produce upon impact of the terrestrial atmosphere over the balloon.

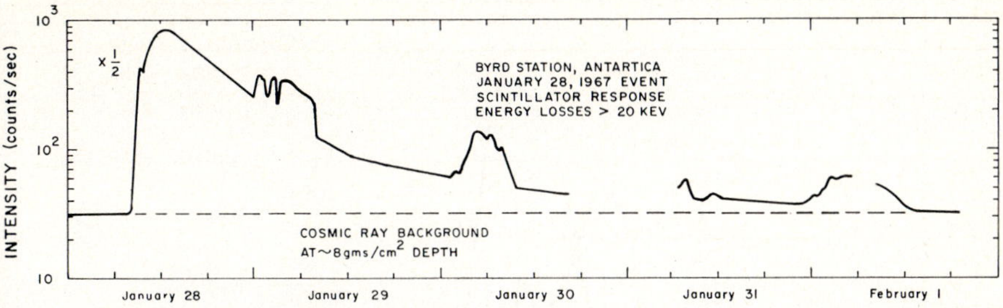

Fig. 3. Scintillation detector response to the January 28, 1967, solar proton event. The diurnal modulation in intensity is due to the variability in the flux of nuclear γ-rays produced by low-energy proton bombardment of the terrestrial atmosphere over Byrd Station.

Figure 3 summarizes the measurements made with a scintillation counter in response to the January 28 event. The diurnal modulation of intensity is quite evident in these measurements, whereas the directly penetrating proton component ($E > 100$ mev) showed only a steady decline after the peak of the event. The scintillator response is therefore dominated by the presence of nuclear γ-rays produced by the intense low-energy proton bombardment. The period of observation was magnetically quiet with the exception of some minor transient substorms so that it proved to be an excellent opportunity to study the diurnal cutoff variation in detail. Moreover, there was no evidence for any similar time variations in the flux of low-energy protons detected by satellite outside the magnetosphere, so that one can be quite sure that the diurnal variation observed close to the earth truly reflects the axially asymmetric aspect of the magnetosphere, that is, daytime compression and nighttime extension of the field.

A relative comparison of some of the nuclear γ-ray results with the diurnal intensity variation which would be predicted on the basis of one theoretical model in the cutoff at a magnetic latitude such as Byrd Station is shown in Figure 4. The assumptions involved in making the comparison are sufficiently realistic to allow some tentative conclusions to be drawn. First of all, agreement would be better if the theoretical curve were to be centered on geomagnetic midnight (2200 hours local time at Byrd Station) rather than on local midnight. Even so, the transition takes place much more rapidly than predicted. Also, comparison of the absolute magnitudes of the measured and predicted effects suggests that the cutoff at Byrd Station is probably less than 4 mev at night and is certainly below 50 mev in the daytime—the minimum and

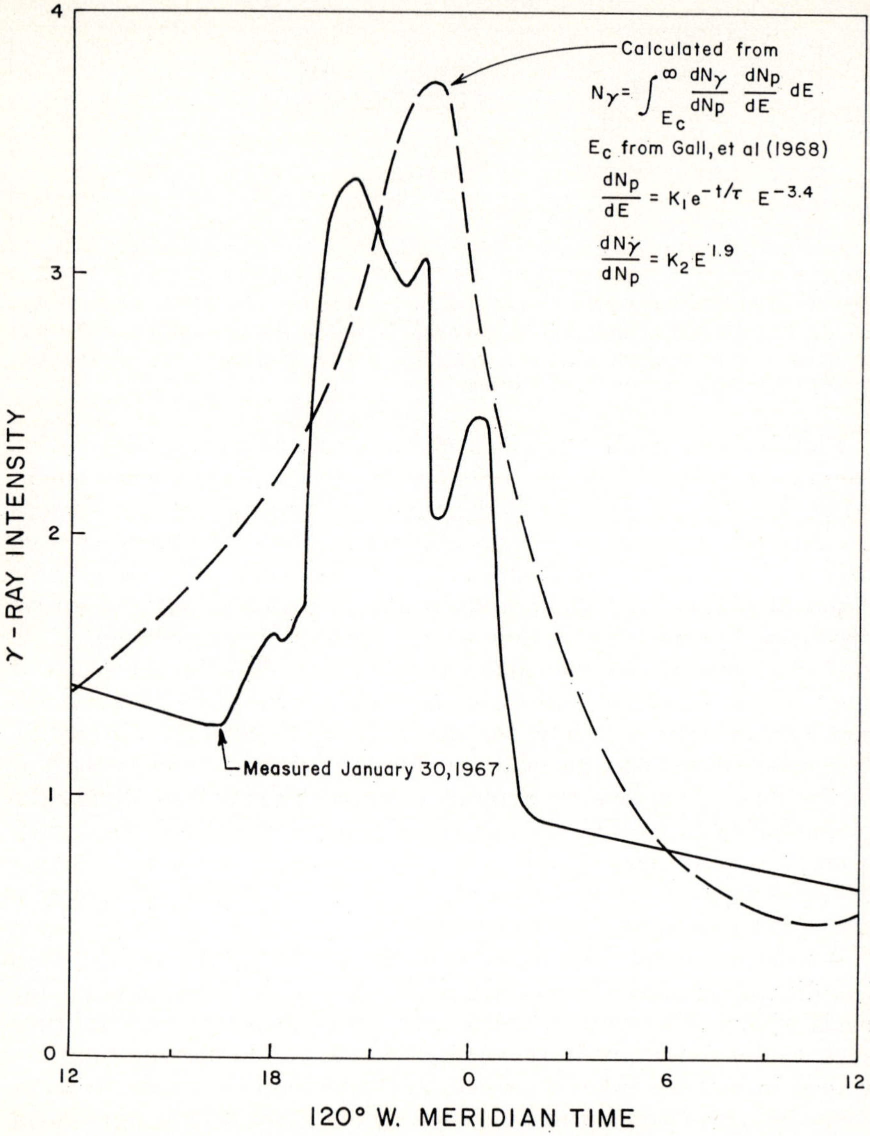

Fig. 4. Comparison of the local-time variation in the nuclear γ-ray flux observed on January 30, 1967, with that predicated on the basis of the diurnal variation in proton cutoff calculated by Gall *et al.* (1968). dN_p/dE is the incident proton spectrum and $dN\gamma/dN_p$ gives the γ-ray production.

maximum values predicted from the simple magnetospheric model used. Though still preliminary, new calculations by Gall (personal communication), using a more realistic model for the internal field, indicate that the cutoff at Byrd Station is probably less than 1 mev at night and would not exceed 25 mev in the daytime.

There are at least three important factors that need to be incorporated into a more satisfactory theoretical model. These are: (1) the inclination of the geomagnetic dipole with the solar ecliptic plane (Roederer, 1968), (2) partial ring currents within the magnetosphere (Cummings *et al.*, 1968), and (3) transient alterations of the field configuration (Heppner *et al.*, 1967). Each of these factors might easily lead to substantial conjugate or hemispheric asymmetries in the cutoffs and their diurnal variations at high latitudes.

PROTON INTENSITY AFFECTED BY SMALL MAGNETOSPHERIC SUBSTORMS

On certain occasions during the January 28, 1968, solar proton event the nighttime increase in the γ-ray intensity, which reflects the low value of the cutoff, was observed to recover almost completely for transient periods of time (Barcus, 1969c). These recoveries were found to be in approximate time coincidence with the occurrence of small magnetospheric substorms (Akasofu, 1964) as evidenced by the characteristic disturbance in the local magnetic field at Byrd Station.

Three examples of the effect are shown in Figure 5. The decrease in the nuclear γ-ray intensity, or increase in the proton cutoff, is delayed some 10 to 15 minutes from the first appearance of micropulsations in the horizontal component of the local field. These pulsations are a characteristic signature of the "triggering" of the substorm in the magnetosphere (Rostoker, 1967), whereas the subsequent depression of the local field is indicative of development of overhead ionospheric current systems. Protons in the energy range involved here almost certainly arrive over Byrd Station only after passing some distance through the magnetotail, perhaps entering the tail some distance downstream in the solar plasma flow past earth. The mechanism of entry is not clear at this time, but, assuming the particles follow well-defined trajectories once in the tail rather than diffusive propagation, the region of entry ought to be roughly where the tail becomes fragmented and even possibly where the terrestrial lines of force merge with

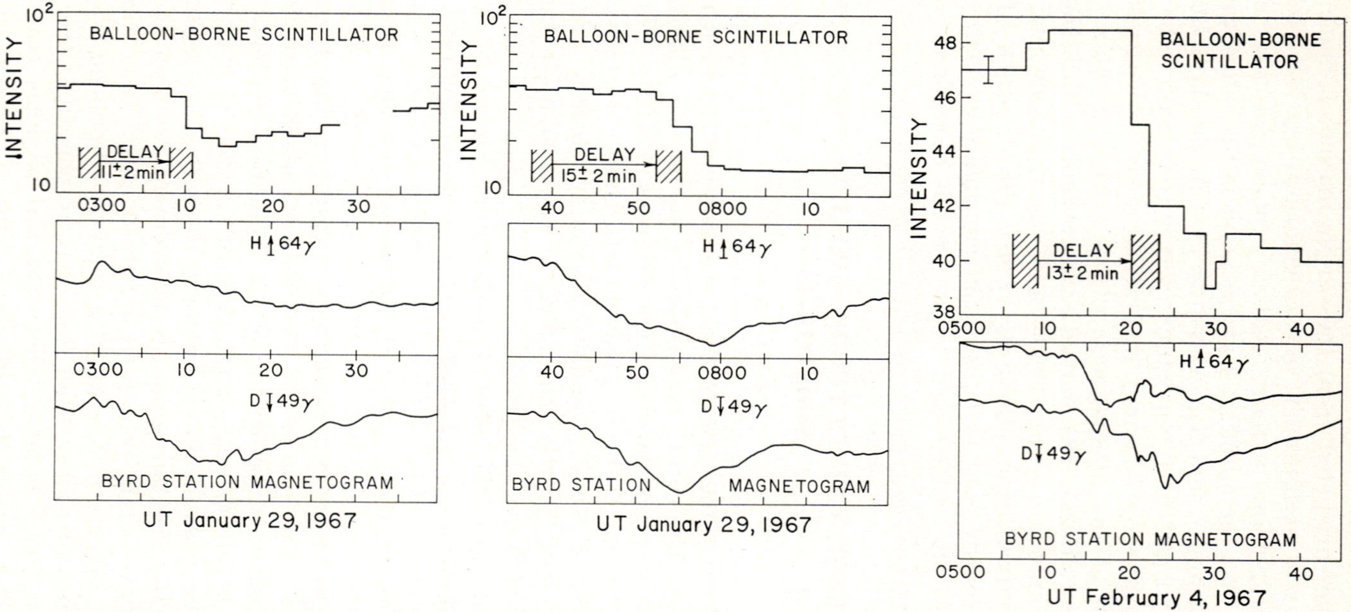

Fig. 5. Examples of the recovery in the nuclear γ-ray flux (increased proton cutoff) associated with small magnetospheric substorms. Increases in the cutoff over Byrd Station appear delayed some 10 to 15 minutes from the first appearance of micropulsations in the local magnetic field.

those embedded in the interplanetary plasma. There is some evidence (Heppner *et al.,* 1967; Dessler, 1968) which suggests that the substorm involves a partial and transient collapse of the tail field and therefore acts to increase the field strength close to the earth, at some 6 to 10 earth radii, at the expense of the more distant portion. If this is the case, then the cutoffs would be necessarily increased. Also, since the collapse would take a finite amount of time to propagate down the tail, a delay should be expected between the onset of the substorm and the appearance of increased cutoffs at high latitudes. Proceeding on this basis, it has been estimated that the point of entry for low-energy protons into the magnetotail could be 200 times earth radius. This estimate agrees surprisingly well with expectations (Behannon, 1968) based on the rate of decrease of intensity in the tail field as observed by satellites out to the lunar orbit ($\approx$ 80 earth radii).

The principal importance of these observations is to demonstrate that the cutoffs may be seriously altered during sporadic substorms of even modest intensity. Further, substorm-related changes of the distant magnetosphere may act to increase the apparent cutoffs at high latitudes. The effect is the opposite of that sometimes seen in middle and high latitudes where, during magnetic storms, the local cutoff is depressed for extended periods (Hofmann and Sauer, 1968). Bewick *et al.* (1970) have argued for this latter effect during even small substorms from a study of trapped particle data obtained onboard a low-altitude polar-orbiting satellite. Coordinated experiments would be of enormous value here.

MAGNETIC CONJUGACY: A DYNAMIC CONCEPT

Ground-based observations (Wescott, 1966) have shown that a number of geophysical phenomena occurring in the auroral zones display similar characteristics, on a real-time basis, between areas in the Northern and Southern Hemispheres which were formerly thought to be linked by specified geomagnetic field lines. Such areas are commonly referred to as magnetically conjugate regions. When it was recognized that energetic electron precipitation out of the magnetosphere generated bremsstrahlung X-rays in sufficient intensity to be easily detected at balloon altitudes, another method of investigation, more simply related to the primary electrons, became possible and was put to use (Anderson *et al.,* 1962; Brown *et al.,* 1965). These results and the early satellite measurements of the distant field topology and its distortions forced considerable revision of the older concepts of a static magnetic conjugacy.

As a part of the 1968 expedition to Byrd Station it was planned to coordinate balloon flights with similar releases from the conjugate region near Hudson's Bay in Canada (Fig. 6). The best location appeared to be at Great Whale River on the eastern side of the bay. At the outset of the field operations extreme surface conditions of weather and the high-velocity stratospheric winds prevailing in the northern winter vortex forced the launch operations to be transferred to Fort Churchill on the western side of the bay. In spite of this, a downwind receiving station remained at Great Whale River.

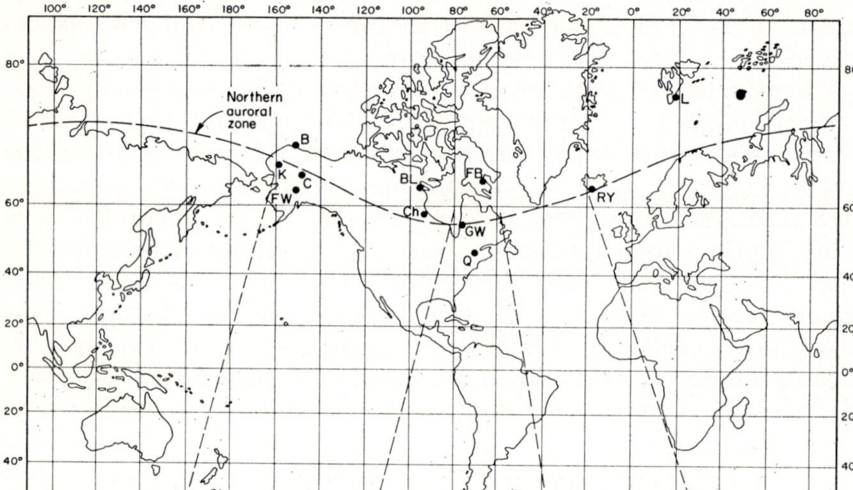

Fig. 6. Map showing the locations of some of the pairs of stations which have been used in conjugate auroral zone studies. Conjugate balloon programs have been conducted using (1) College (C), Alaska, and Macquarie Island (MI), Australia; (2) Fort Churchill (Ch) and Great Whale River (GW), Canada, and the U. S. base at Byrd Station (BY), Anarctica; and (3) Reykjavik (RY), Iceland, and the Japanese base, Syowa Base (SB), Antarctica.

One of the interesting features of auroral zone electron precipitation which was observed during the program was an observation concerned with the poleward expansion phase of a substorm. Working principally with all-sky-camera pictures and magnetograms, Akasofu (1964) has emphasized that the evolution of individual auroral substorms, as seen in the midnight sector of the auroral zone, may be best organized in terms of two characteristic phases—an expansive initial phase lasting some five to ten minutes characterized by the rapid poleward motion ($\approx$20 to 100 km/min) of active auroral bands and the simultaneous depression of the magnetic field, then followed by a gradual recovery phase which lasts some 30 minutes to an hour. These features reflect, predominantly, the behavior of electrons in the 1 to 10 kev range. Our particular interest was focused on the question: to what extent might the more energetic electron precipitation in conjugate regions follow a similar pattern of motion?

Our conjugate balloon observations relating to the poleward expansion feature are shown in Figure 7. The energetic electron precipitation, detected by bremsstrahlung X-rays, was similar in intensity and approximately simultaneous in the two hemispheres. The similarity in onset, cessation, and fine structure of the radiation between 0600 and 0604 UT is most apparent if the records are displaced relatively, as shown, by almost 20 seconds.

The initial phase of the substorm, 0600–0605 UT, is evidenced by the rapid depression of the local magnetic field at Byrd Station. An abrupt increase in ionospheric absorption of galactic radio noise reflects the influx of ionizing radiation. Similar records were obtained in northern Canada at both Great Whale River and Fort Churchill. Additionally, low time resolution all-sky-camera pictures from Fort Churchill showed a stable arc near the southern horizon at about 0601 UT, then the entire sky filled with aurora by about 0603 UT. A lower limit of some 2 to 3 km/sec for the poleward expansion velocity of luminous aurora in the Northern Hemisphere may be inferred.

To facilitate the discussion of the balloon results, Figure 8 shows recent calculations of Barish and Roederer (private communication) on the antarctic conjugate intersects of field lines from fixed geographic locations in the area of Hudson's Bay. The calculations account for the real internal field, magnetopause currents, the magnetotail, and the variable inclination of the dipole with the solar ecliptic plane. They do not take into account the finite conductivity of earth nor the ionosphere—thus the diurnal "wandering" prob-

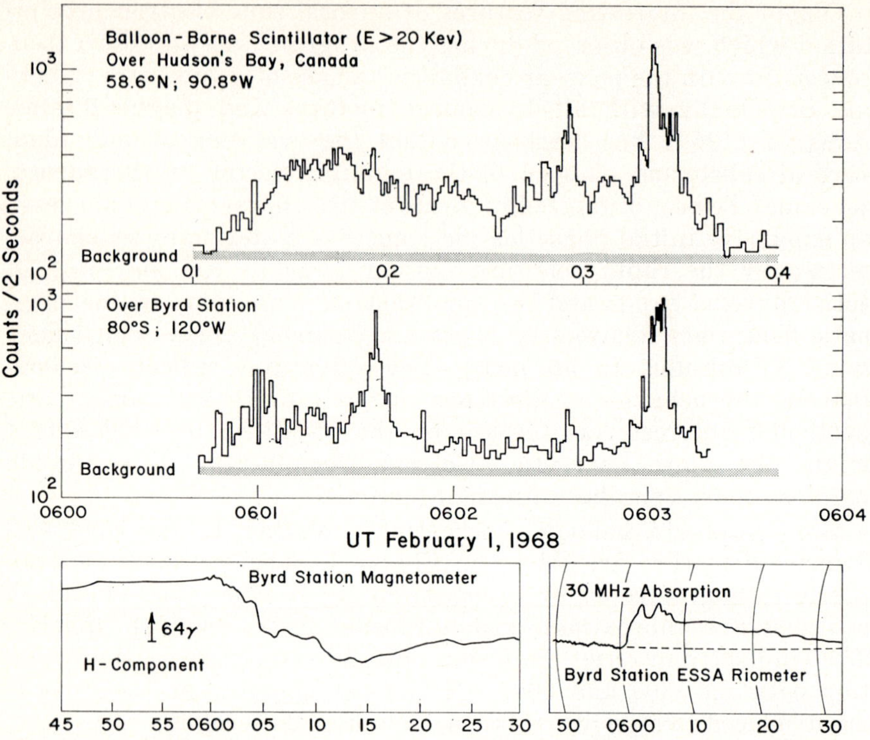

Fig. 7. Balloon observations, in closely conjugate regions, of electron bremsstrahlung accompanying the onset and poleward expansion of a polar substorm. Note that the time scales for the intensity records of the Northern and Southern Hemisphere balloon have been displaced with respect to each other by 20 seconds to emphasize the details of similarity. Also shown are the local geomagnetic disturbance and increase of ionospheric absorption.

ably ought to be considered as an upper limit on the motion of the conjugate intersects for this time of year. For purposes of reference, the corresponding contours of constant L, which are based on the internal field only, are also shown (McIlwain, 1961).

The approximately 20-second delay in the arrival of bursts of energetic electrons over the northern balloon, which had drifted eastward out over Hudson's Bay from Fort Churchill, as compared with their arrival over the Byrd Station balloon, can be interpreted in terms of movements of narrow bands of electron influx aligned approximately parallel to constant L contours in the midnight sector. The observed delay is then assumed to be caused by a polewards motion of the precipitation pattern proceeding to higher L values from $L \leqslant 7$ to $L \geqslant 8.75$ as shown in Figure 8. This distance is in the range of 100 to 400 km, and thus the inferred rate of over-

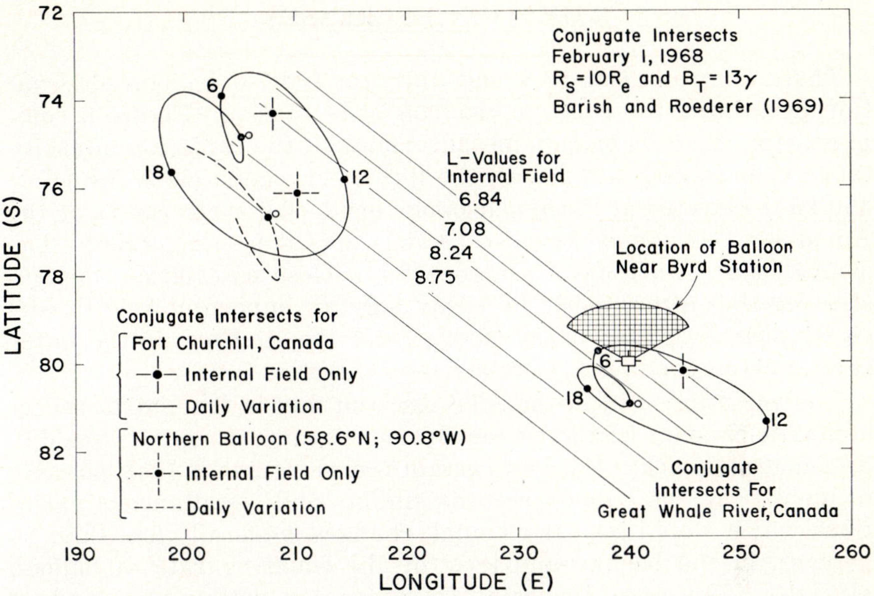

Fig. 8. Conjugate intersects in Antarctica of magnetic field lines from fixed geographic locations in the vicinity of Hudson's Bay, Canada (calculations by Barish and Roederer, private communication). The daily "wandering" of the intersects reflects the effect of the variable inclination of the geomagnetic dipole with the solar ecliptic plane at this time of year. Static conjugate points and constant L-contours, based on the internal field alone, are also shown. The shortest possible distance, across contours of constant L, between the Byrd Station balloon and the conjugate intersect for the northern balloon is about 100 to 400 km.

head motion is approximately 5 to 20 km/sec, somewhat greater than the minimum rate of expansion deduced from the all-sky-camera observations on the poleward boundary of aurora over Fort Churchill for this event. Comparably high speeds for fast auroral waves have been reported recently (Cresswell, 1968; Campbell, 1970).

The present observations are remarkable in themselves; so detailed a correspondence of bremsstrahlung X-rays between hemispheres has not been particularly evident. Perhaps the essential point to be drawn from the observations is a demonstration that energetic electrons may precipitate symmetrically into each hemisphere during the expansion phase of the substorm with the magnetic lines of force on the equatorward side of the expanding poleward boundary remaining closed. Thus, point magnetic conjugacy may be retained as a significant, dynamic concept.

RADIATION DECREASES

There is an entirely new and different type of balloon observation pertaining to energetic electron precipitation. Figure 9 compares simultaneous balloon measurements of the radiation intensity taken over Byrd Station with the flux of energetic electrons ($E > 450$ kev) detected at the synchronous orbit (6.6 earth radii) of the Advanced Technology Satellite (ATS) (Paulikas *et al.*, 1968). The comparison reveals clear evidence for a close association, demonstrating that atmospheric loss may play an important role in correctly assessing the energy budget and the lifetime of the outer zone electron population at relativistic energies.

The variation seen in the ATS electron flux is thought to reflect adiabatic changes brought about by some readjustments in the distant magnetic field. Only on certain occasions has it been possible to identify in the balloon records similar and simultaneous variations which would appear as small changes, generally less than 20 percent, in the background level of the counting rate at balloon altitudes. The most favorable occasions for noting this kind of correspondence appear to exist only whenever the distant field is weak and hence the variations correspond to periods when the field lines from Byrd Station are not drawn out to great distances but, rather, pass close to the orbit of the ATS. At such times, the small changes in the background rates observed at the balloon, and which are correlated with similar intensity changes at the ATS, reflect the variability in the energetic bremsstrahlung produced by those magnetospheric electrons which find themselves in the loss cone. A detailed temporal correspondence cannot be expected because field lines from Byrd Station (120°W) do not pass exactly through the satellite longitude (150°W).

A numerical value for the loss rate cannot be given at this time; work is under way to relate, quantitatively, the measured variation in bremsstrahlung flux to the high-energy spectrum of trapped particles, and this will be reported on in the near future. For the present, a preliminary study of the effect appears to indicate that the loss is probably roughly proportional to the omnidirection electron population.

Another interesting feature revealed in Figure 9 is that the adiabatic effect precedes the onset of a small polar substorm by about 30 minutes. The non-adiabatic changes in the lower-energy ($E > 20$ kev) electron population (substorm effects) are evidenced

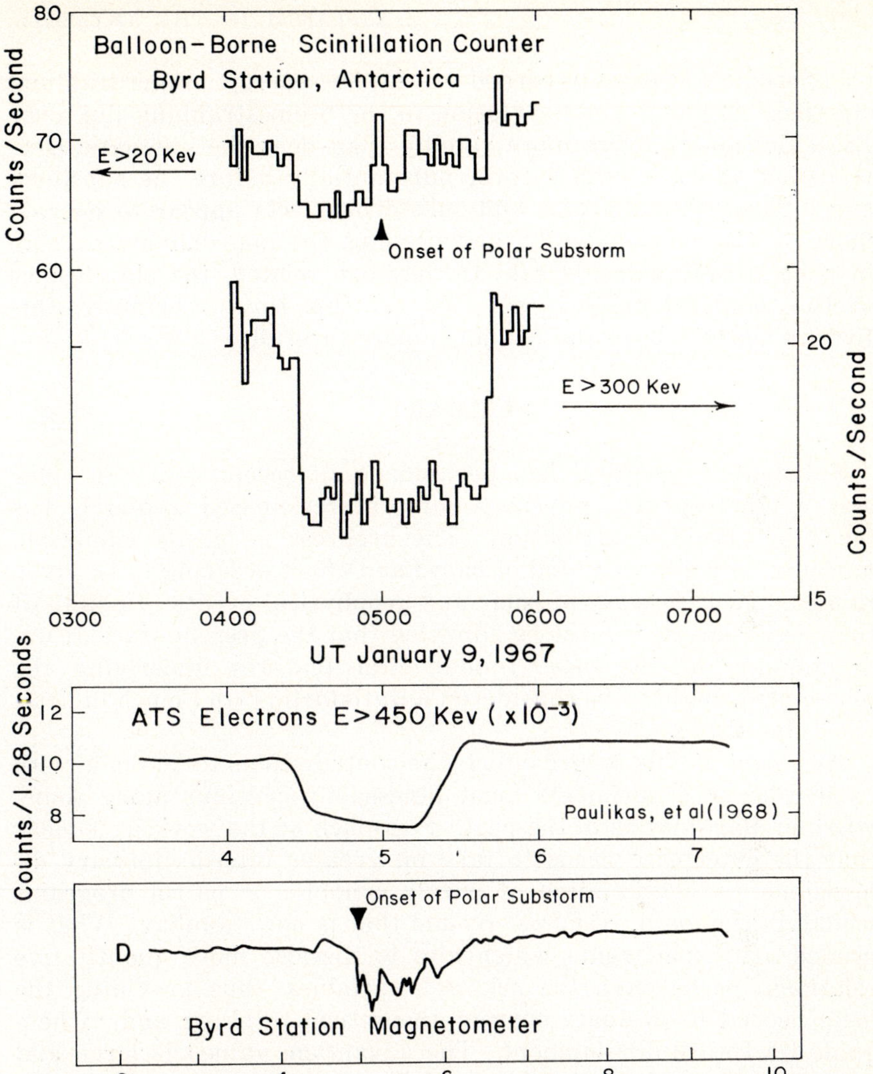

Fig. 9. Small changes in the background counting rate of a scintillation counter at balloon altitudes correlated with similar variations in the quasi-trapped electron (E >450 kev) population sampled by a geostationary satellite at the synchronous orbit of 6.6 earth radii. Those electrons in the loss cone may give rise to energetic bremsstrahlung in the atmosphere over the balloon—such loss would seem to be taking place more or less continuously. The variation in electron flux at ATS is thought to be of an adiabatic nature, a bulk transport of particles due to large-scale readjustments of the distant field. The onset of a small polar substorm (which involves non-adiabatic changes in the lower-energy electron population) reveals its effect by the sporadic increase seen on the balloon at 20 kev (low-energy bremsstrahlung) but not at 300 kev.

by sporadic increases recorded in the low-energy bremsstrahlung channel. Although the depression in the bremsstrahlung flux over Byrd Station recovers more rapidly than does the energetic electron flux at ATS, both recover substantially before the substorm ends. Thus, the adiabatic and substorm effects appear to operate more or less independently, and perhaps the approximate overlap in time is only coincidental. If they are related, the significance of the temporal delay is not clear at this time. Certainly, this feature needs to be examined much more carefully.

SUMMARY

Substantial progress has been made in recent years in solar and magnetospheric physics, and Antarctic-based research has made its special contribution. The progress is mostly empirical, however, and allows a kind of cause-and-effect ordering to be given to a complicated array of solar and geophysical events. In spite of this achievement, it must be admitted that the present state of understanding of the most fundamental features underlying the phenomena ought to be considered unsatisfactory and much difficult work lies ahead.

As a part of this future effort, the contributions to be made with balloon-borne experiments must necessarily continue along somewhat similar lines as in the past. For much of the work, it is clear that the enterprise needs to take on greater interdisciplinary dimensions. A continuation of purely synoptic or patrol programs would, in the main, resurvey ground that is now familiar. What is needed are experiments which aim to disclose more quantitative relationships between the relevant variables, thus providing the tests needed to evaluate current theoretical thinking and to help guide its future development. The advantage gained is large and this shifting emphasis is already reflected both in the planning of future experiments and in the analysis of observations already in hand.

Besides these attempts to resolve some well-defined problems, the Antarctic is admirably suited to a wider range of exploratory balloon-borne experiments than has been attempted thus far. Two such deal with problems which are certain to be of central importance during the next five years: (1) high-resolution measurements of galactic and solar X- and γ-ray sources and (2) high sensitivity measurements of the high Z portion of the cosmic ray spectrum.

Author's Note: The balloon program was supported by the Upper Atmospheric Physics Section, Office of Polar Programs, National Science Foundation. A very special commendation is due F. E. White and P. R. Williamson who so ably and enthusiastically assisted with the operations at Byrd Station, often under extremely adverse conditions of wind and weather.

References

Akasofu, S. I., 1964. The development of the auroral substorm. *Planetary Space Sci., 12:* 273–282.

Anderson, K. A., 1965. Balloon observations of X-rays in the auroral zone. In *Auroral Phenomena,* edited by M. Walt; pp. 46–83. Stanford Univ. Press, Palo Alto, Calif.

Anderson, K. A., C. D. Anger, R. R. Brown, and D. S. Evans, 1962. Simultaneous electron precipitation in the northern and southern auroral zones. *J. Geophys. Res., 67:* 4076–4077.

Bailey, D. K., R. R. Brown, and M. H. Rees, 1970. Simultaneous forward-scatter, riometer, and bremsstrahlung observations of a daytime electron precipitation event in the auroral zone. *J. Atmospheric Terrest. Phys., 32:* 149–170.

Barcus, J. R., F. E. White, and P. R. Williamson, 1967. Study of particle precipitation and magnetospheric phenomena using balloon-borne instrumentation. *Antarctic J. U. S., 2:* 124.

Barcus, J. R., F. E. White, and P. R. Williamson, 1968. Magnetospheric studies using balloon-borne instrumentation. *Antarctic J. U. S., 3:* 127.

Barcus, J. R., 1969a. Solar protons E >100 mev incident over Antarctica during January–February 1967. *Solar Physics, 8:* 186–203.

Barcus, J. R., 1969b. Diurnal variations in low-energy cosmic ray cutoffs. *Planetary Space Sci., 17:* 1173–1181.

Barcus, J. R., 1969c. Increase in cosmic ray cutoffs at high latitudes during magnetospheric substorms. *J. Geophys. Res., 74:* 4694–4700.

Behannon, K. W., 1968. Mapping of earth's bow shock and magnetic tail by Explorer 33. *J. Geophys. Res., 73:* 907–930.

Bewick, A., G. P. Haskell, and R. J. Hynds, 1970. Penetration of low-energy solar protons to low geomagnetic latitudes. *J. Geophys. Res., 75:* 4605–4612.

Brown, R. R., 1966. Electron precipitation in the auroral zone. *Space Sci. Rev., 5:* 311–387.

Brown, R. R., J. R. Barcus, and N. R. Parsons, 1965. Balloon observations of auroral zone X-rays in conjugate regions, 1; Slow time variations. *J. Geophys. Res., 70:* 2579–2598, 2; Microbursts and pulsations. *J. Geophys. Res., 70:* 2599–2612.

Bryant, D. A., T. L. Cline, U. D. Desai, and F. B. McDonald, 1965. Studies of solar protons with Explorers 12 and 14. *Astrophys. J., 141:* 478–499.

Burlaga, L. F., 1967. Anisotropic diffusion of solar cosmic rays. *J. Geophys. Res., 72:* 4449–4466.

Campbell, W. H., 1970. Rapid auroral luminosity fluctuations and geomagnetic pulsations. *J. Geophys. Res., 75:* 6182–6208.

Cresswell, G. R., 1968. Fast temporal and spatial changes in auroras, Ph. D. thesis. Univ. Alaska, College.

Cummings, W. D., J. N. Barfield, and P. J. Coleman, Jr., 1968. Magnetospheric substorms observed at the synchronous orbit. *J. Geophys. Res., 73:* 6687–6698.

Dessler, A. J., 1968. Magnetic merging in the geomagnetic tail. *J. Geophys. Res., 73:* 209–214.

Forbush, S. E., 1946. Three unusual cosmic ray increases possibly due to charged particles from the sun. *Phys. Rev., 70:* 771–772.

Gall, R., J. Jimenez, and L. Comacho, 1968. Arrival of low-energy cosmic rays via magnetospheric tail. *J. Geophys. Res., 73:* 1593–1605.

Heppner, J. P., M. Sugiura, T. L. Skillman, B. G. Ledley, and M. Campbell, 1967. OGO-A magnetic field observations. *J. Geophys. Res., 72:* 5417–5472.

Hofmann, D. J., and H. H. Sauer, 1968. Magnetospheric cosmic-ray cutoffs and their variations. *Space Sci. Res., 8:* 750–803.

Jokipii, J. R., 1966. Cosmic ray propagation. 1. Charged particles in a random magnetic field. *Astrophys. J., 146:* 480–487.

Jokipii, J. R., 1967. Cosmic ray propagation. 2. Diffusion in the interplanetary magnetic field. *Astrophys. J., 149:* 405–415.

Jokipii, J. R., 1968. Addendum and erratum to cosmic ray propagation. 1. *Astrophys. J., 152:* 671–672.

Lally, V. E., 1967. *Superpressure balloons, NCAR-TN-28.* National Center for Atmospheric Research, Boulder, Colo.

McDonald, F. B. (Editor), 1963. *Solar Proton Manual; NASA Technical Manual TR R-169.* N.A.S.A., Washington, D. C.

McIlwain, C. E., 1961. Coordinates for mapping the distribution of magnetically trapped particles. *J. Geophys. Res., 66:* 3681–3691.

Meyer, P., E. N. Parker, and J. A. Simpson, 1956. Solar cosmic rays of Februrary, 1956 and their propagation through interplanetary space. *Phys. Rev., 104:* 768–783.

Michel, F. C., 1965. Effect of magnetospheric tail on cosmic ray cutoffs. *Planetary Space Sci., 13:* 753–760.

Ness, N. F., 1965. The earth's magnetic tail. *J. Geophys. Res., 70:* 2989–3006.

Parker, E. N., 1963. *Interplanetary Dynamical Processes.* Interscience Publishers, N. Y.

Parker, E. N., 1968. The role of stochastic fields in admitting low-energy cosmic rays to the solar system. *J. Geophys. Res., 73:* 6842–6845.

Paulikas, G. A., J. B. Blake, S. C. Freden, and S. S. Imamoto, 1968. Observations of energetic electrons at synchronous altitude, 1. General features and diurnal variations. *J. Geophys. Res., 73:* 4915–4926.

Reid, G. C., and H. H. Sauer, 1967. The influence of the geomagnetic tail on low-energy cosmic-ray cutoffs. *J. Geophys. Res., 72:* 197–208.

Roederer, J. G., 1968. *Quantitative models of the magnetosphere.* Paper presented at the International Symposium of the Magnetosphere, Washington, D. C.

Rostoker, G., 1967. The polarization characteristics of Pi-2 micropulsations and their relation to the determination of possible source mechanisms for the production of nighttime impulsive micropulsation activity. *Can. J. Phys., 45:* 1319–1335.

Störmer, C., 1955. *The Polar Aurora.* Oxford Univ. Press, London.

Wescott, E. M., 1966. Magnetoconjugate phenomena. *Space Sci. Rev., 5:* 507–561.

Winckler, J. R., 1960. Balloon study of high-altitude radiations during the International Geophysical Year. *J. Geophys. Res., 65:* 1331–1359.

Particle Precipitation in the Antarctic Ionosphere

George C. Reid

National Oceanic and Atmospheric Administration, Boulder, Colorado

For seven years observations have been made of the precipitation of energetic particles into the antarctic ionosphere. The technique employs a *riometer* (Little and Leinbach, 1959), a ground-based instrument which provides long-term and essentially continuous measurements that are impossible to obtain with equipment carried aloft by rockets or balloons.

The simplest way of detecting energetic charged particles is by using an ionization chamber in which a particle enters a confined volume of gas and leaves a trail of ions and electrons that can be detected and measured by various conventional methods. The upper atmosphere is often heavily ionized at high geomagnetic latitudes by particles of solar and auroral origin, and a great deal of information about these particles can be obtained by observing and measuring this ionization. The riometer is a relatively simple instrument for carrying out measurements of this kind and has yielded a large quantity of information in the twelve years or so that it has been available.

THE RIOMETER

When the region of the upper atmosphere that lies roughly between altitudes of 30 and 100 km is ionized it causes attenuation of radio signals in the HF and lower VHF bands that traverse it; the free electrons absorb energy from the radio waves and transfer it through collisions to the neutral gas of the atmosphere, where it appears as a minute increase in temperature. At heights above 100 km the atmosphere is sufficiently attenuated that collisions are rare, and at heights below about 30 km collisions are so frequent that the electrons do not pick up much energy. The riometer is a fairly sophisticated radio receiver that continuously monitors the amount of radio-wave absorption by measuring the strength of the radio signal received from the galaxy—the so-called galactic or cosmic noise—which has a constant power level in any given direction in space. The signal strength observed by a fixed antenna on the earth changes throughout the day, but the effects of these changes can be removed by constructing a "quiet-day" signal level and measuring departures from this reference level as indications of absorption produced in the lower ionosphere. Riometers generally operate at a frequency in the neighborhood of 30 MHz, although frequencies as low as 5 MHz and as high as a few hundred MHz have been used for special purposes. The antenna used is normally a rather simple broad-beam array pointing vertically upward. Figure 1 shows a diagram of the antenna used in the majority of our observations; the width of the beam for this particular array is about 60° between half-power points at all azimuths.

Figure 2 shows examples of the three principal types of absorption events that are recorded by riometers (Reid and Collins, 1959). The first event (a) is not produced by particles, and when it occurs it can be seen over the entire sunlit hemisphere of the earth. It is due to the ionization created by X-rays generated by a solar flare, and will not be discussed further in this paper. The

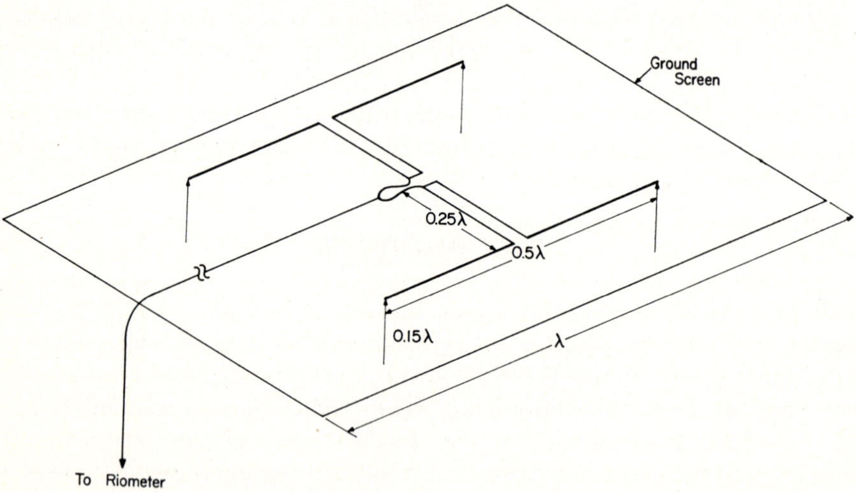

Fig. 1. Sketch of the antenna used for observations of vertical-incidence absorption in Antarctica.

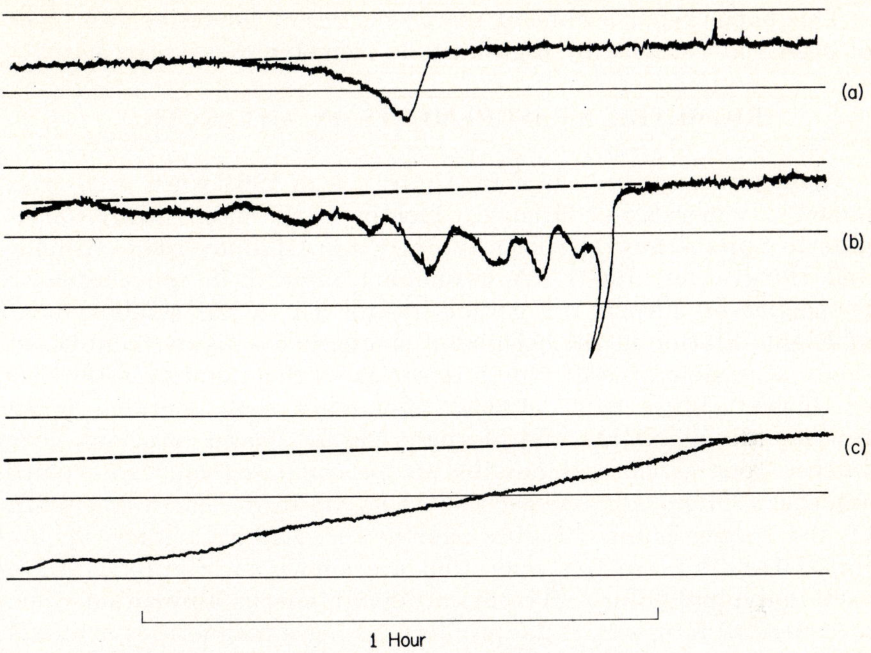

Fig. 2. Examples of the three types of absorption events recorded by riometers at high latitudes. The broken line in each case shows the quiet-day signal, i.e., the signal that would have been recorded in the absence of the event. Example (a) shows the response to solar-flare X-radiation; and (b) and (c) are respectively examples of auroral and polar-cap absorption events.

second event (b) is an example of auroral absorption, and is related to the energetic electrons that produce the visible aurora. Its visual appearance on a riometer record is usually quite highly structured in time, and sharp spikes and quasi-oscillatory forms are common. When auroral absorption occurs at night it is generally accompanied by auroral displays and a considerable amount of disturbance in the geomagnetic field. It is most common in the region known as the auroral oval, and is very rare at magnetic latitudes higher than about 78°. The third example (c), polar-cap absorption (PCA), is caused by energetic protons released by certain intense solar flares, and funneled by the geomagnetic field into regions of high magnetic latitude at and well above the latitude of the auroral oval. The absorption is characteristically smooth and slowly varying, and individual events typically last for two or three days; the onset of a major event is shown in the example.

This paper reports some of the properties of the latter two types of events as revealed by high-latitude riometer observations.

RIOMETER MEASUREMENTS IN ANTARCTICA

Riometers were first used in Antarctica in 1961 when a 30-MHz model was operated at Mirnyy, which is nearly magnetically conjugate to Spitzbergen (Eriksen *et al.*, 1964; Gillmor, 1963; Gillmor and Hargreaves, 1963). A developing interest in the conjugate properties of auroral absorption events led to the establishment of Eights Station at the calculated magnetic conjugate point to an easily accessible area of North America in the vicinity of the city of Quebec (Little *et al.*, 1965). Riometers were operated for a few months at Eights and at three closely spaced locations near Quebec—one as close as possible to the computed conjugate point (Quebec Center) and one each about 80 km to the north and south of the center point (Quebec North and South). Some of the initial results from this operation are shown in Figure 3. Here each individual point represents an instantaneous absorption value measured at intervals of 2.5 minutes during a magnetic storm, and the correlation between various pairs of stations can be seen by

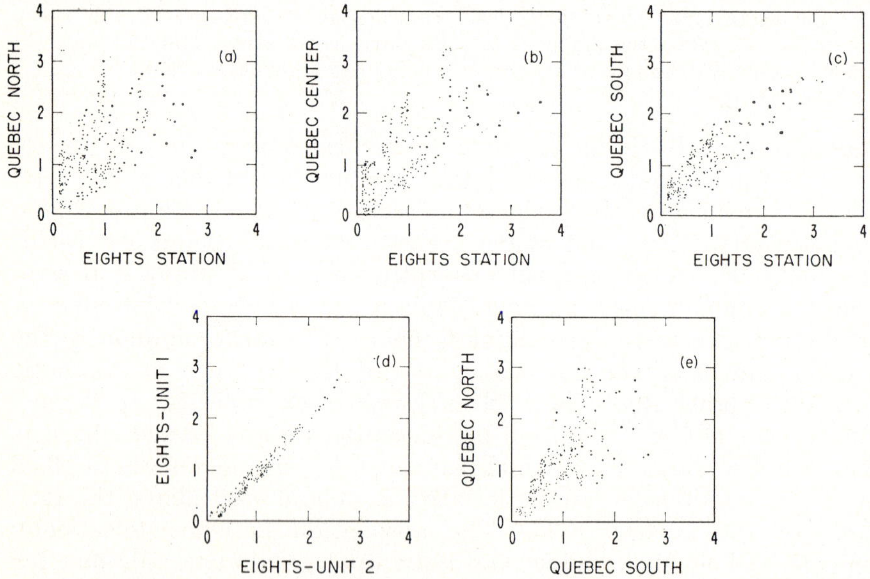

Fig. 3. Scatter plots of absorption recorded at Eights Station and Quebec during a magnetic storm on January 10, 1962 (Little *et al.*, 1965).

the extent to which the points appear to lie on a straight line. Two completely independent units at the same location (Fig. 3d) show extremely good correlation, which establishes the validity of the technique. The best correlation among the other plots is between Quebec South and Eights (Fig. 3c) ; in fact, it is considerably better than that between Quebec South and Quebec North (Fig. 3e) which are only 160 km apart. This certainly appears to establish the existence of conjugacy in a general sense, but note two other facts: first, the best correlation is not between the computed conjugate points, but rather between Eights and a station that is 80 km south of the computed conjugate; and second, the slope of the best-fit straight line is not unity, but there is an apparent tendency for more absorption to occur at the northern station. This particular series of observations was carried out during the northern winter months, and the latter tendency has since been well established from subsequent measurements at higher latitudes. There is invariably more absorption statistically at the station in the local winter hemisphere than at the station in the summer hemisphere (Hargreaves and Chivers, 1965).

A more complete study of the conjugate properties of auroral absorption was begun in 1963 with the establishment of riometer sites at three computed nearly conjugate pairs; Eights Station and Baie St. Paul (near Quebec), on the low-latitude side of the auroral zone; Byrd Station and Great Whale River, close to the maximum of the auroral zone; and South Pole Station and Frobisher Bay, on the high-latitude side of the auroral zone. These observations showed that the winter asymmetry in auroral absorption was much more pronounced at the higher latitudes. An example of the effect at the high-latitude pair of stations is shown in Figure 4. The events here have been grouped into a "day" and a "night" group, since these have quite different characteristics, but the winter asymmetry is quite evident in both groups.

There could be three possible explanations for this asymmetry: (1) since the absorption is produced by atmospheric ionization, differences in chemical composition between the winter and summer hemispheres could give rise to a systematic difference; (2) there could exist such a major seasonal distortion in the geomagnetic field that two stations that are accurately conjugate during one season are farther from conjugacy at other seasons; (3) the mechanism of electron precipitation into the atmosphere could cause more electrons to be precipitated into the winter hemisphere. The first of these possibilities, that of systematic differ-

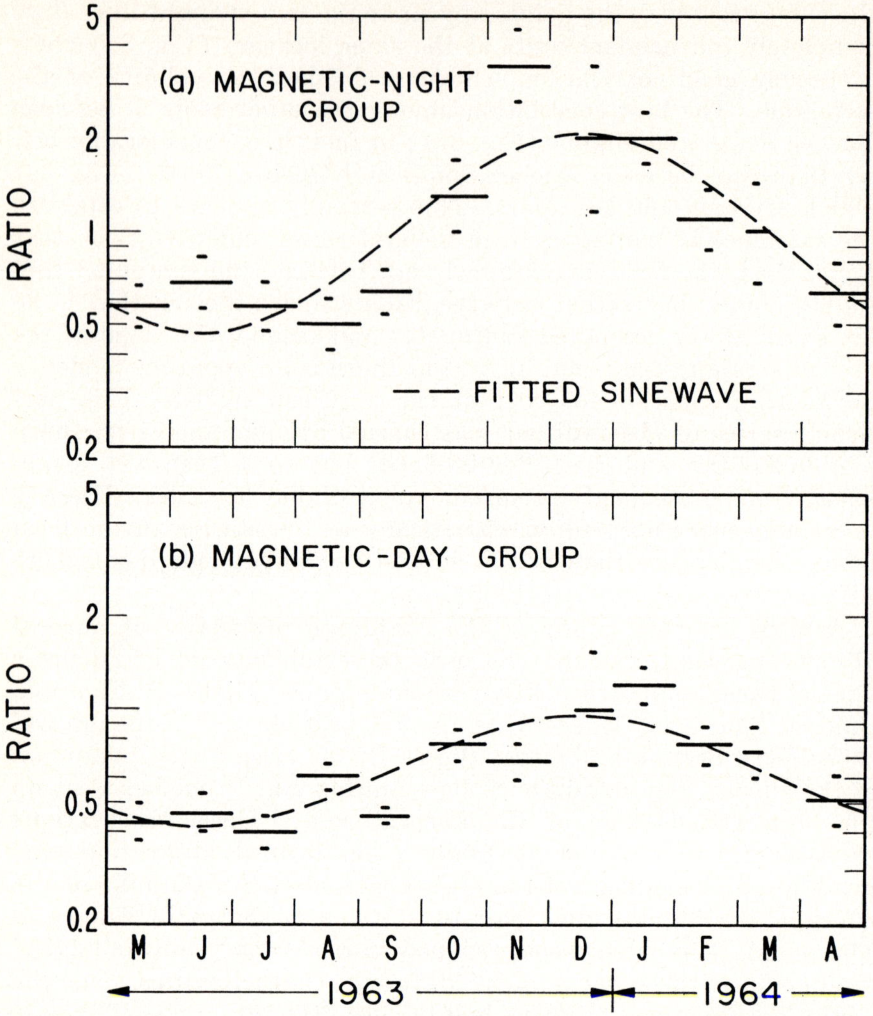

Fig. 4. Monthly median ratio of absorption observed at Frobisher Bay and South Pole Station during 1963–1964 (From Hargreaves and Chivers, 1965).

ences in chemical composition, does not appear to be likely, but it is still an open question. Present knowledge of the ion chemistry of the lower ionosphere indicates that minor chemical species of the neutral atmosphere play an extremely important role. Several of these minor constituents for example (O_3, O, NO, and H_2O) show systematic seasonal variations. One observation that argues against the chemical interpretation, however, is the absence of any systematic seasonal asymmetry in measurements of PCA, which is caused by energetic solar protons, for which the precipitation mechanism is quite different from that influencing the auroral electrons. The second possibility, that of a gross seasonal distortion of the geomagnetic field, would have important consequences on our understanding of the outer geomagnetic field and its interaction with the solar wind. The phenomenon was examined in more detail by locating four riometers at each of two conjugate stations. Each riometer was connected to an obliquely pointing antenna, so that a spatial survey of the absorption could be carried out over distances of about 200 km to the north, south, east, and west. The antennas used were corner reflectors, and a sketch of the system as operated at Byrd Station and Great Whale River for a period of two years is shown in Figure 5. A great deal of data has been produced by this experiment and the analysis is still far from complete. It appears, however, that there is no systematic displacement of the conjugate points large enough to explain the winter asymmetry. The events appear to be larger during winter all over the antenna system, often with similar gradients in absorption at both stations, especially for daytime events. Apparent motions of conjugacy on a smaller spatial scale, however, have been observed (Hargreaves, 1969).

In addition to the winter asymmetry, the statistical properties of auroral absorption events and their variation with geomagnetic activity and with latitude have been investigated in some detail (Hargreaves, 1966; Hargreaves and Cowley, 1967). The correla-

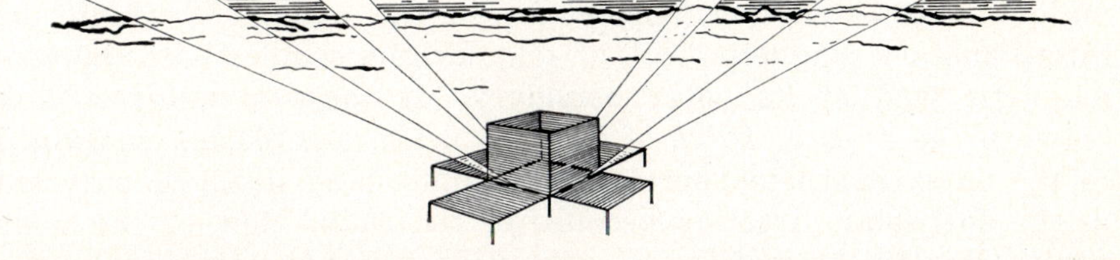

Fig. 5. Sketch of the assembly of four corner-reflector antennas used to study the spatial variation of absorption events at Byrd Station and Great Whale River (After Chivers and Hargreaves, 1965).

tion between individual auroral absorption events and bursts of energetic electrons observed by satellites in the outer magnetosphere has also been studied (Reid and Parthasarathy, 1966; Parthasarathy and Reid, 1967; Hargreaves *et al.,* 1968). Extremely good correlation has been observed on occasion and has provided direct evidence of a close causal relationship between the auroral substorm effect observed at the earth and conditions in the tail of the magnetosphere.

POLAR-CAP ABSORPTION

Polar-cap absorption (PCA) presents a quite different physical situation from that of auroral absorption. PCA is caused by the intense ionization created by solar protons with energies in the range from 1 to 500 Mev, whereas auroral absorption is produced by electrons with some tens of kev energy. The protons are channeled into the polar regions of the earth because, energetic though they are, they do not have the cosmic-ray energies necessary to penetrate deeply into the geomagnetic field. PCA observations can yield important information on three distinct aspects of geophysics: (1) the properties of the proton fluxes themselves and the manner in which they propagate from the sun to the earth; (2) the effect of the geomagnetic field in determining the precipitation pattern of the protons, a question that has a direct bearing on our understanding of the important but poorly understood processes that are involved in the interaction between the outer geomagnetic field and the solar wind; and (3) the physical and chemical properties of the lower ionosphere, the region in which the ionization is created. The first of these areas is best covered by satellite observations, since deductions made using absorption measurements are at best only indirect, but in the other two areas a combination of absorption measurements and satellite observations is already proving to be a powerful technique. One of the major unanswered questions concerns the extent to which the interplanetary magnetic field, of solar origin, couples with the geomagnetic field at its outer boundary. If there is a direct link between the lines of force of the two fields, the plasma contained in the outer magnetosphere will be continually dragged outward in the anti-solar direction because of the radial flow of the solar wind. This steady motion can explain many of the features of the high-latitude ionosphere (Dungey, 1961).

Figure 6 shows a sketch of the appearance of the lines of force

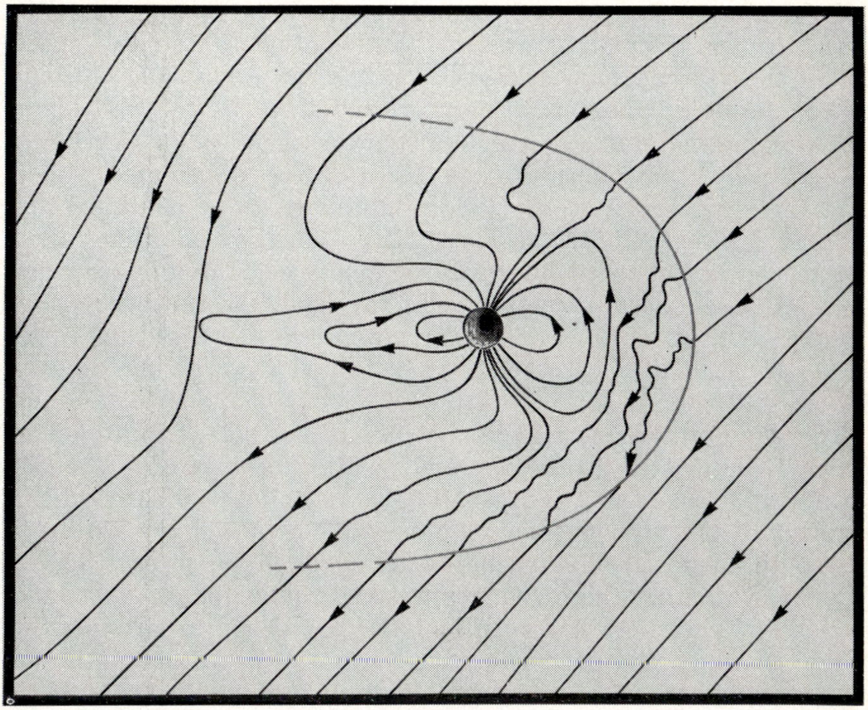

Fig. 6. Sketch of the possible interconnection between the interplanetary and geomagnetic fields for the case of a southward-pointing interplanetary field.

in the vicinity of the earth if a direct coupling exists. The geomagnetic field is compressed on the sunward side by the pressure of the solar wind and is drawn out into a long tail in the antisolar direction. On the sunward side of the geomagnetic-field boundary, or magnetopause, a standing shock wave effectively transforms the supersonic flow of the solar wind into a subsonic flow which eventually accelerates back to a supersonic flow. Direct interconnection of field lines occurs at the magnetopause where the two field regimes come into contact. The connected lines of force are then dragged across the polar caps and stretched out into the tail until they ultimately disconnect at some fairly distant point. In this situation, imagine a beam of protons approaching from the sun with energy low enough to confine the protons to a tube of the interplanetary field. Obviously the protons have direct access to the northern polar cap, but the "conjugate" region in the Southern Hemisphere is totally inaccessible because the solid earth and the atmosphere prevent them from reaching this region. We thus have an interesting case of "anti-conjugacy," in the sense that if the protons appear in one hemisphere, they should be completely absent in the other.

A pronounced enhancement in PCA was observed in February, 1965, by the riometer at Vostok for a period of about an hour near the peak of the event (Reid and Sauer, 1967). Satellite observations near the north geomagnetic pole at the same time failed to see such an enhancement, although enhanced proton fluxes were observed near the auroral zone. In this case the southern polar cap was evidently connected to the sun, unlike the case illustrated in Figure 6. Other cases of similar behavior are being investigated.

There is also the question of the edge of the polar-cap region in which PCA exists. The shape and position of this edge are determined by the energy spectrum of the incoming particles and the topology of the outer geomagnetic field. They often vary diurnally and with magnetic disturbance and it would be interesting to determine whether these changes are accurately conjugate or not. A chain of riometers has been installed in Alaska to straddle the region in which the polar-cap edge normally occurs, but it is not now practical to install a similar chain in Antarctica since much of the important latitude region is covered by ocean and there are too few stations in the land areas to be useful. The problem may again be answered, however, by a combination of ground-based observations from the Arctic with satellite measurements made over the inaccessible antarctic regions. Evidence for major departures from conjugacy observed at the auroral-zone stations has been presented for the PCA events of September, 1966, and January, 1967 (Sauer, 1968); these observations are not readily explainable at present.

With regard to the properties of the atmosphere itself, we are forced to consider a situation of great physical complexity. The absorption measured by a riometer is determined by the altitude profile of free electrons in the atmosphere and this is, in turn, determined by a delicate balance between the rate of production by the energetic protons and the rate of removal by the complex set of ionic reactions that take place in the height range from 30 to 100 km. This is where high-latitude riometer observations of PCA can supply some helpful insight into the important features of the entire lower ionosphere. Major advances have recently been taking place in our understanding of atmospheric chemical reactions that involve negative ions, and these reactions are vitally important in determining the rate of loss of free electrons in the lower ionosphere. The new advances have proven difficult to test in their applicability to the lower ionosphere at mid-latitudes, because the lower ionosphere is only very weakly ionized there and the ionizing source itself (solar electromagnetic radiation) undergoes a pronounced diurnal variation. During PCA events, however, the same region of the atmosphere is very strongly ionized and the solar protons producing the ionization do not vary diurnally in intensity; furthermore, the rate at which they produce free electrons can be rather easily calculated once their energy spectrum is known. Observations of these events are now beginning to provide us with a means of checking the validity of the new ion chemistry as it applies to the ionosphere. A definite upward displacement of the PCA ionization in going from daytime to nighttime conditions has been discovered during the major PCA event of September, 1966 (Reid, 1969), and is consistent with the possible role of associative-detachment reactions involving atomic oxygen. Further results are too preliminary at this time to be discussed in detail here. There appears to be a real prospect, however, of a solution to this extremely complex and important problem of the ion chemistry of the lower ionosphere, and the findings will have a major influence on our understanding of the physics of this region of the atmosphere at all latitudes.

Antarctica is an extremely valuable laboratory for the study of energetic-particle precipitation in the earth's atmosphere, and important results have been obtained concerning the behavior of the particles themselves and of the structure of the atmosphere. The combination of a synoptic program of continuous ground-based observations at several fixed latitudes with satellite observations of a range of latitudes at essentially fixed times is likely to prove a powerful tool in furthering our understanding of the earth's particle environment and its influence on the atmosphere.

Author's Note: The work described here has been carried out with the partial support of the National Science Foundation through its Office of Polar Programs. It represents the combined effort of a large number of individuals, too numerous to mention here, but the author wishes to acknowledge in particular the efforts of Dr. C. G. Little and Dr. H. J. A. Chivers in initiating the program.

References

Chivers, H. J. A., and J. K. Hargreaves, 1965. The use of multiple antennas in studies of absorption at conjugate points. In *High Latitude Particles and the Ionosphere,* edited by B. Maehlum; pp. 257–264. Logos Press Ltd., London.

Dungey, J. W., 1961. Interplanetary magnetic field and the auroral zones. *Phys. Rev. Letters, 6:* 47–48.

Eriksen, K. W., C. S. Gillmor, and J. K. Hargreaves, 1964. Some observations of short duration cosmic noise absorption events in conjugate regions at high magnetic latitude. *J. Atmospheric Terrest. Phys., 26:* 77–90.

Gillmor, C. S., 1963. The day-to-night ratio of cosmic noise absorption during polar-cap absorption events. *J. Atmospheric Terrest. Phys., 25:* 263–266.

Gillmor, C. S., and J. K. Hargreaves, 1963. The occurrence of short duration cosmic noise absorption events inside the southern auroral zone. *J. Atmospheric Terrest. Phys., 25:* 311–317.

Hargreaves, J. K., 1966. On the variation of auroral radio absorption with geomagnetic activity. *Planetary Space Sci., 14:* 991–1006.

Hargreaves, J. K., 1969. Conjugate and closely spaced observations of auroral radio absorption. 1. Seasonal and diurnal behavior. *Planetary Space Sci., 17:* 1459–1484.

Hargreaves, J. K., and H. J. A. Chivers, 1965. A study of auroral absorption events at the South Pole. 2. Conjugate properties. *J. Geophys. Res., 70:* 1093–1102.

Hargreaves, J. K., and F. C. Cowley, 1967. Studies of auroral radio absorption events at three magnetic latitudes. *Planetary Space Sci., 15:* 1571–1597.

Hargreaves, J. K., E. W. Hones, and S. Singer, 1968. Relations between bursts of energetic electrons at 17 earth-radii in the magnetotail and radio absorption events in the ionospheric D region. *Planetary Space Sci., 16:* 567–580.

Little, C. G., and H. Leinbach, 1959. The riometer—a device for the continuous measurement of ionospheric absorption. *Proc. Inst. Radio Engrs., 47:* 315–320.

Little, C. G., E. R. Schiffmacher, H. J. A. Chivers, and K. W. Sullivan, 1965. Cosmic noise absorption events at geomagnetically conjugate stations. *J. Geophys. Res., 70:* 639–648.

Parthasarathy, R., and G. C. Reid, 1967. Magnetospheric activity and its consequences in the auroral zone. *Planetary Space Sci., 15:* 917–929.

Reid, G. C., 1969. Associative detachment in the mesosphere and the diurnal variation of polar-cap absorption. *Planetary Space Sci., 17:* 731–736.

Reid, G. C., and C. Collins, 1959. Observations of abnormal VHF radio wave absorption at medium and high latitudes. *J. Atmospheric Terrest. Phys., 14:* 63–81.

Reid, G. C., and R. Parthasarathy, 1966. Ionospheric effects of energetic electron bursts in the tail of the magnetosphere. *J. Geophys. Res., 71:* 3267–3272.

Reid, G. C., and H. H. Sauer, 1967. Evidence of nonuniformity of solarproton precipitation over the polar caps. *J. Geophys. Res., 72:* 4383–4389.

Sauer, H. H., 1968. Nonconjugate aspects of recent polar-cap absorption events. *J. Geophys. Res., 73:* 3058–3062.

Interhemispheric Phase Shift for PC-1 Micropulsations at Kotzebue and Macquarie Island

JOHN O. ANNEXSTAD

Manned Spacecraft Center, National Aeronautics and Space Administration, Houston, Texas

CHARLES R. WILSON

Geophysical Institute, University of Alaska, College

The Geophysical Institute of the University of Alaska established conjugate point observatories at Kotzebue, Alaska, and Macquarie Island in late 1966. The geomagnetic coordinates of these observatories are latitude (Φ_g) of 63.7°N, longitude (Λ_g) of 242.1° for Kotzebue and Φ_g = 61.1°S, Λ_g = 243.1° for Macquarie Island. The stations are located at opposite ends of the dipole field line which extends to 5.23 earth radii (R_E) into the magnetosphere. The Kotzebue station is serviced and staffed by a part-time Geophysical Institute employee who resides in the village. The Macquarie Island observatory is manned and operated by personnel from the Australian National Antarctic Research Expedition (ANARE) under a cooperative agreement. Each observatory is equipped with identical three-component induction-loop magnetometers, Esterline Angus chart recorders, slow-speed tape recorders (2.5 inches/hour), and Sprengnether crystal clocks. A brief description of the equipment, installation, and operation of these stations has been reported by Annexstad (1967).

The Kotzebue-Macquarie conjugate stations were established for the purpose of studying geomagnetic micropulsations at high latitudes. This is an extension of work done by Annexstad and Wilson (1968) who studied the conjugate relationships of pulsations, giant (P_g). The authors used records from the University of

Alaska and Macquarie Island in their study. Since these areas are not closely conjugate it was decided that Kotzebue (the intersect of Macquarie Island computed by Roederer *et al.,* 1965) should be established. It was hoped that the information obtained from the Kotzebue-Macquarie pair would be more useful in testing the theories of micropulsation characteristics at conjugate points. The most promising type of micropulsation event for study was the pulsations continuous, Range 1 (PC-1) (1.0 to 0.2 Hz). This report covers the features of the PC-1 micropulsations as observed at the Kotzebue-Macquarie conjugate observatories during 1967.

PC-1 MICROPULSATIONS

The PC-1 micropulsation has been extensively studied by many workers and its general characteristics are well known. Excellent references on the properties of PC-1's are contained in the review works of Troitskaya (1964), Wescott (1966), and Campbell (1967). The PC-1 is believed to be caused by hydromagnetic wave energy which is guided along the lines of force and bounces between opposite hemispheres. This theory was presented by Jacobs and Watanabe (1964) and Obayashi (1965) to explain the alternate arrival of energy packets at conjugate points. According to Kenney *et al.* (1968), this explanation provides an adequate basis for a description of PC-1 characteristics.

Figure 1 shows a PC-1 micropulsation displayed as a sonagram, a "three-dimensional" plot of an event with real time as the abscissa, frequency as the ordinate, and darkness as the relative amplitude. This event appeared simultaneously at Kotzebue and Macquarie on February 28, 1967. This figure shows the horizontal (H) component observed at both stations between 0000 and 0300 hours UT. The clear separation of the energy packets as black dots within the event plus the general decrease of frequency over the entire event are evident. Mid-frequency of this event was approximately 0.4 Hz. Figure 1 is a clear example of the conjugate nature of the PC-1 micropulsation. Gokberg *et al.* (1967) have reported that the periods and frequency-time structure of PC-1's are identical at conjugate points. The identical character of PC-1 micropulsations recorded simultaneously at conjugate points was also demonstrated by Tepley (1964). When Tepley compared the arrival times of energy bursts at conjugate stations he discovered that this fine structure was displaced by a half period at each station. The author compared sonagrams of simul-

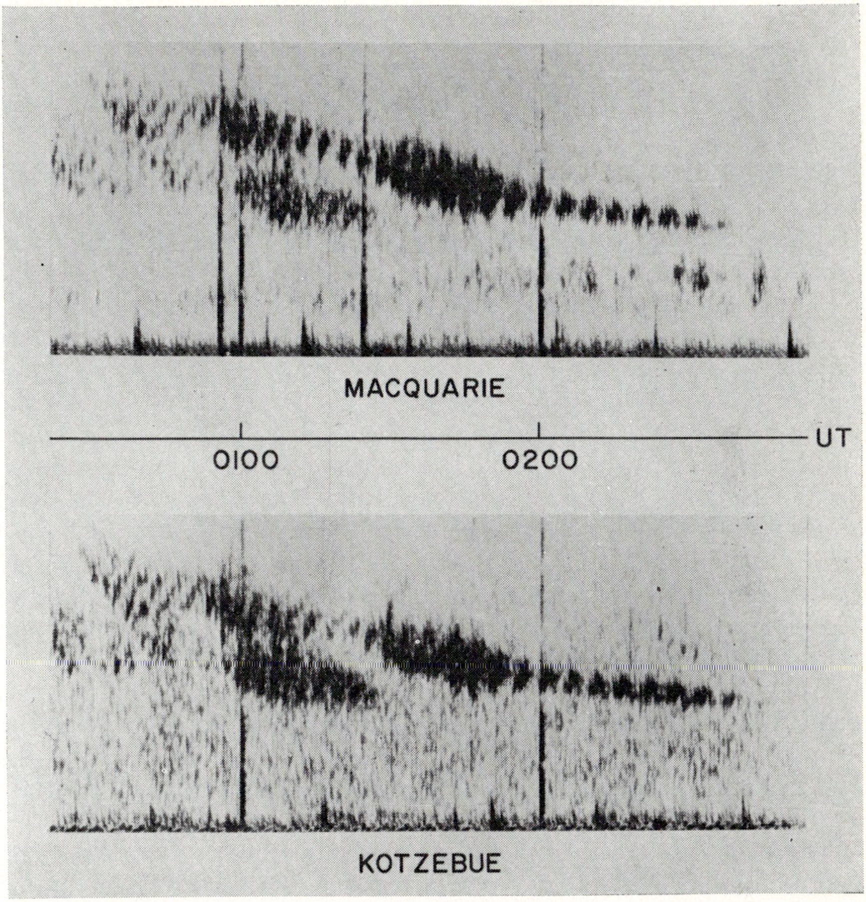

Fig. 1. Sonagrams of PC-1 micropulsations recorded at Kotzebue and Macquarie Island, February 28, 1967, at 0100–0200 UT.

taneous events recorded at Kauai and Tongatapu and found that the wave groups appeared alternately at each station. This characteristic was called the 180° interhemispheric phase shift. A further check of this feature by Gendrin and Troitskaya (1965) and Annexstad and Wilson (1968) indicated that the phase shift was not always 180°. Unfortunately, the time error inherent in sonagram analysis is too great to determine accurately the degree of phase shift or interhemispheric travel time of the PC-1 hydromagnetic wave packets.

To help establish a more positive criterion for this property of

PC-1's, a total of 28 simultaneous events were selected from the 1967 Kotzebue-Macquarie records for detailed analysis.

DATA ANALYSIS

The Kotzebue-Macquarie stations are equipped with identical Esterline Angus Curvilinear chart recorders and slow-speed AM magnetic tape recorders. Since most PC-1 events, even at high-latitude stations, are low-amplitude phenomena, the chart records do not show all the events clearly. Therefore, to obtain the greatest number of events for analysis it was necessary to use the AM tape records. The AM tape speed was set at 2.5 inches per hour for recording to provide a speed-up factor of 5,000 at normal playback speeds. The speed-up factor brings a 1-Hz signal into the audio range so that a PC-1 event can be heard or reproduced on a sonagram. The Macquarie and Kotzebue tapes were searched audibly to locate simultaneous events. The process is tedious and time consuming but it is most fruitful because very low-amplitude events can be easily located. The PC-1 has a characteristic falling frequency tone not unlike a whistler and is easy to discern from other geomagnetic phenomena.

Every audible simultaneous event was reproduced by the sonagram method to determine the best events for further analysis. The sonagram gives a visual picture of the event and enables the researcher to determine event characteristics and time of appearance.

The events selected for detailed analysis were re-recorded from magnetic tape onto Visicorder chart paper. Visicorder chart speeds are so rapid that individual wave forms of PC-1 events can be easily seen. This method provides for each event an expanded time scale not practicable during real time recording.

The Visicorder charts were then scaled for event duration and for the relative amplitude of the envelope of the PC-1 oscillation. Scaling was done on an Oscar F machine with the operator measuring 288 points of envelope amplitude in each record section. Each event was scaled in sections of 24 minutes and the amplitude data was punched on IBM cards. The total accumulative error in picking starting times and scaling intervals by this method is estimated to be five seconds. The digital data from the selected 28 events was used for cross-correlation and power spectral analysis on an IBM-360 computer. The cross-correlation analysis involved shifting the time scale of an event recorded at Kotzebue relative to the time scale of the same event recorded at Macquarie. The output factor is normalized so that when the individual cycles are compared at any time, a correlation value between +1.0 and −1.0 is obtained.

The power spectral density of each event was determined by the method of numerical filters (Gauss, 1964). To obtain a more accurate measure of the 180° interhemispheric phase shift, the method of power spectral density was used to define the frequency of PC-1 wave groups. The error in picking the exact period of the wave packet is estimated to be ±10 seconds.

The PC-1 micropulsation is a geomagnetic oscillation of frequency 1.0 to 0.2 Hz which appears as a string of modulated wave packets. Figure 2 is an analogue record of an event recorded simultaneously at Kotzebue and Macquarie on December 13, 1967. The modulated character of the wave groups as well as the individual wave cycles is easily seen. These wave groups appear as a series of isolated dots on a sonagram as shown in Figure 1.

The 28 simultaneous events recorded at Kotzebue-Macquarie during 1967 and selected for detailed analysis are listed in Table 1. This table gives the date each event occurred, the time of the event in UT, the time of each interval scaled for amplitude, and the value of the geomagnetic index of world magnetic activity (K_p) for the three-hour interval during which the event appeared. Events 2, 9, 12, 15, 17, 22, 23, 24, and 28 were of sufficient duration to warrant two or more sections of scaling. The additional scaling was performed to see if the cross-correlation and power-spectral values changed within an event.

For auroral-zone stations the time of appearance at conjugate points of the same PC-1 wave packet is a measure of the travel time of the anisotropic hydromagnetic wave packet along the line of force connecting the stations. This travel time has been estimated in some studies by the method of transparent overlays of sonagrams (Tepley, 1964). Annexstad and Wilson (1968) used this method for an event recorded at Kotzebue and Macquarie on February 28, 1967. Their sonagrams of this event showed a time shift of 120 seconds even though the vertical time lines were quite broad and resulted in a large error in picking the time shift. However, a reasonable estimate of the time was obtained and the definite line-up of wave packets could be clearly seen in the lower part of their sonagram.

The cross-correlation method of comparing time shifts has been substituted for the sonagram method. The cross-correlation func-

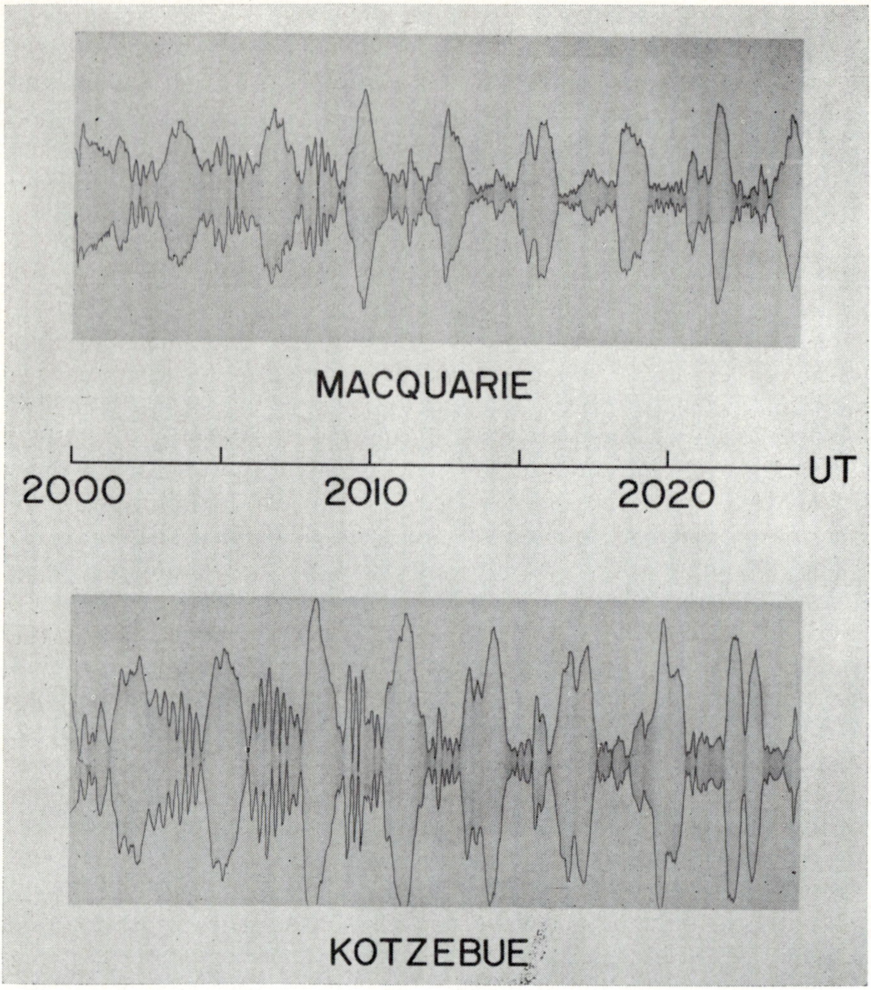

Fig. 2. Amplitude/time record of horizontal (H) component for PC-1 micropulsation at Kotzebue and Macquarie Island, December 13, 1967.

tion from −1.0 to +1.0 was estimated every 5 seconds of time shift from event coincidence to 300 seconds out of phase.

Figure 3 is a plot of the cross-correlation versus time shift of a PC-1 event recorded on February 28, 1967. The analysis section used to produce this figure is between 0130 UT and 0154 UT which corresponds to the midpoint of the sonagram in Annexstad and Wilson (1968). Note in Figure 3 that two correlation peaks are seen, one at 130 seconds and the other at 185 seconds. The

Table 1. Simultaneous PC-1 events recorded at Kotzebue and Macquarie Island during 1967.

Event No.	1967 Date	Time (UT)	Scaling interval	K_p	Event No.	1967 Date	Time (UT)	Scaling interval	K_p
1	Jan 16	0130–0500	0212–0236	3^-	16	July 8–9	2350–0200	0006–0030	0^+
2a	Feb 28	0010–0240	0130–0154	1	17a	July 9–10	2100–0210	2100–2124	1
2b			0200–0224	1	17b			0136–0200	0^+
3	Feb 28–Mar 1	2230–0200	0003–0027	2	18	July 10–11	2100–0200	2300–2324	2^-
4	Mar 9	0000–0100	0003–0027	1	19	Aug 13	0000–0300	0030–0054	1
5	Mar 13	0110–0230	0130–0154	1	20	Aug 14	0010–0130	0024–0048	2^+
6	Mar 13–14	2340–0130	0003–0027	3^-	21	Oct 13–14	2330–0530	0340–0404	2^-
7	Mar 15	1920–2140	2036–2100	0^+	22a	Oct 20–21	2330–0530	0200–0224	0
8	Mar 17–18	2150–0100	2236–2300	1^+	22b			0436–0500	0
9a	Mar 22–23	1650–0630	1654–1718	1^-	23a	Oct 22	0050–0430	0124–0148	0
9b			0324–0348	0	23b			0324–0348	0^+
9c			0512–0536	0	24a	Oct 23	1330–1700	1412–1436	2
10	Apr 27–28	2300–0300	0012–0036	0^+	24b			1524–1548	1^-
11	Apr 28–29	2350–0110	0012–0036	1	25	Nov 18	0100–0310	0236–0300	1
12a	May 6	1810–2200	1906–1930	1^+	26	Nov 18–19	2330–0200	0036–0100	1^-
12b			2136–2200	2	27	Dec 12	1300–1600	1530–1554	2^-
13	May 10–11	2230–0200	0048–0112	4^-	28a	Dec 13	1910–2400	1930–1954	2^-
14	May 22–23	2350–0100	0036–0100	1^-	28b			2000–2024	2^-
15a	July 2–3	1650–0500	1736–1800	0^+	28c			2036–2100	2^-
15b			0200–0224	0^+	28d			2212–2236	1^+
					28e			2300–2324	1^+

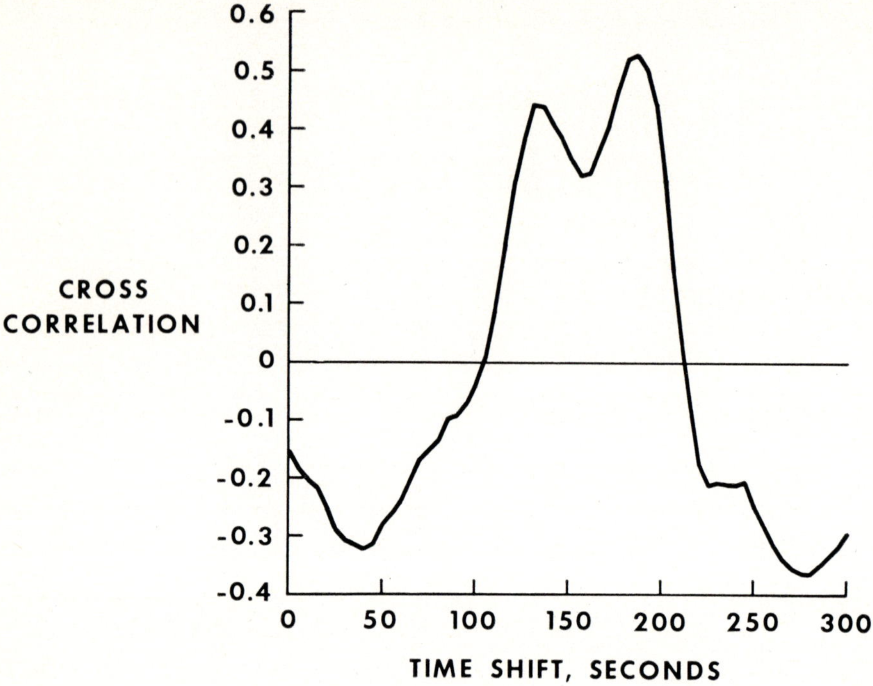

Fig. 3. Cross correlation for PC-1 event, February 28, 1967, at Kotzebue and Macquarie Island at 0130 UT (NASA-S-69-1128).

sonagram method used for the same event showed a single 120-second time shift. The double peaks noticed in the cross-correlation would not be discernible by the sonagram method because of the large error in the visual comparison. The double peak could be due to the superposition of a number of wave trains as expressed by Pope (1964).

In Figure 4, which is the same event 30 minutes later, the predominant time shift period has become 205 seconds. In this figure the secondary peak has leveled out and an almost pure tone remains. The time shift, however, has increased 20 seconds, which indicates that travel time along the force line can change with time.

The 130-second peak which appeared to be significant has now become a slight bump in the curve at 140 seconds. It appears that as this event continues a rather pure tone begins to dominate as if a resonant condition of the line of force is developing.

An interesting feature of the PC-1 micropulsation is the period

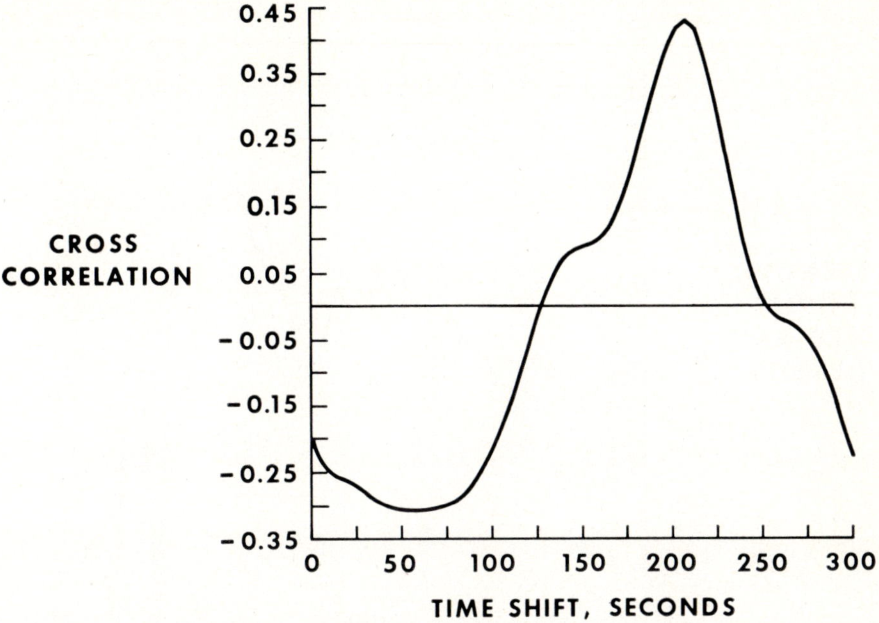

Fig. 4. Cross correlation for PC-1 event, February 28, 1967, at Kotzebue and Macquarie Island at 0200 UT (NASA-S-69-1123).

of the wave packets received at a single station. The period of these repetitive packets has been measured and computed as the relative power spectral density. Figures 5 and 6 are the spectral density plots of the February 28, 1967, event of 0130 UT at Kotzebue and Macquarie, respectively. Although it is difficult to pick a single period, these figures suggest a spectral peak near 200 seconds at both stations. A minor peak at 60 to 70 seconds also appears but this has much less significance due to the uncertainty of this method of analysis at these frequencies.

If the travel time (ΔT) as noted in Figure 3 and the spectral period as in Figures 5 and 6 are combined, it is possible to compute the interhemispheric phase shift.

Let ΔT = travel time between stations

DHT = travel time from a station to its conjugate and return

then $\Phi = \Delta T\ (360°)/DHT$ where Φ = interhemispheric phase shift in degrees

if $DHT/2 = \Delta T$ then the phase shift is 180°.

For the data obtained in Figures 3, 5, and 6 we use the following figures:

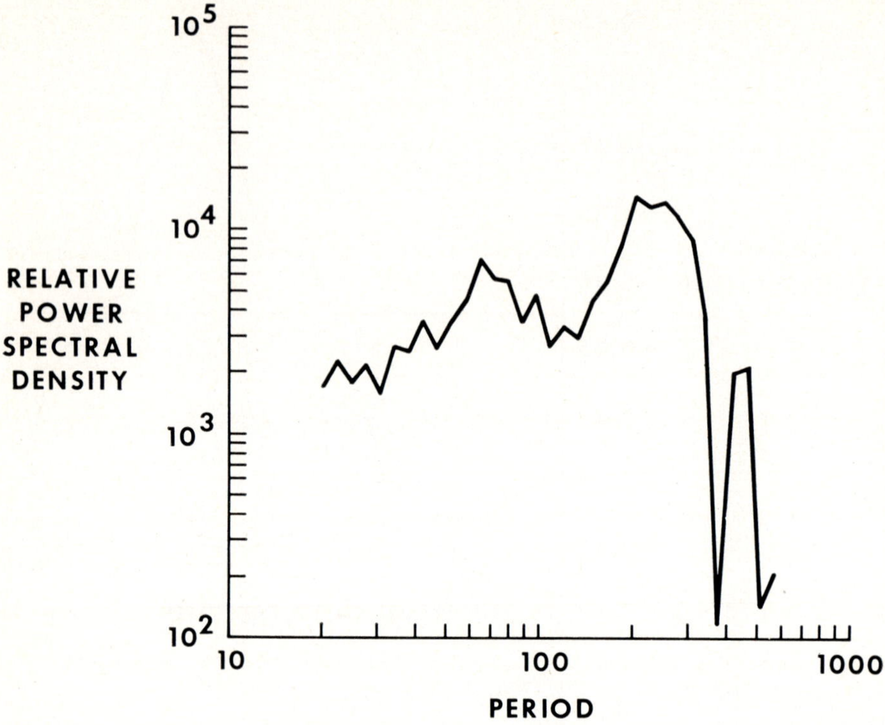

Fig. 5. Relative power spectral density for PC-1 event, February 28, 1967, 0130 UT at Kotzebue (NASA-S-69-1131).

ΔT	DHT Kotzebue	DHT Macquarie
130	200	222
185		

from which we find:

	Kotzebue		Macquarie Island	
ΔT	DHT_k	Φ_k	DHT_m	Φ_m
130	200	234	222	211
185	200	333	222	300

The value of the phase shift Φ ranges between 234° to 333° for Φ_k and 211° to 300° for Φ_m depending upon the values of ΔT and DHT used. Using the ΔT = 185 seconds and the major DHT peak at both stations, the phase shift is Φ = 333° for Kotzebue and 300° for Macquarie. To obtain an interhemispheric phase shift value nearer 180° it is necessary to use ΔT = 130

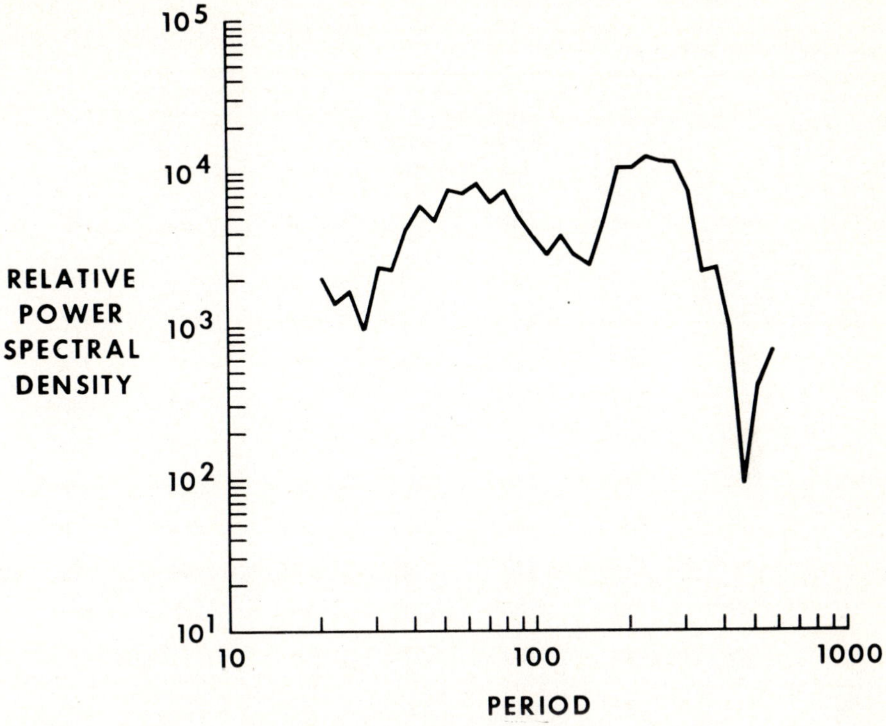

Fig. 6. Relative power spectral density for PC-1 event, February 28, 1967, 0200 UT at Macquarie Island (NASA-S-69-1126).

seconds. This value is not predominant and appears to represent a harmonic or secondary correlation peak besides producing a Φ value that is far from 180°.

This event is too complicated to give a clear picture of cross-correlation or power spectral density. However, by exercising judgment and taking the most outstanding values, the phase shift is shown to be considerably greater than 180°.

In Table 2, each event is presented with the cross-correlation value, ΔT in seconds, and the DHT in seconds from Kotzebue and Macquarie. The phase shift Φ from both stations has been calculated and presented plus the average Φ. Missing values are the result of inconclusive data. For some events, more than one value of DHT and Φ is listed for either or both stations. These values and their averages are computed separately to give the appropriate phase shift values. In most cases, as in event 9a, the average values agree rather well between Kotzebue and Macquarie.

Table 2. Kotzebue and Macquarie Island, 1967. Cross-correlation values, travel time between stations (ΔT), double hop time (DHT) and interhemispheric phase shift (Φ).

Event No.	Cross-correl. value	ΔT (seconds)	DHT Kotzebue (seconds)	DHT McQ (seconds)	Φ_k	Φ_m	$\frac{\Phi_k+\Phi_m}{2}$
1	.24	65	58	63	43	11	27
2a	.53	185	247	247	270	270	270
2b	.43	205	330	304	223	243	233
3	.41	210	218	217	347	348	348
4	.28	265	304	375	314	254	284
5	.52	245	304	304	290	290	290
6	.59	185	245	304	271	219	245
7	.69	175	219	222	287	284	285
8	.48	150	105	107	154	145	149
9a	.76	140	146	146 } 163 180 }	345	345 } 309 280 }	327
9b	.44	130	274	180	171	260	216
9c	.50	80	156	158	185	182	184
10	.42	120	222	200	195	216	206
11	.73	145	247	271	211	193	202
12a	.57	55	107	107	185	185	185
12b	.35	80	180	107 135	160	269 213	215 187
13	.34	120	243	246	178	176	177
14	.54	135	246	200	198	243	221
15a	.31	60	132	107 200	164	202 108	183 136
15b	.52	85	130	146	235	210	223
16	.17	150	128	115 128	62	110 62	86 62
17a	.32	70	162	118 145 165	156	214 174 153	185 165 155

Table 2. (continued)

Event No.	Cross-correl. value	ΔT (seconds)	DHT Kotzebue (seconds)	DHT McQ (seconds)	Φ_k	Φ_m	$\frac{\Phi_k+\Phi_m}{2}$
17b	.50	90	180	200	180	162	171
18	.37	100	118	220	305	164	235
19	.46	150	181	182	298	297	298
20	.41	85	146	200	210	153	182
21	.41	120	132	117 180	327	9	168
22a	.38	105	87 120	87	74 53	74	74 64
22b	.82	160	132		76		
23a	.52	95	162 211 } 186	222	211 162 } 184	154	183 158 } 169
23b	.57	115	200	222	207	186	197
24a	.33	100	107	118	336	305	321
24b	.63	100	63 146 } 104	63 132 } 88	211 247 } 346	211 273 } 49	211 260 } 198
25	.59	185	180	247	10	270	320
26	.54	115	220	178	188	233	211
27			338	304			
28a	.62	95	162	146 180 } 163	211	234 190 } 210	211
28b	.78	90	180	180	180	180	180
28c	.84	95	180	180	190	190	190
28d	.81	115	200	222	207	186	197
28e	.58	140	304	107 338	166	149	158

Legend $\Phi = \Delta T\ (360°)/\text{DHT}$.

Total accumulative error in calculating Φ is estimated to be ± 10 percent. The value of ΔT is estimated every 5 seconds with a gross error of 5 percent for an average $\Delta T = 130$ seconds. The power spectral density error is about 5 percent for any particular value of DHT.

The numbers presented in Table 2 cover a wide range. It is instructive, however, to look at some specific values. The average value of ΔT is about 130 seconds and the average DHT is nearly 200 seconds. The calculated phase shift using these values is 232°. Assuming a 10 percent error in calculation, the value of 232° is still far greater than the expected 180° shift. This average value for DHT agrees rather well with Obayashi's (1965) value for a geomagnetic latitude of 65°.

Event No. 28 in Table 2 was broken into 5 sections in an attempt to determine how cross-correlation and phase shift changed within an event. The values of Φ_k (phase shift, Kotzebue) and Φ_m (phase shift, Macquarie) are very close to 180° in sections 28b, c, and d. In fact, the highest correlation figures of all 28 events are noted when these same values of Φ are near 180°. This event was surprisingly stable in frequency and is an excellent indicator of the travel time along a line of force. If there is any indication of K_p influencing travel time, it is apparent from this event. Note that the value of ΔT during event No. 28 increases from 90 to 140 seconds between 28b and 28e. The value K_p as listed in Table 1 decreases from 2^- to 1^+ during the course of event 28. If the travel time along the line of force depends solely on the length of the line, then the value of ΔT should change inversely with K_p. This is the case in event 28. In event 9a, b, and c, however, this is not the case. In fact we see here after checking Tables 1 and 2 that the value of ΔT decreases as K_p decreases. Hence the travel time in this event is probably more dependent upon plasma density than field-line length.

At best, the K_p values as listed in Table 1 are only indicators of the level of geomagnetic activity. A brief check of these values shows K_p ranging from 0 to 4^- during PC-1 events. The majority of events, however, occur when K_p is 1^+ or less.

The PC-1 events presented in Tables 1 and 2 are really too few to help determine a seasonal or local time distribution. All 28 events were recorded near 0000 hours UT or about local noon at Macquarie and Kotzebue. No significant seasonal effect can be determined.

Author's Note: This research was supported by NSF grant GA-726. We would like to thank the Australian National Antarctic Research Expedition personnel who provided logistical support and operated the Macquarie Island micropulsation equipment.

References

Annexstad, J. O., 1967. Kotzebue, Alaska-Macquarie Island conjugate point micropulsation experiment. *Antarctic J. U. S., 2* (5) :165.

Annexstad, J. O., and C. R. Wilson, 1968. PC-1 fine structure phase shift at high latitude conjugate points. *J. Geophys. Res., 73* (9) : 3063–3065.

Campbell, W. H., 1967. *Geomagnetic Pulsations, Physics of Geomagnetic Phenomena.* Academic Press, New York.

Gauss, E. J., 1964. Estimation of power spectral density by filters. *J. Assoc. Computing Machinery, 11* (1) : 98–103.

Gendrin, R. E., and V. A. Troitskaya, 1965. Preliminary results of a micropulsation experiment at conjugate points. *Radio Sci., 69 D:* 1107–1116.

Gokberg, M. B., A. L. Kolisher, V. A. Troitskaya, R. Gendrin, and S. Lacourly, 1967. Peculiarities of PC-1 propagation in conjugate points. (Abstract IAGA 1961). *Intern. Assoc. Geomagnetism Aeronomy, Bull. 24.*

Jacobs, J. A., and T. Watanabe, 1964. Micropulsation whistlers. *J. Atmospheric Terrest. Phys., 26:* 825–829.

Kenney, J. F., H. B. Knaflick, and H. B. Liemohn, 1968. Magnetospheric parameters determined from structured micropulsations. *J. Geophys. Res., 73* (21) : 6737–6749.

Obayashi, T., 1965. Hydromagnetic whistlers. *J. Geophys. Res., 70* (5) : 1069–1078.

Pope, J. H., 1964. An explanation for the apparent polarization of some geomagnetic micropulsations (pearls). *J. Geophys. Res., 69* (3) : 399–405.

Roederer, J. G., W. N. Hess, and E. G. Stassinopoulos, 1965. Conjugate intersects to selected geophysical stations. *NASA Tech. Rept., X-642-65-182.*

Tepley, L., 1964. Low latitude observations of fine structured hydromagnetic emissions. *J. Geophys. Res., 69* (11) : 2273–2290.

Troitskaya, V. A., 1964. Rapid variations of the electromagnetic field of the earth. In *Research in Geophysics, Vol. I, Sun, Upper Atmosphere and Space.* M.I.T. Press, Cambridge, Mass.

Wescott, E. M., 1966. Magnetoconjugate phenomena. *Space Sci. Rev., 5:* 507–561.

Cosmic Ray Intensity Variations

MARTIN A. POMERANTZ

Bartol Research Foundation of The Franklin Institute, Swarthmore, Pennsylvania

Cosmic rays are predominantly electrically charged particles, mostly protons, that impinge upon the earth's atmosphere from outer space. They may arrive from sources far beyond the solar system (galactic cosmic rays) or they may originate at the sun (solar cosmic rays). Because they interact with magnetic fields, cosmic rays serve as unique probes for studying the terrestrial environment, interplanetary space, and the nature of the control exercised over these regions by the sun.

Cosmic ray research in the Antarctic plays a crucial role in investigating the electromagnetic conditions in space. In particular, cosmic ray intensity measurements at polar stations afford the only means for probing regions that lie appreciably outside the ecliptic plane and are not likely to become accessible to spacecraft for some time. Furthermore, notwithstanding the current capabilities for making sophisticated *in situ* measurements in space, observations of the time variations in the flux of galactic cosmic rays reaching the earth make it possible to derive a vast amount of information concerning the gross features, during both quiet and disturbed periods, of the far-reaching solar plasma regime, extending well beyond the orbit of earth. In addition, solar cosmic rays are subject to local magnetic configurations in the immediate vicinity of the sun, as well as to the disturbed conditions prevailing in the interplanetary medium and in the earth's magnetosphere in the aftermath of great solar eruptions.

DIRECTIONAL AND ENERGY RESPONSE OF DETECTORS

The unique character of cosmic ray stations in the polar regions resides in the optical properties of cosmic ray instruments dictated by their location within the earth's magnetic field. The geomagnetic field acts both as a momentum spectrometer and as a complicated system of lenses.

The spectrometer action imposes a minimum value of the energy (rigorously, the momentum per unit charge or magnetic rigidity $R = pc/Ze$ where p is the momentum, c is the velocity of light, Z is the charge number, and e is the charge on the electron) that a particle must have to reach a particular location. This threshold below which the arrival of particles is forbidden is greatest at the geomagnetic equator, and decreases toward the poles where it becomes zero. Thus, at high latitudes, the earth's atmosphere, rather than the geomagnetic field, determines the minimum energy of particles that can propagate their effects down to ground-based detectors. Consequently, primary protons (the original cosmic rays that impinge on the top of the atmosphere) with energies as low as a few hundred Mev can be detected through their progeny that are able to penetrate to sea level.

The complications introduced by the lens action is illustrated in Figure 1, which shows the computed trajectory of a particular cosmic ray as it approaches the earth. It is clear that, when this quasi-trapped particle eventually strikes the earth, as indeed it

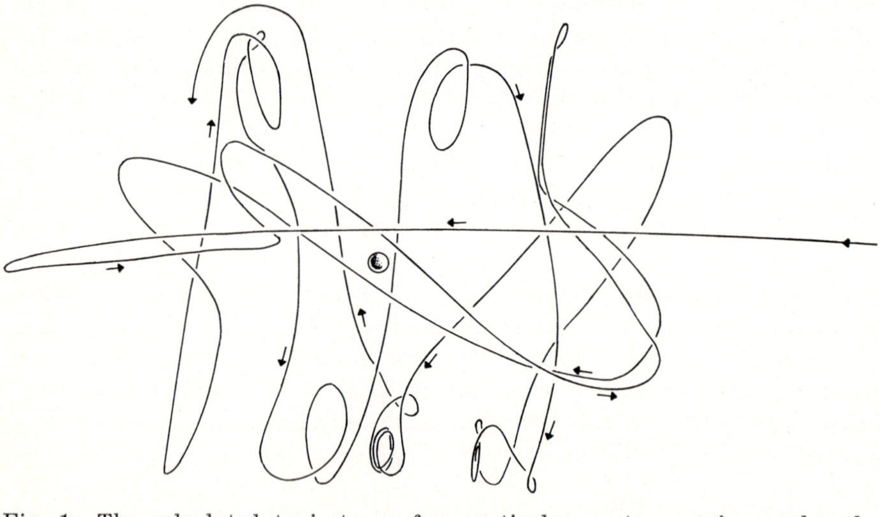

Fig. 1. The calculated trajectory of a particular proton moving under the influence of the earth's magnetic field after arrival from a distant source. Although this orbit is not necessarily typical, it serves to indicate the importance of calculating individual trajectories in evaluating the directional response of a cosmic ray detector located at a particular point on the earth.

will, the direction toward which the detector recording its arrival happens to be pointing bears no relation to the direction in space from whence the particle came prior to its encounter with the terrestrial magnetic field.

Fortunately, the problem is somewhat more tractable than Figure 1, which represents an extreme situation, suggests. It is possible, albeit with the expenditure of vast amounts of computer time, to calculate the asymptotic directions (Fig. 2) as a function of magnetic rigidity of cosmic rays arriving at a specified point on the earth's surface (McCracken *et al.*, 1968). Figure 3 shows the only possible directions from which particles with the indicated rigidities can come in order for them to reach the polar stations marked by asterisks.

Proceeding further with the analysis, and taking into account both the primary energy spectrum and the dependence of the response characteristics of the particular detector upon primary energy, leads to the determination of the asymptotic cones of acceptance depicted in Figure 4. The shaded regions are the portions of the celestial sphere (in geographic coordinates) from which those cosmic rays making the principal contribution to the count-

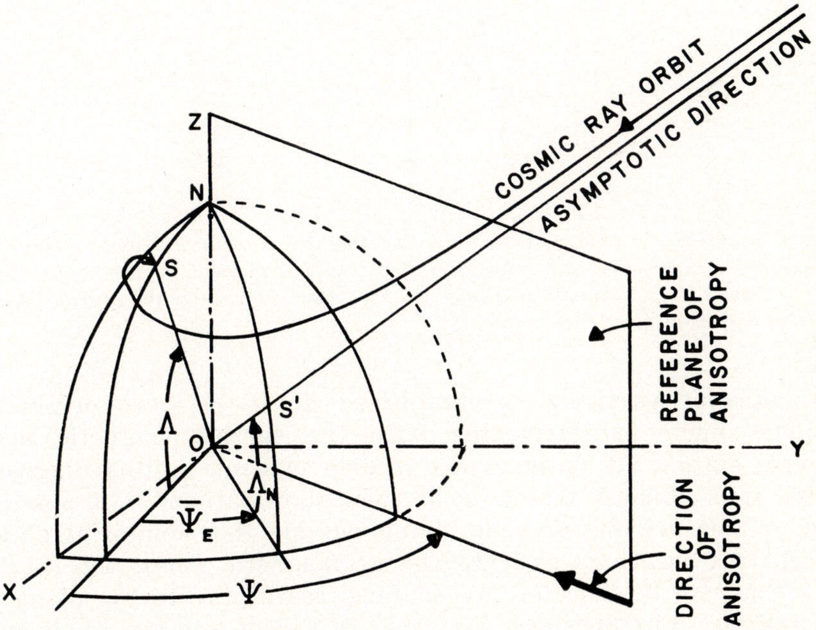

Fig. 2. Definition of asymptotic direction, and the direction of anisotropy.

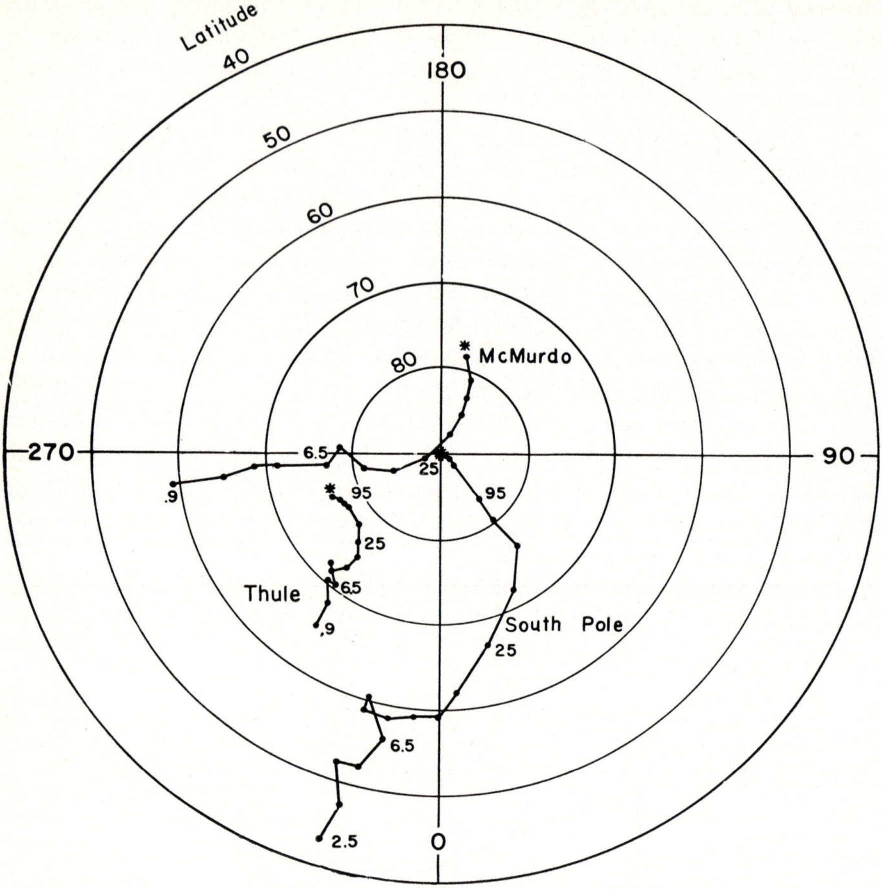

Fig. 3. Asymptotic arrival directions for the three polar stations designated by asterisks. Each dot represents the point on the celestial sphere from which all particles of the indicated rigidity (in Gv) that can reach the station in the vertical direction must have come.

ing rates of particular ground-based detectors were originally incident prior to interacting with the earth's magnetic field. Several significant features are clearly evident in this diagram. First, it is obvious that only at the polar stations is it possible to view the regions of space lying outside the equatorial plane. Except for locations close to the geomagnetic poles, the cosmic rays that can be detected are confined essentially to the plane of the ecliptic. Furthermore, the cones of acceptance are small only for polar stations. Finally, it is obvious that any attempt to

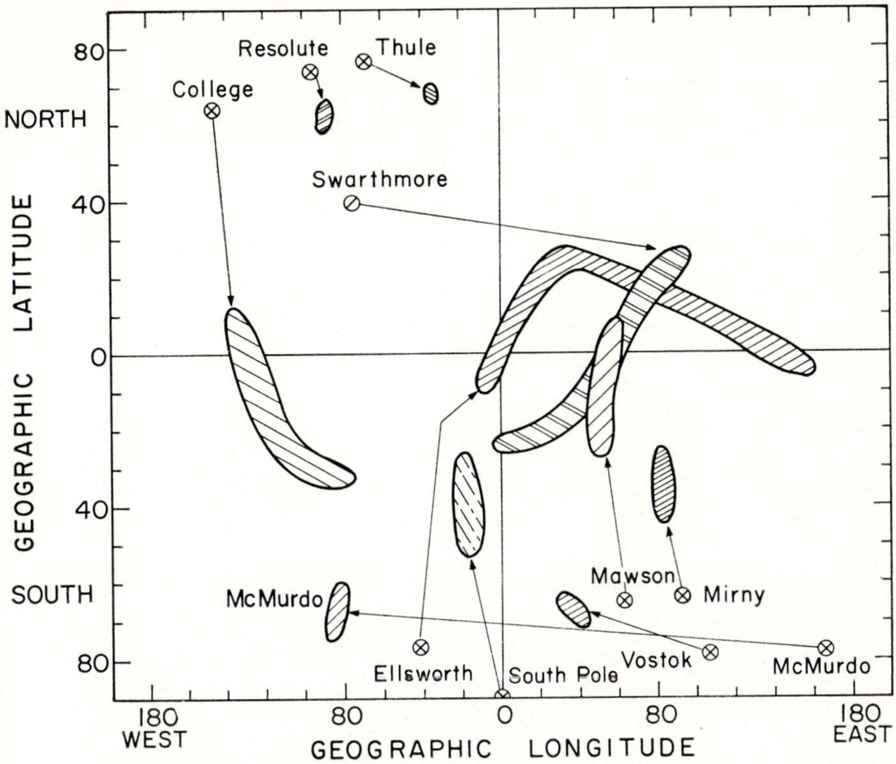

Fig. 4. Cones of acceptance, or directions of viewing, of cosmic ray detectors located at each point indicated by a circled ×.

correlate cosmic ray intensity measurements with specific directions in space must involve detailed consideration of these effects.

A further complication is introduced by the atmosphere, since, by various nuclear interactions, the incoming primary cosmic ray is rapidly converted into secondaries, some of which ultimately reach detectors on the ground. The situation is shown schematically in Figure 5. Here, the three modes whereby a sufficiently energetic primary may elect to propagate its effects through the atmosphere are represented. Lower energy particles (~1–10 Bev) mainly spawn the nucleonic component, through a cascade process. Comprising a few percent of the net particle flux at sea level, the nucleons are selectively detected by a device called a neutron monitor. More energetic primaries (~10–100 Bev) are responsible for the muons that are observed with a meson telescope. Finally, the higher-energy cosmic rays (~10^3–10^{11} Bev) give rise to extensive air showers.

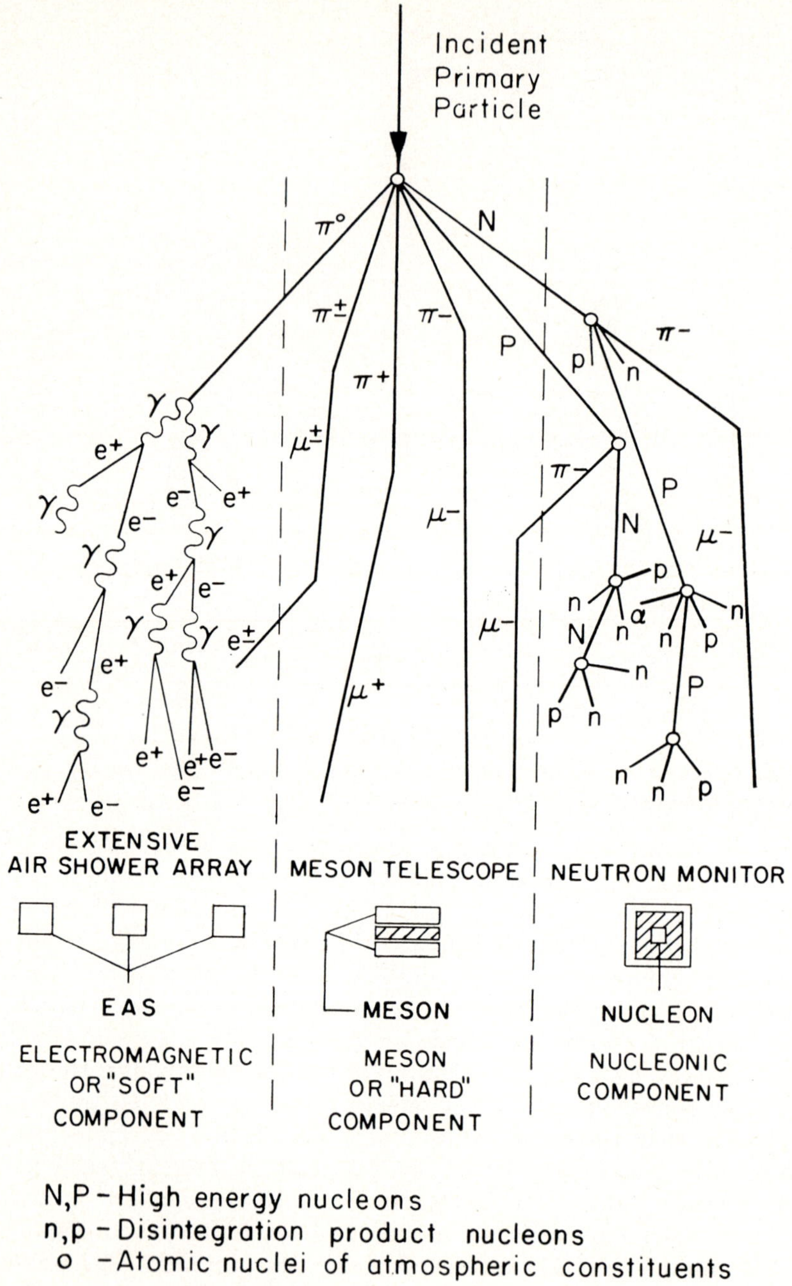

Fig. 5. Schematic representation of the various modes whereby an incident cosmic ray primary propagates its effects through the atmosphere down to ground level. The three types of detector respond to primaries with increasingly higher energies from right to left in this diagram.

The gyroradius of a 1,000 Bev proton in the 5×10^{-5} gauss interplanetary magnetic field is 5 astronomical units (AU). The solar magnetic regime extends out to a distance variously estimated to be between 5 and 100 AU; hence this is the extreme upper limit of the energy of cosmic rays whose motion is dominated by solar processes. Consequently, studies of solar effects upon the cosmic radiation involve the first two components only, and a crude energy resolution is attained by utilizing both neutron monitors and meson telescopes.

MODULATIONS AND ANISOTROPIES

Spatial anisotropies and intensity modulations are studied with ground-based detectors by relating observed time variations in the rate of arrival of cosmic rays to specific directions in space by highly sophisticated analytical procedures. These intensity fluctuations span time scales ranging from minutes to two solar cycles. It is possible in this review only to exemplify the preeminent role of cosmic ray observations in the Antarctic by very brief reference to one or two of the wide variety of phenomena that are of current interest.

SOLAR DIURNAL VARIATION

The cosmic ray intensity varies as a function of local solar time. As is shown in Figure 6, this solar diurnal variation can be represented vectorially on a so-called harmonic dial as the hand of a 24-hour clock, pointing toward the time at which maximum intensity is observed. The length of this vector is proportional to the amplitude of the first harmonic wave. When the appropriate correction for geomagnetic bending is applied to the vector determined from the observations at each station, the true local solar time of maximum is found to be around 1800 hours in every case.

A theoretical model that accounts for such features as the magnitude of the average daily vector and its dependence upon the location of the station envisages the Archimedean spiral interplanetary magnetic field as corotating with the sun, in the manner sketched schematically in Figure 7, just as though it were rigidly connected. The twisted and kinked magnetic irregularities superposed by solar disturbances upon the quiet-time field lines act as scattering centers from which the cosmic ray particles effectively bounce. Since this entire structure is like a huge paddle wheel,

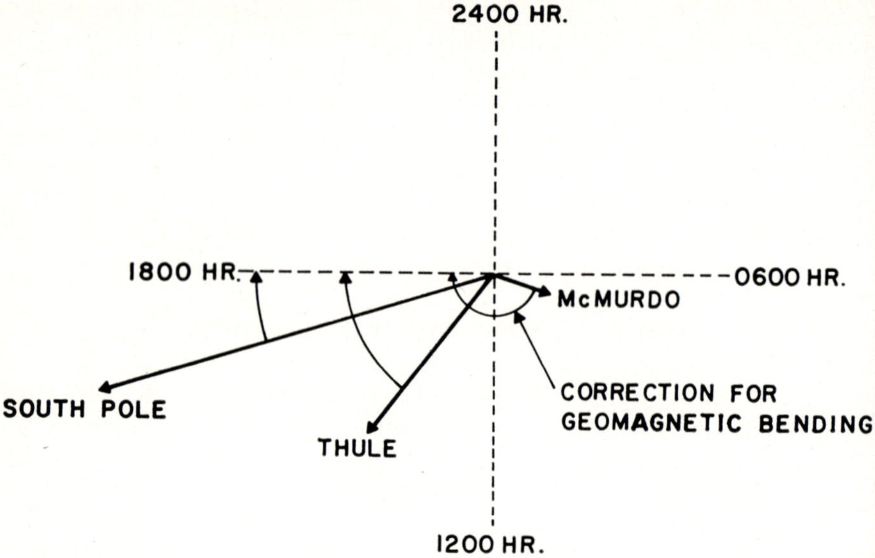

Fig. 6. Twenty-four hour harmonic dial, or clock diagram, showing the vectors representing the solar diurnal anisotropy, and the calculated corrections for geomagnetic bending, for several polar stations.

it stirs up the cosmic ray gas in such a manner that there is more flow from 90° east of the sun-earth line (6:00 PM), whereas particles attempting to reach the earth at dawn are discouraged by the oncoming blades. Many details concerning the character, density, and size of the irregularities, as well as other important properties of the interplanetary medium, can be deduced from the quantitative analysis of the observational data on the basis of the relevant theoretical model.

NORTH-SOUTH ASYMMETRY

It has now been well established that there is a radial space gradient in the cosmic ray intensity in the plane of the ecliptic, as a consequence of the convective removal of cosmic rays by the sun's outwardly expanding corona — the solar wind. This gives rise to an inverse relationship between the cosmic ray intensity and the level of solar activity. Moreover, quite recent theoretical discussions have postulated the existence of a cosmic ray intensity gradient perpendicular to the ecliptic plane.

As Figure 8 shows, measurements obtained at stations in the two polar regions do not provide any evidence for a large-scale

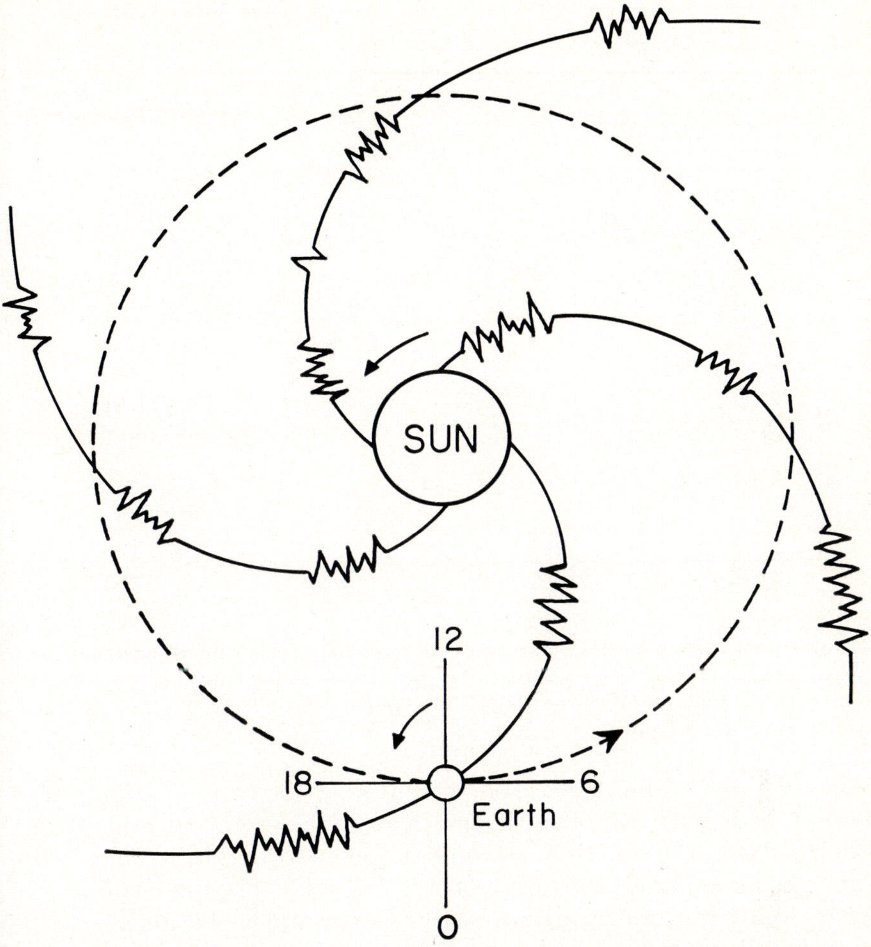

Fig. 7. Schematic model of the mechanism that produces the solar daily variation.

steady-state north-south asymmetry. However, similar observations have revealed that, at least during limited periods, such an effect does, in fact, occur. This phenomenon was discovered in the records of the cosmic ray storm shown in Figures 9 and 10. A detailed analysis of data from many stations, based upon a theoretical model (Nagashima *et al.*, 1968) developed to account for this transient axial intensity gradient during a Forbush decrease, led to the result plotted in Figure 11. The agreement between the predicted solid line and the observed experimental

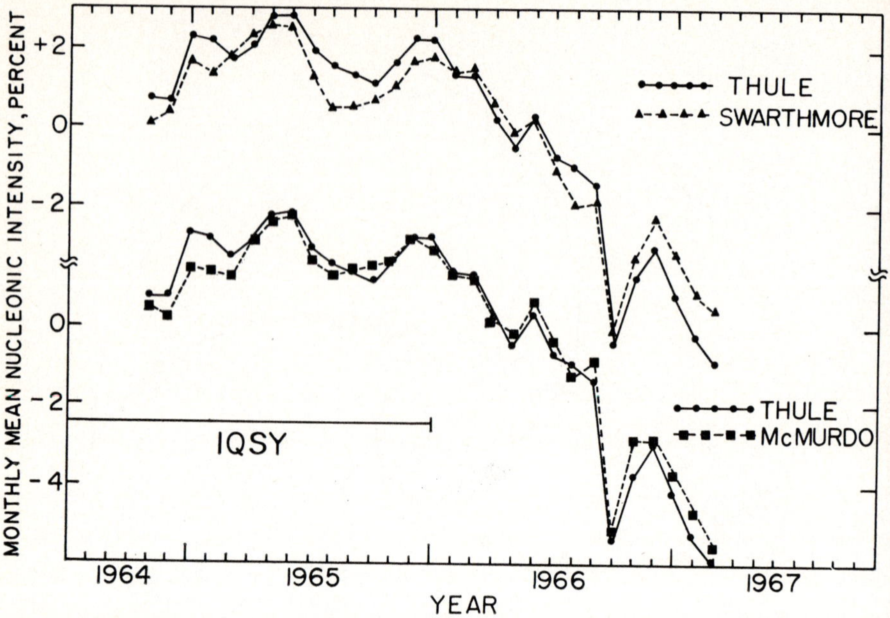

Fig. 8. Comparisons of the monthly mean nucleonic intensity as observed over several years at stations viewing directions north and south of the ecliptic plane (Thule and McMurdo), and in and perpendicular to the ecliptic plane (Swarthmore and Thule).

points confirms the picture sketched in a greatly oversimplified manner in Figure 12. The three-dimensional vector of anisotropy, which pointed almost (but not quite) toward the South Pole, arose from the unsymmetrical distribution of solar plasma around the earth following an unusual solar disturbance, because of the geometrical configuration of the active region on the sun and the earth. Like the invisible shield of old TV commercials, this giant bubble blown out from the sun tended to reduce the flux of cosmic rays reaching the earth in an asymmetrical manner.

A number of other north-south asymmetry events have since been identified, and we now know that roughly one out of three Forbush decreases displays this phenomenon (Duggal and Pomerantz, 1969).

SOLAR COSMIC RAYS

The emission by the sun of nuclear particles having energies as high as several hundred Mev is a rare phenomenon, which, on

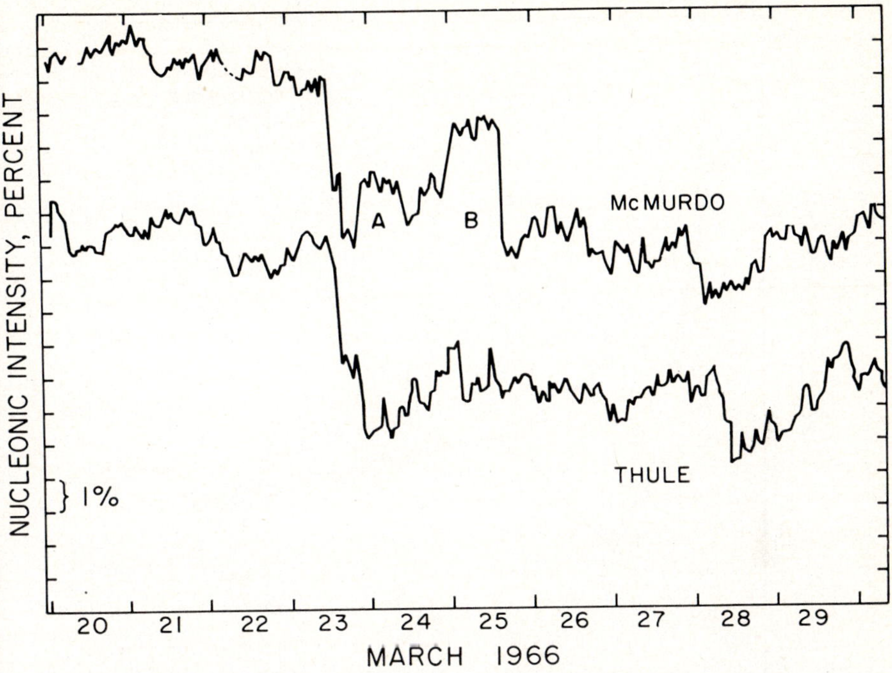

Fig. 9. Nucleonic intensity, in hourly intervals, at Thule and McMurdo Stations during March, 1966. Pronounced north-south differences are clearly indicated at A and B.

the average, happens only once in two years. Thus, the arrival from the sun of "newborn" cosmic rays having sufficient energy to propagate their effects through the earth's atmosphere is by far the most spectacular phenomenon that we can hope to observe with ground-based detectors.

According to earlier theories (e.g., Firor, 1954) energetic charged particles traveling to the earth from the sun, through what was then regarded as completely empty interplanetary space, could penetrate through the dipole geomagnetic field, as it was pictured at that time, only in well-defined impact zones. Since these did not encompass high latitudes, the calculations indicated that the arrival of solar cosmic rays at polar stations was precluded. However, cosmic ray flux increases have been observed during every so-called ground-level event and, in fact, their magnitude has generally been greater than that at lower-latitude stations having directions of viewing in the equatorial plane. Studies of these events have revealed that diffusion mechanisms play an

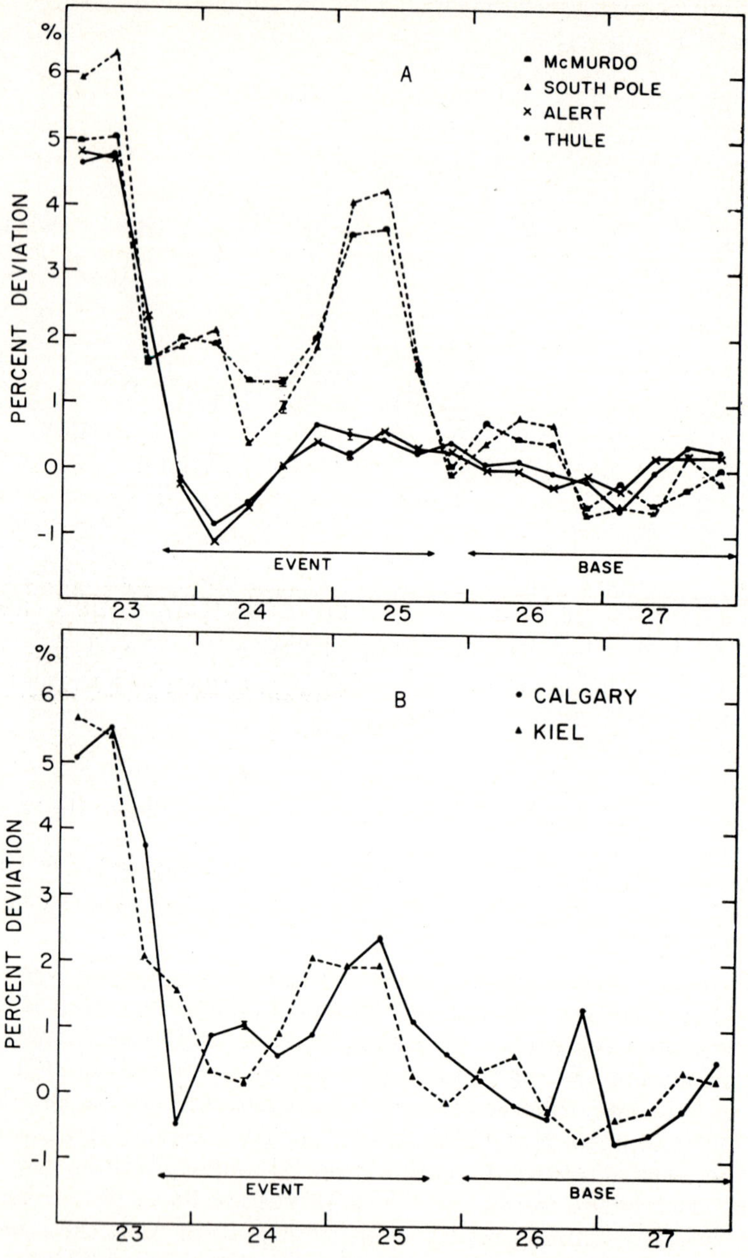

Fig. 10. Six-hour averages (March, 1966) of the intensity deviations from the mean level (BASE) (a) at antarctic and arctic stations, and (b) at a pair of stations having asymptotic directions of viewing that differ only in longitudes. This confirms that the direction of anisotropy was perpendicular to the equatorial plane.

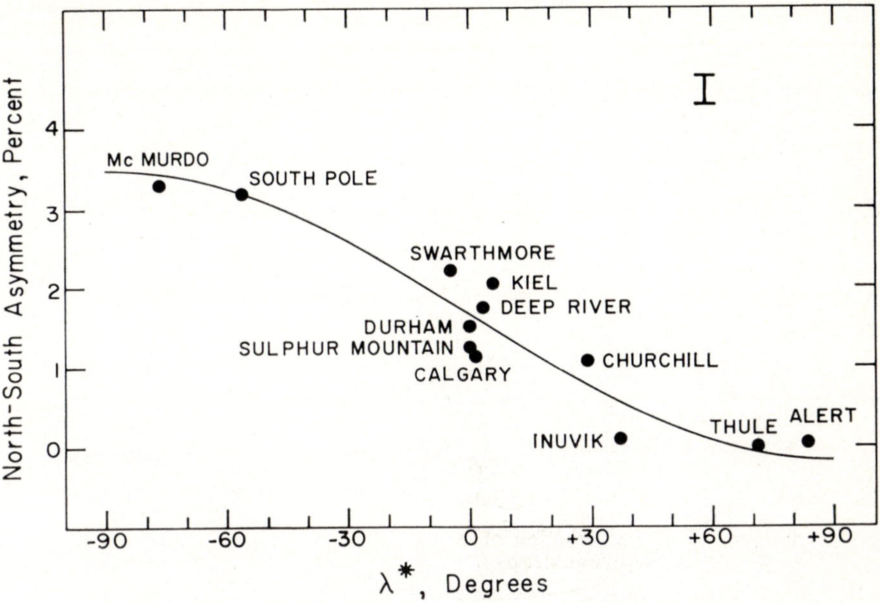

Fig. 11. North-south asymmetry plotted as a function of λ*, the effective asymptotic latitude. Determined by analysis, λ* represents as a point on the celestial sphere the entire asymptotic cone for a particular detector, rigidity spectrum, and location.

important role in the transport of particles from the sun to the earth (Baird *et al.*, 1967; Pomerantz *et al.*, 1961a, b, c; Pomerantz and Duggal, 1961).

The morphology of a solar particle event is indicated in Figure 13, which shows the temporal relationships of the various phenomena that may follow a great explosion on the sun. Figure 14 shows the cosmic ray observations at the North and South Polar stations during an unusual period when two such events occurred in rapid succession.

A historic event is shown in Figure 15. This represents the first of only two occasions out of about 23 observed thus far upon which a flare on the back side of the sun produced energetic particles that reached the earth.

The characteristics of the intensity profiles, and other evidence, suggest that the propagation of the solar particles that arrived on January 28, 1967, was controlled by a diffusion mechanism. An example of the comparison of the measurements with the predictions of a theoretical model (Pomerantz *et al.*, 1961a) is shown in

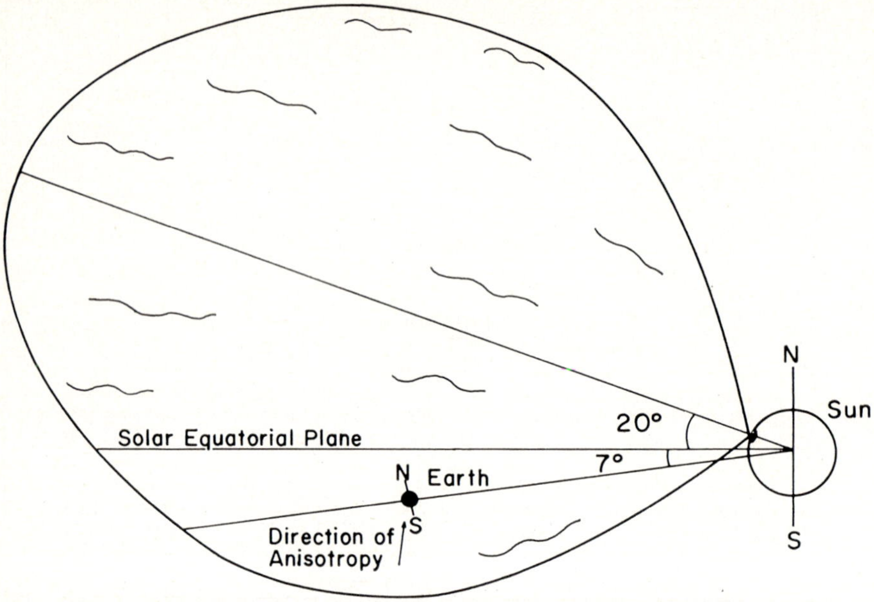

Fig. 12. Schematic representation of the solar plasma regions that produced the observed north-south asymmetry. The direction of the anisotropy in space, almost perpendicular to the plane of the ecliptic, is also indicated.

Figure 16. Here, the data are represented in appropriately normalized units of intensity R and time τ. The solid lines are derived from the solution of the diffusion equations. This plot covering the post-maximum period reveals the dimensionality of the source, i.e., whether it may be regarded as a point ($n = 3$), an infinite line ($n = 2$), or an infinite plane ($n = 1$). The points lie closest to the line corresponding to the three-dimensional case ($n = 3$) but deviate because of the finite extent of the diffusing region.

Finally, it is interesting to consider in some detail the event that occurred on November 18, 1968, since it exemplifies the other extreme among the possible modes of propagation of solar cosmic rays. This is, in fact, the first case in which immediate impact of solar particles in the polar regions has been observed with the new, high counting-rate neutron monitors.

As is evident in Figure 17 (Pomerantz, 1970), the statistical uncertainty in the data recorded with the type of apparatus (Simpson, 1957) that was first introduced at the time of the International Geophysical Year (1957–1958) was appreciably larger than that characterizing the present arrangement (Car-

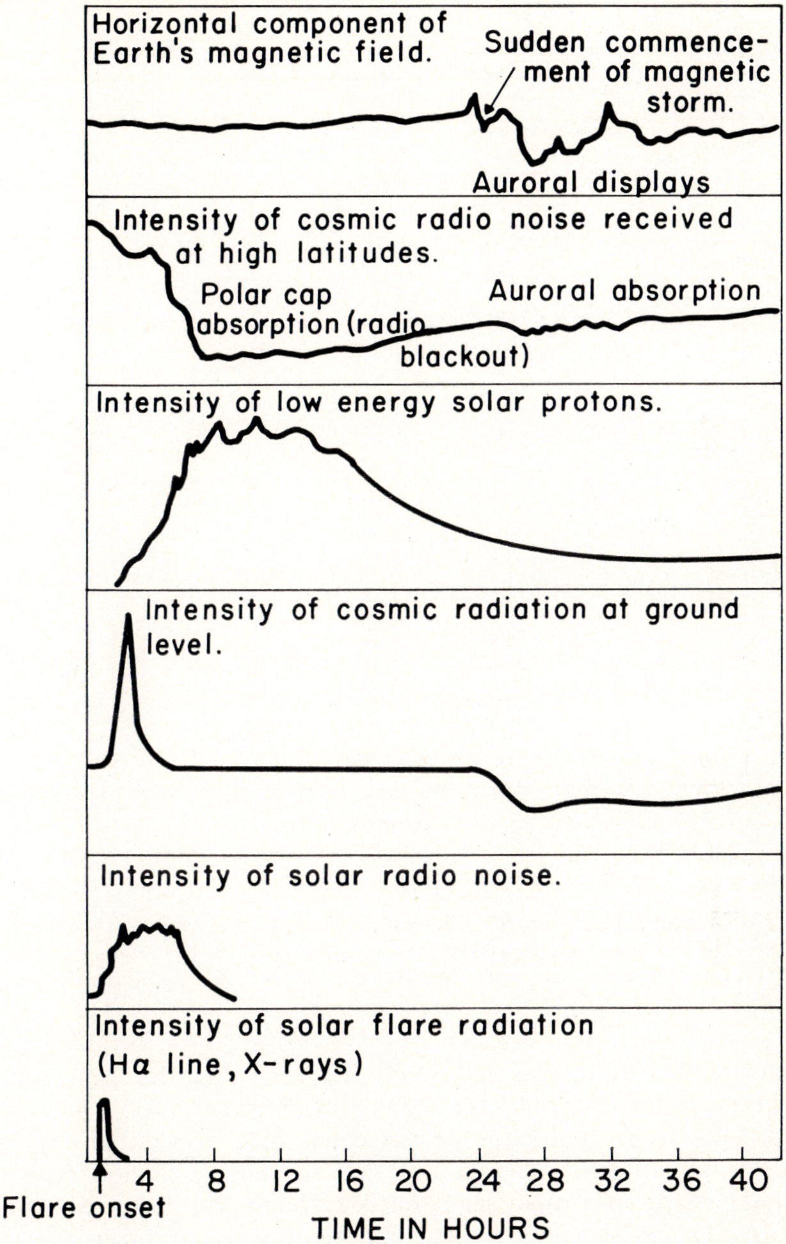

Fig. 13. Time pattern of various effects observed when very energetic solar cosmic rays are emitted during a great solar flare. Lesser flares may be accompanied by some of these phenomena.

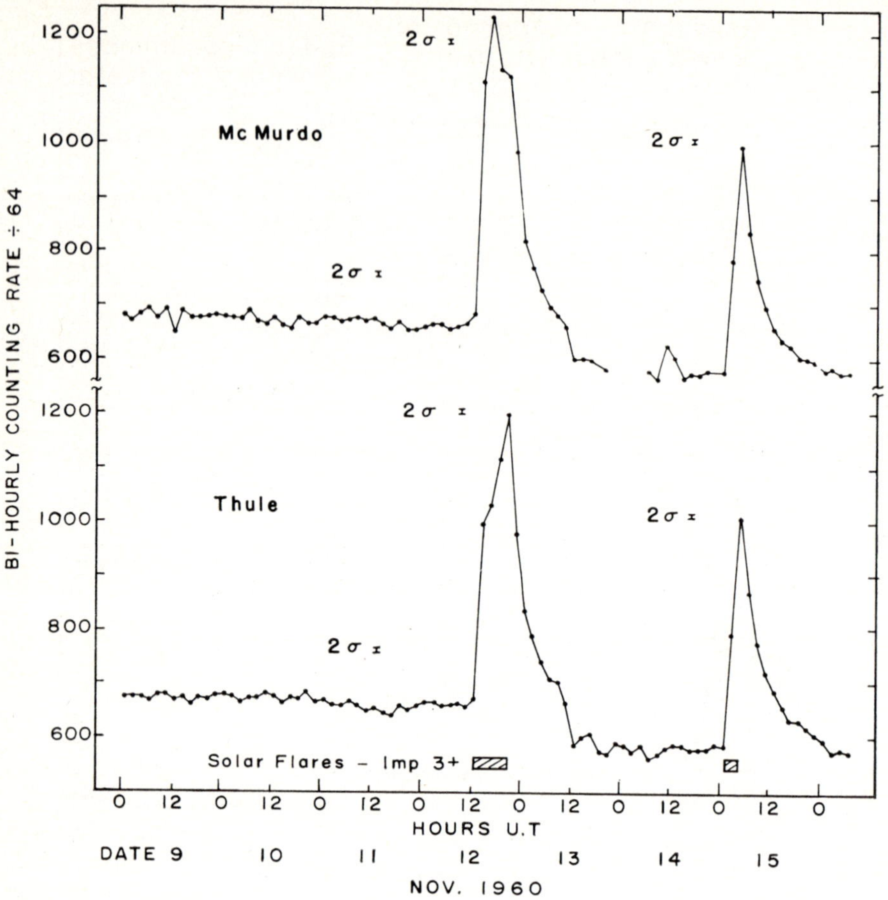

Fig. 14. Energetic particle events in which solar cosmic rays with sufficiently high energies to make their effects felt at sea level were detected near the North and South Poles, on two different occasions. The 2σ marks represent statistical standard deviations.

michael, 1968) that was originally adopted for the program of the International Years of the Quiet Sun (1964–1965). The earlier instruments would not have provided the high resolution required for the quantitative analysis that led to the conclusion that the dominant mode of propagation on November 18, 1968, was guidance directly from the sun along magnetic lines of force.

Figure 18 shows the intensity of solar cosmic rays as recorded by the Bartol neutron monitors at McMurdo and South Pole Stations, as well as at the arctic station at Thule, Greenland, and at

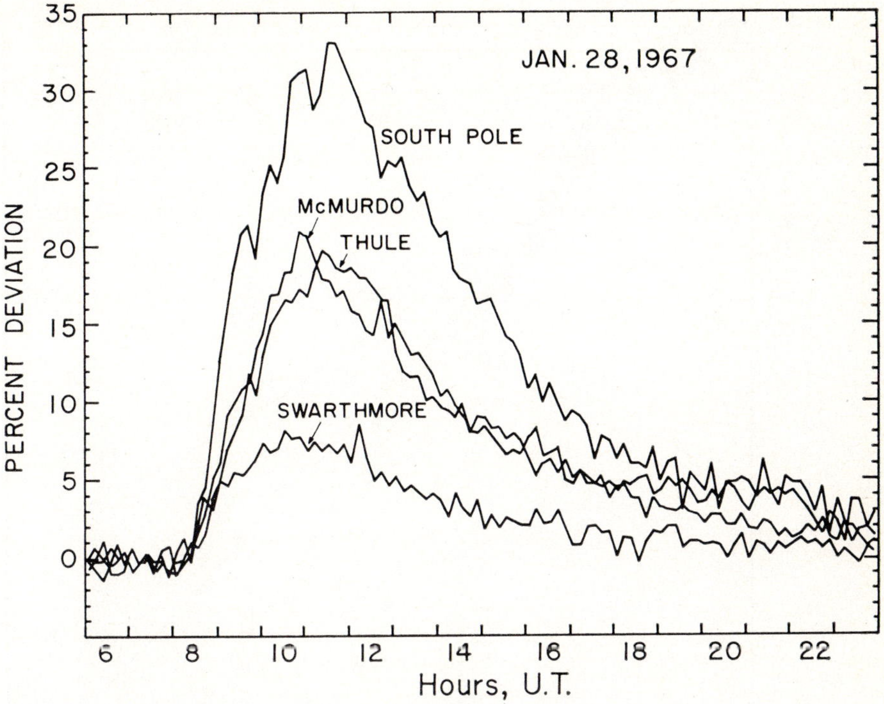

Fig. 15. First observation of the arrival of very energetic solar cosmic rays from the back side of the sun. Percentage deviations from the average pre-flare level at Thule, McMurdo, South Pole, and Swarthmore on January 28, 1967, are plotted. The data are averaged over 10-minute intervals.

Swarthmore. At the last-named station, solar particles can arrive only from the equatorial plane. Because of its altitude, the South Pole detector responds to lower-energy primary particles than do the other stations, hence the magnitude of the increase is enhanced.

The most striking feature is the sharp rise time, in marked contrast to the slower-developing previous events, particularly the one shown in Figure 15. Maximum intensity was attained 10 minutes after onset, and the major activity subsided in about 2 hours. This event, which occurred while the galactic intensity was recovering from the effects of a cosmic ray storm, was associated with a relatively minor (1B) limb flare at 29°N, 87°W on the solar disk. The spectrum, deduced from an analysis of data from 18 stations, was of the form $I = k \exp(-R/550)$, where R is the magnetic rigidity in units of MV.

After normalizing the data to remove the effects of differences

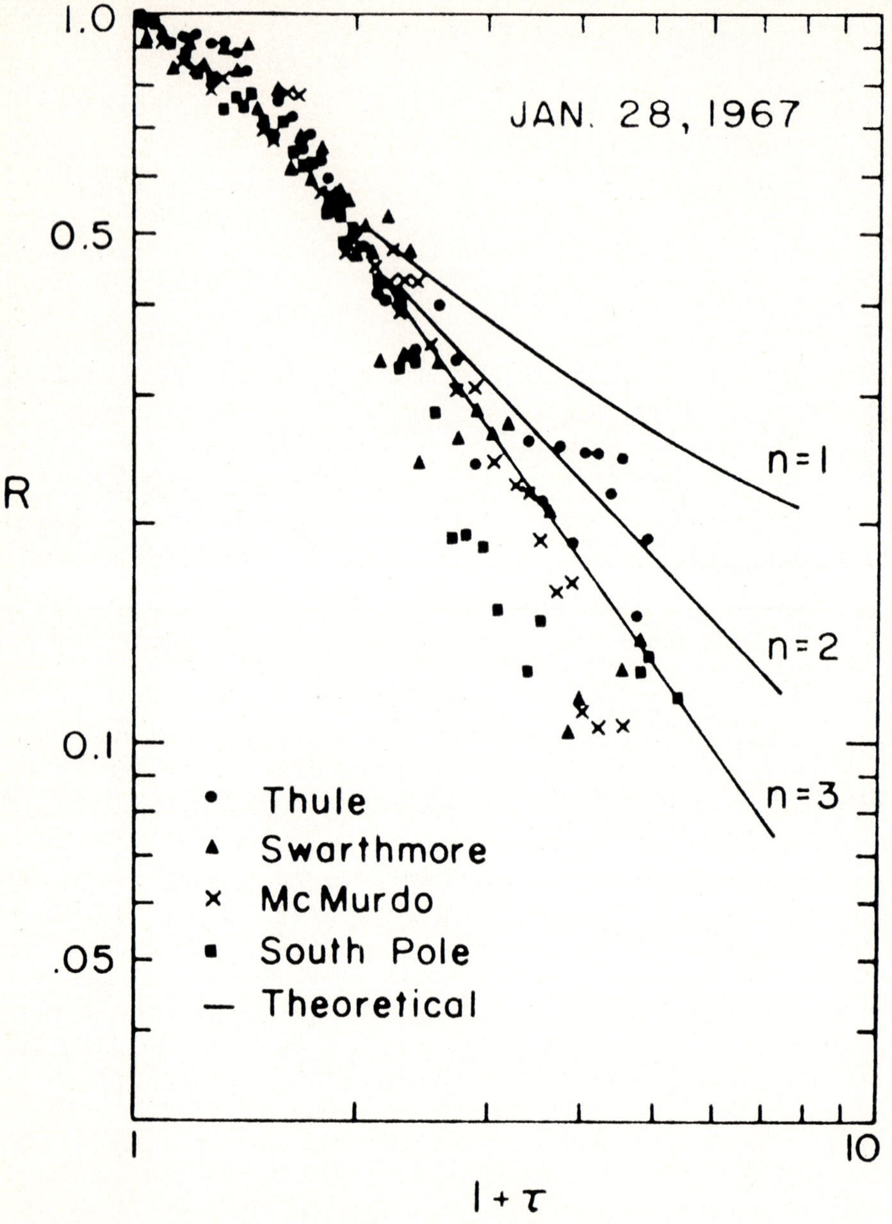

Fig. 16. Plot, in normalized units, of the intensity at various stations as a function of time during the post-maximum period on January 28, 1967. (Theoretical curves correspond to n-dimensional diffusion.)

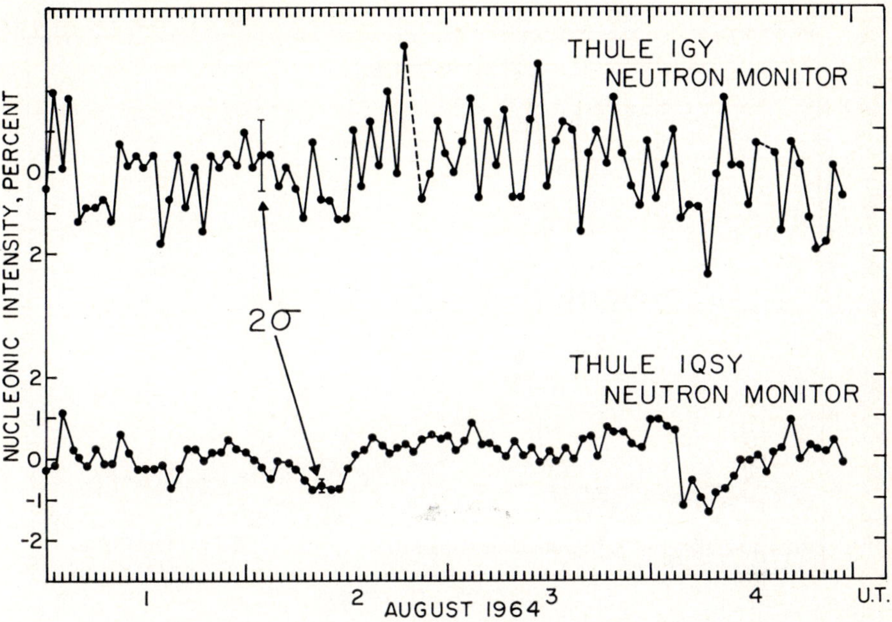

Fig. 17. Comparison of data recorded simultaneously by an IGY and an IQSY neutron monitor operating side by side. The data points represent percentage deviations of the hourly counting rates from the respective means over the entire indicated period. The reduction in the magnitude of the statistical "noise" is clearly evident.

in altitude and geomagnetic threshold rigidity, a large variance remains in the magnitude of the increase as recorded at different stations near the peak of this event. For example, the percentage increase observed at Thule (76.6°N, 291.6°E) was twice that at Alert (82.5°N, 297.7°E), while no enhancement was recorded by the Soviet station at Tiksi Bay (71.6°N, 128.9°E).

In Figure 19, the normalized maximum percentage increases during a 20-minute interval are indicated in circles representing the approximate asymptotic direction of arrival of the solar particles to which the detectors at the specified locations (X) respond. Our analysis reveals that the intensity increase was symmetric with respect to a point on the celestial sphere with geographic coordinates 20°S, 40°W (12h right ascension, −20° declination). This location was 50° west of the position of the sun at that time, which conforms with the Archimedean spiral structure of the interplanetary magnetic field, thus confirming the hypothesis, based upon the exceedingly rapid rise to maximum, that the solar

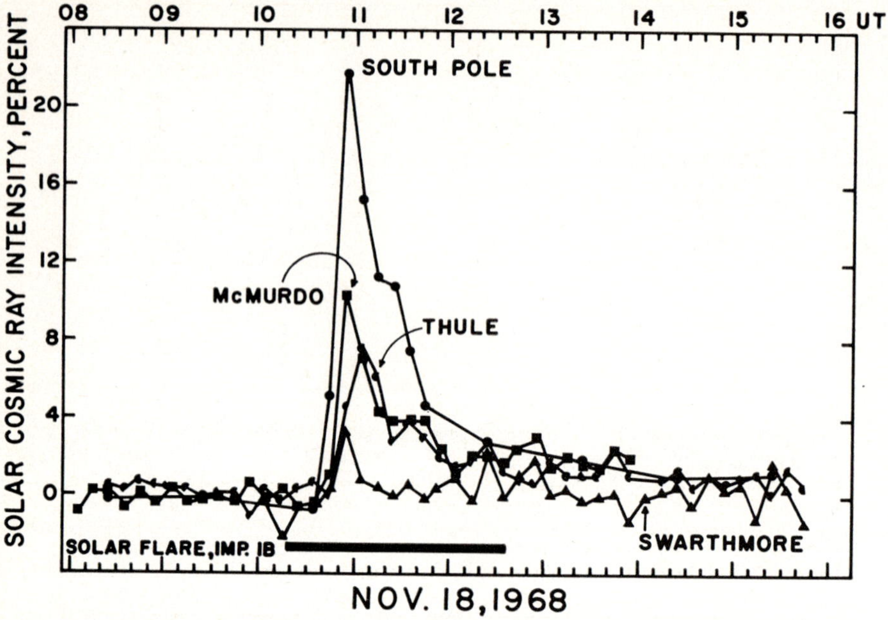

Fig. 18. Solar cosmic ray event of November 18, 1968, as observed by Bartol neutron monitor stations. The ordinates are percentage increase in intensity above the galactic cosmic ray background. South Pole Station recorded the largest flux detected anywhere on the earth's surface.

particles were magnetically guided from the source along the lines of force as illustrated in Figure 20.

CONCLUSION

Cosmic rays have a great deal to tell us about a wide variety of physical phenomena ranging from nuclear forces to the evolution of the universe. In this brief review, we have limited our attention to just a single facet of cosmic ray research — studies in which ground-based detectors in the Antarctic play a key role. But it seems appropriate to note in closing that the impact of cosmic rays upon antarctic research is not confined to that portion of the program that is usually designated upper atmospheric physics. For, through the isotopes they produce, these subatomic visitors from afar also contribute to such seemingly unrelated fields as geology, glaciology, meteorology, and oceanography (Pomerantz, 1971).

Author's Note: It is a pleasure to express my appreciation to the National Science Foundation for its continuing support in carrying out the antarctic cosmic ray program.

References

Baird, G. A., G. G. Bell, S. P. Duggal, and M. A. Pomerantz, 1967. Neutron monitor observations of high-energy solar particles during the new cycle. *Solar Phys., 2:* 491–501.

Carmichael, H., 1968. Cosmic rays (instruments). In *Annals of the IQSY, Geophysical Measurements: Techniques, Observational Schedules and Treatment of Data,* edited by C. M. Minnis; vol. 1, pp. 178–197. M.I.T. Press, Cambridge, Mass.

Duggal, S. P., and M. A. Pomerantz, 1970. Transient north-south asymmetries of cosmic radiation. In *Acta Physica Hungarica, Proceedings of the Eleventh International Conference on Cosmic Rays, Budapest, Hungary, August 24–September 4, 1969;* vol. 29, suppl. 2.

Firor, J., 1954. Cosmic radiation intensity-time variations and their origin. IV. Increases associated with solar flares. *Phys. Res., 94:* 1017–1028.

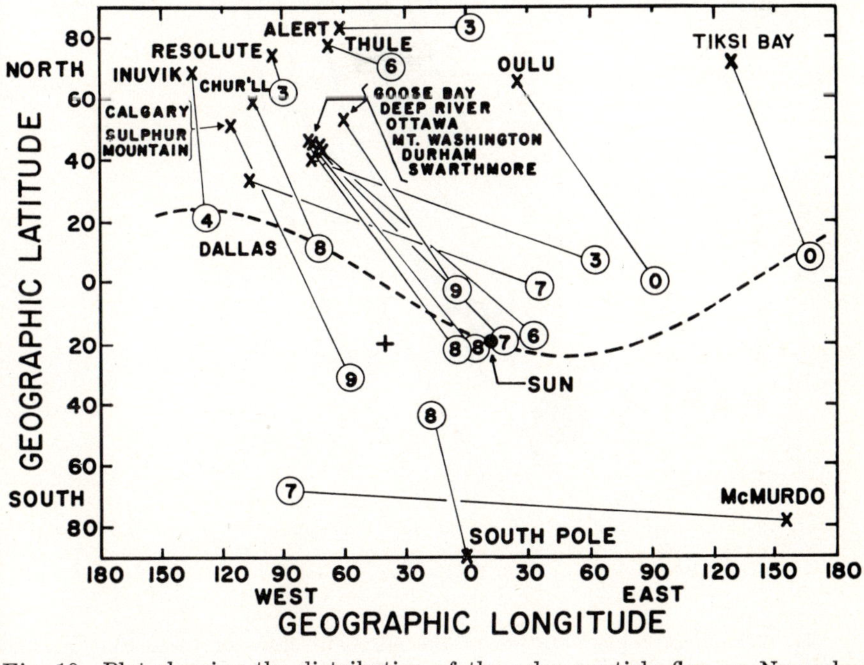

Fig. 19. Plot showing the distribution of the solar particle flux on November 18, 1968, about the axis of symmetry, +, which represents the position of the apparent source. The number in each circle indicates the percentage enhancement (appropriately normalized to remove the effects of altitude and geomagnetic cutoff differences) above the galactic cosmic ray background.

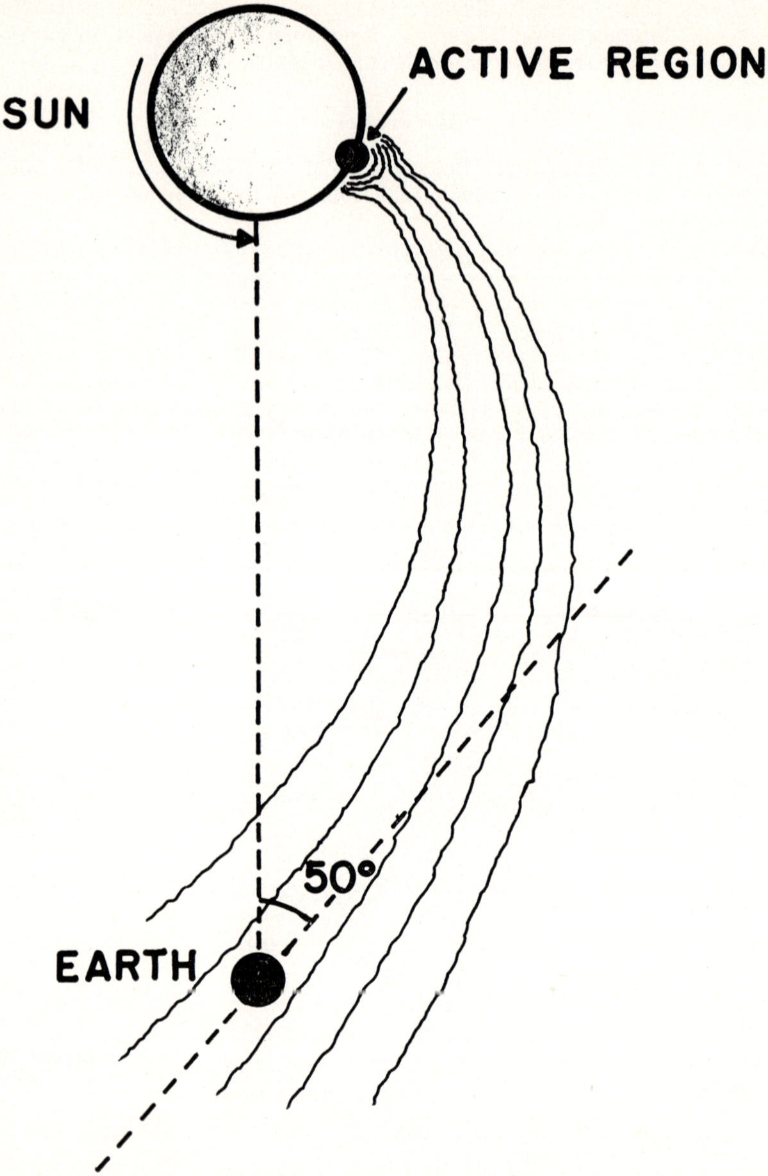

Fig. 20. Schematic representation of the magnetic lines of force that guided the solar cosmic rays from the sun to the earth on November 18, 1968.

McCracken, K. G., U. R. Rao, B. C. Fowler, M. A. Shea, and D. F. Smart, 1968. Cosmic rays (asymptotic directions, etc.). In *Annals of the IQSY, Geophysical Measurements: Techniques, Observational Schedules and Treatment of Data,* edited by C. M. Minnis; vol. 1, pp. 198–214. M.I.T. Press, Cambridge, Mass.

Nagashima, K., S. P. Duggal, and M. A. Pomerantz, 1968. Cosmic ray anisotropy in three-dimensional space. *Planetary Space Sci., 16:* 29–46.

Pomerantz, M. A., 1969. IQSY Data Review: Cosmic Rays. In *Annals of the IQSY, Survey of IQSY Observations and Bibliography,* edited by C. M. Minnis; vol. 6, pp. 211–223. M.I.T. Press, Cambridge, Mass.

Pomerantz, M. A., 1971. *Cosmic Rays.* Van Nostrand Reinhold Co., New York.

Pomerantz, M. A., and S. P. Duggal, 1961. Unusual increase in the cosmic ray intensity on November 20, 1960. *J. Franklin Inst., 271:* 327–335.

Pomerantz, M. A., and S. P. Duggal, 1962. Anisotropy in solar particles incident on polar regions during July, 1961. *J. Franklin Inst., 273:* 242–248.

Pomerantz, M. A., S. P. Duggal, and K. Nagashima, 1961a. Observation near the North and South Poles of bursts of cosmic rays from the sun. *J. Franklin Inst., 271:* 317–326.

Pomerantz, M. A., S. P. Duggal, and K. Nagashima, 1961b. Solar-produced cosmic rays near the North and South Poles. *Phys. Rev. Letters, 6:* 123–125.

Pomerantz, M. A., S. P. Duggal, and K. Nagashima, 1961c. The unusual cosmic ray intensity increases on November 12, 1960. *Space Res., 2:* 788–802.

Simpson, J. A., 1957. Cosmic-radiation neutron intensity monitor. In *Annals of the International Geophysical Year, Cosmic Radiation,* edited by Sir Harold Spencer Jones; vol. *4,* part 7, pp. 351–373. Pergamon Press, London.

PART VI

Ocean Dynamics

PART VI

Ocean Dynamics

Antarctic oceanography is unique because of the influence of the Southern Ocean on the continents and the world ocean. The Atlantic, Pacific, Indian, and Arctic Oceans are joined to each other by narrow straits and canals, but their common bond is the almost uninterrupted sweep of water from 1,000 to 3,000 km wide that surrounds Antarctica. Although it connects with the other great oceans, it is distinctly different.

The rotation of the earth wheels this mass and its Circumpolar Current clockwise around Antarctica, but the movements of the world ocean are also driven by the great temperature differences between the polar and tropical waters. As the shallower waters in the south cool, become denser, and sink, they are joined by waters of higher salinity caused by the freezing of the sea ice and also from the freezing and melting of ice on the undersides of the ice shelves. These dense, cold bottom waters flow northward to beyond the Equator where they have a direct effect on the climate and fisheries far into the Northern Hemisphere.

The importance of these complex flows of great masses of water has been recognized by the National Science Foundation which has sponsored research in the physical oceanography around Antarctica for more than ten years. Earlier oceanographic observations have been made by various expeditions into these waters since at least the time of Captain Cook in the eighteenth century. It has certainly been the most continuously active of the antarctic scientific disciplines.

In February, 1962, the *Eltanin* (See Preface) began a systematic survey of the oceanography, geology, geophysics, and biology of the ocean around Antarctica. In the following eight years she has operated in the Southern Ocean almost continuously: first in the South Atlantic, Scotia Sea, and southeastern Pacific; and then, moving progressively westward, she covered the southern and southwestern Pacific, the Tasman Sea, and the southeastern Indian Ocean between Australia and Antarctica. These multidisciplinary, multi-institutional survey cruises were interspersed with special-purpose cruises in biology, geology, and geophysics. In late 1970 the *Eltanin* was operating along a series of tracks that will survey the southern Indian Ocean, and her survey of the Southern Ocean should be completed by 1975.

Each of the authors of Part VI of this volume has covered different aspects of our present knowledge and the needs for future research on the characteristics of the Southern Ocean.

An introduction to the overall complexity of the physical oceanography of the Southern Ocean is to be seen in Arnold Gordon's paper. His work on the *Eltanin* has resulted in significant contributions to the study of ocean dynamics and has particularly helped to outline the location, volume, and dynamics of the Circumpolar Current and the physical and chemical characteristics of the southern water masses as they change throughout the year.

A more detailed study of the Circumpolar Current is to be found in the paper by John L. Bowen and Henry Stommel. They have taken previously unanalyzed data collected by the *Discovery II*, south and southwest of the southern tip of Africa in 1938 and 1939 and interpreted from them the dynamics of the current. They found that the Circumpolar Current is relatively stable in its latitudinal position as it flows through this region.

The volume of antarctic water moving northward out of the Southern Ocean and into the rest of the world ocean is discussed by Bruce Warren. He combines the work of others with the results of two *Eltanin* cruises which were primarily directed to studying the physical oceanography of the middle latitudes of the southern Pacific. The main effort of these cruises was to locate and measure the major deep currents of Antarctic Bottom Water.

Extensive research was also carried out in the Weddell Sea by the icebreaker USCGC *Glacier* as part of the Weddell Sea Oceanographic Expedition; Robert Elder and James Seabrooke, who were aboard, report on the sources of Atlantic Bottom Water. Cold Antarctic Bottom Water, found as far north as the major fishing areas of the North Atlantic, has major economic significance.

Many other oceanographic problems are being actively attacked by these and other marine scientists. Their work is not only valuable to those who are directly concerned with antarctic research but has direct worldwide scientific, economic, and social importance.

MORT D. TURNER

Earth Sciences Programs
Office of Polar Programs
National Science Foundation
Washington, D.C.

Recent Physical Oceanographic Studies of Antarctic Waters

ARNOLD L. GORDON

Lamont-Doherty Geological Observatory of Columbia University, Palisades, New York

ANTARCTIC CIRCUMPOLAR CURRENT

The antarctic waters flow around the continent in a clockwise direction. The current, called the Antarctic Circumpolar Current, is deep with little attenuation with depth. Surface velocities are generally less than 0.5 knots (25 cm/sec), according to the charts of the U. S. Naval Oceanographic Office (Neumann and Pierson, 1966) although values between 0.5 and 1.0 knots are suggested for the Pacific sector of antarctic waters by Bolgurtsev (1966). The current accelerates when transversing relatively narrow channels, as in the Drake Passage. Such constrictions of streamlines are also observed in the open ocean whenever the current is directly above a deep fracture in north-south ridges. The current turns northward on approaching a ridge and southward over a basin, but the magnitude of the deflection is apparently influenced by the angle of the axis of flow to the axis of the ridge.

The East-Wind Drift is a westward-flowing current along the coastlines of Antarctica. This flow is not completely circumpolar, but at various points it is diverted northward and causes a string of clockwise gyres in the large embayments of the Weddell, the Ross, and the Bellingshausen Seas. The intersection of these gyres with the Antarctic Circumpolar Current and the vertical motions of the water masses within the gyres present many interesting problems. The Antarctic Divergence (Kort, 1968), the region between the Circumpolar Current and the East-Wind Drift, may be broken into segments centered within each gyre. The lack of winter data in the ice-covered regions now permits only a one-season study.

The Antarctic Circumpolar Current is generally considered to be zonal although it has large latitudinal variations. Figure 1 shows the position of the axis of this current. Its axis is not so well defined as other major ocean currents, with the exception of segments of its course where it transverses a constriction, as over the U. S. Antarctic Research Program (USARP) Fracture Zone (Gordon, 1967a). Barcilon (1966, 1967) suggested a seasonal variation in the magnitude of the current due to the slowing of the current by the summer peripheral freshwater discharge from

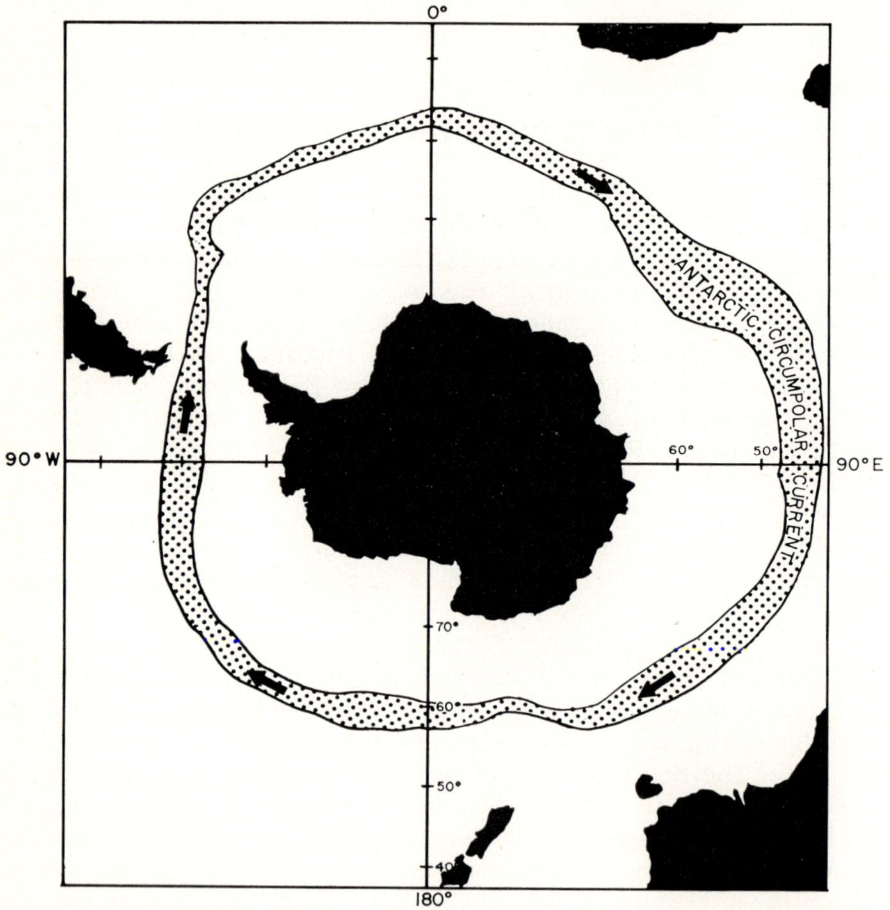

Fig. 1. The region of maximum sea surface slope. The axis of the Antarctic Circumpolar Current should coincide with this maximum in the sea surface slope (from Plate 103, Part 1, USSR Antarctic Atlas, 1966).

Antarctica. No evidence to support a summer slowing of the current is available, however, and the existing information suggests, in fact, a maximum speed in late summer (Gordon, 1968a). Perhaps a summer speedup of the East-Wind Drift results from the peripheral freshwater discharge, but absence of data for the winter velocities does not permit the evaluation of the summer values as either a minimum or a maximum.

The transport of the Antarctic Circumpolar Current is estimated from its geostrophic relationship. The success of this method depends on the choice of a zero reference level (a level of zero horizontal geostrophic velocity). This choice is difficult or impossible over much of the antarctic waters because the current direction appears not to vary from the sea surface to the sea floor. This uniformity of current direction is deduced from evidence of bottom currents as shown in photographic and sedimentation studies (Heezen *et al.*, 1968; Hollister and Heezen, 1967; Hollister and Elder, 1969), and the lack of baroclinicity of antarctic waters which is needed to yield a significant shear. Because of the minor attenuation of the current with depth, the use of a deep isobaric surface for a zero reference level, as is often done in geostrophic studies, can lead to large errors in calculation of the total volume transports. Using such a method, transport values of 86 to 134×10^6 m^3/sec relative to the 3,000 decibar level (3,000 m) are calculated (Gordon, 1967b).

In the southern Drake Passage, the water mass structure suggests a deep and bottom flow toward the Pacific Ocean (Gordon, 1966, 1967a) and hence a zero reference layer within the water column in this region. This layer was extrapolated northward across the Drake Passage by Gordon (1967b) using an equivalent barotropic assumption. Such a reference layer penetrated to depths greater than the sea floor; however, it yields a velocity field which is consistent with descriptive oceanographic results and with various theoretical models (Gill, 1968). The axis of the Antarctic Circumpolar Current is confined to the northern Drake Passage (mainly between 56° and 57°S). The small countercurrent confined to the deep water of the southern Drake Passage continues along the continental margin of Antarctica in the Bellingshausen Sea. The origin of this water is the spillover from the Weddell Sea to the Scotia Sea at a passage near 39°W (Gordon, 1966). Therefore, an Atlantic to Pacific transport of Weddell Sea water occurs but is far less than the eastward transport of the central and northern Drake Passage.

The total geostrophic volume transport through the Drake Passage based on the above reference layer is 218×10^6 m^3/sec. This is the largest value yet proposed for the Drake Passage transport. It is interesting that a value of 216×10^6 m^3/sec was arrived at by the numerical solution of the wind-driven ocean (O'Brien, 1969). Direct current measurements for extended periods are needed to test the results of the geostrophic calculations (Capurro, 1968).

WATER MASSES

The influence of the antarctic waters on the world ocean and atmosphere is a result of the large meridional flow (Fig. 2). The southward-flowing Circumpolar Deep Water is warm, salty, low in oxygen, but high in nutrients. This water eventually is converted at the sea-air interface into the fresher, colder, highly oxygenated Antarctic Surface Water. Part of the deep water is altered near the coast to a dense cold water mass which sinks and entrains more deep water to produce the Antarctic Bottom Water. Both the Antarctic Surface Water and Bottom Water masses flow northward, compensating for the southward-flowing deep water. The surface water sinks on reaching the slightly less

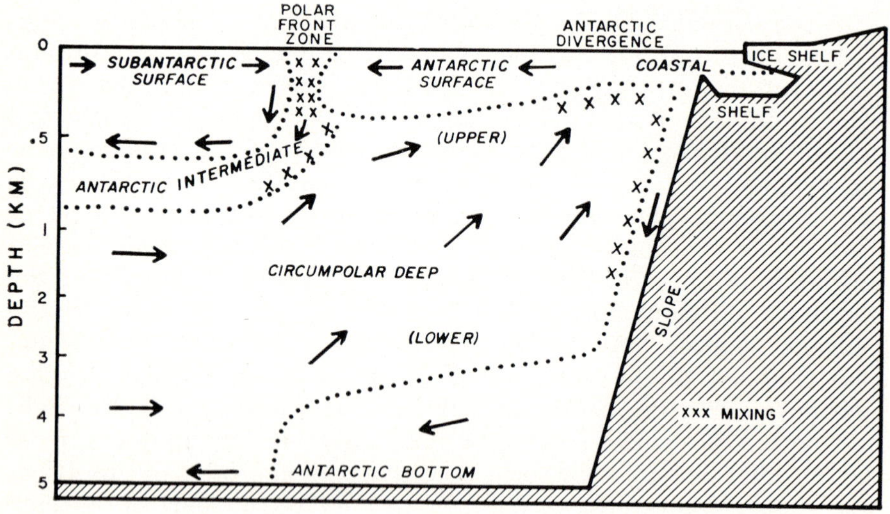

Fig. 2. Schematic representation of antarctic water masses and meridional flow.

dense Subantarctic Surface Water where it comprises the bulk of the Antarctic Intermediate Water which, in turn, influences most of the oceans of the Southern Hemisphere.

Both the northward-flowing antarctic water masses are eventually altered; they are warmed by heat flux from the surface and the sea floor and their oxygen is consumed by biological activity and salt introduced from the North Atlantic Ocean and the Mediterranean Sea. They enter the deep water and flow southward to start the cycle over again. Therefore, the conversion of deep water to surface and bottom water and their subsequent transformation to deep water farther north represents an oceanic overturning or "breathing" of the deep ocean for which the Antarctic Ocean plays a key role (Gordon, 1970a).

The Circumpolar Deep Water is characterized by a salinity maximum (S_{max}). This maximum is considered the core of the lower Circumpolar Deep Water (Gordon, 1967a). The upper deep water is characterized by a temperature maximum (found only below the Antarctic Surface Water) and an oxygen minimum. The salinity along the S_{max} core layer is shown in Figure 3 and the temperature-salinity maximum (T/S_{max}) relationship in Figure 4.

The Circumpolar Deep Water moves eastward as part of the Antarctic Circumpolar Current and recirculates around Antarctica. As it does this, it loses water to the surface and bottom water masses and is resupplied from the north. The resupply probably is accomplished around the entire continent but the introduction of highly saline water from the Atlantic Ocean, because of the injection of North Atlantic Deep Water (NADW), stands out as a separate feature in both Figures 3 and 4.

The rapid increase in salinity from the Drake Passage to the Indian Ocean is no doubt due to the influx of NADW. This influx occurs between the longitudes of 10°W and 70°E, between the South Sandwich Trench region and Kerguelan Island, where the salinity of the S_{max} increases steadily to the north indicating a diffusive salt transport southward. In the southeastern Indian Ocean and South Pacific an axis of salinity within the S_{max} core layer is found and the diffusive salt transport is probably directed both north and south of the axis. Therefore it appears likely that the integration of highly saline NADW into Circumpolar Deep Water is completed to the west of 70°E. The S_{max} may be thought of as an axis of spreading although not necessarily an axis of flow. Along the axis of spreading, the salinity decreases from 34.76 ‰

Fig. 3. Salinity distribution on the salinity maximum core layer.

near Kerguelan to 34.73 ‰ in Drake Passage which is a decrease of only .03 ‰ in a distance of roughly 12,800 kilometers measured along the 60°S parallel.

Figure 5 is a plot of the observations within the axis of spreading from 70°E eastward to Drake Passage. The drop in salinity is hardly perceptible amid the scatter of points. Much of the decrease, however, occurs in the vicinity of the 180° meridian and the deep northward-flowing western boundary current reported by Reid *et al.* (1968) and Warren (this volume) begins in the vicinity of this longitudinal zone where the current is characterized by a high salinity core. It may be possible, therefore, that the Circumpolar Current divides into two sections after passing

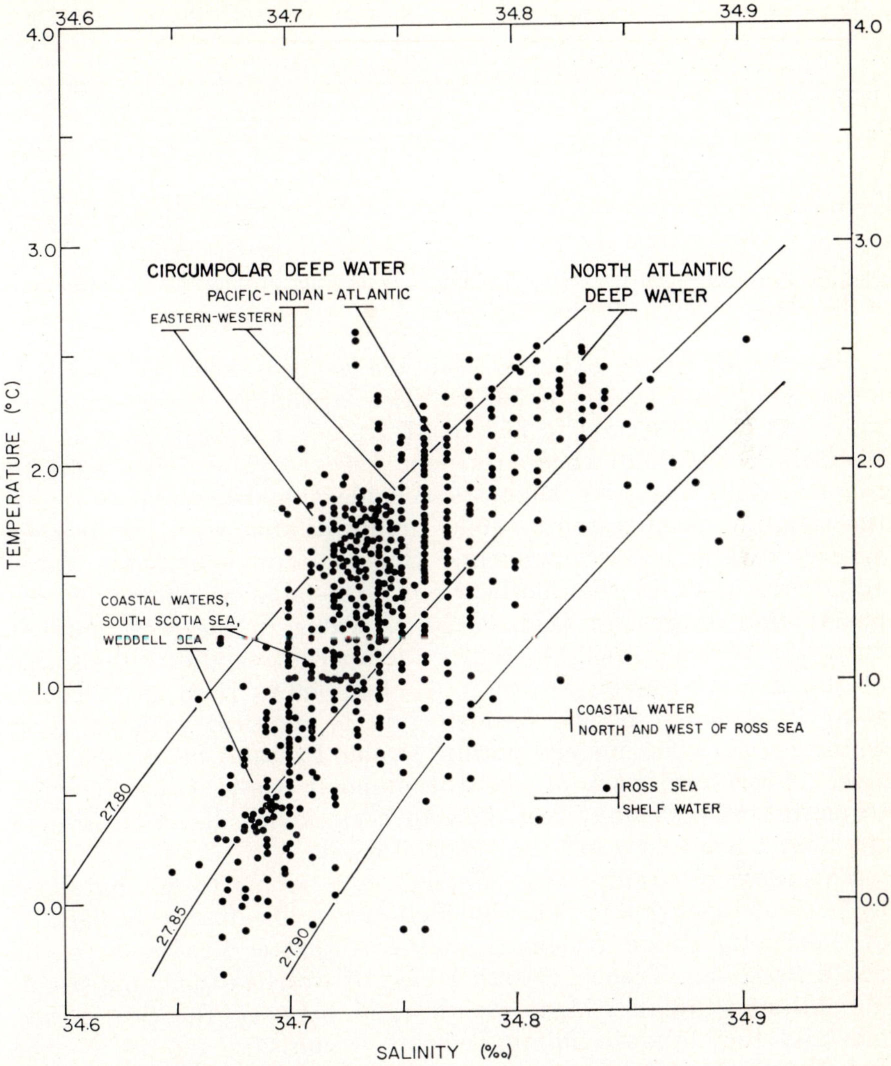

Fig. 4. Temperature-salinity relation at the core layer of the lower Circumpolar Deep Water.

the Macquarie Ridge south of New Zealand where one branch may flow northward and the other may continue in its circumpolar course. The lower salinity of the latter suggests that either it is not derived from the center of the S_{max} axis, or that it combines with antarctic water flowing northward from the Ross Sea-Balleny Island region.

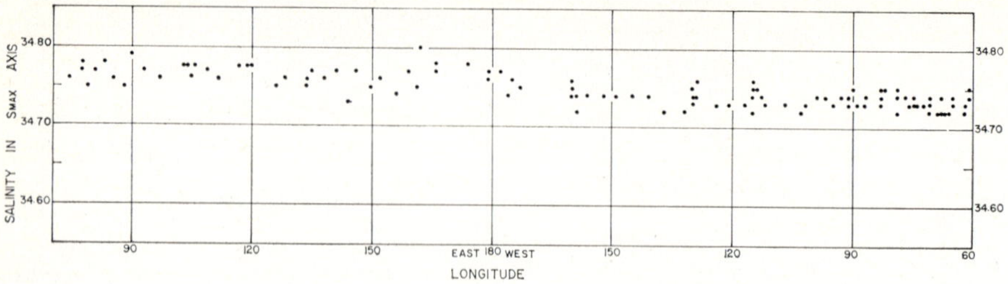

Fig. 5. Salinity variation as a function of longitude of the axis of spreading within the salinity-maximum core layer.

The Weddell gyre extends from the eastern coast of the Antarctic Peninsula to 25° to 30°E. The latitudinal extent is from the coast of Antarctica to 55° to 57°S; this northern limit is the Weddell-Scotia Confluence (Gordon, 1967a). The lower salinity found within the gyre suggests considerable recirculation since the influx of deep water becomes highly diluted with the fresher antarctic water mass components. Some Circumpolar Deep Water enters the gyre in the southeastern extremity as shown by the penetration of greater than 34.70 ‰ water in the west current along the 63°S parallel. A study of temperature-salinity diagrams of the Atlantic Ocean (Gordon, 1971a) shows that the Circumpolar Deep Water of the Weddell gyre is identical with the deep water below 3,000 meters within Drake Passage below the S_{max} level. Therefore, part of the Circumpolar Deep Water flowing through Drake Passage may flow in a clockwise direction around the Scotia Sea and enter the Weddell gyre.

The eastern extent of the Weddell gyre seems to be controlled by bottom topography. The Weddell-Scotia Confluence is parallel to the Scotia Ridge system from the Antarctic Peninsula to the South Sandwich Trench. Farther east, it overlies the zonal-trending Atlantic-Indian Ridge. At the gap between the Scotia system and the Atlantic-Indian Ridge between 25° and 10°W, the isohalines penetrate farther south. At 25° to 30°E another gap appears in the Atlantic-Indian Ridge. Here the isohalines of the lower Circumpolar Deep Water turn sharply to the south, giving rise to the eastern boundary of the Weddell gyre. It appears that the bottom topography prohibits the saltier Circumpolar Deep Water from penetrating south of 57°S until the zonal ridge is broken in the vicinity of 25° to 30°E.

The T/S_{max} points for the sections other than the Weddell gyre or coastal areas fall mostly in the 27.80–27.85 σ_T density unit interval, indicating nearly isentropic circulation. The T/S_{max} points shift to lower the temperature and salinity segments of the diagram as the geographic position of the water they represent shifts eastward from the South Atlantic. The temperature-salinity points within the Weddell Sea have higher density but lower salinity. This condition is caused by the recirculation within the gyre and the mixing with the colder Antarctic Bottom Water. The T/S_{max} points in the Ross Sea area have a higher salinity and density than the S_{max} water in the circumpolar open ocean belt. This condition can only occur as a result of coastal freezing. The Ross Sea and adjacent coastal areas have topographic depressions which trap this water and prevent its escape and dilution in the open oceans. Therefore, the S_{max} within these coastal areas do not represent the lower Circumpolar Deep Water, but a separate continental shelf water mass, which may be of importance in bottom water production.

The depths of the S_{max} layer (Fig. 3) reveal the decreasing depth of the core layer to the south; this depth change, however, is not a smooth function of latitude; great variations with longitude are also found. Fairly shallow depths (<500 m) are found in the Weddell Sea gyre and northeast of the Ross Sea. In addition, there are a few areas of a very rapid depth change: within the Weddell-Scotia Confluence region, near 145°W and 57°S and near 170°E, 63°S. In the first case, the relationship of this oceanographic feature to bottom topography has already been discussed. In the second case, a close relationship with a fracture zone occurs (Gordon, 1967a). The last case may be related to the mid-ocean ridge which parallels the Circumpolar Current in this vicinity. Perhaps it bears the same relationship to a Ross Sea gyre as does the Weddell-Scotia Confluence to the Weddell gyre.

The northward penetration of lower-salinity water in the vicinity of 120°E is puzzling. In the Weddell and Ross Sea regions, such a feature can be associated with a north-south ridge system. There is no such system shown in topographic maps for the 120°E region. Perhaps there is some relation to a fracture in the mid-ocean ridge in the vicinity of 120°E.

MERIDIONAL TRANSPORTS OF WATER MASSES

The introduction of the saline deep water into the surface layer would cause a constant salinity increase of the Antarctic Surface Water. While seasonal oscillations of surface salinity occur, there appears to be no overall trend to higher salinities. The introduction of salt must be balanced by the introduction of fresh water because of the predominance of precipitation over evaporation and continental runoff (icebergs, blown snow, and freshwater runoff). A salt budget was studied by Gordon (1971a) in order to determine the deep water input to the surface and bottom water masses.

Table 1 summarizes the freshwater input to the Antarctic Surface Water which is considered to extend from the southern limits of the polar front zone to the continent, a total area of 20×10^6 km^2. (For a complete discussion, see Gordon, 1971a.)

After taking into account the seasonal variations in the surface salinity, it was determined that the deep water enters the surface water at a rate of 60×10^6 m^3/sec during the summer months. This value must be considered a first approximation as the error is estimated to be $\pm 20 \times 10^6$ m^3/sec. However, it agrees fairly well with a 54×10^6 m^3/sec value found by calculation of the Ekman layer divergence of the Antarctic Surface Water.

The winter months pose a further problem since salt is lost from the surface layer by production of Antarctic Bottom Water. Assuming that surface water sinks when reaching a salinity of 34.6 ‰ and assuming that the upwelling of deep water at a rate of 60×10^6 m^3/sec continues during the winter, it is found that surface water sinks to the sea floor at a rate of 34×10^6 m^3/sec during the winter months. This water mixes with an additional 34×10^6 m^3/sec of deep water at a depth to produce bottom water at a rate of 68×10^6 m^3/sec during the winter months.

The yearly average values of meridional transport across the polar front zone are shown in Table 2.

Table 1. Freshwater input to Antarctic Surface Water. Minus sign indicates a freshwater withdrawal.

Source	Summer	Winter	Reference
Excess precipitation over evaporation	$+ 4.0 \times 10^{15}$ kg	$+ 4.0 \times 10^{15}$ kg	Wüst *et al.*, 1954
Continental runoff	$+ 2.1 \times 10^{15}$ kg	0	Giovinetto, 1964
Sea ice	$+ 2.3 \times 10^{15}$ kg	$- 2.3 \times 10^{15}$ kg	Munk, 1966

Table 2. Values of meridional transport across the polar front zone.

Antarctic Surface Water	43×10^6 m^3/sec to the north
Circumpolar Deep Water	77×10^6 m^3/sec to the south
Antarctic Bottom Water	34×10^6 m^3/sec to the north

The Antarctic Surface Water value reflects both the quantity of water mixing across the polar front zone into the Subantarctic Surface Water and the quantity contributing to the production of Antarctic Intermediate Water. The deep water value contains the amount which enters the surface layer and also the quantity which is entrained by the sinking brine during the winter months in the production of Antarctic Bottom Water. Figure 6 shows the average meridional transports in the world ocean. The production of North Atlantic Deep Water is approximately 15×10^6 m³/sec. This amount represents a transfer from warm to cold water components of the ocean. The compensating transfer from cold to warm water is accomplished by upwelling in the main thermocline and mixing across the antarctic polar front zone.

Since 60×10^6 m³/sec of deep water enters the Antarctic Surface Water and the surface water is about 1.5° to 2°C colder than the upper deep water, there is a 90 to 120×10^{12} cal per sec loss of heat to the atmosphere or approximately 14–19 kcal/cm² per year. This value represents the total heat transport by currents from the deep to surface layers. It should be balanced by the heat transfer across the sea-air interface by the following equation:

$$T = E + H - (Q_s - Q_b)$$

where T = heat transport by currents
E = heat loss by evaporation
H = heat loss by turbulent heat exchange from sea to air
Q_s = heat gain by solar radiation (short wave)
Q_b = heat loss by terrestrial back radiation (long wave).

The values of the terms on the right side of the equation can be approximated using Plates 109 and 75 of the U.S.S.R. *Antarctic Atlas* (1966). The evaporation loss south of the polar front zone is about 30 kcal/cm² per year. The turbulent heat loss is about 5 kcal/cm² per year. The difference between the incoming and outgoing radiation is approximately 20 kcal/cm² per year. Therefore, the value of T found from the heat budget terms is 15 kcal/cm² per year which agrees well with the 14–19 kcal/cm² per year value arrived at by salt budget consideration. Kort (1962, 1964) stated that the deep water carries into antarctic waters 30.2×10^{18} kcal/year (150 kcal/cm² per year) which is much greater than the amount suggested from the heat balance. The high value results from the large northward transport of deep water of 800×10^6 m³/sec which Kort arbitrarily used.

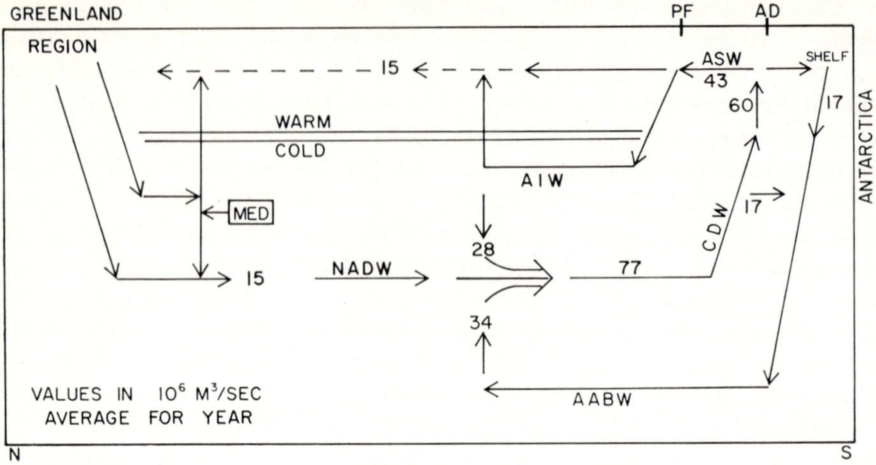

Fig. 6. Meridional transports of the world ocean (Gordon, 1971a).

The meridional input of 77×10^6 m^3/sec of deep water with 60×10^6 m^3/sec of this entering the surface layer appears to be a reasonable magnitude. This indicates a ratio of approximately 2:1 of zonal to meridional transports.

ANTARCTIC BOTTOM WATER

The intense climatic conditions of the antarctic atmosphere cause thermohaline changes of water near the surface. The dense water mixes to varying degrees with deep water resulting in the production of a dense water that sinks to the sea floor. This Antarctic Bottom Water then spreads northward influencing vast areas of the world ocean. There are three processes which can produce the dense surface water. The resulting water masses will be called Antarctic Bottom Water I, II, and III (AABW I, AABW II, and AABW III).

AABW I: Produced by formation of sea ice during the winter months (Brennecke, 1921; Mosby, 1934; Fofonoff, 1956). During the sea-ice formation, brine increases the salinity of the surface water on the continental shelf. When a sufficiently high salinity is attained the water drops off the shelf and mixes with the upper Circumpolar Deep Water to form a solution denser than either parent, because of the non-linearity in the sea water equation of state. This process is usually considered the most important method of bottom water production in the Weddell Sea, where it is believed most bottom water is produced. The salinity of the bottom water formed by this method would be slightly less than the salinity of the lower deep water. This condition is found in the bottom water leaving the Weddell Sea (Gordon, 1971a).

AABW II: Produced by freezing of sea water to or melting from the bottom of the large ice shelves. This method is suggested by Gordon (1971a) based on the occurrence of subsurface water with temperatures below the one atmosphere freezing point of sea water in the Ross Sea and Weddell Sea. Values as low as −2.13°C have been recorded on *Eltanin.* These cold temperatures are found at the upper boundary of the saline Ross Sea Shelf Water. A schematic drawing of this process is shown in Figure 7. These "supercooled" (or perhaps "supercold") highly saline waters must be a result of freezing below the surface. The freezing point of sea water decreases with increasing depth. Therefore, the resultant brine may have temperatures below that of brine produced by surface freezing. It is generally accepted that freezing occurs under the interior of the Ross Ice Shelf and the cold high-salinity shelf water (up to 34.97 ‰) trapped in the topographic depression of the Ross Sea may be the product of this process. The shelf water escapes over the northern sill of the Ross Sea depression and sinks to the bottom of the open ocean. It is possible that melting of shelf ice (S. S. Jacobs, A. F. Amos, and P. Bruchhausen, study in preparation) may also contribute to bottom water formation. Perhaps the AABW II should be reserved for any bottom water production related to contact with shelf ice.

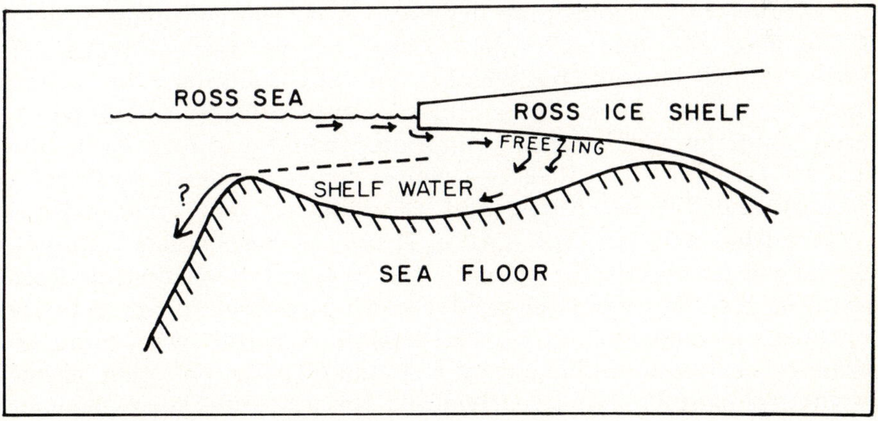

Fig. 7. Schematic of proposed formation of Ross Sea Shelf Water by a process of freezing to bottom of ice shelf (Gordon, 1971a).

AABW III: Produced by the intense cooling and evaporation imposed on the surface water by the katabatic winds. This process occurs in polynyas which commonly extend over 600 to 700 square miles in winter and much more in the summer months. Ledenev (1963) mentioned the intense thermohaline alterations produced by katabatic winds, and attributed the formation of the supercooled water to this action. Perhaps the alterations may be great enough to create a water mass capable of reaching the continental shelf floor and ultimately the bottom of the open ocean.

Any or all of these three types of bottom water may be important in a particular area. The major bottom water source areas are the Weddell Sea and the Ross Sea. The water coming from the Weddell area appears to have the greater influence on the world ocean. Its salinity is a little less than the salinity of the deep water, while the bottom water originating in the Ross Sea is detected as a bottom salinity maximum (Gordon, 1971a). The Ross Sea bottom water (believed to contain AABW II) was found on *Eltanin* Cruise 37 (Gordon, 1969) west of the Balleny Islands, entering this area by way of a passage between the Balleny Islands and Antarctica. The bottom salinity in this area is over 34.7 ‰. It is displaced northward in the vicinity of 142°E by what appears to be a locally produced bottom water of low salinity, possibly of AABW III type. The region off Adélie Coast is characterized by high katabatic winds and large polynyas. The locally produced bottom water has salinities of less than 34.7 ‰ with oxygen above 7.0 ml/liter (representing over 90 percent of the saturation level).

The numerous topographic depressions on the continental shelf of the Ross Sea and off Adélie Coast act as natural traps for newly formed dense water which eventually contribute to bottom water formation. These offer opportunities to sample winter-produced water or perhaps fairly undiluted water resulting from the ice shelf freezing. The Ross Sea depression is discussed by Gordon (1971a) and Jacobs, Amos, and Bruchhausen (in preparation).

The author believes that AABW II may be responsible for some bottom water production in both the Weddell Sea and the Ross Sea. The AABW I would be produced where sea ice forms in fairly nonturbulent embayments where the surface salinity can build up to the critical value indicated by Fofonoff (1956). In other areas, the critical salinity is not reached and the ice-produced water cannot penetrate the thick Circumpolar Deep Water. In this case, the water sinks to the base of the Antarctic Surface Water, that is, within the transition zone from surface to deep water. This process may be responsible for the production of the minimum temperature water layer at the base of the surface water; this layer is called the winter water (Mosby, 1934). The AABW III variety forms in moderate amounts where polynyas occur. It may represent the locally produced bottom water which influences the continental shelf and slope, but is not produced in amounts capable of influencing major deep ocean areas.

A comprehensive study of the coastal and ice shelf conditions should be made with long-term bottom current and temperature measurements. In addition, data on the water layer under the ice shelves should be collected by unmanned probes through the ice or projectile probes introduced from the open water area, or perhaps by manned nuclear submersibles.

ANTARCTIC POLAR FRONT ZONE

The Antarctic and Subantarctic Surface Water masses are separated by a zone of relatively rapid temperature and salinity change. Numerous crossings of this zone show that the details of the structure can vary widely and it is difficult to make generalizations, but it is believed to be a zone of convergence. Here the Antarctic Surface Water sinks and entrains some Subantarctic Surface Water and Circumpolar Deep Water to produce the Antarctic Intermediate Water. The zone is sometimes called the Antarctic Convergence (Deacon, 1933, 1937; Mackintosh, 1946) to indicate this process. Individual crossings of the zone, however, often show no signs of convergence and occasionally signs of divergence (Wexler, 1959). Models of wind field can be constructed which can lead to either convergent or divergent fields of motion (Wyrtki, 1960). Because of the complicated processes at this zone, the author prefers to call it the antarctic polar front zone, analagous to the atmospheric polar front, which separates the polar from the subpolar air masses, and implies neither convergence nor divergence.

Various authors have defined the frontal zone differently (Gordon, 1971b). The "surface expression" is the manifestation of the front at the sea surface. The front is often masked during the summer months by the heating of the surface layer. The "subsurface expression" is usually a better way of defining the front since the influence of weather is not so great at depth as it is at the immediate surface. The surface and subsurface expressions can be separated by as much as two degrees of latitude (Gordon, 1971a). Therefore, the entire Antarctic Surface Water, which is 200 to 300 meters thick at its northern terminus, does not terminate at the same position but may extend farther at a particular level. A surface expression south of the subsurface expression is more common. This situation results from a thin stratum of Subantarctic Surface Water overriding the Antarctic Surface Water.

The polar front is also believed to form meanders and eddies (Mackintosh, 1946). During Cruise 33 of the *Eltanin* (March-May, 1968) an isolated patch of Antarctic Surface Water was found near the USARP Fracture Zone of the Pacific-Antarctic Ridge. It is believed that this was a detached eddy. The exact form of the polar front zone and its variations in time and space are difficult to study with a single ship. It would be more productive to study the frontal region by adopting a multiship program similar to that used in the Gulf Stream studies.

Some studies on the seasonal variability of the frontal zone have been carried out. Botnikov (1963, 1964) showed a seasonal oscillation of 1° to 2° of latitude (farthest north in the southern winter) and long-term oscillations of 4° of latitude from 1901 to 1960. Gordon (1967a) showed a polar front zone with a width of 2° to 4° of latitude; the instantaneous front position lies somewhere within this zone. Ostapoff (1962a, b) indicated an even broader 5° zone. The position of the polar front zone may be controlled by bottom topography or by the northward position of the Antarctic Bottom Water, which is also controlled by bottom topography. The seasonal and shorter-period oscillations as well as the sharpness of the zone are most likely the result of wind and thermohaline conditions.

Within the South Pacific sector of antarctic waters, the polar front is often broken into a series of subdivisions (Gordon, 1967a, 1971b). This region, called the double polar front zone, extends from the Macquarie Island Ridge, south of New Zealand, to a longitude of approximately 110°W. Figure 8 shows an example of the double polar front zone. A similar structure was noted by Wexler (1959), Burling (1961), Ostapoff (1962a, b), and Houtman (1967). The following section describes the subdivisions (Gordon, 1971b).

Proceeding from south to north, the sections encountered are:

1. *Stable zone* in which the cold Antarctic Surface Water mass lies uniformly above the upper Circumpolar Deep

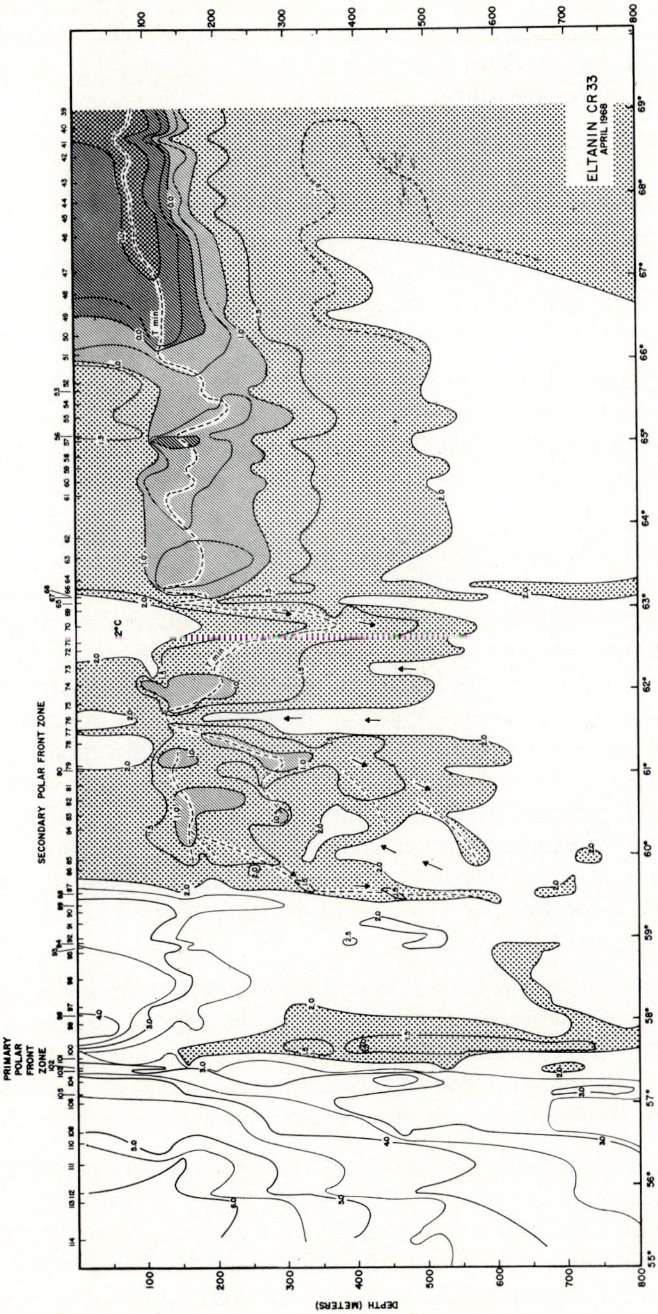

Fig. 8. Thermal structure of the upper 800 meters along 125°W (Gordon, 1971b).

Water. The isotherms tend to be horizontal with a large gradient in temperature at the boundary of the surface and deep water. Toward the northern end, the T_{min} layer is variable in strength and depth.

2. *Secondary polar front zone* is separated from the stable zone by a drop in the depth of the T_{min} layer and an increase in the surface temperature. Within the secondary zone, the T_{min} layer shows great variability, but remains well defined. The isotherms tend to slope at a very steep angle with occasional evidence of filaments or streams of T_{min} penetrating to fairly deep levels.

3. *Warm water zone* is the area in which the T_{min} weakens to become discontinuous or absent. This zone is relatively warm, with the surface layers demonstrating higher stability than found in the zones to the immediate north and south.

4. *Primary polar front zone* is relatively narrow and shows much vertical stretching of the water properties. This feature is vertically elongated only relative to other ocean features and not in the absolute sense. In this zone, the water is cold and is marked by a reestablishment of the T_{min} layer. A patch of cold water is generally isolated in a north-south plane from the main body of T_{min} water to the south. The influence of the cold water of this cell occasionally extends to the surface where it lowers the surface temperature below that of the surface of the more southerly warm zone. At the surface of the northern boundary of the primary zone, there is a fairly rapid temperature change.

5. *Subantarctic Surface Water* is the northernmost zone. This zone is warmer than the other zones: it is always above 3° and usually above 5° C. The isotherms slope steeply toward the north. Occasional reversals of the slope of the isotherm surfaces are found.

The cause of the double polar front zone is not known, although numerous speculative proposals can be made. The polar front zone, like the Antarctic Bottom Water production, represents numerous problems which are difficult to solve using data from a single moving oceanographic ship. A multiship program and long-term measurements from anchored buoy arrays are needed.

Author's Notes: The physical oceanography program aboard the USNS *Eltanin* has been supported by the National Science Foundation Office of Polar Programs through numerous grants since 1962. The grant effective during the preparation of this paper is GA 10794.

This paper is Lamont-Doherty Geological Observatory Contribution No. 1500.

References

Atlas of Antarctica, 1966. Edited by Bakayer; vol. 1. Moscow. In: *Soviet Geography, May–June, 1967.* Translation of legend matter and explanatory text by Am. Geograph. Soc., New York.

Barcilon, V., 1966. On the influence of the peripheral antarctic water discharge on the dynamics of the Circumpolar Current. *J. Marine Res., 24* (3): 269–275.

Barcilon, V., 1967. Further investigation of the influence of the peripheral antarctic water discharge on the Circumpolar Current. *J. Marine Res., 25* (1): 1–9.

Bolgurtsev, B. N., 1966. Calculation of currents in the Pacific sector of the Antarctic. English Transl., Izvestia. *Atmos. Oceanic Phys., 2* (11): 716–722.

Botnikov, V. N., 1963. Geographical position of the Antarctic Convergence Zone in the Antarctic Ocean. *Inform. Bull. Sov. Antarctic Exped. No. 41 (Eng. Ed.), 4* (6): 324–327.

Botnikov, V. N., 1964. Seasonal and long term fluctuations of the Antarctic Convergence Zone. *Inform. Bull. Sov. Antarctic Exped. No. 45 (Eng. Ed.), 5* (2): 92–95.

Brennecke, W., 1921. Die ozeanographischen Arbeiten der Deutschen Antarktischen Exped., 1911–1912. *Arch. Dtsch. Siewarte, 39* (1): 1–216.

Burling, R. W., 1961. Hydrology of circumpolar waters south of New Zealand. *New Zealand Dept. Sci. Ind. Res. Bull. 143, Memoir 10:* 9–61.

Capurro, L. R. A., 1968. Velocity measurements in the Southern Ocean. In *Symposium on Antarctic Oceanography, Santiago, Chile, Sept. 13–16, 1966;* pp. 58–66. Scott Polar Res. Inst., Cambridge, England.

Deacon, G. E. R., 1933. A general account of the hydrology of the South Atlantic Ocean. *Discovery Repts., 7:* 171–238.

Deacon, G. E. R., 1937. The hydrology of the Southern Ocean. *Discovery Repts., 15:* 1–124.

Deacon, G. E. R., 1963. The Southern Ocean. In *The Sea,* edited by M. N Hill; vol. 2, pp. 281–296. Interscience, New York.

Fofonoff, N. P., 1956. Some properties of sea water influencing the formation of Antarctic bottom water. *Deep-Sea Res., 4:* 32–35.

Gill, A. E., 1968. A linear model of the Antarctic Circumpolar Current. *J. Fluid Mech., 32* (3): 465–488.

Giovinetto, M. B., 1964. Estimate of mass flux in Antarctica. *Geol. Soc. Am. Spec. Paper, 76:* 309.

Gordon, A. L., 1966. Potential temperature, oxygen and circulation of bottom water in the Southern Ocean. *Deep-Sea Res., 13:* 1125–1138.

Gordon, A. L., 1967a. Structure of antarctic waters between 20°W and 170°W. In *Antarctic Map Folio Series, Folio 6,* edited by V. Bushnell. Am. Geograph. Soc., New York.

Gordon, A. L., 1967b. Geostrophic transport through the Drake Passage. *Science, 156* (3783) : 1732–1734.

Gordon, A. L., 1968a. Comment on the peripheral antarctic water discharge. *J. Marine Res., 26* (1) : 78–79.

Gordon, A. L., 1968b. Spreading and mixing within the main core layers and bottom circulation in the Southern Ocean. In *Symposium on Antarctic Oceanography, Santiago, Chile, Sept. 13–16, 1966;* pp. 69–72. Scott Polar Res. Inst., Cambridge, England.

Gordon, A. L., 1969. Preliminary analyses of the bottom circulation off the Adélie coast, Antarctica (*Eltanin* Cruise No. 37). In *Mixing, Diffusion and Circulation Rates in Ocean Waters;* pp. 1–11. Atomic Energy Commission, Washington, D.C.

Gordon, A. L., 1971a. Oceanography of antarctic waters. In *Antarctic Research Series 15, Antarctic Oceanology I,* edited by J. L. Reid. Am. Geophys. Union, Washington, D.C.

Gordon, A. L., 1971b. Antarctic polar front zone. In *Antarctic Research Series 15, Antarctic Oceanology I,* edited by J. L. Reid. Am. Geophys. Union, Washington, D.C.

Heezen, B. C., M. Tharp, and C. D. Hollister, 1968. Illustrations of the marine geology of the Southern Ocean. In *Symposium on Antarctic Oceanography, Santiago, Chile, Sept. 13–16, 1966;* pp. 101–109. Scott Polar Res. Inst., Cambridge, England.

Hollister, C. D., and R. B. Elder, 1969. Contour currents in the Weddell Sea. In *Deep-Sea Photography,* edited by J. B. Hersey; pp. 177–189. Johns Hopkins Press, Baltimore.

Hollister, C. D., and R. B. Elder, 1969. Contour currents in the Weddell Sea. *Deep-Sea Res., 16:* 99–101.

Houtman, T. J., 1964. Surface temperature gradients at the Antarctic Convergence. *New Zealand J. Geol. Geophys., 7* (2) : 245–270.

Houtman, T. J., 1967. Water masses and fronts in the Southern Ocean south of New Zealand, *Bull. 174 New Zealand Dept. Sci. Indust. Res.* and *New Zealand Oceanogr. Inst. Mem. 36.*

Kort, V. G., 1962. On heat exchange of the antarctic waters. *Am. Geophys. Union Monograph, 7:* 163–167.

Kort, V. G., 1964. Antarctic oceanography. In *Research in Geophysics;* vol. 2, pp. 309–333. M.I.T. Press, Cambridge, Mass.

Kort, V. G., 1968. Frontal zones of the Southern Ocean. In *Symposium on Antarctic Oceanography, Santiago, Chile, Sept. 13–16, 1966;* pp. 3–7. Scott Polar Res. Inst., Cambridge, England.

Ledenev, V. G., 1963. Influence of evaporation on the formation of cold antarctic water. *Soviet Antarctic Exped. Inform. Bull., 5* (1) : 50–52.

Mackintosh, N. A., 1946. The Antarctic Convergence and the distribution of surface temperatures in antarctic waters. *Discovery Repts., 23:* 177–212.

Mosby, H., 1934. The waters of the Atlantic Antarctic Ocean. *Sci. Res. Norwegian Antarctic Exped. 1927–28, No. 11.* Norske Videnskaps-Akad, Oslo.

Mosby, H., 1968. Bottom water formation. In *Symposium on Antarctic Oceanography, Santiago, Chile, Sept. 13–16, 1966;* pp. 47–57. Scott Polar Res. Inst., Cambridge, England.

Munk, W. H., 1966. Abyssal recipes. *Deep-Sea Res., 13:* 707–730.

Neumann, G., and W. J. Pierson, Jr., 1966. *Principles of Physical Oceanography.* Prentice-Hall, Englewood Cliffs, N. J.

O'Brien, J. J., 1969. A numerical study of the entire wind-driven Pacific Ocean. *Trans. Am. Geophys. Union, 50* (4) : 203.

Ostapoff, F., 1962a. On the frictionally induced transverse circulation of the Antarctic Circumpolar Current. *Deut. Hydr. Z., 15* (3) : 103–113.

Ostapoff, F., 1962b. The salinity distribution at 200 meters and the antarctic frontal zones. *Deut. Hydr. Z., 15* (4) : 113–142.

Reid, J., H. Stommel, E. D. Stroup, and B. A. Warren, 1968. Detection of a deep boundary current in the western South Pacific. *Nature, 217:* 937.

Warren, B., 1971. Antarctic contributions to water circulation. In *Research in the Antarctic,* edited by L. O. Quam; pp. 630–643. Am. Assoc. Advan. Sci., Washington, D.C.

Wexler, H., 1959. The Antarctic convergence or divergence? In *Atmosphere and the Sea in Motion,* edited by B. Bolin; pp. 107–120. Rockefeller Inst. Press, N.Y.

Wüst, G., W. Brogmus, and E. Noodt, 1954. Die Zonale Verteilung von Salzgehalt, Niederschlag, Verdunstrung, Temperatur und Dichte un der Oberfläche der Ozeans. *Kiel. Meeresforsch., 10:* 137–161.

Wyrtki, F., 1960. The Antarctic Circumpolar Current and the Antarctic Polar Front. *Deut. Hydr. Z., 13* (4) : 153–173.

Antarctic Deep Water Contribution to the World Ocean

Bruce A. Warren

Woods Hole Oceanographic Institution, Woods Hole, Massachusetts

The essential contribution of the Antarctic to the general ocean circulation has been recognized since the end of the last century: it is simply that water from the Antarctic is largely responsible for keeping the rest of the deep sea cold. This fact was realized very soon after the first few deep-temperature soundings were made in temperate latitudes, and, since we are inclined at times to forget the perceptions of our forebears, I should like to quote two paragraphs from a long article on oceanic circulation which Alexander Buchan (1895) appended to the final volume of the *Challenger* Reports. Buchan drew up a series of charts, based on all available data (mainly the *Challenger* observations), showing the distribution of temperature at various levels in the world ocean. Among other things, he had this to say about them:

> The striking fact is that the deep-sea temperatures in all latitudes, equatorial as well as polar, are uniformly low, and, except in a few restricted regions, do not differ from each other more than about two degrees. . . . It is also to be noted that the lowest deep-sea temperatures are found in those parts of the ocean which lie in the Southern hemisphere, and that, on the whole, higher temperatures are encountered as we recede from the Antarctic region. It may also be pointed out that the lower deep-sea temperatures extend farther to the north from the Southern Ocean, just over those depths of the sea which appear to have, and probably do have, a direct communication with the south; that is, are not cut off by any intervening submarine ridge separating them from the cold waters of Antarctica.

> There can be no doubt that these very low deep-sea temperatures have their origin in the Southern or Antarctic Ocean, the icy cold waters of which are propagated northwards, the rate of propagation being so slight as to be regarded rather as a slow creep than as a distinctly recognizable movement of the water. It is evident that the increase of temperature from the bottom of the ocean to the surface is due to the slow descent of the warmer water of the surface carrying downwards their higher temperatures to greater depths.

On the whole, considering the time at which it was written, Buchan's statement is quite a good interpretative summary. There has been progress in oceanography in the last seventy years, however, which has both given better documentation to some aspects of Buchan's picture and required qualitative modification to other aspects. In this paper I should like to review how our information and ideas on the antarctic contribution to the deep circulation has developed since Buchan's original interpretation.

VOLUME AND DISTRIBUTION OF ANTARCTIC WATER

An early change in the picture was actually a reduction in the importance ascribed to the Antarctic in maintaining the low deep temperature of the ocean. Examination of deep salinity and dissolved-oxygen data, notably by Merz and Wüst (1922) and Wüst (1935), showed that deep water in the North Atlantic was nearly all "formed" at the surface of the subpolar North Atlantic rather than the Antarctic. This North Atlantic Deep Water reaches into the South Atlantic as well, where it lies over the denser bottom water from the Antarctic, and small traces of it can be detected by its high salinity all around Antarctica in the Circumpolar Current.

Curiously, however, the distribution of dissolved-oxygen concentration demonstrates that there is no analogous sinking of surface water to great depths in the North Pacific, nor is deep water formed in the North Indian Ocean. The arrangement of continental masses thus brings it about that both the deep Pacific and Indian Oceans are filled by water deriving immediately from the Antarctic, even though this water is somewhat mixed with North Atlantic Deep Water, rather than being entirely the bottom water which sinks from the surface of the Weddell and Ross Seas.

The amount of water in the world ocean which comes directly from the Antarctic is therefore a substantial portion of the total. It is difficult and perhaps pointless to try to define "antarctic water" precisely, but, for the purpose of rough volume estimates, it is probably safe to regard as antarctic water all water in the Indian and Pacific Oceans of potential temperature less than 3°C and all water in the Atlantic of potential temperature less than 2°C (except that in the Arctic and Greenland-Norwegian Seas). These criteria, unfortunately, do admit small, spurious amounts of North Pacific Intermediate Water, as well as some Norwegian Sea overflow water in the North Atlantic, but they also exclude most of the Antarctic Intermediate Water in the world ocean; thus, on balance, they seem suitable for a rough global delineation. On this basis, water from the Antarctic would comprise 24 percent of the Atlantic Ocean (Montgomery, 1958), 70 percent of the Indian Ocean (Pollak, 1958), 71 percent of the Pacific Ocean (Cochrane, 1958), and 59 percent of the entire world ocean. These figures all include the Southern Ocean, which by definition is filled with antarctic water, but even if one excludes that part of the ocean south of the 55th parallel, the approximate mean latitude of the Antarctic Convergence, one still finds that the Antarctic contributes about 54 percent of the water in the rest of the world ocean.

The only respect in which Buchan's interpretation is entirely contradicted by modern ideas is in his notion that the decrease of temperature with depth in the deep water implies downward advection of the warmer water above. Indeed, it would be difficult to construct a kinematically consistent picture of deep motions composed only of downward flow from above and northward flow from the Antarctic. It seems likely that the rise in temperature away from the ocean bottom is a result, instead, of downward, turbulent *diffusion* of heat, and that the deep temperature distribution is held stationary by a balancing *upward* advection of colder deep water. For example, this advection-diffusion balance is remarkably consistent with the vertical temperature variation in the North Pacific below the upper kilometer (Munk, 1966). The upward vertical velocity required by the rate of change of temperature in the deep water there is a few centimeters per day; if this value is extrapolated over the full area of the world ocean, one can calculate a net upward flux in the abyssal water of a few tens of millions of cubic meters per second, a figure comparable to the horizontal volume transports of the subtropical western boundary currents. This upward movement of deep water must be supplied by the influx from subpolar regions, which, as we have seen from the global statistics, is largely antarctic water. Thus, by this indirect means, we arrive at an order-of-magnitude estimate of the rate at which water from the Antarctic must be entering the rest of the world ocean.

In one way or another, modern theories of the oceanic thermocline (recently reviewed and extended by Veronis, 1969) include an upward velocity at the base of the thermocline. This is of the same magnitude as that inferred in the deep water, and must again be supported by the flow of deep water from subpolar regions. Thus water from the Antarctic probably has a far-reaching effect, through playing a role in the maintenance of the thermocline over large areas of the ocean.

PATTERN OF FLOW

Buchan seems to have believed, as other writers in the first half of this century did more explicitly, that the northward movement of water from the Antarctic was distributed fairly uniformly over the full breadth of the ocean basins, being obstructed only by the submarine ridge systems. The dynamics of motions which are very slow in comparison with the earth's rotation are rather peculiar, however, and their pattern may actually be radically different from this simplest, intuitive interpretation of the large-scale distribution of properties. As far as is known today, the mean deep flow in the central regions of the oceans really is of the magnitude of the "slow creep" conjectured by Buchan, and a creep of such large horizontal scale, that the motion must be exactly geostrophic. Stommel (1958), and later Stommel and Arons (1960), have shown that if such motion is accompanied by the upward component we have just discussed, then the flow must be directed *away* from the equator, rather than *toward* it, in both the Southern and Northern Hemispheres. Therefore, the northward flow which must be coming from the Antarctic has to be confined to deep currents which are so swift and narrow as not to be dominated by the constraint of exact geostrophic balance; and it works out further that such currents must be western boundary currents. Thus, in contrast to Buchan's flow pattern, the dynamically consistent picture seems to be of antarctic water flowing northward in narrow currents along the western boundaries of oceans, filling the central ocean basins from their western sides rather than their southern sides, and having a mean poleward rather than equatorward component of velocity in the central regions. For vertical velocity components of the order of a few centimeters per day, as estimated above, these poleward velocity components come out to be of the order of fractions of a millimeter per second, and the volume transports of the boundary currents are of the order of ten million cubic meters per second.

Stommel's (1958) schematic picture of the horizontal pattern of deep flow is given in Figure 1. The heavy black dots are supposed to indicate sinking of surface water to great depth in the Weddell Sea and the subpolar North Atlantic, and the heavy black lines indicate the hypothesized deep western boundary currents. The light lines are intended to suggest streamlines of the flow elsewhere, as fed by the boundary currents, and the arrows show the sense of the motion. The upward flux of water out of the abyssal depths is not included in this representation, and the picture is qualitatively wrong as regards the real ocean, through its omission of the northward-flowing antarctic water in the middle- and low-latitude regions of the South Atlantic. This theoretical pattern, however, is based on an idealized model of plane-

Fig. 1. Schematic theoretical pattern of deep circulation in the world ocean (After Stommel, 1958). Heavy black dots indicate sinking regions, and heavy black lines indicate predicted deep boundary currents.

tary flow which precludes boundary currents lying one above the other and flowing in opposite directions; presumably, if one could solve a more realistic model, one would find a northward-flowing boundary current of antarctic water along the east coast of South America as well. The remainder of this paper is devoted to a review of the observational material bearing on the verification of this theoretical scheme for the movement of antarctic water.

DEEP WESTERN BOUNDARY CURRENTS

One might first consider which elements of the theory *can* be verified. The determining factor is really the assumed upward velocity in the deep water, but the estimates of its magnitude are so low as to put it utterly beyond the reach of any measurement technique now available. The small mean horizontal velocities in the central ocean, of the order of a mm/sec, are probably just barely accessible to a long-term program with moored current meters, but the program would have to be so elaborate for significance that it would be far too expensive to undertake. In fact, the only elements feasible to observe at the present time are the postulated western boundary currents. Their existence should at least be noticeable in the distribution of tracer properties, while their estimated speeds are large enough, and their widths small enough, to allow determinations of their velocities and transports, either by existing techniques of direct current measurement or by geostrophic calculation from the density field. It may well be, of course, that this particular theory is not unique in its prediction of deep boundary currents, and that other, quite different theories might require them as well, but since their presence is a necessary ingredient of the Stommel-Arons theory, they have considerable bearing on its oceanographic value. It is this one aspect of the theory, therefore, which we shall consider.

In the South Atlantic, deep boundary currents had in fact been reported by Wüst in 1955, before the abyssal circulation theory had been devised. As an example, Figure 2 is a profile (After Wüst, 1955) of specific volume anomaly at 15° to 18°S between Brazil and Angola, as based on observations made during the *Meteor* expedition of 1925–1927. In the deep water on the Brazilian side of the profile we see the pronounced slope in isopycnals which is characteristic of permanent ocean currents, whereas elsewhere the distribution is rather featureless.

The geostrophic velocities which Wüst calculated from these

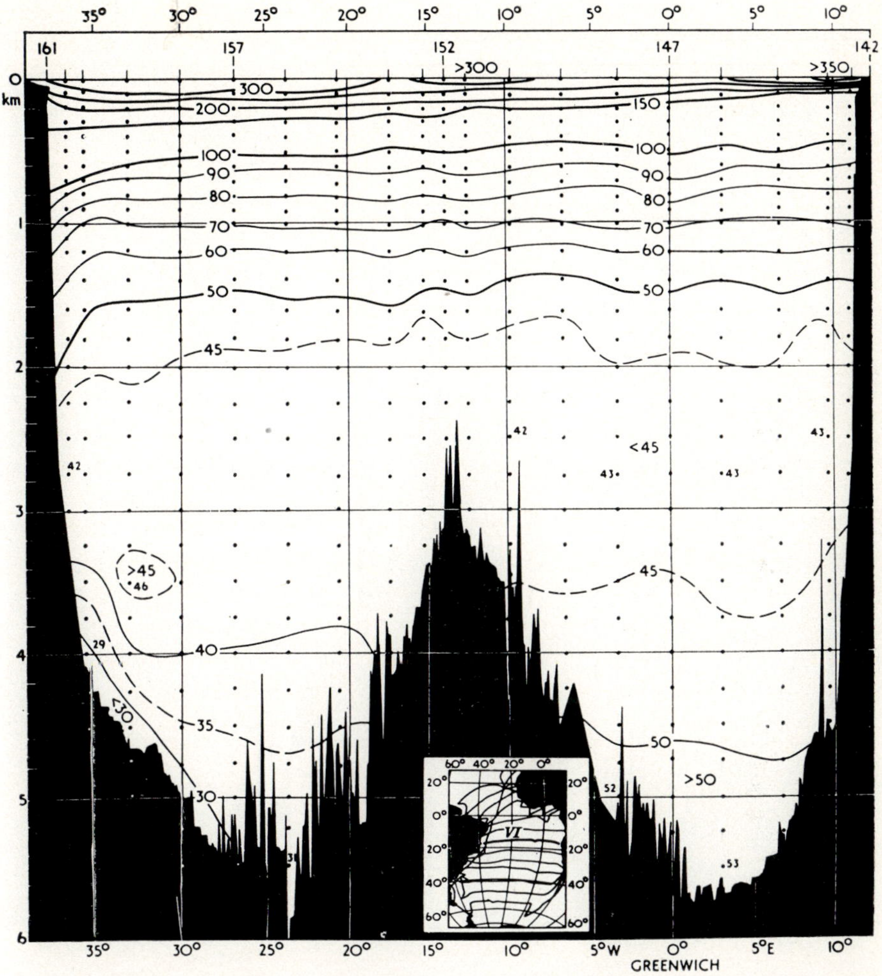

Fig. 2. Vertical section of specific volume anomaly (cl/ton) along *Meteor* Profile VI (May–June, 1926) at 15° to 18°S between Brazil and Angola (After Wüst, 1955). Inset shows section location.

specific volume data are illustrated in Figure 3. To make the calculations Wüst assumed zero horizontal velocity near the 1 km level, along the line connecting the open circles; this assumption is plausible because the line lies close to the interface between Antarctic Intermediate Water above, and North Atlantic Deep Water below. The contours of flow speed are labeled in cm/sec. The calculated velocities are of course slight, except in the zone

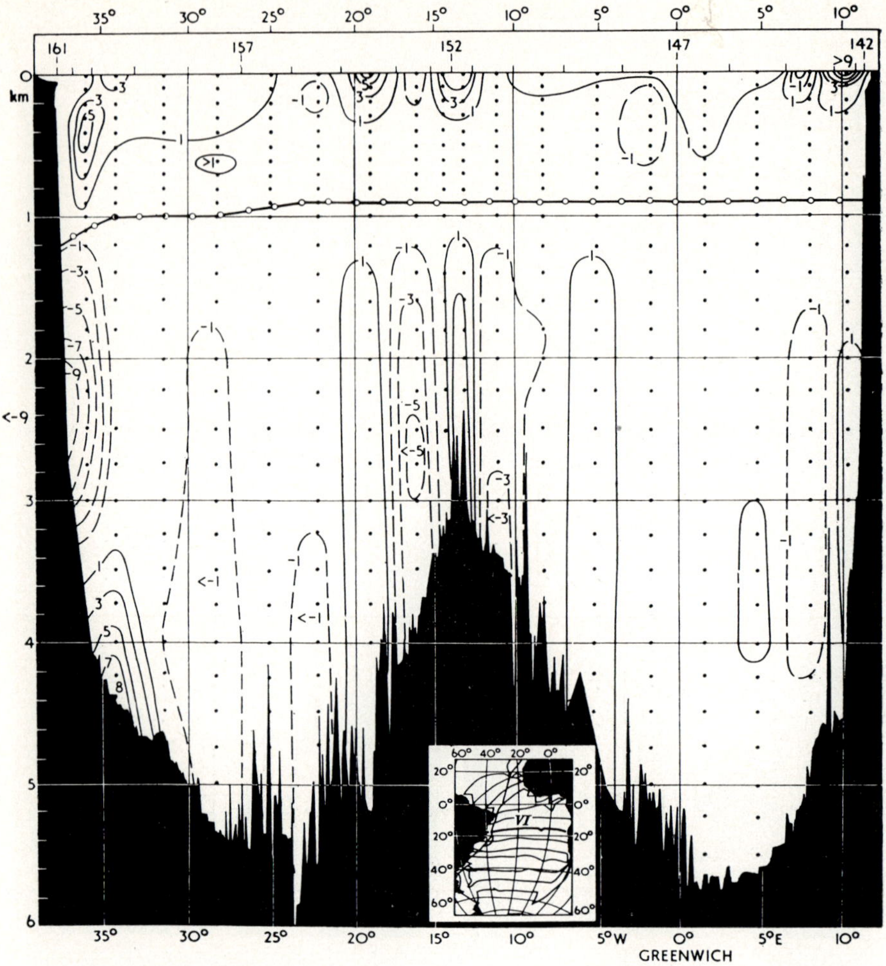

Fig. 3. Vertical section of calculated geostrophic velocity (cm/sec) normal to *Meteor* Profile VI, between Brazil and Angola (After Wüst, 1955). Solid contours denote northward flow, dashed contours, southward flow. Velocity assumed zero along line of open circles near 1-km level.

of sloping isopycnals against the western boundary. At depths of 1 to 3 km there is a pronounced southward-flowing current of North Atlantic Deep Water, with speeds exceeding 9 cm/sec; this corresponds to the boundary current explicitly shown in Figure 1. Below this feature there is a northward-flowing current of Antarctic Bottom Water, about 500 km wide, having its maximum speed of 8 cm/sec at the bottom. The estimated volume transport of antarctic water here is about 12×10^6 m^3/sec (Wüst, 1957). This would be the current which we have already noted as missing from the flow scheme in Figure 1.

In the South Pacific, the observations were inadequate until very recently to tell whether a comparable current existed. In 1967, however, two transpacific hydrographic sections were made by the *Eltanin,* the research vessel of the U. S. Antarctic Research Program, one at 28°S, the other at 43°S. One of the objects of these cruises was to make the closely spaced observations near the western boundary of the deep South Pacific which were needed to verify the predicted current. The work was successful and a deep current was indeed detected on both sections (Reid *et al.,* 1968).

The positions of these hydrographic stations are shown in Figure 4. Since the Tasman Sea is closed off to the north at depths greater than 3,000 m, the western boundary of the deep Pacific really lies off New Zealand and the Tonga-Kermadec Ridge, rather than Australia, and the discussion will be limited to that portion of the profile along 28°S, specifically Stations 134 to 156.

The distribution of temperature between the Tonga-Kermadec Ridge and the foot of the East Pacific Rise is given in Figure 5. The Tonga-Kermadec Trench, nearly 9,000 m deep at this crossing, is continued in the inset. At depths greater than 3,000 m the isotherms all slope downward away from the Ridge, indicating the existence of some sort of boundary current. The width of the full zone of sloping isotherms is nearly 1,000 km, about twice the width of the deep currents on the South Atlantic profile. One suspects, although it hasn't been proved, that the very intense slope over the flank of the Tonga-Kermadec Ridge, as well as the reverse slope on the opposite side of the Trench, are both local effects of the Trench on geostrophic flow.

The corresponding salinity distribution is given in Figure 6. The small salinity maximum at a depth of about 4,000 m in the zone of sloping isotherms is proof that the water here is indeed flowing northward from the Antarctic, because this maximum results from the slight entrainment of relatively saline North Atlantic Deep Water into the Antarctic Circumpolar Current.

Full velocity profiles such as Wüst calculated for the *Meteor* sections in the South Atlantic are not yet available for these two *Eltanin* sections, but Figure 7 illustrates the general decrease in current speed eastward from the Tonga-Kermadec Ridge at the

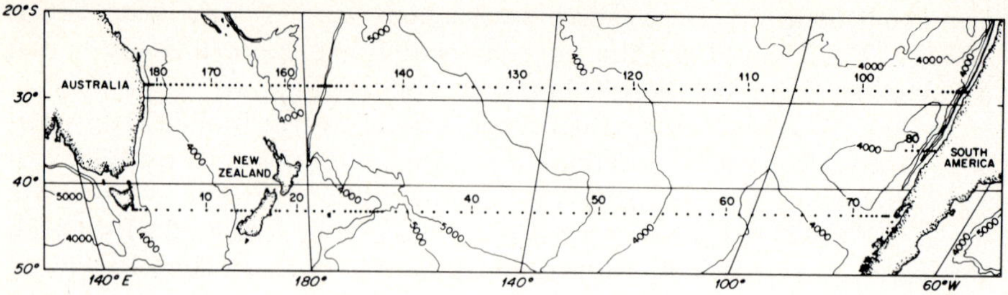

Fig. 4. Positions of hydrographic stations occupied by *Eltanin,* March–July, 1967.

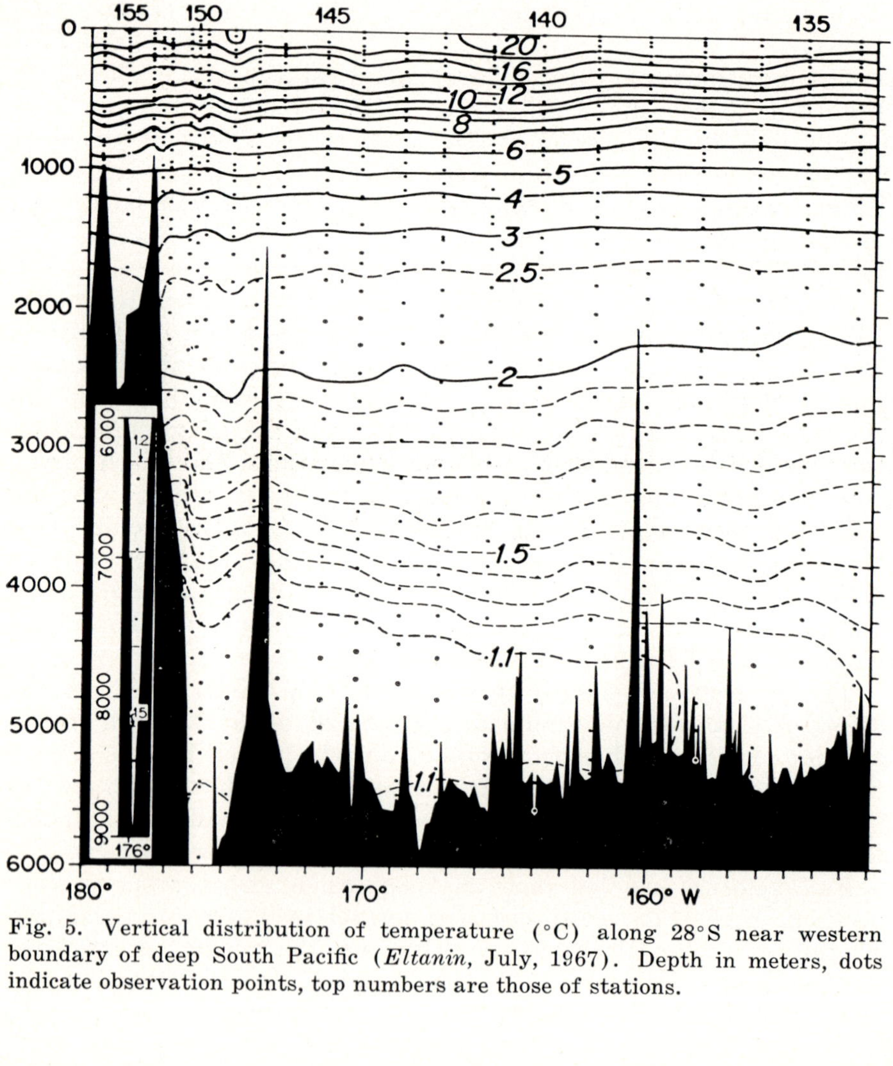

Fig. 5. Vertical distribution of temperature (°C) along 28°S near western boundary of deep South Pacific (*Eltanin,* July, 1967). Depth in meters, dots indicate observation points, top numbers are those of stations.

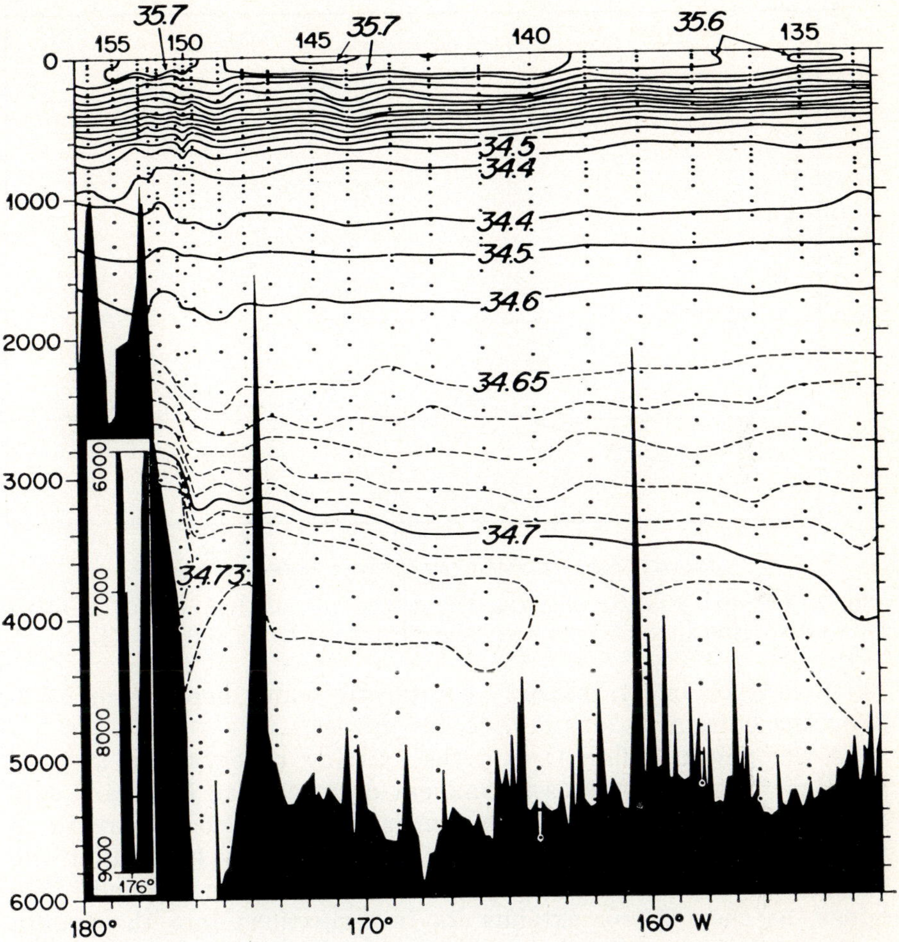

Fig. 6. Vertical distribution of salinity (‰) along 28°S near western boundary of deep South Pacific (*Eltanin*, July, 1967). Depth in meters, dots indicate observation points.

4-km level. The curve represents a calculation of geostrophic velocity from the density field, on the assumption that the horizontal velocity is zero at a depth of 2,500 m, just above the sloping deep isolines in Figures 4 and 5. The current speed reaches 17 cm/sec in the region of intensely sloping isotherms on the flank of the ridge, but otherwise is only a few centimeters per second. There is a countercurrent, as noted above, in the vicinity of the Trench, and at distances of more than 900 km from the Ridge, the general speed is so small as not to be detectible. The

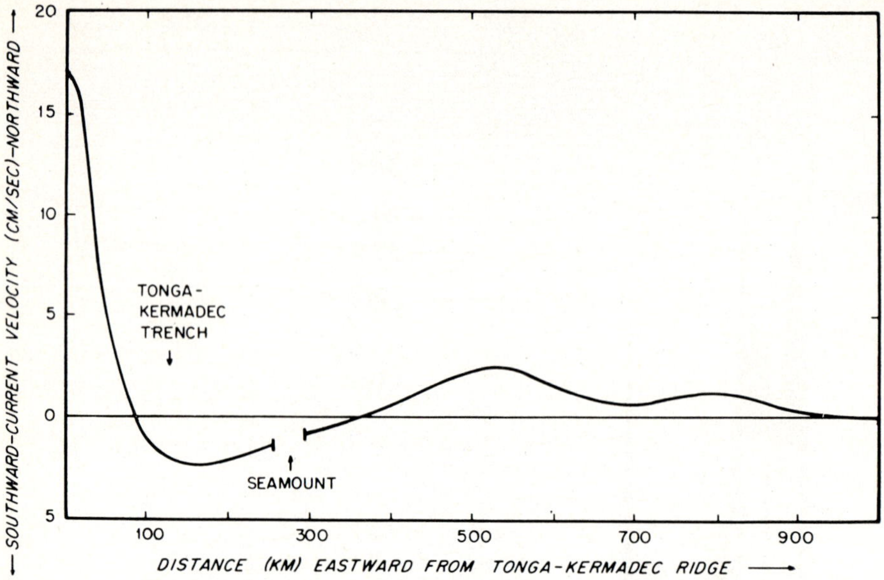

Fig. 7. Calculated geostrophic velocity at 4,000 m relative to 2,500 m along 28°S near western boundary of deep South Pacific (*Eltanin*, July, 1967).

northward volume transport of antarctic water here, from 2,500 m to the bottom, is about 17×10^6 m^3/sec.

In the South Indian Ocean, the existing observations are not sufficient to tell whether a permanent deep western boundary current is present or not. Given the existence of such currents in the Atlantic and Pacific, however, it seems highly likely that one will eventually be discovered in the Indian Ocean as well. One hopes, as the *Eltanin* extends its investigations into the Indian sector of the Antarctic, that it will be possible to make the critical, closely spaced observations in the southwestern Indian Ocean that are needed to detect such a feature.

Nevertheless, the unambiguous presence of the deep boundary currents in the Atlantic and Pacific Oceans, with volume transports of the right order of magnitude, gives considerable observational support to the abyssal circulation theory of Stommel and Arons (1960). It seems probable, therefore, that the filling of the deep ocean through an ocean-wide northward creep of antarctic water, as envisioned by Buchan and his immediate successors, is not correct, but that the antarctic water actually does flow northward in narrow, relatively swift currents, and fills the deep basins from their western sides.

Author's Note: This paper is Contribution No. 2251 from the Woods Hole Oceanographic Institution.

This work was supported by the Office of Polar Programs, National Science Foundation, under Contract GA 10824.

References

Buchan, A., 1895. Report on oceanic circulation. In *Report on the Scientific Results of the Voyage of H.M.S. Challenger, 1872–76,* Summary of Results, Second Part, Appendix (Physics and Chemistry, Part VIII). H. M. Stationery Office, Eyre and Spottiswoode, London.

Cochrane, J. D., 1958. The frequency distribution of water characteristics in the Pacific Ocean. *Deep-Sea Res., 5:* 111–127.

Merz, A., and G. Wüst, 1922. Die atlantische Vertikalzirkulation. *Zeitschrift der Gesellschaft für Erdkunde zu Berlin, 1:* 1–35.

Montgomery, R. B., 1958. Water characteristics of Atlantic Ocean and of world ocean. *Deep-Sea Res., 5:* 134–148.

Munk, W. H., 1966. Abyssal recipes. *Deep-Sea Res., 13* (4) : 707–730.

Pollak, M. J., 1958. Frequency distribution of potential temperatures and salinities in the Indian Ocean. *Deep-Sea Res., 5:* 128–133.

Reid, J., Jr., H. Stommel, E. D. Stroup, and B. A. Warren, 1968. Detection of deep boundary current in the western South Pacific. *Nature, 217:* 937.

Stommel, H., 1958. The abyssal circulation. *Deep-Sea Res., 5:* 80–82.

Stommel, H., and A. B. Arons, 1960. On the abyssal circulation of the world ocean-II. An idealized model of the circulation pattern and amplitude in oceanic basins. *Deep-Sea Res., 6:* 217–233.

Veronis, G., 1969. On theoretical models of the thermohaline circulation. *Deep-Sea Res. (Suppl.), 16:* 301–323.

Wüst, G., 1935. Die Stratosphäre. In *Wissenschaftliche Ergebnisse der Deutschen Atlantischen Expedition auf dem Forschungs-und Vermessungsschiff "Meteor" 1925–1927;* vol. 6, no. 1, pp. 109–288. Gruyter, Berlin.

Wüst, G., 1955. Stromgeschwindigkeiten im Tiefenund Bodenwasser des Atlantischen Ozeans auf Grund dynamischer Berechnung der *Meteor*—Profile der Deutschen Atlantischen Expedition 1925/27. *Deep-Sea Res. (Suppl.), 3:* 373–397.

Wüst, G., 1957. Stromgeschwindigkeiten und Strommengen in den Tiefen des Atlantischen Ozeans. In *Wissenschaftliche Ergebnisse der Deutschen Atlantischen Expedition auf dem Forschungs-und Vermessungsschiff "Meteor" 1925–1927;* vol. 6, no. 2, pp. 261–420. Gruyter, Berlin.

How Variable is the Antarctic Circumpolar Current?

JOHN L. BOWEN and HENRY STOMMEL

Department of Meteorology, Massachusetts Institute of Technology, Cambridge

It is often suggested that the dynamics of the Antarctic Circumpolar Current differ from those of other portions of the world ocean because of the lack of complete meridional boundaries. The Sverdrup dynamics which govern subtropical gyres seem to give its baroclinic structure remarkable steadiness. On the other hand, a predominantly zonal jet might be more free to wander in latitude, as in the atmosphere. Because of the uncertainty of the dynamics of the Antarctic Circumpolar Current, it is interesting to examine several lateral hydrographic sections to see if there are noticeable fluctuations in the latitude of the axis of flow. Our analysis of the series of sections in the *Discovery II* data shows the current to be stable in position. Its latitude varies less than the spacing between successive stations.

THE *DISCOVERY II* SECTIONS, 1938–1939

The data were collected by the Royal Research Vessel *Discovery II* (Anon., 1947). Between April, 1938, and March, 1939, the Antarctic Circumpolar Current was crossed completely or partially 16 times. Half of the crossings were made along 0° longitude, the other half along 20°E (Fig. 1).

The stations used are listed in Table 1. The two north-south sections (Nos. 1 and 2) that were made in April, 1938, were the last part of a circumpolar cruise that the *Discovery II* began in October, 1937. The first section begins near 50°S, 0°, and runs south to approximately 65°S. After zigzagging eastward along the ice pack to approximately 20°E, the ship headed north to the South

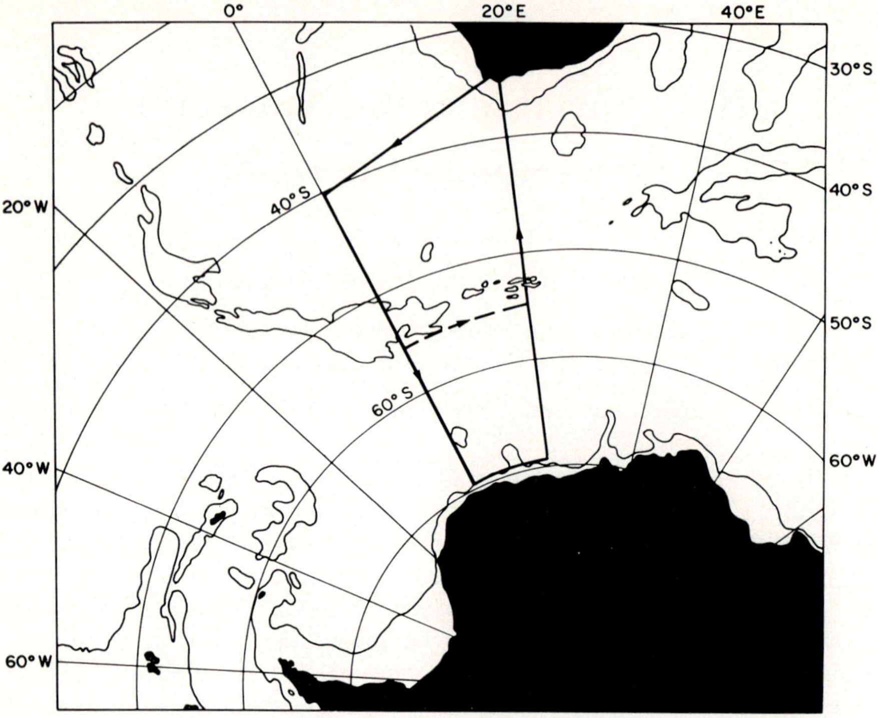

Fig. 1. Approximate location of the two sets of *Discovery II* sections on 0° and 20°E longitude. The bottom contours are drawn only to a depth of 3,000 meters in order to show the location of major ridges.

African coast, making a section crossing the Circumpolar Current.

In July, 1938, after a two-month stay in port, the *Discovery II* began the first of seven cruises during which 14 sections across the current were made. Each cruise consisted of two sections. The first section, called the 0° longitude section, had four or five deep hydrographic stations between Cape Town and a position 40°S, 0°, and deep stations every 3° or 4° southward along 0° longitude to either the ice pack or the Antarctic Continent. The second section, called the 20°E section, had deep stations every 3° or 4° northward along 20°E from as far south as possible to Cape Town. These 14 sections (Nos. 3 to 16) along with Nos. 1 and 2 gave 16 north-south sections during a period of one year by which the Antarctic Circumpolar Current might be examined to determine whether or not there was a discernible variation.

Five of the sections, those made during the summer months, covered the entire distance between Africa and the Antarctic

Table 1. List of stations.

Section	Stations	Dates	Latitude (South)
1	2311 – 2323	11 Apr. – 18 Apr. 1938	50°05′ – 65°04′
2	2335 – 2350	22 Apr. – 2 May 1938	67°10′ – 39°11′
3	2351 – 2362	2 July – 12 July 1938	35°31′ – 54°59′
4	2374 – 2380	19 July – 25 July 1938	55°42′ – 39°51′
5	2381 – 2394	6 Aug. – 18 Aug. 1938	35°30′ – 57°18′
6	2411 – 2419	23 Aug. – 30 Aug. 1938	56°25′ – 38°46′
7	2420 – 2432	15 Sep. – 25 Sep. 1938	35°11′ – 56°37′
8	2447 – 2453	1 Oct. – 6 Oct. 1938	54°47′ – 37°51′
9	2454 – 2465	18 Oct. – 27 Oct. 1938	35°36′ – 55°17′
10	2478 – 2486	2 Nov. – 9 Nov. 1938	54°17′ – 34°38′
11	2487 – 2501	23 Nov. – 5 Dec. 1938	34°40′ – 55°30′
12	2517 – 2525	12 Dec. – 18 Dec. 1938	56°57′ – 34°29′
13	2526 – 2547	7 Jan. – 22 Jan. 1939	34°20′ – 69°30′
14	2559 – 2576	27 Jan. – 5 Feb. 1939	68°50′ – 40°12′
15	2578 – 2601	16 Feb. – 4 Mar. 1939	35°08′ – 69°44′
16	2606 – 2626	5 Mar. – 18 Mar. 1939	69°40′ – 37°47′

Continent, crossing the Circumpolar Current completely. Of the other sections, all but No. 1, which was mainly to the south, crossed the major portion of the current. All of the sections except No. 1 crossed the Antarctic Convergence, as determined by Mackintosh (1946) to be between 49°24′ and 51°36′S for the 0° longitude sections and between 48°24′ and 50°48′S for the 20°E sections.

From the surface current chart of Schott (1942) it can be seen that sections are not exactly perpendicular to the current. North of 40°S the 0° longitude sections are parallel to the current. (A complication in the northern area is the Subtropical Convergence near the African Coast.) Between 40° and 50°S these sections are nearly perpendicular to the current while south of 50°S to the Antarctic Divergence near 65°S they again become nearly parallel to the current. The 20°E longitude sections cross the current perpendicularly except near the African continent, where the Agulhas Current complicates the flow, and south of the Antarctic Divergence, near 60°S.

ANALYSIS OF THE SECTIONS

Our first task was to draw isotherms of all the sections. An example of such a section (No. 13) is shown in Figure 2. The

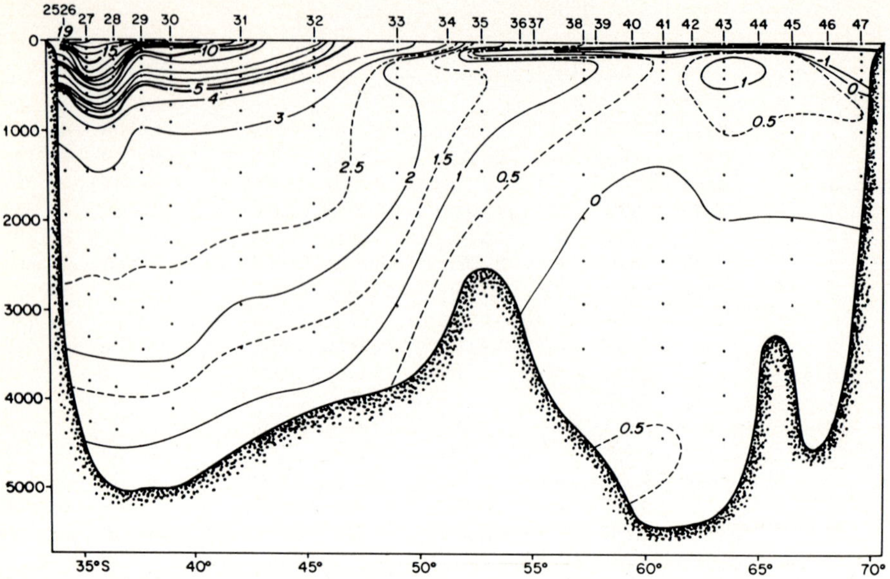

Fig. 2. A sample temperature section (No. 13) on 0° longitude.

section was made along 0° longitude. Other sections are similar except for the surface layers where there is a seasonal influence. The center of the current is at approximately 50°S. Unlike other ocean currents the isotherms in this current undergo extreme changes in depth across the section. Thus the 1°C isotherm changes in depth by more than 4,000 meters in 12° of latitude. In this region there is really no main thermocline limiting the depth of the current. The vertical profile of the geostrophic current is nearly linear, as in Couette motion. The axis of the current seems to move along the northern slope of the great mid-ocean ridge which at that point runs nearly parallel to 53°S.

Figures 3 and 4 show the magnitude of variation of the position of sloping isotherms and show the temperature at 2,000 meters on a time and latitude plane. Figure 3 shows all cruises along 0° longitude and Figure 4, all cruises along 20°E. The lines sloping from left to right connect points of observation and represent the different cruises. The black dots represent the points of observation. The waviness of the isotherms is mostly within the station spacing, and therefore cannot be regarded as well determined. It is clear, however, that the position of these isotherms is notably steady, and that there is no indication of major wave disturbances such as one might expect to find in a major zonal baroclinic current.

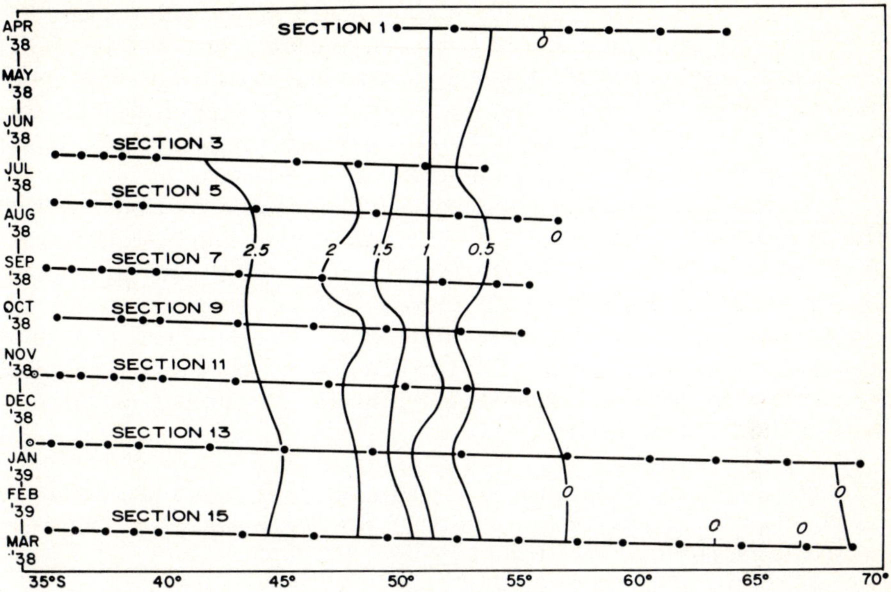

Fig. 3. Temperature contours at 2,000 meters depth along 0° longitude. Straight lines show the locations of sections observed. Solid dots designate the location of the individual deep stations.

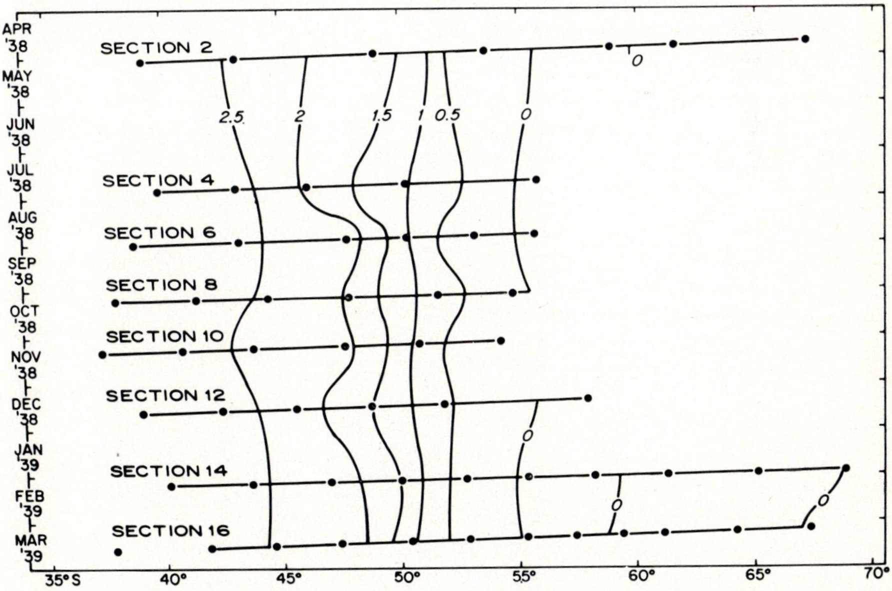

Fig. 4. Same as Figure 3, but sections are along 20°E.

The very cold water at 5,000 meters south of the ridge (Fig. 2) may possibly be a flow direct from the Weddell Sea, and it would be interesting to see if this has a seasonal variation. Unfortunately, this region could not be visited at enough times of the year to sample it sufficiently, and we must await records from recording instruments and submarines in the future.

It seems doubtful that repeated hydrographic sections across the Antarctic Circumpolar Current will reveal much statistically significant information on variability unless stations are more closely spaced. Because such closely spaced stations would be time-consuming and unusually difficult to obtain, there does not appear to be any reason for instituting a regularly occupied hydrographic section across the Antarctic Circumpolar Current within the foreseeable future.

Author's Note: This work was sponsored, in part, by the Office of Polar Programs of the National Science Foundation, under Grant GA 1295.

References

Anonymous, 1947. Station lists of *Discovery II* reports. *Discovery Repts., 24:* 1–422.

Mackintosh, N. A., 1946. The Antarctic Convergence and the distribution of surface temperature in antarctic waters. *Discovery Repts., 23:* 177–212.

Schott, G., 1942. Grundlagen einer Weltkarte der Meerestromungen. *Ann. Hydrol. Mar. Mat., Meteorol., 70:* 247.

The Formation of Antarctic Bottom Water

ROBERT B. ELDER and JAMES M. SEABROOKE

Polar Projects Section, U. S. Coast Guard Oceanographic Unit, Washington, D. C.

The Weddell Sea is the largest single ocean area in the Antarctic with perennial ice cover. This area is generally believed to be the source of most of the Antarctic Bottom Water that flows into northerly latitudes. There are varying opinions on the extent of the northward migration of Antarctic Bottom Water. Dietrich (1963) traced it as far north as 50°N in the Pacific and 45°N in the Atlantic while Defant (1961) indicated that it can be traced to 25°N in the Pacific and 8°N in the Atlantic. Both judgments indicate the importance of Antarctic Bottom Water in oceanic circulation.

Despite the importance of the oceanographic processes in the Weddell Sea, much of it remained unstudied until the austral summer of 1968–1969 because no ship with a suitable combination of ice breaking and scientific support capability had ever been available. An appropriate research facility became available when the U. S. Coast Guard modified the icebreaker USCGC *Glacier* for oceanographic research. The *Glacier's* equipment included five oceanographic laboratories, two oceanographic winches, a satellite photo receiving system, and satellite navigational equipment; a winch and crane system for piston coring and dredging were added for the 1969 operation.

The first phase of the International Weddell Sea Oceanographic Expedition, conducted during February and March, 1968 (IWSOE 68), was a cooperative multidisciplinary expedition and the National Science Foundation was the general coordinator of the scientific work. The major purpose of the expedition was to study the formation of the Antarctic Bottom Water. A second phase of the program (IWSOE 69) was conducted during February and March, 1969.

IWSOE 68 PROGRAMS

The U. S. Coast Guard Oceanographic Unit conducted a program to obtain physical, nutrient and pH data, bottom cores, and photographs. Analysis of the physical and nutrient data permitted a more complete understanding of the formation of Antarctic Bottom Water. The bottom photographs in the southern and western Weddell Sea supplemented others taken on the research ship *Eltanin* in the northern Antarctic Peninsula area and together their analysis allowed the pattern of contour currents to be established (Hollister and Elder, 1969).

A program to investigate currents related to the formation of Antarctic Bottom Water was directed by Dr. Thor Kvinge of the University of Bergen. Antarctic Bottom Water is formed by the mixing of warm deep water from northern latitudes with cold dense water from the continental shelf. One of the theories related to its formation (Fofonoff, 1956; Mosby, 1966) is that owing to the nonlinear relationship of density to temperature and salinity, the cold dense water formed on the shelf through freezing is prevented from sinking until a certain critical density is reached. Therefore, according to this theory, the flow of Antarctic Bottom Water down the continental slope is presumably periodic. To investigate this theory, four submerged instrumented buoy systems were installed during IWSOE 68 to operate throughout the following austral winter. Ice conditions during IWSOE 69 prevented recovery, but the system is expected to remain intact for at least an additional year.

A program to study the zonation of the Weddell Sea benthos was directed by Dr. John S. Rankin of the University of Connecticut. Samples of the benthic organisms were obtained by using a variety of bottom sampling gear, primarily the epibenthic sled. All sediment samples were washed through sieves and the macroscopic organisms were classified and preserved. The preliminary analysis indicated two primary zones: (1) at water depths of 400 to 1,000 meters, a great number and variety of relatively large animals were found; and (2) at water depths greater than 1,000 meters, relatively small animals, characterized by few numbers and kinds, were found. An exception was the foraminifera observed, some of which were about ¾ inch long.

The productivity of the Weddell Sea was examined by Texas A&M University under the direction of Dr. Sayed Z. El-Sayed. The studies included light penetration, chlorophyll and phaeophytin concentration, photosynthesis (by the C^{14} uptake method), and plankton which were collected with vertical tows and by filtering large water samples. A preliminary analysis indicated conspicuous variations in the productivity of the areas visited. In general, El-Sayed found the southwest and western regions of the Weddell Sea to be far more productive than the central and southern regions.

The microalgae and protozoa of antarctic pack ice were investigated by the Institute of Marine Science, University of Miami. Observations and measurements were made and samples obtained within and under the pack ice by scuba divers and correlated with observations obtained by other investigators.

A program to study the population dynamics of antarctic seals was conducted by Dr. Donald B. Sinniff of the University of Minnesota. Seals within one-fourth of a mile of the ship for a two-hour period were counted at selected times throughout the day and blood samples were collected. The samples were processed for later analysis by electrophoresis to show if racial differences exist. Helicopters landed on ice floes, the seals on them were anesthetized by a dart gun, and blood samples were drawn. A similar population study of penguins was also carried out.

IWSOE 69 PROGRAMS

The program conducted aboard USCGC *Glacier* in 1969 was essentially the same as that conducted in 1968, except that a piston coring program was conducted under the direction of the University of California, Los Angeles, and because of scheduling problems the productivity program was dropped.

During both the 1968 and 1969 expeditions, concurrent oceanographic research programs were also conducted by the Argentine icebreaker *San Martin* in the northeastern portion of the Weddell Sea. The two ships met twice, once just prior to entering the Weddell Sea and again at about the midpoint of the survey. Ideas and data were informally exchanged.

FORMATION OF ANTARCTIC BOTTOM WATER

One theory of Antarctic Bottom Water formation in the Weddell Sea is that it is formed during winter by the mixing of cold water which acquires its temperature-salinity characteristics on the continental shelf and warm deep water which originates in northern latitudes. This theory has been described in detail by Fofonoff (1956) and Mosby (1966). Data collected during the International Weddell Sea Oceanographic Expedition indicated that another, possibly more important, method of formation occurs.

According to Fofonoff, two critical salinities of shelf water are 34.51 and 34.63‰ (freezing temperatures are assumed). Any mixture of 34.51‰ shelf water and warm deep water will result in a mixture with a density lighter than the warm deep water and a mixture of 34.63‰ shelf water will have a density heavier than the warm deep water. Mixtures of warm deep water and shelf water with salinities between 34.51 and 34.63‰ will be heavier than either type because of the nonlinearities in the temperature-salinity-density relationship. As Fofonoff stated, "Shelf water in this salinity range cannot float freely over the warm deep water and is also prevented from sinking by its heavier mixtures. It is, therefore, found only on the continental shelf and has not been observed in the open sea." Therefore, in what is somewhat like an iterative freezing process at the surface, the salinity of the nearly homogeneous shelf water gradually increases until the critical salinity is reached, and as Mosby stated, ". . . a sudden flow along the bottom may be imagined to start, perhaps emptying the whole reservoir of homogeneous shelf water."

A complete evaluation of this theory will have to await data collected during the austral winter. It is hoped that recovery of the University of Bergen's buoys will provide suitable data. Since this is a winter phenomenon, the data collected during IWSOE 68 and IWSOE 69 cannot be used as a basis either to prove or disprove the theory; however, the data collected shows evidence that formation of Antarctic Bottom Water is not limited to the mechanism just described.

Analysis of the data indicated that water of sufficient density to mix with warm deep water and form Antarctic Bottom Water is present during the summer on the shelf in the southwestern Weddell Sea. Analysis of the data further indicated that this dense shelf water is not formed at the air-sea interface or transported into the southwestern Weddell Sea from other areas. Furthermore, it is not believed to be formed in winter and prevented from flowing off the shelf by bottom topography. Consequently, it is concluded that the dense shelf water is formed on the continental shelf and results from the water's exposure to the immense ice shelves extending around the southwest sector of the Weddell Sea.

TEMPERATURE-SALINITY STUDIES

Water of sufficient density to mix with warm deep water and form Antarctic Bottom Water is present below approximately 200 meters on the continental shelf in the southwestern Weddell Sea, based on an analysis of the temperature and salinity data from 58 stations collected during IWSOE 68, sixteen of which were on the continental shelf. Analysis procedures were similar to those used by Fofonoff (1956) to indicate the salinity at which shelf water would mix with warm deep water to form Antarctic Bottom Water.

Figure 1 is a potential temperature-salinity diagram which includes all temperature and salinity data collected during IWSOE 68. The data were summarized by averaging the salinities from all stations in each one-tenth degree interval of potential temperature. The maximum range of salinities in each interval is indicated by the horizontal lines drawn through Θ-S points. Salinities were averaged up to the level of the salinity maximum only. Points without lines through them show the minimum temperature of each station.

Analysis of the IWSOE 68 data indicated somewhat different temperature and salinity characteristics from those presented by Fofonoff. Fofonoff concluded that Antarctic Bottom Water consisted of a mixture of warm deep water with a temperature and salinity of 0.6°C and 34.70‰, and shelf water at freezing temperature (approximately −1.89°C) and 34.63‰ salinity. None of the warm deep water observed during IWSOE 68 was higher than 0.4°C and the average temperature and salinity of the layer near the shelf was approximately 0.2°C and 34.67‰.

A line drawn from this point (0.2°C and 34.67‰) through the values representing Antarctic Bottom Water and extended to the freezing point (Fig. 2) indicates the shelf water having an appropriate salinity (approximately 34.60‰) to mix with warm deep water and form Antarctic Bottom Water, assuming approximately linear mixing between two types. Plots of observed data collected at all 10 stations on the continental shelf in the Weddell Sea include only observations having salinity values greater than 34.50‰. This cluster of points near freezing temperatures with salinity values of 34.60‰ or greater represents an extensive amount of shelf water having sufficient density to mix with warm deep water and form Antarctic Bottom Water, or to flow down the slope without mixing. Since water having the characteristics of dense shelf

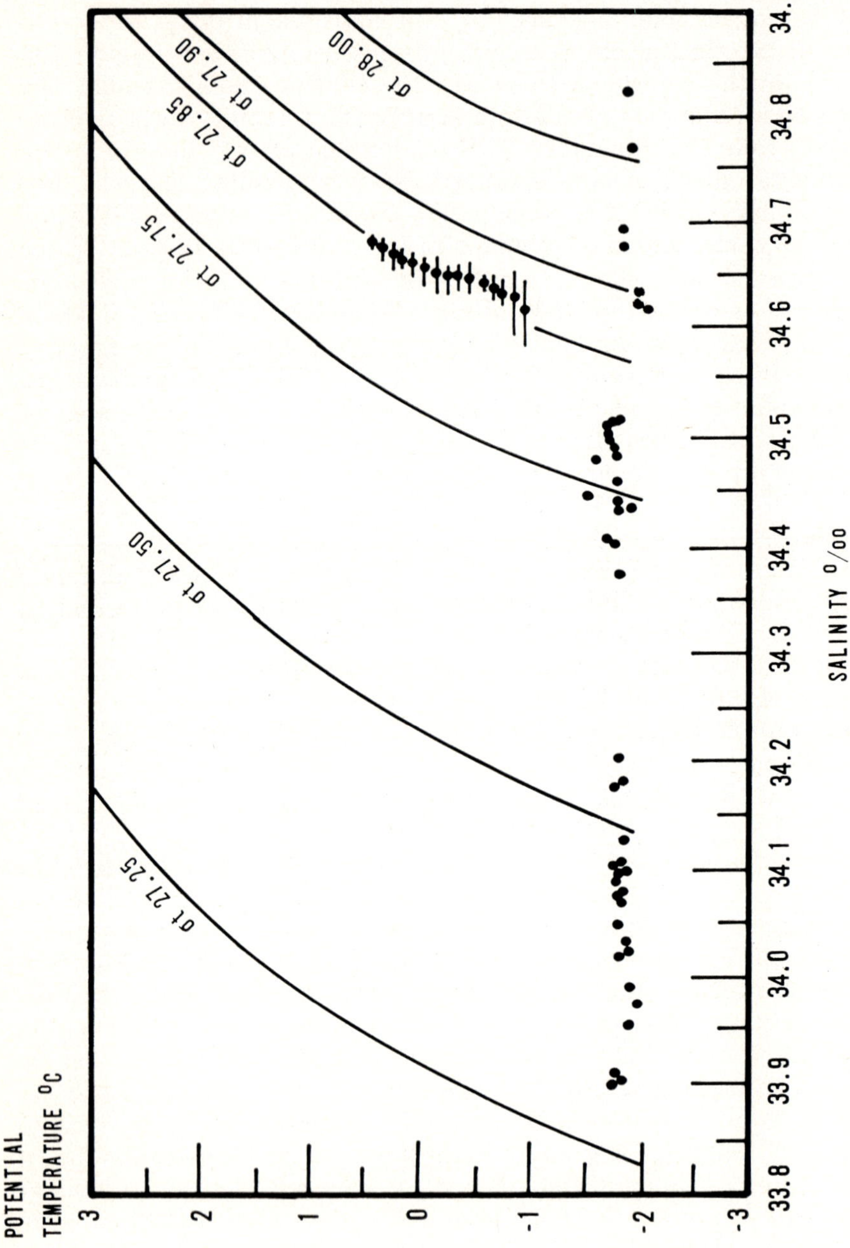

Fig. 1. Potential temperature (Θ)-salinity (S) diagram (IWSOE 68 data).

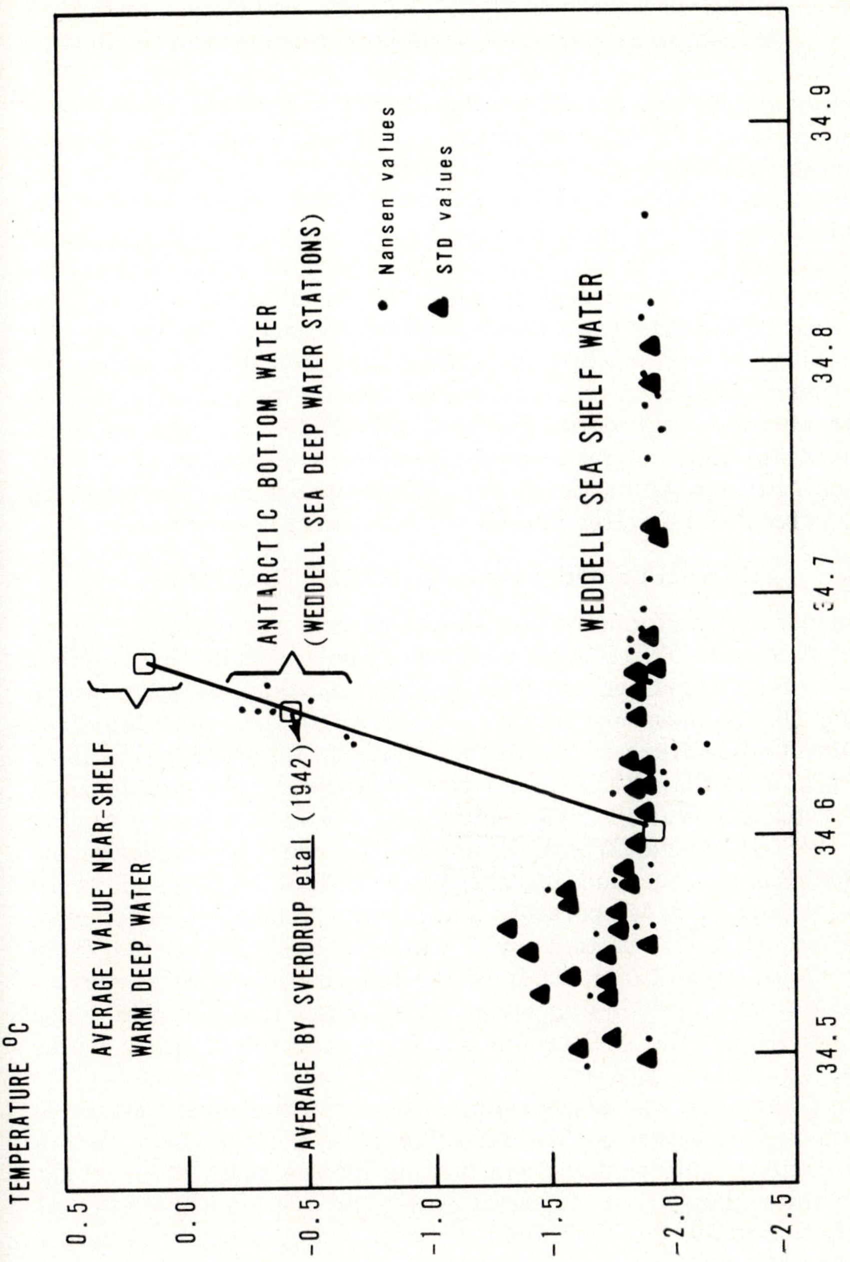

Fig. 2. Temperature-salinity characteristics of Weddell Sea water masses (IWSOE 68 data).

water ($T \cong 1.9°C$, $S > 34.6$) was not found off the shelf, such water apparently mixed with less dense shelf water before flowing off the shelf to mix with warm deep water to form Antarctic Bottom Water.

Sverdrup, Johnson, and Fleming (1942) defined the characteristics of Antarctic Bottom Water as −0.4°C and 34.66‰. This agrees with the data collected during IWSOE 68. The temperature and salinity data obtained near the bottom at the deeper stations in the Weddell Sea are shown in Figure 2 to be concentrated near Sverdrup's value for Antarctic Bottom Water. This point also represents a mixture of warm deep water of the observed characteristics with bottom shelf water at a seven- to three-part ratio. The plausibility of this mixture is further enhanced by comparing the preformed phosphate and preformed nitrate values of the three water masses. Seabrooke, Hufford, and Elder (in preparation) using mean values of preformed phosphate and preformed nitrate determined that Antarctic Bottom Water was a mixture made up of 35 percent shelf water and 65 percent warm deep water.

SOURCES OF BOTTOM SHELF WATER

Various explanations of the source of cold bottom shelf water were examined. There is no evidence from the data that surface shelf water is modified by atmospheric conditions to form water having the temperature-salinity characteristics of that found at greater depths. Much of the surface water on the shelf had salinity values of less than 34.00‰ and temperatures several tenths of a degree above freezing. Examinations of the data collected during both IWSOE 68 and IWSOE 69 and during previous cruises in the Weddell Sea and surrounding areas fail to show evidence of water having comparable temperature and salinity values. It is believed, therefore, that the bottom shelf water is not transported from other areas. In addition, study of the temperature-salinity characteristics of the surrounding water types shows that the cold dense water found on the shelf could not be a mixture of other water types.

The possibility was also examined that the cold dense water is formed in the winter as the result of air-sea interaction and in some manner is prevented from flowing off the shelf. This is not likely since the bottom topography of the shelf in the area of operation is quite flat and could not entrap the quantity of water present (Fig. 3).

The most plausible explanation of the mechanism by which the cold dense subsurface shelf water is formed is that it is a result

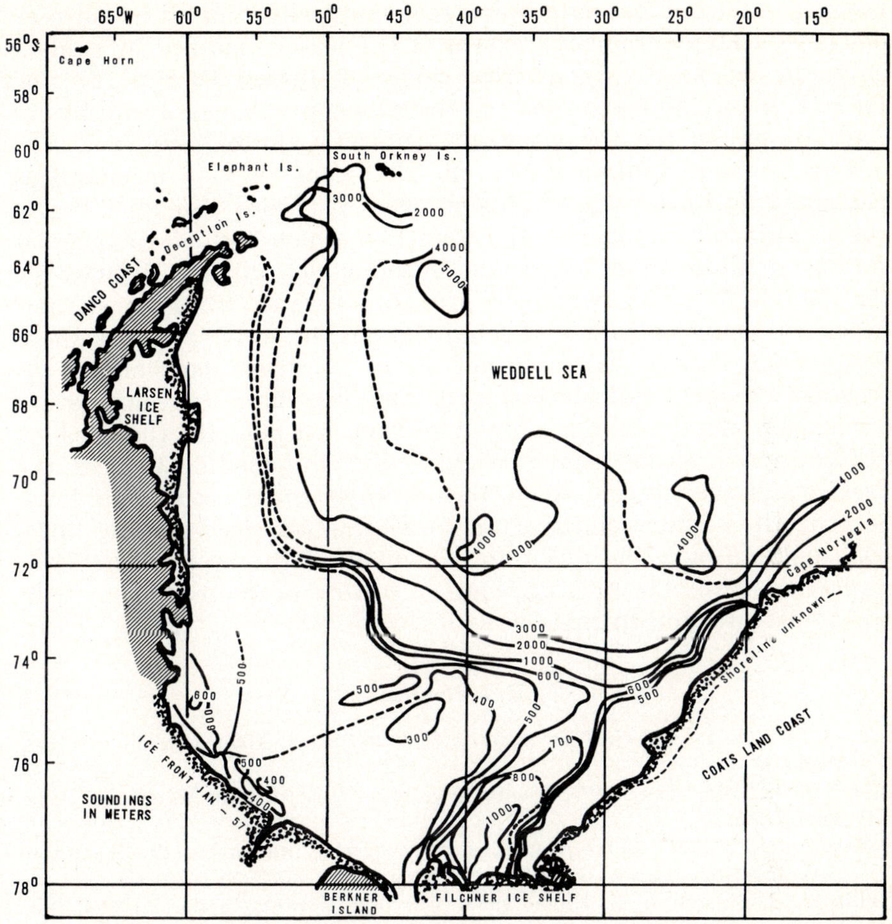

Fig. 3. Weddell Sea bottom topography (After Kvinge, 1968).

of its contact with the underside of the ice shelf surrounding the area and extending seaward great distances. The process of forming cold dense water by this method was well described by Lusquinos (1963). Wexler (1960) measured the vertical distribution of temperature in an ice shelf at Little America within five meters of the ice-sea interface. The temperature at that point was approximately −5°C. As Lusquinos stated, "It must be assumed that the water in contact with the underside of the shelf ice will be kept at its freezing point. As heat flows upwards through the ice, the contact water is continuously being renewed from the surrounding water masses by vertical convection and horizontal advection." Lusquinos' data were geographically limited so he may not have been aware of the extent of the water modified by contact with the ice shelf. From data collected during IWSOE 68 and IWSOE 69, it appears that the described process is a significant contribution to the formation of Antarctic Bottom Water.

This process would not prevent the occurrence of mechanisms described by Fofonoff and Mosby. Mosby (1966) discussed water observed in the summer in the Ross Sea which had characteristics similar to those observed in the Weddell Sea during IWSOE 68. He stated, "... this water is probably formed by a 'secondary' process by sinking of water from the shallower part of the shelf. But in any case, it can only act as an 'artificial' bottom for the seasonal effect in the surface layer and can therefore not prevent a bottom water formation similar to that accepted for the Weddell Sea." In the southwestern Weddell Sea the modification of the shelf water due to cooling by the ice shelf could occur simultaneously in the winter months with the mechanism described by Fofonoff and Mosby. The question of which of the two processes is more important in forming Antarctic Bottom Water must await additional data for an answer.

References

Defant, A., 1961. *Physical Oceanography;* vol. 1, p. 150. Macmillan, New York.

Dietrich, G., 1963. *General Oceanography;* pp. 477–480. John Wiley and Sons, New York.

Fofonoff, N. P., 1956. Some properties of sea-water influencing the formation of Antarctic bottom water. *Deep-Sea Res., 4:* 32–35.

Hollister, C. D., and R. B. Elder, 1969. Contour currents in the Weddell Sea. *Deep-Sea Res., 16:* 99.

Kvinge, T., 1968. *Technical Report on Project to Measure Currents Related to the Formation of Antarctic Bottom Water in the Weddell Sea.* Geof. Inst. Univ. Bergen.

Lusquinos, A. J., 1963. Extreme temperature in the Weddell Sea. *Mat.-Naturv. Serie, Univ. Bergen, No. 23.*

Mosby, H., 1966. Bottom water formation. *SCAR/SCOR/IAPO/IUBS Symposium on Antarctic Oceanography; Santiago, Chile, 13–16 Sept. 1966.* Section 2, Review Paper 1. (Unpublished manuscript) Dr. Mosby's present address is Geophysical Institute, Univ. Bergen, Norway.

Seabrooke, J. M., G. L. Hufford, and R. B. Elder, 1971. *Formation of Antarctic Bottom Water in the Weddell Sea. J. Geophys. Res.* (In press).

Sverdrup, H. V., M. W. Johnson, and R. H. Fleming, 1942. *The Oceans; Their Physics, Chemistry and General Biology;* pp. 611–613. Prentice-Hall, Englewood Cliffs, N.J.

Wexler, H., 1960. Heating and melting of floating ice shelves. *J. Glaciol., 3* (27) : 626.

PART VII

Gondwanaland

PART VII

Gondwanaland

Although the near match of the coasts of the Americas to those of Africa and Europe caused speculation by many early scientists and philosophers such as Francis Bacon (1620) and P. Placet (1668) as to the possibility that they had been joined in the past, it was the discovery of the similarity of certan rock formations and especially of fossil plants associated with coal measures that lead Antonio Snider in 1858 to propose that all continents had once been joined. The Austrian geologist, Eduard Suess, after finding a remarkably similar sequence of rock formations containing coal measures and a distinctive *Glossopteris* flora in India, South Africa, South America, and Australia, concluded early in this century that all lands of the Southern Hemisphere had been a single continent which he called Gondwanaland from the province in India where he had first studied the rock series.

Two decades later, in 1937, Du Toit of South Africa summarized the research of Southern Hemisphere geologists displaying a most exciting array of evidence for the Gondwanaland thesis. Most compelling are the extensive beds of tillite and glacial polish and striae on the hard rocks on which they lie, unquestioned evidence of the action of extensive glaciation. In all parts of the Southern Hemisphere the tillites are found not only in the same geologic periods but also in a sequence of sediments bearing fossils of identical plant species—the *Glossopteris* flora. There are also great resemblances in the land fauna, especially reptiles and amphibians found in the Gondwana beds of South America and South Africa. To account for the similarity of the rocks of all the southern land masses and also account for extensive glaciation on lands which are now astride the tropics, Du Toit considered that Gondwanaland drifted in the southern polar region and then separated into several parts which drifted back toward the tropics leaving only Antarctica stranded at the pole.

The major objections to the theory of continental drift have been the absence of a motive force of sufficient power, a cause for initiating the drift and the theoretical orogeny that curved the Pacific mountain belts by crimpling of the forward edge of the drifting blocks.

How does the new evidence relate to these objections? The idea of spreading ocean floors expressed by Dietz and Hess, but based on the ideas expressed earlier (in the late 1930's) by the Dutch geophysicist Vening Meinesz, is now generally considered an adequate mechanism. The concept is that beneath the mid-ocean ridges are rising convection currents in the earth's mantle; from this axis the currents spread laterally, widening the ocean basins while forcing the continents apart. Vening Meinesz based his idea on gravity anomalies over the ridges and the deep-sea trenches. Dietz and Hess referred to the thermal anomalies over the mid-ocean ridges. When Vine and Matthews combined these ideas with the magnetic reversal patterns, the jigsaw-puzzle pieces fell in place and a clear picture emerged. The ocean basins have apparently been formed by an ever-widening fracture in the mid-ocean ridges, and the rocks of the ocean floor are progressively older with distance from the ridge.

Antarctic research is adding new bits of evidence. Pitman and Heirtzler, aboard the USARP research ship *Eltanin* in 1965, found linearity of pattern and symmetry of magnetic anomalies on both sides of the Pacific-Antarctic Ridge and time scale indications that the spreading rate is 4.5 cm per year averaged over the past ten million years.

And how does Antarctica fit into Gondwanaland? Du Toit fit Antarctica into Gondwanaland largely on the basis of its shape and the known mountain ranges of West Antarctica. Hamilton has shown that current knowledge of the rocks and geologic structure is consistent with Du Toit's pattern. The rocks of Antarctica are very similar to those of Australia, South Africa, the Falkland Islands, South America, and India. Halpern shows that radiometric ages of igneous rock from West Antarctica and neighboring Southern Hemisphere land masses are consistent with Du Toit's "Samfrau Geosyncline" hypothesis. That *Glossopteris* flora occur in Antarctica has been known since Scott's first expedition of 1901, and in 1959 Long found tillites similar to those of the other Southern Hemisphere lands. Frakes and Crowell of UCLA have concluded that the tillites represent shallow and deep marine glacial deposits as well as terrestrial drifts. They are now studying the tillites of other areas to establish more accurately the geography of Gondwanaland at the time of breakup. During the last field season in Antarctica (1967–1968), Peter Barrett of Ohio State University found a fragment of bone which Edwin Colbert of the American Museum of Natural History identified as part of the jaw bone of a labyrinthodont, an amphibian of Late Paleozoic age. Fossils of this animal have been found in South Africa, Madagascar, and Australia. A tropical creature unable to tolerate salt water could have become distributed over such widespread places only if the lands were once connected.

LOUIS O. QUAM

Office of Polar Programs
National Science Foundation
Washington, D.C.

The Evolution of the Southern Oceans

J. R. HEIRTZLER

Woods Hole Oceanographic Institution, Woods Hole, Massachusetts

Within the last few years much marine geophysical data has been interpreted in terms of sea-floor spreading. As a result it is now possible to reconstruct the relative positions of many continents, especially those of the Southern Hemisphere, for the last 200 million years. Most continental reconstructions using marine data have been made for those continents bordering the Atlantic Ocean although marine data are adequate for nearly all of the southern continents. Such reconstructions confirm many of the early generalities about continental drift.

It is not possible to review here the evidence supporting the hypothesis of sea-floor spreading (See Anon., 1968; Heirtzler, 1968; Phinney, 1969). For most oceans of the world, however, it has been determined that material from the deep earth upwells at the axis of the mid-ocean ridge system and moves out to both sides of the ridge at a rate of up to about 6 cm per year. While so doing the ocean floor becomes magnetized in strips, approximately parallel to the axis and symmetric about it, by reversals of the geomagnetic field. Seismic activity is related to such motion. The spreading causes characteristic bathymetric features. The extent of data and experience is now nearly sufficient for one to distinguish continental from oceanic sections of the earth's crust by their surficial expression, although final confirmation of the thicker continental crust usually requires exploration by seismic refraction. In most areas where the mid-ocean ridge does not go under continents the axis of upwelling, or spreading, is characterized by a peaked undersea mountain range. The ruggedness of the topography is suppressed by an irregular thickness of sediments increasing away from the ridge crest and across the ocean basins. Near the continents there is usually a very thick sedimentary layer caused by material washed from the continents. The peaked center line of the mid-ocean ridge is frequently offset laterally by a fracture with the linear extent of the fracture extending far across the ocean basins.

Marine data have thus far only been able to provide information about the *relative* motion of the bordering continents. It has provided some general information about past climatic conditions through studies of glacial detritus, palynology, etc., but this information has not been specific enough to permit firm conclusions about past absolute positions of parts of the ocean basins. To obtain information about past latitudes (for example) one must turn to continental studies, particularly the paleomagnetism of continental rocks.

The paleomagnetic analysis of volcanic rock samples can determine the direction in which the rock is magnetized and thus determine the direction of the magnetic field at the time the volcanic rock originally cooled. If the direction at the time the rock cooled is not the same as the direction today, the formation from which the sample was taken must have moved by a known amount. If the age of the rock is determined by an independent method, one can determine the *latitudinal* change of the formation (continent) by the dip of the magnetization, although it is not possible to determine the longitudinal change of the formation with as great confidence.

By combining information on relative motion from the oceans with the information on latitude from paleomagnetism one can detail the evolution of the southern oceans.

BATHYMETRIC FEATURES

The physiographic charts of the Atlantic and Indian Oceans (Heezen and Tharp, 1961, 1964) have been of great value in illustrating the shape of bathymetric features of those oceans. Although some distortion is inherent in the physiographic method of presentation and although there were little actual bathymetric data in some areas these two charts show the shape of the important bathymetric features, many of which are linear. The linear features were read from the original Mercator charts and Figure 1 shows them projected to a polar plot by azimuthal equidistant projection for latitudes south of 30°S.

Although no such diagrams have yet been published for the Pacific-Antarctic Ocean nor south of 58°S in the Atlantic several important features can be noticed in Figures 1 and 2. Midway between South America and Africa and extending south of Africa, the broken and offset axis of the ridge can be distinguished. At approximately right angles to this axis and crossing at the offsets in the ridge axis, the fractures can be identified. One of the longest of these fractures in the Atlantic extends westward towards South America with a southerly offset at its westerly end where it parallels the northern edge of the Scotia Arc. Linear features paralleling the ridge axis and some distance to the east and west of it are of unknown origin.

As the ridge axis passes south of Africa it is increasingly difficult to identify and is easily confused with the northward-trending Mozambique, Prince Edward, and Malagasy Fracture Zones (Fig. 3). The feature south of Africa is the Agulhas Plateau. The two easternmost of the longer fracture zones (Prince Edward and Malagasy) continue to the north and are nearly the east and west boundaries of the Madagascar Ridge south of Madagascar. The Diamantina Fracture Zone is immediately southwest of Australia and it approximately parallels the axis of the ridge shown south of that fracture zone. This unusual configuration of the Diamentina Fracture Zone can be explained in terms of sea-floor spreading, as will be seen in a following section. The ridge axis south of Australia is terminated on the west by the Amsterdam Fracture Zone. The Diamentina Fracture Zone is terminated on the west by the Ninetyeast Ridge which extends nearly due north. Just north of the Diamentina Fracture Zone and off southwest Australia is the Naturaliste Plateau and just north of the Diamentina Fracture Zone and at its juncture with Ninetyeast Ridge a feature called Broken Ridge is located. The Kerguelen Plateau is approximately parallel to the ridge south of Australia and is located about as far south of the ridge axis as the Diamentina Fracture. Naturaliste Ridge and Broken Ridge are located north of the ridge. On its eastern end the Kerguelen Plateau abuts the Antarctic Continent just as the Naturaliste Plateau abuts Australia. On its western end it terminates near the Amsterdam Fracture Zone. Other important bathymetric features of the Indian Ocean which play an important part in the opening of the southern oceans are the Rodriguez Fracture Zone, which is east-west trending and intersects the mid-Indian Ridge due east of Madagascar, and the Chagos-Laccadive and Seychelles-Mascarene Ridges which parallel the axis of the mid-Indian Ridge as it continues northward and to the Gulf of Aden.

The Indian Ocean is clearly the most bathymetrically complex of

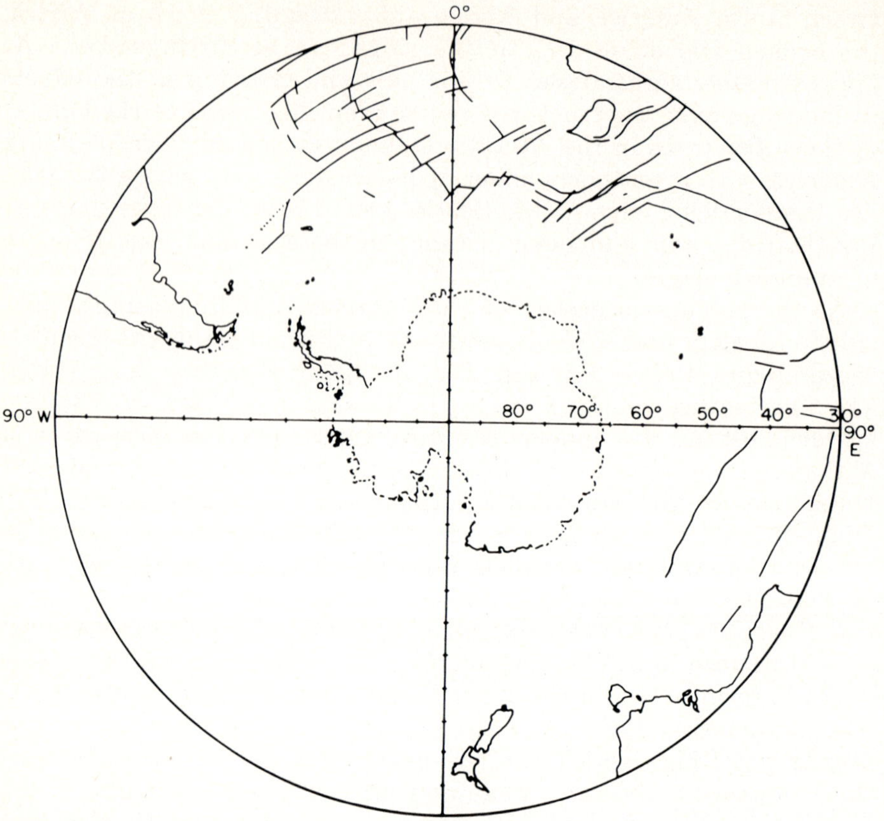

Fig. 1. Bathymetric features and lineations of the South Atlantic and Indian Oceans (After Heezen and Tharp, 1961, 1964).

the present day southern oceans. Heezen and Tharp (1965) refer to many of the plateaus and ridges just named in the Indian Ocean as "micro-continents." Francis and Raitt (1967) showed by seismic refraction studies that the Broken Ridge is continental in structure. Granite has been found in the Seychelles Islands and those islands and Madagascar are known to be quite old (Miller and Mudie, 1961). It is probable that the other ridges and plateaus named are of a similar nature.

East of New Zealand over the broad New Zealand Plateau Houtz *et al.* (1967) have reported the results of seismic profiling. They give evidence that Paleozoic material underlies much of the Chatham Rise which is the northern portion of the New Zealand Plateau. The islands of the Campbell Plateau, which is the south-

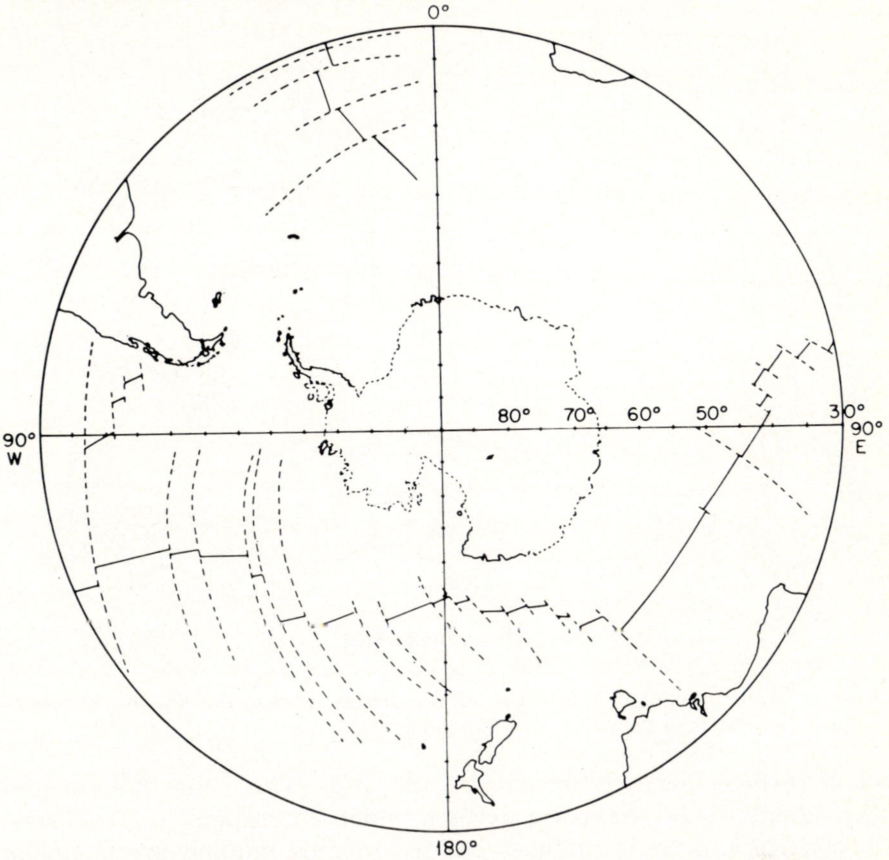

Fig. 2. Mid-ocean ridge axes (solid line) and fracture zones (dashed line) indicated by marine magnetic data (After LePichon and Heirtzler, 1968; Pitman *et al.*, 1968; Dickson *et al.*, 1968).

ern portion of the New Zealand Plateau also have continental-type rocks.

Officer (1955) showed that the floor of the Tasman Sea is oceanic crust rather than continental but that Lord Howe Rise is continental. Studies of earthquake waves by Press and Dewart (1959) and by Evison *et al.* (1960) show the Ross Sea to be most probably continental.

MARINE MAGNETIC FEATURES

As part of their magnetic study of the various southern oceans, LePichon and Heirtzler (1968), Pitman *et al.* (1968), and Dickson

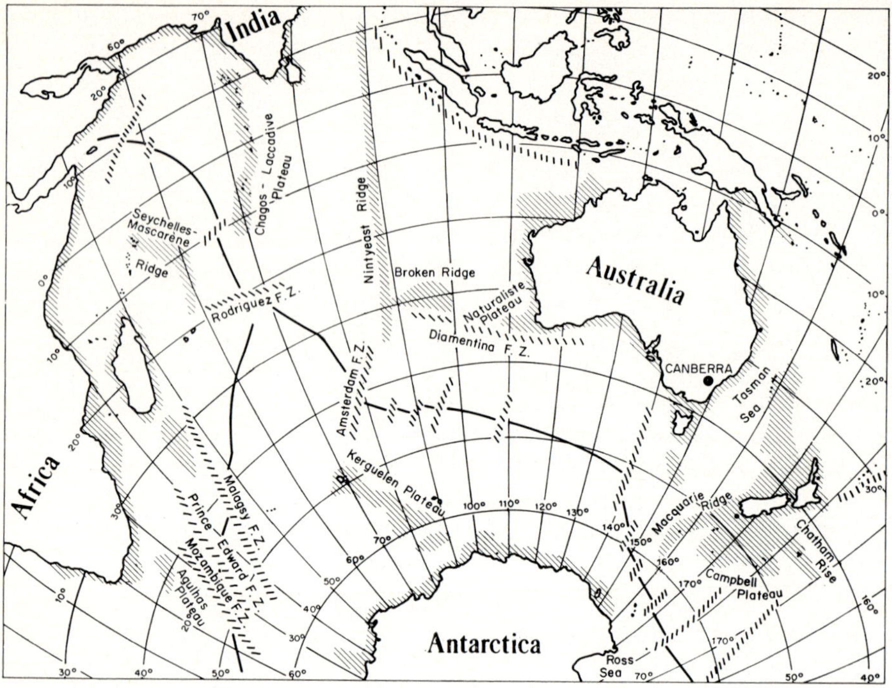

Fig. 3. Main topographic features of the Indian Ocean and Pacific-Antarctic Ocean south and southeast of New Zealand.

et al. (1968) located the axis of the mid-ocean ridge system and the offsets in the magnetic pattern which correspond to fractures. The ridge axis and fractures defined by this method are sketched in Figure 2. Where these magnetic studies overlap the existing physiographic diagrams they show essentially the same ridge axis and fractures. The magnetic work south of New Zealand and throughout the Pacific-Antarctic Ocean, however, provides information about the ridge and fracture system where nearly no data existed before. It also shows (Herron and Hayes, 1969) that the Chile Ridge, west of Chile, is also a spreading ridge with a fracture system.

A very important result of the magnetic analyses that is not shown in Figure 2 is the precise age of the various parts of the ocean floor, increasing in age with distance from the ridge axis. The papers mentioned and Heirtzler *et al.* (1968) show the ages. Those ages determine the sequential relative positions of the continents and the times these positions were occupied. The magnetic data show that the Southern Hemisphere continents and India were once a single supercontinent and that the various continents separated at different times with South America moving to the west and overriding the Pacific Ocean floor which is moving to the east.

Although magnetic data were somewhat meager in the Indian Ocean, LePichon and Heirtzler (1968) believed that they saw evidence for two major episodes of spreading there. The first began sometime in Permian to Triassic. The second occurred in about the Eocene and it was in this episode that India started traveling from south of the equator to its present position.

In the South Atlantic Ocean magnetic ages could be determined only about half-way across the ocean basins but extrapolation indicated an initial separation of South America from Africa about 200 million years (m.y.) ago (Dickson *et al.*, 1968), with possibly some minor change in the direction of spreading about 75 to 80 million years ago.

A well established 80 m.y. magnetic isochron line against the New Zealand Plateau led Pitman *et al.* (1968) to infer that the plateau separated from the Antarctic Continent at about that time. A magnetic isochron line against the southern continental margin of Australia indicated that it separated from Antarctica 40 m.y. ago. The fact that the Broken Ridge is continental and symmetrically located about the ridge with respect to the Kerguelen Plateau suggests that the Naturaliste Plateau and Broken Ridge moved northward with Australia and separated from the Kerguelen Plateau—Antarctic block.

EARTHQUAKE EPICENTERS

In recent years the number of seismological observatories has increased and the reporting of earthquakes has become more thorough. This has permitted a large number of earthquake epicenters to be located more accurately. All epicenter locations recorded with the U.S. Coast and Geodetic Survey for quakes occurring during the period 1961–1967 and south of 30°S are shown in Figure 4. Sykes (1967) has shown that shallow epicenters occur along the crest of the mid-ocean ridge or along fracture zones between offset sections of the ridge axis. Isaacs *et al.* (1968) discussed the role of earthquakes in sea-floor spreading. They emphasized that deep epicenters are found at trenches such as the Peru-Chile Trench off the west coast of South America, at the eastern edge of the Scotia Arc and at the Kermadec Trench north of New Zealand.

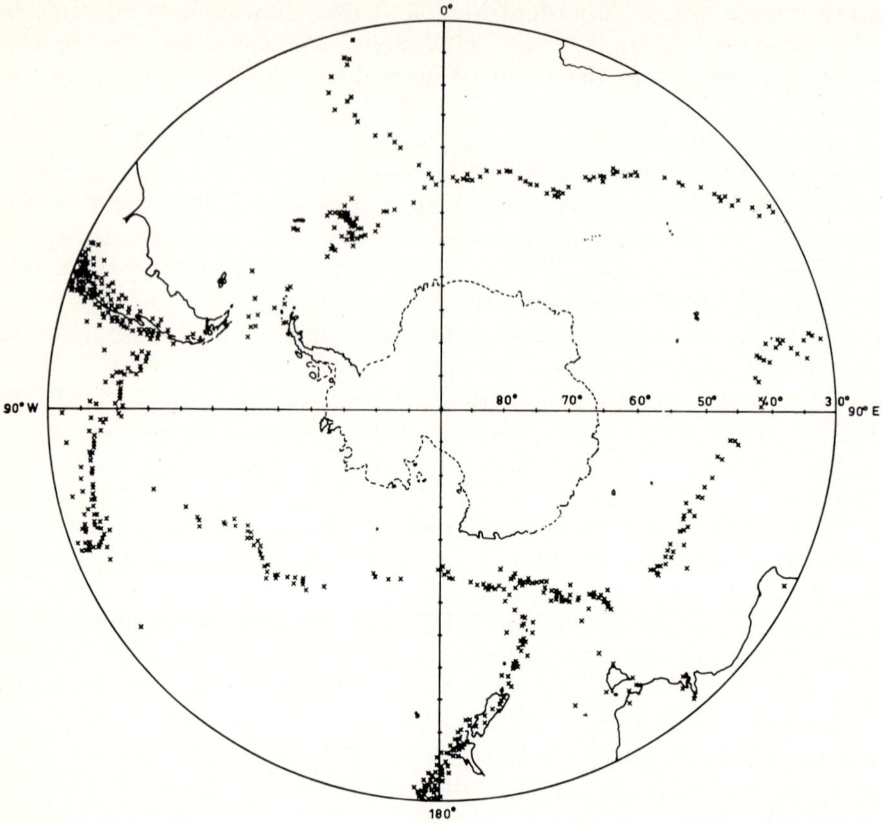

Fig. 4. Earthquake epicenters that occurred during the period 1961–1967 and south of 30°S (for epicenters on file with the U.S. Coast and Geodetic Survey, from plot supplied by Laverty and Dorman). Some epicenters have been omitted in areas of numerous epicenters.

Sykes (1963) used the location of epicenters in the Pacific-Antarctic to identify the large offset in the ridge axis at about 56°S. By first-motion studies of epicenters south of New Zealand, Sykes (1967) showed that the Macquarie Ridge is a compressional rather than a tensional feature. In the South Atlantic, epicenters indicate the presence of a fracture running from the ridge axis to the southern edge of the Scotia Arc. That fracture has not been noted in the few shipboard cruises in that area.

Epicenters, being so numerous, define the ridge and fracture zones in many areas better than can be done from shipboard data.

Epicenter studies can only indicate what has happened in the last few years, however, and not over geologic time. Thus the shipboard and epicenter studies complement each other.

On the Antarctic Continent earthquakes are essentially nonexistent today; but volcanic activity in the Balleny Islands and in Victoria Land of East Antarctica exists today or has existed in the recent past and rather widespread fumarolic activity is believed to exist in Marie Byrd Land of West Antarctica (LeMasurier and Wade, 1968).

PALEOMAGNETISM

Recent reviews of paleomagnetic work include those of Irving *et al.* (1963), Gough *et al.* (1964), Irving (1964), Creer (1965), Irving (1966), and McElhinny *et al.* (1968). McElhinny's paper (1968) concerns the change in latitude of India and McElhinny (1967) is a review of all paleomagnetic results on the Gondwanaland continents.

Rocks from southern continents which have been analyzed have come mainly from Africa and Australia. Very few have come from Antarctica or South America or from the islands of the southern oceans and almost none have come from New Zealand. Of the rocks that have been analyzed most either predate the breakup of Gondwanaland or were magnetized quite recently in their present locations.

Some of the main conclusions reached, as they apply to material emplaced since the late Paleozoic (Permian) or early Mesozoic (Triassic-Jurassic) times, are:

1. There has not been an appreciable change in the latitude of South America since the Paleozoic (about 200 m.y. ago).
2. There is good reason to believe that Africa remained fixed in location during the period from 180 to 100 m.y. ago.
3. Canberra, Australia, has moved from a latitude of about 70°S to its present latitude of about 35°S since the Cretaceous (100 m.y. ago).
4. The Deccan traps of India moved from 30°S to 20°N from the time that they were formed in the Eocene (42–65 m.y. ago) to the present. Very likely India had completed its northerly movement by the Miocene (20 m.y. ago), so it moved with a speed of at least 10 cm per yr.

THE FITTING OF THE NEW ZEALAND PLATEAU TO ANTARCTICA

Attempting to match any continental mass to the Antarctic coast is difficult because of the Antarctic ice cover, which makes the land inaccessible to study except in a few outcrop areas. The weight of the ice is believed to depress and fracture the continental shelves (Zhivago, 1962), and the ice severely restricts the operation of marine geophysical investigations near the shores. Atmospheric conditions prohibit accurate navigation by vessels not equipped with the new satellite navigation equipment, and thus limit a ship's ability to do accurate surveys.

Attempts to fit the coast of the New Zealand Plateau have previously been difficult because of the limited knowledge of its structure. The Alpine Fault runs the length of North and South Islands. To make a proper fit to the Antarctic Continent 80 m.y. ago one must restore motions that have occurred along this fault since that time.

Figure 5 shows, by arrows, similar ancient features that were once together but have now been separated by 300 miles. The differential motion along this fault today is about 6 miles per m.y. This velocity, if it has been constant, would indicate that the features were together about 50 m.y. ago, shortly after the New Zealand Plateau separated from Antarctica.

Figure 5 shows the reconstructed position of the New Zealand Plateau along with the commonly accepted position of Australia at the time. The magnetic data show that Australia did not separate from Antarctica until about 40 m.y. ago and thus some 40 m.y. after the New Zealand Plateau had separated and was drifting away. The fact that Australia was still in place when New Zealand separated must have set up a strain within the New Zealand block. It is understandable that shear may have occurred along some plane such as the Alpine Fault so the New Zealand block could be accommodated against the Australian one. It would also be expected that the nature of faulting along the primitive Alpine Fault would have changed when Australia separated, although one has not attempted to find field evidence for that event. A hiatus in the sea-floor spreading seems to have occurred south of New Zealand at that time (Christoffel and Ross, 1970).

In this figure no reconstruction of North and South Islands has been made along the Alpine Fault, but it is clear that some attempt might be made. It would not be surprising if additional faults were

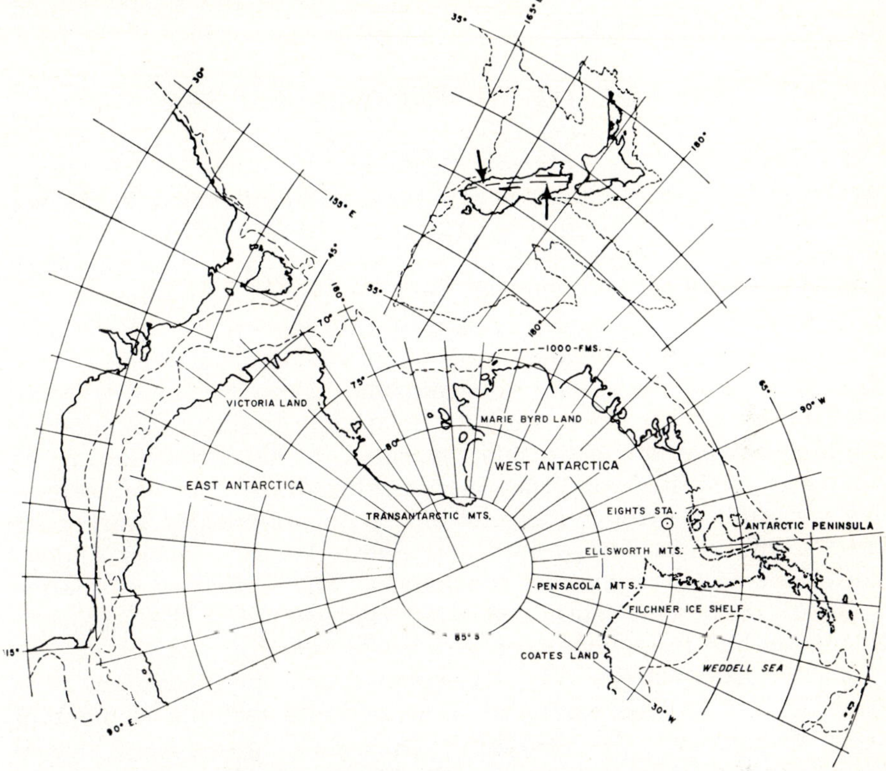

Fig. 5. Reconstruction of Antarctica, Australia, and New Zealand. The early motion along the Alpine Fault of New Zealand and the early motion of the Antarctic Peninsula have not been restored.

found underwater on the Campbell Plateau. In fact such fractures have been found just to the east of North Island and west of the Hikurangi Trench (Houtz *et al.*, 1967).

It is interesting to speculate about the possible relationship between the Macquarie Ridge and the Kermadec Trench. It would seem that the New Zealand Plateau block has drifted over a trench or sink resulting in compressional strain and some displacement along the vertical line over the trench, with volcanic activity in North and South Islands. The strained continental crust over the trench line would be weakened and horizontal motion along an Alpine Fault at this position would be facilitated.

Wade (1967) reported that a Cretaceous orogeny formed the Rockefeller Mountains of Marie Byrd Land. The time of that event could well have been simultaneous with the separation of the New Zealand block.

THE OPENING OF THE WEDDELL SEA

The position of the Antarctic Peninsula in Figure 5 is shown by the dashed line because there is a good possibility that it did not occupy that position with respect to the remainder of the Antarctic Continent at that time. The unique shape of the coasts on either side of the Weddell Sea suggests that the Antarctic Peninsula was once against the Antarctic coast to the east (Coats Land and Western Queen Maud Land), and there was then no Weddell Sea. This position of the Antarctic Peninsula makes the reconstruction much easier and does not seem to violate any geologic evidence. It would seem that this peninsula separated in the initial breakup of Gondwanaland in about Triassic times. It is likely that the present-day peninsula was in contact not only with present-day Antarctica but also in contact with present-day South America, so the Andean Cordillera was straight and continuous. The similarity of the geology of the lower South American continent and the Antarctic Peninsula has frequently been noticed by many geologists.

Wasilewski (1967) said, "Ellsworth Land, specifically the area from Eights Station eastward, is a separate tectonic element of West Antarctica." He also said, "A geologic province which is bounded on the west at 80°W, on the south at 76°S, and on the east at the boundary of the Filchner Ice Shelf, breaks West Antarctica into distinct provinces." Williams and Ford (1968), in referring to certain intrusive formations, stated, "The dikes are considered (by A. B. Ford) to place a probable minimum age of Jurassic on the post-Permian deformation in the Pensacola Mountains. Post-Permian deformation is unrecorded elsewhere in the Transantarctic Mountains, except possibly in northern Victoria Land, but was extensive in the Ellsworth Mountains of West Antarctica." All of these geologic observations suggest the pivoting of the Antarctic Peninsula about a fulcrum located approximately at Eights Station.

Figure 6 indicates how this may have occurred, probably with oversimplification. There have been attempts to include the bending of continental masses in the continental drift theory as in the proposed opening of the Bay of Biscay (Matthews and Williams, 1968). The bending of structures around island arcs has been suggested and may seem a bit more plausible than the bending of continental structures elsewhere. It is possible that the Antarctic Peninsula was separated from the remainder of the continent by

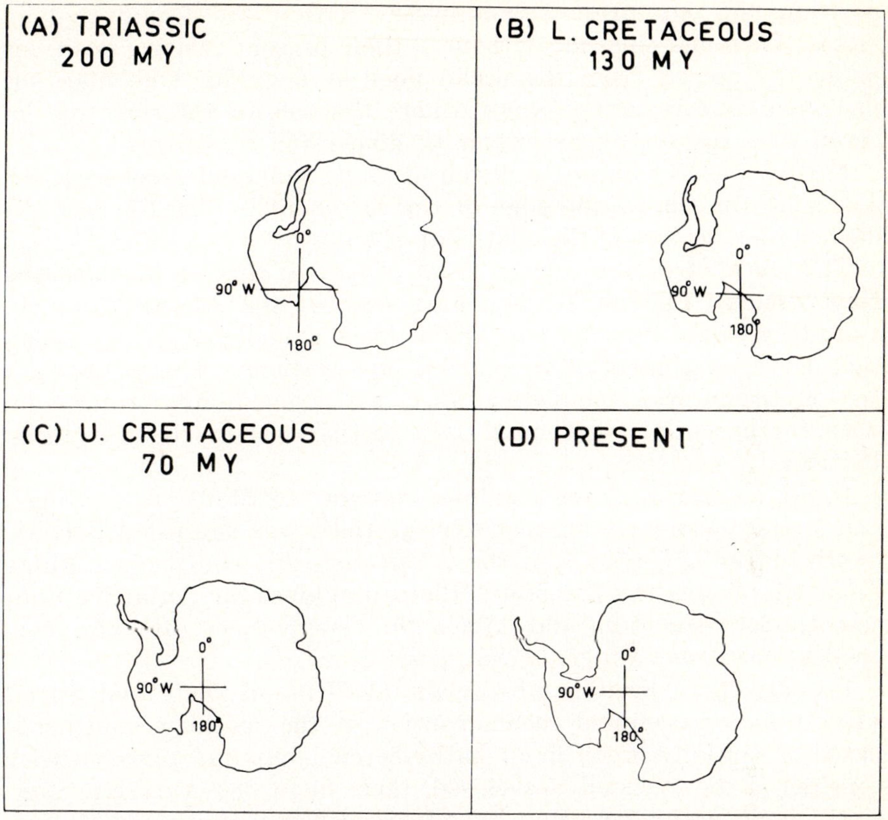

Fig. 6. Drift of the Antarctic Continent accompanied by the opening of the Weddell Sea.

some now extinct axis of spreading or by some set of fracture zones. Until more is known of the geophysics of the ocean floor in the Weddell Sea, the ocean floor off Ellsworth and Marie Byrd Lands, and the Ross Sea, it will not be known if that is a probability.

Since the initial presentation of this paper, Schopf (1969) has independently made a somewhat similar suggestion. He proposed that West Antarctica has been laterally shifted with respect to larger East Antarctica by sea-floor spreading.

SEPARATION OF THE GONDWANALAND CONTINENTS AND THE OPENING OF THE SOUTHERN OCEANS

A display of the sequential positions of the Gondwanaland continents can now be made. One must first determine the relative positions of our present landmasses within the Gondwanaland block. Then one must move them to their present relative positions using the record from the ocean floor as a guide. One may use paleomagnetic results to know where the pole of rotation was located with respect to the swarm of dispersing continents.

Figure 7 (left) shows a sketch of Gondwanaland reconstructed. The solid line shows the edge of the continent in Triassic and the dashed lines sectors of the continent of today.

This reconstruction differs from others in that it includes the New Zealand Plateau (shown here without the Alpine Fault restored), a closed Weddell Sea, and a closed primordial Indian Ocean that is in agreement with marine observations. The primordial Indian Ocean was completely filled with known microcontinents with the exception of a small area to the west of the Kerguelen Plateau.

It can be seen that the Agulhas Plateau, the Madagascar Ridge, and Madagascar were against Africa. India was against Australia. South of India, Ceylon and the Naturaliste Plateau-Broken Ridge followed, placing the Kerguelen Plateau against the Antarctic Continent. Between India and Africa the Chagos-Laccadive and Seychelles-Mascarene Ridges were fused.

Recently both Smith and Hallam (1970) and Dietz and Sproll (1970) have attempted reconstruction of the southern continents based, essentially, upon fit of bathymetric contours. Since neither considered the Weddell Sea closed, their fit of the Antarctic Continent is different from that hypothesized here. Smith and Hallam also have a different fit between India and Australia from that shown here. Those authors did not consider various microcontinents in their reconstruction. On the other hand, Crawford (1969), after a study of the ages of old rocks in India and Australia, positioned India and Australia approximately as shown here. It would seem that the simple fitting of bathymetric contours for continental reconstruction is inadequate for the Indian Ocean.

The fitting of what is now northwest India against the horn of Africa presents problems in every reconstruction. Until more is known of the quasi-continental Somali Basin, it is not possible to make a good fit there.

The pole of rotation is essentially that given by Irving *et al.* (1963). It is not entirely clear whether this reconstruction is in any disagreement with the distribution of tillite deposits from the late Paleozoic. The location of the pole, as shown, places all the Southern Hemisphere continents on one side of the earth.

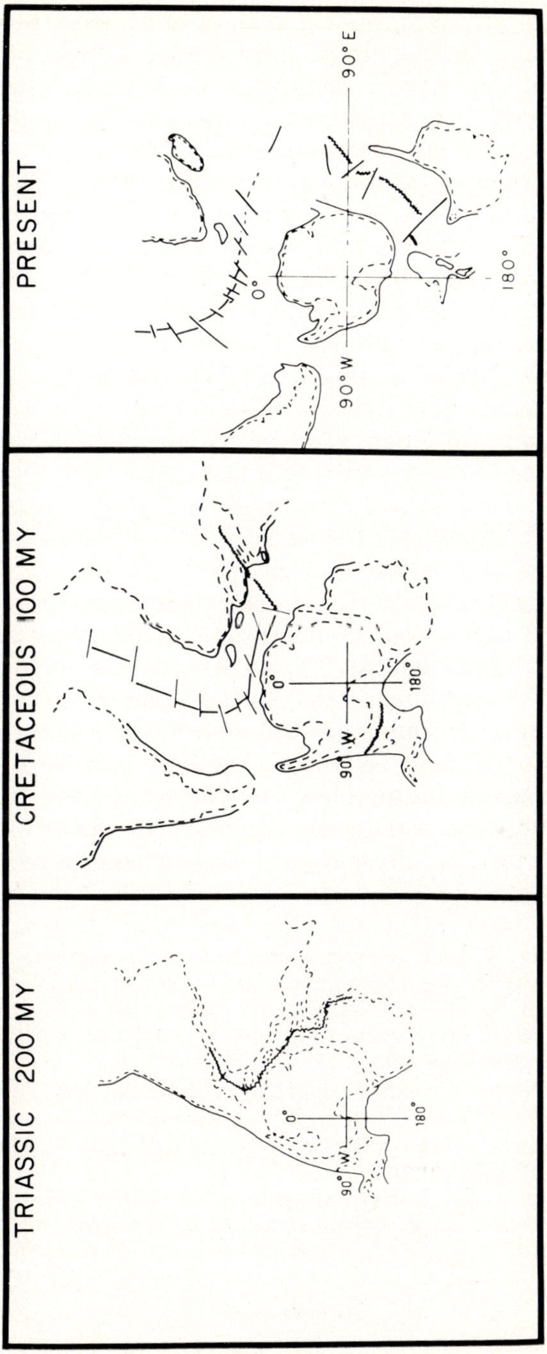

Fig. 7. Drift of southern continents and the opening of the southern oceans since the breakup of Gondwanaland.

The sawtooth line shows the line of first separation with all relative motions being nearly at right angles to that line. In terms of absolute motion Africa remained nearly stationary and the other pieces drifted southeast and southwest away from Africa, with the ridges moving in a similar direction.

Figure 7 (center) shows the relative position of the landmasses about 100 m.y. ago. Canberra was 70°S, the Deccan trap area of India approached 30°S, and South America changed longitude but not latitude. After this time the active spreading ridge shifted from between India and Australia to between India and Africa. The Scotia Arc, and the Prince Edward and Malagasy Fracture Zones could be identified at this stage. The Rodriguez and Diamantina Fracture Zones were probably a single fracture zone extending completely across the then existing ridge. The Naturaliste and Kerguelen Plateaus were still one mass. The split between India and Africa separated the Laccadive-Maldive and Seychelles-Mascarene Ridges. Also a short time later the separation of the New Zealand Plateau from Antarctica occurred.

Figure 7 (right) shows the present configuration after India has disappeared rapidly to the north and Australia, with the Naturaliste-Broken Ridge, separated from Antarctica, with the Kerguelen Plateau. The paleomagnetic pole, or pole of rotation, is also shown. The continents have drifted as a whole (polar wandering) and have separated relative to one another (sea-floor spreading). Under this combined motion New Zealand has moved from a Triassic configuration, where the North Island had the same latitude as South Island, to the present position where South Island is southernmost.

Author's Notes: Much of the data utilized in writing the basic geophysical papers on the marine areas surrounding Antarctica were acquired by the USNS *Eltanin*. National Science Foundation grants were instrumental in the acquisition, reduction, and interpretation of these data.

Office of Naval Research contracts Nonr-266(48) and Nonr-266(88) with Columbia University and contract Nonr-4029(00) with the Woods Hole Oceanographic Institution supported the preparation of this paper.

The comments of A.B. Ford on parts of the paper are appreciated.

This is Woods Hole Oceanographic Institution Contribution No. 2409.

References

Anonymous, 1968. Gondwanaland revisited: New evidence for continental drift. *Proc. Am. Phil. Soc., 112,* No. 5.

Christoffel, D. A., and D. I. Ross, 1970. A fracture zone in the Southwest Pacific Basin south of New Zealand and its implications for sea-floor spreading. *Earth Planetary Sci. Letters, 8:* 125–130.

Crawford, A. R., 1969. India, Ceylon and Pakistan: New age data and comparisons with Australia. *Nature, 223:* 380–382.

Creer, K. M., 1965. A symposium on continental drift, III, paleomagnetic data from the gondwanic continents. *Phil. Trans. Roy. Soc. London, Ser. A, 258:* 27–40.

Dickson, G. O., W. C. Pitman, III, and J. R. Heirtzler, 1968. Magnetic anomalies in the South Atlantic and ocean floor spreading. *J. Geophys. Res., 73:* 2087–2100.

Dietz, R. S., and W. P. Sproll, 1970. Fit between Africa and Antarctica: A continental drift reconstruction. *Science, 167:* 1612–1614.

Evison, F. F., R. E. Ingham, R. H. Orr, and J. H. LeFort, 1960. Thickness of the earth's crust in Antarctica and surrounding oceans. *Geophys. J., 3:* 289–306.

Francis, T. J. G., and R. W. Raitt, 1967. Seismic refraction measurements in the South Indian Ocean. *J. Geophys. Res., 72:* 3015.

Gough, D. I., N. D. Opdyke, and M. W. McElhinny, 1964. The significance of paleomagnetic results from Africa. *J. Geophys. Res., 69:* 2509–2519.

Heezen, B. C., and M. Tharp, 1961. *Physiographic Diagram of the South Atlantic Ocean, the Caribbean Sea, the Scotia Sea and the Eastern Margin of the South Pacific Ocean.* Geol. Soc. Am., Boulder, Colorado.

Heezen, B. C., and M. Tharp, 1964. *Physiographic Diagram of the Indian Ocean.* Geol. Soc. Am., Boulder, Colorado.

Heezen, B. C., and M. Tharp, 1965. Tectonic fabric of the Atlantic and Indian Oceans and continental drift, a symposium on continental drift. *Phil. Trans. Roy. Soc. London, Ser. A, 1088:* 90.

Heirtzler, J. R., 1968. Sea-floor spreading. *Sci. Am., 219:* 60–70.

Heirtzler, J. R., G. O. Dickson, E. M. Herron, W. C. Pitman, III, and X. LePichon, 1968. Marine magnetic anomalies, geomagnetic field reversals, and motions of the ocean floor and continents. *J. Geophys. Res., 73:* 2119–2136.

Herron, E. M., and D. E. Hayes, 1969. A geophysical study of the Chile Ridge. *Earth Planetary Sci. Letters, 6:* 77–83.

Houtz, R., J. Ewing, M. Ewing, and A. G. Lonardi, 1967. Seismic reflection profiles on the New Zealand Plateau. *J. Geophys. Res., 72:* 4713–4729.

Irving, E., 1964. *Paleomagnetism and Its Application to Geological and Geophysical Problems.* J. Wiley and Sons, New York.

Irving, E., 1966. Paleomagnetism of some carboniferous rocks from New South Wales and its relation to geological events. *J. Geophys. Res., 71:* 6025–6051.

Irving, E., W. A. Robertson, and P. M. Scott, 1963. The significance of the paleomagnetic results from mesozoic rocks of Eastern Australia. *J. Geophys. Res., 68:* 2313–2317.

Isaacs, B., J. Oliver, and L. R. Sykes, 1968. Seismology and the new global tectonics. *J. Geophys. Res., 73:* 5855–5899.

LeMasurier, W. E., and F. A. Wade, 1968. Fumarolic activity in Marie Byrd Land, Antarctica. *Science, 162:* 352.

LePichon, X., and J. R. Heirtzler, 1968. Magnetic anomalies in the Indian Ocean and sea-floor spreading. *J. Geophys. Res., 73:* 2101–2117.

Matthews, D. H., and C. A. Williams, 1968. Linear magnetic anomalies in the Bay of Biscay: A qualitative interpretation. *Earth Planetary Sci. Letters, 4:* 315.

McElhinny, M. W., 1967. The paleomagnetism of the southern continents—a survey and analysis. *Int. Un. of Geol. Sciences UNESCO Symposium on Continental Drift.* Montevideo.

McElhinny, M. W., 1968. Northward drift of India—examination of recent paleomagnetic results. *Nature, 217:* 342–344.

McElhinny, M. W., J. C. Briden, and D. L. Jones, 1968. Geological and geophysical implications of paleomagnetic results from Africa. *Rev. Geophys., 6:* 201–258.

Miller, J. A., and J. D. Mudie, 1961. Potassium-argon age determinations on granite from the island of Mahé in the Seychelles Archipelago. *Nature, 194:* 1174–1175.

Officer, C. B., 1955. Southwest Pacific crustal structure. *Trans. Am. Geophys. Union, 36:* 449–459.

Phinney, R. A., 1969. *History of the Earth's Crust.* Princeton Univ. Press, Princeton, N. J.

Pitman, W. C., III, E. M. Herron, and J. R. Heirtzler, 1968. Magnetic anomalies in the Pacific and sea-floor spreading. *J. Geophys. Res., 73:* 2069–2085.

Press, F., and G. Dewart, 1959. Extent of the Antarctic Continent. *Science, 129:* 462.

Schopf, J. M., 1969. Ellsworth Mountains: Position in West Antarctica due to sea-floor spreading. *Science, 164:* 63–66.

Smith, A. G., and A. Hallam, 1970. The fit of the southern continents. *Nature, 225:* 139–144.

Sykes, L. R., 1963. Seismicity of the South Pacific Ocean. *J. Geophys. Res., 68:* 5999–6006.

Sykes, L. R., 1967. Mechanism of earthquakes and nature of faulting on the mid-oceanic ridge. *J. Geophys. Res., 72:* 2131–2153.

Wade, A. F., 1967. Geology of the Marie Byrd Land coastal sector of West Antarctica. *Antarctic J. U.S., 2:* 93–94.

Wasilewski, P. J., 1967. Magnetic signature of rocks from Ellsworth Land. *Antarctic J. U.S., 2:* 179–181.

Williams, P. L., and A. B. Ford, 1968. Pensacola Mountains Project. *Antarctic J. U.S., 3:* 181.

Zhivago, A. V., 1962. Outlines of Southern Ocean geomorphology. In *Antarctic Research,* edited by H. Wexler, M. J. Rubin, and J. E. Caskey; pp. 74–80. *Geophys. Monograph Ser., No. 7.* Am. Geophys. Union, Washington, D.C.

Antarctic Fossil Vertebrates and Gondwanaland

EDWIN H. COLBERT

Museum of Northern Arizona, Flagstaff

One of the most crucial subjects in the study of geology today is that of the past relationships of continents. The possibility of continental drift has engaged the minds of geologists, paleontologists, and biologists with increasing intensity during the past decade, especially as the result of recent evidence. Drift, once almost summarily dismissed by most American geologists (although greatly favored by many European authorities and particularly by geologists in the Southern Hemisphere, has found increasing support during these past few years as the result of evidence that would seem more and more to tip the scales in favor of the theory.

The evidence that has been brought together has come from a wide range of scientific disciplines. Among the accumulation of facts that would seem to point toward drift, the distributions of certain fossil vertebrates are of particular importance. These patterns of distribution can be studied without the accompaniment of any basic assumptions; they are the fixed points around which interpretations for their existence can be developed.

Of particular significance as evidence concerning the past geographical relationships of ancient continents are the distributions of those vertebrates that were confined to the continental masses. Among these are the larger terrestrial vertebrates: the remains of animals that were definitely wedded to the earth, that lived on the ground, and that moved about over the ground. Such animals could not be carried across considerable distances by high winds and storms as can insects or birds or the seeds of plants. They could not leap barriers of their own volition as can flying animals. They could not drift as waifs on floating logs as can small animals. They could not swim across wide stretches of the sea as can aquatic animals. In short, the wide distribution of such animals can mean only that at one time they were enabled to move from one continental area to another over dry land.

In addition there are the widely distributed freshwater fishes. These fishes, particularly the ones that Myers has designated as *primary* or *obligatory* freshwater types, because of their intolerance to salt water are contained perhaps even more by marine barriers than are the land-living vertebrates. As Myers (1967) has said, "Their dispersal patterns are thus far more conservative than those of other vertebrates." And what applies to modern freshwater fishes, based upon our knowledge of their physiological limitations, must apply to fossil forms when these latter are known to have lived in freshwater environments.

Any theory of past continental relationships that ignores these facts and is contrary to the evidence of the fossils must be suspect.

THE POSITION OF ANTARCTICA

The Antarctic Continent today is an isolated landmass, separated from its nearest continental neighbors by great expanses of open ocean. If Antarctica, now so isolated from other continents, was once a part of Gondwanaland, then either it must have been connected to at least one or possibly more of the southern continental blocks by long land bridges, or it must have had a position of contiguity to one or more of them from which, during millions of years of geologic times, it has subsequently drifted.

There now appears to be convincing evidence for a close geologic relationship between East Antarctica and other southern continents. Such evidence includes the geographical fit between a part of the East Antarctic coastline with the southeastern border of Africa and the southern border of Australia (Smith and Hallam, 1970; Dietz and Sproll, 1970) ; the alignment of the Precambrian—early Paleozoic geosyncline of Antarctica with the Adelaide geosyncline of eastern Australia (Hurley, 1968) ; the late Paleozoic and early Mesozoic stratigraphic sequences in Antarctica and other southern continents, characterized by basal Carboniferous and Permian tillites and terminal post-Triassic volcanic flows and intrusions; the accordance of geomagnetic measurements; and the widely spread occurrences of the Carboniferous to Triassic plant *Glossopteris* and of the Triassic plant, *Dicroidium*.

But what is the evidence of the fossil vertebrates?

ANTARCTIC MESOZOIC VERTEBRATES

Until quite recently there was no record of continental vertebrates of any significant geologic age in the sediments of Antarctica. Then some discoveries were made in rather quick succession, indicating the presence of Mesozoic vertebrates in East Antarctica. The first of these discoveries was made in the field season of 1966–1967 when some fragmentary remains of fishes were found in thin sedimentary interbeds within the Kirkpatrick Basalts near the summit of Mount Kirkpatrick, and on Blizzard Heights, about 26 miles or 42 kilometers to the southwest of Mount Kirkpatrick. Then, during the field season of 1967–1968, a small fragment of an amphibian lower jaw was found in the Fremouw Formation at Graphite Peak, about 66 miles or 106 kilometers southeast of Mount Kirkpatrick. Finally, as a result of an intensive field program carried on during the 1969–1970 season, a considerable collection of fossil amphibians and reptiles was secured from the Fremouw Formation at Coalsack Bluff, a nunatak about 85 miles or 136 kilometers northwest of Graphite Peak*. The fishes are of Jurassic age; the amphibians and reptiles can be placed within the early phases of the Triassic (Fig. 1).

To consider first the fishes, the following remarks were written by Dr. David Elliot, who made the discovery, in a letter to Dr. Bobb Schaeffer of the American Museum of Natural History.

> These samples come from a thin sedimentary interbed within the Kirkpatrick Basalts near the northwest summit of Mount Kirkpatrick at an elevation of approximately 13,900 feet. This unit is 1–2 feet thick. It is approximately 1,140 feet above the base of the lava pile and about 1,620 feet above the top of the sandstones of the Triassic

---

* Since this contribution went to press a field party working at McGregor Glacier, about 150 miles to the southeast of Coalsack Bluff, made a collection of Fremouw tetrapods that augments and expands the original collection from Coalsack Bluff. The new materials include, in addition to amphibians, *Lystrosaurus* and thecodonts, articulated skeletons of the cynodont therapsid, *Thrinaxodon,* good fossils of the cotylosaur, *Procolophon,* and rather abundant remains of prolacertid eosuchians. These are all elements characteristic of the South African *Lystrosaurus* zone. Thus the Antarctic-African connection in early Triassic time is immeasurably strengthened on the basis of these new fossil discoveries. This point should be kept in mind when reading the text of the present paper.

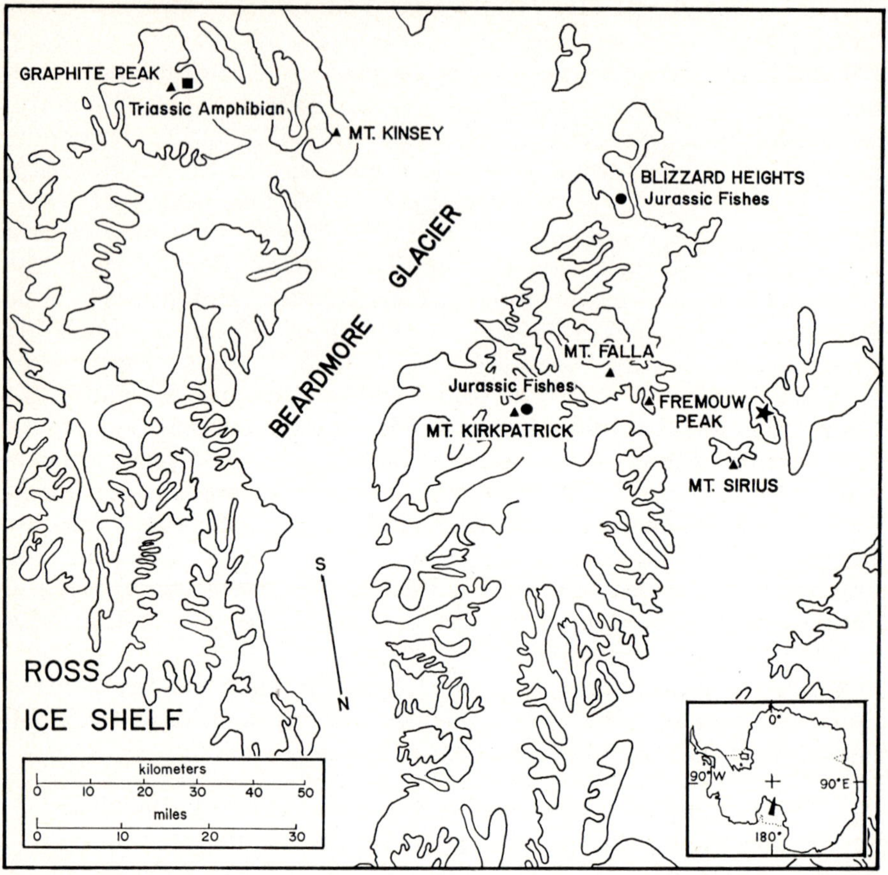

Fig. 1. A portion of the Beardmore Glacier area showing the localities for the Triassic labyrinthodont amphibian found at Graphite Peak, the Triassic amphibians and reptiles collected at Coalsack Bluff, and the Jurassic fishes found at Mount Kirkpatrick and at Blizzard Heights. The star (center, right) indicates the location of Coalsack Bluff.

Falla Formation. The Triassic age of the Falla Formation was proved last year by the discovery of elements of the *Dicroidium* flora in several beds, and the Jurassic age of the basalts confirmed by the conchostracans which have been identified by Dr. Paul Tasch of Wichita State University. Other sedimentary interbeds have more and better preserved conchostracans and ostracods, and all the interbeds found are at about the same stratigraphic level—as far as can be determined in a succession of basalts.

In a subsequent letter to Schaeffer, Elliot described the other locality at which fishes were found. This site, southwest of Mount Kirkpatrick, and about 26 miles distant,

> . . . crops out at an elevation of 10,425 feet, approximately 215 feet below the summit and 1,415 feet above the base of the lavas, though a fault with a throw of about 150 feet gives a true stratigraphic thickness of about 1,780 feet. At this section no other sedimentary interbeds occur and the lavas probably rest directly on the Prebble Formation, a volcanic mudflow, agglomerate and tuff unit which separates the Kirkpatrick Basalts and the Falla Formation.

In a recent letter Elliot stated that, "The age of the basalts (containing the interbeds in which are preserved the fossil fishes) has been confirmed by K/A age determinations."

Since these discoveries were made, additional fishes have been recovered from the Jurassic interbeds in the Beardmore region (Fig. 2). The materials are presently being studied by Dr. Schaeffer, and a published account of their morphological characters and their taxonomic relationships will appear in the near future.

Although the analysis and identification of these fishes has not as yet been published, it can be concluded with good reason that they were probably freshwater types. This judgment is based upon several facts. It has already been pointed out that these sediments are limited interbeds within the basalts, an indication that they were deposited in small ponds or lakes, rather than in extended marine environments. None of these deposits, according to Dr. Elliot, could be traced laterally for more than about a hundred yards. Furthermore, the sediments are frequently finely laminated, such lamination apparently caused by secondary calcite replacement of the original siliceous rock. Although there is much indication of secondary alteration, nevertheless the basic evidence of these sediments as deposits in small basins of limited extent remains clear. They contain numerous conchostracans and plant remains, also indications of a freshwater environment. Finally, the basalts do not show any evidence of eruption into water, as might be expected if they were associated with extensive marine sediments.

A preliminary description of the amphibian bone from Graphite Peak has recently appeared, from which the following account of the location and stratigraphic relationships of the fossil may be quoted (Barrett *et al.*, 1968).

Fig. 2. A fragment of rock from Blizzard Heights, containing bones and scales of fossil fishes. The upper photograph was made under daylight; the lower under ultraviolet light. The circular objects in the lower photograph, enclosed in the rectangle, and enlarged to the right, are vertebral centra, in end views. The smallest divisions of the scale are each .5 mm.

The bone was found at 85°3.3′S and 172°19′E, at an elevation of 2780 m, about three quarters of the way up a west-facing ridge 4 km west of Graphite Peak. Stratigraphically, the bone comes from 76 m above the base of the new unit that will be named the Fremouw Formation, a unit 600 m thick consisting mainly of sandstone and greenish grey mudstone, which disconformably overlies the Buckley Formation and underlies the Falla Formation in the Beardmore area.

The precise location of the find was 1 m below the top of a coarse-grained, quartzose sandstone unit, 16 m thick, in an extensive pebbly lens generally less than 1 m thick. The sandstone unit dips at 23° to the south east and forms the higher of two hogbacks on the ridge. The bone-bearing pebbly lens is exposed over about 20 m^2; this and other pebbly strata within the sandstone were searched for about three hours, and although no vertebrate remains were found, the internal mold of a gastropod was discovered at the upper contact of the unit.

The Fremouw Formation, which is the lower of two Triassic formations in the Beardmore Glacier region, is dated in part by the presence within it of the very characteristic Triassic plant, *Dicroidium,* which is found in the uppermost part of the formation. Because the Fremouw Formation, containing *Dicroidium,* immediately succeeds the Buckley Formation, which contains *Glossopteris* but not *Dicroidium,* one may assume that the basal portion of the Fremouw Formation may represent an early stage of Triassic history in Antarctica. Therefore the fossil amphibian which occurs in the Fremouw Formation might be expected to show affinities with lower Triassic amphibians from other continents (Fig. 3).

Unfortunately this single fossil is so fragmentary that it reveals little definite evidence as to what its relationships on lower taxonomic levels might be. That it is a labyrinthodont is obvious. As shown in the preliminary description of the fossil, this fragment of bone, some 7 cm in length, shows the rugose external surface (here displayed on the outer surface of the surangular bone) so characteristic of the labyrinthodont skull and mandibular elements. This is the back portion of a left ramus with the articular region and a part of the retroarticular process preserved. Some of the grooves of the lateral line system, so typical of the labyrinthodonts,

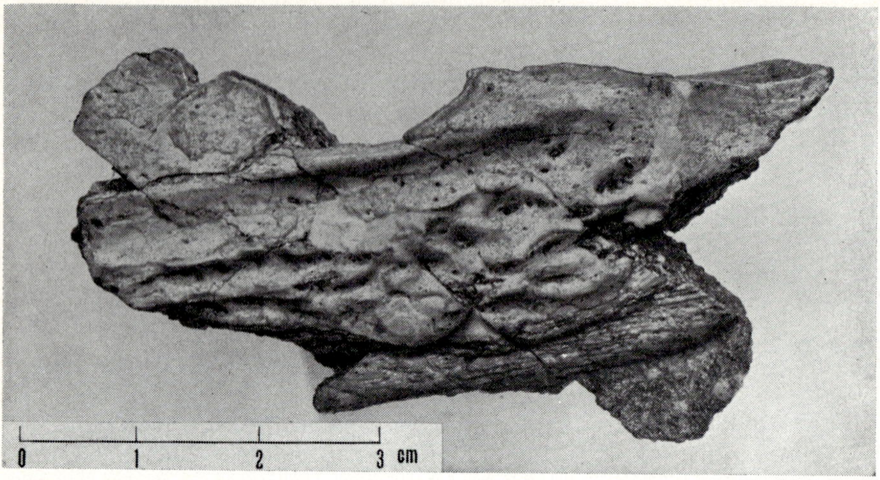

Fig. 3. External view of a fragment from the posterior portion of the left mandibular ramus of a labyrinthodont amphibian found at Graphite Peak (American Museum of Natural History, New York, No. 9301). This figure shows the characteristic rugose sculpture on the external surface of the surangular bone. The course of the sulcus mandibularis can be distinguished, running from the high retroarticular process on the right, down and to the left to the lower border of the bone. Branching to the left from it are the sulcus accessorius just beneath the strong horizontal ridge that borders the lower rim of the articular surface, and the sulcus oralis below and parallel to it. On the lower right edge of the bone is some adhering matrix.

may be discerned: namely the sulcus mandibularis and sulcus oralis. On the inner side of the bone a portion of the adductor fossa is preserved, containing two prominent surangular foramina. Also preserved is the foramen chorda tympani, occupying a position along the junction between the prearticular and surangular bones. That portion of the retroarticular process which is preserved shows that the complete process must have been relatively large, with a horizontal upper border (See Romer, 1947; Watson, 1962).

These are the clues with which one has to work, and they are admittedly meager (Fig. 4).

Fortunately the amphibian jaw fragment found at Graphite Peak, which was little more than an indication of things to come, has been augmented by the collection of amphibian and reptilian bones made at Coalsack Bluff in the season of 1969–1970 (Elliot *et al.*, 1970). This collection, consisting of at least 450 specimens, has not been studied in detail, but as a result of preliminary examinations it is possible to say that it contains labyrinthodont am-

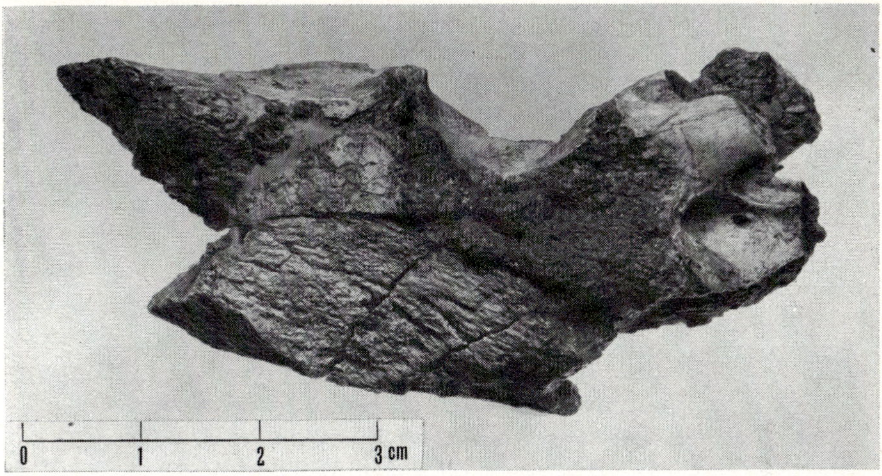

Fig. 4. The same bone fragment as shown in Figure 3, in internal view. The articular surface is plainly visible, with the large retroarticular surface to the left. The foramen chorda tympani is visible near the junction on the left side of the two broken edges. To the right is the posterior portion of the adductor fossa, with two prominent surangular foramina.

phibians, and therapsid and thecodont reptiles. And among the therapsids, the genus *Lystrosaurus* has been identified, upon the basis of numerous bones, beyond any shadow of doubt (Colbert, 1970). Moreover, the specimens of *Lystrosaurus* from Coalsack Bluff would seem to be virtually identical with *Lystrosaurus murrayi,* a form especially characteristic of the Lower Triassic *Lystrosaurus* Zone of South Africa. Thus a close paleontological link has been established between Antarctica and southern Africa—a link based upon a reptilian genus that clearly inhabited land areas within these now-separated continents, and that undoubtedly migrated from one region to another over terrestrial routes. Moreover, the association of labyrinthodont amphibians and thecodont reptiles with *Lystrosaurus* in Antarctica reflects the similar associations that are so typical of the *Lystrosaurus* fauna as it occurs, not only in the Beaufort beds of southern Africa, but also in the Panchet beds of India, as well as in the Tunghungshan Formation of western China (Figs. 5 and 6). In addition, the amphibian materials now known from Antarctica would seem to show (among other resemblances) definite affinities with the Lower Triassic amphibian, *Deltasaurus,* from Australia (John Cosgriff, personal communication).

Consequently, even before there has been the time and oppor-

Fig. 5. Right maxilla of *Lystrosaurus,* contained in matrix, from Coalsack Bluff (American Museum of Natural History, New York, No. 9302). Note the tip of the erupting tooth.

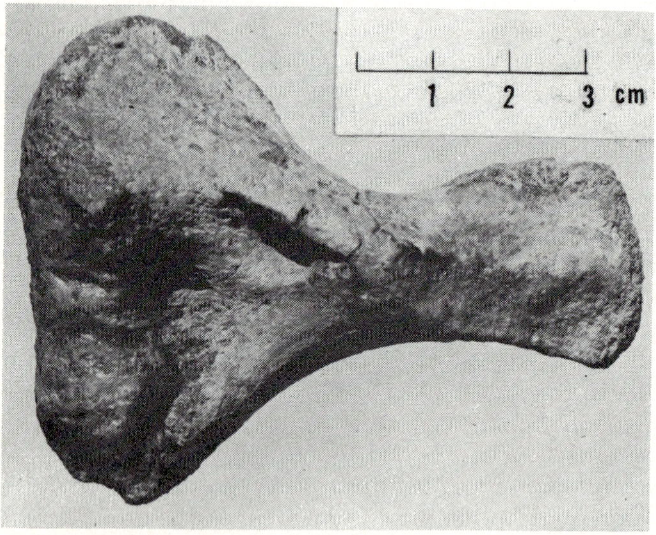

Fig. 6. Distal portion of left humerus of *Lystrosaurus* from Coalsack Bluff (American Museum of Natural History, New York, No. 9304). The entepicondylar foramen is visible, above the distal articular surface.

tunity to study the antarctic fossils in detail, it is abundantly clear that an extraordinarily close paleontological link exists between Lower Triassic Antarctica and Africa. And this link extends beyond these confines to include India, adjacent portions of Asia, and Australia.

On the basis of such evidence, still in the preliminary stages of its interpretation, but nonetheless clear as to its implications, we may base our conclusions as to the significance of Mesozoic vertebrates, particularly tetrapods, that have been found in Antarctica.

TRIASSIC TETRAPODS AND SOUTHERN CONTINENTS

There are four principal Gondwana areas (exclusive of Antarctica) in which tetrapod faunas of early Triassic age are to be found. These are South Africa, and contiguous regions in southern Africa, where abundant assemblages of reptiles and amphibians occur in the underlying *Lystrosaurus* and overlying *Cynognathus* zones of the Middle and Upper Beaufort beds in the Karroo sequence (Haughton and Brink, 1954; Haughton, 1963; Kitching, 1968); peninsular India, where the Panchet and the Yerrapalli Formations yield tetrapods extraordinarily close to those of the African sequence (Robinson, 1967); northwestern Argentina, where reptiles recently discovered in the Puesto Viejo Formation show close similarities to the reptiles in the *Cynognathus* zone (Bonaparte, 1967); and Australia, where in the western part of the continent, amphibians from the Blina shales of the Erskine Range may be related to some of the amphibians in the *Cynognathus* zone, and where, in New South Wales and Tasmania, amphibians indicate further extensions of such relationships (Cosgriff, 1965).

The Lower Triassic tetrapods of South Africa occur in extraordinary abundance, and afford a rather comprehensive and varied view of what the land-living vertebrates of Gondwanaland were like during that particular phase of geologic history. Here is a great array of reptiles, and to a lesser degree of amphibians, that lived across broad continental areas interspersed with numerous lakes and frequent streams. The amphibians are labyrinthodonts of various kinds. The reptiles are overwhelmingly dominated by the dicynodonts, those strange, heavy-bodied, beaked, and essentially toothless reptiles that apparently were herbivores, feeding upon the abundant vegetation in their environment. In addition there are varied carnivorous reptiles, for the most part mammal-like theriodonts. The amphibians and the dicynodonts formed the broad base of a food pyramid surmounted by an apex of widely adapted carnivorous reptiles. It was a viable ecological relationship, for it persisted throughout early Triassic history.

Lystrosaurus, which gives its name to the earliest South African Triassic horizon, was probably a freshwater dicynodont, inhabiting streams and lakes in company with various amphibians. In the succeeding horizon, the *Cynognathus* zone, is the dicynodont *Kannemeyeria,* a large, heavy, land-living reptile. Here also is found *Cynognathus,* perhaps the most characteristic mammal-like carnivore of this zone, a medium to rather large, aggressive, "wolf-like" predatory reptile.

Some of these very same reptiles are found in peninsular India, where *Lystrosaurus,* virtually identical with the African prototype, occurs in the Panchet Formation, and a kannemeyerian, of the genus *Wadiasaurus,* is typical of the Yerrapalli Formation. Obviously there was a close connection between Africa and India during early Triassic time.

Crossing to South America, it is especially revealing to learn, as a result of very recent work by Bonaparte, that in the Puesto Viejo Formation there are, among other things, *Kannemeyeria* and *Cynognathus,* closely allied to representatives of these same genera in the *Cynognathus* zone of South Africa, while another cynodont genus, *Pascualgnathus,* characterized by broad molar teeth, is obviously closely related to the *Cynognathus* zone broad-toothed form *Diademodon.* Thus an early Triassic connection between Africa and South America becomes apparent.

Coming now to Australia, we see as a result of recent work by Cosgriff that the Blina shales near the northwestern coast of today's island continent contain fossil trematosaurian amphibians which have been placed in a new genus, *Deltasaurus,* that shows close relationships to the genus *Rhytidosteus* of the South African *Cynognathus* zone. (The Blina sediments evidently represent an aquatic facies in which reptiles as yet have not been found; hence the comparison between amphibians.) Therefore a connection between Australia and Africa would seem to be indicated. (*Deltasaurus* is also obviously related to the trematosaur *Peltostega* found in the lower Triassic sediments of Spitzbergen.)

These close faunal relationships obliquely northeast and southwest between southern Africa and India, and east and west between Africa, South America, and Australia certainly indicate a free interchange of land-living vertebrates during early Triassic history. This fact would seem to reinforce the recent physical evidence (geophysical, geomagnetic, paleogeographic, and structural) for an early Mesozoic Gondwana continent, large blocks of which later were to fragment and drift apart. Yet the evidence of the fossils up to now has not been absolute. One can always invoke passages back and forth the "long way around" between continental blocks occupying approximately their present positions; from Africa through Asia Minor to India, on to the southeast through the Indies (then supposedly a solid landmass) to Australia, and on to the northeast across a Bering connection, down through North America, through an isthmus and into South America. It can be objected that this is a long and tortuous route but such an objection cannot be advanced as a strong counterargument. Migrations of active, land-living vertebrates across half the circumference of the globe have happened time and again, and in relatively short spans of time. Witness the spread of the Western Hemisphere cougar, *Felis concolor,* from northern Canada to the tip of South America within the limits of Pleistocene history.

A more telling counterargument is found in the close taxonomic relationships that now are apparent between early Triassic reptiles in South Africa and South America as exemplified by the genera *Kannemeyeria* and *Cynognathus,* present in both continents, as well as by *Pascualgnathus* in South America and its close counterpart, *Diademodon,* in South Africa. There is a singular absence of these forms in northeast Asia and North America along the migration route that they would have had to follow.

ANTARCTIC TETRAPODS AND GONDWANALAND

Now, however, we have at hand labyrinthodont amphibians, *Lystrosaurus,* and other reptiles from Triassic sediments of Antarctica. How does this bear upon Gondwanaland and the distribution of early Triassic tetrapods?

The chances against the migration of early Triassic labyrinthodonts and reptiles into Antarctica by swimming across a wide stretch of open ocean would appear to be beyond the realm of probability. Modern amphibians are characteristically intolerant to salt water, and it would seem likely that the same was true for amphibians of past geologic ages. It is true that certain species within one group of labyrinthodonts, the trematosaurs, have been found in Spitzbergen in typical marine deposits of early Triassic age, thus indicating that perhaps these particular labyrinthodonts had departed from the amphibian norm. But there are some niggling questions concerning these supposed marine labyrinthodonts. Were the animals truly marine, or were their remains washed into the oceans from nearby land? If marine, did they venture into the open ocean, or did they stay close to continental margins as do modern sea lions? Even though the adults may have lived in the sea, they certainly must have entered fresh waters to breed, and thus were in this way tied to the land. The antarctic fossils, however, are found in very characteristic freshwater sediments, and so the chances are strong that the amphibians were the usual continental-type labyrinthodonts.

The reptiles of Gondwana aspect (*Lystrosaurus* and others) found in the Triassic sediments of Antarctica indicate that the former existence of a connection whereby these animals invaded the polar continent is beyond question. The occurrence of closely related amphibians and reptiles in Africa, South America, and Australia does not absolutely prove the theory, although it is in strong agreement with the theory of drift. There were always the "long way around" migrations to explain the distribution of these tetrapods. But there was no "long way around" to Antarctica; tetrapods must have reached the continent, either by way of a land bridge, or at a time when the Antarctic was an integral portion of Gondwanaland.

The only possibility of a land bridge upon the basis of present evidence would seem to be along the Scotia Arc. Recent work on mid-ocean ridges and sea-floor spreading indicates that the Scotia Arc is at its oldest of early Cenozoic age. This is shown, for example, by the presence in South Georgia of granitic intrusions cutting Aptian sediments, thus indicating that the present position of the island based upon the data of sea-floor spreading is a post-intrusion movement. Such an event would have started at its earliest in late Cretaceous time (Data furnished by Elliot). All of which indicates that there would seem to have been no possible land connection between Antarctica and South America during the Mesozoic era. Therefore a direct early Triassic ligation between Antarctica and Africa would appear to afford the most plausible avenue for the entrance of early Mesozoic tetrapods into the south polar continent. A joining of the eastern border of Antarctica, from the Ross Sea to about the ninetieth meridian east, to the Great Australian Bight, and in turn of the northwestern border of Australia to the eastern margin of peninsular India, the western border of the latter being contiguous with the eastern margin of Africa as shown in the Hurley reconstruction of 1968, would provide broad corridors for the movement of early Triassic tetrapods from a central Gondwana area of evolution into an outlying antarctic region of settlement (Hurley, 1968). An alternative reconstruction, involving the same relationships between Antarctica and Australia, but with this whole conjoined landmass rotated in such a way as to link Antarctica with the southeastern border of Africa, thereby satisfying Du Toit's concept of the Samfrau Geosyncline, would likewise provide the necessary broad corridors for the invasion of Antarctica by Triassic tetrapods. This latter reconstruction has been strengthened within the past year as a result of computerized studies of the fit between the southeastern border of the African block and the Weddell Sea region of Antarctica (Fig. 7) (Smith and Hallam, 1970; Dietz and Sproll, 1970).

With Antarctica revealing early Triassic tetrapods, the case for a Gondwana continent is immeasurably strengthened. There is no point in thinking of Antarctica joined to a southern landmass, as would seem to be necessary to provide it with Triassic tetrapods, without having the other southern continents also participate in the great supercontinental Gondwana block.

CONCLUSIONS

The discoveries of Jurassic fishes and of Triassic amphibians and reptiles in the Beardmore Glacier region of the Transantarctic Mountains open new vistas in our understanding of the Mesozoic history of the Southern Hemisphere. These fossils point very strongly to the ligation of Antarctica with the Gondwanaland block at the beginning of Mesozoic history, and reinforce the growing evidence of early Triassic land-living vertebrates, to show that at that time Antarctica and Africa were contiguous, as were Africa and South America, while India, if not contiguous with South Africa, was at least connected to it by a broad, continental migration route. These antarctic fossils offer some of the strongest evidence as yet obtained to indicate the probability, if not the absolute proof, of the existence of a late Paleozoic-early Mesozoic Gondwanaland—a southern continent that subsequently rifted, its separate parts drifting away from each other during the course of late Mesozoic and Cenozoic history to form the Southern Hemisphere continents (and peninsular India) as they exist today.

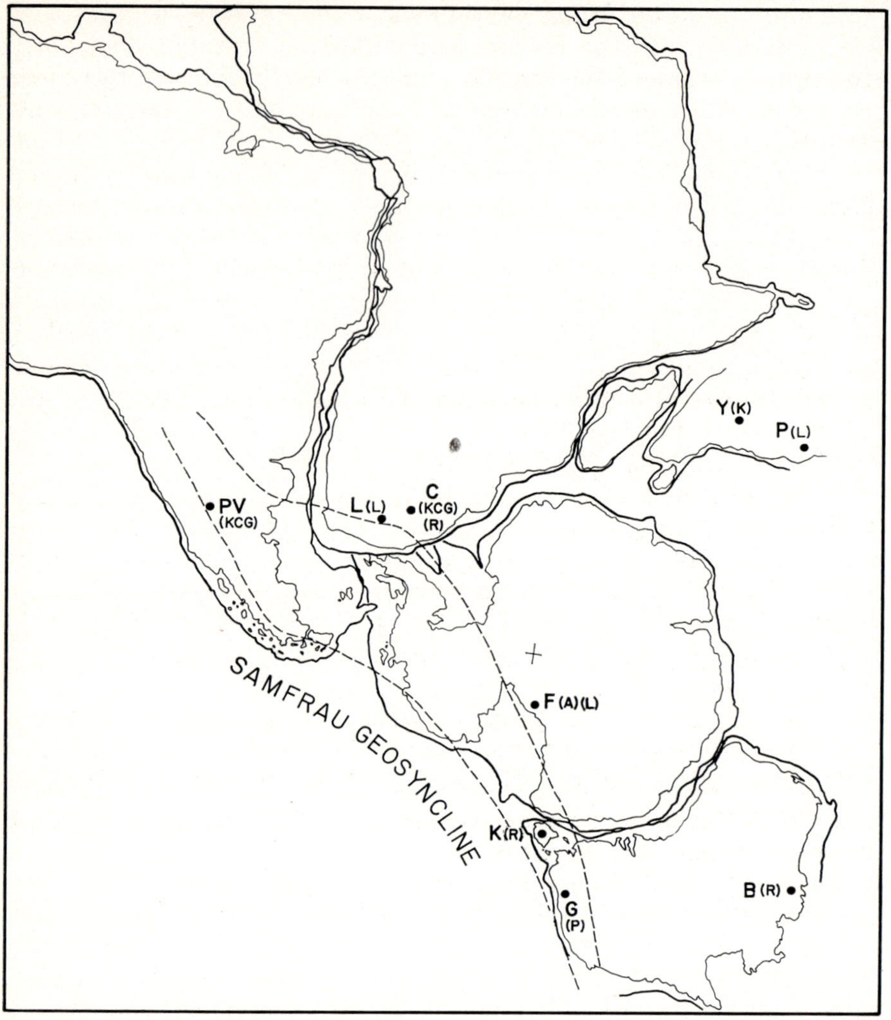

Fig. 7. A portion of Gondwanaland, following the Du Toit reconstruction, with the Samfrau orogenic belt as defined by Halpern, based upon Du Toit's Samfrau Geosyncline, indicated by dashed lines. This shows the relationships of various localities where Lower Triassic tetrapods have been found, when the continents are so reassembled.

Antarctica. F: Fremouw Formation with labyrinthodont amphibians (A), therapsid reptiles including *Lystrosaurus* (L) and other reptiles.

Australia. K: Knocklofty Formation with rhytidosteid labyrinthodont (R). G: Gosford Formation with *Parotosaurus* (P). B: Blina Formation with rhytidosteid labyrinthodont, *Deltasaurus* (R).

References

Barrett, P. J., R. J. Baillie, and E. H. Colbert, 1968. Triassic amphibian from Antarctica. *Science, 161:* 460–462.

Bonaparte, J. F., 1967. New vertebrate evidence for a southern transatlantic connection during the Lower or Middle Triassic. *Palaeontology, 10:* 554–563.

Colbert, E. H., 1970. The fossil tetrapods of Coalsack Bluff. *Antarctic J. U. S., 5:* 57–61.

Cosgriff, J. W., 1965. A new genus of temnospondyli from the Triassic of Western Australia. *J. Roy. Soc. Western Australia, 48:* 65–90.

Dietz, R. S. and W. P. Sproll, 1970. Fit between Africa and Antarctica: a continental drift reconstruction. *Science, 167:* 1612–1614.

Elliot, D. H., E. H. Colbert, W. J. Breed, J. A. Jensen and J. S. Powell, 1970. Triassic tetrapods from Antarctica: Evidence for continental drift. *Science, 169* (3951): 1197–1201.

Haughton, S. H. and A. S. Brink, 1954. A bibliographical list of Reptilia from the Karroo beds of Africa. *Pal. Africana, 2:* 1–187.

Haughton, S. H., 1963. Note on the distribution of fossil Reptilia of Karroo age. *Pal. Africana, 8:* 1–11.

Hurley, P. M., 1968. The confirmation of continental drift. *Sci. Am., 218:* 52–64.

Kitching, J. W., 1968. On the *Lystrosaurus* zone and its fauna with special reference to some immature Lystrosauridae. *Pal. Africana, 11:* 61–76.

Myers, G. S., 1967. Zoogeographical evidence of the age of the South Atlantic Ocean. *Studies in Tropical Oceanography, Miami, No. 5:* 614–621.

Robinson, P. L., 1967. The Indian Gondwana formations—a review. *First Symp. Gondwana Stratigr., Buenos Aires;* pp. 202–268.

Romer, A. S., 1947. Review of the labyrinthodontia. *Bull. Museum Comparative Zool., Harvard College, 99:* 1–368.

Smith, A. G. and A. Hallam, 1970. The fit of the southern continents. *Nature, 225:* 139–144.

Watson, D. M. S., 1962. The evolution of the labyrinthodonts. *Phil. Trans. Roy. Soc. London, Ser. B, No. 723, 245:* 219–265.

Fig. 7. Continued.

Peninsular India. P: Panchet Formation with *Lystrosaurus* (L). Y: Yerrapalli Formation with *Kannemeyerian* (K).

South Africa. L: *Lystrosaurus* zone of Middle Beaufort beds, with *Lystrosaurus* (L). C: *Cynognathus* zone of Upper Beaufort beds with *Rhytidosteus* (R), *Kannemeyeria* (K), *Cynognathus* (C), and broad-toothed cynodont, *Diademodon* (G).

South America. PV: Puesto Viejo Formation with *Kannemeyeria* (K), *Cynognathus* (C), and broad-toothed cynodont, *Pascualgnathus* (G).

Invertebrate Fossil Record and Continental Drift

PAUL TASCH

Department of Geology, Wichita State University, Wichita, Kansas

Cumulative data on Gondwanaland fossil invertebrates now permit reconstruction of some faunal distribution patterns, intercontinental migratory routes, paleosalinities, as well as other analyses. Such information importantly supplements the vertebrate fossil record and contributes an independent paleobiological evaluation of purely physical interpretations of continental displacement.

The fossil records of antarctic invertebrates have been extended during the past five years, particularly because of the collections from the Cambrian (Webers, 1970), Devonian (Boucot *et al.*, 1967; Doumani *et al.*, 1965; White, 1968), Permian (Carpenter, 1969; Doumani and Tasch, 1965; Plumstead, 1964; Tasch, 1968, 1969; Tasch and Gafford, 1968; Tasch and Riek, 1969), Jurassic (Carpenter, 1969; Elliot and Tasch, 1967; Quilty, 1970; Stevens, 1967; Williams, 1970), and Cretaceous (Taylor, 1970; Thomson, 1970).

Somewhat older data on Mesozoic fossils from West Antarctica support the newer findings (Ball, 1960; Behrendt and Laudon, 1964; Cox, 1953; Howarth, 1958; Zeuner, 1959). All or portions of these data can be interpreted to support the theory of continental drift. Observations that support the hypothesis of continental proximity have been the result of investigations of living and fossil biotas of the Southern Hemisphere (e.g., Adie, 1952; Bond, 1955; Darlington, 1965; Evans, 1958a; Haughton, 1924; Krömmelbein, 1966; Riek, 1962; Tillyard, 1917, 1922; Zeuner, 1959, 1960).

The most prominent fossil invertebrates in pertinent antarctic collections are brachiopods (articulates and inarticulates), mollusks (pelecypods and cephalopods), and arthropods (conchostracans, insects, and ostracods). Gastropods, isopods, and decapods occur with less prominence in Mesozoic beds although in the Upper

Cambrian, mollusks such as the monoplacophorans appear to have been important. Serpulid worms constitute significant faunal elements at a few Mesozoic sites. Fossil spoor occur especially in Devonian through Permian beds and include trails, tracks, burrows, castings, eggs, and other trace fossils. Thus far, archeocyathids and trilobites comprise the chief Cambrian faunal components.

MARINE FAUNAS

An interesting Upper Cambrian fauna from the Heritage Range, Ellsworth Mountains, includes twelve species of agnostid and other trilobites, several mollusks, brachiopods, archeocyathids, and pelmatozoans. Trilobites are reported to show Australian-Asiatic affinities (Webers, 1970). Older work on archeocyathids from Antarctica established equivalent affinities for several species (Hill, 1964).

Lower Devonian brachiopods from the Horlick Mountains in Antarctica include species of the following genera: *Pleurothyrella,* which is confined to the austral province, and *Australospirifer.* Both of these genera have close affinities to equivalent austral forms of South America and South Africa. Presence of another genus, *Tanerhynchia,* suggests likely communication between Antarctica and New Zealand (Boucot *et al.,* 1967). Inarticulates (large orbiculoids) found in both East and West Antarctica are characteristic of the Lower Devonian of the Southern Hemisphere (A. J. Rowell in Doumani *et al.,* 1965).

These data point to restricted migratory routes between Antarctica and other Southern Hemisphere continents during portions of Devonian time. Such restrictions might be attributed to the closer proximity of continents.

A recent report of late Middle Devonian freshwater fish beds in the Mawson-Mulock area of the Lashly Mountains (White, 1968), in which conchostracan fossils occur, may bring new evidence to support this inference. Thus, in an effort to explain the occurrence of the freshwater fossil fish *Bothriolepsis,* White (1968) concluded that "river-capture and swamps seem to have been the only means of migration" unless one postulates a saline-tolerant phase for which there is no evidence. Regarding the poorly preserved conchostracan material which the writer is in the process of studying, one can inquire as to its possible origin. The Devonian conchostracan fauna of the Buchan Cave limestone, Victoria, Australia, recently sampled by the writer, would be the nearest likely source in light of a recent Antarctica-Australia computer fit (Sproll and Dietz, 1969).

Other marine forms include faunas from the Upper Jurassic and Lower Cretaceous of West Antarctica (Lyon Nunataks, Johnson Nunataks, Alexander Island, and Graham Land). The Lyon Nunataks fauna consists of molluscan coleoids, *Conodicoelites;* serpulid worms, *Rotularia;* two pelecypod pectinaceans, *Variasmussium;* and one undetermined species. Similar forms are found in the Johnson Nunataks. The coleoid has strong affinities to a New Zealand belemnite. The serpulid also has apparent equivalents in the Upper Jurassic of New Zealand.

Upper Jurassic and Lower Cretaceous faunas from Alexander Island and the Upper Cretaceous of Graham Land include mollusks (gastropods, ammonites, lamellibranchs), annelid worms (serpulids), and arthropods (decapods). Study of them has led to some significant observations:

1. The Upper Cretaceous ammonite faunas from West Antarctica contain some genera that are found in western Madagascar.
2. The lamellibranch, *Ancellina,* abundant in Cretaceous beds of Alexander Island as well as the serpulid, *Rotularia australis,* also occur in strata of the same lithology in Patagonia, among other places.
3. Another serpulid species, *Rotularia callosa,* from the Upper Cretaceous of Graham Land has representatives in India, New Zealand, and Patagonia (Stevens, 1967).

More recently, Middle Jurassic ammonites from the Behrendt Mountains in Ellsworth Land were described (Quilty, 1970). Associated with a large sample of ammonites were some belemnites, bivalves, brachiopods, gastropods, trace fossils, rare crustaceans, fish, and plants. A rich marine fauna (including abundant ammonites as well as other mollusks, annelid worms, and plants), presumably Jurassic, has been reported from the mountainous Lassiter Coast which borders the Weddell Sea at the south end of the Antarctic Peninsula (Williams, 1970).

One interpretation of data from West Antarctica would support the view that certain marine migration routes between Southern Hemisphere continents became available by continents drifting apart. Greater geographic spread of Gondwanaland marine Jurassic compared to marine Triassic (Teichert, 1970) apparently reflected this situation. Such routes were probably shallow (Quilty, 1970).

NONMARINE FAUNAS

Permian

The Permian (Lower Beaufort) of the antarctic Ohio Range, Mount Glossopteris Formation, consists essentially of a single major faunal component, fossil branchiopod crustaceans—the conchostracans. In a very thin zone of restricted horizontal spread there occur successive multiple generations of the ribbed clam shrimp, *Leaia gondwanella,* a few of the unribbed *Cyzicus (Lioestheria) doumanii,* recently discovered insects, as well as *Glossopteris* flora.

Ribbed conchostracans equivalent to the antarctic forms have been found in the Rio do Rasto formation of Brazil, the Madumabisa shale of Southern Rhodesia, the Lower Beaufort of Natal, the Newcastle Coal Measures of New South Wales, and the Upper Bowen Coal Measures of Queensland. Of these the most likely source for antarctic Ohio Range leaiids is the Newcastle Coal Measures fauna which were systematically sampled by the writer during the summer of 1970 (Figs. 1 and 2).

Jurassic

Interbeds of the Queen Alexandra Range Kirkpatrick basalts bear Jurassic fossil conchostracans. Conchostracans and ostracods also occur in Mauger Nunatak (85°44′S, 176°40′E). Beds of apparently equivalent age in Victoria Land, Brimstone Peak (Ricker, 1964), and Carapace Nunatak (Gunn and Warren, 1962, and the writer's collection, 1969–1970) also yield similar nonmarine fossils. Included in the Carapace Nunatak biota are isopods, ostracods (H. W. Ball, personal communication, 1966), and insects (Carpenter, 1969). Common to all of the above sites is the conchostracan *Cyzicus (Lioestheria)* sp.

The conchostracans from the Jurassic Lebombo volcanic sequence of Mozambique, collected by Dr. Reinhold Förster of the University of Munich, are particularly interesting. During the summer of 1968 the writer examined these specimens, and compared them with the above-mentioned collections. They all shared the characteristic of hachure-type markings between growth bands which is

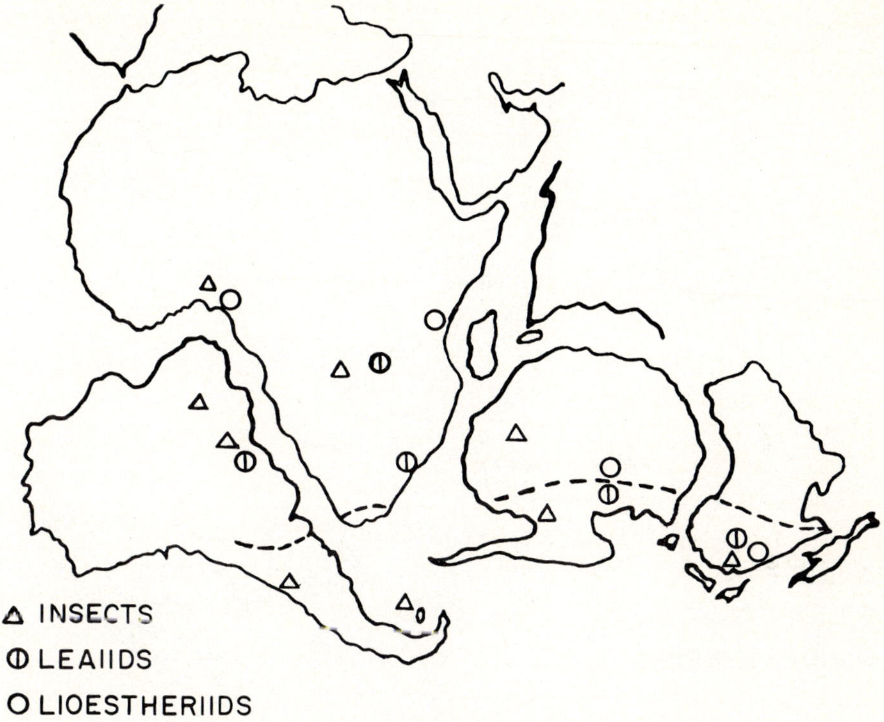

Fig. 1. Restoration of continents to inferred Paleozoic (Permian) positions. Dashed line represents Samfrau Geosyncline. If continental shelves were included, proximity would be considerably enhanced. Leaiids and lioestheriids are ribbed and unribbed conchostracans respectively.

typically lioestheriid. The duration of the freshwater bodies in which they lived, as reflected in multiple growth bands, was also similar.

Mozambique merits further comment. Besides having forms that are related to the antarctic Jurassic lioestheriids, its Permian (Lower Beaufort) is probably a correlate of the Madumabisa shale of Southern Rhodesia (Borges, 1952). Professor Geoffrey Bond (personal communication, 1969) noted that while the Rhodesian Madumabisa shale itself does not reach into Mozambique the formation is probably a time-correlate of the entire South African Beaufort. The Mozambique Permian yields *Cyzicus (Euestheria)* cf *minuta* at one locality and *Cyzicus (Lioestheria) borgesi* at another (Teixeira, 1943). Both species were associated with a *Glossopteris* flora. Since the antarctic Permian also has lioestheriids,

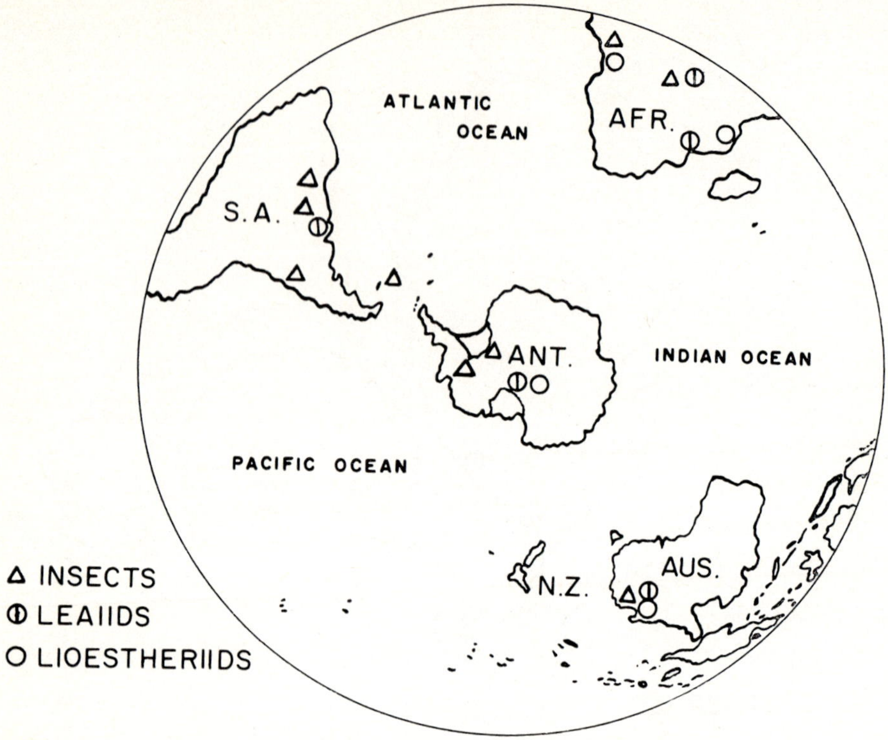

Fig. 2. Present-day disposition of continents. Permian insect and conchostracan distribution in context of present arrangement of continents.

conchostracan equivalences are shared by the Permian as well as the Jurassic of Mozambique and Antarctica. This suggests the availability of Paleozoic and Mesozoic fresh- and brackish-water routes which restoration of continents to presumed Gondwanaland positions seems to provide between East Africa and Antarctica (Fig. 1).

FOSSIL INSECT RECORD

Superimposed on *Glossopteris* leaf venation, the venation of two insect wings of Lower Permian age occur in a sample from the middle horizon, Theron Mountains (Plumstead, 1964). These insects which were to have been described by Zeuner are lost. They are regarded as homopterous as interpreted from a published photograph (Carpenter, 1969).

Fossil insects have been found in the writer's antarctic samples from the Polarstar Formation, Sentinel Mountains, and the Mount Glossopteris Formation, Ohio Range, both Permian in age. The Sentinel Mountain form appears to have homopteran affinities (Tasch and Riek, 1969), but familial assignment will require more data (Carpenter, 1969). The Ohio Range insects occur in the leaiid conchostracan beds and consist of numerous fragments, chiefly of the abdomen. Carpenter assigns this material to *Uralonympha,* and possibly to the species of this genus he recently described from another collection, in which it was represented by a nearly complete specimen that lacked only the abdomen (Carpenter, 1969).

There are now three widely separated Permian insect sites in Antarctica. A new Jurassic insect site is also known from Carapace Nunatak (Carpenter, 1969). The most abundant remains are fragments of mayfly nymphs, although a dragonfly wing and possibly a few other insects are also represented. Occurrence of beetles has long been on record at the Jurassic Mount Flora, near Hope Bay (Zeuner, 1959). These freshwater forms were assigned to two genera, *Grahamelytra* and *Ademosynoides.* The last named form is closest to Australian Triassic beetles. Zeuner interpreted the resemblance as indicative of paleogeographic connections to Australia during the Jurassic.

Insect fossils, while not abundant, are widespread throughout the Gondwana area. Upper Permian insect wings related to *Paleodictyoptera* are recorded from the Falkland Islands. They occur in association with *Glossopteris* (Adie, 1952; Holm, 1911). Tillyard (1928) reported on a Permian damselfly (Odonata) from the same area.

Carboniferous, Permian, and Triassic insects from the South American mainland include blattids and three species of *Phyloblatta* from the Brazilian Carboniferous (Carpenter, 1930; Comacho, 1966); *Protohymenoptera*(?) from the Permian of the Paraná Basin (Oliviera, 1930) and the Lower Permian of Argentina (Comacho, 1966); and a homopterous genus, *Sanctipaulus,* from the Triassic of Rio Grande do Sul, Brazil (Beltrão, 1965; Pinto, 1956). Insects assignable to the suborder Archizygoptera, known from the Australian Triassic, have been described from the Triassic of Mendoza, Argentina (Carpenter, 1960).

One can add to the South American occurrences the Permo-Triassic insects of New South Wales (Evans, 1943, 1956, 1958b; Riek, 1953; Tillyard, 1917, 1922). In particular, numerous insects of the New South Wales Permian (Evans, 1943, 1958b) and the Triassic of New South Wales and Queensland (Evans, 1956) are homopterous. Postulated repositioning of continents (Fig. 1) can help to explain the distribution of homopterous insects during the Permian and Triassic.

Tillyard reported mecopterans—scorpion flies—in abundance among other insects, in the New South Wales Permian (Riek, 1953). They were fossilized in association with a *Glossopteris* flora and ribbed conchostracans—leaiids.

A Triassic blattid, *Triassoblatta,* and a homopteran assigned to the family Scytinopteridae are shown from the plant-bearing beds of the New Town Coal Measures of Hobart, Tasmania (Riek, 1962). Unribbed conchostracans also occur in these beds that were sampled by the writer in the summer of 1970.

More Gondwana insects are known from the African Permian. The Karroo beds (Lower Beaufort) of the Lunda region, Portuguese Angola, contained a complete fossil insect with paired membranous wings. It was poorly preserved in red marly shales, and was assigned to *Paleodictyoptera* (?) (Teixeira, 1960). Associated with the Angolan insect were fishes and unribbed conchostracans of several genera, including *Cyzicus (Euestheria)*.

A wing of a blattid insect, *Rhodesiomylacris bondi* Zeuner, was found together with the ribbed conchostracan, *Leaia sesami,* and an unribbed *Cyzicus* sp. in the Madumabisa shale of Southern Rhodesia. Other leaiids and cyzicids, but no insects, were reported in younger beds of the same shale (Bond, 1955). One or another of the Madumabisa shale leaiid beds are probably correlates of the Ohio Range *Leaia* zone as well as the Mozambique Lower Beaufort.

In the Triassic Stormberg Series of South Africa, a shale band near the base of the Cave Sandstone has yielded fossil insects assignable to three orders: Coleoptera, Plectoptera, and Orthoptera (Haughton, 1924). The Middle Triassic Molteno beds of Natal also have several species of coleopterans and one blattid associated with plant fossils (Zeuner, 1960).

The only relevant indication of fossil insects from India is a mention of unnamed forms as biotic associates of the unribbed conchostracan, *Cyzicus (Lioestheria) kotahensis* from the Lower Jurassic of Kotá, India (Jones, 1862). This Indian estheriid appears to have been a contemporary of the lioestheriids of the Queen Alexandra Range (Elliot and Tasch, 1967). The writer's collections from this range are now being scanned for possible insect associates of the dominant lioestheriid fauna.

Antarctic, South American, Falkland Islands, Angolan, Southern Rhodesian, South African, Indian, and Australian insects of the Permian, Triassic, and Jurassic have been cited. These are indicators of many others that could have migrated across a transantarctic land connection between continents of the Southern Hemisphere.

GAPS AND THEORETICAL CONSIDERATIONS

Gaps

Some lacunae remain in the Southern Hemisphere distribution of Permo-Carboniferous ribbed (leaiid) conchostracans. This distribution bears on migratory routes to and from the Antarctic of the time. Since the leaiid conchostracans carried the same bioprogram, these ribbed types, now separated by oceanic distances, must have originated from a common gene pool. Fractionation of the original population by migration and wind transport of eggs within and between regional and nearby land areas, could then account for the observed distribution.

Important lacunae for which data are needed include:

1. The lack of reports of Carboniferous ribbed conchostracans from South America, eastern Australia, and Tasmania.
2. No *Leaia* types have been recorded thus far from the Permo-Carboniferous of India, Madagascar, or Tasmania.
3. Still undocumented is the source of the Western Australian leaiids (Carboniferous, Fitzroy Range).

Ribbed forms from the antarctic Permian (Ohio Range) are thought to have derived from the Newcastle Coal Measures of eastern Australia, where similar types abound. In turn, the Newcastle leaiids are likely derivatives of Fitzroy Range migrants. Two possibilities remain for pinpointing the origin of the Fitzroy Range ribbed conchostracans: either they may be traced back to a stock from the African Carboniferous, where such forms are known, or from the Indian Coal Measures, where none has been reported. Determination of which of the alternatives is to be preferred will require more field data, particularly in India.

Migratory Routes

Another consideration is the postulate of a transantarctic migratory route for insects and conchostracans. Until recently data on fossil insects in Antarctica were sparse. Even so, more than a decade ago, based solely on certain modern insect distributions, one worker suggested a Mesozoic transantarctic route for Southern Hemisphere insects (Evans, 1958a). With the newer data on antarctic and other Southern Hemisphere fossil insects and conchostracans reviewed earlier, a Paleozoic as well as a Mesozoic trans-antarctic migratory route for terrestrial and freshwater faunas seems much more plausible.

Paleosalinity

Availability of shallow, fresh-to-brackish water routes between Southern Hemisphere continents seems to be a requirement in order to account for the Permo-Carboniferous and Jurassic distributions of conchostracans and other nonmarine crustaceans (Gislén, 1936; Krömmelbein, 1966).

There are several different, but related approaches to paleosalinity. One postulate that is considered to be plausible would reduce normal oceanic salinity from 35‰ to 30‰ during Permo-Triassic time. This would have been achieved by withdrawal of 7×10^{15} tons of salt (Fischer, 1964). During the late Paleozoic, *Glossopteris* floral distribution is thought to indicate a narrow gap of water between continents (Darlington, 1965) which is consistent with the salt-withdrawal postulate. Several geochemical studies of the Ohio Range leaiid zone led to the determination of a paleosalinity range of 29 to 31‰ (with a −4‰ correction factor) (Tasch and Gafford, 1968). These data were supported by the fossil faunal evidence. Where salinity increased by 2 to 33‰ in the section, recurring nonmarine crustacean branchiopods (*Leaia*) first disappeared. It is reasonable to conclude that suitable shallow-water routes were available for non-halophilic forms during the indicated times.

Transport

Log, leaf, or animal transport of leaiid eggs between continents can be ruled out because it is unlikely that salt-water wetting of eggs could be avoided in traversing oceanic distances separating continents. Wetting or immersion of this type would render conchostracan eggs infertile or inhibit hatching, as determined by the writer's experiments with modern forms. One type of animal transport to which the above statements would not apply would be by birds. Birds might pick up pond muds containing conchostracan eggs as they walk over dried-out ponds and pools—but birds had not yet evolved in Permian time.

Although modern conchostracan eggs on floodplains such as that of the Missouri River can be dispersed by wind over a fair-sized local area, this dispersal is all inland, all on the same floodplain for example, ordinarily in a serial way from one dried-out pond or pool to a neighboring one. This mode of dispersal is relatively restricted in an areal sense. Conchostracan egg transport by wind dispersal, across oceanic distances presently separating continents, is unknown and from all available data of negligible probability.

The existence of aerial plankton has long been established (Gislén, 1948). For present purposes, data on airborne insects trapped over the Pacific-Antarctica region are of special interest. The likelihood is slight for such forms remaining alive (Gressitt, 1961). Even if survival occurs, the probability of reaching Antarctica from Australia, for example, is also most limited. Finally, should the Antarctic Continent be attained, the viability of such insects has never been demonstrated. By contrast, nymphs of the Ohio Range fossil insect fauna (Permian) and from the Carapace Nunatak (Jurassic) reflect reproducing populations (Carpenter, 1969).

Wind dispersal has not brought any conchostracan eggs to the Antarctic Continent or to the subantarctic islands in recent times, as indicated in pond and lake surveys. There are no fossil conchostracans younger than Jurassic presently known from Antarctica.

An interpretation which seems best to fit available fossil data would attribute the absence of antarctic post-Jurassic nonmarine branchiopod crustaceans to the disappearance of suitable, nearby, and shallow, fresh-to-brackish water migratory routes. A coastal swamp area might be such a route, for example. At low water, isolated pools would appear and subsequently evaporate, allowing bottom muds, some with crustacean branchiopod eggs, to be windblown to a nearby water patch. Continental displacement can explain the destruction of such routes in late or post-Jurassic time. That could account for the consequent intermingling of species populations of Mesozoic marine forms between continents of the Southern Hemisphere (Stevens, 1967).

SUMMARY

The concept of Gondwanaland and continental displacement ties together numerous, otherwise disparate, independently acquired bits of marine and nonmarine invertebrate fossil evidence into a coherent whole. Recent vertebrate fossil data on antarctic freshwater fish, terrestrial reptiles, and amphibians which require nonmarine routes and land connections between Southern Hemisphere continents, are effectively concordant with the interpretations set forth here.

References

Adie, R. J., 1952. Iles Falkland et Antarctique. In *Symposium sur les Séries de Gondwana,* edited by C. Teichert; pp. 384–399. XIX Congr. Geol. Intern., Alger.

Ball, H. W., 1960. Upper Cretaceous Decapoda and Serpulidae from James Ross Island, Grahamland. *Falkland Islands Dependencies Surv., Sci. Repts., 24.*

Behrendt, J. C., and T. S. Laudon, 1964. Cretaceous fossils collected at Johnson Nunatak, Antarctica. *Science, 143:* 353–354.

Beltrão, R., 1965. Paleontologia do Santa Maria e São, Pedro do Sul, Brasil. Universidade Federal de Santa Maria. *Inst. Ciencias Nat. Bol., 2:* 70.

Bond, G., 1955. The Madumabisa (Karroo) shale in the Middle Zambesi region. *Trans. Proc. Geol. Soc. South Africa, 58:* 71–99.

Borges, A., 1952. Le Système du Karroo au Moçambique. In *Symposium sur les Séries de Gondwana,* edited by C. Teichert; p. 232. XIX Congr. Geol. Intern., Alger.

Boucot, A. J., G. A. Doumani, J. G. Johnson, and G. F. Webers, 1967. Devonian of Antarctica. In *International Symposium on the Devonian System,* edited by D. H. Oswald; vol. 1, pp. 639–648. Alberta Soc. Petrol. Geol., Calgary, Alberta.

Carpenter, F. M., 1930. Un blattide permiano do Brasil. *Brasil. Serv. Geol. Min. Bol., 50:* 1–9.

Carpenter, F. M., 1960. A Triassic odonate from Argentina. *Psyche, 67* (3) : 71–75.

Carpenter, F. M., 1969. Fossil insects from Antarctica. *Psyche, 76* (4) : 418–424.

Camacho, H. H., 1966. *Invertebrados fósiles;* pp. 487–490. Editorial Univ. Buenos Aires (Eudeba), Buenos Aires.

Cox, L. R., 1953. Lower Cretaceous Gastropoda, Lamellibranchia and Annelida from Alexander I Land. *Falkland Islands Dependencies Surv., Sci. Repts., 4.*

Darlington, Jr., P. J., 1965. *Biogeography of the Southern End of the World.* Harvard Univ. Press, Cambridge, Mass.

Doumani, G. A., and P. Tasch, 1965. A leaiid conchostracan zone in the Ohio Range, Horlick Mountains, Antarctica. In *Antarctic Research Series 6, Geology and Paleontology of the Antarctic,* edited by J. B. Hadley; pp. 229–239. Am. Geophys. Union, Washington, D. C.

Doumani, G. A., R. S. Boardman, A. J. Rowell, A. T. Boucot, J. G. Johnson, D. W. Fisher, and R. S. Miles, 1965. Lower Devonian fauna of the Horlick Formation, Ohio Range, Antarctica. In *Antarctic Research Series 6, Geology and Paleontology of the Antarctic,* edited by J. B. Hadley; pp. 241–274. Am. Geophys. Union, Washington, D. C.

Elliot, D. H., and P. Tasch, 1967. Lioestheriid conchostracans: a new Jurassic locality and regional and Gondwana correlations. *J. Paleontol., 41* (6) : 1561–1563.

Evans, J. W., 1943. Upper Permian Homoptera from New South Wales. *Records Australian Museum (Sydney), 21* (4) : 180–198.

Evans, J. W., 1956. Paleozoic and Mesozoic Hemiptera (Insecta). *Australian J. Zool., 4* (2) : 166–258.

Evans, J. W., 1958a. Insect evolution and continental drift. In *Continental Drift Symposium,* edited by S. W. Carey; pp. 134–161. Univ. Tasmania, Hobart.

Evans, J. W., 1958b. New Upper Permian Homoptera from the Belmont beds. *Records Australian Museum, 24* (9) : 109–114.

Fischer, A. G., 1964. Brackish oceans as the cause of the Permo-Triassic marine faunal crisis. In *Problems of Paleoclimatology,* edited by A. E. M. Nairn; pp. 566–577. Interscience, London.

Gislén, T., 1936. Contributions to the ecology of *Limnadia. Lunds Univ. Arss. Avd. 2, 32* (9) : 3–19.

Gislén, T., 1948. Aerial plankton and its condition of life. *Biol. Rev., 23:* 109–126.

Gressitt, J. L., 1961. Problems in the zoogeography of Pacific and antarctic insects. *Pacific Insects Monograph, 2:* 1–94.

Gunn, B. M., and G. Warren, 1962. Geology of Victoria Land between the Mawson and Mulock Glaciers, Antarctica. *New Zealand Geol. Surv. Bull., 71:* 1–143.

Haughton, S. H., 1924. The fauna and stratigraphy of the Stormberg Series. *Ann. So. African Mus., 12:* 1–300.

Hill, D., 1964. Archeocyatha from loose material at Plunket Point at the head of Beardmore Glacier. In *Antarctic Geology,* edited by R. J. Adie; pp. 609–619. North Holland Publ. Co., Amsterdam.

Holm, G., 1911. Insect remains. In Halle, T. G.: On the geological structure and history of the Falkland Islands. *Geol. Inst. Univ. Upsala Bull., 11:* 183–184.

Howarth, M. K., 1958. Upper Jurassic and Cretaceous ammonite faunas of Alexander I Land and Graham Land. *Falkland Islands Dependencies Surv., Sci. Repts., 21.*

Jones, T. R., 1862. *Fossil Estheriae;* pp. 81–83. The Palaeontographical Soc., London.

Krömmelbein, K., 1966. Gondwana Wealden Ostracoda from N. E. Brazil and West Africa. In *Proceedings Second West African Micropaleontological Colloquium, Ibadan,* edited by J. E. Van Hinte; pp. 113–118. E. J. Brill, Leiden.

Oliveira, E. P., 1930. Insectos permianos do Estado do Paraná. *Annais Acad. Brasil Ciencias, 2* (4) : 215–218.

Pinto, I. D., 1956. Artropódos da Formação Santa Maria (Triássico Superior) do Rio Grande do Sul, Com Noticias sôbre alguns restos vegetais. *Bol. Soc. Brasil Geol., 5* (1) : 75–87

Plumstead, E. P., 1964. Paleobotany of Antarctica. In *Antarctic Geology,* edited by R. J. Adie; pp. 637–654. North Holland Publ. Co., Amsterdam.

Quilty, P. G., 1970. Jurassic ammonites from Ellsworth Land, Antarctica. *J. Paleontol., 44* (1) : 110–116.

Ricker, J., 1964. Outline of the geology between Mawson and Priestly Glaciers, Victoria Land. In *Antarctic Geology,* edited by R. J. Adie; pp. 265–275. North Holland Publ. Co., Amsterdam.

Riek, E. F., 1953. Fossil mecopterid insects from the Upper Permian of New South Wales. *Records Australian Museum (Sydney), 23:* 55–87.

Riek, E. F., 1962. Fossil insects from the Triassic at Hobart, Tasmania. *Papers Proc. Roy. Soc. Tasmania, 96:* 39–40.

Sproll, W. P., and R. S. Dietz, 1969. Morphological continental drift fit of Australia and Antarctica. *Nature, 222:* 345–348.

Stevens, G. R., 1967. Upper Jurassic fossils from Ellsworth Land, West Antarctica and notes on Upper Jurassic biogeography of the South Pacific region. *New Zealand J. Geol. Geophys., 10*(2): 345–386.

Tasch, P., 1968. Trace fossils from the Permian Polarstar Formation, Sentinel Mountains, Antarctica. *Kansas Acad. Sci. Trans., 71*(2): 184–194.

Tasch, P., 1969. Antarctic leaiid zone: seasonal events; Gondwana correlations. In *Gondwana Stratigraphy,* edited by A. J. Amos; pp. 185–194. I. U. G. S. Symposium Buenos Aires 1–15 October, 1967. UNESCO, Paris.

Tasch, P., and E. L. Gafford, 1968. Paleosalinity of Permian nonmarine deposits in Antarctica. *Science, 160:* 1221–1222.

Tasch, P., and E. F. Riek, 1969. Permian insect wing from Antarctic Sentinel Mountains. *Science, 164:* 1529–1530.

Taylor, B. J., 1970. Stratigraphical correlation in South-East Alexander Island. In *Abstracts of Papers, Symposium on Antarctic Geology and Solid Earth Geophysics, Oslo, 6–15 August, 1970;* p. 31. Sci. Comm. Antarctic Res., Intern. Union Geol. Sci.

Teichert, C., 1970. Marine fossil invertebrate faunas of the Gondwana region. *Second I. U. G. S. Symposium on the Stratigraphy and Paleontology of the Gondwana System, Capetown and Johannesburg, South Africa.* Council Sci. Ind. Res. (Graphic Arts Division), Pretoria, South Africa.

Teixeira, C., 1943. Notas para o estudo do "Karroo" de Região de Tete, Na África Oriental Portuguesa. *Bol. Soc. Geol. Portugal, 2:* 1–13.

Teixeira, C., 1960. Sur quelques fossiles du Karroo de la Lunda, Angola. In *Publicações Culturais No. 50.* Companhia de Diamantes de Angola (Diamang); pp. 79–116. Museu do Dundo, Lisboa.

Thomson, M. R. A., 1970. Ammonite faunas of South-Eastern Alexander Island and their stratigraphical significance. In *Abstracts of Papers, Symposium on Antarctic Geology and Solid Earth Geophysics, Oslo, 6–15 August, 1970;* p. 32. Sci. Comm. Antarctic Res., Intern. Union Geol. Sci.

Tillyard, R. J., 1917. Permian and Triassic insects from New South Wales in the collection of Mr. John Mitchell. *Linnean Soc. New South Wales Proc., 42*(168): 720–756.

Tillyard, R. J., 1922. Some new Permian insects from Belmont, N. S. W., in the collection of Mr. John Mitchell. *Linnean Soc. New South Wales Proc., 47*(187): 279–292.

Tillyard, R. J., 1928. A Permian damselfly wing from the Falkland Islands. *Trans. Entomol. Soc., 76:* 53–63.

Webers, G. F., 1970. An unusual Upper Cambrian fauna from West Australia. In *Abstracts of Papers, Symposium on Antarctic Geology and Solid Earth Geophysics, Oslo, 6–15 August, 1970;* p. 44. Sci. Comm. Antarctic Res., Intern. Union Geol. Sci.

White, E. I., 1968. Devonian fishes of the Mawson-Mulock area, Victoria Land, Antarctica. *Trans-Antarctic Exp., 1955–1958, Sci. Repts., No. 16, Geology 5.* Trans-Antarctic Expedition Comm., London.

Williams, P. L., 1970. Geology of the Lassiter Coast. *Antarctic J. U. S., 5*(4): 98–99.

Zeuner, F. E., 1959. Jurassic beetles from Graham Land, Antarctica. *Paleontology, 1*(4): 407–409.

Zeuner, F. E., 1960. A Triassic insect fauna from the Molteno beds of South Africa. *XI Inter. Kongres f. Entomologie, Wien, 1:* 304–306.

Evidence for Gondwanaland from a Review of West Antarctic Radiometric Ages

MARTIN HALPERN

The University of Texas at Dallas

Alexander L. Du Toit (1937) suggested that during the Paleozoic evolution of Gondwanaland a major geosyncline directly connected South America, Africa, Antarctica, and Australia. He called this belt the "Samfrau Geosyncline." The radiometric ages reported from West Antarctica and neighboring Southern Hemisphere land masses were considered in their relationship to DuToit's concept and to the post-Samfrau Cretaceous plutonic igneous suite which rings the Pacific margin of Antarctica.

RADIOMETRIC AGES FROM WEST ANTARCTICA

West Antarctica is a province of the earth's crust where geochronology plays an important role. Only within about the past five years have radiometric ages been available from West Antarctica. Figure 1 illustrates those areas from which rocks have been radiometrically dated as of 1968; their ages are listed in Table 1.

SAMFRAU OROGENIC BELT

The Samfrau orogenic belt as used in this paper includes Du Toit's Paleozoic Samfrau Geosyncline (Du Toit, 1937) and a Devonian through Triassic geochronologic province as outlined in Figure 2. The distribution of radiometric ages of igneous and metamorphic rocks (Fig. 2) indicates the presence of a nearly continuous approximately 200-to-400-million-year geochronologic province extending from South America to Australia. Radiometric ages of rocks from South America and Australia relating to the

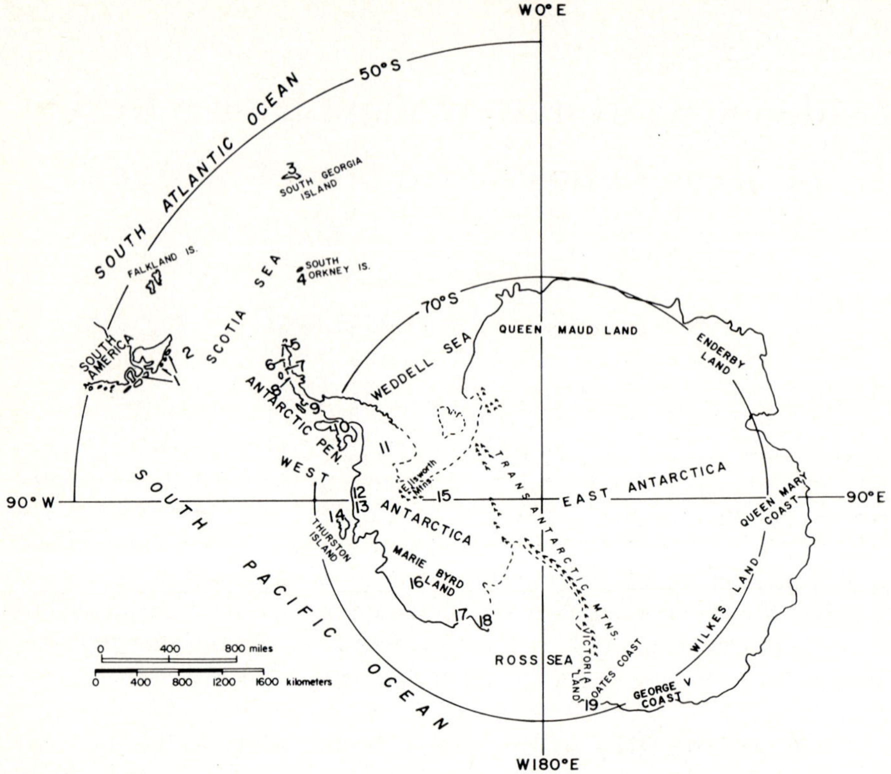

Fig. 1. Geographic location of radiometrically dated samples referred to in Table 1.

existence of this province are shown in Figure 2 and Table 2. The geochronologic province passes through most of West Antarctica, and the Oates Coast (see Fig. 1) of East Antarctica. The South America-Africa fit to the Antarctic is in northern West Antarctica where the stratigraphically oldest crystalline rocks have minimum ages of 199 million years (m.y.) in the Jones Mountains (Craddock *et al.,* 1964a) (Fig. 2, area E) and 280 m.y. in the Thurston Island area (Craddock *et al.,* 1964b) (Fig. 2, area F). The Australia fit is in East Antarctica where plutonic igneous rocks from the Oates Coast (Fig. 2, area H) have been dated at 305 to 355 m.y. (Ravich and Krylov, 1964; Webb *et al.,* 1964).

A generally linear feature, the geochronologic province postulated in Figure 2 occupies a position tangential to the older, more

Table 1. Compilation of West Antarctic and related radiometric ages.

Number in Figure 1	Location	Material	Decay scheme	Calculated age in m.y.*	Reference
1	Cascade Bay, Sts. of Magellan, Chile	Biotite from diorite	K-Ar	77	Halpern, 1962
1	Bahia Tres Brazos, Beagle Canal, Chile	Biotite-whole rock from quartz monzonite	Rb-Sr	72	Halpern, In press
1	Pta. Hope, Sts. of Magellan, Chile	Biotite-whole rock from quartz diorite	Rb-Sr	74	Halpern, In press
1	Est. Santa Rosa, Beagle Canal, Chile	Biotite-whole rock from dioritic gabbro	Rb-Sr	77	Halpern, In press
2	Drake Strait (S. of Cape Horn) 30 m from shore, 393m depth	Gravel with sand and pebbles	K-Ar	178	Krylov *et al.*, 1961
3	Near Stromness Bay, South Georgia Island	Whole rock-mylonitized argillaceous rock	K-Ar	67	Grikurov *et al.*, 1967
4	Signy and Moe Islands, South Orkney Islands	8 biotite concentrates 1 muscovite concentrate from quartz-mica schist	K-Ar	176–199	Miller, 1960
4	Signy Island, South Orkney Islands[a]	plagioclase-actinolite schist	K-Ar	224	Grikurov *et al.*, 1967
		garnet-quartz-mica schist	K-Ar	214	Grikurov *et al.*, 1967
		muscovite from preceding garnet-quartz-mica schist	K-Ar	195	Grikurov *et al.*, 1967

Table 1. (continued)

Number in Figure 1	Location	Material	Decay scheme	Calculated age in m.y.*	Reference
5	Cape Legoupil area, Antarctic Peninsula	biotite from granodiorite	K-Ar	75	Halpern, 1962
		pyroxene from gabbro	K-Ar	100	Halpern, 1962
6	Tisné Point, Antarctic Peninsula	biotite-whole rock from granodiorite	Rb-Sr	90	Halpern, 1967
7	Canelo Point, Antarctic Peninsula	biotite from diorite	K-Ar	94	Scott, 1965
8	Doumer Island, Antarctic Peninsula	biotite from quartz diorite	K-Ar	52.5	Scott, 1965
		quartz diorite	Pb-α	45	Scott, 1965
9	Marguerite Bay, Antarctic Peninsula[b]	Melanocratic gneissic rock of diorite composition	K-Ar	105	Grikurov *et al.*, 1966
		Biotite from quartz-plagioclase-biotite xenolith in granite dike	K-Ar	110	Grikurov *et al.*, 1966
		Granite dike which cuts gneissic rocks of diorite composition	K-Ar	90	Grikurov *et al.*, 1966
		Biotite from diorite	K-Ar	110	Grikurov *et al.*, 1966
		Biotite from gneissic diorite	K-Ar	119	Grikurov *et al.*, 1966
		Cataclastic gneissic granite	K-Ar	90	Grikurov *et al.*, 1966

Table 1. (continued)

Number in Figure 1	Location	Material	Decay scheme	Calculated age in m.y.*	Reference
		Amphibole from biotitic amphibolite	K-Ar	133	Grikurov *et al.*, 1966
		Biotite from biotitic amphibolite	K-Ar	110	Grikurov *et al.*, 1966
		Biotitic amphibolite	K-Ar	114	Grikurov *et al.*, 1966
		Amphibole from amphibolite	K-Ar	105	Grikurov *et al.*, 1966
		Gneissic granite	K-Ar	90	Grikurov *et al.*, 1966
		Mesocratic gneissic granodiorite	K-Ar	105	Grikurov *et al.*, 1966
		Granite porphyry	K-Ar	81	Grikurov *et al.*, 1966
		Porphyroblastic granite	K-Ar	95	Grikurov *et al.*, 1966
		Porphyroblastic granite	K-Ar	95	Grikurov *et al.*, 1966
		Potassium keratophyre	K-Ar	95	Grikurov *et al.*, 1966
		Biotite granite	K-Ar	95	Grikurov *et al.*, 1966
		Biotite granite	K-Ar	86	Grikurov *et al.*, 1966
		Granite porphyry dike	K-Ar	81	Grikurov *et al.*, 1966
		Quartz-albite porphyry dike	K-Ar	86	Grikurov *et al.*, 1966
10	Alexander Island, Antarctic Peninsula[c]	Biotite from lithic clastic tuff	K-Ar	67	Grikurov *et al.*, 1967
		Polymictic sandstone	K-Ar	100	Grikurov *et al.*, 1967
		Polymictic sandstone	K-Ar	105	Grikurov *et al.*, 1967

Table 1. (continued)

Number in Figure 1	Location	Material	Decay scheme	Calculated age in m.y.*	Reference
11	Eastern Ellsworth Land nunataks[d]	Arkosic sandstone	K-Ar	157	Grikurov *et al.*, 1967
		Schistose arkosic sandstone	K-Ar	157	Grikurov *et al.*, 1967
		Biotite concentrates-whole rocks from quartz monzonite, quartz diorite, granodiorite	Rb-Sr isochron	96	Halpern, 1967
		Whole rock basalt	K-Ar	6	Halpern, this paper
12	Eights Coast area	Biotite from quartz diorite	K-Ar	97	Drake *et al.*, 1964
		Zircon from same quartz diorite	Pb-α	150	Drake *et al.*, 1964
13	Jones Mountains area	Muscovite from granite	K-Ar	199	Craddock *et al.*, 1964a
		Quartz-latite porphyry	K-Ar	104	Craddock *et al.*, 1964a
14	Thurston Island	Biotite from garnetiferous quartz diorite gneiss	Rb-Sr	280	Craddock *et al.*, 1964b
15	Mt. Byerly, interior West Antarctica	Biotite-whole rock from granite	Rb-Sr	167	Halpern, 1966
16	Mt. Sidley	Crystalline lava boulder	K-Ar	6	Doumani, 1964
17	Phillips Mountains, Ford Ranges	Biotite concentrates-whole rocks from quartz diorite	Rb-Sr isochron	352	Halpern, 1968

Table 1. (continued)

Number in Figure 1	Location	Material	Decay scheme	Calculated age in m.y.*	Reference
17	Ford Ranges	Whole rock monzonite, quartz diorite, granodiorite, adamellite	Rb-Sr isochron	98	Halpern, 1968
17	Mt. Atwood, Clark Mountains, Ford Ranges	Biotite from adamellite	K-Ar	143	Boudette *et al.*, 1966
		K-feldspar from adamellite	Rb-Sr	137	Boudette *et al.*, 1966
		Whole rock from adamellite	Rb-Sr	116	Boudette *et al.*, 1966
18	Rockefeller Mountains	Granites		Cretaceous	Wade, 1967
		Biotite schist		Cretaceous	Wade, 1967
19	Sputnik Islands, Oates Coast	Biotite-plagiogranite	K-Ar	305	Ravich and Krylov, 1964
19	Anamenskiy Island, Oates Coast	Biotite-plagiogranite	K-Ar	314	Ravich and Krylov, 1964
19	Nella Island, Oates Coast	Biotite from adamellite	K-Ar	343	Webb *et al.*, 1964
19	Thala Island, Oates Coast	Biotite from adamellite	K-Ar	355	Webb *et al.*, 1964

* Rb-Sr: Ages have been adjusted to λ_β $Rb^{87} = 1.47 \times 10^{-11}$ yr^{-1}.

* K-Ar: Ages have been adjusted to $\lambda_\beta = 4.72 \times 10^{-10}$ yr^{-1} and $\lambda_\epsilon = 5.85 \times 10^{-11}$ yr^{-1}.
$K^{40} = 1.22 \times 10^{-4}$ g/g K, when listed in referenced article.

(Footnotes cont'd, following page)

Footnotes for Table 1 (continued)

[a] Triassic metamorphism is chronologically consistent with the Cape folding in the Cape of Good Hope region of South Africa. It is the present writer's speculation that the basement terrain of the South Orkney Islands represents a fragment of continental crust of the late Paleozoic Samfrau orogenic belt as reconstructed in Figure 2.

[b] The K-Ar analyses include samples of the Marguerite Bay region "Basement Complex" and associated plutonic bodies which have been assigned Precambrian and early Paleozoic ages by Adie (1954). The intrusive bodies are considered by Grikurov *et al.* (1966) as Cretaceous; ages from the metamorphic complex are possible minimum ages associated with Cretaceous Andean orogeny.

[c] Grikurov *et al.* (1967) consider the K-Ar ages representative of the ages of the source material of the sedimentary rocks as well as the effects of a very late metamorphism of the sedimentary strata. To the south of Alexander Island, nunataks in eastern Ellsworth Land consist of Cretaceous intrusive rocks cutting folded, fossiliferous Jurassic sedimentary rocks (Halpern, 1967). No pre-Mesozoic sedimentary rocks containing a *faunal* assemblage of reliable stratigraphic age designation have yet been discovered on the Antarctic Peninsula. However, recent Russian palynology studies of rocks from the Trinity Peninsula Series of Alexander Island and the north Antarctic Peninsula reported *miospores* of early and middle Carboniferous age (Grikurov and Dibner, 1968).

[d] The whole rock basalt sample is from a single small nunatak of partly vesicular basalt which crops out to the east of Mount Boyer (Halpern, 1967).

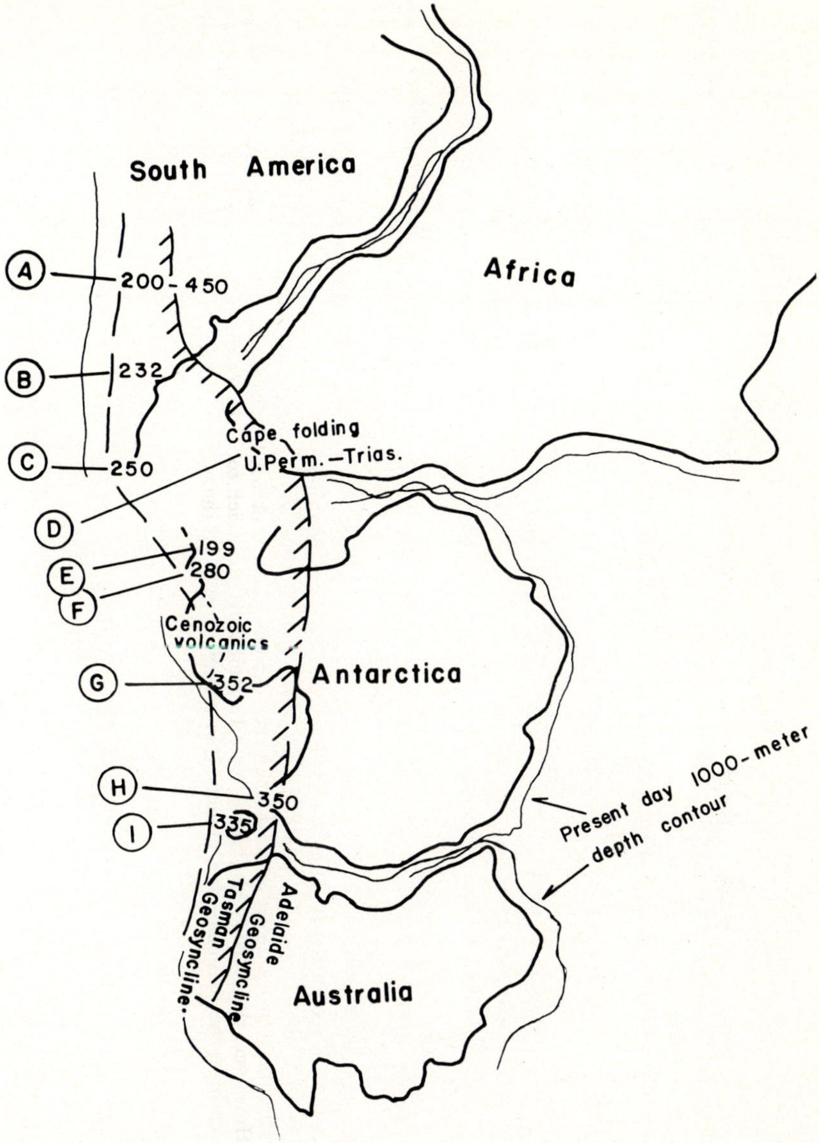

Fig. 2. Distribution of radiometric ages of igneous and metamorphic rocks within the reconstructed Samfrau orogenic belt. Diagonal ruling shows the Samfrau Geosyncline essentially as drawn by Du Toit, 1937. All dates are in millions of years.

Table 2. Gondwanaland Samfrau radiometric ages excluding Antarctica.

Continent	Location	Position on Figure 2	Age (m.y.)	Reference
South America	Pampean Ranges	A	200–450	Stipanicic and Linares, 1969
	North Patagonia	B	232	Halpern, 1968
	Magellan Basin	C	250[b]	Halpern, In press
Africa	Cape of Good Hope[a]	D		Allsopp and Kolbe, 1965 Du Toit, 1954
Australia	Tasmania	I	335[b]	Brooks and Compston, 1965
	Tasman Geosyncline		260–400	Richards *et al.*, 1966

[a] Late Paleozoic plutonic igneous rocks are not known to intrude the Devonian to Carboniferous Cape System of South Africa. However, the strong folding of the Cape System, which took place during Late Permian to Triassic time (Du Toit, 1954), is considered supporting evidence for placing the southern tip of Africa within the late Paleozoic Samfrau orogenic belt.

[b] Age adjusted to $\lambda_\beta = 1.47 \times 10^{-11}$ yr^{-1}.

stable Gondwanaland mass. It extends from South America to Australia, through much of the present western interior of Argentina, the eastern Straits of Magellan region of southern Chile, parts of West and East Antarctica, and the Tasman geosynclinal region of Tasmania and Queensland.

The most valid paleogeographic reconstructions are those which attempt a fit of geologic features which are themselves more or less normal to the line of supposed separation, as, for example, the fit of northeastern Brazil and West Africa (Hurley *et al.*, 1967). The Devonian through Triassic igneous and metamorphic events of the Samfrau orogenic belt fulfill this requirement. Continental polar wander paths, plotted from the measurement of the remnant magnetism of rocks, are not restricted to the sampling of features perpendicular to the line of separation, and thus provide a means of testing proposed reconstructions.

Reconstructions of Gondwanaland generally find difficulty in positioning the Antarctic Peninsula of West Antarctica. In the reconstruction of McElhinny *et al.* (1968), drawn mainly from the results of paleomagnetic measurements of African rocks, the Mesozoic-Cenozoic Andean orogenic belt of the Antarctic Peninsula trends into Paleozoic rocks of southern Africa. If, however, the northern Antarctic Peninsula in its present position is considered a relatively young feature which postdates the breakup of the Samfrau orogenic belt, the Paleozoic reconstructions drawn from paleomagnetic (McElhinny *et al.*, 1968) and geochronologic (Fig. 2) results are consistent.

CRETACEOUS PLUTONIC IGNEOUS SUITE

Marginal to or superimposed upon the fragmented Samfrau orogenic belt is the circum-Pacific Andean orogenic belt. Radiometric ages of plutonic igneous rocks from the Andean suites of South America and West Antarctica are shown in Figure 1 and Table 1. North of the Ford Ranges of West Antarctica (Fig. 1, location 17), the circum-Pacific Cretaceous igneous suite crops out on the South Island of New Zealand (Aronson, 1968).

At the southeastern end of South Georgia Island (Fig. 1, location 3), igneous rocks of presumed Andean affinity intrude the Cretaceous Cumberland Bay-type sedimentary rocks (Adie, 1964). If South Georgia Island is assumed to have always existed at its present location relative to South America and the Antarctic Peninsula, this would necessitate igneous plutonic activity at one small locality at present some 2,000 km from the South America-Antarctica Cretaceous igneous suite.

Paleocurrent measurements at South Georgia Island indicate that sediments were transported by northerly- and southerly-flowing currents (Frakes, 1966). The mineralogy of the sedimentary strata indicate derivation from a continental terrain. Even if one assumes a 90° rotation of South Georgia Island, there is no bathymetric indication of the past existence of a continental block capable of supplying the quartz-rich Cumberland Bay-type detrital material.

The general linearity of the Cretaceous igneous intrusive suite of Chile and north Antarctic Peninsula and sedimentologic data are consistent with the Hawkes (1962) hypothesis that South Georgia Island once formed part of a continental strip joining South America and Antarctica. The post-Cretaceous disruption of this segment of continental crust is probably intimately related to sea-floor spreading in the South Atlantic.

Author's Notes: A number of summary papers listing antarctic radiometric ages has been published recently, e.g., Picciotto and Coppez (1962, 1964), and Ravich and Krylov (1964). The majority of antarctic radiometric ages are for East Antarctic rocks of Precambrian and Cambrian age. As they are not germane to the discussion of Samfrau or Andean orogenic belts, they have been omitted from Figure 1 and Table 1, and have not been discussed in this paper. The reader is referred to a recent paper by Hurley (1968) which briefly discusses the relevance of East Antarctic geology and geochronology to Gondwanaland.

Additional radiometric age data from West Antarctica (Halpern, M., Rb-Sr total rock and mineral ages from the Marguerite Bay area, Kohler Range and Fosdick Mountains, *Proceedings SCAR/IUGS Symposium on Antarctic Geology and Solid Earth Geophysics, Oslo, Norway, August, 1970*) and southern South America (Halpern, M., M. Umpierre, U. and E. Linares, Radiometric ages of crystalline rocks from southern South America as related to Gondwana and Andean geologic provinces, *Proceedings International Upper Mantle Project Conference on Solid Earth Problems, Buenos Aires, Argentina, October, 1970*) are consistent with the geochronologic reconstruction presented in this review paper.

The argon and potassium analyses of eastern Ellsworth Land nunataks (Table 1) were carried out by W. H. Burke and J. B. Otto, Mobil Oil Corporation Field Research Laboratory, Dallas, Texas.

The research by the writer has been largely supported by the Office of Polar Programs of the National Science Foundation.

This paper is Contribution No. 83, Geosciences Division, Southwest Center for Advanced Studies, Dallas, Texas.

References

Adie, R. J., 1954. The petrology of Graham Land. I. The Basement Complex; early Paleozoic plutonic and volcanic rocks. *Falkland Islands Dependencies Surv. Sci. Repts. 11.* Colonial Office, H. M. Stationary Office, London, England.

Adie, R. J., 1964. Geological history. In *Antarctic Research,* edited by Sir Raymond Priestley, R. J. Adie and G. de Q. Robin; pp. 118–162. Butterworths, London.

Allsopp, H. L., and P. Kolbe, 1965. Isotopic age determinations on the Cape Granite and intruded Malmesbury sediments, Cape Peninsula, South Africa. *Geochim. Cosmochim. Acta, 29:* 1115–1130.

Aronson, J. L., 1968. Regional geochronology of New Zealand. *Geochim. Cosmochim. Acta, 32:* 669–697.

Boudette, E. L., R. F. Marvin, and C. E. Hedge, 1966. Biotite, potassium-feldspar, and whole-rock ages of adamellite, Clark Mountains, West Antarctica. In *United States Geological Survey Professional Paper, 550-D;* pp. D190-D194. U. S. Dept. Interior. Government Printing Office, Washington, D. C.

Brooks, C., and W. Compston, 1965. The age and initial Sr^{87}/Sr^{86} of the Heemskirk Granite, Western Tasmania. *J. Geophys. Res., 70* (24): 6249–6262.

Craddock, C., T. W. Bastien, and R. H. Rutford, 1964a. Geology of the Jones Mountains area. In *Antarctic Geology,* edited by R. J. Adie; pp. 171–189. North Holland Publishing Company, Amsterdam.

Craddock, C., P. W. Gast, G. N. Hanson, and H. Linder, 1964b. Rubidium-strontium ages from Antarctica. *Geol. Soc. Am. Bull., 75* (3): 237–240.

Doumani, G. A., 1964. Volcanoes of the Executive Committee Range, Byrd Land. In *Antarctic Geology,* edited by R. J. Adie; pp. 666–675. North Holland Publishing Company, Amsterdam.

Drake, A. A., Jr., T. W. Stern, and H. H. Thomas, 1964. Radiometric ages of zircon and biotite in quartz diorite, Eights Coast, Antarctica. In *United States Geological Survey Professional Paper, 501-D;* pp. D50-D-53. U. S. Dept. Interior. Government Printing Office, Washington, D. C.

Du Toit, A. L., 1937. *Our Wandering Continents.* Oliver and Boyd, Edinburgh.

Du Toit, A. L., 1954. *The Geology of South Africa;* 3rd edition. Oliver and Boyd, London.

Frakes, L. A., 1966. Geologic setting of South Georgia Island. *Geol. Soc. Am. Bull., 77* (12): 1463–1468.

Grikurov, G. E., A. Y. Krylov, and Y. I. Silin, 1966. Radiometric dating of some rocks from the Marguerite Bay region of the Antarctic Peninsula. *Akad. Nauk. SSSR. Dokl., 171* (6): 1399–1401.

Grikurov, G. E., A. Y. Krylov, and Y. I. Silin, 1967. Radiometric dating of some rocks from the Scotia Arc and Alexander I Land (West Antarctica). *Akad. Nauk. SSSR. Dokl., 172* (1): 168–171.

Grikurov, G. E., and A. F. Dibner, 1968. New data on Trinity Peninsula Series (S_{1-3}) in West Antarctica. *Akad. Nauk. SSSR. Dokl., 179* (2): 410–412.

Halpern, M., 1962. Potassium-argon dating of plutonic bodies in Palmer Peninsula and southern Chile. *Science, 138* (3546): 1261–1262.

Halpern, M., 1966. Rubidium-strontium date from Mt. Byerly, West Antarctica. *Earth Planetary Sci. Letters, 1:* 455–457.

Halpern, M., 1967. Rubidium-strontium isotopic age measurements of plutonic igneous rocks in eastern Ellsworth Land and northern Antarctic Peninsula, Antarctica. *J. Geophys. Res., 72* (20): 5133–5142.

Halpern, M., 1968. Ages of Antarctic and Argentine rocks bearing on continental drift. *Earth Planetary Sci. Letters, 5:* 159–167.

Halpern, M., In press. Geologic significance of isotopic age measurements of rocks from Tierra del Fuego, Chile. In *Symposium on Continental Drift in the South Atlantic Region,* edited by J. Tuzo Wilson. UNESCO, Paris.

Hawkes, D. D., 1962. The structure of the Scotia Arc. *Geol. Mag., 99*(1): 85–91.

Hurley, P. M., F. F. M. de Alemeida, G. C. Melcher, U. G. Cordani, J. R. Rand, K. Kawashita, P. Vandoros, W. H. Pinson, Jr., and H. W. Fairbairn, 1967. Test of continental drift by comparison of radiometric ages. *Science, 157* (3788): 495–500.

Hurley, P. M., 1968. The confirmation of continental drift. *Sci. Am., 218*(4): 53–64.

Krylov, A. Y., A. P. Lisitsin, and Y. I. Silin, 1961. Significance of the argon-potassium ratio in oceanic oozes. *Akad. Nauk. SSSR. Izvestiia,* Geology Series *(3):* 66–78.

McElhinny, M. W., J. C. Briden, D. L. Jones, and A. Brock, 1968. Geological and geophysical implications of paleomagnetic results from Africa. *Rev. Geophys., 6* (2): 201–238.

Miller, J. A., 1960. Potassium-argon ages of some rocks from the South Atlantic. *Nature, 187* (4742): 1019–1020.

Picciotto, E., and A. Coppez, 1962. *Bibliographie des mesures d'ages absolus en Antarctique.* Universite Libre de Bruxelles, Belgium.

Picciotto, E., and A. Coppez, 1964. Bibliography of absolute age determinations in Antarctica (Addendum). In *Antarctic Geology,* edited by R. J. Adie; pp. 563–569. North Holland Publishing Company, Amsterdam.

Ravich, M. G., and A. J. Krylov, 1964. Absolute ages of rocks from East Antarctica. In *Antarctic Geology,* edited by R. J. Adie; pp. 579–589. North Holland Publishing Company, Amsterdam.

Richards, J. R., D. A. White, A. W. Webb, and C. D. Branch, 1966. Chronology of the acid igneous rocks of North Queensland, Australia. *Earth Planetary Sci. Letters, 1:* 107–109.

Scott, K. M., 1965. Geology of the southern Gerlache Strait region, Antarctica. *J. Geol., 73* (3): 518–527.

Stipanicic, P. N., and E. Linares, 1969. Edades radimétricas determinadas para la República Argentina y su significado geológico. *Acad. Nac. Ciencias, 47:* 51–96. Cordoba, Argentina.

Wade, F. A., 1967. Geology of the Marie Byrd Land coastal sector of West Antarctica. *Antarctic J. U. S., 2* (4): 93–94.

Webb, A. W., I. McDougall, and J. A. Cooper, 1964. Potassium-argon dates from the Vincennes Bay region and Oates Land. In *Antarctic Geology,* edited by R. J. Adie; pp. 597–600. North Holland Publishing Company, Amsterdam.

The Position of Antarctica in Gondwanaland

LAWRENCE A. FRAKES* and JOHN C. CROWELL

Departments of Geology, University of California, Los Angeles and Santa Barbara

The continent of Antarctica has long been viewed as a moving segment of Gondwanaland, a drifting portion of the giant supercontinent which has now arrived over the South Rotational Pole. Even when only the first limited geologic observations were available, such as those made by Scott and his ill-fated companions, coal and fossil fragments suggested that the now frigid region in the past had supported a verdant temperate or subtropical flora. Details of the geology, hard won from a hostile environment during the present century, reveal the broad outlines of the geologic history of the continent. Comparisons of rocks of the Gondwanaland system, bathymetric and topographic observations, geophysical and geochronological information, and paleomagnetic data now support the fragmentation concept. Many rocks are very similar to those on now-distant continents of Africa, South America, and Australia. Such observations and correlations, growing rapidly in coverage and significance in recent years, are made even more plausible and acceptable through our recent understanding of crustal tectonic processes beneath the sea. During the past decade, a mechanism for continental fragmentation and drift has been discovered in the processes of sea-floor spreading (Hess, 1962; Vine and Matthews, 1963; Vine, 1968). The record of sea-floor spreading as revealed in subsea topography and magnetic patterns shows that most of the oceanic floor between Antarctica and Australia was formed within the last 40 million years,

* Present address: Department of Geology, The Florida State University, Tallahassee.

and between Antarctica and New Zealand within the last 80 million years (Heirtzler, 1968).

Under the hypotheses of continental drift and sea-floor spreading for a globe as mobile as our earth, the motion of any segment probably has been long and variable. Although we lack a reference system to determine *absolute* motion, we can find the *relative* motions of plates with reference to other plates or with regard to the poles of the geomagnetic field. We can match the shapes of crustal plates and find the rotational poles for two adjacent plates by means of intersecting normals from transform faults (McKenzie and Parker, 1967; Morgan, 1968; Le Pichon, 1968). Where a plate has moved relative to the dipole magnetic field of the earth, the paleomagnetic data for any continent can be used to construct the positions of magnetic poles and the paleolatitudes through time on the plate. It is *not* possible to determine the coordinates of the plate or of a point from the paleomagnetic method because we lack evidence that the geomagnetic field has remained in a fixed position through geologic time. Although the value of knowing relative motions is much less than knowing absolute movements for understanding the history of crustal plates, relative motions in themselves tell us much about earth history; and, perhaps most importantly, their use in various combinations offers the prospect of eventually solving absolute movements of plates on the globe.

As for most crustal plates, relative motion of the antarctic plate through geologic time is shown by three lines of evidence. First, utilizing the hypothesis of sea-floor spreading, it has moved relative to the spreading ocean ridges and parallel to the transform faults. Moreover, since the ridge surrounds the continent almost continuously, its circumference or length has been enlarging through time. That is, the median line of the ridge has moved systematically away from Antarctica as new crust has been formed along its axis. Second, disrupted geologic trends show that Antarctica has probably moved relative to other Gondwanaland fragments, in particular Australia and Africa. Third, because the position of the South Magnetic Pole, as determined from antarctic rocks, has varied through time, there has been motion of Antarctica relative to the magnetic field of the earth. By comparing this movement of Antarctica with that of other Gondwanaland fragments, we can derive relative motions between continents; but the data on paleomagnetism for Antarctica unfortunately are very sparse. Here we attempt to determine relative motions by fitting Antarctica into a reconstruction of Gondwanaland using broken geologic trends and paleomagnetism. In particular, we use evidence derived from studies of late Paleozoic glaciation of the southern continents.

CONTINENTAL FITTING

Continents may be assembled into their likely pre-drift positions by matching similar opposing features such as coast-lines or bathymetry, trends or linear elements, and traces derived from the analysis of rock aspects such as metamorphic isograds, paleocurrent transport directions, and from paleomagnetic studies. Comparison of continental-slope geometry, as was undertaken for continents bordering the Atlantic by Bullard *et al.* (1965) is a first step in continental fitting. Without some limitation imposed by continental shape, it is difficult to proceed to a more detailed analysis of probability of fit. The matching of geology on opposed coasts (Hurley, 1968; Allard and Hurst, 1969; Webb, 1968) follows sequentially as a secondary approach in an appraisal. Such comparisons are usually, but not necessarily, based on first-order reconstructions or suggestions. If these secondary comparisons are deemed satisfactory, the probability increases that the now-separated continents were once joined. Although at present it is not possible to quantify these probabilities because they are based on qualitative judgments, they very significantly strengthen the correlation. Similarly, third-order matching of trends within comparable rock units can add data to improve the second-order fitting. Much is therefore to be gained from making use of such comparisons as are available, and a few studies of this kind have been attempted (Martin, 1961; Creer, 1965; Crowell and Frakes, 1968).

FITTING ANTARCTICA AND AUSTRALIA

Since continental outlines at the present shoreline or at the outer margin of the continental shelf are subject to the variable effects of erosion and deposition, Bullard and others (1965) chose instead to use the 500 fathom ($\approx$1,000 m) isobath, which is well down the continental slope. In the case of the Atlantic continents, they showed that this level in fact gave the best fit. It is more difficult to decide whether the 500 fathom isobath is best for antarctic fitting because the bathymetry is still poorly known there. Other factors, moreover, such as the isostatic depression due to the weight of the ice, may in time require selection of another or several depths. For the time being we have assumed that the 500 fathom line is as well located as any other on the Antarctic periphery and have used it to construct first-order fits. It was first necessary to draw distortion-free polar projections, one on each of the two fitted continents and centered on a common point positioned midway along the 500 fathom isobath. The central points of each map were then superposed to yield a single polar projection of the fitted continents.

Because the coastline and the 500 fathom isobath of both East Antarctica and Australia are nearly coincident with small circles of the same size, a unique fit based on shape for these two continents is largely ruled out. However, extending the southward salient of the Australia 500 fathom line to include Tasmania places some constraint on the fitting. The most logical fit therefore is as shown in Figure 1, with Tasmania inserted into the margin of the Ross Sea. The fit is reinforced by the fact that orogenic trends of Antarctica (Hamilton, 1962) are aligned across the continental boundaries with those of Australia. In a general way, there is also similarity of rock types within orogens on both continents. For example, rocks in both places include metasediments and granitic basement rocks, although late Precambrian glacials of South Australia are not known in Antarctica. Such secondary matching is quite subjective, however, because older orogens, in particular, have undergone several periods of deformation and metamorphism; and the radiometric dates of most provinces accordingly have a wide and overlapping range. Nonetheless, the boundaries of the Adelaide and Tasman Geosynclines of Australia (Wilson *et al.*, 1960) seem well established, as do those of the Ross Geosyncline in Antarctica. Similarities of lesser structural trends (Fig. 1) are considered as supporting the former juxtaposition of the two continents, but considerably more data and testing are needed.

Third-order evidence comes from detailed paleogeographic studies of late Paleozoic glacial strata of Antarctica and Australia. These are well dated by fossils as late Carboniferous and early Permian in South Australia and Tasmania (Banks, 1962) and fall in the same range in Victoria Land, Antarctica (Frakes and Crowell, 1968). In Tasmania, Banks (1962) has shown that glacial ice flowed from a source area located west and southwest of the island; in South Australia and Victoria, flow was from

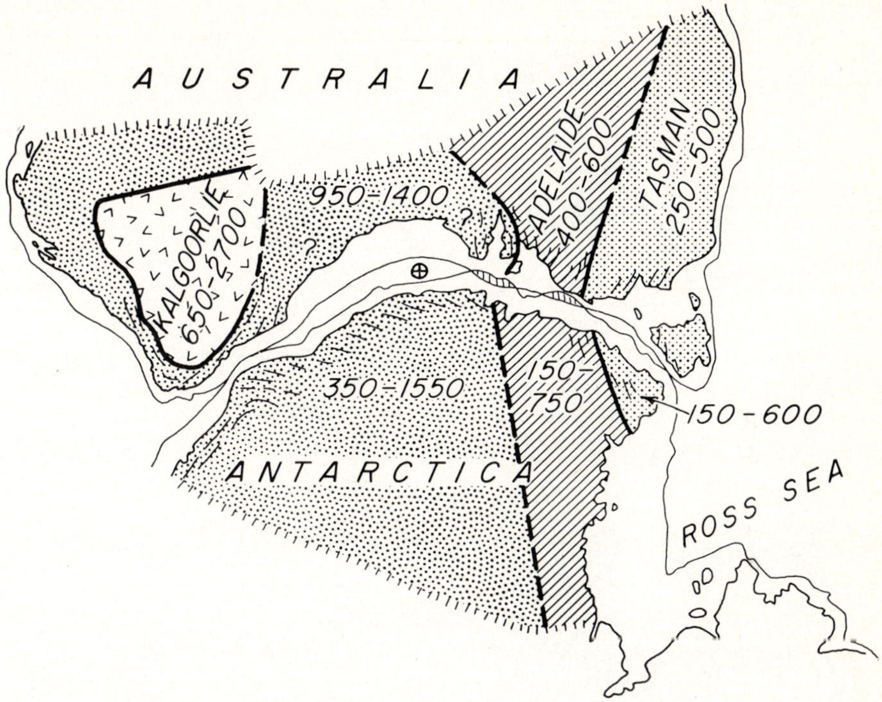

Fig. 1. Orogens in the Ross Sea sector of East Antarctica (Hamilton, 1962) and southeastern Australia (Wilson *et al.*, 1960). Structural trends are represented by fine lines near continental margins. The cross-and-circle represents the center of the polar projection. Ages are in millions of years.

the south and southeast (Brown *et al.*, 1968). Under the present arrangement of continents this source would now be somewhere in the southern ocean south of the Great Australian Bight, in a region now beneath deep water and underlain by young basaltic oceanic floor with no evidence of sialic rocks at hand. In the Ross Sea sector of Antarctica, a major source area of late Paleozoic ice was positioned in northern Victoria Land (Frakes and Crowell, 1968); and the ice flow was in a southerly direction. The Victoria Land source area is located south of Tasmania and South Australia when the continents are juxtaposed (Fig. 2). This arrangement suggests that Victoria Land may have served as the source area for the Australian tillites, also. Rock types among clasts are similar in tillites of both continents, but unique kinds have not yet been found.

Paleolatitudes determined from magnetic samples on both con-

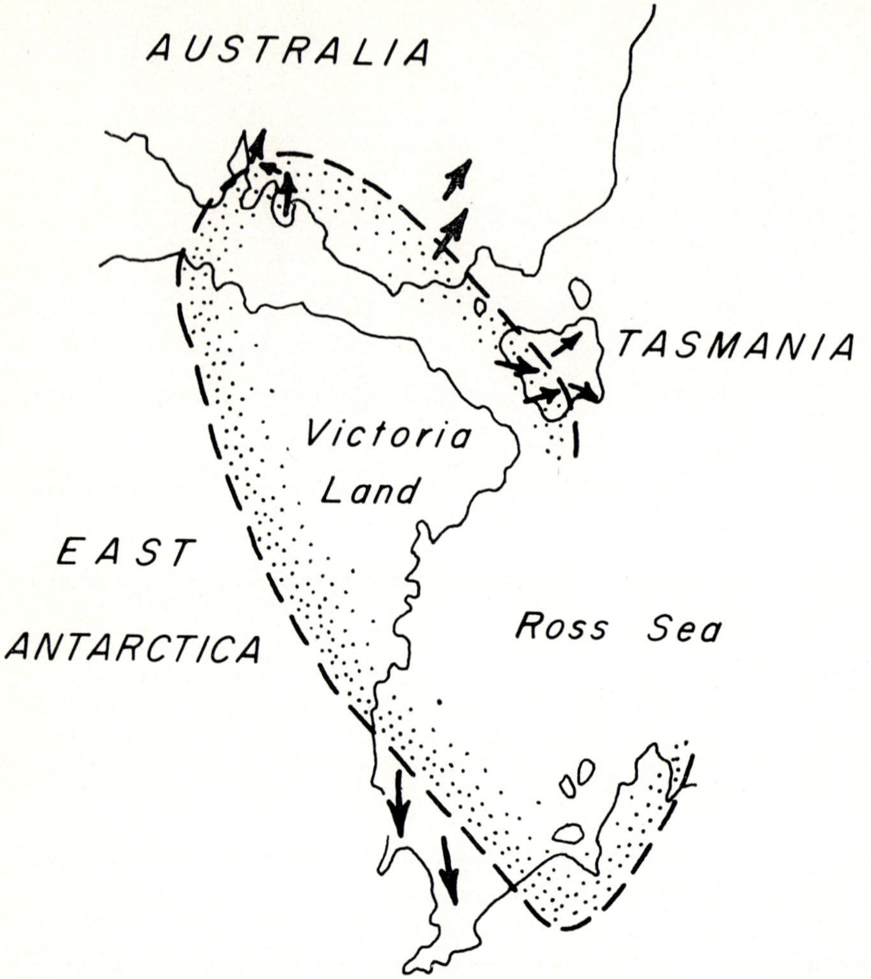

Fig. 2. Paleogeography of late Paleozoic glaciation in East Antarctica and southeastern Australia. Stippled area represents glacial source area, arrows depict directions of ice flow from sedimentary structures.

tinents may be used to find relative motions through time. By use of paleomagnetic data from antarctic rocks, it is possible to chart the change in latitude of a point now over the South Rotational Pole. The data, taken from a paleomagnetic summary by Creer (1965) and from Zijderveld (1968), are shown in Figure 3A. Because magnetic samples are lacking for the interval from the Jurassic to the Ordovician, that segment of the curve, as

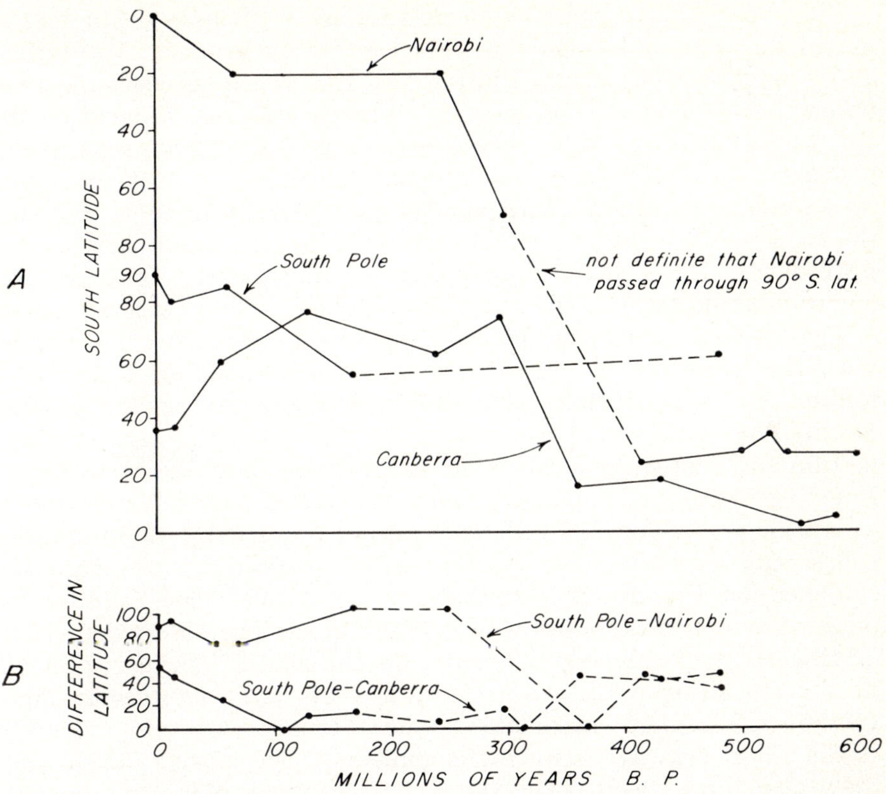

Fig. 3. A. Latitude through time for points represented by the South Rotational Pole, Canberra, and Nairobi. B. Latitudinal differences through time between South Pole and Canberra, and South Pole and Nairobi. Lines are dashed where data points are widely spaced.

well as the Proterozoic portion, is indefinite, but may be estimated eventually from paleoclimatic indicators, such as fossil faunas, floras, tillites, and biostromal limestones.

The paleolatitude curve from Australian rocks, following Irving (1964), shows the paleolatitudinal change for Canberra and, together with the antarctic data, has been utilized to estimate the *difference* in latitude between terrain positioned over the present South Rotational Pole and Canberra through time (Fig. 3B). All data used in this study have been magnetically cleaned in alternating current and have $\alpha < 15°$ (the half-angle of the cone of projection for degree of confidence 95 percent is less than 15°).

This South Pole-Canberra curve in Figure 3B provides a measure of the time and amount of relative motion between Antarctica and Australia. The present latitudinal difference between the two points is 55° and the great-circle difference before separation of the two continents was about 30° (Fig. 1). Thus, separation probably occurred when the latitudinal difference first exceeded 30°, about 45 million years ago (Fig. 3B). Prior to that time, the continents were joined, as indicated by the small latitudinal differences. Differences approaching 50° in the early Paleozoic are not reliable because of the scarcity of data for the antarctic curve.

The time of separation deduced from this approach corresponds with the initiation of spreading from the mid-Indian Ridge (40 million years ago; Heirtzler, 1968); but the divergence of the South Pole and Canberra curves in Figure 3A suggests that motion may have been initiated as early as late Mesozoic time. Thus, separation of Australia from Antarctica may have occurred as long ago as about 120 million years, or as recently as 40 million years ago, depending on whether one favors the paleomagnetic evidence or the sea-floor-spreading hypothesis. One additional piece of evidence casts light on this problem. The oldest definitely marine strata bordering Australia on the south, in the region of its juxtaposition with Antarctica, are of early Cretaceous age (~ 100-130 million years old). These rocks constitute evidence of the oldest seaway between the continents (Teichert, 1958), and they also agree well with the evidence from diverging curves beginning at about 120 million years ago. Initial separation therefore may have been gradual, beginning in the early Cretaceous and becoming more rapid in the Eocene.

FITTING ANTARCTICA AND AFRICA

A variation of the method was used in fitting Antarctica to Africa. Since a unique fit based on coastal configuration is not obvious, the matching was done by aligning the antarctic Ross Orogen with the Cape Fold Belt of southern Africa. The results give a good match for the 500 fathom isobath, but there is only fair alignment of smaller structural features (Fig. 4). The reconstruction suffers, moreover, from a lack of good dating information in the region of the Weddell Sea. At present it is not known whether orogenic regions corresponding to the Natal belt and the Swazi shield of Africa occur in Antarctica.

Late Paleozoic glacial rocks of both continents provide addi-

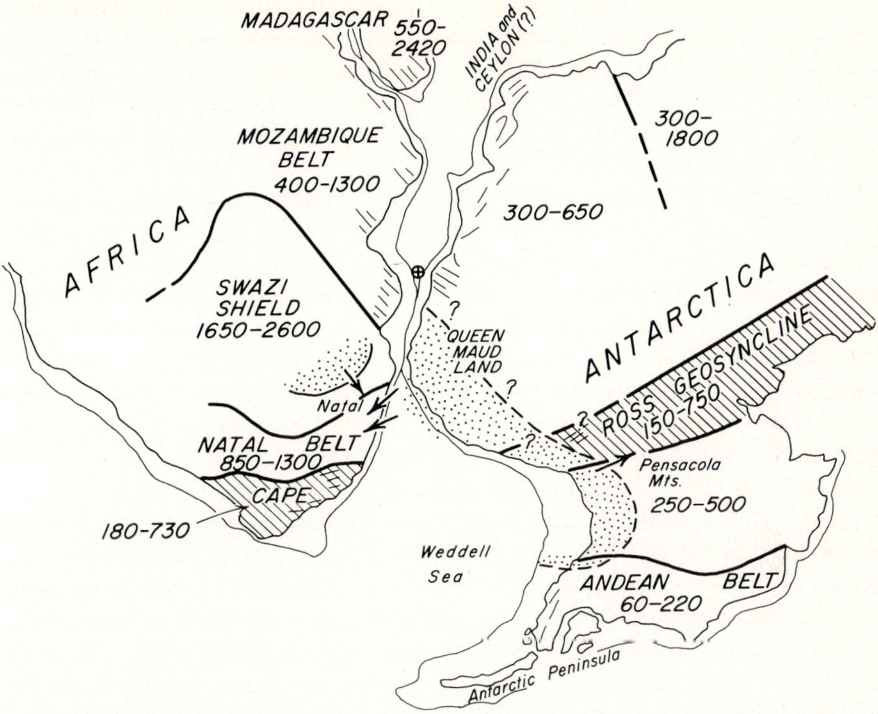

Fig. 4. Orogens in the Weddell Sea section of Antarctica (Hamilton, 1962) and southern Africa (Nicolaysen, 1962). Structural trends are represented by fine lines near continental margins. Lined areas correspond to Ross Geosyncline and Cape Fold Belt. Stipple represents glacial source area, arrows depict directions of ice flow from sedimentary structures. Cross-and-circle represents center of polar projection. Numbers represent ages in millions of years.

tional evidence bearing on the suggested fit. In the Weddell Sea sector of Antarctica, detailed studies of the Gale Mudstone of the Pensacola Mountains (Frakes *et al.*, 1966) and of the Crashsite Conglomerate of the Sentinel Range (Matthews *et al.*, 1967) indicate that sedimentation of glacial debris took place in a subaqueous environment. This distinctive facies of thick tillite with rare shale and turbidite interbeds is also developed in the Karroo basin of South Africa; the only other occurrences known among the late Paleozoic glacials are in the eastern Falkland Islands and the Sierra de la Ventana of eastern Argentina (Frakes and Crowell, 1967; Coates, 1967). Juxtaposition of these facies in our reconstruction strongly supports these former positions of Antarctica and Africa.

A major source area for the Pensacola tillites may also have served as a source for glacial debris in southern Africa. Du Toit (1921) pointed out that the directions of ice movement on glaciated floors of the Natal region demand an ice center in the present Indian Ocean during the late Paleozoic. The center postulated for the Pensacola glacials is positioned in the Weddell Sea region (Frakes and Crowell, 1968); the suggested reconstruction places this region adjacent to and up-glacier from the striated floors of Natal (Fig. 4). Again, clast types in tillites of both continents are similar, but unique types have not been recognized. Here the problem is more complicated than in the Antarctica-Australia match because the postulated source area, based on ice and current directional indicators, is now partially covered by ice and partially submerged on the continental shelf so that the rock types are not known.

Matching by difference of paleolatitudes between the points beneath the present South Rotational Pole and Nairobi, Kenya, is illustrated in Figure 3. These points at present lie 91 degrees of latitude apart. The African data are based on paleomagnetic results summarized by Girdler (1968), but there is a long gap in the record between about 300 and 410 million years. In our reconstruction (Fig. 4) Nairobi lies at a great circle distance of about 35°–40° from the South Pole point; paleolatitude differences less than this indicate that the continents probably were together, and differences greater than this indicate that they were separated. However, the sparsity of data means that the latitudinal differences are unreliable before about 170 million years ago. Paleolatitudinal differences are consistently greater than 70° since that time and were less than 40° in the Ordovician. This indicates that relative motion between Antarctica and Africa was initiated at some indefinite time between 170 and 480 million years ago. A clue to the exact timing comes from paleogeographic studies of the middle Permian Ecca Formation of South Africa. A source area similar to that for the glacials of Natal is necessary to explain the paleocurrents, which flowed from the region of the Indian Ocean (Ryan, 1967). Slightly younger strata do not reflect such a source area. Thus, separation of Antarctica and Australia may have taken place during or after the late Permian (230-250 million years ago).

This approach to the relative motion problem offers no answer to when spreading took place on the Southwest Indian Ridge between Antarctica and Africa, if indeed it occurred (Le Pichon and Heirtzler, 1968). Motion deduced for the 230- to 250-million-year interval may have resulted from spreading on the ridge or it may have been in response to spreading along a completely different locus. Nor is it possible to state that because the paleolatitudinal differences have been relatively constant (<30° variability) for the last 170 million years, there has been no relative motion between the two continents. Oscillating motions parallel to lines of latitude might not be apparent on our diagram, and they could perhaps explain the 30° variability. Nevertheless, large latitudinal motions would seem to be ruled out by the data.

A test of the fits examined here can be made by placing the continents in their fitted positions and then showing curves that plot the respective positions of poles determined from paleomagnetism. If the curves for two continents coincide over a portion of their length, the acceptability of the fit is markedly strengthened (Creer, 1965). At times of divergence after a period of coincidence of curves, relative motion between continents is indicated. This interpretation is independent of polar motion, since movement of the pole affects curves of all continents in like amount and direction.

The positions of Antarctica, Australia, and Africa from our reconstruction, together with their polar curves, are shown in Figure 5. The curves lie together for most of the Paleozoic, although relative positions by age are not ordered in every case. Coincidence of the curves for much of the Paleozoic supports the fits suggested here. Divergence of the antarctic curve from the African one seems to begin in the late Paleozoic, probably in late Permian time, and the Antarctic-Australian divergence may have taken place in the early Tertiary.

ADDITIONAL FITTING

One significant result of constructing polar projections for Gondwanaland fragments is that peninsular India is not easily fitted to Antarctica unless Ceylon had a different position with respect to India. The west coast of India, on the other hand, coincides nicely with the east coast of Madagascar; and a second-order matching can be made by comparison of the shield rocks of the two subcontinents. These crystalline complexes, repeatedly mobilized, range in age back to about 2,400 million years, are lithologically similar, and display matching structural trends on reconstruction. Similar matching can be attained between western

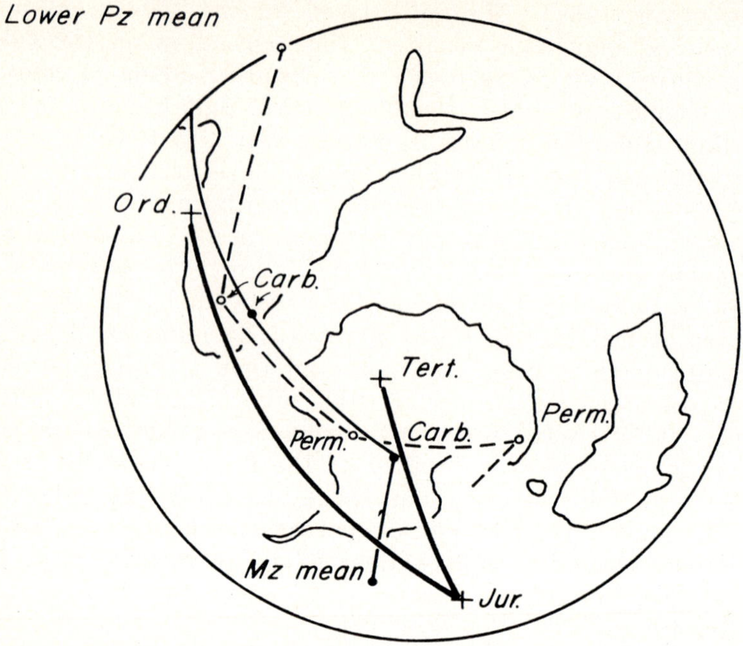

Fig. 5. A portion of Gondwanaland reassembled, with superposed curves depicting relative motions between the pole and the continental fragments. From paleomagnetic data (Creer, 1965, 1968). Heavy line = antarctic data; solid line = African data; dashed line = Australian data.

Madagascar and the rocks of the Mozambique belt in coastal Tanzania.

It is not certain that the assembly discussed above had a direct connection to Antarctica; if it did, Madagascar and India may have constituted a southward-pointing wedge partially located between Africa and Antarctica, with necessary readjustment of the position of Ceylon. Third-order lines of evidence for fitting this block to Antarctica are lacking.

Polar projections also show that our fit leaves a significant gap between the east coast of peninsular India and the west coast of Australia. Other types of projections (Du Toit, 1937) apparently allow this gap to be closed, but this must result from distortion or non-polar projections. It is likely that through most of the Paleozoic a seaway lay to the west of Australia, in view of the development of thick Paleozoic marine sections of the Australian west coast and continental shelf (Teichert, 1958).

The matching of South America is similarly not considered in detail here because it appears not to have a direct connection to Antarctica, except through the late Mesozoic-Tertiary structure of the Scotia Arc (Frakes, 1966). Relationships between South America and Africa have been discussed adequately elsewhere (Du Toit, 1937; Creer, 1965).

CONCLUSIONS

Matching of Antarctica to Australia and Africa can be accomplished by fitting, at the 500 fathom isobath, alignments of geochronologic and orogenic belts and other structural features, comparison of paleogeographic trends deduced from late Paleozoic glacial deposits, evaluation of paleolatitude differences through time for points on separate continents, and coincidence of poles from paleomagnetic data. Taken together, these results constitute strong evidence that Antarctica abutted Australia so that Tasmania occupied part of the Ross Sea, and also that the Weddell Sea region lay next to the Natal Coast of Africa. On coastal matching and aligned structural trends, Madagascar, prior to the opening of the Mozambique Channel in middle Permian time, lay adjacent to the east African coast and was bracketed on the east by peninsular India. A large gap separated India from western Australia, probably representing a salient of the Tethys Sea.

Australia was separated from Antarctica about 40 to 45 million years ago; but an initial restricted breakup may have occurred somewhat earlier, in Cretaceous time. Antarctica and Africa probably separated in the late Permian or somewhat later, and significant relative motion between the two ceased long ago. It seems likely that until the late Mesozoic, peninsular India was juxtaposed with Antarctica in view of the fact that the same and related reptile and amphibian genera occur in all the southern continents (Colbert, 1964), but the location of this connection is not certain.

The technique of using paleolatitudinal differences between continents to determine times of relative continental motion has some value, but this is limited at present because the paleomagnetic data do not allow reconstruction of reasonably complete curves for some continent pairs. With additional information, it may be possible to determine the motion between India and Madagascar and other Gondwanaland segments.

Authors' Note: This work was supported by grants from the National Science Foundation, Office of Polar Programs.

References

Allard, G. O., and V. J. Hurst, 1969. Brazil-Gabon geologic link supports continental drift. *Science, 163:* 528–532.

Banks, M. R., 1962. Permian. The geology of Tasmania. *J. Geol. Soc. Australia, 9* (2): 189–215.

Brown, D. A., K. S. W. Campbell, and K. A. W. Crook, 1968. *The Geological Evolution of Australia and New Zealand.* Pergamon, Oxford.

Bullard, Sir Edward, J. E. Everett, and A. G. Smith, 1965. The fit of the continents around the Atlantic. In *A Symposium on Continental Drift,* organized by P. M. S. Blackett, Sir Edward Bullard, and S. K. Runcorn; pp. 41–51. *Roy. Soc. Phil. Trans. No. 1088.* London.

Coates, D. A., 1967. Stratigraphy and sedimentation of the Sauce Grande Formation, Sierra de la Ventana, southern Buenos Aires Province, Argentina. *Simp. Intern. Estratigrafia Palaeontol. Gondwana, Resumenes;* p. 28. Mar del Plata, Argentina.

Colbert, E. H., 1964. Climatic zonation and terrestrial faunas. In *Problems in Palaeoclimatology,* edited by A. E. M. Nairn; pp. 617–637. Interscience, London.

Creer, K. M., 1965. Palaeomagnetic data from the Gondwanic continents. In *A Symposium on Continental Drift,* organized by P. M. S. Blackett, Sir Edward Bullard, and S. K. Runcorn; pp. 27–40. *Roy. Soc. Phil. Trans. No. 1088.* London.

Creer, K. M., 1968. Arrangement of the continents during the Palaeozoic Era. *Nature, 219:* 41–44.

Crowell, J. C., and L. A. Frakes, 1968. Late Paleozoic glacial facies and the origin of the South Atlantic Ocean. In *Other Subjects;* vol. 13, pp. 291–302. XXIIIrd Intern. Geol. Congr., Prague.

Du Toit, A. L., 1921. The Carboniferous glaciation of South Africa. *Trans. Geol. Soc. South Africa, 24:* 188–227.

Du Toit, A. L., 1937. *Our Wandering Continents.* Oliver and Boyd, Edinburgh.

Frakes, L. A., 1966. Geologic setting of South Georgia Island. *Geol. Soc. Am. Bull., 77:* 1463–1468.

Frakes, L. A., and J. C. Crowell, 1967. Facies and paleography of Late Paleozoic Lafonian Diamictite, Falkland Islands. *Geol. Soc. Am. Bull., 78* (1): 37–58.

Frakes, L. A., and J. C. Crowell, 1968. Late Paleozoic glacial geography of Antarctica. *Earth Planetary Sci. Letters, 4* (3): 253–256.

Frakes, L. A., J. L. Matthews, I. R. Neder, and J. C. Crowell, 1966. Movement directions in late Paleozoic glacial rocks, Horlick and Pensacola Mountains, Antarctica. *Science, 153:* 746–749.

Girdler, R. W., 1968. Drifting and rifting of Africa. *Nature, 217:* 1102–1106.

Hamilton, W., 1962. Antarctic tectonics and continental drift. In *Polar Wandering and Continental Drift,* edited by A. C. Munyan; pp. 74–93. *Soc. Econ. Paleontol. Mineral., Tulsa, Spec. Publ. No. 10.*

Heirtzler, J. R., 1968. Sea-floor spreading. *Sci. Am., 219* (6) : 60–73.

Hess, H. H., 1962. History of ocean basins. In *Petrologic Studies, A Volume in Honor of A. F. Buddington,* edited by A. E. J. Engel, H. L. James, and B. F. Leonard; pp. 599–621. Geol. Soc. Am., New York.

Hurley, P. M., 1968. The confirmation of continental drift. *Sci. Am., 218* (4) : 53–64.

Irving, E., 1964. *Paleomagnetism and Its Application to Geological and Geophysical Problems.* Wiley, New York.

Le Pichon, X., 1968. Sea-floor spreading and continental drift. *J. Geophys. Res., 73* (12) : 3661–3698.

Le Pichon, X., and J. R. Heirtzler, 1968. Magnetic anomalies in the Indian Ocean and sea-floor spreading. *J. Geophys. Res., 73* (6) : 2101–2118.

Martin, H., 1961. The hypothesis of continental drift in the light of recent advances of geological knowledge in Brazil and in South-West Africa. *Geol. Soc. South Africa, Trans., Annexure, 64:* 1–47.

Matthews, J. L., J. C. Crowell, D. A. Coates, I. R. Neder, and L. A. Frakes, 1967. Late Paleozoic glacial rocks in the Sentinel and Queen Alexandra Ranges. *Antarctic J. U. S., 2:* 108.

McKenzie, D. P., and R. L. Parker, 1967. The North Pacific: an example of tectonics on a sphere. *Nature, 216:* 1276–1280.

Morgan, W. J., 1968. Rises, trenches, great faults, and crustal blocks. *J. Geophys. Res., 73* (6) : 1959–1982.

Nicolaysen, L. O., 1962. Stratigraphic interpretation of age measurements in southern Africa. In *Petrologic Studies, A Volume in Honor of A. F. Buddington,* edited by A. E. J. Engel, H. L. James, and B. F. Leonard; pp. 569–598. Geol. Soc. Am., New York.

Ryan, P. J., 1967. Stratigraphy of the Ecca Series and lowermost Beaufort beds (Permian) in the Great Karroo basin of South Africa. *Simp. Intern. Estratigrafia Paleontol. Gondwana, Resumenes;* pp. 41–42. Mar del Plata, Argentina.

Teichert, C., 1958. Australia and Gondwanaland. *Geol. Rundschau, 47:* 562–590.

Vine, F. J., 1968. Magnetic anomalies associated with mid-ocean ridges. In *The History of the Earth's Crust,* edited by R. A. Phinney; pp. 73–89. Princeton Univ. Press, Princeton, N.J.

Vine, F. J., and D. H. Matthews, 1963. Magnetic anomalies over oceanic ridges. *Nature, 199:* 947–949.

Webb, G. W., 1968. Palinspastic restoration suggesting late Paleozoic North Atlantic rifting. *Science, 159:* 875–878.

Wilson, A. F., W. Compston, P. M. Jeffery, and G. H. Riley, 1960. Radioactive ages from the Precambrian rocks in Australia. *J. Geol. Soc. Australia, 6:* 179–195.

Zijderveld, J. D. A., 1968. Natural remnant magnetizations of some intrusive rocks from the Sør Rondane Mountains, Queen Maud Land, Antarctica. *J. Geophys. Res., 73:* 3773–3786.

INDEX